Neural Networks for Pattern Recognition

Neural Networks for Pattern Recognition

CHRISTOPHER M. BISHOP

*Department of Computer Science
and Applied Mathematics
Aston University
Birmingham, UK*

CLARENDON PRESS · OXFORD

Oxford University Press, Great Clarendon Street, Oxford OX2 6DP

Oxford New York
Athens Auckland Bangkok Bogota Bombay Buenos Aires
Calcutta Cape Town Dar es Salaam Delhi Florence Hong Kong
Istanbul Karachi Kuala Lumpur Madras Madrid Melbourne
Mexico City Nairobi Paris Singapore Taipei Tokyo Toronto Warsaw

and associated companies in
Berlin Ibadan

Oxford is a trade mark of Oxford University Press

Published in the United States
by Oxford University Press Inc., New York

First published 1995
Reprinted 1996 (twice), 1997 (twice)

A catalogue record for this book is available from the British Library

Library of Congress Cataloging in Publication Data
Bishop, Chris (Chris M.)
Neural networks for pattern recognition / Chris Bishop.
1. Neural networks (Computer science). 2. Pattern recognition
systems. I. Title.
QA76.87.B574 1994 006.4—dc20 95-40465

ISBN 0 19 853864 2 (Pbk)

Printed in Great Britain by
Bookcraft (Bath) Ltd, Midsomer Norton, Somerset

To Jenna

FOREWORD

Geoffrey Hinton

Department of Computer Science
University of Toronto

For those entering the field of artificial neural networks, there has been an acute
need for an authoritative textbook that explains the main ideas clearly and con-
sistently using the basic tools of linear algebra, calculus, and simple probability
theory. There have been many attempts to provide such a text, but until now,
none has succeeded. Some authors have failed to separate the basic ideas and
principles from the soft and fuzzy intuitions that led to some of the models as
well as to most of the exaggerated claims. Others have been unwilling to use the
basic mathematical tools that are essential for a rigorous understanding of the
material. Yet others have tried to cover too many different kinds of neural network without going into enough depth on any one of them. The most successful
attempt to date has been "Introduction to the Theory of Neural Computation"
by Hertz, Krogh and Palmer. Unfortunately, this book started life as a graduate
course in statistical physics and it shows. So despite its many admirable qualities
it is not ideal as a general textbook.

Bishop is a leading researcher who has a deep understanding of the material
and has gone to great lengths to organize it into a sequence that makes sense. He
has wisely avoided the temptation to try to cover everything and has therefore
omitted interesting topics like reinforcement learning, Hopfield Networks and
Boltzmann machines in order to focus on the types of neural network that are
most widely used in practical applications. He assumes that the reader has the
basic mathematical literacy required for an undergraduate science degree, and
using these tools he explains everything from scratch. Before introducing the
multilayer perceptron, for example, he lays a solid foundation of basic statistical
concepts. So the crucial concept of overfitting is first introduced using easily
visualised examples of one-dimensional polynomials and only later applied to
neural networks. An impressive aspect of this book is that it takes the reader all
the way from the simplest linear models to the very latest Bayesian multilayer
neural networks without ever requiring any great intellectual leaps.

Although Bishop has been involved in some of the most impressive applications of neural networks, the theme of the book is principles rather than applications. Nevertheless, it is much more useful than any of the applications-oriented
texts in preparing the reader for applying this technology effectively. The crucial
issues of how to get good generalization and rapid learning are covered in great
depth and detail and there are also excellent discussions of how to preprocess

the input and how to choose a suitable error function for the output.

It is a sign of the increasing maturity of the field that methods which were once justified by vague appeals to their neuron-like qualities can now be given a solid statistical foundation. Ultimately, we all hope that a better statistical understanding of artificial neural networks will help us understand how the brain actually works, but until that day comes it is reassuring to know why our current models work and how to use them effectively to solve important practical problems.

PREFACE

Introduction

In recent years neural computing has emerged as a practical technology, with successful applications in many fields. The majority of these applications are concerned with problems in pattern recognition, and make use of feed-forward network architectures such as the multi-layer perceptron and the radial basis function network. Also, it has also become widely acknowledged that successful applications of neural computing require a principled, rather than *ad hoc*, approach. My aim in writing this book has been to provide a more focused treatment of neural networks than previously available, which reflects these developments. By deliberately concentrating on the pattern recognition aspects of neural networks, it has become possible to treat many important topics in much greater depth. For example, density estimation, error functions, parameter optimization algorithms, data pre-processing, and Bayesian methods are each the subject of an entire chapter.

From the perspective of pattern recognition, neural networks can be regarded as an extension of the many conventional techniques which have been developed over several decades. Indeed, this book includes discussions of several concepts in conventional statistical pattern recognition which I regard as essential for a clear understanding of neural networks. More extensive treatments of these topics can be found in the many texts on statistical pattern recognition, including Duda and Hart (1973), Hand (1981), Devijver and Kittler (1982), and Fukunaga (1990). Recent review articles by Ripley (1994) and Cheng and Titterington (1994) have also emphasized the statistical underpinnings of neural networks.

Historically, many concepts in neural computing have been inspired by studies of biological networks. The perspective of statistical pattern recognition, however, offers a much more direct and principled route to many of the same concepts. For example, the sum-and-threshold model of a neuron arises naturally as the optimal discriminant function needed to distinguish two classes whose distributions are normal with equal covariance matrices. Similarly, the familiar logistic sigmoid is precisely the function needed to allow the output of a network to be interpreted as a probability, when the distribution of hidden unit activations is governed by a member of the exponential family.

An important assumption which is made throughout the book is that the processes which give rise to the data do not themselves evolve with time. Techniques for dealing with non-stationary sources of data are not so highly developed, nor so well established, as those for static problems. Furthermore, the issues addressed within this book remain equally important in the face of the additional complication of non-stationarity. It should be noted that this restriction does not mean that applications involving the prediction of time series are excluded. The key consideration for time series is not the time variation of the signals themselves, but whether the underlying process which generates the data is itself evolving with time, as discussed in Section 8.4.

Use as a course text

This book is aimed at researchers in neural computing as well as those wishing to apply neural networks to practical applications. It is also intended to be used used as the primary text for a graduate-level, or advanced undergraduate-level, course on neural networks. In this case the book should be used sequentially, and care has been taken to ensure that where possible the material in any particular chapter depends only on concepts developed in earlier chapters.

Exercises are provided at the end of each chapter, and these are intended to reinforce concepts developed in the main text, as well as to lead the reader through some extensions of these concepts. Each exercise is assigned a grading according to its complexity and the length of time needed to solve it, ranging from ($\star$) for a short, simple exercise, to ($\star\star\star$) for a more extensive or more complex exercise. Some of the exercises call for analytical derivations or proofs, while others require varying degrees of numerical simulation. Many of the simulations can be carried out using numerical analysis and graphical visualization packages, while others specifically require the use of neural network software. Often suitable network simulators are available as add-on tool-kits to the numerical analysis packages. No particular software system has been prescribed, and the course tutor, or the student, is free to select an appropriate package from the many available. A few of the exercises require the student to develop the necessary code in a standard language such as C or C++. In this case some very useful software modules written in C, together with background information, can be found in Press *et al.* (1992).

Prerequisites

This book is intended to be largely self-contained as far as the subject of neural networks is concerned, although some prior exposure to the subject may be helpful to the reader. A clear understanding of neural networks can only be achieved with the use of a certain minimum level of mathematics. It is therefore assumed that the reader has a good working knowledge of vector and matrix algebra, as well as integral and differential calculus for several variables. Some more specific results and techniques which are used at a number of places in the text are described in the appendices.

Overview of the chapters

The first chapter provides an introduction to the principal concepts of pattern recognition. By drawing an analogy with the problem of polynomial curve fitting, it introduces many of the central ideas, such as parameter optimization, generalization and model complexity, which will be discussed at greater length in later chapters of the book. This chapter also gives an overview of the formalism of statistical pattern recognition, including probabilities, decision criteria and Bayes' theorem.

Chapter 2 deals with the problem of modelling the probability distribution of a set of data, and reviews conventional parametric and non-parametric methods, as well as discussing more recent techniques based on mixture distributions. Aside from being of considerable practical importance in their own right, the concepts of probability density estimation are relevant to many aspects of neural computing.

Neural networks having a single layer of adaptive weights are introduced in Chapter 3. Although such networks have less flexibility than multi-layer networks, they can play an important role in practical applications, and they also serve to motivate several ideas and techniques which are applicable also to more general network structures.

Chapter 4 provides a comprehensive treatment of the multi-layer perceptron, and describes the technique of error back-propagation and its significance as a general framework for evaluating derivatives in multi-layer networks. The Hessian matrix, which plays a central role in many parameter optimization algorithms as well as in Bayesian techniques, is also treated at length.

An alternative, and complementary, approach to representing general nonlinear mappings is provided by radial basis function networks, and is discussed in Chapter 5. These networks are motivated from several distinct perspectives, and hence provide a unifying framework linking a number of different approaches.

Several different error functions can be used for training neural networks, and these are motivated, and their properties examined, in Chapter 6. The circumstances under which network outputs can be interpreted as probabilities are discussed, and the corresponding interpretation of hidden unit activations is also considered.

Chapter 7 reviews many of the most important algorithms for optimizing the values of the parameters in a network, in other words for network training. Simple algorithms, based on gradient descent with momentum, have serious limitations, and an understanding of these helps to motivate some of the more powerful algorithms, such as conjugate gradients and quasi-Newton methods.

One of the most important factors in determining the success of a practical application of neural networks is the form of pre-processing applied to the data. Chapter 8 covers a range of issues associated with data pre-processing, and describes several practical techniques related to dimensionality reduction and the use of prior knowledge.

Chapter 9 provides a number of insights into the problem of generalization, and describes methods for addressing the central issue of model order selection. The key insight of the bias–variance trade-off is introduced, and several techniques for optimizing this trade-off, including regularization, are treated at length.

The final chapter discusses the treatment of neural networks from a Bayesian perspective. As well as providing a more fundamental view of learning in neural networks, the Bayesian approach also leads to practical procedures for assigning error bars to network predictions and for optimizing the values of regularization coefficients.

Some useful mathematical results are derived in the appendices, relating to the properties of symmetric matrices, Gaussian integration, Lagrange multipliers, calculus of variations, and principal component analysis.

An extensive bibliography is included, which is intended to provide useful pointers to the literature rather than a complete record of the historical development of the subject.

Nomenclature

In trying to find a notation which is internally consistent, I have adopted a number of general principles as follows. Lower-case bold letters, for example $\mathbf{v}$, are used to denote vectors, while upper-case bold letters, such as $\mathbf{M}$, denote matrices. One exception is that I have used the notation $\vec{y}$ to denote a vector whose elements y^n represent the values of a variable corresponding to different patterns in a training set, to distinguish it from a vector $\mathbf{y}$ whose elements y_k correspond to different variables. Related variables are indexed by lower-case Roman letters, and a set of such variables is denoted by enclosing braces. For instance, $\{x_i\}$ denotes a set of input variables x_i, where $i = 1, \ldots, d$. Vectors are considered to be column vectors, with the corresponding row vector denoted by a superscript T indicating the transpose, so that, for example, $\mathbf{x}^{\mathrm{T}} \equiv (x_1, \ldots, x_d)$. Similarly, $\mathbf{M}^{\mathrm{T}}$ denotes the transpose of a matrix $\mathbf{M}$. The notation $\mathbf{M} = (M_{ij})$ is used to denote the fact that the matrix $\mathbf{M}$ has the elements M_{ij}, while the notation $(\mathbf{M})_{ij}$ is used to denote the ij element of a matrix $\mathbf{M}$. The Euclidean length of a vector $\mathbf{x}$ is denoted by $\|\mathbf{x}\|$, while the magnitude of a scalar x is denoted by $|x|$. The determinant of a matrix $\mathbf{M}$ is written as $|\mathbf{M}|$.

I typically use an upper-case P to denote a probability and a lower-case p to denote a probability density. Note that I use $p(x)$ to represent the distribution of x and $p(y)$ to represent the distribution of y, so that these distributions are denoted by the same symbol p even though they represent different functions. By a similar abuse of notation I frequently use, for example, y_k to denote the outputs of a neural network, and at the same time use $y_k(\mathbf{x}; \mathbf{w})$ to denote the non-linear mapping function represented by the network. I hope these conventions will save more confusion than they cause.

To denote functionals (Appendix D) I use square brackets, so that, for example, $E[f]$ denotes functional of the function $f(\mathbf{x})$. Square brackets are also used in the notation $\mathcal{E}[Q]$ which denotes the expectation (i.e. average) of a random variable Q.

I use the notation $\mathcal{O}(N)$ to denote that a quantity is *of order N*. Given two functions $f(N)$ and $g(N)$, we say that $f = \mathcal{O}(g)$ if $f(N) < Ag(N)$, where A is a constant, for all values of N (although we are typically interested in large N). Similarly, we will say that $f \sim g$ if the ratio $f(N)/g(N) \to 1$ as $N \to \infty$.

I find it indispensable to use two distinct conventions to describe the weight parameters in a network. Sometimes it is convenient to refer explicitly to the weight which goes *to* a unit labelled by j *from* a unit (or input) labelled by i.

Such a weight will be denoted by w_{ji}. In other contexts it is more convenient to label the weights using a single index, as in w_k, where k runs from 1 to W, and W is the total number of weights. The variables w_k can then be gathered together to make a vector $\mathbf{w}$ whose elements comprise all of the weights (or more generally all of the adaptive parameters) in the network.

The notation δ_{ij} denotes the usual Kronecker delta symbol, in other words $\delta_{ij} = 1$ if $i = j$ and $\delta_{ij} = 0$ otherwise. Similarly, the notation $\delta(x)$ denotes the Dirac delta function, which has the properties $\delta(x) = 0$ for $x \neq 0$ and

$$\int_{-\infty}^{\infty} \delta(x)\, dx = 1.$$

In d-dimensions the Dirac delta function is defined by

$$\delta(\mathbf{x}) \equiv \prod_{i=1}^{d} \delta(x_i).$$

The symbols used for the most commonly occurring quantities in the book are listed below:

c	number of outputs; number of classes
$\mathcal{C}_k$	kth class
d	number of inputs
E	error function
$\mathcal{E}[Q]$	expectation of a random variable Q
$g(\cdot)$	activation function
i	input label
j	hidden unit label
k	output unit label
M	number of hidden units
n	pattern label
N	number of patterns
$P(\cdot)$	probability
$p(\cdot)$	probability density function
t	target value
τ	time step in iterative algorithms
W	number of weights and biases in a network
x	network input variable
y	network output variable
z	activation of hidden unit
$\ln$	logarithm to base e
$\log_2$	logarithm to base 2

Acknowledgements

Finally, I wish to express my considerable gratitude to the many people who, in one way or another, have helped with the process of writing this book. The first of these is Jenna, who has displayed considerable patience and good humour, notwithstanding my consistent underestimates of the time and effort required to complete this book. I am particularly grateful to a number of people for carefully reviewing draft material for this book, and for discussions which in one way or another have influenced parts of the text: Geoff Hinton, David Lowe, Stephen Luttrell, David MacKay, Alan McLachlan, Martin Møller, Radford Neal, Cazhaow Qazaz, Brian Ripley, Richard Rohwer, David Saad, Iain Strachan, Markus Svensén, Lionel Tarassenko, David Wallace, Chris Williams, Peter Williams and Colin Windsor. I would also like to thank Richard Lister for providing considerable assistance while I was typesetting the text in LATEX. Finally, I wish to thank staff at Oxford University Press for their help in the final stages of preparing this book.

Several of the diagrams in the book have been inspired by similar diagrams appearing in published work, as follows:

Figures 1.15, 2.3, 2.5, and 3.1 .... (Duda and Hart, 1973)
Figure 2.13 .... (Luttrell, 1994)
Figures 3.10 and 3.14 .... (Minsky and Papert, 1969)
Figure 4.4 .... (Lippmann, 1987)
Figure 5.8 .... (Lowe, 1995)
Figures 5.9 and 5.10 .... (Hartman *et al.*, 1990)
Figure 8.3 .... (Ghahramani and Jordan, 1994a)
Figure 9.12 .... (Fahlman and Lebiere, 1990)
Figure 9.14 .... (Jacobs *et al.*, 1991)
Figure 9.19 .... (Hertz *et al.*, 1991)
Figures 10.1, 10.10, 10.11 and 10.15 .... (MacKay, 1994a)
Figures 10.3, 10.4, 10.5 and 10.6 .... (MacKay, 1995a)
Figures 9.3 and 10.12 .... (MacKay, 1992a)

Chris Bishop

CONTENTS

1

STATISTICAL PATTERN RECOGNITION

The term pattern recognition encompasses a wide range of information processing problems of great practical significance, from speech recognition and the classification of handwritten characters, to fault detection in machinery and medical diagnosis. Often these are problems which many humans solve in a seemingly effortless fashion. However, their solution using computers has, in many cases, proved to be immensely difficult. In order to have the best opportunity of developing effective solutions, it is important to adopt a principled approach based on sound theoretical concepts.

The most general, and most natural, framework in which to formulate solutions to pattern recognition problems is a statistical one, which recognizes the probabilistic nature both of the information we seek to process, and of the form in which we should express the results. Statistical pattern recognitionis a well established field with a long history. Throughout this book, we shall view neural networks as an extension of conventional techniques in statistical pattern recognition, and we shall build on, rather than ignore, the many powerful results which this field offers.

In this first chapter we provide a gentle introduction to many of the key concepts in pattern recognition which will be central to our treatment of neural networks. By using a simple pattern classification example, and analogies to the problem of curve fitting, we introduce a number of important issues which will re-emerge in later chapters in the context of neural networks. This chapter also serves to introduce some of the basic formalism of statistical pattern recognition.

1.1 An example – character recognition

We can introduce many of the fundamental concepts of statistical pattern recognition by considering a simple, hypothetical, problem of distinguishing handwritten versions of the characters 'a' and 'b'. Images of the characters might be captured by a television camera and fed to a computer, and we seek an algorithm which can distinguish as reliably as possible between the two characters. An image is represented by an array of pixels, as illustrated in Figure 1.1, each of which carries an associated value which we shall denote by x_i (where the index i labels the individual pixels). The value of x_i might, for instance, range from 0 for a completely white pixel to 1 for a completely black pixel. It is often convenient to gather the x_i variables together and denote them by a single vector $\mathbf{x} = (x_1, \ldots, x_d)^{\mathrm{T}}$ where d is the total number of such variables, and the

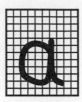

Figure 1.1. Illustration of two hypothetical images representing handwritten versions of the characters 'a' and 'b'. Each image is described by an array of pixel values x_i which range from 0 to 1 according to the fraction of the pixel square occupied by black ink.

superscript T denotes the transpose. In considering this example we shall ignore a number of detailed practical considerations which would have to be addressed in a real implementation, and focus instead on the underlying issues.

The goal in this classification problem is to develop an algorithm which will assign any image, represented by a vector $\mathbf{x}$, to one of two classes, which we shall denote by $\mathcal{C}_k$, where $k = 1, 2$, so that class $\mathcal{C}_1$ corresponds to the character 'a' and class $\mathcal{C}_2$ corresponds to 'b'. We shall suppose that we are provided with a large number of examples of images corresponding to both 'a' and 'b', which have already been classified by a human. Such a collection will be referred to as a *data set*. In the statistics literature it would be called a *sample*.

One obvious problem which we face stems from the high dimensionality of the data which we are collecting. For a typical image size of 256 × 256 pixels, each image can be represented as a point in a d-dimensional space, where $d = 65\,536$. The axes of this space represent the grey-level values of the corresponding pixels, which in this example might be represented by 8-bit numbers. In principle we might think of storing every possible image together with its corresponding class label. In practice, of course, this is completely impractical due to the very large number of possible images: for a 256 × 256 image with 8-bit pixel values there would be $2^{8 \times 256 \times 256} \simeq 10^{158\,000}$ different images. By contrast, we might typically have a few thousand examples in our training set. It is clear then that the classifier system must be designed so as to be able to classify correctly a previously unseen image vector. This is the problem of *generalization*, which is discussed at length in Chapters 9 and 10.

As we shall see in Section 1.4, the presence of a large number of input variables can present some severe problems for pattern recognition systems. One technique to help alleviate such problems is to combine input variables together to make a smaller number of new variables called *features*. These might be constructed 'by hand' based on some understanding of the particular problem being tackled, or they might be derived from the data by automated procedures. In the present example, we could, for instance, evaluate the ratio of the height of the character to its width, which we shall denote by $\widetilde{x}_1$, since we might expect that characters

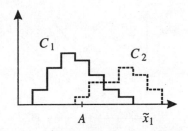

Figure 1.2. Schematic plot of the histograms of the feature variable $\tilde{x}_1$ given by the ratio of the height of a character to its width, for a data set of images containing examples from classes $\mathcal{C}_1 \equiv$ 'a' and $\mathcal{C}_2 \equiv$ 'b'. Notice that characters from class $\mathcal{C}_2$ tend to have larger values of $\tilde{x}_1$ than characters from class $\mathcal{C}_1$, but that there is a significant overlap between the two histograms. If a new image is observed which has a value of $\tilde{x}_1$ given by A, we might expect the image is more likely to belong to class $\mathcal{C}_1$ than $\mathcal{C}_2$.

from class $\mathcal{C}_2$ (corresponding to 'b') will typically have larger values of $\tilde{x}_1$ than characters from class $\mathcal{C}_1$ (corresponding to 'a'). We might then hope that the value of $\tilde{x}_1$ alone will allow new images to be assigned to the correct class. Suppose we measure the value of $\tilde{x}_1$ for each of the images in our data set, and plot their values as histograms for each of the two classes. Figure 1.2 shows the form which these histograms might take. We see that typically examples of the character 'b' have larger values of $\tilde{x}_1$ than examples of the character 'a', but we also see that the two histograms overlap, so that occasionally we might encounter an example of 'b' which has a smaller value of $\tilde{x}_1$ than some example of 'a'. We therefore cannot distinguish the two classes perfectly using the value of $\tilde{x}_1$ alone.

If we suppose for the moment that the only information available is the value of $\tilde{x}_1$, we may wish to know how to make best use of it to classify a new image so as to minimize the number of misclassifications. For a new image which has a value of $\tilde{x}_1$ given by A as indicated in Figure 1.2, we might expect that the image is more likely to belong to class $\mathcal{C}_1$ than to class $\mathcal{C}_2$. One approach would therefore be to build a classifier system which simply uses a threshold for the value of $\tilde{x}_1$ and which classifies as $\mathcal{C}_2$ any image for which $\tilde{x}_1$ exceeds the threshold, and which classifies all other images as $\mathcal{C}_1$. We might expect that the number of misclassifications in this approach would be minimized if we choose the threshold to be at the point where the two histograms cross. This intuition turns out to be essentially correct, as we shall see in Section 1.9.

The classification procedure we have described so far is based on the evaluation of $\tilde{x}_1$ followed by its comparison with a threshold. While we would expect this to give some degree of discrimination between the two classes, it suffers from the problem, indicated in Figure 1.2, that there is still significant overlap of the histograms, and hence we must expect that many of the new characters on which we might test it will be misclassified. One way to try to improve the

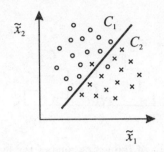

Figure 1.3. A hypothetical classification problem involving two feature variables $\tilde{x}_1$ and $\tilde{x}_2$. Circles denote patterns from class C_1 and crosses denote
patterns from class C_2. The decision boundary (shown by the line) is able to
provide good separation of the two classes, although there are still a few patterns which would be incorrectly classified by this boundary. Note that if the
value of either of the two features were considered separately (corresponding
to a projection of the data onto one or other of the axes), then there would be
substantially greater overlap of the two classes.

situation is to consider a second feature $\tilde{x}_2$ (whose actual definition we need not
consider) and to try to classify new images on the basis of the values of $\tilde{x}_1$ and
$\tilde{x}_2$ considered together. The reason why this might be beneficial is indicated in
Figure 1.3. Here we see examples of patterns from two classes plotted in the
$(\tilde{x}_1, \tilde{x}_2)$ space. It is possible to draw a line in this space, known as a *decision
boundary*, which gives good separation of the two classes. New patterns which lie
above the decision boundary are classified as belonging to class C_1 while patterns
falling below the decision boundary are classified as C_2. A few examples are still
incorrectly classified, but the separation of the patterns is much better than if
either feature had been considered individually, as can be seen by considering all
of the data points projected as histograms onto one or other of the two axes.

We could continue to consider ever larger numbers of (independent) features
in the hope of improving the performance indefinitely. In fact, as we shall see in
Section 1.4, adding too many features can, paradoxically, lead to a worsening of
performance. Furthermore, for many real pattern recognition applications, it is
the case that some overlap between the distributions of the classes is inevitable.
This highlights the intrinsically probabilistic nature of the pattern classification
problem. With handwritten characters, for example, there is considerable vari-
ability in the way the characters are drawn. We are forced to treat the measured
variables as random quantities, and to accept that perfect classification of new
examples may not always be possible. Instead we could aim to build a classifier
which has the smallest probability of making a mistake.

1.2 Classification and regression

The system considered above for classifying handwritten characters was designed to take an image and to assign it to one of the two classes C_1 or C_2. We can represent the outcome of the classification in terms of a variable y which takes the value 1 if the image is classified as C_1, and the value 0 if it is classified as C_2. Thus, the overall system can be viewed as a mapping from a set of input variables $x_1, \ldots, x_d$, representing the pixel intensities, to an output variable y representing the class label. In more complex problems there may be several output variables, which we shall denote by y_k where $k = 1, \ldots, c$. Thus, if we wanted to classify all 26 letters of the alphabet, we might consider 26 output variables each of which corresponds to one of the possible letters.

In general it will not be possible to determine a suitable form for the required mapping, except with the help of a data set of examples. The mapping is therefore modelled in terms of some mathematical function which contains a number of adjustable parameters, whose values are determined with the help of the data. We can write such functions in the form

$$y_k = y_k(\mathbf{x}; \mathbf{w}) \tag{1.1}$$

where $\mathbf{w}$ denotes the vector of parameters. A neural network model, of the kind considered in this book, can be regarded simply as a particular choice for the set of functions $y_k(\mathbf{x}; \mathbf{w})$. In this case, the parameters comprising $\mathbf{w}$ are often called *weights*. For the character classification example considered above, the threshold on $\tilde{x}$ was an example of a parameter whose value was found from the data by plotting histograms as in Figure 1.2. The use of a simple threshold function, however, corresponds to a very limited form for $y(\mathbf{x}; \mathbf{w})$, and for most practical applications we need to consider much more flexible functions. The importance of neural networks in this context is that they offer a very powerful and very general framework for representing non-linear mappings from several input variables to several output variables, where the form of the mapping is governed by a number of adjustable parameters. The process of determining the values for these parameters on the basis of the data set is called *learning* or *training*, and for this reason the data set of examples is generally referred to as a *training set*. Neural network models, as well as many conventional approaches to statistical pattern recognition, can be viewed as specific choices for the functional forms used to represent the mapping (1.1), together with particular procedures for optimizing the parameters in the mapping. In fact, neural network models often contain conventional approaches as special cases, as discussed in subsequent chapters.

In classification problems the task is to assign new inputs to one of a number of discrete classes or categories. However, there are many other pattern recognition tasks, which we shall refer to as *regression* problems, in which the outputs represent the values of continuous variables. Examples include the determination of the fraction of oil in a pipeline from measurements of the attenuation of gamma beams passing through the pipe, and the prediction of the value of a currency exchange rate at the some future time, given its values at a number of recent times. In fact, as discussed in Section 2.4, the term 'regression' refers to a specific kind of function defined in terms of an average over a random quantity. Both regression and classification problems can be seen as particular cases of *function approximation*. In the case of regression problems it is the regression function (defined in Section 6.1.3) which we wish to approximate, while for classification problems the functions which we seek to approximate are the probabilities of membership of the different classes expressed as functions of the input variables. Many of the key issues which need to be addressed in tackling pattern recognition problems are common both to classification and regression.

1.3 Pre-processing and feature extraction

Rather than represent the entire transformation from the set of input variables $x_1, \ldots, x_d$ to the set of output variables $y_1, \ldots, y_c$ by a single neural network function, there is often great benefit in breaking down the mapping into an initial *pre-processing* stage, followed by the parametrized neural network model itself. This is illustrated schematically in Figure 1.4. For many applications, the outputs from the network also undergo *post-processing* to convert them to the required form. In our character recognition example, the original input variables, given by the pixel values x_i, were first transformed to a single variable $\tilde{x}_1$. This is an example of a form of pre-processing which is generally called *feature extraction*. The distinction between the pre-processing stage and the neural network is not always clear cut, but often the pre-processing can be regarded as a fixed transformation of the variables, while the network itself contains adaptive parameters whose values are set as part of the training process. The use of pre-processing can often greatly improve the performance of a pattern recognition system, and there are several reasons why this may be so, as we now discuss.

In our character recognition example, we know that the decision on whether to classify a character as 'a' or 'b' should not depend on where in the image that character is located. A classification system whose decisions are insensitive to the location of an object within an image is said to exhibit *translation invariance*. The simple approach to character recognition considered above satisfies this property because the feature $\tilde{x}_1$ (the ratio of height to width of the character) does not depend on the character's position. Note that this feature variable also exhibits *scale invariance*, since it is unchanged if the size of the character is uniformly re-scaled. Such invariance properties are examples of *prior knowledge*, that is, information which we possess about the desired form of the solution which is additional to the information provided by the training data. The inclusion of prior knowledge into the design of a pattern recognition system can improve its performance dramatically, and the use of pre-processing is one important way of achieving this. Since pre-processing and feature extraction can have such a significant impact on the final performance of a pattern recognition system, we have devoted the whole of Chapter 8 to a detailed discussion of these topics.

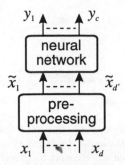

Figure 1.4. The majority of neural network applications require the original input variables $x_1, \ldots, x_d$ to be transformed by some form of pre-processing to give a new set of variables $\widetilde{x}_1, \ldots, \widetilde{x}_{d'}$. These are then treated as the inputs to the neural network, whose outputs are denoted by $y_1, \ldots, y_c$.

1.4 The curse of dimensionality

There is another important reason why pre-processing can have a profound effect on the performance of a pattern recognition system. To see this let us return again to the character recognition problem, where we saw that increasing the number of features from 1 to 2 could lead to an improvement in performance. This suggests that we might use an ever larger number of such features, or even dispense with feature extraction altogether and simply use all 65 536 pixel values directly as inputs to our neural network. In practice, however, we often find that, beyond a certain point, adding new features can actually lead to a *reduction* in the performance of the classification system. In order to understand this important effect, consider the following very simple technique (not recommended in practice) for modelling non-linear mappings from a set of input variables x_i to an output variable y on the basis of a set of training data.

We begin by dividing each of the input variables into a number of intervals, so that the value of a variable can be specified approximately by saying in which interval it lies. This leads to a division of the whole input space into a large number of boxes or cells as indicated in Figure 1.5. Each of the training examples corresponds to a point in one of the cells, and carries an associated value of the output variable y. If we are given a new point in the input space, we can determine a corresponding value for y by finding which cell the point falls in, and then returning the average value of y for all of the training points which lie in that cell. By increasing the number of divisions along each axis we could increase the precision with which the input variables can be specified. There is, however, a major problem. If each input variable is divided into M divisions, then the total number of cells is M^d and this grows *exponentially* with the dimensionality of the input space. Since each cell must contain at least one data point, this implies that the quantity of training data needed to specify the mapping also grows exponentially. This phenomenon has been termed the *curse of dimensionality*

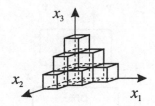

Figure 1.5. One way to specify a mapping from a d-dimensional space $x_1, \ldots, x_d$
to an output variable y is to divide the input space into a number of cells, as
indicated here for the case of $d = 3$, and to specify the value of y for each of
the cells. The major problem with this approach is that the number of cells,
and hence the number of example data points required, grows exponentially
with d, a phenomenon known as the 'curse of dimensionality'.

(Bellman, 1961). If we are forced to work with a limited quantity of data, as we
are in practice, then increasing the dimensionality of the space rapidly leads to
the point where the data is very sparse, in which case it provides a very poor
representation of the mapping.

Of course, the technique of dividing up the input space into cells is a particularly inefficient way to represent a multivariate non-linear function. In subsequent chapters we shall consider other approaches to this problem, based on
feed-forward neural networks, which are much less susceptible to the curse of
dimensionality. These techniques are able to exploit two important properties of
real data. First, the input variables are generally correlated in some way, so that
the data points do not fill out the entire input space but tend to be restricted to
a sub-space of lower dimensionality. This leads to the concept of *intrinsic dimensionality* which is discussed further in Section 8.6.1. Second, for most mappings
of practical interest, the value of the output variables will not change arbitrarily
from one region of input space to another, but will typically vary smoothly as
a function of the input variables. Thus, it is possible to infer the values of the
output variables at intermediate points, where no data is available, by a process
similar to interpolation.

Although the effects of dimensionality are generally not as severe as the example of Figure 1.5 might suggest, it remains true that, in many problems, reducing
the number of input variables can sometimes lead to improved performance for
a given data set, even though information is being discarded. The fixed quantity
of data is better able to specify the mapping in the lower-dimensional space, and
this more than compensates for the loss of information. In our simple character
recognition problem we could have considered all 65 536 pixel values as inputs
to our non-linear model. Such an approach, however, would be expected to give
extremely poor results as a consequence of the effects of dimensionality coupled
with a limited size of data set. As we shall discuss in Chapter 8, one of the important roles of pre-processing in many applications is to reduce the dimensionality

of the data before using it to train a neural network or other pattern recognition system.

1.5 Polynomial curve fitting

Many of the important issues concerning the application of neural networks can be introduced in the simpler context of polynomial curve fitting. Here the problem is to fit a polynomial to a set of N data points by the technique of minimizing an error function. Consider the Mth-order polynomial given by

$$y(x) = w_0 + w_1 x + \cdots + w_M x^M = \sum_{j=0}^{M} w_j x^j. \tag{1.2}$$

This can be regarded as a non-linear mapping which takes x as input and produces y as output. The precise form of the function $y(x)$ is determined by the values of the parameters $w_0, \ldots w_M$, which are analogous to the weights in a neural network. It is convenient to denote the set of parameters $(w_0, \ldots, w_M)$ by the vector $\mathbf{w}$. The polynomial can then be written as a functional mapping in the form $y = y(x; \mathbf{w})$ as was done for more general non-linear mappings in (1.1).

We shall label the data with the index $n = 1, \ldots, N$, so that each data point consists of a value of x, denoted by x^n, and a corresponding desired value for the output y, which we shall denote by t^n. These desired outputs are called *target* values in the neural network context. In order to find suitable values for the coefficients in the polynomial, it is convenient to consider the error between the desired output t^n, for a particular input x^n, and the corresponding value predicted by the polynomial function given by $y(x^n; \mathbf{w})$. Standard curve-fitting procedures involve minimizing the square of this error, summed over all data points, given by

$$E = \frac{1}{2} \sum_{n=1}^{N} \{y(x^n; \mathbf{w}) - t^n\}^2. \tag{1.3}$$

We can regard E as being a function of $\mathbf{w}$, and so the polynomial can be fitted to the data by choosing a value for $\mathbf{w}$, which we denote by $\mathbf{w}^*$, which minimizes E. Note that the polynomial (1.2) is a linear function of the parameters $\mathbf{w}$ and so (1.3) is a quadratic function of $\mathbf{w}$. This means that the minimum of E can be found in terms of the solution of a set of linear algebraic equations (Exercise 1.5). Functions which depend linearly on the adaptive parameters are called linear models, even though they may be non-linear functions of the original input variables. Many concepts which arise in the study of such models are also of direct relevance to the more complex non-linear neural networks considered in Chapters 4 and 5. We therefore present an extended discussion of linear models (in the guise of 'single-layer networks') in Chapter 3.

The minimization of an error function such as (1.3), which involves target values for the network outputs, is called *supervised learning* since for each input pattern the value of the desired output is specified. A second form of learning in neural networks, called *unsupervised learning*, does not involve the use of target data. Instead of learning an input–output mapping, the goal may be to model the probability distribution of the input data (as discussed at length in Chapter 2) or to discover clusters or other structure in the data. There is a third form of learning, called *reinforcement learning* (Hertz *et al.*, 1991) in which information is supplied as to whether the network outputs are good or bad, but again no actual desired values are given. This is mainly used for control applications, and will not be discussed further.

We have introduced the sum-of-squares error function from a heuristic viewpoint. Error functions play an important role in the use of neural networks, and the whole of Chapter 6 is devoted to a detailed discussion of their properties. There we shall see how the sum-of-squares error function can be derived from some general statistical principles, provided we make certain assumptions about the properties of the data. We shall also investigate other forms of error function which are appropriate when these assumptions are not valid.

We can illustrate the technique of polynomial curve fitting by generating synthetic data in a way which is intended to capture some of the basic properties of real data sets used in pattern recognition problems. Specifically, we generate training data from the function

$$h(x) = 0.5 + 0.4\sin(2\pi x) \tag{1.4}$$

by sampling the function $h(x)$ at equal intervals of x and then adding random noise with a Gaussian distribution (Section 2.1.1) having standard deviation $\sigma = 0.05$. Thus for each data point a new value for the noise contribution is chosen. A basic property of most data sets of interest in pattern recognition is that the data exhibits an underlying systematic aspect, represented in this case by the function $h(x)$, but is corrupted with random noise. The central goal in pattern recognition is to produce a system which makes good predictions for *new* data, in other words one which exhibits good generalization. In order to measure the generalization capabilities of the polynomial, we have generated a second data set called a *test set*, which is produced in the same way as the training set, but with new values for the noise component. This reflects the basic assumption that the data on which we wish to use the pattern recognition system is produced by the same underlying mechanism as the training data. As we shall discuss at length in Chapter 9, the best generalization to new data is obtained when the mapping represents the underlying systematic aspects of the data, rather capturing the specific details (i.e. the noise contribution) of the particular training set. We will therefore be interested in seeing how close the polynomial $y(x)$ is to the function $h(x)$.

Figure 1.6 shows the 11 points from the training set, as well as the function

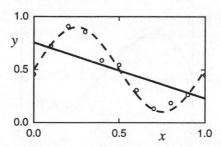

Figure 1.6. An example of a set of 11 data points obtained by sampling the function $h(x)$, defined by (1.4), at equal intervals of x and adding random noise. The dashed curve shows the function $h(x)$, while the solid curve shows the rather poor approximation obtained with a linear polynomial, corresponding to $M = 1$ in (1.2).

$h(x)$ from (1.4), together with the result of fitting a linear polynomial, given by (1.2) with $M = 1$. As can be seen, this polynomial gives a poor representation of $h(x)$, as a consequence of its limited flexibility. We can obtain a better fit by increasing the order of the polynomial, since this increases the number of *degrees of freedom* (i.e. the number of free parameters) in the function, which gives it greater flexibility. Figure 1.7 shows the result of fitting a cubic polynomial ($M = 3$) which gives a much better approximation to $h(x)$. If, however, we increase the order of the polynomial too far, then the approximation to the underlying function actually gets worse. Figure 1.8 shows the result of fitting a 10th-order polynomial ($M = 10$). This is now able to achieve a perfect fit to the training data, since a 10th-order polynomial has 11 free parameters, and there are 11 data points. However, the polynomial has fitted the data by developing some dramatic oscillations. Such functions are said to be *over-fitted* to the data. As a consequence, this function gives a poor representation of $h(x)$.

1.5.1 *Generalization*

In order to assess the capability of the polynomial to generalize to new data, it is convenient to consider the root-mean-square (RMS) error given by

$$E^{\mathrm{RMS}} = \sqrt{\frac{1}{N} \sum_{n=1}^{N} \{y(x^n; \mathbf{w}^*) - t^n\}^2} \qquad (1.5)$$

where $\mathbf{w}^*$ represents the vector of coefficients corresponding to the minimum of the error function, so that $y(x; \mathbf{w}^*)$ represents the fitted polynomial. For the purpose of evaluating the effectiveness of the polynomial at predicting new data, this is a more convenient quantity to consider than the original sum-of-squares error (1.3) since the strong dependence on the number of data points has been

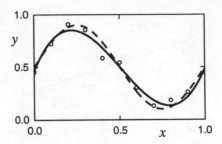

Figure 1.7. This shows the same data set as in Figure 1.6, but this time fitted by a cubic ($M = 3$) polynomial, showing the significantly improved approximation to $h(x)$ achieved by this more flexible function.

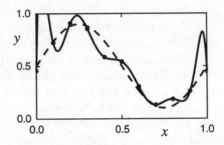

Figure 1.8. The result of fitting the same data set as in Figure 1.6 using a 10th-order ($M = 10$) polynomial. This gives a perfect fit to the training data, but at the expense of a function which has large oscillations, and which therefore gives a poorer representation of the generator function $h(x)$ than did the cubic polynomial of Figure 1.7.

removed. Figure 1.9 shows a plot of E^{RMS} for both the training data set and the test data set, as a function of the order M of the polynomial. We see that the training set error decreases steadily as the order of the polynomial increases. The test set error, however, reaches a minimum at $M = 3$, and thereafter increases as the order of the polynomial is increased.

The ability of the polynomial to generalize to new data (i.e. to the test set) therefore reaches an optimum value for a polynomial of a particular degree of complexity. Generalization is treated at greater length in Chapter 9, where we discuss the trade-off between the *bias* and the *variance* of a model. A model which has too little flexibility, such as the linear polynomial of Figure 1.6, has a high bias, while a model which has too much flexibility, such as the 10th-order polynomial of Figure 1.8, has a high variance. The point of best generalization is determined by the trade-off between these two competing properties, and occurs

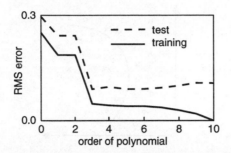

Figure 1.9. Plots of the RMS error (1.5) as a function of the order of the polynomial for both training and test sets, for the example problem considered in the previous three figures. The error with respect to the training set decreases monotonically with M, while the error in making predictions for new data (as measured by the test set) shows a minimum at $M = 3$.

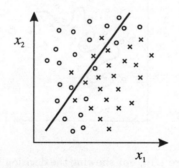

Figure 1.10. A schematic example of vectors in two dimensions (x_1, x_2) belonging to two classes shown by crosses and circles. The solid curve shows the decision boundary of a simple model which gives relatively poor separation of the two classes.

when the number of degrees of freedom in the model is relatively small compared to the size of the data set (4 free parameters for $M = 3$, compared with 11 data points in this example).

The problem of over-fitting is one which also arises in classification tasks. Figures 1.10–1.12 show a succession of decision boundaries for a schematic example of a classification problem involving two classes, and two input variables. As the complexity of the model is increased, so the decision boundary can become more complex and hence give a better fit to the training data. For many applications, however, the best generalization performance is again obtained from a model with an intermediate level of flexibility.

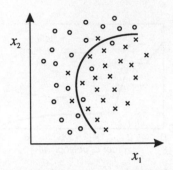

Figure 1.11. As in Figure 1.10, but showing the decision boundary corresponding to a more flexible model, which gives better separation of the training data.

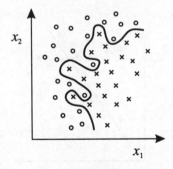

Figure 1.12. As in Figure 1.10, but showing the decision boundary corresponding to a highly flexible model which is able to achieve perfect separation of the training data. In many applications the distributions of data from different classes overlap, and the best generalization performance is then achieved by a model with intermediate complexity, corresponding to the decision boundary in Figure 1.11.

1.6 Model complexity

Using an example of polynomial curve fitting, we have seen that the best generalization performance is achieved by a model whose complexity (measured here by the order of the polynomial) is neither too small nor too large. The problem of finding the optimal complexity for a model provides an example of *Occam's razor*, named after William of Occam (1285–1349). This is the principle that we should prefer simpler models to more complex models, and that this preference should be traded off against the extent to which the models fit the data. Thus a highly complex model which fits the data extremely well (such as the 10th-order polynomial above) actually gives a poorer representation of the systematic aspects of the data than would a simpler model (such as the 3rd-order polynomial). A model which is too simple, however, as in the 1st-order polynomial, is also not prefered as it gives too poor a fit to the data. The same considerations apply to neural network models, where again we can control the complexity of the model by controlling the number of free parameters which it possesses.

An alternative approach to optimizing the generalization performance of a model is to control its *effective complexity*. This can be achieved by considering a model with many adjustable parameters, and then altering the training procedure by adding a penalty term Ω to the error function. The total error then becomes

$$\widetilde{E} = E + \nu\Omega \tag{1.6}$$

where Ω is called a *regularization* term. The value of Ω depends on the mapping function $y(x)$, and if the functional form of Ω is chosen appropriately, it can be used to control over-fitting. For example, if we examine the function represented by the 10th-order polynomial in Figure 1.8, we see that it has large oscillations, and hence the function $y(x)$ has regions of large curvature. We might therefore choose a regularization function which is large for functions with large values of the second derivative, such as

$$\Omega = \frac{1}{2} \int \left(\frac{d^2 y}{dx^2} \right)^2 dx. \tag{1.7}$$

The parameter ν in (1.6) controls the extent to which the regularization term influences the form of the solution, and hence controls the effective complexity of the model. Regularization is discussed in greater detail in Sections 5.4, 9.2 and 10.1.5.

We have seen that, for a fixed size of data set, it is important to achieve the optimum level of complexity for the model in order to minimize the combination of bias and variance. By using a sequence of successively larger data sets, however, and a corresponding set of models with successively greater complexity, it is possible in principle to reduce both bias and variance simultaneously and hence to improve the generalization performance of the network. The ultimate generalization achievable will be limited by the intrinsic noise on the data.

1.7 Multivariate non-linear functions

The role of neural networks, as we have already indicated, is to provide general parametrized non-linear mappings between a set of input variables and a set of output variables. Polynomials provide such mappings for the case of one input variable and one output variable. Provided we have a sufficiently large number of terms in the polynomial, we can approximate any reasonable function to arbitrary accuracy. This suggests that we could simply extend the concept of a polynomial to higher dimensions. Thus, for d input variables, and again one output variable, we could consider higher-order polynomials up to, say, order 3, given by

$$y = w_0 + \sum_{i_1=1}^{d} w_{i_1} x_{i_1} + \sum_{i_1=1}^{d} \sum_{i_2=1}^{d} w_{i_1 i_2} x_{i_1} x_{i_2} + \sum_{i_1=1}^{d} \sum_{i_2=1}^{d} \sum_{i_3=1}^{d} w_{i_1 i_2 i_3} x_{i_1} x_{i_2} x_{i_3}. \quad (1.8)$$

For an Mth-order polynomial of this kind, the number of independent adjustable parameters would grow like d^M (Exercise 1.8). While this now has a power law dependence on d, rather than the exponential dependence of the model represented in Figure 1.5, it still represents a dramatic growth in the number of degrees of freedom of the model as the dimensionality of the input space increases. For medium to large applications, such a model would need huge quantities of training data in order to ensure that the adaptive parameters (the coefficients in the polynomial) were well determined.

There are in fact many different ways in which to represent general non-linear mappings between multidimensional spaces. The importance of neural networks, and similar techniques, lies in the way in which they deal with the problem of scaling with dimensionality. Generally, these models represent non-linear functions of many variables in terms of superpositions of non-linear functions of a single variable, which we might call 'hidden functions' (also called hidden units). The key point is that the hidden functions are themselves adapted to the data as part of the training process, and so the number of such functions only needs to grow as the complexity of the problem itself grows, and not simply as the dimensionality grows. The number of free parameters in such models, for a given number of hidden functions, typically only grows linearly, or quadratically, with the dimensionality of the input space, as compared with the d^M growth for a general Mth-order polynomial. We devote Chapters 4 and 5 to a study of two of the most popular such models, known respectively as the *multi-layer perceptron* and the *radial basis function* network.

Barron (1993) has studied the way in which the residual sum-of-squares error decreases as the number of parameters in a model is increased. For neural networks he showed that this error falls as $\mathcal{O}(1/M)$ where M is the number of hidden units in the network, irrespective of the number of input variables. By contrast, the error only decreases as $\mathcal{O}(1/M^{2/d})$, where d is the dimensionality of input space, for polynomials or indeed any other series expansion in which it is the coefficients of linear combinations of fixed functions which are adapted. We see that neural networks therefore offer a dramatic advantage for function approximation in spaces of many dimensions.

The price which we pay for this efficient scaling with dimensionality is that the network functions are now necessarily non-linear functions of the adaptive parameters. Unlike polynomial curve fitting, the procedure for determining the values of the parameters is now a problem in non-linear optimization, which is computationally intensive and which presents a number of additional complications, such as the presence of multiple minima in the error function. Chapter 7 is therefore concerned with the important topic of finding efficient algorithms for performing this optimization.

1.8 Bayes' theorem

In the remainder of this chapter we introduce some of the basic concepts of the statistical approach to pattern recognition, in preparation for later chapters. For readers interested in a more detailed account of these topics there are many standard textbooks which specialize in this area, including Duda and Hart (1973), Hand (1981), Devijver and Kittler (1982), and Fukunaga (1990). Rather than present these concepts in an abstract fashion, we let them unfold naturally in the context of the character recognition problem introduced at the start of this chapter.

We begin by supposing that we wish to classify a new character but as yet we have made no measurements on the image of that character. The goal is to classify the character in such a way as to minimize the probability of misclassification. If we had collected a large number of examples of the characters, we could find the fractions which belong in each of the two classes. We formalize this by introducing the *prior* probabilities $P(C_k)$ of an image belonging to each of the classes C_k. These correspond to the fractions of characters in each class, in the limit of an infinite number of observations. Thus, if the letter 'a' occurs three times as often as the letter 'b', we have $P(C_1) = 0.75$ and $P(C_2) = 0.25$.

If we were forced to classify a new character without being allowed to see the corresponding image, then the best we can do is to assign it to the class having the higher prior probability. That is, we assign the image to class C_1 if $P(C_1) > P(C_2)$, and to class C_2 otherwise. In the character recognition example, this means we would always classify a new character as 'a'. This procedure minimizes the probability of misclassification, even though we know that some of the images will correspond to the character 'b'.

Now suppose that we have measured the value of the feature variable $\tilde{x}_1$ for the image. It is clear from Figure 1.2 that this gives us further information on which to base our classification decision, and we seek a formalism which allows this information to be combined with the prior probabilities which we already possess. To begin with, we shall suppose that $\tilde{x}_1$ is assigned to one of a discrete set of values $\{X^l\}$, as was done for the histogram plot of Figure 1.2. We can represent this information in a slightly different way, as an array of cells, as in Figure 1.13. The *joint* probability $P(C_k, X^l)$ is defined to be the probability that the image has the feature value X^l *and* belongs to class C_k. This corresponds to the fraction of the images which fall into a particular cell (in row C_k and column X^l) in the limit of an infinite number of images. The prior probabilities $P(C_k)$ introduced earlier correspond to the total fraction of images in the corresponding row of the array.

Next we introduce the *conditional* probability $P(X^l|C_k)$ which specifies the probability that the observation falls in column X^l of the array *given* that it

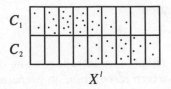

Figure 1.13. Data from the histogram of Figure 1.2 represented as an array. The feature variable $\widetilde{x}_1$ can take one of the discrete values X^l and each image is assigned to one of the two classes $\mathcal{C}_1$ or $\mathcal{C}_2$. The number of dots in each cell represents the number of images having the corresponding value of X^l and the corresponding class label. Various probabilities are defined in the text in terms of the fraction of points falling in different regions of the array.

belongs to class $\mathcal{C}_k$. It is given by the fraction of the images in row $\mathcal{C}_k$ which fall in cell X^l (in the limit of an infinite number of images).

We now note that the fraction of the total number of images which fall into cell $(\mathcal{C}_k, X^l)$ is given by the fraction of the number of images in row $\mathcal{C}_k$ which fall in cell $(\mathcal{C}_k, X^l)$ times the fraction of the total number of images which fall in row $\mathcal{C}_k$. This is equivalent to writing the joint probability in the form

$$P(\mathcal{C}_k, X^l) = P(X^l|\mathcal{C}_k)P(\mathcal{C}_k). \tag{1.9}$$

By a similar argument, we can see that the joint probability can also be written in the form

$$P(\mathcal{C}_k, X^l) = P(\mathcal{C}_k|X^l)P(X^l) \tag{1.10}$$

where $P(\mathcal{C}_k|X^l)$ is the probability that the class is $\mathcal{C}_k$ *given* that the measured value of $\widetilde{x}_1$ falls in the cell X^l. The quantity $P(X^l)$ is the probability of observing a value X^l with respect to the whole data set, irrespective of the class membership, and is therefore given by the fraction of the total number of images which fall into column X^l. The two expressions for the joint probabilities in (1.9) and (1.10) must, however, be equal. Thus, we can write

$$P(\mathcal{C}_k|X^l) = \frac{P(X^l|\mathcal{C}_k)P(\mathcal{C}_k)}{P(X^l)}. \tag{1.11}$$

This expression is referred to as *Bayes' theorem* (after the Revd. Thomas Bayes, 1702–1761). The quantity on the left-hand side of (1.11) is called the *posterior* probability, since it gives the probability that the class is $\mathcal{C}_k$ after we have made a measurement of $\widetilde{x}_1$. Bayes' theorem allows the posterior probability to be expressed in terms of the prior probability $P(\mathcal{C}_k)$, together with the quantity $P(X^l|\mathcal{C}_k)$ which is called the *class-conditional* probability of X^l for class $\mathcal{C}_k$.

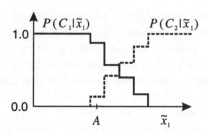

Figure 1.14. Histogram plot of posterior probabilities, corresponding to the histogram of observations in Figure 1.2, for prior probabilities $P(\mathcal{C}_1) = 0.6$ and $P(\mathcal{C}_2) = 0.4$.

The denominator in Bayes' theorem, $P(X^l)$, plays the role of a normalization factor, and ensures that the posterior probabilities sum to unity. As we shall see shortly, the posterior probability is a quantity of central interest since it allows us to make optimal decisions regarding the class membership of new data. In particular, assigning a new image to the class having the largest posterior probability minimizes the probability of misclassification of that image.

The denominator in Bayes' theorem can be expressed in terms of the prior probabilities and the class-conditional probabilities. To do this we note that any new measurement must be assigned to one of the two classes $\mathcal{C}_1$ or $\mathcal{C}_2$. Thus

$$P(\mathcal{C}_1|X^l) + P(\mathcal{C}_2|X^l) = 1. \tag{1.12}$$

Substituting (1.11) into (1.12) we obtain

$$P(X^l) = P(X^l|\mathcal{C}_1)P(\mathcal{C}_1) + P(X^l|\mathcal{C}_2)P(\mathcal{C}_2). \tag{1.13}$$

1.8.1 Inference and decision

The importance of Bayes' theorem lies in the fact that it re-expresses the posterior probabilities in terms of quantities which are often much easier to calculate. We have seen in our character recognition example that the prior probabilities can be estimated from the proportions of the training data which fall into each of the classes. Similarly, the class-conditional probabilities $P(X^l|\mathcal{C}_k)$ could be estimated from the histograms of Figure 1.2. From these quantities we can also find the normalization factor in Bayes' theorem, by use of (1.13), and hence evaluate the posterior probabilities. Figure 1.14 shows the histograms of posterior probability, corresponding to the class-conditional probabilities in Figure 1.2, for prior probabilities $P(\mathcal{C}_1) = 0.6$ and $P(\mathcal{C}_2) = 0.4$.

For a new image, having feature value X^l, the probability of misclassification is minimized if we assign the image to the class $\mathcal{C}_k$ for which the posterior probability $P(\mathcal{C}_k|X^l)$ is largest, as we shall demonstrate in Section 1.9. Thus, if we observe a new image with feature value A, as shown in Figure 1.14, it should be assigned to class $\mathcal{C}_1$.

In some cases the prior probabilities can be estimated directly from the training data itself. However, it sometimes happens (often by design) that the fractions of examples from different classes in the training data set differ from the probabilities expected when our trained pattern recognition system is applied to new data. As an example, consider the problem of designing a system to distinguish between normal tissue (class $\mathcal{C}_1$) and tumours (class $\mathcal{C}_2$) on medical X-ray images, for use in mass screening. From medical statistics we may know that, in the general population, the probability of observing a tumour is 1% and so we should use prior probabilities of $P(\mathcal{C}_1) = 0.99$ and $P(\mathcal{C}_2) = 0.01$. In collecting a training data set, however, we might choose to include equal numbers of examples from both classes to ensure that we get a reasonable number of representatives of tumours, without having to use a huge number of images in total. We can still use the images in our data set to estimate the class-conditional probabilities $P(X^l|\mathcal{C}_k)$ and then use Bayes' theorem to calculate the correct posterior probabilities using the known prior probabilities. Note that in practice these prior probabilities could be obtained from medical statistics without the need to collect images or determine their class. In this example, failure to take correct account of the prior probabilities would lead to significantly sub-optimal results.

One approach to statistical pattern recognition is therefore to evaluate the class-conditional probabilities and the prior probabilities separately and then combine them using Bayes' theorem to give posterior probabilities, which can then be used to classify new examples. An alternative approach is to estimate the posterior probability functions directly. As we shall see in Chapter 6, the outputs of a neural network can be interpreted as (approximations to) posterior probabilities, provided the error function used to train the network is chosen appropriately.

It is important to distinguish between two separate stages in the classification process. The first is *inference* whereby data is used to determine values for the posterior probabilities. These are then used in the second stage which is *decision making* in which those probabilities are used to make decisions such as assigning a new data point to one of the possible classes. So far we have based classification decisions on the goal of minimizing the probability of misclassification. In Section 1.10 we shall discuss more general decision criteria, and introduce the concept of a loss matrix.

As we have indicated, the minimum probability of misclassification is obtained by assigning each new observation to the class for which the posterior probability is largest. In the literature this is sometimes referred to as the "Bayes' rule". We avoid this terminology, however, since the role of Bayes' theorem is in the evaluation of posterior probabilities, and this is quite distinct from any subsequent decision procedure.

1.8.2 *Bayesian versus frequentist statistics*

Until now we have defined probabilities in terms of fractions of a set of observations in the limit where the number of observations tends to infinity. Such a view of probabilities is known as *frequentist*. There is, however, a totally different way of viewing the same formalism. Consider, for example, the problem of predicting the winner of a bicycle race. The 'probability' of a particular cyclist winning does not sit naturally within the frequentist framework since the race will take place only once, and so it will not be possible to perform a large number of trials. Nevertheless, it would not seem unusual to hear someone say that a particular cyclist has a 30% probability of winning. In this case we are using the term 'probability' to express a subjective 'degree of belief' in a particular outcome.

Suppose we try to encode these subjective beliefs as real numbers. In a key paper, Cox (1946) showed that, provided we impose some simple, and very natural, consistency requirements, we are led uniquely to the Bayesian formalism. If we use a value of 1 to denote complete certainty that an event will occur, and 0 to denote complete certainty that the event will not occur (with intermediate values representing corresponding degrees of belief), then these real values behave exactly like conventional probabilities. Bayes' theorem then provides us with a precise quantitative prescription for updating these probabilities when we are presented with new data. The prior probability represents our degree of belief before the data arrives. After we observe the data, we can use Bayes' theorem to convert this prior probability into a posterior probability. Jaynes (1986) gives an enlightening review of the fascinating, and sometimes controversial, history of Bayesian statistics.

1.8.3 *Probability densities*

So far we have treated the feature variable $\tilde{x}_1$ by discretizing it into a finite set of values. In many applications it will be more appropriate to regard the feature variables as continuous. Probabilities for discrete variables are then replaced by probability *densities*. From now on we shall omit the $\tilde{\ }$ symbol and suppose that the variables x_i now refer to input quantities after any pre-processing and feature extraction have been performed.

A probability density function $p(x)$ specifies that the probability of the variable x lying in the interval between any two points $x = a$ and $x = b$ is given by

$$P(x \in [a, b]) = \int_a^b p(x)\, dx. \tag{1.14}$$

The function $p(x)$ is normalized so that $P(x \in [a, b]) = 1$ if the interval $[a, b]$ corresponds to the whole of x-space. Note that we use upper-case letters for probabilities and lower-case letters for probability densities. For continuous variables, the class-conditional probabilities introduced above become class-conditional probability density functions, which we write in the form $p(x|\mathcal{C}_k)$. The histograms plotted in Figure 1.2 effectively provide unnormalized, discretized estimates of the two functions $p(x|\mathcal{C}_1)$ and $p(x|\mathcal{C}_2)$.

If there are d variables $x_1, \ldots, x_d$, we may group them into a vector $\mathbf{x} = (x_1, \ldots, x_d)^{\mathrm{T}}$ corresponding to a point in a d-dimensional space. The distribution of values of $\mathbf{x}$ can be described by probability density function $p(\mathbf{x})$, such that the probability of $\mathbf{x}$ lying in a region $\mathcal{R}$ of $\mathbf{x}$-space is given by

$$P(\mathbf{x} \in \mathcal{R}) = \int_{\mathcal{R}} p(\mathbf{x}) \, d\mathbf{x}. \tag{1.15}$$

We define the *expectation*, or *expected* (i.e. average) value, of a function $Q(\mathbf{x})$ with respect to a probability density $p(\mathbf{x})$ to be

$$\mathcal{E}[Q] \equiv \int Q(\mathbf{x}) p(\mathbf{x}) \, d\mathbf{x} \tag{1.16}$$

where the integral is over the whole of $\mathbf{x}$-space. For a finite set of data points $\mathbf{x}^1, \ldots, \mathbf{x}^N$, drawn from the distribution $p(\mathbf{x})$, the expectation can be approximated by the average over the data points

$$\mathcal{E}[Q] \equiv \int Q(\mathbf{x}) p(\mathbf{x}) \, d\mathbf{x} \simeq \frac{1}{N} \sum_{n=1}^{N} Q(\mathbf{x}^n). \tag{1.17}$$

1.8.4 *Bayes' theorem in general*

For continuous variables the prior probabilities can be combined with the class-conditional densities to give the posterior probabilities $P(\mathcal{C}_k|x)$ using Bayes' theorem, which can now be written in the form

$$P(\mathcal{C}_k|x) = \frac{p(x|\mathcal{C}_k)P(\mathcal{C}_k)}{p(x)}. \tag{1.18}$$

Here $p(x)$ is the *unconditional* density function, that is the density function for x irrespective of the class, and is given by

$$p(x) = p(x|\mathcal{C}_1)P(\mathcal{C}_1) + p(x|\mathcal{C}_2)P(\mathcal{C}_2). \tag{1.19}$$

Again this plays the role of a normalizing factor in (1.18) and ensures that the posterior probabilities sum to 1

$$P(\mathcal{C}_1|x) + P(\mathcal{C}_2|x) = 1 \tag{1.20}$$

as can be verified by substituting (1.18) into (1.20) and using (1.19).

A large part of Chapter 2 is devoted to the problem of modelling probability density functions on the basis of a set of example data. One application for such techniques is for estimating class-conditional densities for subsequent use in Bayes' theorem to find posterior probabilities.

In most practical pattern classification problems it is necessary to use more than one feature variable. We may also wish to consider more than two possible classes, so that in our character recognition problem we might consider more than two characters. For c different classes $C_1, \ldots, C_c$, and for a continuous feature vector $\mathbf{x}$, we can write Bayes' theorem in the form

$$P(C_k|\mathbf{x}) = \frac{p(\mathbf{x}|C_k)P(C_k)}{p(\mathbf{x})} \tag{1.21}$$

where the unconditional density $p(\mathbf{x})$ is given by

$$p(\mathbf{x}) = \sum_{k=1}^{c} p(\mathbf{x}|C_k)P(C_k) \tag{1.22}$$

which ensures that the posterior probabilities sum to unity

$$\sum_{k=1}^{c} P(C_k|\mathbf{x}) = 1. \tag{1.23}$$

In practice, we might choose to model the class-conditional densities $p(\mathbf{x}|C_k)$ by parametrized functional forms. When viewed as functions of the parameters they are referred to as *likelihood* functions, for the observed value of $\mathbf{x}$. Bayes' theorem can therefore be summarized in the form

$$\text{posterior} = \frac{\text{likelihood} \times \text{prior}}{\text{normalization factor}}. \tag{1.24}$$

1.9 Decision boundaries

The posterior probability $P(C_k|\mathbf{x})$ gives the probability of the pattern belonging to class C_k once we have observed the feature vector $\mathbf{x}$. The probability of mis-classification is minimized by selecting the class C_k having the largest posterior probability, so that a feature vector $\mathbf{x}$ is assigned to class C_k if

$$P(C_k|\mathbf{x}) > P(C_j|\mathbf{x}) \qquad \text{for all } j \neq k. \tag{1.25}$$

We shall examine the justification for this rule shortly. Since the unconditional density $p(\mathbf{x})$ is independent of the class, it may be dropped from the Bayes'

formula for the purposes of comparing posterior probabilities. Thus, we can use
(1.21) to write the criterion (1.25) in the form

$$p(\mathbf{x}|\mathcal{C}_k)P(\mathcal{C}_k) > p(\mathbf{x}|\mathcal{C}_j)P(\mathcal{C}_j) \qquad \text{for all } j \neq k. \tag{1.26}$$

A pattern classifier provides a rule for assigning each point of feature space
to one of c classes. We can therefore regard the feature space as being divided
up into c *decision regions* $\mathcal{R}_1, \ldots, \mathcal{R}_c$ such that a point falling in region $\mathcal{R}_k$ is
assigned to class $\mathcal{C}_k$. Note that each of these regions need not be contiguous,
but may itself be divided into several disjoint regions all of which are associated
with the same class. The boundaries between these regions are known as *decision
surfaces* or *decision boundaries*.

In order to find the optimal criterion for placement of decision boundaries,
consider again the case of a one-dimensional feature space x and two classes
$\mathcal{C}_1$ and $\mathcal{C}_2$. We seek a decision boundary which minimizes the probability of
misclassification, as illustrated in Figure 1.15. A misclassification error will occur
if we assign a new pattern to class $\mathcal{C}_1$ when in fact it belongs to class $\mathcal{C}_2$, or vice
versa. We can calculate the total probability of an error of either kind by writing
(Duda and Hart, 1973)

$$P(\text{error}) = P(x \in \mathcal{R}_2, \mathcal{C}_1) + P(x \in \mathcal{R}_1, \mathcal{C}_2)$$

$$= P(x \in \mathcal{R}_2|\mathcal{C}_1)P(\mathcal{C}_1) + P(x \in \mathcal{R}_1|\mathcal{C}_2)P(\mathcal{C}_2)$$

$$= \int_{\mathcal{R}_2} p(x|\mathcal{C}_1)P(\mathcal{C}_1)\, dx + \int_{\mathcal{R}_1} p(x|\mathcal{C}_2)P(\mathcal{C}_2)\, dx \tag{1.27}$$

where $P(x \in \mathcal{R}_1, \mathcal{C}_2)$ is the joint probability of x being assigned to class $\mathcal{C}_1$ and
the true class being $\mathcal{C}_2$. Thus, if $p(x|\mathcal{C}_1)P(\mathcal{C}_1) > p(x|\mathcal{C}_2)P(\mathcal{C}_2)$ for a given x, we
should choose the regions $\mathcal{R}_1$ and $\mathcal{R}_2$ such that x is in $\mathcal{R}_1$, since this gives a
smaller contribution to the error. We recognise this as the decision rule given by
(1.26) for minimizing the probability of misclassification. The same result can be
seen graphically in Figure 1.15, in which misclassification errors arise from the
shaded region. By choosing the decision boundary to coincide with the value of x
at which the two distributions cross (shown by the arrow) we minimize the area
of the shaded region and hence minimize the probability of misclassification. This
corresponds to classifying each new pattern x using (1.26), which is equivalent
to assigning each pattern to the class having the largest posterior probability.

A similar justification for this decision rule may be given for the general case
of c classes and d-dimensional feature vectors. In this case it is easier to calculate
the probability of a new pattern being correctly classified (Duda and Hart, 1973)

$$P(\text{correct}) = \sum_{k=1}^{c} P(\mathbf{x} \in \mathcal{R}_k, \mathcal{C}_k)$$

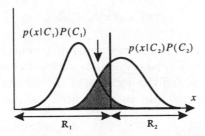

Figure 1.15. Schematic illustration of the joint probability densities, given by $p(x, C_k) = p(x|C_k)P(C_k)$, as a function of a feature value x, for two classes C_1 and C_2. If the vertical line is used as the decision boundary then the classification errors arise from the shaded region. By placing the decision boundary at the point where the two probability density curves cross (shown by the arrow), the probability of misclassification is minimized.

$$= \sum_{k=1}^{c} P(\mathbf{x} \in \mathcal{R}_k | C_k) P(C_k)$$

$$= \sum_{k=1}^{c} \int_{\mathcal{R}_k} p(\mathbf{x}|C_k) P(C_k) \, d\mathbf{x}. \tag{1.28}$$

This probability is maximized by choosing the $\{\mathcal{R}_k\}$ such that each $\mathbf{x}$ is assigned to the class for which the integrand is a maximum, which is equivalent to (1.26).

1.9.1 *Discriminant functions*

Although we have focused on probability distribution functions, the decision on class membership in our classifiers has been based solely on the relative sizes of the probabilities. This observation allows us to reformulate the classification process in terms of a set of *discriminant functions* $y_1(\mathbf{x}), \ldots, y_c(\mathbf{x})$ such that an input vector $\mathbf{x}$ is assigned to class C_k if

$$y_k(\mathbf{x}) > y_j(\mathbf{x}) \qquad \text{for all } j \neq k. \tag{1.29}$$

The decision rule for minimizing the probability of misclassification may easily be cast in terms of discriminant functions, simply by choosing

$$y_k(\mathbf{x}) = P(C_k|\mathbf{x}). \tag{1.30}$$

If we use Bayes' theorem, and note that the unconditional density $p(\mathbf{x})$ in the denominator does not depend on the class label C_k, and therefore does not affect the classification decision, we can write an equivalent discriminant function in the form

$$y_k(\mathbf{x}) = p(\mathbf{x}|\mathcal{C}_k)P(\mathcal{C}_k). \tag{1.31}$$

Since it is only the relative magnitudes of the discriminant functions which are important in determining the class, we can replace $y_k(\mathbf{x})$ by $g(y_k(\mathbf{x}))$, where $g(\cdot)$ is any monotonic function, and the decisions of the classifier will not be affected. By taking logarithms for example, we could write our discriminant functions in the form

$$y_k(\mathbf{x}) = \ln p(\mathbf{x}|\mathcal{C}_k) + \ln P(\mathcal{C}_k). \tag{1.32}$$

In general the decision boundaries are given by the regions where the discriminant functions are equal, so that if $\mathcal{R}_k$ and $\mathcal{R}_j$ are contiguous then the decision boundary separating them is given by

$$y_k(\mathbf{x}) = y_j(\mathbf{x}). \tag{1.33}$$

The locations of the decision boundaries are therefore unaffected by monotonic transformations of the discriminant functions.

Discriminant functions for two-class decision problems are traditionally written in a slightly different form. Instead of using two discriminant functions $y_1(\mathbf{x})$ and $y_2(\mathbf{x})$, we introduce a single discriminant function

$$y(\mathbf{x}) = y_1(\mathbf{x}) - y_2(\mathbf{x}) \tag{1.34}$$

and we now use the rule that $\mathbf{x}$ is assigned to class $\mathcal{C}_1$ if $y(\mathbf{x}) > 0$ and to class $\mathcal{C}_2$ if $y(\mathbf{x}) < 0$. From the remarks above it follows that we can use several forms for $y(\mathbf{x})$ including

$$y(\mathbf{x}) = P(\mathcal{C}_1|\mathbf{x}) - P(\mathcal{C}_2|\mathbf{x}) \tag{1.35}$$

or alternatively

$$y(\mathbf{x}) = \ln \frac{p(\mathbf{x}|\mathcal{C}_1)}{p(\mathbf{x}|\mathcal{C}_2)} + \ln \frac{P(\mathcal{C}_1)}{P(\mathcal{C}_2)}. \tag{1.36}$$

It may not appear that we have gained a great deal by introducing discriminant functions, but as we shall see it is often possible to determine suitable discriminant functions from our training data without having to go through the intermediate step of probability density estimation. However, by relating the discriminant functions to the probabilities, we retain the link to the optimal criteria of decision theory introduced above. There are also important links between discriminant functions and neural networks, and these will be explored in subsequent chapters.

1.10 Minimizing risk

So far we have based our classification decisions on the desire to minimize the probability of misclassifying a new pattern. In many applications this may not be the most appropriate criterion. Consider for instance the medical screening problem discussed on page 20. There may be much more serious consequences if we classify an image of a tumour as normal than if we classify a normal image as that of a tumour. Such effects may easily be taken into account as follows.

We define a *loss matrix* with elements L_{kj} specifying the penalty associated with assigning a pattern to class $\mathcal{C}_j$ when in fact it belongs to class $\mathcal{C}_k$. Consider all the patterns $\mathbf{x}$ which belong to class $\mathcal{C}_k$. Then the *expected* (i.e. average) loss for those patterns is given by

$$R_k = \sum_{j=1}^{c} L_{kj} \int_{\mathcal{R}_j} p(\mathbf{x}|\mathcal{C}_k) \, d\mathbf{x}. \tag{1.37}$$

Thus, the overall expected loss, or *risk*, for patterns from all classes is

$$R = \sum_{k=1}^{c} R_k P(\mathcal{C}_k) \tag{1.38}$$

$$= \sum_{j=1}^{c} \int_{\mathcal{R}_j} \left\{ \sum_{k=1}^{c} L_{kj} p(\mathbf{x}|\mathcal{C}_k) P(\mathcal{C}_k) \right\} d\mathbf{x}.$$

This risk is minimized if the integrand is minimized at each point $\mathbf{x}$, that is if the regions $\mathcal{R}_j$ are chosen such that $\mathbf{x} \in \mathcal{R}_j$ when

$$\sum_{k=1}^{c} L_{kj} p(\mathbf{x}|\mathcal{C}_k) P(\mathcal{C}_k) < \sum_{k=1}^{c} L_{ki} p(\mathbf{x}|\mathcal{C}_k) P(\mathcal{C}_k) \qquad \text{for all } i \neq j \tag{1.39}$$

which represents a generalization of the usual decision rule for minimizing the probability of misclassification. Note that, if we assign a loss of 1 if the pattern is placed in the wrong class, and a loss of 0 if it is placed in the correct class, so that $L_{kj} = 1 - \delta_{kj}$ (where δ_{kj} is the Kronecker delta symbol defined on page xiii), then (1.39) reduces to the decision rule for minimizing the probability of misclassification, given by (1.26). In an application such as the medical image classification problem, the values of the coefficients L_{kj} would probably be chosen by hand, based on the views of experienced medical staff. For other applications, in finance for example, it may be possible to choose values for the L_{kj} in a more systematic fashion since the risks can be more easily quantified.

1.10.1 *Rejection thresholds*

In general we expect most of the misclassification errors to occur in those regions of x-space where the largest of the posterior probabilities is relatively low, since there is then a strong overlap between different classes. In some applications it may be better not to make a classification decision in such cases. This is sometimes called the reject option. For the medical classification problem for example, it may be better not to rely on an automatic classification system in doubtful cases, but to have these classified instead by a human expert. We then arrive at the following procedure

$$
\text{if}\quad \max_k P(\mathcal{C}_k|\mathbf{x}) \quad
\begin{cases}
\geq \theta, & \text{then classify } \mathbf{x} \\
< \theta, & \text{then reject } \mathbf{x}
\end{cases}
\tag{1.40}
$$

where θ is a threshold in the range $(0, 1)$. The larger the value of θ, the fewer points will be classified. One way in which the reject option can be used is to to design a relatively simple but fast classifier system to cover the bulk of the feature space, while leaving the remaining regions to a more sophisticated system which might be relatively slow.

The reject option can be applied to neural networks by making use of the result, to be discussed in Chapter 6, that the outputs of a correctly trained network approximate Bayesian posterior probabilities.

Exercises

1.1 ($\star$) The first four exercises explore the failure of common intuition when dealing with spaces of many dimensions. In Appendix B it is shown that

$$
\int_{-\infty}^{\infty} \exp\left\{-\frac{\lambda}{2}x^2\right\} dx = \left(\frac{2\pi}{\lambda}\right)^{1/2}.
\tag{1.41}
$$

Consider the following identity involving the transformation from Cartesian to polar coordinates

$$
\prod_{i=1}^{d} \int_{-\infty}^{\infty} e^{-x_i^2} dx_i = S_d \int_0^{\infty} e^{-r^2} r^{d-1}\, dr
\tag{1.42}
$$

where S_d is the surface area of the unit sphere in d dimensions. By making use of (1.41) show that

$$
S_d = \frac{2\pi^{d/2}}{\Gamma(d/2)}
\tag{1.43}
$$

where $\Gamma(x)$ is the gamma function defined by

$$
\Gamma(x) \equiv \int_0^{\infty} u^{x-1} e^{-u}\, du.
\tag{1.44}
$$

Using the results $\Gamma(1) = 1$ and $\Gamma(3/2) = \sqrt{\pi}/2$, verify that (1.43) reduces to the well-known expressions when $d = 2$ and $d = 3$.

1.2 ($\star$) Using the result (1.43), show that the volume of a hypersphere of radius a in d-dimensions is given by

$$V_d = \frac{S_d a^d}{d}. \tag{1.45}$$

Hence show that the ratio of the volume of a hypersphere of radius a to the volume of a hypercube of side $2a$ (i.e. the circumscribed hypercube) is given by

$$\frac{\text{volume of sphere}}{\text{volume of cube}} = \frac{\pi^{d/2}}{d2^{d-1}\Gamma(d/2)}. \tag{1.46}$$

Using Stirling's approximation

$$\Gamma(x+1) \simeq (2\pi)^{1/2}e^{-x}x^{x+1/2} \tag{1.47}$$

which is valid when x is large, show that, as $d \to \infty$, the ratio (1.46) goes to zero. Similarly, show that the ratio of the distance from the centre of the hypercube to one of the corners, divided by the perpendicular distance to one of the edges, is $\sqrt{d}$, and therefore goes to ∞ as $d \to \infty$. These results show that, in a high dimensional space, most of the volume of a cube is concentrated in the large number of corners, which themselves become very long 'spikes'.

1.3 ($\star$) Consider a sphere of radius a in d dimensions. Use the result (1.45) to show that the fraction of the volume of the sphere which lies at values of the radius between $a - \epsilon$ and a, where $0 < \epsilon < a$, is given by

$$f = 1 - \left(1 - \frac{\epsilon}{a}\right)^d. \tag{1.48}$$

Hence show that, for any fixed ϵ no matter how small, this fraction tends to 1 as $d \to \infty$. Evaluate the ratio f numerically, with $\epsilon/a = 0.01$, for the cases $d = 2$, $d = 10$ and $d = 1000$. Similarly, evaluate the fraction of the volume of the sphere which lies inside the radius $a/2$, again for $d = 2$, $d = 10$ and $d = 1000$. We see that, for points which are uniformly distributed inside a sphere in d dimensions where d is large, almost all of the points are concentrated in a thin shell close to the surface.

1.4 ($\star\star$) Consider a probability density function $p(\mathbf{x})$ in d dimensions which is a function only of radius $r = \|\mathbf{x}\|$ and which has a Gaussian form

$$p(\mathbf{x}) = \frac{1}{(2\pi\sigma^2)^{1/2}} \exp\left(-\frac{\|\mathbf{x}\|^2}{2\sigma^2}\right). \tag{1.49}$$

By changing variables from Cartesian to polar coordinates, show that the probability mass inside a thin shell of radius r and thickness ϵ is given by $\rho(r)\epsilon$ where

$$\rho(r) = \frac{S_d r^{d-1}}{(2\pi\sigma^2)^{1/2}} \exp\left(-\frac{r^2}{2\sigma^2}\right) \tag{1.50}$$

where S_d is the surface area of a unit sphere in d dimensions. Show that the function $\rho(r)$ has a single maximum which, for large values of d, is located at $\widehat{r} \simeq \sqrt{d}\sigma$. Finally, by considering $\rho(\widehat{r} + \epsilon)$ where $\epsilon \ll \widehat{r}$ show that for large d

$$\rho(\widehat{r} + \epsilon) = \rho(\widehat{r}) \exp\left(-\frac{3\epsilon^2}{2\sigma^2}\right). \tag{1.51}$$

Thus, we see that $\rho(r)$ decays exponentially away from its maximum at $\widehat{r}$ with length scale σ. Since $\sigma \ll \widehat{r}$ at large d, we see that most of the probability mass is concentrated in a thin shell at large radius. By contrast, note that the value of the probability density itself is $\exp(d/2)$ times *bigger* at the origin than at the radius $\widehat{a}$, as can be seen by comparing $p(\mathbf{x})$ in (1.49) for $\|\mathbf{x}\|^2 = 0$ with $p(\mathbf{x})$ for $\|\mathbf{x}\|^2 = \widehat{r}^2 = \sigma^2 d$. Thus, the bulk of the probability mass is located in a different part of space from the region of high probability density.

1.5 (⋆) By differentiating of the sum-of-squares error function (1.3), using the form of the polynomial given in (1.2), show that the values of the polynomial coefficients which minimize the error are given by the solution of the following set of linear simultaneous equations

$$\sum_{j=1}^{M} A_{jj'} w_j = T_{j'} \tag{1.52}$$

where we have defined

$$A_{jj'} = \sum_n (x^n)^{j+j'} \qquad T_{j'} = \sum_n t^n (x^n)^{j'}. \tag{1.53}$$

1.6 (⋆) Consider the second-order terms in a higher-order polynomial in d dimensions, given by

$$\sum_{i=1}^{d} \sum_{j=1}^{d} w_{ij} x_i x_j. \tag{1.54}$$

Show that the matrix w_{ij} can be written as the sum of a symmetric matrix $w_{ij}^{S} = (w_{ij} + w_{ji})/2$ and an anti-symmetric matrix $w_{ij}^{A} = (w_{ij} - w_{ji})/2$. Verify that these satisfy $w_{ij}^{S} = w_{ji}^{S}$ and $w_{ij}^{A} = -w_{ji}^{A}$. Hence show that

$$\sum_{i=1}^{d} \sum_{j=1}^{d} w_{ij} x_i x_j = \sum_{i=1}^{d} \sum_{j=1}^{d} w_{ij}^{S} x_i x_j \tag{1.55}$$

so that the contribution from the anti-symmetric matrix vanishes. This demonstrates that the matrix w_{ij} can be chosen to be symmetric without loss of generality. Show that, as a consequence of this symmetry, the number of independent parameters in the matrix w_{ij} is given by $d(d+1)/2$.

1.7 (⋆⋆) Consider the Mth-order term in a multivariate polynomial in d dimensions, given by

$$\sum_{i_1=1}^{d} \sum_{i_2=1}^{d} \cdots \sum_{i_M=1}^{d} w_{i_1 i_2 \cdots i_M} x_{i_1} x_{i_2} \cdots x_{i_M}. \tag{1.56}$$

The M-dimensional array $w_{i_1 i_2 \cdots i_M}$ contains d^M elements, but many of these are related as a consequence of the many interchange symmetries of the factor $x_{i_1} x_{i_2} \cdots x_{i_M}$. Show that the redundancy in the coefficients can be removed by rewriting (1.56) in the form

$$\sum_{i_1=1}^{d} \sum_{i_2=1}^{i_1} \cdots \sum_{i_M=1}^{i_{M-1}} w_{i_1 i_2 \cdots i_M} x_{i_1} x_{i_2} \cdots x_{i_M}. \tag{1.57}$$

Hence show that the number of independent parameters $n(d, M)$ which appear at order M satisfies the relation

$$n(d, M) = \sum_{i=1}^{d} n(i, M-1). \tag{1.58}$$

Use this relation to show, by induction, that

$$n(d, M) = \frac{(d + M - 1)!}{(d - 1)! \, M!}. \tag{1.59}$$

To do this, first show that the result is true for $M = 2$, and any value of $d \geq 1$, by comparing (1.59) with the result of Exercise 1.6. Now use (1.58) to show that, if the result holds at order $M - 1$, then it will also hold at order M provided the following relation is satisfied:

$$\sum_{i=1}^{d} \frac{(i + M - 2)!}{(i - 1)! \, (M - 1)!} = \frac{(d + M - 1)!}{(d - 1)! \, M!}. \tag{1.60}$$

Finally, use induction to prove (1.60). This can be done by first showing that (1.60) is correct for $d = 1$ and arbitrary M (making use of the result $0! = 1$), then assuming it is correct for dimension d and verifying that it is correct for dimension $d + 1$.

1.8 (⋆⋆) In the previous exercise we considered the Mth-order term in a generalized polynomial. Now consider all of the terms up to and including the Mth order. Show that the total number $N(d, M)$ of independent parameters satisfies

$$N(d, M) = \sum_{j=0}^{M} n(d, j).$$ (1.61)

Hence, using the expression (1.59), show by induction that

$$N(d, M) = \frac{(d + M)!}{d! \, M!}.$$ (1.62)

To do this, first show that the result (1.62) holds for $M = 0$ and arbitrary $d \geq 1$. Then, by assuming that (1.62) holds at order M, show that it holds at order $M + 1$. Use Stirling's approximation in the form $\ln n! \simeq n \ln n - n$ to show that, for large d, the quantity $N(d, M)$ grows like d^M. For the general cubic ($M = 3$) polynomial in d-dimensions, evaluate numerically the total number of independent parameters for (i) $d = 10$ and (ii) $d = 100$, which correspond to typical small-scale and medium-scale applications.

1.9 ($\star$) Suppose we have a box containing 8 apples and 4 oranges, and we have a second box containing 10 apples and 2 oranges. One of the boxes is chosen at random (with equal probability) and an item is selected from the box and found to be an apple. Use Bayes' theorem to find the probability that the apple came from the first box.

1.10 ($\star$) Consider two non-negative numbers a and b, and show that, if $a \leq b$ then $a \leq (ab)^{1/2}$. Use this result to show that, if the decision regions are chosen to minimize the probability of misclassification, this probability will satisfy

$$P(\text{error}) \leq \int \{p(\mathbf{x}|\mathcal{C}_1)P(\mathcal{C}_1)p(\mathbf{x}|\mathcal{C}_2)P(\mathcal{C}_2)\}^{1/2} \, d\mathbf{x}.$$ (1.63)

1.11 ($\star$) Verify that the minimum-risk decision criterion (1.39) reduces to the decision rule (1.26) for minimizing the probability of misclassification when the loss matrix is given by $L_{kj} = 1 - \delta_{kj}$.

2

PROBABILITY DENSITY ESTIMATION

In this chapter we consider the problem of modelling a probability density function $p(\mathbf{x})$, given a finite number of data points $\mathbf{x}^n$, $n = 1, \ldots, N$ drawn from that density function. The methods we describe can be used to build classifier systems by considering each of the classes $\mathcal{C}_k$ in turn, and estimating the corresponding class-conditional densities $p(\mathbf{x}|\mathcal{C}_k)$ by making use of the fact that each data point is labelled according to its class. These densities can then be used in Bayes' theorem (Section 1.8) to find the posterior probabilities corresponding to a new measurement of $\mathbf{x}$, which can in turn be used to make a classification of $\mathbf{x}$.

Density estimation can also be applied to unlabelled data (that is data without any class labels) where it has a number of applications. In the context of neural networks it can be applied to the distribution of data in the input space as part of the training process for radial basis function networks (Section 5.9), and to provide a method for validating the outputs of a trained neural network (Bishop, 1994b).

In Chapter 6, techniques for density estimation are combined with neural network models to provide a general framework for modelling *conditional* density functions.

Here we consider three alternative approaches to density estimation. The first of these involves *parametric* methods in which a specific functional form for the density model is assumed. This contains a number of parameters which are then optimized by fitting the model to the data set. The drawback of such an approach is that the particular form of parametric function chosen might be incapable of providing a good representation of the true density. By contrast, the second technique of *non-parametric* estimation does not assume a particular functional form, but allows the form of the density to be determined entirely by the data. Such methods typically suffer from the problem that the number of parameters in the model grows with the size of the data set, so that the models can quickly become unwieldy. The third approach, sometimes called *semi-parametric* estimation, tries to achieve the best of both worlds by allowing a very general class of functional forms in which the number of adaptive parameters can be increased in a systematic way to build ever more flexible models, but where the total number of parameters in the model can be varied independently from the size of the data set. We shall focus on semi-parametric models based on *mixture distributions*. Feed-forward neural networks can be regarded as semi-parametric models for conditional density estimation, as discussed further in Chapter 6.

It should be emphasized that accurate modelling of probability densities from finite data sets in spaces of high dimensionality (where high could be as low as $d = 10$) is, in general, extremely difficult. In Exercise 1.4 it was shown that most of the probability mass associated with a Gaussian distribution in a space of high dimensionality occurs in a thin shell at large radius. With a finite data set, there may be few, if any, data points associated with the region of high probability density near the origin. This is another example of the 'curse of dimensionality' discussed in Section 1.4.

The techniques described in this chapter are not only of great interest in their own right, but they also provide an excellent introduction to many of the central issues which must be addressed when using neural networks in practical applications. More extensive discussions of density estimation can be found in Duda and Hart (1973), Titterington *et al.* (1985), Silverman (1986), McLachlan and Basford (1988), Fukunaga (1990) and Scott (1992).

2.1 Parametric methods

One of the most straightforward approaches to density estimation is to represent the probability density $p(\mathbf{x})$ in terms of a specific functional form which contains a number of adjustable parameters. The values of the parameters can then be optimized to give the best fit to the data. The simplest, and most widely used, parametric model is the *normal* or *Gaussian* distribution, which has a number of convenient analytical and statistical properties. Since our aim is to explain the basic principles of parametric density estimation, we shall limit our discussion to normal distributions.

We shall also describe the two principal techniques for determining the parameters of the model distribution, known respectively as *maximum likelihood* and *Bayesian inference*. As an illustration of the Bayesian approach, we consider the problem of finding the mean of a normal distribution. Bayesian methods are also considered in Chapter 10 where they are applied to the more complex problem of learning in neural networks. We shall also consider stochastic techniques for on-line learning in which the data values arrive sequentially and must be discarded as soon as they are used.

2.1.1 *The normal distribution*

The normal density function, for the case of a single variable, can be written in the form

$$p(x) = \frac{1}{(2\pi\sigma^2)^{1/2}} \exp\left\{ -\frac{(x-\mu)^2}{2\sigma^2} \right\} \tag{2.1}$$

where μ and σ^2 are called the *mean* and *variance* respectively, and the parameter σ (which is the square root of the variance) is called the *standard deviation*. The coefficient in front of the exponential in (2.1) ensures that $\int_{-\infty}^{\infty} p(x)\,dx = 1$, as can easily be verified using the results derived in Appendix B. The mean and variance of the one-dimensional normal distribution satisfy

$$\mu = \mathcal{E}[x] = \int_{-\infty}^{\infty} x p(x) \, dx \tag{2.2}$$

$$\sigma^2 = \mathcal{E}[(x - \mu)^2] = \int_{-\infty}^{\infty} (x - \mu)^2 p(x) \, dx \tag{2.3}$$

where $\mathcal{E}[\cdot]$ denotes the expectation.

In d dimensions the general multivariate normal probability density can be written

$$p(\mathbf{x}) = \frac{1}{(2\pi)^{d/2}|\Sigma|^{1/2}} \exp\left\{-\frac{1}{2}(\mathbf{x} - \boldsymbol{\mu})^{\mathrm{T}} \Sigma^{-1} (\mathbf{x} - \boldsymbol{\mu})\right\} \tag{2.4}$$

where the mean $\boldsymbol{\mu}$ is now a d-dimensional vector, Σ is a $d \times d$ *covariance matrix*, and $|\Sigma|$ is the determinant of Σ. The pre-factor in (2.4) ensures that $\int_{-\infty}^{\infty} p(\mathbf{x}) \, d\mathbf{x} = 1$, as can again be verified using the results derived in Appendix B. The density function $p(\mathbf{x})$ is governed by the parameters $\boldsymbol{\mu}$ and Σ, which satisfy

$$\boldsymbol{\mu} = \mathcal{E}[\mathbf{x}] \tag{2.5}$$

$$\Sigma = \mathcal{E}[(\mathbf{x} - \boldsymbol{\mu})(\mathbf{x} - \boldsymbol{\mu})^{\mathrm{T}}]. \tag{2.6}$$

From (2.6) we see that Σ is a symmetric matrix, and therefore has $d(d+1)/2$ independent components. There are also d independent elements in $\boldsymbol{\mu}$, and so the density function is completely specified once the values of $d(d+3)/2$ parameters have been determined. The quantity

$$\Delta^2 = (\mathbf{x} - \boldsymbol{\mu})^{\mathrm{T}} \Sigma^{-1} (\mathbf{x} - \boldsymbol{\mu}) \tag{2.7}$$

which appears in the exponent in (2.4), is called the *Mahalanobis* distance from $\mathbf{x}$ to $\boldsymbol{\mu}$. From the results derived in Appendix A for the properties of real symmetric matrices, we see that the surfaces of constant probability density for (2.4) are hyperellipsoids on which Δ^2 is constant, as shown for the case of two dimensions in Figure 2.1. The principal axes of the hyperellipsoids are given by the eigenvectors $\mathbf{u}_i$ of Σ which satisfy

$$\Sigma \mathbf{u}_i = \lambda_i \mathbf{u}_i \tag{2.8}$$

and the corresponding eigenvalues λ_i give the variances along the respective principal directions.

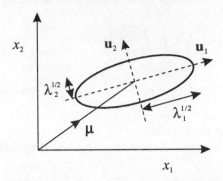

Figure 2.1. A normal distribution in two dimensions is governed by a mean vector μ and a covariance matrix with eigenvectors $\mathbf{u}_1$ and $\mathbf{u}_2$, and corresponding eigenvalues λ_1 and λ_2. The ellipse corresponds to a contour of constant probability density on which the density is smaller by a factor $e^{-1/2}$ than it is at the point μ.

It is sometimes convenient to consider a simplified form of Gaussian distribution in which the covariance matrix is diagonal,

$$(\mathbf{\Sigma})_{ij} = \delta_{ij}\sigma_j^2, \tag{2.9}$$

which reduces the total number of independent parameters in the distribution to $2d$. In this case the contours of constant density are hyperellipsoids with the principal directions aligned with the coordinate axes. The components of $\mathbf{x}$ are then said to be *statistically independent* since the distribution of $\mathbf{x}$ can be written as the product of the distributions for each of the components separately in the form

$$p(\mathbf{x}) = \prod_{i=1}^{d} p(x_i). \tag{2.10}$$

Further simplification can obtained by choosing $\sigma_j = \sigma$ for all j, which reduces the number of parameters still further to $d + 1$. The contours of constant density are then hyperspheres. A surface plot of the normal distribution for this case is shown in Figure 2.2. Although these simplified distributions have fewer parameters, they also clearly have less generality.

2.1.2 *Properties of the normal distribution*

The normal distribution has a number of important properties which make it a common choice for use in parametric density estimation:

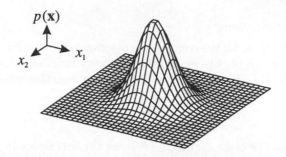

Figure 2.2. Surface plot of a normal distribution in two dimensions for a diagonal covariance matrix governed by a single variance parameter σ^2.

1. It has relatively simple analytical properties allowing many useful results to be obtained explicitly. For instance, any moment of the distribution can be expressed as a function of μ and Σ.

2. The *central limit theorem* states that, under rather general circumstances, the mean of M random variables tends to be distributed normally, in the limit as M tends to infinity. The main condition is that the variance of any one variable should not dominate. A common application is to the sum of a set of variables drawn independently from the same distribution. In practice, convergence tends to be very rapid, so that for values of M as small as 10 the approximation to a normal distribution can be very good. We might hope that measurements of naturally occurring phenomena have several constituent components, leading to a distribution which is close to normal.

3. Under any non-singular linear transformation of the coordinate system, the Mahalanobis distance keeps its quadratic form and remains positive definite. Thus, after such a transformation, the distribution is again normal, but with different mean and covariance parameters.

4. The *marginal* densities of a normal distribution, obtained by integrating out some of the variables, are themselves normal. Similarly, the *conditional* densities, obtained by setting some of the variables to fixed values, are also normal.

5. There exists a linear transformation which diagonalizes the covariance matrix. This leads to a new coordinate system, based on the eigenvectors of Σ, in which the variables are statistically independent, so that the density function for the vector $\mathbf{x}$ factors into the product of the densities for each of the component variables separately (Exercise 2.2).

6. For given values of the mean and the covariance matrix, the normal density function maximizes the entropy. This point is discussed further in Section 6.10.

In practice, the main reason for choosing a normal distribution is usually its analytical simplicity.

2.1.3 *Discriminant functions*

In Section 1.9.1 we introduced the concept of a discriminant function, and showed how it could be related to the class-conditional density functions through Bayes' theorem. This led to a particular form of discriminant function given by

$$y_k(\mathbf{x}) = \ln p(\mathbf{x}|\mathcal{C}_k) + \ln P(\mathcal{C}_k) \tag{2.11}$$

where $\mathcal{C}_k$ denotes the kth class, and $P(\mathcal{C}_k)$ denotes the corresponding prior probability. Each new input vector $\mathbf{x}$ is assigned to the class $\mathcal{C}_k$ which gives the largest value for the corresponding discriminant $y_k(\mathbf{x})$. This choice of classification criterion minimizes the probability of misclassification. If each of the class-conditional density functions $p(\mathbf{x}|\mathcal{C}_k)$ in (2.11) is taken to be an independent normal distribution, then from (2.4) we have

$$y_k(\mathbf{x}) = -\frac{1}{2}(\mathbf{x} - \boldsymbol{\mu}_k)^{\mathrm{T}}\boldsymbol{\Sigma}_k^{-1}(\mathbf{x} - \boldsymbol{\mu}_k) - \frac{1}{2}\ln|\boldsymbol{\Sigma}_k| + \ln P(\mathcal{C}_k) \tag{2.12}$$

where we have dropped constant terms. The decision boundaries, along which $y_k(\mathbf{x}) = y_j(\mathbf{x})$, are therefore general quadratic functions in d-dimensional space.

An important simplification occurs if the covariance matrices for the various classes are equal, so that $\boldsymbol{\Sigma}_k = \boldsymbol{\Sigma}$. Then the $|\boldsymbol{\Sigma}_k|$ terms are class independent and may be dropped from (2.12). Similarly, the quadratic term $\mathbf{x}^{\mathrm{T}}\boldsymbol{\Sigma}^{-1}\mathbf{x}$ is also class independent and can be dropped. Since $\boldsymbol{\Sigma}$ is a symmetric matrix, its inverse must also be symmetric (Appendix A). It therefore follows that $\mathbf{x}^{\mathrm{T}}\boldsymbol{\Sigma}^{-1}\boldsymbol{\mu}_k = \boldsymbol{\mu}_k^{\mathrm{T}}\boldsymbol{\Sigma}^{-1}\mathbf{x}$. This gives a set of discriminant functions which can be written in the form

$$y_k(\mathbf{x}) = \mathbf{w}_k^{\mathrm{T}}\mathbf{x} + w_{k0} \tag{2.13}$$

where

$$\mathbf{w}_k^{\mathrm{T}} = \boldsymbol{\mu}_k^{\mathrm{T}}\boldsymbol{\Sigma}^{-1} \tag{2.14}$$

$$w_{k0} = -\frac{1}{2}\boldsymbol{\mu}_k^{\mathrm{T}}\boldsymbol{\Sigma}^{-1}\boldsymbol{\mu}_k + \ln P(\mathcal{C}_k) \tag{2.15}$$

The functions in (2.13) are an example of *linear* discriminants, since they are linear functions of $\mathbf{x}$. Decision boundaries, corresponding to $y_k(\mathbf{x}) = y_j(\mathbf{x})$, are then hyperplanar. This result is illustrated for a two-class problem with two variables, in which the two classes have equal covariance matrices, in Figure 2.3. Linear discriminants are closely related to neural network models which have a single layer of adaptive weights, as will be discussed in Section 3.1.

Another simplification of the discriminant functions is possible if again the

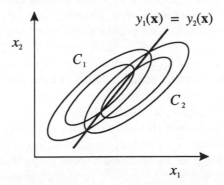

Figure 2.3. For two classes having normal probability densities with equal co-variance matrices, the decision boundary corresponding to the contour along which the discriminant functions are equal, is linear. Here the ellipses correspond to contours of constant class-conditional density, while the straight line represents the decision boundary which minimizes the probability of misclassification for equal prior probabilities $P(\mathcal{C}_1) = P(\mathcal{C}_2)$.

covariance matrices for all of the classes are equal, and in addition all of the variables are statistically independent, so that $\boldsymbol{\Sigma}$ becomes a diagonal matrix. Then $\boldsymbol{\Sigma} = \sigma^2\mathbf{I}$ (where $\mathbf{I}$ denotes the unit matrix) and the discriminant functions in (2.12) can be written

$$y_k(\mathbf{x}) = -\frac{\|\mathbf{x} - \boldsymbol{\mu}_k\|^2}{2\sigma^2} + \ln P(\mathcal{C}_k) \qquad (2.16)$$

where the class-independent term $-d\ln\sigma$ has been dropped. If the classes have equal prior probabilities $P(\mathcal{C}_k)$ then the decision rule takes a particularly simple form: measure the Euclidean distance to each of the class means $\boldsymbol{\mu}_k$ and assign the vector to the class with the nearest mean. In this case the mean vectors act as *templates* or *prototypes* and the decision rule corresponds to simple template matching. If the prior probabilities are not equal then this template matching rule becomes modified as indicated by (2.16). The concept of a prototype also arises in connection with radial basis function networks, as discussed in Chapter 5.

2.2 Maximum likelihood

Having decided on a parametric form for a density function $p(\mathbf{x})$, the next stage is to use the data set to find values for the parameters. In this section and the next we review briefly the two principal approaches to this problem, known respectively as *maximum likelihood* and *Bayesian inference*. Although these methods often lead to similar results, their conceptual basis is rather different. Maximum likelihood seeks to find the optimum values for the parameters by maximizing a likelihood function derived from the training data. By contrast, in the Bayesian approach the parameters are described by a probability distribution. This is initially set to some prior distribution, which is then converted to a posterior distribution, through the use of Bayes' theorem, once the data has been observed. The final expression for the desired probability density of input variables is then given by an integral over all possible values of the parameters, weighted by their posterior distribution. Note that the Bayesian approach does not involve setting the parameters to specific values, unlike the maximum likelihood method. Since our aim in this chapter is to give an overview of conventional pattern recognition techniques, we shall restrict our attention to the case of the normal density function for which the results are relatively straightforward.

We begin our discussion of parameter estimation by considering the maximum likelihood procedure. Suppose we consider a density function $p(\mathbf{x})$ which depends on a set of parameters $\boldsymbol{\theta} = (\theta_1, \ldots, \theta_M)^{\mathrm{T}}$. In a classification problem we would take one such function for each of the classes. Here we shall omit the class labels for simplicity, but essentially the same steps are performed separately for each class in the problem. To make the dependence on the parameters explicit, we shall write the density function in the form $p(\mathbf{x}|\boldsymbol{\theta})$. We also have a data set of N vectors $\mathcal{X} \equiv \{\mathbf{x}^1, \ldots, \mathbf{x}^N\}$. If these vectors are drawn independently from the distribution $p(\mathbf{x}|\boldsymbol{\theta})$, then the joint probability density of the whole data set $\mathcal{X}$ is given by

$$p(\mathcal{X}|\boldsymbol{\theta}) = \prod_{n=1}^{N} p(\mathbf{x}^n|\boldsymbol{\theta}) \equiv \mathcal{L}(\boldsymbol{\theta}) \tag{2.17}$$

where $\mathcal{L}(\boldsymbol{\theta})$ can be viewed as a function of $\boldsymbol{\theta}$ for fixed $\mathcal{X}$, in which case it is referred to as the *likelihood* of $\boldsymbol{\theta}$ for the given $\mathcal{X}$. The technique of maximum likelihood then sets the value of $\boldsymbol{\theta}$ by maximizing $\mathcal{L}(\boldsymbol{\theta})$. This corresponds to the intuitively reasonable idea of choosing the $\boldsymbol{\theta}$ which is most likely to give rise to the observed data. A more formal discussion of the origins of the maximum likelihood procedure is given in Akaike (1973). In practice, it is often more convenient to consider the negative logarithm of the likelihood

$$E = -\ln \mathcal{L}(\boldsymbol{\theta}) = -\sum_{n=1}^{N} \ln p(\mathbf{x}^n|\boldsymbol{\theta}) \tag{2.18}$$

and to find a minimum of E. This is equivalent to maximizing $\mathcal{L}$ since the negative logarithm is a monotonically decreasing function. The negative log-likelihood can be regarded as an *error function*, as discussed at greater length in Chapter 6.

For most choices of density function, the optimum $\boldsymbol{\theta}$ will have to be found by an iterative numerical procedure of the kind described in Chapter 7. However, for the special case of a multivariate normal density, we can find the maximum likelihood solution by analytic differentiation of (2.18), with $p(\mathbf{x}|\boldsymbol{\theta})$ given by (2.4). Some straightforward but rather involved matrix algebra (Anderson, 1958;

Tatsuoka, 1971) then leads to the following results

$$\widehat{\boldsymbol{\mu}} = \frac{1}{N} \sum_{n=1}^{N} \mathbf{x}^n \qquad (2.19)$$

$$\widehat{\boldsymbol{\Sigma}} = \frac{1}{N} \sum_{n=1}^{N} (\mathbf{x}^n - \widehat{\boldsymbol{\mu}})(\mathbf{x}^n - \widehat{\boldsymbol{\mu}})^{\mathrm{T}} \qquad (2.20)$$

which represents the intuitive result that the maximum likelihood estimate $\widehat{\boldsymbol{\mu}}$ of the mean vector $\boldsymbol{\mu}$ is given by the *sample average* (i.e. the average with respect to the given data set). We recall from (2.5) that, for data generated from a normal distribution, the expectation of $\mathbf{x}$ (i.e. the average value of $\mathbf{x}$ over an infinite sample) gives the true mean $\boldsymbol{\mu}$. Similarly, the maximum likelihood estimate $\widehat{\boldsymbol{\Sigma}}$ of the covariance matrix $\boldsymbol{\Sigma}$ is given by the sample average of the outer product $(\mathbf{x}^n - \widehat{\boldsymbol{\mu}})(\mathbf{x}^n - \widehat{\boldsymbol{\mu}})^{\mathrm{T}}$. Again, from (2.6), we note that, for data generated from a normal distribution, the expectation of this quantity (with $\widehat{\boldsymbol{\mu}}$ replaced by $\boldsymbol{\mu}$) gives the true covariance matrix $\boldsymbol{\Sigma}$.

Although the maximum likelihood approach seems intuitively reasonable, we should point out that it can suffer from some deficiencies. Consider the maximum likelihood estimates for the mean and variance of a normal distribution in one dimension, given from (2.19) and (2.20), by

$$\widehat{\mu} = \frac{1}{N} \sum_{n=1}^{N} x^n, \qquad (2.21)$$

$$\widehat{\sigma}^2 = \frac{1}{N} \sum_{n=1}^{N} (x^n - \widehat{\mu})^2. \qquad (2.22)$$

If we consider the expectation, defined in (1.16), of the estimate for $\widehat{\sigma}^2$, then we obtain (Exercise 2.4)

$$\mathcal{E}[\widehat{\sigma}^2] = \frac{N-1}{N} \sigma^2 \qquad (2.23)$$

where σ^2 is the true variance of the distribution from which the data set was generated. An estimate such as this, whose expected value differs from the true value, is said to exhibit *bias*. In the limit $N \to \infty$, we see that the bias disappears, and indeed for moderate values of N the maximum likelihood estimator gives a reasonable approximation. The problem has arisen because, in the expression (2.22) for $\widehat{\sigma}^2$, we have used our estimate $\widehat{\mu}$ for the mean, rather than the true value μ. In Chapter 10 a similar effect is discussed in the context of learning

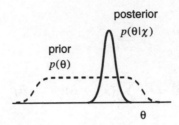

Figure 2.4. Schematic illustration of Bayesian inference for a parameter θ. The prior distribution reflects our initial belief in the range of values which θ might take, before we have observed any data, and is typically very broad. Once we have observed the data set $\mathcal{X}$, we can calculate the corresponding posterior distribution using Bayes' theorem. Since some values of the parameter will be more consistent with the data than others, this leads to posterior distribution which is narrower than the prior distribution.

in neural networks. In this case the consequences are potentially much more serious, as a result of the much larger number of parameters which have to be determined.

2.3 Bayesian inference

In the maximum likelihood method described above, the goal is to find the single most likely value for the parameter vector θ given the observed data. The Bayesian approach, however, is rather different. Our uncertainty in the values of the parameters is represented by a probability density function, as discussed in Section 1.8.2. Before we observe the data, the parameters are described by a *prior* probability density, which is typically very broad to reflect the fact that we have little idea of what values the parameters should take. Once we observe the data, we can make use of Bayes' theorem to find the corresponding *posterior* probability density. Since some values of the parameters are more consistent with the data than others, we find that the posterior distribution is narrower than the prior distribution. This phenomenon is known as *Bayesian learning*, and is illustrated schematically in Figure 2.4.

We first give a formal discussion of Bayesian learning in general terms, and then consider a very simple example to see how it operates in practice. In Chapter 10 we apply Bayesian techniques to the much more complex problems of determining the parameters in a neural network, and of comparing different network models.

We begin by writing the desired density function for the vector $\mathbf{x}$, given the training data set $\mathcal{X}$, as an integral over a joint distribution of the form

$$p(\mathbf{x}|\mathcal{X}) = \int p(\mathbf{x}, \theta|\mathcal{X}) \, d\theta. \tag{2.24}$$

From the definition of conditional probability densities, we can then write

$$p(\mathbf{x}, \boldsymbol{\theta}|\mathcal{X}) = p(\mathbf{x}|\boldsymbol{\theta}, \mathcal{X})p(\boldsymbol{\theta}|\mathcal{X}).$$ (2.25)

The first factor, however, is independent of $\mathcal{X}$ since it is just our assumed form for the parametrized density, and is completely specified once the values of the parameters $\boldsymbol{\theta}$ have been set. We therefore have

$$p(\mathbf{x}|\mathcal{X}) = \int p(\mathbf{x}|\boldsymbol{\theta})p(\boldsymbol{\theta}|\mathcal{X})\, d\boldsymbol{\theta}.$$ (2.26)

Thus, instead of choosing a specific value for $\boldsymbol{\theta}$, the Bayesian approach performs a weighted average over all values of $\boldsymbol{\theta}$. The weighting factor $p(\boldsymbol{\theta}|\mathcal{X})$, which is the posterior distribution of $\boldsymbol{\theta}$, is determined by starting from some assumed prior distribution $p(\boldsymbol{\theta})$ and then updating it using Bayes' theorem to take account of the data set $\mathcal{X}$. Since the data points $\{\mathbf{x}^1, \ldots, \mathbf{x}^N\}$ are assumed to be drawn independently from the same underlying distribution, we can write

$$p(\mathcal{X}|\boldsymbol{\theta}) = \prod_{n=1}^{N} p(\mathbf{x}^n|\boldsymbol{\theta})$$ (2.27)

which is precisely the likelihood function introduced in (2.17). Using Bayes' theorem we can then write the posterior distribution for $\boldsymbol{\theta}$ in the form

$$p(\boldsymbol{\theta}|\mathcal{X}) = \frac{p(\mathcal{X}|\boldsymbol{\theta})p(\boldsymbol{\theta})}{p(\mathcal{X})} = \frac{p(\boldsymbol{\theta})}{p(\mathcal{X})} \prod_{n=1}^{N} p(\mathbf{x}^n|\boldsymbol{\theta})$$ (2.28)

where the normalization factor in the denominator is given by

$$p(\mathcal{X}) = \int p(\boldsymbol{\theta}') \prod_{n=1}^{N} p(\mathbf{x}^n|\boldsymbol{\theta}')\, d\boldsymbol{\theta}'$$ (2.29)

and ensures that $\int p(\boldsymbol{\theta}|\mathcal{X})\, d\boldsymbol{\theta} = 1$. Typically, the evaluation of integrals such as (2.26) and (2.29) is a very complex undertaking, and, in general, it is only analytically feasible for the class of density functions for which the posterior density in (2.28) has the same functional form as the prior. For a given choice of density $p(\mathbf{x}|\boldsymbol{\theta})$, a prior $p(\boldsymbol{\theta})$ which gives rise to a posterior $p(\boldsymbol{\theta}|\mathcal{X})$ having the same functional form is said to be a *conjugate prior*. If we were to update the distribution of $\boldsymbol{\theta}$ using a succession of data points, with the posterior at each stage forming the prior at the next stage, then the distribution would retain the same functional form throughout. Such functions are known as *reproducing densities* (Duda and Hart, 1973), and include the normal distribution as the most commonly encountered example.

In order to illustrate the technique of Bayesian learning, we consider a simple example involving a one-dimensional input space governed by a single variable x. We shall suppose that the data is generated from a normal distribution for which the standard deviation σ is assumed to be known. The goal is to find the mean μ of the distribution, given a set of data points $\{x^1, \ldots, x^N\}$. We shall take the prior density for μ to be a normal distribution having mean μ_0 and standard deviation σ_0, given by

$$p_0(\mu) = \frac{1}{(2\pi\sigma_0^2)^{1/2}} \exp\left\{-\frac{(\mu - \mu_0)^2}{2\sigma_0^2}\right\}. \tag{2.30}$$

This expresses our prior knowledge of the mean μ, and so if we are very uncertain as to its value we would choose a large value for σ_0. Once we have observed a given set of N data points, we can calculate the posterior density $p(\mu|\mathcal{X}) = p_N(\mu|x_1, \ldots, x_N)$ using Bayes' theorem. It is important to distinguish clearly between the distribution of x, which we are trying to model, and the distributions $p_0(\mu)$ and $p_N(\mu|\mathcal{X})$, which describe our uncertainty in the value of μ. In this particular example, all of these distributions are normal.

Using (2.28) we can write the posterior distribution in the form

$$p_N(\mu|\mathcal{X}) = \frac{p_0(\mu)}{p(\mathcal{X})} \prod_{n=1}^{N} p(x^n|\mu). \tag{2.31}$$

Then, using the form (2.1) for the normal distribution for $p(x|\mu)$, it is straightforward to show (Exercise 2.5) that the posterior distribution $p_N(\mu|\mathcal{X})$ is also normal, with mean μ_N and variance σ_N^2 given by

$$\mu_N = \frac{N\sigma_0^2}{N\sigma_0^2 + \sigma^2}\overline{x} + \frac{\sigma^2}{N\sigma_0^2 + \sigma^2}\mu_0 \tag{2.32}$$

$$\frac{1}{\sigma_N^2} = \frac{N}{\sigma^2} + \frac{1}{\sigma_0^2} \tag{2.33}$$

where $\overline{x}$ is the sample mean

$$\overline{x} = \frac{1}{N} \sum_{n=1}^{N} x^n. \tag{2.34}$$

From (2.32) and (2.33) we see that, as the number of data points N increases, the mean of the posterior distribution for μ approaches the sample mean $\overline{x}$. Similarly, the standard deviation σ_N approaches zero. This result is illustrated for a particular set of parameter values in Figure 2.5.

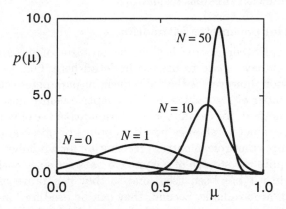

Figure 2.5. An illustration of Bayesian inference for the case of data drawn from a normal density function. The plot shows the posterior density for the mean μ, which is itself also given by a normal distribution in this example. As the number N of data points increases, the posterior density becomes more sharply peaked. In this example, the prior distribution was chosen to have a mean of 0.0 and standard deviation of 0.3 to reflect the fact that we have little idea of what value μ should have. The true mean of the distribution of x from which the data was generated, was 0.8 (with a standard deviation of 0.3 which is assumed to be known). Note that, as the size N of the sample increases, the posterior distribution concentrates around the true value of the mean.

There is a simple relationship between the technique of Bayesian inference and the maximum likelihood method. From (2.17) and (2.28) we have, omitting the denominator since it is independent of $\boldsymbol{\theta}$,

$$p(\boldsymbol{\theta}|\mathbf{x}^1, \ldots, \mathbf{x}^N) \propto \mathcal{L}(\boldsymbol{\theta})p(\boldsymbol{\theta}). \tag{2.35}$$

If we have little prior information about $\boldsymbol{\theta}$ then $p(\boldsymbol{\theta})$ will be relatively flat. The likelihood function by definition peaks at the maximum likelihood value $\widehat{\boldsymbol{\theta}}$. If the peak is relatively sharp, then the integral in (2.26) will be dominated by the region around $\widehat{\boldsymbol{\theta}}$, and the integral in (2.26) will be given approximately by

$$p(\mathbf{x}|\mathcal{X}) \simeq p(\mathbf{x}|\widehat{\boldsymbol{\theta}}) \int p(\boldsymbol{\theta}|\mathcal{X}) \, d\boldsymbol{\theta} = p(\mathbf{x}|\widehat{\boldsymbol{\theta}}) \tag{2.36}$$

where we have used $\int p(\boldsymbol{\theta}|\mathcal{X}) \, d\boldsymbol{\theta} = 1$. Thus, the distribution is just given by the maximum likelihood expression. We have seen that, as the number N of observations increases, the posterior probability density for $\boldsymbol{\theta}$ tends to become more and more sharply peaked. For large numbers of observations, therefore, the Bayesian representation of the density $p(\mathbf{x})$ approaches the maximum likelihood solution. For a limited number of observations, however, the two approaches will tend to give somewhat different results.

2.4 Sequential parameter estimation

There are several other approaches to the problem of parameter estimation, which we do not have space to discuss in detail here. One technique which is worthy of mention, however, is that of sequential parameter estimation, since it underpins a number of algorithms used in adaptive neural networks.

Sequential methods for parameter estimation make use of iterative techniques to update the parameter values as new data points or observations are acquired. They play an important role in pattern recognition for a number of reasons. First, they do not require the storage of a complete data set since each data point can be discarded once it has been used, and so they can prove useful when large volumes of data are available. Second, they can be used for 'on-line' learning in real-time adaptive systems. Finally, if the underlying process which generates the data has a slow time variation, the parameter values can adapt to 'track' the behaviour of the system.

In simple cases it may be possible to take a standard 'batch' technique for parameter estimation and separate out the contribution from the $(N + 1)$th data point to give a sequential update formula. For instance, from the maximum likelihood expression for the mean of a normal distribution, given by (2.19), we obtain

$$\widehat{\boldsymbol{\mu}}_{N+1} = \widehat{\boldsymbol{\mu}}_N + \frac{1}{N+1}(\mathbf{x}^{N+1} - \widehat{\boldsymbol{\mu}}_N). \tag{2.37}$$

We see that it is only necessary to store the values of $\widehat{\boldsymbol{\mu}}$ and N, and so each data point is used once and can then be discarded. Note that the contribution of each successive data point decreases as a consequence of the $1/(N + 1)$ coefficient. Although this heuristic procedure seems reasonable, we would like to find some formal assurance that it will converge satisfactorily. To do this, we turn to a more general view of sequential parameter estimation.

2.4.1 *The Robbins–Monro algorithm*

The iterative formula of (2.37) is a particular example of a more general procedure for finding the roots of functions which are defined stochastically. Consider a pair of random variables g and θ which are correlated, as indicated in Figure 2.6. The average value of g for each value of θ defines a function $f(\theta)$

$$f(\theta) = \mathcal{E}[g|\theta] \tag{2.38}$$

where $\mathcal{E}[\cdot|\theta]$ denotes the expectation for the given value of θ. Thus, if we could make several measurements of the value of g for a given value of θ we would obtain a set of random values whose average value (in the limit of an infinite sample) defines the value of the function f at that value of θ. Functions which have this

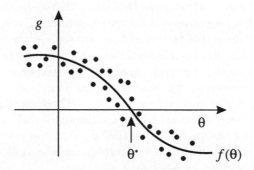

Figure 2.6. The regression function $f(\theta)$ is defined to be the expectation of a random variable g for each value of θ. The root θ^* of $f(\theta)$ can be found by the Robbins–Monro algorithm.

general form are referred to as *regression* functions, and a general procedure for finding the roots of such functions was given by Robbins and Monro (1951).

The goal is to find a value θ^* for which $f(\theta^*) = 0$. We shall assume that g has finite variance

$$\mathcal{E}[(g - f)^2|\theta] < \infty \tag{2.39}$$

and we shall also assume, without loss of generality, that $f(\theta) > 0$ for $\theta < \theta^*$ and $f(\theta) < 0$ for $\theta > \theta^*$ as indicated in Figure 2.6. The Robbins–Monro procedure then specifies a sequence of successive estimates for the root given by

$$\theta_{N+1} = \theta_N + a_N g(\theta_N) \tag{2.40}$$

where $g(\theta_N)$ is a value for the random variable g obtained when θ takes the value θ_N. The coefficients $\{a_N\}$ represent a sequence of positive numbers which satisfy the following three conditions:

$$\lim_{N \to \infty} a_N = 0 \tag{2.41}$$

$$\sum_{N=1}^{\infty} a_N = \infty \tag{2.42}$$

$$\sum_{N=1}^{\infty} a_N^2 < \infty. \tag{2.43}$$

It can then be shown that the sequence of estimates θ_N does indeed converge to the root θ^* with probability 1 (Robbins and Monro, 1951). For a simple proof of this result, see Fukunaga (1990).

The first condition (2.41) ensures that successive corrections tend to decrease in magnitude so that the process converges to a limiting value, while the second condition (2.42) ensures that the corrections are sufficiently large that the root is eventually found. The final condition (2.43) ensures that the accumulated noise has finite variance so that the noise does not spoil the convergence to the root.

An analogous procedure for finding the minimum of a regression function has been given by Kiefer and Wolfowitz (1952). These stochastic approximation schemes have also been extended to the multidimensional case by Blum (1954).

We can formulate the maximum likelihood parameter estimate as a sequential update method using the Robbins–Monro formula as follows. The maximum likelihood value $\widehat{\theta}$ is given by a solution of

$$\frac{\partial}{\partial \theta} \left\{ \prod_{n=1}^{N} p(x^n|\theta) \right\} \Bigg|_{\widehat{\theta}} = 0. \tag{2.44}$$

Since we can equally well seek a maximum of the logarithm of the likelihood function, we can also write

$$\frac{1}{N} \frac{\partial}{\partial \theta} \left\{ \sum_{n=1}^{N} \ln p(x^n|\theta) \right\} \Bigg|_{\widehat{\theta}} = 0 \tag{2.45}$$

where we have introduced an extra factor of $1/N$, which allows us to take the limit $N \to \infty$ and hence obtain the expectation

$$\lim_{N \to \infty} \frac{1}{N} \sum_{n=1}^{N} \left\{ \frac{\partial}{\partial \theta} \ln p(x^n|\theta) \right\} = \mathcal{E} \left[\frac{\partial}{\partial \theta} \ln p(x|\theta) \right] \tag{2.46}$$

Thus, the maximum likelihood solution is asymptotically equivalent to finding a solution of

$$\mathcal{E} \left[\frac{\partial}{\partial \theta} \ln p(x|\theta) \right] = 0. \tag{2.47}$$

From the Robbins–Monro formula (2.40) this can be solved using an iterative scheme of the form

$$\theta_{N+1} = \theta_N + a_N \frac{\partial}{\partial \theta} \ln p(x^{N+1}|\theta) \Bigg|_{\theta_N} \tag{2.48}$$

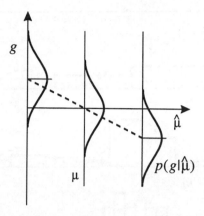

Figure 2.7. This figure shows the specific form taken by the diagram in Figure 2.6, for the particular case of data drawn from an assumed normal distribution in which the variable g corresponds to the derivative of the log-likelihood function, and is given by $(x - \widehat{\mu})/\sigma^2$. The dashed line represent the regression function $(\mu - \widehat{\mu})/\sigma^2$, and its root gives the required maximum likelihood estimate $\widehat{\mu}$ of the mean in the limit of an infinite set of data.

This is a very straightforward scheme to implement, once we have chosen a functional form for the density $p(x|\theta)$.

As a specific example, consider the case where $p(x|\theta)$ is taken to be a normal distribution, with known standard deviation σ and unknown mean μ. It is then a few lines of algebra (Exercise 2.6) to show that, if we choose $a_N = \sigma^2/(N+1)$, we recover the one-dimensional version of (2.37). This choice of a_N satisfies the criteria (2.41) – (2.43), and so convergence is assured. In this case, the random variable θ of Figure 2.6 is given by the estimate $\widehat{\mu}$ of the mean, and the random variable g is given by $(x - \widehat{\mu})/\sigma^2$. The corresponding regression function $f(\theta)$ is then $\mathcal{E}[(x - \widehat{\mu})/\sigma^2] = (\mu - \widehat{\mu})/\sigma^2$, and the root of this regression function gives the required maximum likelihood estimate $\widehat{\mu} = \mu$ of the mean, in the limit of an infinite supply of data, as shown in Figure 2.7. Similar stochastic learning schemes are discussed in the context of adaptive neural networks in later chapters.

2.5 Non-parametric methods

In this section we consider some of the more important non-parametric techniques for probability density estimation. The term non-parametric is used to describe probability density functions for which the functional form is not specified in advance, but which depends on the data itself. We begin with a discussion of simple histogram methods, and then move onto kernel-based approaches which, as discussed in Chapter 5, have a close connection with radial basis function neural networks. We then discuss another important non-parametric estimation

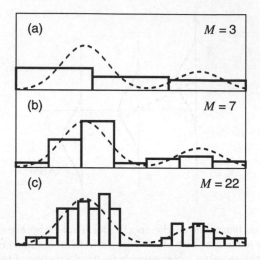

Figure 2.8. An illustration of the histogram approach to density estimation. A set of thirty data points was generated by sampling a density function given by the sum of two normal distributions with means $\mu_1 = 0.3$, $\mu_2 = 0.8$, standard deviations $\sigma_1 = \sigma_2 = 0.1$, and amplitudes of 0.7 and 0.3 respectively. The original distribution is shown by the dashed curve, and the histogram estimates are shown by the solid curves. The number M of histogram bins within the given interval determines the width of the bins, which in turn controls the smoothness of the estimated density.

technique called K-nearest-neighbours and show how this approach can be used both for density estimation and to provide classification decisions directly. Finally, we consider the role of the smoothing parameters which govern the degree of smoothness of the estimated density and which arise in any non-parametric technique. Determination of suitable values for such parameters is an important part of the density estimation process.

2.5.1 *Histograms*

The basic problem of non-parametric density estimation is very simple. Given a set of data points, we wish to model the probability distribution which generated the data, without making any prior assumption about the form of the distribution function (except for some general smoothness properties, which we shall discuss shortly). In Section 1.1 we considered a histogram of hypothetical values for a feature $\tilde{x}_1$ for each of two classes. The histogram is obtained simply by dividing the $\tilde{x}_1$-axis into a number of bins, and approximating the density at each value of $\tilde{x}_1$ by the fraction of the points which fall inside the corresponding bin. This procedure represents a simple form of non-parametric density estimation.

In Figure 2.8 we show a simple example of density estimation using the histogram approach. Note that we can choose both the number of bins M, and their starting position on the axis. The results are often not too sensitive to the starting position, but the parameter M plays a crucial role. Figure 2.8 shows the histograms which result from values of M of 3, 7 and 22. We see that the number of bins (or more precisely the bin width) is acting as a smoothing parameter. If the bin width is too small then the estimated density is very spiky, while if its value is too large then some of the true structure in the density (in this case the bimodal nature of the distribution) is smoothed out. In general we expect there to be some optimum value for the bin width which represents the best compromise between these problems. This situation is closely related to that encountered in Section 1.5 in the context of curve fitting with polynomials. There we saw the importance of choosing a suitable number of terms in the polynomial in order to capture the underlying structure in the data, without over-fitting to the noise on the individual data points. Similarly, in the case of density estimation, we do not know the true underlying density, and so we are faced with the problem of how to choose a suitable value for the parameter M. We shall see that this is a key issue which will arise in a number of different guises, both in the context of conventional techniques and of neural networks. For the moment we defer the problem of finding the optimal value for parameters such as M while we examine alternative approaches to non-parametric density estimation.

One advantage of the histogram method is that, once the histogram has been constructed, the data can be discarded and only the information on the sizes and locations of the histogram bins need be retained. (In this sense, the histogram representation should strictly be regarded as a semi-parametric technique). Indeed, the histogram may be constructed sequentially in which data points are considered one at a time and then discarded. The benefits of sequential techniques were discussed in Section 2.4. However, the simple histogram suffers from a number of difficulties which make it unsuitable for use in most practical applications, except for rapid visualization of data in one or two dimensions. One problem is that the estimated density function is not smooth but has discontinuities at the boundaries of the histogram bins. Since these boundaries were selected by hand in advance of observing the data, it is unlikely that they represent true structure in the distribution. A second very serious problem becomes apparent when we consider the generalization to higher dimensions. If we divide each variable into M intervals, then a d-dimensional feature space will be divided into M^d bins. This exponential growth with d is an example of the 'curse of dimensionality' discussed in Section 1.4. In high dimensions we would either require a huge number of data points to obtain a density estimate, or most of the bins would be empty, corresponding to an estimated density of zero.

2.5.2 *Density estimation in general*

So far we have given a rather heuristic discussion of density estimation based on the idea of histograms. To proceed further we return to the basic definition of probability density functions. The probability that a new vector $\mathbf{x}$, drawn from the unknown density function $p(\mathbf{x})$, will fall inside some region $\mathcal{R}$ of $\mathbf{x}$-space is, by definition, given by

$$P = \int_{\mathcal{R}} p(\mathbf{x}') \, d\mathbf{x}'. \tag{2.49}$$

If we have N data points drawn independently from $p(\mathbf{x})$ then the probability that K of them will fall within the region $\mathcal{R}$ is given by the binomial law

$$\Pr(K) = \frac{N!}{K!\,(N-K)!} P^K (1-P)^{N-K}. \tag{2.50}$$

The mean fraction of points falling in this regions is given by $\mathcal{E}[K/N] = P$ and the variance around this mean is given by $\mathcal{E}[(K/N - P)^2] = P(1-P)/N$. Thus the distribution is sharply peaked as $N \to \infty$. We therefore expect that a good estimate of the probability P can be obtained from the mean fraction of the points which fall within $\mathcal{R}$, so that

$$P \simeq K/N. \tag{2.51}$$

If we assume that $p(\mathbf{x})$ is continuous and does not vary appreciably over the region $\mathcal{R}$, then we can approximate (2.49) by

$$P = \int_{\mathcal{R}} p(\mathbf{x}') \, d\mathbf{x}' \simeq p(\mathbf{x}) V \tag{2.52}$$

where V is the volume of $\mathcal{R}$, and $\mathbf{x}$ is some point lying inside $\mathcal{R}$. From (2.51) and (2.52) we obtain the intuitive result

$$p(\mathbf{x}) \simeq \frac{K}{NV}. \tag{2.53}$$

Note that to obtain this estimate we have had to make two assumptions, the validity of which is governed by the choice of the region $\mathcal{R}$. In order for (2.51) to hold accurately we require $\mathcal{R}$ to be relatively large, so that P will be large and the binomial distribution will be sharply peaked. However, the approximation in (2.52) is most accurate when $\mathcal{R}$ is relatively small, so that $p(\mathbf{x})$ is approximately constant inside the integration region. Once again, we see that there is a choice to be made regarding the degree of smoothing to be performed, and for a given size of data set we expect that there will be some optimum value for the size of $\mathcal{R}$ which will give the best estimate of $p(\mathbf{x})$. We shall return to this problem shortly.

In applying (2.53) to practical density estimation problems there are two basic approaches we can adopt. The first is to choose a fixed value of K and determine the corresponding volume V from the data. This gives rise to the K-nearest-neighbour approach discussed later. Alternatively we can fix the volume V and determine K from the data. This leads to the class of kernel-based density estimation techniques, which we describe next.

We expect that, in the limit of an infinite number of data points, our estimation procedure should become exact, since the volume of $\mathcal{R}$ can be shrunk to zero, thereby ensuring that (2.52) becomes increasingly accurate, while also improving the accuracy of (2.51) by ensuring that $\mathcal{R}$ contains an ever increasing number of points. It can be shown that both kernel methods and K-nearest-neighbour methods do indeed converge to the true probability density in the limit of infinite N, provided that V shrinks with N, and K grows with N, in a suitable way (Duda and Hart, 1973).

2.5.3 Kernel-based methods

Suppose we take the region $\mathcal{R}$ to be a hypercube with sides of length h centred on the point $\mathbf{x}$. Its volume is then given by

$$V = h^d. \tag{2.54}$$

We can find an expression for K, the number of points which fall within this region, by defining a *kernel function* $H(\mathbf{u})$, also known as a *Parzen window* (Rosenblatt, 1956; Parzen, 1962) given by

$$H(\mathbf{u}) = \begin{cases} 1 & |u_j| < 1/2 \quad j = 1,\ldots,d \\ 0 & \text{otherwise} \end{cases} \tag{2.55}$$

so that $H(\mathbf{u})$ corresponds to a unit hypercube centred at the origin. Thus, for all data points $\mathbf{x}^n$, the quantity $H((\mathbf{x} - \mathbf{x}^n)/h)$ is equal to unity if the point $\mathbf{x}^n$ falls inside a hypercube of side h centred on $\mathbf{x}$, and is zero otherwise. The total number of points falling inside the hypercube is then simply

$$K = \sum_{n=1}^{N} H\left(\frac{\mathbf{x} - \mathbf{x}^n}{h}\right). \tag{2.56}$$

If we substitute (2.56) and (2.54) into (2.53) we obtain the following estimate for the density at the point $\mathbf{x}$:

$$\widetilde{p}(\mathbf{x}) = \frac{1}{N} \sum_{n=1}^{N} \frac{1}{h^d} H\left(\frac{\mathbf{x} - \mathbf{x}^n}{h}\right) \tag{2.57}$$

where $\widetilde{p}(\mathbf{x})$ denotes the model density. We can regard this density estimate as consisting of the superposition of N cubes of side h, with each cube centred on one of the data points. This is somewhat reminiscent of the histogram approach, except that, instead of bins which are defined in advance, we have cells whose locations are determined by the data points. Nevertheless, we still have an estimate which has discontinuities.

We can smooth out the estimate by choosing different forms for the kernel function $H(\mathbf{u})$. For instance, a common choice is a multivariate normal kernel, for which

$$\widetilde{p}(\mathbf{x}) = \frac{1}{N} \sum_{n=1}^{N} \frac{1}{(2\pi h^2)^{d/2}} \exp\left\{ -\frac{\|\mathbf{x} - \mathbf{x}^n\|^2}{2h^2} \right\} \tag{2.58}$$

In general, if the kernel functions satisfy

$$H(\mathbf{u}) \geq 0 \tag{2.59}$$

and

$$\int H(\mathbf{u})\, d\mathbf{u} = 1 \tag{2.60}$$

then the estimate in (2.57) will satisfy $\widetilde{p}(\mathbf{x}) \geq 0$ and $\int \widetilde{p}(\mathbf{x})\, d\mathbf{x} = 1$, as required.

As a simple example of kernel density estimation, we return to the data set used to construct the histograms of Figure 2.8. In Figure 2.9 we plot the results of density estimation using a Gaussian kernel function, with values of the width parameter h given by 0.2, 0.08 and 0.01 respectively. This shows that h is acting as a smoothing parameter, and that an appropriate choice for the value of h is important if a good approximation to the true density is to be obtained. When the kernel width h is too large the estimated density is over-smoothed and the bimodal nature of the underlying distribution is lost. Conversely, when h is too small, a great deal of structure is present in the estimated density which represents the properties of the particular data set rather than true structure in the underlying distribution.

Some insight into the role of the kernel function can be obtained by computing the expectation of the estimated density, in other words the average value of the model density at some given point $\mathbf{x}$, where the average is taken over different possible selections of the data points $\mathbf{x}^n$. Making use of (2.57) we have

$$\mathcal{E}[\widetilde{p}(\mathbf{x})] = \frac{1}{N} \sum_{n=1}^{N} \mathcal{E}\left[\frac{1}{h^d} H\left(\frac{\mathbf{x} - \mathbf{x}'}{h} \right) \right]$$

$$= \mathcal{E}\left[\frac{1}{h^d} H\left(\frac{\mathbf{x} - \mathbf{x}'}{h} \right) \right]$$

$$= \int \frac{1}{h^d} H\left(\frac{\mathbf{x} - \mathbf{x}'}{h} \right) p(\mathbf{x}')\, d\mathbf{x}' \tag{2.61}$$

where, in the third line, we have used the fact that the vectors $\mathbf{x}^n$ are drawn independently from the density $p(\mathbf{x})$, and so the expectation is simply given by an

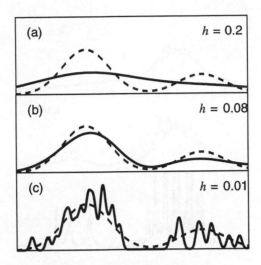

Figure 2.9. An example of the kernel approach to density estimation, using the same data as in Figure 2.8. Gaussian kernel functions have been used with various values for the kernel width h.

integral weighted by this density. We see that the expectation of the estimated density is a convolution of the true density with the kernel function, and so represents a smoothed version of the true density. Here the kernel width h plays the role of the smoothing parameter. For $h \to 0$, the kernel approaches a delta function and $\widetilde{p}(\mathbf{x})$ approaches the true density. For a finite sample size, however, a small value of h leads to a noisy representation for $\widetilde{p}(\mathbf{x})$ which approaches a set of delta functions centred on the data points. Once again, we see that we must choose a compromise value for the smoothing parameter h.

The kernel-based method suffers from the drawback of requiring all of the data points to be stored, which can make evaluation of the density very slow if the number of data points is large. One solution is to use fewer kernel functions and to adapt their positions and widths in response to the data. Methods for doing this, based on maximum likelihood, will be described in Section 2.6.

Another problem with the kernel-based estimator is that it gives a biased estimate of the density. In fact, Rosenblatt (1956) showed that, for a finite data set, there is no non-negative estimator which is unbiased for all continuous density functions.

The use of kernel methods to estimate regression functions is discussed in Chapter 5, which also demonstrates the close link with radial basis function networks.

2.5.4 *K-nearest-neighbours*

One of the potential problems with the kernel-based approach to density estimation arises from the use of a fixed width parameter h for all of the data points.

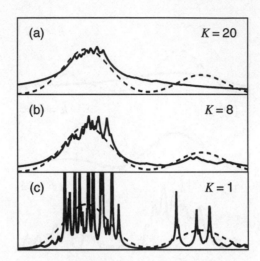

Figure 2.10. The K-nearest-neighbour approach to density estimation, again using the same data as in Figure 2.8, for various values of K.

If h is too large there may be regions of x-space in which the estimate is over-smoothed. Reducing h may, however, lead to problems in regions of lower density where the model density $\tilde{p}$ will become noisy. Thus, the optimum choice of h may be a function of position. This difficulty is addressed in the K-nearest-neighbour approach to density estimation.

We again return to (2.53) as our starting point, but we now fix K and allow the volume V to vary. Thus, we consider a small hypersphere centred at a point x, and allow the radius of the sphere to grow until it contains precisely K data points. The estimate of the density at the point x is then given by (2.53), where V is the volume of the sphere. In Figure 2.10 we show the result of the K-nearest-neighbour approach, for the same data set as used in Figures 2.8 and 2.9, for the values $K = 20$, 8 and 1. We see that K acts as a smoothing parameter and that there is an optimum choice for the value of K.

One disadvantage of the K-nearest-neighbour technique is that the resulting estimate is not a true probability density since its integral over all x-space diverges. A disadvantage of both kernel and K-nearest-neighbour methods is that all of the training data points must be retained. This might lead to problems of computer storage, and can require large amounts of processing to evaluate the density for new values of x. More sophisticated versions of these algorithms allow fewer data points to be used (Hart, 1968; Gates, 1972; Hand and Batchelor, 1978). There also exist tree search techniques which speed up the process finding the near neighbours of a point (Fukunaga and Narendra, 1975).

As we have already indicated, one of the applications of density estimation is in the construction of classifiers through the use of Bayes' theorem. This involves modelling the class-conditional densities for each class separately, and then combining them with priors to give models for the posterior probabilities which can then be used to make classification decisions. We can use this approach to find a classifier based directly on the K-nearest-neighbour technique by the following slight modification. Suppose our data set contains N_k points in class C_k and N points in total, so that $\sum_k N_k = N$. We then draw a hypersphere around the point x which encompasses K points irrespective of their class label. Suppose this sphere, of volume V, contains K_k points from class C_k. Then we can use (2.53) to give approximations for the class-conditional densities in the form

$$p(x|C_k) = \frac{K_k}{N_k V}. \tag{2.62}$$

The unconditional density can be similarly estimated from

$$p(x) = \frac{K}{NV} \tag{2.63}$$

while the priors can be estimated using

$$P(C_k) = \frac{N_k}{N}. \tag{2.64}$$

We now use Bayes' theorem to give

$$P(C_k|x) = \frac{p(x|C_k)P(C_k)}{p(x)} = \frac{K_k}{K}. \tag{2.65}$$

Thus, to minimize the probability of misclassifying a new vector x, it should be assigned to the class C_k for which the ratio K_k/K is largest. This is known as the *K-nearest-neighbour classification rule*. It involves finding a hypersphere around the point x which contains K points (independent of their class), and then assigning x to the class having the largest number of representatives inside the hypersphere. For the special case of $K = 1$ we have the *nearest-neighbour rule*, which simply assigns a point x to the same class as that of the nearest point from the training set. Figure 2.11 shows an example of the decision boundary corresponding to the nearest-neighbour classification rule.

2.5.5 *Smoothing parameters*

For all of the density estimation techniques discussed in this section we have seen that there is always some form of smoothing parameter governing the nature of the estimated density. For histograms it is the width of the bins, for kernel methods it is the kernel width h, and for K-nearest-neighbours it is the value of K. If the model density is over-smoothed, the *bias* becomes large and leads to a relatively poor estimator. However, with insufficient smoothing the *variance* is

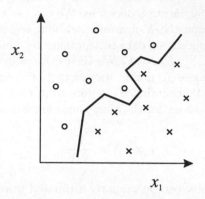

Figure 2.11. Example of the decision boundary produced by the nearest-neighbour classification rule. Note that the boundary is piecewise linear, with each segment corresponding to the perpendicular bisector between two data points belonging to different classes.

high, so that the model density is noisy and very sensitive to the individual data points. (Bias and variance are defined more precisely in Section 9.1). The choice of a suitable value for the smoothing parameter is analogous to the problem of choosing the number of terms in a polynomial used in curve fitting, discussed in Section 1.5. Similar smoothing parameters will appear in our discussions of neural networks. For instance, the number of hidden units in a layered feed-forward network can play a similar role to the number of terms in a polynomial.

It is important to realize that we cannot simply pick the value of the smoothing parameter which gives the largest value for the likelihood, as the likelihood can always be increased indefinitely by choosing ever smaller values for the smoothing parameter. Consider for instance the case of kernel estimators. The likelihood function can be written as

$$\mathcal{L}(h) = \prod_{n=1}^{N} p(\mathbf{x}^n | h; \mathbf{x}^1, \dots \mathbf{x}^N) \qquad (2.66)$$

where $p(\mathbf{x} | \dots)$ is given by (2.58) for the case of Gaussian kernels. It is easily verified that unconstrained maximization of $\mathcal{L}(h)$ leads to $h \to 0$ so that the resulting density estimate consists of a delta function at each data point, with zero density elsewhere.

The goal in selecting smoothing parameters is to produce a model for the probability density which is as close as possible to the (unknown) true density $p(\mathbf{x})$. It is often convenient to have a formal measure of the difference, or 'distance', between two density functions. If $\tilde{p}(\mathbf{x})$ is our model of the density function, then the average negative log-likelihood per data point, in the limit as the number of data points goes to infinity, can be written as an expectation in the form

$$\mathcal{E}\left[-\ln \mathcal{L}\right] = -\lim_{N\to\infty} \frac{1}{N} \sum_{n=1}^{N} \ln \widetilde{p}(\mathbf{x}^n) \tag{2.67}$$

$$= -\int p(\mathbf{x}) \ln \widetilde{p}(\mathbf{x}) \, d\mathbf{x} \tag{2.68}$$

which can be regarded as a measure of the extent to which the model density and the true density agree. When $\widetilde{p}(\mathbf{x}) = p(\mathbf{x})$ this measure has a residual value given by

$$-\int p(\mathbf{x}) \ln p(\mathbf{x}) \, d\mathbf{x} \tag{2.69}$$

which is known as the *entropy* of $p(\mathbf{x})$ (Section 6.10). It is convenient to subtract off this residual value to give a measure of the 'distance' between $\widetilde{p}(\mathbf{x})$ and $p(\mathbf{x})$ in the form

$$L = -\int p(\mathbf{x}) \ln \frac{\widetilde{p}(\mathbf{x})}{p(\mathbf{x})} \, d\mathbf{x} \tag{2.70}$$

which is known as the *Kullback–Leibler distance* or *asymmetric divergence* (Kullback and Leibler, 1951; Kullback, 1959). It is easily shown (Exercise 2.10) that $L \geq 0$ with equality if, and only if, the two density functions are equal. Note that L is not symmetric with respect to the two probability distributions. This is reasonable since it is more important for the model distribution $\widetilde{p}(\mathbf{x})$ to be close to the true distribution $p(\mathbf{x})$ in regions where data is more likely to be found. Thus the integral in (2.70) is weighted by the true distribution.

In a practical density estimation problem we are therefore faced with the difficulty of deciding a suitable value for the smoothing parameter. This is an example of a very general, and very important, issue which is concerned with choosing the optimal level of complexity, or flexibility, of a model for a given data set. Rather than consider this problem in the framework of density estimation, we defer further discussion until Chapters 9 and 10, where we consider the analogous issue in the context of neural network models. There we shall discuss two general approaches for dealing with model complexity, based respectively on cross-validation and Bayesian inference.

2.6 Mixture models

So far in this chapter we have considered two general approaches to density estimation, parametric and non-parametric, each of which has its merits and limitations. In particular, the parametric approach assumes a specific form for the density function, which might be very different from the true density. Usually, however, parametric models allow the density function to be evaluated very rapidly for new values of the input vector. Non-parametric methods, by contrast, allow very general forms of density function, but suffer from the fact that the number of variables in the model grows directly with the number of training data points. This leads to models which can be very slow to evaluate for new input vectors.

In order to combine the advantages of both parametric and non-parametric methods we need to find techniques which are not restricted to specific functional forms, and yet where the size of the model only grows with the complexity of the problem being solved, and not simply with the size of the data set. This leads us to a class of models which we shall call *semi-parametric*. The price we have to pay is that the process of setting up the model using the data set (i.e. the training of the model) is computationally intensive compared to the simple procedures needed for parametric or non-parametric methods (which in some cases involve little more than evaluating a few expressions for parameter values, or even just storing the training data).

In this section we shall restrict attention to one particular form of density function, called a *mixture model*. As well as providing powerful techniques for density estimation, mixture models find important applications in the context of neural networks, for example in configuring the basis functions in radial basis function networks (Section 5.9), in techniques for conditional density estimation (Section 6.4), in the technique of soft weight sharing (Section 9.4), and in the mixture-of-experts model (Section 9.7). Here we discuss three training methods for mixture models, all of which are based on maximum likelihood, involving respectively non-linear optimization, re-estimation (leading to the EM algorithm) and stochastic sequential estimation.

In the non-parametric kernel-based approach to density estimation, the density function was represented as a linear superposition of kernel functions, with one kernel centred on each data point. Here we consider models in which the density function is again formed from a linear combination of basis functions, but where the number M of basis functions is treated as a parameter of the model and is typically much less than the number N of data points. We therefore write our model for the density as a linear combination of component densities $p(\mathbf{x}|j)$ in the form

$$p(\mathbf{x}) = \sum_{j=1}^{M} p(\mathbf{x}|j)P(j). \tag{2.71}$$

Such a representation is called a *mixture distribution* (Titterington *et al.*, 1985; McLachlan and Basford, 1988) and the coefficients $P(j)$ are called the *mixing parameters*. Notice that there is a strong similarity between (2.71) and the expression given in equation (1.22) for the unconditional density of data taken from a mixture of several classes. This similarity has been emphasized by our choice of notation. We shall call $P(j)$ the *prior* probability of the data point having been generated from component j of the mixture. These priors are chosen to satisfy the constraints

$$\sum_{j=1}^{M} P(j) = 1 \qquad (2.72)$$

$$0 \leq P(j) \leq 1. \qquad (2.73)$$

Similarly, the component density functions $p(\mathbf{x}|j)$ are normalized so that

$$\int p(\mathbf{x}|j)\, d\mathbf{x} = 1 \qquad (2.74)$$

and hence can be regarded as class-conditional densities. To generate a data point from the probability distribution (2.71), one of the components j is first selected at random with probability $P(j)$, and then a data point is generated from the corresponding component density $p(\mathbf{x}|j)$. An important property of such mixture models is that, for many choices of component density function, they can approximate any continuous density to arbitrary accuracy provided the model has a sufficiently large number of components, and provided the parameters of the model are chosen correctly.

The key difference between the mixture model representation and a true classification problem lies in the nature of the training data, since in this case we are not provided with any 'class labels' to say which component was responsible for generating each data point. This represents an example of *incomplete data*, and we shall discuss this problem at greater length when we consider the EM algorithm in Section 2.6.2. As with any of the other density estimation techniques discussed in this chapter, the technique of mixture modelling can be applied separately to each class $\mathcal{C}_k$ in a true classification problem. In this case, each class-conditional density $p(\mathbf{x}|\mathcal{C}_k)$ is represented by an independent mixture model of the form (2.71).

Having made the link with prior probabilities and conditional densities, we can introduce the corresponding *posterior* probabilities, which we can express using Bayes' theorem in the form

$$P(j|\mathbf{x}) = \frac{p(\mathbf{x}|j)P(j)}{p(\mathbf{x})} \qquad (2.75)$$

where $p(\mathbf{x})$ is given by (2.71). These posterior probabilities satisfy

$$\sum_{j=1}^{M} P(j|\mathbf{x}) = 1. \qquad (2.76)$$

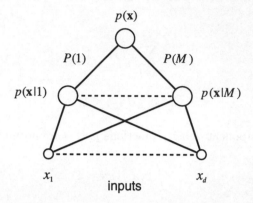

Figure 2.12. Representation of the mixture model (2.71) in terms of a network diagram. For Gaussian component densities $p(\mathbf{x}|j)$ given by (2.77), the lines connecting the inputs x_i to the components $p(\mathbf{x}|j)$ represent the elements μ_{ji} of the corresponding mean vectors $\boldsymbol{\mu}_j$.

The value of $P(j|\mathbf{x})$ represents the probability that a particular component j was responsible for generating the data point $\mathbf{x}$.

In this section, we shall limit our attention to mixture models in which the individual component densities are given by Gaussian distribution functions. We shall further assume that the Gaussians each have a covariance matrix which is some scalar multiple of the identity matrix so that $\boldsymbol{\Sigma}_j = \sigma_j^2 \mathbf{I}$ (where $\mathbf{I}$ is the identity matrix) and hence

$$p(\mathbf{x}|j) = \frac{1}{(2\pi\sigma_j^2)^{d/2}} \exp\left\{ -\frac{\|\mathbf{x} - \boldsymbol{\mu}_j\|^2}{2\sigma_j^2} \right\}. \tag{2.77}$$

In fact, the techniques we shall describe are easily extended to general Gaussian component densities having full covariance matrices as discussed in Section 2.1.1 in the context of parametric distributions.

The mixture model can be represented in terms of a network diagram as shown in Figure 2.12. This is simply a diagrammatic representation of a mathematical function, in this case the mixture model in (2.71). Such diagrams prove particularly useful when considering complex neural network structures, as discussed in later chapters.

2.6.1 *Maximum likelihood*

Various procedures have been developed for determining the parameters of a Gaussian mixture model from a set of data. In the remainder of this chapter we consider three approaches, all of them based on maximizing the likelihood of the parameters for the given data set. A review of maximum likelihood techniques in this context has been given by Redner and Walker (1984).

For the case of Gaussian components of the form (2.77), the mixture density contains the following adjustable parameters: $P(j)$, μ_j and σ_j (where $j = 1, \ldots, M$). The negative log-likelihood for the data set is given by

$$E = -\ln\mathcal{L} = -\sum_{n=1}^{N}\ln p(\mathbf{x}^n) = -\sum_{n=1}^{N}\ln\left\{\sum_{j=1}^{M}p(\mathbf{x}^n|j)P(j)\right\} \tag{2.78}$$

which can be regarded as an error function. Maximizing the likelihood $\mathcal{L}$ is then equivalent to minimizing E.

It is important to emphasize that minimizing this error function is non-trivial in a number of respects. First of all, there exist parameter values for which the likelihood goes to infinity (Day, 1969). These arise when one of the Gaussian components collapses onto one of the data points, as can be seen by setting $\mu_j = \mathbf{x}$ in (2.77) and then letting $\sigma_j \to 0$. In addition, small groups of points which are close together can give rise to local minima in the error function which may give poor representations of the true distribution. In practical problems we wish to avoid the singular solutions and the inappropriate local minima. Several techniques for dealing with the problems of singularities have been proposed. One approach is to constrain the components to have equal covariance matrices (Day, 1969). Alternatively, when one of the variance parameters shrinks to a small value during the course of an iterative algorithm, the corresponding Gaussian can be replaced with one having a larger width.

Since the error function is a smooth differentiable function of the parameters of the mixture model, we can employ standard non-linear optimization techniques, such as those described in Chapter 7, to find its minima. We shall see in Chapter 7, that there are considerable computational advantages in making use of gradient information provided it can be evaluated efficiently. In the present case the derivatives of E can be found analytically.

For the centres μ_j of the Gaussian components we find, by simple differentiation of (2.78), and making use of (2.75) and (2.77),

$$\frac{\partial E}{\partial \mu_j} = \sum_{n=1}^{N}P(j|\mathbf{x}^n)\frac{(\mu_j - \mathbf{x}^n)}{\sigma_j^2}. \tag{2.79}$$

Similarly, for the width parameter σ_j we obtain

$$\frac{\partial E}{\partial \sigma_j} = \sum_{n=1}^{N}P(j|\mathbf{x}^n)\left\{\frac{d}{\sigma_j} - \frac{\|\mathbf{x}^n - \mu_j\|^2}{\sigma_j^3}\right\}. \tag{2.80}$$

The minimization of E with respect to the mixing parameters $P(j)$ must be carried out subject to the constraints (2.72) and (2.73). This can be done by representing the mixing parameters in terms of a set of M auxiliary variables $\{\gamma_j\}$ such that

$$P(j) = \frac{\exp(\gamma_j)}{\sum_{k=1}^{M} \exp(\gamma_k)}. \tag{2.81}$$

The transformation given by (2.81) is called the *softmax* function, or normalized exponential, and ensures that, for $-\infty \le \gamma_j \le \infty$, the constraints (2.72) and (2.73) are satisfied as required for probabilities. We can now perform an unconstrained minimization of the error function with respect to the $\{\gamma_j\}$. To find the derivatives of E with respect to γ_j we make use of

$$\frac{\partial P(k)}{\partial \gamma_j} = \delta_{jk} P(j) - P(j) P(k) \tag{2.82}$$

which follows from (2.81). Using the chain rule in the form

$$\frac{\partial E}{\partial \gamma_j} = \sum_{k=1}^{M} \frac{\partial E}{\partial P(k)} \frac{\partial P(k)}{\partial \gamma_j} \tag{2.83}$$

together with (2.75) and (2.78), we then obtain the required derivatives in the form

$$\frac{\partial E}{\partial \gamma_j} = -\sum_{n=1}^{N} \{P(j|\mathbf{x}^n) - P(j)\} \tag{2.84}$$

where we have made use of (2.76). The complete set of derivatives of the error function with respect to the parameters of the model, given by (2.79), (2.80) and (2.84), can then be used in the non-linear optimization algorithms described in Chapter 7 to provide practical techniques for finding minima of the error function.

Some insight into the nature of the maximum likelihood solution can be obtained by considering the expressions for the parameters at a minimum of E. Setting (2.79) to zero we obtain

$$\widehat{\boldsymbol{\mu}}_j = \frac{\sum_n P(j|\mathbf{x}^n)\mathbf{x}^n}{\sum_n P(j|\mathbf{x}^n)} \tag{2.85}$$

which represents the intuitively satisfying result that the mean of the jth component is just the mean of the data vectors, weighted by the posterior probabilities that the corresponding data points were generated from that component. Similarly, setting the derivatives in (2.80) to zero we find

$$\widehat{\sigma}_j^2 = \frac{1}{d} \frac{\sum_n P(j|\mathbf{x}^n)\|\mathbf{x}^n - \widehat{\boldsymbol{\mu}}_j\|^2}{\sum_n P(j|\mathbf{x}^n)} \tag{2.86}$$

which again represents the intuitive result that the variance of the jth component is given by the variance of the data with respect to the mean of that component, again weighted with the posterior probabilities. Finally, setting the derivative in (2.84) to zero we obtain

$$\widehat{P}(j) = \frac{1}{N} \sum_{n=1}^{N} P(j|\mathbf{x}^n) \tag{2.87}$$

so that, at the maximum likelihood solution, the prior probability for the jth component is given by the posterior probabilities for that component, averaged over the data set.

2.6.2 *The EM algorithm*

While the formulae given in (2.85), (2.86) and (2.87) provide useful insight into the nature of the maximum likelihood solution, they do not provide a direct method for calculating the parameters. In fact they represent highly non-linear coupled equations, since the parameters occur implicitly on the right-hand sides by virtue of (2.75). They do, however, suggest that we might seek an iterative scheme for finding the minima of E. Suppose we begin by making some initial guess for the parameters of the Gaussian mixture model, which we shall call the 'old' parameter values. We can then evaluate the right-hand sides in (2.85), (2.86) and (2.87), and this will give a revised estimate for the parameters, which we shall call the 'new' parameter values, for which we might hope the value of the error function is smaller. These parameter values then become the 'old' values, and the process is repeated. We shall show that, provided some care is taken over the way in which the updates are performed, an algorithm of this form can be found which is guaranteed to decrease the error function at each iteration, until a local minimum is found. This provides a simple, practical method for estimating the mixture parameters which avoids the complexities of non-linear optimization algorithms. We shall also see that this is a special case of a more general procedure known as the *expectation–maximization*, or EM, algorithm (Dempster *et al.*, 1977).

From (2.78) we can write the change in error when we replace the old parameter values by the new values in the form

$$E^{\text{new}} - E^{\text{old}} = -\sum_n \ln \left\{ \frac{p^{\text{new}}(\mathbf{x}^n)}{p^{\text{old}}(\mathbf{x}^n)} \right\} \tag{2.88}$$

where $p^{\text{new}}(\mathbf{x})$ denotes the probability density evaluated using the new values for the parameters, while $p^{\text{old}}(\mathbf{x})$ represents the density evaluated using the old parameter values. Using the definition of the mixture distribution given by (2.71), we can write this in the form

$$E^{\text{new}} - E^{\text{old}} = -\sum_n \ln \left\{ \frac{\sum_j P^{\text{new}}(j) p^{\text{new}}(\mathbf{x}^n|j)}{p^{\text{old}}(\mathbf{x}^n)} \frac{P^{\text{old}}(j|\mathbf{x}^n)}{P^{\text{old}}(j|\mathbf{x}^n)} \right\} \qquad (2.89)$$

where the last factor inside the brackets is simply the identity. We now make use of Jensen's inequality (Exercise 2.13) which says that, given a set of numbers $\lambda_j \geq 0$ such that $\sum_j \lambda_j = 1$,

$$\ln \left(\sum_j \lambda_j x_j \right) \geq \sum_j \lambda_j \ln(x_j). \qquad (2.90)$$

Since the probabilities $P^{\text{old}}(j|\mathbf{x})$ in the numerator of (2.89) sum to unity, they can play the role of the λ_j in (2.90). This gives

$$E^{\text{new}} - E^{\text{old}} \leq -\sum_n \sum_j P^{\text{old}}(j|\mathbf{x}^n) \ln \left\{ \frac{P^{\text{new}}(j) p^{\text{new}}(\mathbf{x}^n|j)}{p^{\text{old}}(\mathbf{x}^n) P^{\text{old}}(j|\mathbf{x}^n)} \right\}. \qquad (2.91)$$

We wish to minimize E^{new} with respect to the 'new' parameters. If we let Q be the right-hand side in (2.91) then we have $E^{\text{new}} \leq E^{\text{old}} + Q$ and so $E^{\text{old}} + Q$ represents an upper bound on the value of E^{new}. We can therefore seek to minimize this bound with respect to the 'new' values of the parameters, as illustrated in Figure 2.13 (Luttrell, 1994). Minimizing Q will necessarily lead to a decrease in the value of the E^{new} unless E^{new} is already at a local minimum.

If we now drop terms which depend only on the 'old' parameters, we can write the right-hand side of (2.91) in the form

$$\widetilde{Q} = -\sum_n \sum_j P^{\text{old}}(j|\mathbf{x}^n) \ln \left\{ P^{\text{new}}(j) p^{\text{new}}(\mathbf{x}^n|j) \right\} \qquad (2.92)$$

and the smallest value for the upper bound is found by minimizing this quantity. If we consider the specific case of a Gaussian mixture model then we have

$$\widetilde{Q} = -\sum_n \sum_j P^{\text{old}}(j|\mathbf{x}^n) \left\{ \ln P^{\text{new}}(j) - d \ln \sigma_j^{\text{new}} - \frac{\|\mathbf{x}^n - \boldsymbol{\mu}_j^{\text{new}}\|^2}{2(\sigma_j^{\text{new}})^2} \right\} + \text{const.} \qquad (2.93)$$

We can now minimize this function with respect to the 'new' parameters. For the parameters $\boldsymbol{\mu}_j$ and σ_j this minimization is straightforward. However, for the mixing parameters $P^{\text{new}}(j)$ we must take account of the constraint $\sum_j P^{\text{new}}(j) = 1$. This is easily done by introducing a Lagrange multiplier λ and minimizing the function

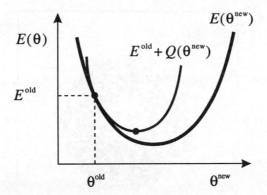

Figure 2.13. Schematic plot of the error function E as a function of the new value θ^{new} of one of the parameters of the mixture model. The curve $E^{\text{old}} + Q(\theta^{\text{new}})$ provides an upper bound on the value of E^{new} and the EM algorithm involves finding the minimum value of this upper bound.

$$\widetilde{Q} + \lambda \left(\sum_j P^{\text{new}}(j) - 1 \right). \tag{2.94}$$

Setting the derivatives of (2.94) with respect to $P^{\text{new}}(j)$ to zero we obtain

$$0 = -\sum_n \frac{P^{\text{old}}(j|\mathbf{x}^n)}{P^{\text{new}}(j)} + \lambda. \tag{2.95}$$

The value of λ can be found by multiplying both sides of (2.95) by $P^{\text{new}}(j)$ and summing over j. Using $\sum_j P^{\text{new}}(j) = 1$ and $\sum_j P^{\text{old}}(j|\mathbf{x}^n) = 1$ we obtain $\lambda = N$. We then finally obtain the following update equations for the parameters of the mixture model:

$$\boldsymbol{\mu}_j^{\text{new}} = \frac{\sum_n P^{\text{old}}(j|\mathbf{x}^n)\mathbf{x}^n}{\sum_n P^{\text{old}}(j|\mathbf{x}^n)} \tag{2.96}$$

$$(\sigma_j^{\text{new}})^2 = \frac{1}{d} \frac{\sum_n P^{\text{old}}(j|\mathbf{x}^n)\|\mathbf{x}^n - \boldsymbol{\mu}_j^{\text{new}}\|^2}{\sum_n P^{\text{old}}(j|\mathbf{x}^n)} \tag{2.97}$$

$$P(j)^{\text{new}} = \frac{1}{N} \sum_n P^{\text{old}}(j|\mathbf{x}^n). \tag{2.98}$$

Notice carefully where the 'new' and 'old' parameters appear on the right-hand

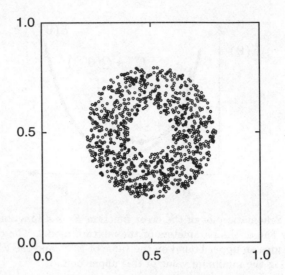

Figure 2.14. Example of the application of the EM algorithm to mixture density estimation showing 1000 data points drawn from a distribution which is
uniform inside an annular region.

sides of these expressions. These should be compared with the corresponding
maximum likelihood results (2.85)–(2.87). The algorithm is readily extended to
include Gaussian functions with full covariance matrices.

As a simple example of the use of the EM algorithm for density estimation,
we consider a set of 1000 data points generated from a distribution which is
uniform within an annular-shaped region, as shown in Figure 2.14. A Gaussian
mixture model, with seven components of the form (2.77), was then fitted to
this data. The initial configuration of the model is shown in Figure 2.15. After
20 cycles of the EM algorithm the Gaussians had evolved to the form shown
in Figure 2.16. The corresponding contours of probability density are shown in
Figure 2.17.

Further insight into the EM algorithm can be obtained by returning to our
earlier remarks concerning the similarities between a mixture density model and
the representation for the unconditional density in a classification problem. In
the latter case, the data points $\mathbf{x}^n$ all carry a class label indicating which component density function was responsible for generating them. This allows each
class-conditional density function to be considered separately, and its parameters
found by maximizing the likelihood using only the data points from that class.
If the class-conditional densities are given by Gaussian functions, then we saw in
Section 2.2 that the corresponding maximum likelihood problem could be solved
analytically to give expressions such as (2.19) and (2.20) for the parameters of
the Gaussians.

For the problem of unconditional density estimation using a mixture model we

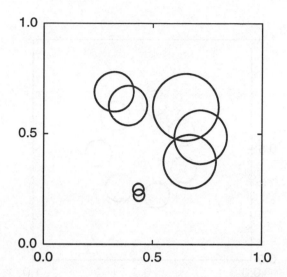

Figure 2.15. This shows the initial configuration of seven Gaussians of a mixture model which has been initialized using the data in Figure 2.14. Each circle represents the line along which $\|\mathbf{x} - \boldsymbol{\mu}_j\| = \sigma_j$ for the corresponding Gaussian component. The parameters of the mixture model were initialized by first setting the centres $\boldsymbol{\mu}_j$ to a random subset of the data points. The width parameter σ_j for each component was initialized to the distance to the nearest other component centre, and finally the priors $P(j)$ were all set to $1/M$, where $M = 7$ in this example.

do not have corresponding 'class' labels. The data set is said to be *incomplete*, and the maximum likelihood procedure leads to a non-linear optimization problem which does not have an analytic solution. A very general treatment of such incomplete-data problems was given by Dempster *et al.* (1977), who developed the EM algorithm as an elegant and powerful approach to their solution. It can also be applied to problems in which incompleteness of the data takes the form of missing values for some of the variables in the training set. The example of re-estimating the parameters of a Gaussian mixture model discussed above is a special case of the EM algorithm.

We have already remarked that the problem of determining the parameters in the mixture model would be very straightforward if we knew which component j was responsible for generating each data point. We therefore consider a hypothetical *complete* data set in which each data point is labelled with the component which generated it. Thus, for each data point $\mathbf{x}^n$, we can introduce a variable z^n, which is an integer in the range $(1, M)$ specifying which component of the mixture generated the data point. The negative log-likelihood (or error function) for the complete data problem, for 'new' parameter values, is given by

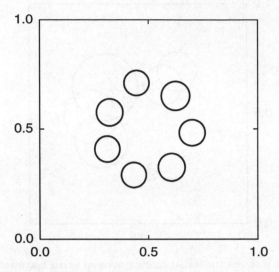

Figure 2.16. Final configuration of the Gaussians from Figure 2.15 after 20 cycles of the EM algorithm using the data set from Figure 2.14.

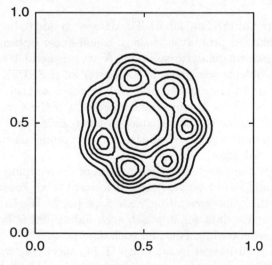

Figure 2.17. Contours of constant probability density corresponding to the Gaussian mixture model of Figure 2.16.

$$E^{\text{comp}} = -\ln \mathcal{L}^{\text{comp}} \tag{2.99}$$

$$= -\sum_{n=1}^{N} \ln p^{\text{new}}(\mathbf{x}^n, z^n) \tag{2.100}$$

$$= -\sum_{n=1}^{N} \ln \{P^{\text{new}}(z^n) p^{\text{new}}(\mathbf{x}^n|z^n)\}. \tag{2.101}$$

If we knew which component was responsible for generating each data point, then $P^{\text{new}}(z^n) = 1$ and the complete-data error function decomposes into a sum of independent terms, one for each component of the mixture, each of which only involves the data points generated by that component. This sum is then easily minimized with respect to the parameters of the component distributions. The problem, however, is that we do not know which component is responsible for each data point, and hence we do not know the distribution of the z^n. We therefore adopt the following procedure. First we guess some values for the parameters of the mixture model (the 'old' parameter values) and we then use these, together with Bayes' theorem, to find the probability distribution of the $\{z^n\}$. We then compute the expectation of E^{comp} with respect to this distribution. This is the *expectation* or E-step of the EM algorithm. The 'new' parameter values are then found by minimizing this expected error with respect to the parameters. This is the *maximization* or M-step of the EM algorithm (since minimizing an error function is equivalent to maximizing the corresponding likelihood).

The probability for z^n, given the value of $\mathbf{x}^n$ and the 'old' parameter values, is just $P^{\text{old}}(z^n|\mathbf{x}^n)$. Thus, the expectation of E^{comp} over the complete set of $\{z^n\}$ values is obtained by summing (2.101) over all possible values of the $\{z^n\}$ with a weighting factor given by the probability distribution for the $\{z^n\}$ to give

$$\mathcal{E}[E^{\text{comp}}] = \sum_{z^1=1}^{M} \cdots \sum_{z^N=1}^{M} E^{\text{comp}} \prod_{n=1}^{N} P^{\text{old}}(z^n|\mathbf{x}^n). \tag{2.102}$$

It is convenient to rewrite E^{comp} from (2.101) in the equivalent form

$$E^{\text{comp}} = -\sum_{n=1}^{N} \sum_{j=1}^{M} \delta_{jz^n} \ln \{P^{\text{new}}(j) p^{\text{new}}(\mathbf{x}^n|j)\}. \tag{2.103}$$

We now substitute (2.103) into (2.102), and perform the sums over the $\{z^n\}$ variables by making use of the identity

$$\sum_{z^1=1}^{M} \cdots \sum_{z^N=1}^{M} \delta_{jz^n} \prod_{n'=1}^{N} P^{\text{old}}(z^{n'}|\mathbf{x}^{n'}) = P^{\text{old}}(j|\mathbf{x}^n) \tag{2.104}$$

which can be proved using

$$\sum_{z=1}^{M} P^{\text{old}}(z|\mathbf{x}^n) = 1.$$ (2.105)

This gives the expectation of the complete-data likelihood in the form

$$\mathcal{E}[E^{\text{comp}}] = -\sum_{n=1}^{N}\sum_{j=1}^{M} P^{\text{old}}(j|\mathbf{x}^n)\ln\left\{P^{\text{new}}(j)p^{\text{new}}(\mathbf{x}^n|j)\right\}.$$ (2.106)

We now note that (2.106) is identical to (2.92). Thus, minimization of (2.106) leads to the form of the EM algorithm derived above.

2.6.3 *Stochastic estimation of parameters*

As a third approach to the determination of the parameters of a Gaussian mixture model we consider the technique of stochastic on-line optimization (Tråvén, 1991). Again we seek to minimize the error function, but now we suppose that the data points are arriving one at a time and we wish to find a sequential update scheme. Consider the minimum-error expression (2.85) for the mean $\boldsymbol{\mu}_j$ of the jth component of the mixture for a data set consisting of N points

$$\boldsymbol{\mu}_j^N = \frac{\sum_{n=1}^{N} P(j|\mathbf{x}^n)\mathbf{x}^n}{\sum_{n=1}^{N} P(j|\mathbf{x}^n)}.$$ (2.107)

From the corresponding expression for $N+1$ data points, we can separate off the contribution from $\mathbf{x}^{N+1}$ in order to obtain an expression for $\boldsymbol{\mu}_j^{N+1}$ in terms of $\boldsymbol{\mu}_j^N$. This is analogous to the procedure we adopted for stochastic estimation of the parameters of a single Gaussian function in Section 2.4. After some simple algebra we obtain

$$\boldsymbol{\mu}_j^{N+1} = \boldsymbol{\mu}_j^N + \eta_j^{N+1}(\mathbf{x}^{N+1} - \boldsymbol{\mu}_j^N)$$ (2.108)

where the parameter η_j^{N+1} is given by

$$\eta_j^{N+1} = \frac{P(j|\mathbf{x}^{N+1})}{\sum_{n=1}^{N+1} P(j|\mathbf{x}^n)}.$$ (2.109)

As it stands this does not constitute a useful algorithm since the denominator in (2.109) contains an ever increasing number of terms, all of which would have to be re-estimated every time the parameter values were changed. It would therefore require the storage of all previous data points, in conflict with the goal of a stochastic learning procedure. One approach is to note that, if the model had already converged to the maximum likelihood solution, we could use (2.87) to write (2.109) in the form

$$\eta_j^{N+1} = \frac{P(j|\mathbf{x}^{N+1})}{(N+1)P(j)} \tag{2.110}$$

and then to use this as an approximation for the η_j. Alternatively, the parameters η_j can themselves also be estimated stochastically, using the update formula

$$\frac{1}{\eta_j^{N+1}} = \frac{P(j|\mathbf{x}^N)}{P(j|\mathbf{x}^{N+1})} \frac{1}{\eta_j^N} + 1 \tag{2.111}$$

which follows directly from the definition (2.109). If the data is arriving on-line, as distinct from being taken from a fixed training set with replacement, then the problem of singular solutions, discussed in Section 2.6.1, will not arise since an individual data point is used once only and then discarded.

Exercises

2.1 ($\star$) Using the form (2.1) for the normal distribution in one dimension, and the results derived in Appendix B, show that $\int p(x)\,dx = 1$, and verify (2.2) and (2.3).

2.2 ($\star\star$) Consider the Gaussian distribution in d dimensions given by (2.4). By using the properties of symmetric matrices derived in Appendix A, show that there exists a transformation to a new coordinate system, defined by the eigenvectors of $\mathbf{\Sigma}$, such that the transformed variables $\tilde{x}_i$ become statistically independent, so that the distribution of the $\tilde{x}_i$ can be written as $p(\tilde{x}_1, \ldots, \tilde{x}_d) = \prod_i p(\tilde{x}_i)$. Hence show that show that $\int p(\mathbf{x})\,d\mathbf{x} = 1$. Finally, verify (2.5) and (2.6).

2.3 ($\star$) Using the expression (2.1) for the normal distribution in one dimension, show that values of the mean and variance parameters which minimize the error function (2.18) are given by (2.21) and (2.22).

2.4 ($\star\star$) Using the definition of expected value given by (1.16), and the form of the normal distribution (2.1), derive the result (2.23). Now consider the following estimate of the variance

$$\tilde{\sigma}^2 = \frac{1}{N-1} \sum_{n=1}^{N} (x^n - \hat{\mu})^2 \tag{2.112}$$

where $\hat{\mu}$ is the maximum likelihood estimate for the mean given by (2.21). Show that this estimate has the property that its expected value is equal to the true variance σ^2. Estimators which have this property are said to be *unbiased*. If the mean μ of the distribution is known exactly, instead of being determined from the data, show that the estimate of the variance given by

$$\tilde{\sigma}^2 = \frac{1}{N} \sum_{n=1}^{N} (x^n - \mu)^2 \tag{2.113}$$

is unbiased.

2.5 $(\star)$ Derive the results (2.32) and (2.33) for the mean and variance of the posterior distribution of μ given a set of N observed values of x.

2.6 $(\star)$ Using the maximum likelihood expression (2.19) for the mean $\boldsymbol{\mu}$ of a Gaussian distribution, derive the result (2.37) for the iterative sequential estimation of $\boldsymbol{\mu}$.

2.7 $(\star\star)$ Consider the problem of parametric density estimation for data in one dimension using a normal distribution with mean μ and variance σ^2. Show that the Robbins–Monro formula (2.48) for sequential maximum likelihood gives rise to the heuristic formula (2.37) for the estimation of μ provided we choose the coefficients $a_N = \sigma^2/(N+1)$. Obtain the corresponding formula for iterative estimation of σ^2, analogous to (2.37) for μ, by separating out the contribution from the $(N+1)^{\text{th}}$ data point in the maximum likelihood expression (2.22). Verify that substitution of a normal distribution into the Robbins–Monro formula (2.48) gives the same result, for a suitable choice of the coefficients a_N.

2.8 $(\star)$ Consider two class-conditional densities in d-dimensions, each of which is described by a Gaussian with a covariance matrix given by $\boldsymbol{\Sigma}_k = \sigma_k^2 \mathbf{I}$, where $\mathbf{I}$ is the unit matrix, but with different values of the variance parameter σ_k^2. Show that the decision boundary along which the posterior probabilities for the two classes are equal takes the form of a hypersphere.

2.9 $(\star\star\star)$ This exercise explores numerically the behaviour of the K-nearest-neighbour classification algorithm. Begin by generating data in two dimensions from two classes, each described by a Gaussian distribution having a covariance matrix which is proportional to the unit matrix, but with different variances. Assume equal class priors but use different class means. Plot the data points, using a different symbol for each of the two classes, and also plot the optimal decision boundary given by the result derived in Exercise 2.8. Also plot the decision boundaries predicted by the K-nearest-neighbour classification algorithm for various values of K. One way to do this is to consider a fine grid of points covering the region of interest, and assign each point the value $+1$ or -1 according to the class predicted the K-nearest-neighbour classification described on page 57. Then use a contouring package to plot the contour having value 0. By restricting the number of data points, show that there exists an optimal value for K in order for the decision boundary predicted by the algorithm to be as close as possible to the optimal one, and that smaller or larger values of K give poorer results.

2.10 ($\star$) By sketching graphs of $\ln x$ and $x - 1$ verify the inequality $\ln x \leq x - 1$ with equality if, and only if, $x = 1$. Confirm this result by differentiation of $\ln x - (x - 1)$. Hence show that the Kullback–Leibler distance (2.70) satisfies $L \geq 0$ with equality if, and only if, the two distributions are equal.

2.11 ($\star$) Consider two discrete probability distributions p_i and q_i such that $\sum_i p_i = 1$ and $\sum_i q_i = 1$. The corresponding discrete version of the Kullback–Leibler distance can be written

$$-\sum_i p_i \ln \left(\frac{q_i}{p_i} \right) \tag{2.114}$$

By differentiating (2.114) with respect to q_i, and making use of a Lagrange multiplier (Appendix C) to ensure that the constraint $\sum_i q_i = 1$ is satisfied, show that this distance is minimized when $q_i = p_i$ for all i, and that the corresponding value for the distance is zero.

2.12 ($\star$) Using the result (2.105), verify the identity (2.104).

2.13 ($\star\star$) In discussing the convergence properties of the EM algorithm we made use of Jensen's inequality for convex functions. We can define a convex function $f(x)$ as one for which every chord lies on or below the graph of the function (a chord being a straight line which connects two points on the graph of the function). This is illustrated in Figure 2.18. Use this definition

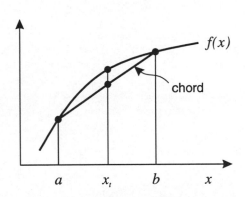

Figure 2.18. Illustration of a convex function $f(x)$ as used to derive Jensen's inequality.

to show that, for a point $x_t = (1-t)a + tb$ part way along the chord, where $0 \leq t \leq 1$, we have

$$f((1-t)a + tb) \geq (1-t)f(a) + tf(b). \tag{2.115}$$

Given a set of points x_j all lying in the interval (a, b), and a set of M

numbers $\lambda_j \geq 0$ such that $\sum_j \lambda_j = 1$, show that the quantity $\sum_j \lambda_j x_j$ also lies in the interval (a, b). Starting from (2.115) use induction to prove Jensen's inequality

$$f\left(\sum_{j=1}^{M} \lambda_j x_j\right) \geq \sum_{j=1}^{M} \lambda_j f(x_j), \qquad (2.116)$$

for any $M \geq 2$. This is the form of Jensen's inequality used in (2.90).

2.14 ($\star\star$) Starting from (2.107), derive the expression (2.108) for the stochastic update of the mean μ_j of the jth component of a Gaussian mixture model. Similarly, starting from the maximum likelihood expression for the variance of a spherical Gaussian given by (2.86), obtain the corresponding expression for $(\sigma_j^2)^{N+1}$. Finally, derive (2.111) from (2.109).

3

SINGLE-LAYER NETWORKS

In Chapter 1 we showed that the optimal decision rule for minimizing the probability of misclassification requires a new pattern to be assigned to the class having the largest posterior probability. We also showed how the posterior probabilities can be related to class-conditional densities through Bayes' theorem, and in Chapter 2 we described several techniques for estimating these densities. An alternative approach, which circumvents the determination of probability densities, is based on the idea of a discriminant function, also introduced in Chapter 1. In a practical application of discriminant functions, specific parametrized functional forms are chosen, and the values of the parameters are then determined from a set of training data by means of a suitable learning algorithm.

The simplest choice of discriminant function consists of a linear combination of the input variables, in which the coefficients in the linear combination are the parameters of the model, and has been considered widely in the literature on conventional approaches to pattern recognition. This simple discriminant can be generalized by transforming the linear combination with a non-linear function (called an activation function) which leads to concepts such as logistic regression and the perceptron. Another extension involves transforming the input variables with fixed non-linear functions before forming the linear combination, to give generalized linear discriminants. As we shall see, these various forms of linear discriminant can be regarded as forms of neural network in which there is a single layer of adaptive weights between the inputs and the outputs.

Various techniques exist for determining the weight values in single-layer networks, and in this chapter we shall consider several of them in detail. In particular, we shall study perceptron learning, least-squares methods and the Fisher discriminant. As well as forming an important class of techniques in their own right, single-layer networks provide many useful insights into the properties of more complex multi-layer networks. Single-layer networks were widely studied in the 1960's, and the history of such networks is reviewed in Widrow and Lehr (1990). Two useful books from this period are Nilsson (1965) and Lewis and Coates (1967).

3.1 Linear discriminant functions

In Chapter 1 we saw that optimal discriminant functions can be determined from class-conditional densities via Bayes' theorem. Instead of performing density estimation, however, we can postulate specific parametrized functional forms for the discriminant functions and use the training data set to determine suitable values for the parameters. In this section we consider various forms of linear discriminant, and discuss their properties.

3.1.1 *Two classes*

We begin by considering the two-category classification problem. In Chapter 1 we introduced the concept of a discriminant function $y(\mathbf{x})$ such that the vector $\mathbf{x}$ is assigned to class $\mathcal{C}_1$ if $y(\mathbf{x}) > 0$ and to class $\mathcal{C}_2$ if $y(\mathbf{x}) < 0$. The simplest choice of discriminant function is one which is linear in the components of $\mathbf{x}$, and which can therefore be written as

$$y(\mathbf{x}) = \mathbf{w}^{\mathrm{T}}\mathbf{x} + w_0 \tag{3.1}$$

where we shall refer to the d-dimensional vector $\mathbf{w}$ as the *weight vector* and the parameter w_0 as the *bias*. Sometimes $-w_0$ is called a *threshold*. Note that the use of the term bias here is quite distinct from the concept of statistical bias which is discussed briefly on page 41, and at length in Section 9.1. From Section 2.1.3 we know that, for class-conditional densities having normal distributions with equal covariance matrices, a linear discriminant of the form (3.1) is optimal.

The expression in (3.1) has a simple geometrical interpretation (Duda and Hart, 1973) as follows. We first note that the decision boundary $y(\mathbf{x}) = 0$ corresponds to a $(d-1)$-dimensional hyperplane in d-dimensional $\mathbf{x}$-space. For the case of a two-dimensional input space, $d = 2$, the decision boundary is a straight line, as shown in Figure 3.1. If $\mathbf{x}^A$ and $\mathbf{x}^B$ are two points on the hyperplane, then $y(\mathbf{x}^A) = 0 = y(\mathbf{x}^B)$ and so, using (3.1), we have $\mathbf{w}^{\mathrm{T}}(\mathbf{x}^B - \mathbf{x}^A) = 0$. Thus, $\mathbf{w}$ is normal to any vector lying in the hyperplane, and so we see that $\mathbf{w}$ determines the orientation of the decision boundary. If $\mathbf{x}$ is a point on the hyperplane then the normal distance from the origin to the hyperplane is given by

$$l = \frac{\mathbf{w}^{\mathrm{T}}\mathbf{x}}{\|\mathbf{w}\|} = -\frac{w_0}{\|\mathbf{w}\|} \tag{3.2}$$

where we have used $y(\mathbf{x}) = 0$ together with (3.1). Thus, the bias w_0 determines the position of the hyperplane in $\mathbf{x}$-space, as indicated in Figure 3.1.

There is a slightly different notation which we can adopt which will often prove convenient. If we define new $(d+1)$-dimensional vectors $\widetilde{\mathbf{w}} = (w_0, \mathbf{w})$ and $\widetilde{\mathbf{x}} = (1, \mathbf{x})$, then we can rewrite (3.1) in the form

$$y(\mathbf{x}) = \widetilde{\mathbf{w}}^{\mathrm{T}}\widetilde{\mathbf{x}}. \tag{3.3}$$

With this notation we can interpret the decision boundary $y(\mathbf{x}) = 0$ as a d-dimensional hyperplane which passes through the origin in $(d+1)$-dimensional $\widetilde{\mathbf{x}}$-space.

We can represent the linear discriminant function in (3.1) or (3.3) in terms

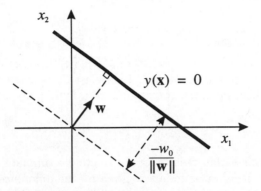

Figure 3.1. A linear decision boundary, corresponding to $y(\mathbf{x}) = 0$, in a two-dimensional input space (x_1, x_2). The weight vector $\mathbf{w}$, which can be represented as a vector in $\mathbf{x}$-space, defines the orientation of the decision plane, while the bias w_0 defines the position of the plane in terms of its perpendicular distance from the origin.

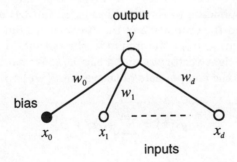

Figure 3.2. Representation of a linear discriminant function as a neural network diagram. Each component in the diagram corresponds to a variable in the linear discriminant expression. The bias w_0 can be considered as a weight parameter from an extra input whose activation x_0 is permanently set to $+1$.

of a network diagram as shown in Figure 3.2. Inputs $x_1, \ldots, x_d$ are shown as circles, which are connected by the weights $w_1, \ldots, w_d$ to the output $y(\mathbf{x})$. The bias w_0 is represented as a weight from an extra input x_0 which is permanently set to unity.

3.1.2 Several classes

Linear discriminants can easily be extended to the case of c classes by following the ideas introduced in Chapter 1 and using one discriminant function $y_k(\mathbf{x})$ for each class C_k of the form

$$y_k(\mathbf{x}) = \mathbf{w}_k^{\mathrm{T}}\mathbf{x} + w_{k0}. \tag{3.4}$$

A new point $\mathbf{x}$ is then assigned to class C_k if $y_k(\mathbf{x}) > y_j(\mathbf{x})$ for all $j \neq k$. The decision boundary separating class C_k from class C_j is given by $y_k(\mathbf{x}) = y_j(\mathbf{x})$ which, for linear discriminants, corresponds to a hyperplane of the form

$$(\mathbf{w}_k - \mathbf{w}_j)^{\mathrm{T}}\mathbf{x} + (w_{k0} - w_{j0}) = 0. \tag{3.5}$$

By analogy with our earlier results for the single discriminant (3.1), we see that the normal to the decision boundary is given by the difference between the two weight vectors, and that the perpendicular distance of the decision boundary from the origin is given by

$$l = -\frac{(w_{k0} - w_{j0})}{\|\mathbf{w}_k - \mathbf{w}_j\|}. \tag{3.6}$$

The multiclass linear discriminant function (3.4) can be expressed in terms of a neural network diagram as shown in Figure 3.3. The circles at the top of the diagram, corresponding to the functions $y_k(\mathbf{x})$ in (3.4) are sometimes called *processing units*, and the evaluation of the discriminant functions can be viewed as a flow of information from the inputs to the outputs. Each output $y_k(\mathbf{x})$ is associated with a weight vector $\mathbf{w}_k$ and a bias w_{k0}. We can express the network outputs in terms of the components of the vectors $\{\mathbf{w}_k\}$ to give

$$y_k(\mathbf{x}) = \sum_{i=1}^{d} w_{ki}x_i + w_{k0}. \tag{3.7}$$

Then each line in Figure 3.3 connecting an input i to an output k corresponds to a weight parameter w_{ki}. As before, we can regard the bias parameters as being weights from an extra input $x_0 = 1$, so that

$$y_k(\mathbf{x}) = \sum_{i=0}^{d} w_{ki}x_i. \tag{3.8}$$

Once the network is trained, a new vector is classified by applying it to the inputs of the network, computing the output unit activations, and assigning the vector to the class whose output unit has the largest activation. This leads to a set of decision regions which are always simply connected and convex. To see

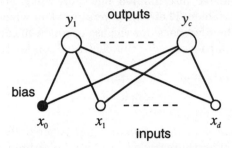

Figure 3.3. Representation of multiple linear discriminant functions $y_k(\mathbf{x})$ as a neural network diagram having c output units. Again, the biases are represented as weights from an extra input $x_0 = 1$.

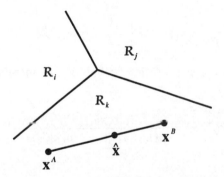

Figure 3.4. Example of decision boundaries produced by a multiclass linear discriminant. If two points $\mathbf{x}^A$ and $\mathbf{x}^B$ both lie in decision region $\mathcal{R}_k$ then every point $\widehat{\mathbf{x}}$ on the line connecting them must also lie in region $\mathcal{R}_k$. It therefore follows that the decision regions must be simply connected and convex.

this, consider two points $\mathbf{x}^A$ and $\mathbf{x}^B$ which both lie in the region $\mathcal{R}_k$ as shown in Figure 3.4. Any point $\widehat{\mathbf{x}}$ which lies on the line joining $\mathbf{x}^A$ and $\mathbf{x}^B$ can be written as

$$\widehat{\mathbf{x}} = \alpha \mathbf{x}^A + (1 - \alpha)\mathbf{x}^B \tag{3.9}$$

where $0 \leq \alpha \leq 1$. Since $\mathbf{x}^A$ and $\mathbf{x}^B$ both lie in $\mathcal{R}_k$, they must satisfy $y_k(\mathbf{x}^A) > y_j(\mathbf{x}^A)$ and $y_k(\mathbf{x}^B) > y_j(\mathbf{x}^B)$ for all $j \neq k$. Using (3.4) and (3.9) it follows that $y_k(\widehat{\mathbf{x}}) = \alpha y_k(\mathbf{x}^A) + (1 - \alpha)y_k(\mathbf{x}^B)$ and hence $y_k(\widehat{\mathbf{x}}) > y_j(\widehat{\mathbf{x}})$ for all $j \neq k$. Thus, all points on the line connecting $\mathbf{x}^A$ and $\mathbf{x}^B$ also lie in $\mathcal{R}_k$ and so the region $\mathcal{R}_k$ must be simply connected and convex.

3.1.3 *Logistic discrimination*

So far we have considered discriminant functions which are simple linear functions of the input variables. There are several ways in which such functions can be generalized, and here we consider the use of a non-linear function $g(\cdot)$ which acts on the linear sum to give a discriminant function for the two-class problem of the form

$$y = g(\mathbf{w}^{\mathrm{T}}\mathbf{x} + w_0) \tag{3.10}$$

where $g(\cdot)$ is called an *activation function* and is generally chosen to be monotonic. The form (3.10) is still regarded as a linear discriminant since the decision boundary which it generates is still linear, as a consequence of the monotonic nature of $g(\cdot)$.

As a motivation for this form of discriminant, consider a two-class problem in which the class-conditional densities are given by Gaussian distributions with equal covariance matrices $\Sigma_1 = \Sigma_2 = \Sigma$, so that

$$p(\mathbf{x}|C_k) = \frac{1}{(2\pi)^{d/2}|\Sigma|^{1/2}} \exp\left\{-\frac{1}{2}(\mathbf{x} - \boldsymbol{\mu}_k)^{\mathrm{T}}\Sigma^{-1}(\mathbf{x} - \boldsymbol{\mu}_k)\right\}. \tag{3.11}$$

Using Bayes' theorem, the posterior probability of membership of class C_1 is given by

$$P(C_1|\mathbf{x}) = \frac{p(\mathbf{x}|C_1)P(C_1)}{p(\mathbf{x}|C_1)P(C_1) + p(\mathbf{x}|C_2)P(C_2)} \tag{3.12}$$

$$= \frac{1}{1 + \exp(-a)} \tag{3.13}$$

$$= g(a) \tag{3.14}$$

where

$$a = \ln \frac{p(\mathbf{x}|C_1)P(C_1)}{p(\mathbf{x}|C_2)P(C_2)} \tag{3.15}$$

and the function $g(a)$ is the *logistic sigmoid* activation function given by

$$g(a) \equiv \frac{1}{1 + \exp(-a)} \tag{3.16}$$

which is plotted in Figure 3.5. If we now substitute expressions for the class-conditional densities from (3.11) into (3.15) we obtain

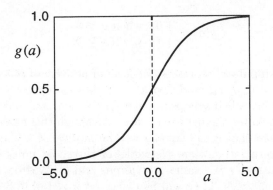

Figure 3.5. Plot of the logistic sigmoid activation function given by (3.16).

$$a = \mathbf{w}^T\mathbf{x} + w_0 \qquad (3.17)$$

where

$$\mathbf{w} = \Sigma^{-1}(\boldsymbol{\mu}_1 - \boldsymbol{\mu}_2) \qquad (3.18)$$

$$w_0 = -\frac{1}{2}\boldsymbol{\mu}_1^T\Sigma^{-1}\boldsymbol{\mu}_1 + \frac{1}{2}\boldsymbol{\mu}_2^T\Sigma^{-1}\boldsymbol{\mu}_2 + \ln\frac{P(\mathcal{C}_1)}{P(\mathcal{C}_2)}. \qquad (3.19)$$

Thus, we see that the use of the logistic sigmoid activation function allows the outputs of the discriminant to be interpreted as posterior probabilities. This implies that such a discriminant is providing more than simply a classification decision, and is potentially a very powerful result. The importance of interpreting the outputs of networks in terms of probabilities is discussed at much greater length in Chapter 6.

The term sigmoid means 'S-shaped', and the logistic form of the sigmoid maps the interval $(-\infty, \infty)$ onto $(0, 1)$. If $|a|$ is small, then the logistic sigmoid function $g(a)$ can be approximated by a linear function, and so in this sense a network with sigmoidal activation functions contains a linear network as a special case. If there are more than two classes then an extension of the previous analysis leads to a generalization of the logistic sigmoid called a *normalized exponential* or *softmax*, which is discussed in detail in Section 6.9.

Linear discriminants with logistic activation functions have been widely used in the statistics literature under the name *logistic discrimination* (Anderson, 1982). Sigmoidal activation functions also play a crucial role in multi-layer neural networks, as discussed in Chapter 4.

Another form of linear discriminant was introduced by McCulloch and Pitts (1943) as a simple mathematical model for the behaviour of a single neuron in a biological nervous system. Again this takes the form (3.10) with an activation function which is the Heaviside step function

$$g(a) = \begin{cases} 0 & \text{when } a < 0 \\ 1 & \text{when } a \geq 0. \end{cases} \tag{3.20}$$

In this model the inputs x_i represent the level of activity of other neurons which connect to the neuron being modelled, the weights w_i represent the strengths of the interconnections, called synapses, between the neurons, and the bias w_0 represents the threshold for the neuron to 'fire'. Although this model has its origins in biology, it is clear that it can equally well be motivated within the framework of statistical pattern recognition. Networks of threshold units were studied by Rosenblatt (1962) under the name *perceptrons* and by Widrow and Hoff (1960) who called them *adalines*. They will be discussed in detail in Section 3.5.

Note that it is sometimes convenient to regard the linear discriminant (3.1) as a special case of the more general form (3.10). In this case the model is said to have a linear activation function, which in fact is just the identity $g(a) \equiv a$.

3.1.4 *Binary input vectors*

Linear discriminants, and the logistic activation function, also arise in a natural way when we consider input patterns in which the variables are binary (so that each x_i can take only the values 0 or 1). Let P_{ki} denote the probability that the input x_i takes the value $+1$ when the input vector is drawn from the class $\mathcal{C}_k$. The corresponding probability that $x_i = 0$ is then given by $1 - P_{ki}$. We can combine these together to write the probability for x_i to take either of its allowed values in the form

$$p(x_i|\mathcal{C}_k) = P_{ki}^{x_i}(1 - P_{ki})^{1-x_i} \tag{3.21}$$

which is called a *Bernoulli* distribution. If we now assume that the input variables are statistically independent, we obtain the probability for the complete input vector as the product of the probabilities for each of the components separately:

$$p(\mathbf{x}|\mathcal{C}_k) = \prod_{i=1}^{d} P_{ki}^{x_i}(1 - P_{ki})^{1-x_i}. \tag{3.22}$$

We now recall from Chapter 1 that we can write a discriminant function which minimizes the probability of misclassifying new inputs in the form

$$y_k(\mathbf{x}) = \ln P(\mathbf{x}|\mathcal{C}_k) + \ln P(\mathcal{C}_k). \tag{3.23}$$

Substituting (3.22) into (3.23) we obtain a linear discriminant function given by

$$y_k(\mathbf{x}) = \sum_{i=1}^{d} w_{ki} x_i + w_{k0} \tag{3.24}$$

in which the weights and bias are given by

$$w_{ki} = \ln P_{ki} - \ln(1 - P_{ki}) \tag{3.25}$$

$$w_{k0} = \sum_{i=1}^{d} \ln(1 - P_{ki}) + \ln P(\mathcal{C}_k). \tag{3.26}$$

We have already seen that, for two classes with normally distributed class-conditional densities, the posterior probabilities can be obtained from the linear discriminant by applying a logistic activation function. A similar result holds also for the Bernoulli distribution. Consider a set of independent binary variables x_i, having Bernoulli class-conditional densities given by (3.22). If we substitute (3.22) into (3.12) we again obtain a single-layer network structure, with a logistic activation function, of the form

$$P(\mathcal{C}_1|\mathbf{x}) = g(\mathbf{w}^{\mathrm{T}}\mathbf{x} + w_0) \tag{3.27}$$

where $g(a)$ is given by (3.16) and

$$w_0 = \sum_i \ln \frac{1 - P_{1i}}{1 - P_{2i}} + \ln \frac{P(\mathcal{C}_1)}{P(\mathcal{C}_2)} \tag{3.28}$$

$$w_i = \ln \frac{P_{1i}}{P_{2i}} - \ln \frac{1 - P_{1i}}{1 - P_{2i}}. \tag{3.29}$$

We have shown that, both for normally distributed and Bernoulli distributed class-conditional densities, the posterior probabilities are obtained by a logistic single-layer network. In fact these are particular instances of a much more general result, which is derived in Section 6.7.1.

3.2 Linear separability

So far in this chapter we have discussed discriminant functions having a decision boundary which is linear, or more generally hyperplanar in higher dimensions. Clearly this is a very restricted class of decision boundary, and we might well expect such systems to have less than optimal performance for many practical applications. Indeed, this provides the principal motivation for using multi-layer networks of the kind discussed in Chapters 4 and 5. The particular nature of the limitation inherent in single-layer systems warrants some careful discussion, however.

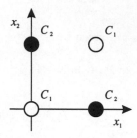

Figure 3.6. The exclusive-OR problem consists of four patterns in a two-dimensional space as shown. It provides a simple example of a problem which is not linearly separable.

Consider for the moment the problem of learning to classify a given data set exactly, where each input vector has been labelled as belonging to one of two classes C_1 and C_2. If all of the points can be a classified correctly by a linear (i.e. hyperplanar) decision boundary, then the points are said to be *linearly separable*. For such a data set there exist weight and bias values such that a linear discriminant will lead to perfect classification. A simple example of a data set which is not linearly separable is provided by the two-dimensional *exclusive-OR* problem, also known as XOR, illustrated in Figure 3.6. The input vectors $\mathbf{x} = (0,0)$ and $(1,1)$ belong to class C_1, while the input vectors $(0,1)$ and $(1,0)$ belong to class C_2. It is clear that there is no linear decision boundary which can classify all four points correctly. This problem can be generalized to d-dimensions when it is known as the d-bit parity problem. In this case the data set consists of all possible binary input vectors of length d, which are classified as class C_1 if there is an even number of 1's in the input vector, and as class C_2 otherwise.

For the case of continuous input variables it is interesting to consider the probability that a random set of patterns will be linearly separable. Suppose we have N data points distributed at random in d dimensions. Note that the particular distribution used to generate the random points is not relevant. All that we require is that there are no accidental degeneracies, i.e. that there is no subset of d or fewer points which are linearly dependent. The points are then said to be in *general position*. Having chosen the points, imagine that we then randomly assign each of the points to one of the two classes C_1 and C_2 with equal probability. Each possible assignment for the complete data set is referred to as a *dichotomy*, and for N points there are 2^N possible dichotomies. We now ask what fraction $F(N, d)$ of these dichotomies is linearly separable. It can be shown (Cover, 1965) that this fraction is given by the expression

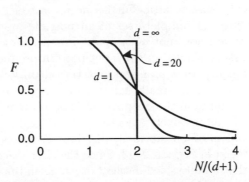

Figure 3.7. Plot of the fraction $F(N, d)$ of the dichotomies of N data points in d dimensions which are linearly separable, as a function of $N/(d+1)$, for various values of d.

$$F(N, d) = \begin{cases} 1 & \text{when } N \leq d + 1 \\ \dfrac{1}{2^{N-1}} \displaystyle\sum_{i=0}^{d} \binom{N-1}{i} & \text{when } N \geq d + 1 \end{cases} \qquad (3.30)$$

which is plotted as a function of $N/(d+1)$ in Figure 3.7 for $d = 1$, $d = 20$ and $d = \infty$. Here the symbol

$$\binom{N}{M} \equiv \frac{N!}{(N-M)!M!} \qquad (3.31)$$

denotes the number of combinations of M objects selected from a total of N. We see from (3.30) that, if the number of data points is fewer than $d+1$, any labelling of the points will always lead to a linearly separable problem. For $N = 2(d+1)$, the probability of linear separability is 0.5 for any value of d (Exercise 3.5). In a practical application, the positions of points from the same class will tend to be correlated, and so the probability that a data set with a much larger number of points than $2(d+1)$ will be linearly separable is higher than (3.30) would suggest.

For the case of binary input patterns, if there are d inputs then there are 2^d possible input patterns and hence 2^{2^d} possible labellings of those patterns between two classes. Those which can be implemented by a perceptron are called *threshold logic functions* and form an extremely small subset (less than $2^{d^2}/d!$) of the total (Lewis and Coates, 1967).

In the neural computing literature a lot of attention is often paid to the inability of single-layer networks to solve simple problems such as XOR. From our statistical pattern recognition perspective, however, we see that the ability of a particular model to provide an exact representation of a given training set is largely irrelevant. We are primarily interested in designing systems with good generalization performance, so that they give the greatest accuracy when presented with previously unseen data. Furthermore, problems such as XOR and parity involve learning the complete set of all possible input patterns, so the concept of generalization does not even apply. Finally, they have the property that the smallest possible change in the input pattern produces the largest possible change in the output. Most practical pattern recognition problems have the opposite characteristic, so that small changes in the inputs do not, for the most part, produce large changes in the outputs, and hence the mapping represented by the network should be relatively smooth.

Consider the problem of two normally-distributed classes with equal covariance matrices, discussed in Section 2.1.3. Since the class distributions overlap it is entirely possible that a finite sized data set drawn from these distributions will not be linearly separable. However, we know that the optimal decision boundary is in fact linear. A single-layer network can therefore achieve the best possible classification performance on unseen data, even though it may not separate the training data exactly.

The key consideration concerns the choice of an appropriate discriminant function for the particular problem in hand. This may involve a combination of prior knowledge of the general form which the solution should take, coupled with an empirical comparison of the performance of alternative models. These issues are considered in more detail in Chapters 8, 9 and 10. Here we simply note that single-layer networks correspond to a very narrow class of possible discriminant functions, and in many practical situations may not represent the optimal choice. Nevertheless, single-layer networks remain of considerable practical importance in providing a benchmark against which the performance of more complex multi-layer networks can be assessed. The fact that single-layer networks can often be trained very quickly, as shown in Section 3.4, gives them a particular advantage over more complex network structures which often require considerable computational effort to train.

3.3   Generalized linear discriminants

One way to generalize the discriminant functions, so as to permit a much larger range of possible decision boundaries, is to transform the input vector $\mathbf{x}$ using a set of M predefined non-linear functions $\phi_j(\mathbf{x})$, sometimes called *basis functions*, and then to represent the output as a linear combination of these functions

$$y_k(\mathbf{x}) = \sum_{j=1}^{M} w_{kj}\phi_j(\mathbf{x}) + w_{k0}. \tag{3.32}$$

This now represents a much larger class of functions $y_k(\mathbf{x})$. In fact, as discussed in Chapters 4 and 5, for a suitable choice of the basis functions $\phi_j(\mathbf{x})$, the function in (3.32) can approximate any continuous functional transformation to arbitrary accuracy. Again, we can absorb the biases as special cases of the weights by defining an extra basis function $\phi_0 = 1$, so that

$$y_k(\mathbf{x}) = \sum_{j=0}^{M} w_{kj}\phi_j(\mathbf{x}). \qquad (3.33)$$

We have assumed that the basis functions $\phi_j(\mathbf{x})$ are fixed, independently of the data. Chapters 4 and 5 discuss multi-layer neural networks, many of which can be regarded as generalized discriminant functions of the form (3.32), but in which the basis functions themselves can be modified during the training process.

3.4 Least-squares techniques

So far in this chapter we have discussed various forms of single-layer network and explored some of their properties. The remainder of the chapter is concerned with techniques for training such networks, and we begin with a discussion of methods based on the minimization of a sum-of-squares error function. This is the simplest form of error function and is most suitable for regression problems. While it can also be used for classification problems, there exist other, more appropriate, error functions, discussed at length in Chapter 6.

3.4.1 *Sum-of-squares error function*

For consistency with the discussions in Chapter 5, we shall consider the error minimization problem in the context of the generalized linear network (3.33). This contains the simple linear discriminant of (3.4) as a special case in which the $\phi_j(\mathbf{x})$ simply correspond to the input variables x_i. The sum-of-squares error function is given by a sum over all patterns in the training set, and over all outputs, of the form

$$E(\mathbf{w}) = \frac{1}{2} \sum_{n=1}^{N} \sum_{k=1}^{c} \{y_k(\mathbf{x}^n; \mathbf{w}) - t_k^n\}^2 \qquad (3.34)$$

where $y_k(\mathbf{x}^n; \mathbf{w})$ represents the output of unit k as a function of the input vector $\mathbf{x}^n$ and the weight vector $\mathbf{w}$, N is the number of training patterns, and c is the number of outputs. The quantity t_k^n represents the target value for output unit k when the input vector is $\mathbf{x}^n$. This error function is a smooth function of the weight parameters w_{kj}, and can be minimized by a variety of standard techniques. Since (3.33) is a linear function of the weights, the error function $E(\mathbf{w})$ is a quadratic function of the weights, and hence its derivatives with respect to the weights are linear functions of the weights. The solution for the weight values at the minimum of the error function can therefore be found exactly in closed form, as we shall see in Section 3.4.3.

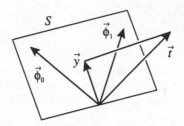

Figure 3.8. Geometrical interpretation of the solution to the least-squares problem, illustrated for the case of 3 training patterns ($N = 3$) and 2 basis functions ϕ_0 and ϕ_1 (corresponding to $M = 1$). The target values t^n are grouped together to form an N-dimensional vector $\vec{t}$ which lives in an N-dimensional Euclidean space. The corresponding network outputs can similarly be represented as a vector $\vec{y}$ which consists of a linear combination of $M + 1$ basis vectors $\vec{\phi}_j$, which themselves span an $(M + 1)$-dimensional Euclidean sub-space S. The least-squares solution for $\vec{y}$ is given by the orthogonal projection of $\vec{t}$ onto S.

3.4.2 *Geometrical interpretation of least squares*

Before deriving a solution for the weights, it is instructive to consider a geometrical interpretation of the least-squares problem. To do this we consider a network having a single output y. There is no loss of generality in doing this as the same discussion applies separately to each output of the network. For a particular input pattern $\mathbf{x}^n$ we can write the network output as

$$y^n = \sum_{j=0}^{M} w_j \phi_j^n \tag{3.35}$$

where $\phi_j^n \equiv \phi_j(\mathbf{x}^n)$. We now group the target values together to form an N-dimensional vector $\vec{t}$ whose elements are given by t^n. This vector can be considered to live in an N-dimensional Euclidean space, as indicated in Figure 3.8. For each basis function $\phi_j(\mathbf{x})$ we can similarly group the N values of ϕ_j^n, corresponding to the N data points, to make a vector $\vec{\phi}_j$, also of dimension N, which can be drawn in the same space as the vector $\vec{t}$. For the moment we shall assume that the number of basis functions (including the bias) is less than the number of patterns, so that $M + 1 < N$. The $M + 1$ vectors $\vec{\phi}_j$, corresponding to the $M + 1$ basis functions, then form a (non-orthogonal) basis set which spans an $(M + 1)$-dimensional Euclidean sub-space S. The network outputs y^n can also be grouped to form a vector $\vec{y}$. From (3.35) we see that $\vec{y}$ is given by a linear combination of the $\vec{\phi}_j$ of the form

$$\vec{y} = \sum_{j=0}^{M} w_j \vec{\phi}_j \qquad (3.36)$$

so that $\vec{y}$ is constrained to lie in the sub-space S, as shown in Figure 3.8. By changing the values of the weights w_j we can change the location of $\vec{y}$ subject to this constraint.

The sum-of-squares error (3.34) can now be written in the form

$$E = \frac{1}{2} \left\| \sum_{j=0}^{M} w_i \vec{\phi}_j - \vec{t} \right\|^2 \qquad (3.37)$$

If we minimize this expression with respect to the weights w_j we find

$$\frac{\partial E}{\partial w_j} = 0 = \vec{\phi}_j^{\mathrm{T}} (\vec{y} - \vec{t}), \qquad j = 1, \ldots, M. \qquad (3.38)$$

This represents a set of coupled equations for the weights, known as the *normal equations* of the least-squares problem, for which we shall find an explicit solution shortly. Before doing so, however, it is useful to consider the geometrical interpretation of (3.38). Let us decompose $\vec{t}$ into the sum of two vectors $\vec{t} = \vec{t}_\perp + \vec{t}_\parallel$ where $\vec{t}_\parallel$ is the orthogonal projection of $\vec{t}$ onto the sub-space S, and $\vec{t}_\perp$ is the remainder. Then $\vec{\phi}_j^{\mathrm{T}} \vec{t}_\perp = 0$ by definition, and hence from (3.38) we have

$$\vec{\phi}_j^{\mathrm{T}} (\vec{y} - \vec{t}_\parallel) = 0, \qquad j = 1, \ldots, M. \qquad (3.39)$$

Since the vectors $\vec{\phi}_i$ form a basis set which span the sub-space S, we can solve (3.39) to give

$$\vec{y} = \vec{t}_\parallel \qquad (3.40)$$

and so the solution vector is just the projection of the vector of target values onto the sub-space spanned by the basis vectors, as indicated in Figure 3.8. This result is intuitively correct, since the process of learning corresponds to choosing a direction for $\vec{y}$ such as to minimize its distance from $\vec{t}$. Since $\vec{y}$ is constrained to lie in the sub-space, the best we can do is choose it to correspond to the orthogonal projection of $\vec{t}$ onto S. This minimizes the length of the error vector $\vec{\epsilon} = \vec{y} - \vec{t}$. Note that the residual error vector $\vec{\epsilon}_{\min} = \vec{t}_\parallel - \vec{t} = -\vec{t}_\perp$ is then orthogonal to S, so that $\vec{\phi}_j^{\mathrm{T}} \vec{\epsilon}_{\min} = 0$.

3.4.3 *Pseudo-inverse solution*

We now proceed to find an exact solution to the least-squares problem. To do this we return to the case of a network having c outputs. Using the expression (3.33), we can write the sum-of-squares error function (3.34) in the form

$$E(\mathbf{w}) = \frac{1}{2} \sum_{n=1}^{N} \sum_{k=1}^{c} \left\{ \sum_{j=0}^{M} w_{kj} \phi_j^n - t_k^n \right\}^2 . \tag{3.41}$$

Differentiating this expression with respect to w_{kj} and setting the derivative to zero gives the normal equations for the least-squares problem in the form

$$\sum_{n=1}^{N} \left\{ \sum_{j'=0}^{M} w_{kj'} \phi_{j'}^n - t_k^n \right\} \phi_j^n = 0. \tag{3.42}$$

In order to find a solution to (3.42) it is convenient to write it in a matrix notation to give

$$(\mathbf{\Phi}^{\mathrm{T}}\mathbf{\Phi})\mathbf{W}^{\mathrm{T}} = \mathbf{\Phi}^{\mathrm{T}}\mathbf{T}. \tag{3.43}$$

Here $\mathbf{\Phi}$ has dimensions $N \times M$ and elements ϕ_j^n, $\mathbf{W}$ has dimensions $c \times M$ and elements w_{kj}, and $\mathbf{T}$ has dimensions $N \times c$ and elements t_k^n. The matrix $\mathbf{\Phi}^{\mathrm{T}}\mathbf{\Phi}$ in (3.43) is a square matrix of dimension $M \times M$. Provided it is non-singular we may invert it to obtain a solution to (3.43) which can be written in the form

$$\mathbf{W}^{\mathrm{T}} = \mathbf{\Phi}^{\dagger}\mathbf{T} \tag{3.44}$$

where $\mathbf{\Phi}^{\dagger}$ is an $M \times N$ matrix known as the *pseudo-inverse* of $\mathbf{\Phi}$ (Golub and Kahan, 1965; Rao and Mitra, 1971) and is given by

$$\mathbf{\Phi}^{\dagger} \equiv (\mathbf{\Phi}^{\mathrm{T}}\mathbf{\Phi})^{-1}\mathbf{\Phi}^{\mathrm{T}} \tag{3.45}$$

Since $\mathbf{\Phi}$ is, in general, a non-square matrix it does not itself have a true inverse, but the pseudo-inverse does have the property (as is easily seen from 3.45) that $\mathbf{\Phi}^{\dagger}\mathbf{\Phi} = \mathbf{I}$ where $\mathbf{I}$ is the unit matrix. Note, however, that $\mathbf{\Phi}\mathbf{\Phi}^{\dagger} \neq \mathbf{I}$ in general. If the matrix $\mathbf{\Phi}^{\mathrm{T}}\mathbf{\Phi}$ is singular then (3.43) does not have a unique solution. However, if the pseudo-inverse is defined by

$$\mathbf{\Phi}^{\dagger} \equiv \lim_{\epsilon \to 0} \ (\mathbf{\Phi}^{\mathrm{T}}\mathbf{\Phi} + \epsilon\mathbf{I})^{-1}\mathbf{\Phi}^{\mathrm{T}} \tag{3.46}$$

then it can be shown that the limit always exists, and that this limiting value minimizes E (Rao and Mitra, 1971).

In practice, the direct solution of the normal equations can lead to numerical difficulties due to the possibility of $\mathbf{\Phi}^T\mathbf{\Phi}$ being singular or nearly singular. This can arise if two of the basis vectors $\vec{\phi}_j$, shown in Figure 3.8, are nearly collinear. The effects of noise and numerical error can then lead to very large values for the weights which give near cancellation between these vectors. Figure 3.9(a) shows two basis vectors $\vec{\phi}_1$ and $\vec{\phi}_2$ which are nearly orthogonal, together with the component $\vec{y}_\parallel$ of $\vec{y}$ which lies in the plane spanned by $\vec{\phi}_1$ and $\vec{\phi}_2$. The corresponding weight values needed to express $\vec{y}_\parallel$ as a linear combination of $\vec{\phi}_1$ and $\vec{\phi}_2$ have relatively small values. By contrast, Figure 3.9(b) shows the corresponding situation when the vectors $\vec{\phi}_1$ and $\vec{\phi}_2$ are nearly collinear. In this case the weights need to adopt large (positive or negative) values in order to represent $\vec{y}_\parallel$ as a linear combination of the basis vectors. In the case where the two basis vectors are exactly collinear, we can write $\vec{\phi}_2 = \lambda\vec{\phi}_1$ for some constant λ. Then $w_1\vec{\phi}_1 + w_2\vec{\phi}_2 = (w_1 + \lambda w_2)\vec{\phi}_1$ and only the combination $(w_1 + \lambda w_2)$ is fixed by the least-squares procedure, with the value of w_2, say, being arbitrary. Near degeneracies will not be uncommon when dealing with real, noisy data sets. In practice, such problems are best resolved by using the technique of *singular value decomposition* (SVD) to find a solution for the weights. A good introduction to SVD, together with a suggested numerical implementation, can be found in Press *et al.* (1992). Such an approach avoids problems due to the accumulation of numerical roundoff errors, and automatically selects (from amongst a set of nearly degenerate solutions) the one for which the length $\|\mathbf{w}_k\|$ of the kth weight vector is shortest.

In the above discussion, the bias parameters were treated as a special case of the weights. We can gain some insight into the role of the biases if we make them explicit. If we consider the minimization of (3.41) with respect to the bias parameters alone we obtain

$$\frac{\partial E}{\partial w_{k0}} = \sum_{n=1}^{N} \left\{ \sum_{j=1}^{M} w_{kj}\phi_j^n + w_{k0} - t_k^n \right\} = 0 \tag{3.47}$$

which can be solved for the biases to give

$$w_{k0} = \bar{t}_k - \sum_{j=1}^{M} w_{kj}\bar{\phi}_j \tag{3.48}$$

where

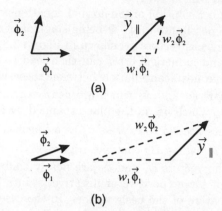

Figure 3.9. In (a) we see two basis vectors $\vec{\phi}_1$ and $\vec{\phi}_2$ which are nearly orthogonal. The least-squares solution vector $\vec{y}_\parallel$ is given by a linear combination of these vectors, with relatively small values for the coefficients w_1 and w_2. In (b) the basis vectors are nearly collinear, and the magnitudes of the corresponding weight values become very large.

$$\bar{t}_k = \frac{1}{N} \sum_{n=1}^{N} t_k^n, \qquad \bar{\phi}_j = \frac{1}{N} \sum_{n=1}^{N} \phi_j^n. \tag{3.49}$$

This result tells us that the role of the bias parameters is to compensate for the difference between the mean (over the training set) of the output vector for the network and the corresponding mean of the target data.

If $\mathbf{\Phi}^{\mathrm{T}}$ is a square non-singular matrix, the pseudo-inverse reduces to the usual inverse. The matrix is square when $N = M$, so that the number of patterns equals the number of basis functions. If we multiply (3.43) by $(\mathbf{\Phi}^{\mathrm{T}})^{-1}$ we obtain

$$\mathbf{\Phi}\mathbf{W}^{\mathrm{T}} = \mathbf{T}. \tag{3.50}$$

If we write this in index notation we have

$$\sum_{j=0}^{M} w_{kj}\phi_j^n = t_k^n \tag{3.51}$$

and we see that, for each input pattern, the network outputs are exactly equal to the corresponding target values, and hence the sum-of-squares error (3.41) will be zero. The condition for $(\mathbf{\Phi}^{\mathrm{T}})^{-1}$ to exist is that the columns ϕ^n of the matrix $\mathbf{\Phi}^{\mathrm{T}}$ be linearly independent. If the vectors ϕ^n are not linearly independent, so that the effective value of N is less than M, then the least-squares problem is under-determined. Similarly, if there are fewer patterns than basis functions, so that $N < M$, then the least-squares problem is again under-determined. In such cases, there is a continuum of solutions for the weights, all of which give zero error. Singular value decomposition leads to a numerically well-behaved algorithm which picks out the particular solution for which the magnitude $\|\mathbf{w}_k\|$ of the weight vector for each output unit k is the shortest. As we have already indicated in Chapter 1, it is desirable to have a sufficiently large training set that the weight values are 'over-determined', so that in practice we arrange that $N > M$, which corresponds to the situation depicted in Figure 3.8.

3.4.4 *Gradient descent*

We have shown how, for a linear network, the weight values which minimize the sum-of-squares error function can be found explicitly in terms of the pseudo-inverse of a matrix. It is important to note that this result is only possible for the case of a linear network, with a sum-of-squares error function. If a non-linear activation function, such as a sigmoid, is used, or if a different error function is considered, then a closed form solution is no longer possible. However, if the activation function is differentiable, as is the case for the logistic sigmoid in (3.16) for instance, the derivatives of the error function with respect to the weight parameters can easily be evaluated. These derivatives can then be used in a variety of gradient-based optimization algorithms, discussed in Chapter 7, for finding the minimum of the error function. Here we consider one of the simplest of such algorithms, known as gradient descent.

It is convenient to group all of the parameters (weights and biases) in the network together to form a single weight vector $\mathbf{w}$, so that the error function can be expressed as $E = E(\mathbf{w})$. Provided E is a differentiable function of $\mathbf{w}$ we may adopt the following procedure. We begin with an initial guess for $\mathbf{w}$ (which might for instance be chosen at random) and we then update the weight vector by moving a small distance in $\mathbf{w}$-space in the direction in which E decreases most rapidly, i.e. in the direction of $-\nabla_{\mathbf{w}} E$. By iterating this process we generate a sequence of weight vectors $\mathbf{w}^{(\tau)}$ whose components are calculated using

$$w_{kj}^{(\tau+1)} = w_{kj}^{(\tau)} - \eta \left. \frac{\partial E}{\partial w_{kj}} \right|_{\mathbf{w}^{(\tau)}} \tag{3.52}$$

where η is a small positive number called the *learning rate* parameter. Under suitable conditions the sequence of weight vectors will converge to a point at which E is minimized. The choice of the value for η can be fairly critical, since if it is too small the reduction in error will be very slow, while, if it is too large, divergent oscillations can result.

In general the error function is given by a sum of terms each of which is calculated using just one of the patterns from the training set, so that

$$E(\mathbf{w}) = \sum_n E^n(\mathbf{w}) \tag{3.53}$$

where the term E^n is calculated using pattern n only. In this case we can update the weight vector using just one pattern at a time

$$w_{kj}^{(\tau+1)} = w_{kj}^{(\tau)} - \eta \frac{\partial E^n}{\partial w_{kj}} \tag{3.54}$$

and this is repeated many times by cycling through all of the patterns used in the definition of E. This form of sequential, or pattern-based, update is reminiscent of the Robbins–Monro procedure introduced in Section 2.4, and many of the same comments apply here. In particular, this technique allows the system to be used in real-time adaptive applications in which data is arriving continuously. Each data point can be used once and then discarded, and if the value of η is chosen appropriately, the system may be able to 'track' any slow changes in the characteristics of the data. If η is chosen to decrease with time in a suitable way during the learning process, then gradient descent becomes precisely the Robbins–Monro procedure for finding the root of the regression function $\mathcal{E}[\partial E^n / \partial w_l]$ where $\mathcal{E}$ denotes the expectation. If the value of η is chosen to be steadily decreasing with time, so that $\eta^{(\tau)} = \eta_0/\tau$ (which satisfies the conditions for the Robbins–Monro theorem stated in Section 2.4), then the weight matrix $\mathbf{W}$ can be shown to converge to a solution of

$$\mathbf{\Phi}^{\mathrm{T}}(\mathbf{\Phi W} - \mathbf{T}) = 0 \tag{3.55}$$

where $\mathbf{\Phi}$ is defined on page 92, irrespective of whether or not $\mathbf{\Phi}^{\mathrm{T}}\mathbf{\Phi}$ is singular. Gradient descent, and its limitations, are discussed at greater length in Chapter 7, along with a variety of more sophisticated optimization algorithms.

In order to implement gradient descent, we need explicit expressions for the derivatives of the error function with respect to the weights. We consider first the pattern-based form of gradient descent given by (3.54). For a generalized linear network function of the form (3.33) the derivatives are given by

$$\frac{\partial E^n}{\partial w_{kj}} = \{y_k(\mathbf{x}^n) - t_k^n\}\phi_j(\mathbf{x}^n) = \delta_k^n \phi_j^n \tag{3.56}$$

where we have defined

$$\delta_k^n \equiv y_k(\mathbf{x}^n) - t_k^n. \tag{3.57}$$

We see that the derivative with respect to a weight w_{kj} connecting basis function j to output k can be expressed as the product of δ_k for the output unit and ϕ_j for the basis function. Thus, the derivative can be calculated from quantities which are 'local' (in the sense of the network diagram) to the weight concerned. This property is discussed at greater length in the context of multi-layer networks in Section 4.8. Combining (3.54) and (3.56) we see that the change in the weights due to presentation of a particular pattern is given by

$$\Delta w_{kj} = -\eta \delta_k^n \phi_j^n. \tag{3.58}$$

This rule, and its variants, are known by a variety of names including the LMS (least mean squares) rule, the adaline rule, the Widrow–Hoff rule (Widrow and Hoff, 1960), and the delta rule.

For networks with differentiable non-linear activation functions, such as the logistic sigmoid shown in Figure 3.5, we can write the network outputs in the form

$$y_k = g(a_k) \tag{3.59}$$

where $g(\cdot)$ is the activation function, and

$$a_k = \sum_{j=0}^{M} w_{kj} \phi_j. \tag{3.60}$$

The derivatives of the error function for pattern n again take the form

$$\frac{\partial E^n}{\partial w_{kj}} = g'(a_k) \delta_k^n \phi_j^n \tag{3.61}$$

in which

$$\delta_k^n = g'(a_k)(y_k(\mathbf{x}^n) - t_k^n). \tag{3.62}$$

For the logistic sigmoid given by (3.16), the derivative of the activation function can be expressed in the simple form

$$g'(a) = g(a)(1 - g(a)). \tag{3.63}$$

For gradient descent based on the total error function (summed over all patterns in the training set) given by (3.52), the derivatives are obtained by computing the derivatives for each pattern separately and then summing over all patterns

$$\frac{\partial E}{\partial w_{kj}} = \sum_n \frac{\partial E^n}{\partial w_{kj}}. \tag{3.64}$$

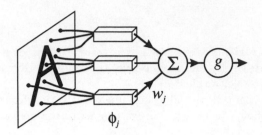

Figure 3.10. The perceptron network used a fixed set of processing elements, denoted ϕ_j, followed by a layer of adaptive weights w_j and a threshold activation function $g(\cdot)$. The processing elements ϕ_j typically also had threshold activation functions, and took inputs from a randomly chosen subset of the pixels of the input image.

3.5 The perceptron

Single-layer networks, with threshold activation functions, were studied by Rosenblatt (1962) who called them *perceptrons*. Rosenblatt also built hardware implementations of these networks, which incorporated learning using an algorithm to be discussed below. These networks were applied to classification problems, in which the inputs were usually binary images of characters or simple shapes. The properties of perceptrons are reviewed in Block (1962).

At the same time as Rosenblatt was developing the perceptron, Widrow and co-workers were working along similar lines using systems known as *adalines* (Widrow and Lehr, 1990). The term adaline comes from ADAptive LINear Element, and refers to a single processing unit with threshold non-linearity (Widrow and Hoff, 1960) of essentially the same form as the perceptron.

We have already seen that a network with a single layer of weights has very limited capabilities. To improve the performance of the perceptron, Rosenblatt used a layer of fixed processing elements to transform the raw input data, as shown in Figure 3.10. These processing elements can be regarded as the basis functions of a generalized linear discriminant. They typically took the form of fixed weights connected to a random subset of the input pixels, with a threshold activation function of the form (3.20). We shall again use the convention introduced earlier of defining an extra basis function ϕ_0 whose activation is permanently set to $+1$, together with a corresponding bias parameter w_0. The output of the perceptron is therefore given by

$$y = g\left(\sum_{j=0}^{M} w_j \phi_j(\mathbf{x})\right) = g(\mathbf{w}^{\mathrm{T}}\boldsymbol{\phi}) \tag{3.65}$$

where $\boldsymbol{\phi}$ denotes the vector formed from the activations $\phi_0, \ldots, \phi_M$. The output unit activation function is most conveniently chosen to be an anti-symmetric version of the threshold activation function of the form

$$g(a) = \begin{cases} -1 & \text{when } a < 0 \\ +1 & \text{when } a \geq 0. \end{cases} \tag{3.66}$$

We now turn to a discussion of the procedures used to train the perceptron.

3.5.1 *The perceptron criterion*

Since our goal is to produce an effective classification system, it would be natural to define the error function in terms of the total number of misclassifications over the training set. More generally we could introduce a loss matrix (Section 1.10) and consider the total loss incurred as a result of a particular classification of the data set. Such error measures, however, prove very difficult to work with in practice. This is because smooth changes in the values of the weights (and biases) cause the decision boundaries to move across the data points resulting in discontinuous changes in the error. The error function is therefore piecewise constant, and so procedures akin to gradient descent cannot be applied. We therefore seek other error functions which can be more easily minimized.

In this section we consider a continuous, piecewise-linear error function called the *perceptron criterion*. As each input vector $\mathbf{x}^n$ is presented to the inputs of the network it generates a corresponding vector of activations ϕ^n in the first-layer processing elements. Suppose we associate with each input vector $\mathbf{x}^n$ a corresponding target value t^n, such that the desired output from the network is $t^n = +1$ if the input vector belongs to class $\mathcal{C}_1$, and $t^n = -1$ if the vector belongs to class $\mathcal{C}_2$. From (3.65) and (3.66) we want $\mathbf{w}^T\phi^n > 0$ for vectors from class $\mathcal{C}_1$, and $\mathbf{w}^T\phi^n < 0$ for vectors from class $\mathcal{C}_2$. It therefore follows that for all vectors we want to have $\mathbf{w}^T(\phi^n t^n) > 0$. This suggests that we try to minimize the following error function, known as the perceptron criterion

$$E^{\text{perc}}(\mathbf{w}) = - \sum_{\phi^n \in \mathcal{M}} \mathbf{w}^T(\phi^n t^n) \tag{3.67}$$

where $\mathcal{M}$ is the set of vectors ϕ^n which are *misclassified* by the current weight vector $\mathbf{w}$. The error function $E^{\text{perc}}(\mathbf{w})$ is the sum of a number of positive terms, and equals zero if all of the data points are correctly classified. From the discussion in Section 3.1 we see that $E^{\text{perc}}(\mathbf{w})$ is proportional to the sum, over all of the input patterns which are misclassified, of the (absolute) distances to the decision boundary. During training, the decision boundary will move and some points which were previously misclassified will become correctly classified (and vice versa) so that the set of patterns which contribute to the sum in (3.67) will change. The perceptron criterion is therefore continuous and piecewise linear with discontinuities in its gradient.

3.5.2 Perceptron learning

If we apply the pattern-by-pattern gradient descent rule (3.54) to the perceptron criterion (3.67) we obtain

$$w_j^{(\tau+1)} = w_j^{(\tau)} + \eta \phi_j^n t^n. \tag{3.68}$$

This corresponds to a very simple learning algorithm which can be summarized as follows. Cycle through all of the patterns in the training set and test each pattern in turn using the current set of weight values. If the pattern is correctly classified do nothing, otherwise add the pattern vector (multiplied by η) to the weight vector if the pattern is labelled class $\mathcal{C}_1$ or subtract the pattern vector (multiplied by η) from the weight vector if the pattern is labelled class $\mathcal{C}_2$. It is easy to see that this procedure tends to reduce the error since

$$-\mathbf{w}^{(\tau+1)\mathrm{T}}(\phi^n t^n) = -\mathbf{w}^{(\tau)\mathrm{T}}(\phi^n t^n) - \eta(\phi^n t^n)^{\mathrm{T}}(\phi^n t^n) < -\mathbf{w}^{(\tau)\mathrm{T}}(\phi^n t^n) \tag{3.69}$$

since $\|\phi^n t^n\|^2 > 0$ and $\eta > 0$.

For the particular case of the perceptron criterion, we see that the value of η is in fact unimportant since a change in η is equivalent to a re-scaling of the weights and bias (assuming the initial parameter values are similarly re-scaled). This leaves the location of the decision boundaries unchanged. To see this, recall that the location of the decision boundary is given by (3.2), and is therefore unchanged if all of the weights, including the bias, are rescaled by the same constant. Thus, when minimizing the perceptron criterion, we can take $\eta = 1$ with no loss of generality. This property does not hold, however, for most other forms of error function.

In Figures 3.11–3.13 we give a simple example of learning in a perceptron, for the case of one basis function ϕ_1, so that, with biases included as special cases of the weights, the data points live in a two-dimensional space (ϕ_0, ϕ_1) with $\phi_0 = 1$.

3.5.3 Perceptron convergence theorem

There is an interesting result which states that, for any data set which is linearly separable, the learning rule in (3.68) is guaranteed to find a solution in a finite number of steps (Rosenblatt, 1962; Block, 1962; Nilsson, 1965; Minsky and Papert, 1969; Duda and Hart, 1973; Hand, 1981; Arbib, 1987; Hertz *et al.*, 1991). This is known as the *perceptron convergence theorem*. Here we give a relatively simple proof, based on Hertz *et al.* (1991).

Since we are considering a data set which is linearly separable, we know that there exists at least one weight vector $\widehat{\mathbf{w}}$ for which all training vectors are correctly classified, so that

$$\widehat{\mathbf{w}}^{\mathrm{T}}\phi^n t^n > 0 \qquad \text{for all } n. \tag{3.70}$$

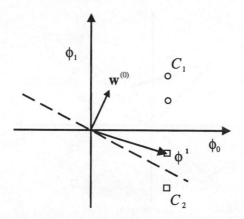

Figure 3.11. A simple example of perceptron learning, for a data set with four patterns. Circles represent patterns belonging to class $\mathcal{C}_1$ and squares represent patterns belonging to class $\mathcal{C}_2$. The initial decision boundary, corresponding to the weight vector $\mathbf{w}^{(0)}$, shown by the dashed curve, leaves one of the points, at ϕ^1, incorrectly classified.

The learning process starts with some arbitrary weight vector which, without loss of generality, we can assume to be the zero vector. At each step of the algorithm, the weight vector is updated using

$$\mathbf{w}^{(\tau+1)} = \mathbf{w}^{(\tau)} + \phi^n t^n \tag{3.71}$$

where ϕ^n is a vector which is misclassified by the perceptron. Suppose that, after running the algorithm for some time, the number of times that each vector ϕ^n has been presented and misclassified is τ^n. Then the weight vector at this point will be given by

$$\mathbf{w} = \sum_n \tau^n \phi^n t^n. \tag{3.72}$$

We now take the scalar product of this equation with $\widehat{\mathbf{w}}$ to give

$$\widehat{\mathbf{w}}^{\mathrm{T}}\mathbf{w} = \sum_n \tau^n \widehat{\mathbf{w}}^{\mathrm{T}} \phi^n t^n$$

$$\geq \tau \min_n \left(\widehat{\mathbf{w}}^{\mathrm{T}} \phi^n t^n \right) \tag{3.73}$$

where $\tau = \sum_n \tau^n$ is the total number of weight updates, and the inequality results from replacing each update vector by the smallest of the update vectors.

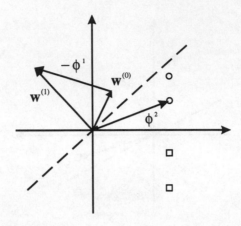

Figure 3.12. To correct for the misclassification of ϕ^1 in Figure 3.11 we add (minus) ϕ^1 onto $\mathbf{w}^{(0)}$ to give a new weight vector $\mathbf{w}^{(1)}$, with the new decision boundary again shown by the dashed curve. The point at ϕ^1 is now correctly classified, but the point at ϕ^2 is now incorrectly classified.

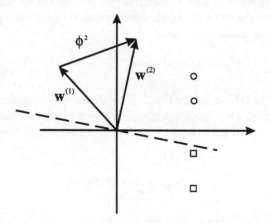

Figure 3.13. To correct for the misclassification of ϕ^2 in Figure 3.12 we add ϕ^2 onto $\mathbf{w}^{(1)}$ to give a new weight vector $\mathbf{w}^{(2)}$ which classifies all the points correctly.

From (3.70) it then follows that the value of $\widehat{\mathbf{w}}^{\mathrm{T}}\mathbf{w}$ is bounded below by a function which grows linearly with τ.

Keeping this result in mind, we now turn to a consideration of the magnitude of the weight vector $\mathbf{w}$. From (3.71) we have

$$\|\mathbf{w}^{(\tau+1)}\|^2 = \|\mathbf{w}^{(\tau)}\|^2 + \|\boldsymbol{\phi}^n\|^2 (t^n)^2 + 2\mathbf{w}^{(\tau)\mathrm{T}}\boldsymbol{\phi}^n t^n$$

$$\leq \|\mathbf{w}^{(\tau)}\|^2 + \|\boldsymbol{\phi}^n\|^2 (t^n)^2 \qquad (3.74)$$

where the inequality follows from the fact that the pattern $\boldsymbol{\phi}^n$ must have been misclassified, and so $\mathbf{w}^{(\tau)\mathrm{T}}\boldsymbol{\phi}^n t^n < 0$. We also have $(t^n)^2 = 1$ since $t^n = \pm 1$, and $\|\boldsymbol{\phi}^n\|^2 \leq \|\boldsymbol{\phi}\|_{\max}^2$ where $\|\boldsymbol{\phi}\|_{\max}$ is the length of the longest input vector. Thus, the change in the value of $\|\mathbf{w}\|^2$ satisfies

$$\Delta\|\mathbf{w}\|^2 \equiv \|\mathbf{w}^{(\tau+1)}\|^2 - \|\mathbf{w}^{(\tau)}\|^2 \leq \|\boldsymbol{\phi}\|_{\max}^2 \qquad (3.75)$$

and so after τ weight vector updates we have

$$\|\mathbf{w}\|^2 \leq \tau\|\boldsymbol{\phi}\|_{\max}^2 \qquad (3.76)$$

and so the length $\|\mathbf{w}\|$ of the weight vector increases no faster than $\tau^{1/2}$. We now recall the previous result that $\widehat{\mathbf{w}}^{\mathrm{T}}\mathbf{w}$ is bounded below by a linear function of τ. Since $\widehat{\mathbf{w}}$ is fixed, we see that for sufficiently large τ these two results would become incompatible. Thus τ cannot grow indefinitely, and so the algorithm must converge in a finite number of steps.

One of the difficulties with the perceptron learning rule is that, if the data set happens not to be linearly separable, then the learning algorithm will never terminate. Furthermore, if we arbitrarily stop the learning process there is no guarantee that the weight vector found will generalize well for new data. Various heuristics have been proposed with a view to giving good performance on problems which are not linearly separable while still ensuring convergence when the problem is linearly separable. For example, the value of the parameter η may be made to decrease during the learning process so that the corrections gradually become smaller. One approach is to take $\eta = K/\tau$ where K is a constant and τ is the step number, by analogy with the Robbins–Monro procedure (Section 2.4.1). An alternative algorithm for finding good solutions on problems which are not linearly separable, called the *pocket algorithm*, is described in Section 9.5.1. As we have already discussed, the issue of linear separability is a somewhat artificial one, and it is more important to develop learning algorithms which can be expected to give good performance across a wide range of problems, even if this means sacrificing the guarantee of perfect classification for linearly separable problems.

3.5.4 *Limitations of the perceptron*

When perceptrons were being studied experimentally in the 1960s, it was found that they could solve many problems very readily, whereas other problems, which superficially appeared to be no more difficult, proved impossible to solve. A critical appraisal of the capabilities of these networks, from a formal mathematical viewpoint, was given by Minsky and Papert (1969) in their book *Perceptrons*.

They showed that there are many types of problem which a perceptron cannot, in any practical sense, be used to solve. In this context a solution is taken to be a correct classification of all of the patterns in the training set.

Many recent textbooks on neural networks have summarized Minsky and Papert's contribution by pointing out that a single-layer network can only classify data sets which are linearly separable, and hence can not solve problems such as the XOR example considered earlier. In fact, the arguments of Minsky and Papert are rather more subtle, and shed light on the nature of multi-layer networks in which only one of the layers of weights is adaptive. Consider the perceptron shown in Figure 3.10. The first layer of fixed (non-adaptive) processing units computes a set of functions ϕ_j whose values depend on the input pattern. Even though the data set of input patterns may not be linearly separable, when viewed in the space of original input variables, it can easily be the case that the same set of patterns becomes linearly separable when transformed into the space of ϕ_j values. Thus a perceptron can solve a linearly inseparable problem, provided it has an appropriate set of first-layer processing elements.

The real difficulty with the perceptron arises from the fact that these processing elements are fixed in advance and cannot be adapted to the particular problem (or data set) which is being considered. As a consequence of this, it turns out that the number, or complexity, of such units must grow very rapidly (typically exponentially) with the dimensionality of the problem if the perceptron is to remain capable in general of providing a solution. It is therefore necessary to limit either the number or the complexity of the first-layer units. Minsky and Papert discuss a range of different forms of perceptron (depending on the form of the functions ϕ_j) and for each of them they provide examples of problems which cannot be solved.

Here we consider one particular form, called a *diameter-limited perceptron*, in which we consider two-dimensional input images as shown in Figure 3.10, and in which each of the ϕ_j takes its inputs only from within a small localized region of the image, called a *receptive field*, having fixed diameter. Minsky and Papert (1969) provide a simple geometrical proof that such a perceptron cannot solve a simple problem involving the determination of whether a binary geometrical image is simply connected. This is illustrated in Figure 3.14. We shall suppose that connected shapes are labelled with targets $+1$ and that disconnected shapes have targets -1. Note that the overall length of the shapes is taken to be much larger than the maximum diameter of the receptive fields (indicated by the dashed circles), so that no single receptive field can overlap both ends of the shape. For the shape in Figure 3.14 (a), the functions ϕ_j and the adaptive weights in the perceptron must be such that the linear sum which forms the input to the threshold function is negative, if this figure is to be correctly classified as 'disconnected'. In going to 3.14 (b), only the left-hand end of the shape has changed, so the receptive fields which lie in this region, and their corresponding weights, must be such that the linear sum is increased sufficiently to make it go positive, since this shape is 'connected'. Similarly, in going from 3.14 (a) to 3.14 (c) the linear sum must also be increased sufficiently to make it positive. However, in going

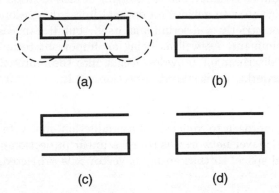

Figure 3.14. An example of a simple problem, involving the determination of whether a geometrical figure is simply connected, which cannot be solved by a perceptron whose inputs are taken from regions of limited diameter.

from 3.14 (a) to 3.14 (d), both ends of the shape have been changed in this way, and so the linear sum must be even more positive. This is inevitable since the diameter limitation means that the response due to the two ends of the shape are independent. Thus, the linear sum cannot be negative for the shape in 3.14 (d), which will therefore be misclassified.

Various alternative approaches to limiting the complexity of the first-layer units can be considered. For instance, in an *order-limited* perceptron, each of the ϕ_j can take inputs only from a limited number of input pixels (which may lie anywhere on the input image). Counter-examples similar to the one presented above can be found also for these other choices of ϕ_j. These difficulties can be circumvented by allowing the number and complexity of the ϕ_j to grow sufficiently rapidly with the dimensionality of the problem. For example, it is shown in Section 4.2.1 that, for networks with binary inputs, there is a simple procedure for constructing the ϕ_j such that any set of input patterns is guaranteed to be linearly separable in the ϕ_j space. The number of such units, however, must grow exponentially with the input dimensionality. Such an approach is therefore totally impractical for anything other than toy problems.

The practical solution to these difficulties is to allow the functions ϕ_j to be *adaptive*, so that they are chosen as part of the learning process. This leads to a consideration of multi-layer adaptive networks, as discussed in Chapters 4 and 5.

3.6   Fisher's linear discriminant

As the final topic of this chapter we consider a rather different approach to linear discriminants, introduced by Fisher (1936). In Section 1.4 we encountered the problem of the 'curse of dimensionality' whereby the design of a good classifier becomes rapidly more difficult as the dimensionality of the input space increases. One way of dealing with this problem is to pre-process the data so as to reduce its dimensionality before applying a classification algorithm. The Fisher discriminant aims to achieve an optimal linear dimensionality reduction. It is therefore not strictly a discriminant itself, but it can easily be used to construct a discriminant. As well as being an important technique in its own right, the Fisher discriminant provides insight into the representations learned by multi-layer networks, as discussed in Section 6.6.1.

3.6.1 *Two classes*

One very simple approach to dimensionality reduction, motivated by our earlier discussion of single-layer networks, is to use a linear projection of the data onto a one-dimensional space, so that an input vector $\mathbf{x}$ is projected onto a value y given by

$$y = \mathbf{w}^{\mathrm{T}}\mathbf{x} \tag{3.77}$$

where, as before, $\mathbf{w}$ is a vector of adjustable weight parameters. Note that this expression does not contain any bias parameter. We shall return to this point shortly. In general, the projection onto one dimension leads to a considerable loss of information, and classes which are well separated in the original d-dimensional space may become strongly overlapping in one dimension. However, by adjusting the components of the weight vector $\mathbf{w}$ we can select a projection which maximizes the class separation. To begin with, consider a two-class problem in which there are N_1 points of class $\mathcal{C}_1$ and N_2 points of class $\mathcal{C}_2$. The mean vectors of the two classes are given by

$$\mathbf{m}_1 = \frac{1}{N_1} \sum_{n \in \mathcal{C}_1} \mathbf{x}^n, \qquad \mathbf{m}_2 = \frac{1}{N_2} \sum_{n \in \mathcal{C}_2} \mathbf{x}^n. \tag{3.78}$$

We might think of defining the separation of the classes, when projected onto $\mathbf{w}$, as being the separation of the projected class means. This suggests that we might choose $\mathbf{w}$ so as to maximize

$$m_2 - m_1 = \mathbf{w}^{\mathrm{T}}(\mathbf{m}_2 - \mathbf{m}_1) \tag{3.79}$$

where

$$m_k = \mathbf{w}^{\mathrm{T}}\mathbf{m}_k \tag{3.80}$$

is the class mean of the projected data from class $\mathcal{C}_k$. However, this expression can be made arbitrarily large simply by increasing the magnitude of $\mathbf{w}$. To solve this problem, we could constrain $\mathbf{w}$ to have unit length, so that $\sum_i w_i^2 = 1$. Using a Lagrange multiplier (Appendix C) to perform the constrained maximization we then find that $\mathbf{w} \propto (\mathbf{m}_2 - \mathbf{m}_1)$. There is still a problem with this approach,

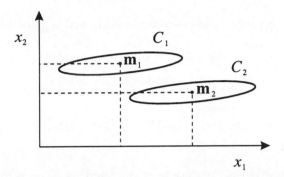

Figure 3.15. A schematic illustration of why it is important to take account of the within-class covariances when constructing the Fisher linear discriminant criterion. Projection of the data onto the x_1-axis leads to greater separation of the projected class means than does projection onto the x_2-axis, and yet it leads to greater class overlap. The problem is resolved by taking account of the within-class scatter of the data points.

however, as illustrated in Figure 3.15. This shows two classes which are well separated in the original two-dimensional space (x_1, x_2). We see that projection onto the x_1-axis gives a much larger separation of the projected class means than does projection onto the x_2-axis. Nevertheless, separation of the projected data is much better when the data is projected onto the x_2-axis than when it is projected onto the x_1-axis. This difficulty arises from the substantial difference of the within-class spreads along the two axis directions. The resolution proposed by Fisher is to maximize a function which represents the difference between the projected class means, normalized by a measure of the within-class scatter along the direction of $\mathbf{w}$.

The projection formula (3.77) transforms the set of labelled data points in $\mathbf{x}$ into a labelled set in the one-dimensional space y. The within-class scatter of the transformed data from class C_k is described the within-class covariance, given by

$$s_k^2 = \sum_{n \in C_k} (y^n - m_k)^2 \tag{3.81}$$

and we can define the total within-class covariance for the whole data set to be simply $s_1^2 + s_2^2$. We therefore arrive at the Fisher criterion given by

$$J(\mathbf{w}) = \frac{(m_2 - m_1)^2}{s_1^2 + s_2^2}. \tag{3.82}$$

We can make the dependence on $\mathbf{w}$ explicit by using (3.77), (3.80) and (3.81) to rewrite the Fisher criterion in the form

$$J(\mathbf{w}) = \frac{\mathbf{w}^\mathrm{T}\mathbf{S}_B\mathbf{w}}{\mathbf{w}^\mathrm{T}\mathbf{S}_W\mathbf{w}} \tag{3.83}$$

where $\mathbf{S}_B$ is the *between-class* covariance matrix and is given by

$$\mathbf{S}_B = (\mathbf{m}_2 - \mathbf{m}_1)(\mathbf{m}_2 - \mathbf{m}_1)^\mathrm{T} \tag{3.84}$$

and $\mathbf{S}_W$ is the total *within-class* covariance matrix, given by

$$\mathbf{S}_W = \sum_{n \in \mathcal{C}_1} (\mathbf{x}^n - \mathbf{m}_1)(\mathbf{x}^n - \mathbf{m}_1)^\mathrm{T} + \sum_{n \in \mathcal{C}_2} (\mathbf{x}^n - \mathbf{m}_2)(\mathbf{x}^n - \mathbf{m}_2)^\mathrm{T}. \tag{3.85}$$

Differentiating (3.83) with respect to $\mathbf{w}$, we find that $J(\mathbf{w})$ is maximized when

$$(\mathbf{w}^\mathrm{T}\mathbf{S}_B\mathbf{w})\mathbf{S}_W\mathbf{w} = (\mathbf{w}^\mathrm{T}\mathbf{S}_W\mathbf{w})\mathbf{S}_B\mathbf{w}. \tag{3.86}$$

From (3.84) we see that $\mathbf{S}_B\mathbf{w}$ is always in the direction of $(\mathbf{m}_2 - \mathbf{m}_1)$. Furthermore, we do not care about the magnitude of $\mathbf{w}$, only its direction. Thus, we can drop any scalar factors. Multiplying both sides of (3.86) by $\mathbf{S}_W^{-1}$ we then obtain

$$\mathbf{w} \propto \mathbf{S}_W^{-1}(\mathbf{m}_2 - \mathbf{m}_1). \tag{3.87}$$

This is known as Fisher's linear discriminant, although strictly it is not a discriminant but rather a specific choice of direction for projection of the data down to one dimension. Note that, if the within-class covariance is isotropic, so that $\mathbf{S}_W$ is proportional to the unit matrix, we find that $\mathbf{w}$ is proportional to the difference of the class means, as discussed above. The projected data can subsequently be used to construct a discriminant, by choosing a threshold y_0 so that we classify a new point as belonging to $\mathcal{C}_1$ if $y(\mathbf{x}) \geq y_0$, and classify it as belonging to $\mathcal{C}_2$ otherwise. In doing this we note that $y = \mathbf{w}^\mathrm{T}\mathbf{x}$ is the sum of a set of random variables, and so we may invoke the central limit theorem (see page 37) and model the class-conditional density functions $p(y|\mathcal{C}_k)$ using normal distributions. The techniques of Chapter 2 can then be used to find the parameters of the normal distributions by maximum likelihood, and the formalism of Chapter 1 then gives an expression for the optimal threshold.

Once we have obtained a suitable weight vector and a threshold, the procedure for deciding the class of a new vector is identical to that of the perceptron network of Section 3.5. We can therefore view the Fisher criterion as a specific procedure for choosing the weights (and subsequently the bias) in a single-layer network. More conventionally, however, it is regarded as a technique for dimensionality reduction, a subject which is discussed at greater length in Chapter 8. In reducing the dimensionality of the data we are discarding information, and this cannot reduce (and will typically increase) the theoretical minimum achievable error rate. Dimensionality reduction may be worthwhile in practice, however, as it alleviates problems associated with the curse of dimensionality. Thus, with finite-sized data sets, reduction of the dimensionality may well lead to overall improvements in the performance of a classifier system.

3.6.2 *Relation to the least-squares approach*

The least-squares approach to the determination of a linear discriminant was based on the goal of making the network outputs as close as possible to a set of target values. By contrast, the Fisher criterion was derived by requiring maximum class separation in the output space. It is interesting to see the relationship between these two approaches. In particular, we shall show that, for the two-class problem, the Fisher criterion can be obtained as a special case of least squares.

So far we have taken the target values to be $+1$ for class C_1 and -1 for class C_2. If, however, we adopt a slightly different target coding scheme then the least-squares solution solution for the weights becomes equivalent to the Fisher solution (Duda and Hart, 1973). In particular, we shall take the targets for class C_1 to be N/N_1, where N_1 is the number of patterns in class C_1, and N is the total number of patterns. This target value approximates the reciprocal of the prior probability for class C_1. For class C_2 we shall take the targets to be $-N/N_2$.

The sum-of-squares error function can be written

$$E = \frac{1}{2} \sum_{n=1}^{N} \left(\mathbf{w}^{\mathrm{T}} \mathbf{x}^n + w_0 - t^n \right)^2 . \tag{3.88}$$

Setting the derivatives of E with respect to w_0 and $\mathbf{w}$ to zero we obtain respectively

$$\sum_{n=1}^{N} \left(\mathbf{w}^{\mathrm{T}} \mathbf{x}^n + w_0 - t^n \right) = 0 \tag{3.89}$$

$$\sum_{n=1}^{N} \left(\mathbf{w}^{\mathrm{T}} \mathbf{x}^n + w_0 - t^n \right) \mathbf{x}^n = 0. \tag{3.90}$$

From (3.89), and making use of our choice of target coding scheme for the t^n, we obtain an expression for the bias in the form

$$w_0 = -\mathbf{w}^{\mathrm{T}} \mathbf{m} \tag{3.91}$$

where $\mathbf{m}$ is the mean of the total data set and is given by

$$\mathbf{m} = \frac{1}{N} \sum_{n=1}^{N} \mathbf{x}^n = \frac{1}{N} (N_1 \mathbf{m}_1 + N_2 \mathbf{m}_2). \tag{3.92}$$

After some straightforward algebra, and again making use of the choice of t^n, the second equation (3.90) becomes

$$\left(\mathbf{S}_W + \frac{N_1 N_2}{N} \mathbf{S}_B\right) \mathbf{w} = N(\mathbf{m}_1 - \mathbf{m}_2) \qquad (3.93)$$

where $\mathbf{S}_W$ is defined by (3.85), $\mathbf{S}_B$ is defined by (3.84), and we have substituted for the bias using (3.91). Using (3.84) we note that $\mathbf{S}_B\mathbf{w}$ is always in the direction of $(\mathbf{m}_2 - \mathbf{m}_1)$. Thus we can write

$$\mathbf{w} \propto \mathbf{S}_W^{-1}(\mathbf{m}_2 - \mathbf{m}_1) \qquad (3.94)$$

where we have ignored irrelevant scale factors. Thus the weight vector coincides with that found from the Fisher criterion. In addition, we have also found an expression for the bias value w_0 given by (3.91). This tells us that a new vector $\mathbf{x}$ should be classified as belonging to class $\mathcal{C}_1$ if $\mathbf{w}^T(\mathbf{x} - \mathbf{m}) > 0$ and class $\mathcal{C}_2$ otherwise.

3.6.3 *Several classes*

We now consider the generalization of the Fisher discriminant to several classes, and we shall assume that the dimensionality of the input space is greater than the number of classes, so that $d > c$. Also, we introduce $d' > 1$ linear 'features' $y_k = \mathbf{w}_k^T\mathbf{x}$, where $k = 1, \ldots, d'$. These feature values can conveniently be grouped together to form a vector $\mathbf{y}$. Similarly, the weight vectors $\{\mathbf{w}_k\}$ can be considered to be the rows of a matrix $\mathbf{W}$, so that

$$\mathbf{y} = \mathbf{W}\mathbf{x} \qquad (3.95)$$

The generalization of the within-class covariance matrix to the case of c classes follows from (3.85) to give

$$\mathbf{S}_W = \sum_{k=1}^{c} \mathbf{S}_k \qquad (3.96)$$

where

$$\mathbf{S}_k = \sum_{n \in \mathcal{C}_k} (\mathbf{x}^n - \mathbf{m}_k)(\mathbf{x}^n - \mathbf{m}_k)^T \qquad (3.97)$$

and

$$\mathbf{m}_k = \frac{1}{N_k} \sum_{n \in \mathcal{C}_k} \mathbf{x}^n \qquad (3.98)$$

where N_k is the number of patterns in class $\mathcal{C}_k$. In order to find a generalization of the between-class covariance matrix, we follow Duda and Hart (1973) and consider first the total covariance matrix

$$\mathbf{S}_T = \sum_{n=1}^{N} (\mathbf{x}^n - \mathbf{m})(\mathbf{x}^n - \mathbf{m})^{\mathrm{T}} \tag{3.99}$$

where $\mathbf{m}$ is the mean of the total data set

$$\mathbf{m} = \frac{1}{N} \sum_{n=1}^{N} \mathbf{x}^n = \frac{1}{N} \sum_{k=1}^{c} N_k \mathbf{m}_k \tag{3.100}$$

and $N = \sum_k N_k$ is the total number of data points. The total covariance matrix can be decomposed into the sum of the within-class covariance matrix, given by (3.96) and (3.97), plus an additional matrix $\mathbf{S}_B$ which we identify as a measure of the between-class covariance

$$\mathbf{S}_T = \mathbf{S}_W + \mathbf{S}_B \tag{3.101}$$

where

$$\mathbf{S}_B = \sum_{k=1}^{c} N_k (\mathbf{m}_k - \mathbf{m})(\mathbf{m}_k - \mathbf{m})^{\mathrm{T}}. \tag{3.102}$$

These covariance matrices have been defined in the original $\mathbf{x}$-space. We can now define similar matrices in the projected d'-dimensional $\mathbf{y}$-space

$$\mathbf{s}_W = \sum_{k=1}^{c} \sum_{n \in \mathcal{C}_k} (\mathbf{y}^n - \boldsymbol{\mu}_k)(\mathbf{y}^n - \boldsymbol{\mu}_k)^{\mathrm{T}} \tag{3.103}$$

and

$$\mathbf{s}_B = \sum_{k=1}^{c} N_k (\boldsymbol{\mu}_k - \boldsymbol{\mu})(\boldsymbol{\mu}_k - \boldsymbol{\mu})^{\mathrm{T}} \tag{3.104}$$

where

$$\boldsymbol{\mu}_k = \frac{1}{N_k} \sum_{n \in \mathcal{C}_k} \mathbf{y}^n, \qquad \boldsymbol{\mu} = \frac{1}{N} \sum_{k=1}^{c} N_k \boldsymbol{\mu}_k. \tag{3.105}$$

Again we wish to construct a scalar which is large when the between-class covariance is large and when the within-class covariance is small. There are now many possible choices of criterion (Fukunaga, 1990). One example is given by

$$J(\mathbf{W}) = \mathrm{Tr}\left\{\mathbf{s}_W^{-1}\mathbf{s}_B\right\} \tag{3.106}$$

where $\mathrm{Tr}\{\mathbf{M}\}$ denotes the trace of a matrix $\mathbf{M}$. This criterion can then be rewritten as an explicit function of the projection matrix $\mathbf{W}$ in the form

$$J(\mathbf{W}) = \mathrm{Tr}\left\{(\mathbf{WS}_W\mathbf{W}^{\mathrm{T}})^{-1}(\mathbf{WS}_B\mathbf{W}^{\mathrm{T}})\right\}. \tag{3.107}$$

Maximization of such criteria is straightforward, though somewhat involved, and is discussed at length in Fukunaga (1990). The weight values are determined by those eigenvectors of $\mathbf{S}_W^{-1}\mathbf{S}_B$ which correspond to the d' largest eigenvalues.

There is one important result which is common to all such criteria, which is worth emphasizing. We first note from (3.102) that $\mathbf{S}_B$ is composed of the sum of c matrices, each of which is an outer product of two vectors and therefore of rank 1. In addition only $(c-1)$ of these matrices are independent as a result of the constraint (3.100). Thus, $\mathbf{S}_B$ has rank at most equal to $(c-1)$ and so there are at most $(c-1)$ non-zero eigenvalues. This shows that the projection down onto the $(c-1)$-dimensional sub-space spanned by the eigenvectors of $\mathbf{S}_B$ does not alter the value of $J(\mathbf{W})$, and so we are therefore unable to find more than $(c-1)$ linear 'features' by this means (Fukunaga, 1990). Dimensionality reduction and feature extraction are discussed at greater length in Chapter 8.

Exercises

3.1 $(\star)$ Consider a point $\hat{x}$ which lies on the plane $y(\hat{\mathbf{x}}) = 0$, where $y(\mathbf{x})$ is given by (3.1). By minimizing the distance $\|\mathbf{x} - \hat{\mathbf{x}}\|$ with respect to $\hat{\mathbf{x}}$ subject to this constraint, show that the value of the linear discriminant function $y(\mathbf{x})$ gives a (signed) measure of the perpendicular distance L of the point $\mathbf{x}$ to the decision boundary $y(\mathbf{x}) = 0$ of the form

$$L = \frac{y(\mathbf{x})}{\|\mathbf{w}\|}. \tag{3.108}$$

3.2 $(\star)$ There are several possible ways in which to generalize the concept of a linear discriminant function from two classes to c classes. One possibility would be to use $(c-1)$ linear discriminant functions, such that $y_k(\mathbf{x}) > 0$ for inputs $\mathbf{x}$ in class $\mathcal{C}_k$ and $y_k(\mathbf{x}) < 0$ for inputs not in class $\mathcal{C}_k$. By drawing a simple example in two dimensions for $c = 3$, show that this approach can lead to regions of $\mathbf{x}$-space for which the classification is ambiguous. Another approach would be to use one discriminant function $y_{jk}(\mathbf{x})$ for each possible pair of classes $\mathcal{C}_j$ and $\mathcal{C}_k$, such that $y_{jk}(\mathbf{x}) > 0$ for patterns in class $\mathcal{C}_j$, and $y_{jk}(\mathbf{x}) < 0$ for patterns in class $\mathcal{C}_k$. For c classes we would need $c(c-1)/2$ discriminant functions. Again, by drawing a specific example in two dimensions for $c = 3$, show that this approach can also lead to ambiguous regions.

3.3 ($\star$) Consider a mixture model of the form (2.71) in which the component densities are given by

$$p(\mathbf{x}|j) = \prod_{i=1}^{d} P_{ji}^{x_i} (1 - P_{ji})^{1-x_i} \qquad (3.109)$$

which is equivalent to (3.22). Show that the maximum likelihood solution for the parameters P_{ji} is given by

$$\widehat{P}_{ji} = \frac{\sum_n P(j|\mathbf{x}^n) x_i^n}{\sum_n P(j|\mathbf{x}^n)} \qquad (3.110)$$

where $P(j|\mathbf{x})$ is the posterior probability for component j corresponding to an input vector $\mathbf{x}$ and is given, from Bayes' theorem, by

$$P(j|\mathbf{x}) = \frac{p(\mathbf{x}|j)P(j)}{\sum_k p(\mathbf{x}|k)P(k)} \qquad (3.111)$$

and $P(j)$ is the corresponding prior probability.

3.4 ($\star\star$) Given a set of data points $\{\mathbf{x}^n\}$ we can define the *convex hull* to be the set of all points $\mathbf{x}$ given by

$$\mathbf{x} = \sum_n \alpha_n \mathbf{x}^n \qquad (3.112)$$

where $\alpha_n \geq 0$ and $\sum_n \alpha_n = 1$. Consider a second set of points $\{\mathbf{z}^n\}$ and its corresponding convex hull. The two sets of points will be linearly separable if there exists a vector $\widehat{\mathbf{w}}$ and a scalar w_0 such that $\widehat{\mathbf{w}}^T\mathbf{x}^n + w_0 > 0$ for all $\mathbf{x}^n$, and $\widehat{\mathbf{w}}^T\mathbf{z}^n + w_0 < 0$ for all $\mathbf{z}^n$. Show that, if their convex hulls intersect, the two sets of points cannot be linearly separable, and conversely that, if they are linearly separable, their convex hulls do not intersect.

3.5 ($\star\star$) Draw all $2^2 = 4$ dichotomies of $N = 2$ points in one dimension, and hence show that the fraction of such dichotomies which are linearly separable is 1.0. By considering the binomial expansion of $2^d = (1+1)^d$, verify that the summation in (3.30) does indeed give $F = 1$ when $N = d+1$ for any d. Similarly, by drawing all $2^4 = 16$ dichotomies of $N = 4$ points in one dimension, show that the fraction of dichotomies which are linearly separable is 0.5. By considering the binomial expansion of $2^{2d+1} = (1+1)^{2d+1}$, show from (3.30) that the fraction of dichotomies which are linearly separable for $N = 2(d+1)$ is given by $F(2d+2, d) = 0.5$ for any N. Verify that these results are consistent with Figure 3.7.

3.6 ($\star\star\star$) Generate and plot a set of data points in two dimensions, drawn from two classes each of which is described by a Gaussian class-conditional density function. Implement the gradient descent algorithm for training a logistic discriminant, and plot the decision boundary at regular intervals

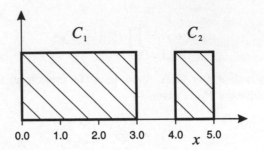

Figure 3.16. Distribution of data in one dimension drawn from two classes, used in Exercise 3.7.

during the training procedure on the same graph as the data. Explore the effects of choosing different values for the learning rate parameter η. Compare the behaviour of the sequential and batch weight update procedures described by (3.52) and (3.54) respectively.

3.7 $(\star\star)$ Consider data in one dimension drawn from two classes having the distributions shown in Figure 3.16. What is the ratio of the prior probabilities for the two classes? Find the linear discriminant function $y(x) = wx + w_0$ which minimizes the sum-of-squares error function defined by

$$E = 3 \int_0^3 \{y(x) - 1\}^2 \, dx + \int_4^5 \{y(x) + 1\}^2 \, dx \qquad (3.113)$$

where the target values are $t = +1$ for class $\mathcal{C}_1$ and $t = -1$ for class $\mathcal{C}_2$. Show that the decision boundary given by $y(x) = 0$ just fails to separate the two classes. Would a single-layer perceptron necessarily find a solution which separates the two classes exactly? Justify your answer. Discuss briefly the advantages and limitations of the least-squares and perceptron algorithms in the light of these results.

3.8 $(\star)$ Prove that, for arbitrary vectors $\mathbf{w}$ and $\widehat{\mathbf{w}}$, the following inequality is satisfied:

$$\frac{(\widehat{\mathbf{w}}^{\mathrm{T}}\mathbf{w})^2}{\|\widehat{\mathbf{w}}\|^2 \|\mathbf{w}\|^2} \leq 1. \qquad (3.114)$$

Hence, using the results (3.73) and (3.76) from the proof of the perceptron convergence theorem given in the text, show that an upper limit on the number of weight updates needed for convergence of the perceptron algorithm is given by

$$\tau_{\max} = \frac{\|\widehat{\mathbf{w}}\|^2 \|\phi\|_{\max}^2}{\min_n (\widehat{\mathbf{w}}^{\mathrm{T}} \phi^n t^n)^2}. \qquad (3.115)$$

3.9 (⋆⋆⋆) Generate a data set consisting of a small number of vectors in two dimensions, each belonging to one of two classes. Write a numerical implementation of the perceptron learning algorithm, and plot both the data points and the decision boundary after every iteration. Explore the behaviour of the algorithm both for data sets which are linearly separable and for those which are not.

3.10 (⋆) Use a Lagrange multiplier (Appendix C) to show that, for two classes, the projection vector which maximizes the separation of the projected class means given by (3.79), subject to the constraint $\|\mathbf{w}\|^2 = 1$, is given by $\mathbf{w} \propto (\mathbf{m}_2 - \mathbf{m}_1)$.

3.11 (⋆⋆) Using the definitions of the between-class and within-class covariance matrices given by (3.84) and (3.85) respectively, together with (3.91) and (3.92) and the choice of target values described in Section 3.6.2, show that the expression (3.90) which minimizes the sum-of-squares error function can be written in the form (3.93).

3.12 (⋆) By making use of (3.98), show that the total covariance matrix $\mathbf{S}_T$ given by (3.99) can be decomposed into within-class and between-class covariance matrices as in (3.101), where the within-class covariance matrix $\mathbf{S}_W$ is given by (3.96) and (3.97), and the between-class covariance matrix $\mathbf{S}_B$ is given by (3.102).

4

THE MULTI-LAYER PERCEPTRON

In Chapter 3, we discussed the properties of networks having a single layer of adaptive weights. Such networks have a number of important limitations in terms of the range of functions which they can represent. To allow for more general mappings we might consider successive transformations corresponding to networks having several layers of adaptive weights. In fact we shall see that networks with just two layers of weights are capable of approximating any continuous functional mapping. More generally we can consider arbitrary network diagrams (not necessarily having a simple layered structure) since any network diagram can be converted into its corresponding mapping function. The only restriction is that the diagram must be *feed-forward*, so that it contains no feedback loops. This ensures that the network outputs can be calculated as explicit functions of the inputs and the weights.

We begin this chapter by reviewing the representational capabilities of multi-layered networks having either threshold or sigmoidal activation functions. Such networks are generally called *multi-layer perceptrons*, even when the activation functions are sigmoidal. For networks having differentiable activation functions, there exists a powerful and computationally efficient method, called *error back-propagation*, for finding the derivatives of an error function with respect to the weights and biases in the network. This is an important feature of such networks since these derivatives play a central role in the majority of training algorithms for multi-layered networks, and we therefore discuss back-propagation at some length. We also consider a variety of techniques for evaluating and approximating the second derivatives of an error function. These derivatives form the elements of the Hessian matrix, which has a variety of different applications in the context of neural networks.

4.1 Feed-forward network mappings

In the first three sections of this chapter we consider a variety of different kinds of feed-forward network, and explore the limitations which exist on the mappings which they can generate. We are only concerned in this discussion with finding fundamental restrictions on the capabilities of the networks, and so we shall for instance assume that arbitrarily large networks can be constructed if needed. In practice, we must deal with networks of a finite size, and this raises a number of important issues which are discussed in later chapters.

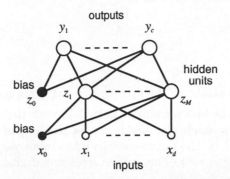

Figure 4.1. An example of a feed-forward network having two layers of adaptive weights. The bias parameters in the first layer are shown as weights from an extra input having a fixed value of $x_0 = 1$. Similarly, the bias parameters in the second layer are shown as weights from an extra hidden unit, with activation again fixed at $z_0 = 1$.

We shall view feed-forward neural networks as providing a general framework for representing non-linear functional mappings between a set of input variables and a set of output variables. This is achieved by representing the non-linear function of many variables in terms of compositions of non-linear functions of a single variable, called activation functions. Each multivariate function can be represented in terms of a network diagram such that there is a one-to-one correspondence between components of the function and the elements of the diagram. Equally, any topology of network diagram, provided it is feed-forward, can be translated into the corresponding mapping function. We can therefore categorize different network functions by considering the structure of the corresponding network diagrams.

4.1.1 *Layered networks*

We begin by looking at networks consisting of successive layers of adaptive weights. As discussed in Chapter 3, single-layer networks are based on a linear combination of the input variables which is transformed by a non-linear activation function. We can construct more general functions by considering networks having successive layers of processing units, with connections running from every unit in one layer to every unit in the next layer, but with no other connections permitted. Such layered networks are easier to analyse theoretically than more general topologies, and can often be implemented more efficiently in a software simulation.

An example of a layered network is shown in Figure 4.1. Note that units which are not treated as output units are called *hidden* units. In this network there are d inputs, M hidden units and c output units. We can write down the analytic function corresponding to Figure 4.1 as follows. The output of the jth hidden unit is obtained by first forming a weighted linear combination of the d input values, and adding a bias, to give

$$a_j = \sum_{i=1}^{d} w_{ji}^{(1)} x_i + w_{j0}^{(1)}. \tag{4.1}$$

Here $w_{ji}^{(1)}$ denotes a weight in the first layer, going *from* input i *to* hidden unit j, and $w_{j0}^{(1)}$ denotes the bias for hidden unit j. As with the single-layer networks of Chapter 3, we have made the bias terms for the hidden units explicit in the diagram of Figure 4.1 by the inclusion of an extra input variable x_0 whose value is permanently set at $x_0 = 1$. This can be represented analytically by rewriting (4.1) in the form

$$a_j = \sum_{i=0}^{d} w_{ji}^{(1)} x_i. \tag{4.2}$$

The activation of hidden unit j is then obtained by transforming the linear sum in (4.2) using an activation function $g(\cdot)$ to give

$$z_j = g(a_j). \tag{4.3}$$

In this chapter we shall consider two principal forms of activation function given respectively by the Heaviside step function, and by continuous sigmoidal functions, as introduced already in the context of single-layer networks in Section 3.1.3.

The outputs of the network are obtained by transforming the activations of the hidden units using a second layer of processing elements. Thus, for each output unit k, we construct a linear combination of the outputs of the hidden units of the form

$$a_k = \sum_{j=1}^{M} w_{kj}^{(2)} z_j + w_{k0}^{(2)}. \tag{4.4}$$

Again, we can absorb the bias into the weights to give

$$a_k = \sum_{j=0}^{M} w_{kj}^{(2)} z_j \tag{4.5}$$

which can be represented diagrammatically by including an extra hidden unit with activation $z_0 = 1$ as shown in Figure 4.1. The activation of the kth output unit is then obtained by transforming this linear combination using a non-linear activation function, to give

$$y_k = \widetilde{g}(a_k). \tag{4.6}$$

Here we have used the notation $\widetilde{g}(\cdot)$ for the activation function of the output units to emphasize that this need not be the same function as used for the hidden units.

If we combine (4.2), (4.3), (4.5) and (4.6) we obtain an explicit expression for the complete function represented by the network diagram in Figure 4.1 in the form

$$y_k = \widetilde{g}\left(\sum_{j=0}^{M} w_{kj}^{(2)} g\left(\sum_{i=0}^{d} w_{ji}^{(1)} x_i\right)\right) \tag{4.7}$$

We note that, if the activation functions for the output units are taken to be linear, so that $\widetilde{g}(a) = a$, this functional form becomes a special case of the generalized linear discriminant function discussed in Section 3.3, in which the basis functions are given by the particular functions z_j defined by (4.2) and (4.3). The crucial difference is that here we shall regard the weight parameters appearing in the first layer of the network, as well as those in the second layer, as being adaptive, so that their values can be changed during the process of network training.

The network of Figure 4.1 corresponds to a transformation of the input variables by two successive single-layer networks. It is clear that we can extend this class of networks by considering further successive transformations of the same general kind, corresponding to networks with extra layers of weights. Throughout this book, when we use the term L-layer network we shall be referring to a network with L layers of adaptive weights. Thus we shall call the network of Figure 4.1 a two-layer network, while the networks of Chapter 3 are called single-layer networks. It should be noted, however, that an alternative convention is sometimes also found in the literature. This counts layers of units rather than layers of weights, and regards the inputs as separate units. According to this convention the networks of Chapter 3 would be called two-layer networks, and the network in Figure 4.1 would be said to have three layers. We do not recommend this convention, however, since it is the layers of adaptive weights which are crucial in determining the properties of the network function. Furthermore, the circles representing inputs in a network diagram are not true processing units since their sole purpose is to represent the values of the input variables.

A useful technique for visualization of the weight values in a neural network is the *Hinton diagram*, illustrated in Figure 4.2. Each square in the diagram corresponds to one of the weight or bias parameters in the network, and the squares are grouped into blocks corresponding to the parameters associated with each unit. The size of a square is proportional to the magnitude of the corresponding

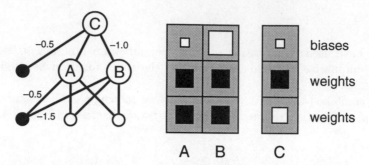

Figure 4.2. Example of a two-layer network which solves the XOR problem, showing the corresponding Hinton diagram. The weights in the network have the value 1.0 unless indicated otherwise.

parameter, and the square is black or white according to whether the parameter is positive or negative.

4.1.2 *General topologies*

Since there is a direct correspondence between a network diagram and its mathematical function, we can develop more general network mappings by considering more complex network diagrams. We shall, however, restrict our attention to the case of *feed-forward* networks. These have the property that there are no feedback loops in the network. In general we say that a network is feed-forward if it is possible to attach successive numbers to the inputs and to all of the hidden and output units such that each unit only receives connections from inputs or units having a smaller number. An example of a general feed-forward network is shown in Figure 4.3. Such networks have the property that the outputs can be expressed as deterministic functions of the inputs, and so the whole network represents a multivariate non-linear functional mapping.

The procedure for translating a network diagram into the corresponding mathematical function follows from a straightforward extension of the ideas already discussed. Thus, the output of unit k is obtained by transforming a weighted linear sum with a non-linear activation function to give

$$z_k = g \left(\sum_j w_{kj} z_j \right) \qquad (4.8)$$

where the sum runs over all inputs and units which send connections to unit k (and a bias parameter is included in the summation). For a given set of values applied to the inputs of the network, successive use of (4.8) allows the activations of all units in the network to be evaluated including those of the output units. This process can be regarded as a *forward propagation* of signals through the

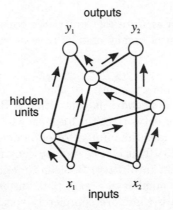

outputs

y_1 y_2

hidden units

x_1 x_2

inputs

Figure 4.3. An example of a neural network having a general feed-forward topology. Note that each unit has an associated bias parameter, which has been omitted from the diagram for clarity.

network. In practice, there is little call to consider random networks, but there is often considerable advantage in building a lot of structure into the network. An example involving multiple layers of processing units, with highly restricted and structured interconnections between the layers, is discussed in Section 8.7.3.

Note that, if the activation functions of all the hidden units in a network are taken to be linear, then for any such network we can always find an equivalent network without hidden units. This follows from the fact that the composition of successive linear transformations is itself a linear transformation. Note, however, that if the number of hidden units is smaller than either the number of input or output units, then the linear transformation which the network generates is not the most general possible since information is lost in the dimensionality reduction at the hidden units. In Section 8.6.2 it is shown that such networks can be related to conventional data processing techniques such as principal component analysis. In general, however, there is little interest in multi-layer linear networks, and we shall therefore mainly consider networks for which the hidden unit activation functions are non-linear.

4.2 Threshold units

There are many possible choices for the non-linear activation functions in a multi-layered network, and the choice of activation functions for the hidden units may often be different from that for the output units. This is because hidden and output units perform different roles, as is discussed at length in Sections 6.6.1 and 6.7.1. However, we begin by considering networks in which all units have Heaviside, or step, activation functions of the form

$$g(a) = \begin{cases} 0 & \text{when } a < 0 \\ 1 & \text{when } a \geq 0. \end{cases} \tag{4.9}$$

Such units are also known as *threshold* units. We consider separately the cases in which the inputs consist of binary and continuous variables.

4.2.1 *Binary inputs*

Consider first the case of binary inputs, so that $x_i = 0$ or 1. Since the network outputs are also 0 or 1, the network is computing a Boolean function. We can easily show that a two-layer network of the form shown in Figure 4.1 can generate any Boolean function, provided the number M of hidden units is sufficiently large (McCulloch and Pitts, 1943). This can be seen by constructing a specific network which computes a particular (arbitrary) Boolean function. We first note that for d inputs the total possible number of binary patterns which we have to consider is 2^d. A Boolean function is therefore completely specified once we have given the output (0 or 1) corresponding to each of the 2^d possible input patterns. To construct the required network we take one hidden unit for every input pattern which has an output target of 1. We then arrange for each hidden unit to respond just to the corresponding pattern. This can be achieved by setting the weight from an input to a given hidden unit to +1 if the corresponding pattern has a 1 for that input, and setting the weight to −1 if the pattern has a 0 for that input. The bias for the hidden unit is set to $1 - b$ where b is the number of non-zero inputs for that pattern. Thus, for any given hidden unit, presentation of the corresponding pattern will generate a summed input of b and the unit will give an output of 1, while any other pattern (including any of the patterns with target 0) will give a summed input of at most $b - 2$ and the unit will have an output of 0. It is now a simple matter to connect each hidden unit to the output unit with a weight +1. An output bias of −1 then ensures that the output of the network is correct for all patterns.

This construction is of little practical value, since it merely stores a set of binary relations and has no capability to generalize to new patterns outside the training set (since the training set was exhaustive). It does, however, illustrate the concept of a *template*. Each hidden unit acts as a template for the corresponding input pattern and only generates an output when the input pattern matches the template pattern.

4.2.2 *Continuous inputs*

We now discuss the case of continuous input variables, again for units with threshold activation functions, and we consider the possible decision boundaries which can be produced by networks having various numbers of layers (Lippmann, 1987; Lonstaff and Cross, 1987). In Section 3.1 it was shown that a network with a single layer of weights, and a threshold output unit, has a decision boundary which is a hyperplane. This is illustrated for a two-dimensional input space in Figure 4.4 (a). Now consider networks with two layers of weights. Again, each hidden units divides the input space with a hyperplane, so that it has activation

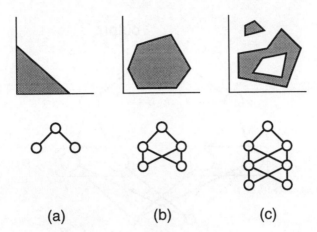

Figure 4.4. Illustration of some possible decision boundaries which can be generated by networks having threshold activation functions and various numbers of layers. Note that, for the two-layer network in (b), a single convex region of the form shown is not the most general possible.

$z = 1$ on one side of the hyperplane, and $z = 0$ on the other side. If there are M hidden units and the bias on the output unit is set to $-M$, then the output unit computes a logical AND of the outputs of the hidden units. In other words, the output unit has an output of 1 only if all of the hidden units have an output of 1. Such a network can generate decision boundaries which surround a single convex region of the input space, whose boundary consists of segments of hyperplanes, as illustrated in Figure 4.4 (b). A convex region is defined to be one for which any line joining two points on the boundary of the region passes only through points which lie inside the region. These are not, however, the most general regions which can be generated by a two-layer network of threshold units, as we shall see shortly.

Networks having three layers of weights can generate arbitrary decision regions, which may be non-convex and disjoint, as illustrated in Figure 4.4 (c). A simple demonstration of this last property can be given as follows (Lippmann, 1987). Consider a particular network architecture in which, instead of having full connectivity between adjacent layers as considered so far, the hidden units are arranged into groups of $2d$ units, where d denotes the number of inputs. The topology of the network is illustrated in Figure 4.5. The units in each group send their outputs to a unit in the second hidden layer associated with that group. Each second-layer unit then sends a connection to the output unit. Suppose the input space is divided into a fine grid of hypercubes, each of which is labelled as class C_1 or C_2. By making the input-space grid sufficiently fine we can approximate an arbitrarily shaped decision boundary as closely as we wish. One group of first-layer units is assigned to each hypercube which corresponds to class C_1,

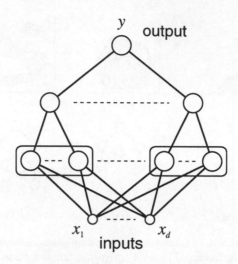

Figure 4.5. Topology of a neural network to demonstrate that networks with three layers of threshold units can generate arbitrarily complex decision boundaries. Biases have been omitted for clarity.

and there are no units corresponding to class C_2. Using the 'AND' construction for two-layer networks discussed above, we now arrange that each second-layer hidden unit generates a 1 only for inputs lying in the corresponding hypercube. This can be done by arranging for the hyperplanes associated with the first-layer units in the block to be aligned with the sides of the hypercube. Finally, the output unit has a bias which is set to -1 so that it computes a logical 'OR' of the outputs of the second-layer hidden units. In other words the output unit generates a 1 whenever one (or more) of the second-layer hidden units does so. If the output unit activation is 1, this is interpreted as class C_1, otherwise it is interpreted as class C_2. The resulting decision boundary then reflects the (arbitrary) assignment of hypercubes to classes C_1 and C_2.

The above existence proof demonstrates that feed-forward neural networks with threshold units can generate arbitrarily complex decision boundaries. The proof is of little practical interest, however, since it requires the decision boundary to be specified in advance, and also it will typically lead to very large networks. Although it is 'constructive' in that it provides a set of weights and thresholds which generate a given decision boundary, it does not answer the more practical question of how to choose an appropriate set of weights and biases for a particular problem when we are given only a set of training examples and we do not know in advance what the optimal decision boundary will be.

Returning to networks with two layers of weights, we have already seen how the AND construction for the output unit allows such a network to generate an arbitrary simply-connected convex decision region. However, by relaxing the

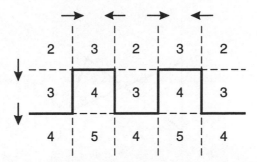

Figure 4.6. Example of a non-convex decision boundary generated by a network having two layers of threshold units. The dashed lines show the hyperplanes corresponding to the hidden units, and the arrows show the direction in which the hidden unit activations make the transition from 0 to 1. The second-layer weights are all set to 1, and so the numbers represent the value of the linear sum presented to the output unit. By setting the output unit bias to −3.5, the decision boundary represented by the solid curve is generated.

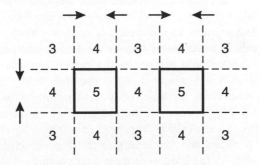

Figure 4.7. As in Figure 4.6, but showing how a disjoint decision region can be produced. In this case the bias on the output unit is set to −4.5.

restriction of an AND output unit, more general decision boundaries can be constructed (Wieland and Leighton, 1987; Huang and Lippmann, 1988). Figure 4.6 shows an example of a non-convex decision boundary, and Figure 4.7 shows a decision region which is disjoint. Huang and Lippmann (1988) give some examples of very complex decision boundaries for networks having a two layers of threshold units.

This would seem to suggest that a network with just two layers of weights could generate arbitrary decision boundaries. This is not in fact the case (Gibson and Cowan, 1990; Blum and Li, 1991) and Figure 4.8 shows an example of a decision region which cannot be produced by a network having just two layers of

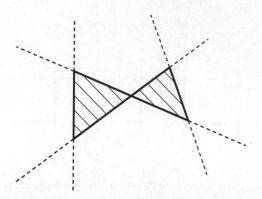

Figure 4.8. An example of a decision boundary which cannot be produced by a network having two layers of threshold units (Gibson and Cowan, 1990).

weights. Note, however, that any given decision boundary can be approximated arbitrarily closely by a two-layer network having sigmoidal activation functions, as discussed in Section 4.3.2.

So far we have discussed procedures for generating particular forms of decision boundary. A distinct, though related, issue whether a network can classify correctly a given set of data points which have been labelled as belonging to one of two classes (a dichotomy). In Chapter 3 it is shown that a network having a single layer of threshold units could classify a set of points perfectly if they were linearly separable. This would always be the case if the number of data points was at most equal to $d + 1$ where d is the dimensionality of the input space. Nilsson (1965) showed that, for a set of N data points, a two-layer network of threshold units with $N - 1$ units in the hidden layer could exactly separate an arbitrary dichotomy. Baum (1988) improved this result by showing that for N points in general position (i.e. excluding exact degeneracies) in d-dimensional space, a network with $\lceil N/d \rceil$ hidden units in a single hidden layer could separate them correctly into two classes. Here $\lceil N/d \rceil$ denotes the smallest integer which is greater than or equal to N/d.

4.3 Sigmoidal units

We turn now to a consideration of multi-layer networks having differentiable activation functions, and to the problem of representing smooth mappings between continuous variables. In Section 3.1.3 we introduced the logistic sigmoid activation function, whose outputs lie in the range $(0, 1)$, given by

$$g(a) \equiv \frac{1}{1 + \exp(-a)} \tag{4.10}$$

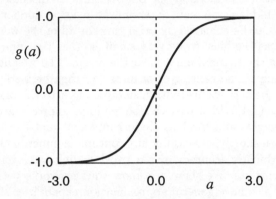

Figure 4.9. Plot of the 'tanh' activation function given by (4.11).

which is plotted in Figure 3.5. We discuss the motivation for this form of activation function in Sections 3.1.3 and 6.7.1, where we show that the use of such activation functions on the network outputs plays an important role in allowing the outputs to be given a probabilistic interpretation.

The logistic sigmoid (4.10) is often used for the hidden units of a multi-layer network. However, there may be some small practical advantage in using a 'tanh' activation function of the form

$$g(a) \equiv \tanh(a) \equiv \frac{e^a - e^{-a}}{e^a + e^{-a}} \tag{4.11}$$

which is plotted in Figure 4.9. Note that (4.11) differs from the logistic function in (4.10) only through a linear transformation. Specifically, an activation function $\widetilde{g}(\widetilde{a}) = \tanh(\widetilde{a})$ is equivalent to an activation function $g(a) = 1/(1 + e^{-a})$ if we apply a linear transformation $\widetilde{a} = a/2$ to the input and a linear transformation $\widetilde{g} = 2g - 1$ to the output. Thus a neural network whose hidden units use the activation function in (4.11) is equivalent to one with hidden units using (4.10) but having different values for the weights and biases. Empirically, it is often found that 'tanh' activation functions give rise to faster convergence of training algorithms than logistic functions.

In this section we shall consider networks with linear output units. As we shall see, this does not restrict the class of functions which such networks can approximate. The use of sigmoid units at the outputs would limit the range of possible outputs to the range attainable by the sigmoid, and in some cases this would be undesirable. Even if the desired output always lay within the range of the sigmoid we note that the sigmoid function $g(\cdot)$ is monotonic, and hence is invertible, and so a desired output of y for a network with sigmoidal output units is equivalent to a desired output of $g^{-1}(y)$ for a network with linear output units. Note, however, that there are other reasons why we might wish to use non-linear activation functions at the output units, as discussed in Chapter 6.

A sigmoidal hidden unit can approximate a linear hidden unit arbitrarily accurately. This can be achieved by arranging for all of the weights feeding into the unit, as well as the bias, to be very small, so that the summed input lies on the linear part of the sigmoid curve near the origin. The weights on the outputs of the unit leading to the next layer of units can then be made correspondingly large to re-scale the activations (with a suitable offset to the biases if necessary). Similarly, a sigmoidal hidden unit can be made to approximate a step function by setting the weights and the bias feeding into that unit to very large values.

As we shall see shortly, essentially any continuous functional mapping can be represented to arbitrary accuracy by a network having two layers of weights with sigmoidal hidden units. We therefore know that networks with extra layers of processing units also have general approximation capabilities since they contain the two-layer network as a special case. This follows from the fact that the remaining layers can be arranged to perform linear transformations as discussed above, and the identity transformation is a special case of a linear transformation (provided there is a sufficient number of hidden units so that no reduction in dimensionality occurs). Nevertheless, it is instructive to begin with a discussion of networks having three layers of weights.

4.3.1 *Three-layer networks*

In Section 4.2 we gave a heuristic proof that a three-layer network with threshold activation functions could represent an arbitrary decision boundary to arbitrary accuracy. In the same spirit we can give an analogous proof that a network with three layers of weights and sigmoidal activation functions can approximate, to arbitrary accuracy, any smooth mapping (Lapedes and Farber, 1988). The required network topology has the same form as in Figure 4.5, with each group of units in the first hidden layer again containing $2d$ units, where d is the dimensionality of the input space. As we did for threshold units, we try to arrange for each group to provide a non-zero output only when the input vector lies within a small region of the input space. For this purpose it is convenient to consider the logistic sigmoid activation function given by (4.10).

We can illustrate the construction of the network by considering a two-dimensional input space. In Figure 4.10 (a) we show the output from a single unit in the first hidden layer, given by

$$z = g(\mathbf{w}^{\mathrm{T}}\mathbf{x} + w_0). \tag{4.12}$$

From the discussion in Section 3.1, we see that the orientation of the sigmoid is determined by the direction of $\mathbf{w}$, its location is determined by the bias w_0, and the steepness of the sigmoid slope is determined by $\|\mathbf{w}\|$. Units in the second hidden layer form linear combinations of these sigmoidal surfaces. Consider the combination of two such surfaces in which we choose the second sigmoid to have the same orientation as the first but displaced from it by a short distance. By

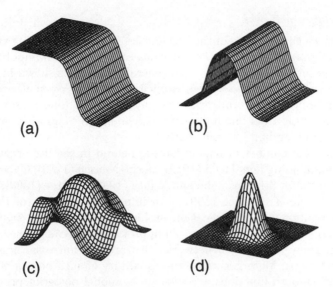

Figure 4.10. Demonstration that a network with three layers of weights, and sigmoidal hidden units, can approximate a smooth multivariate mapping to arbitrary accuracy. In (a) we see the output of a single sigmoidal unit as a function of two input variables. Adding the outputs from two such units can produce a ridge-like function (b), and adding two ridges can give a function with a maximum (c). Transforming this function with another sigmoid gives a localized response (d). By taking linear combinations of these localized functions, we can approximate any smooth functional mapping.

adding the two sigmoids together we obtain a ridge-like function as shown in Figure 4.10 (b). We next construct d of these ridges with orthogonal orientations and add them together to give a bump-like structure as shown in Figure 4.10 (c). Although this has a central peak there are also many other ridges present which stretch out to infinity. These are removed by the action of the sigmoids of the second-layer units which effectively provide a form of soft threshold to isolate the central bump, as shown in Figure 4.10 (d). We now appeal to the intuitive idea (discussed more formally in Section 5.2) that any reasonable function can be approximated to arbitrary accuracy by a linear superposition of a sufficiently large number of localized 'bump' functions, provided the coefficients in the linear combination are appropriately chosen. This superposition is performed by the output unit, which has a linear activation function.

Once again, although this is a constructive algorithm it is of little relevance to practical applications and serves mainly as an existence proof. However, the idea of representing a function as a linear superposition of localized bump functions suggests that we might consider two-layer networks in which each hidden unit generates a bump-like function directly. Such networks are called local basis function networks, and will be considered in detail in Chapter 5.

4.3.2   *Two-layer networks*

We turn next to the question of the capabilities of networks having two layers of weights and sigmoidal hidden units. This has proven to be an important class of network for practical applications. The general topology is shown in Figure 4.1, and the network function was given explicitly in (4.7). We shall see that such networks can approximate arbitrarily well any functional (one–one or many–one) continuous mapping from one finite-dimensional space to another, provided the number M of hidden units is sufficiently large.

A considerable number of papers have appeared in the literature discussing this property including Funahashi (1989), Hecht-Nielsen (1989), Cybenko (1989), Hornik *et al.* (1989), Stinchecombe and White (1989), Cotter (1990), Ito (1991), Hornik (1991) and Kreinovich (1991). An important corollary of this result is that, in the context of a classification problem, networks with sigmoidal non-linearities and two layers of weights can approximate any decision boundary to arbitrary accuracy. Thus, such networks also provide universal non-linear discriminant functions. More generally, the capability of such networks to approximate general smooth functions allows them to model posterior probabilities of class membership.

Here we outline a simple proof of the universality property (Jones, 1990; Blum and Li, 1991). Consider the case of two input variables x_1 and x_2, and a single output variable y (the extension to larger numbers of input or output variables is straightforward). We know that, for any given value of x_1, the desired function $y(x_1, x_2)$ can be approximated to within any given (sum-of-squares) error by a Fourier decomposition in the variable x_2, giving rise to terms of the form

$$y(x_1, x_2) \simeq \sum_s A_s(x_1) \cos(s x_2) \tag{4.13}$$

where the coefficients A_s are functions of x_1. Similarly, the coefficients themselves can be expressed in terms of a Fourier series giving

$$y(x_1, x_2) \simeq \sum_s \sum_l A_{sl} \cos(l x_1) \cos(s x_2) \tag{4.14}$$

We can now use the standard trigonometric identity $\cos\alpha\cos\beta = \frac{1}{2}\cos(\alpha + \beta) + \frac{1}{2}\cos(\alpha - \beta)$ to write this as a linear combination of terms of the form $\cos(z_{sl})$ and $\cos(z'_{sl})$ where $z_{sl} = l x_1 + s x_2$ and $z'_{sl} = l x_1 - s x_2$. Finally, we note that the function $\cos(z)$ can be approximated to arbitrary accuracy by a linear combination of threshold step functions. This can be seen by making an explicit construction, illustrated in Figure 4.11, for a function $f(z)$ in terms of a piecewise constant function, of the form

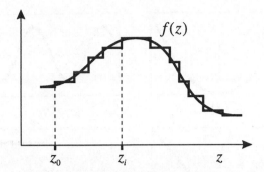

Figure 4.11. Approximation of a continuous function $f(z)$ by a linear superposition of threshold step functions. This forms the basis of a simple proof that a two-layer network having sigmoidal hidden units and linear output units can approximate a continuous function to arbitrary accuracy.

$$f(z) \simeq f_0 + \sum_{i=0}^{N} \{f_{i+1} - f_i\} \, H(z - z_i) \qquad (4.15)$$

where $H(z)$ is the Heaviside step function. Thus we see that the function $y(x_1, x_2)$ can be expressed as a linear combination of step functions whose arguments are linear combinations of x_1 and x_2. In other words the function $y(x_1, x_2)$ can be approximated by a two-layer network with threshold hidden units and linear output units. Finally, we recall that threshold activation functions can be approximated arbitrarily well by sigmoidal functions, simply by scaling the weights and biases.

Note that this proof does not indicate whether the network can simultaneously approximate the derivatives of the function, since our approximation in (4.15) has zero derivative except at discrete points at which the derivative is undefined. A proof that two-layer networks having sigmoidal hidden units can simultaneously approximate both a function and its derivatives was given by Hornik *et al.* (1990).

As a simple illustration of the capabilities of two-layer networks with sigmoidal hidden units we consider mappings from a single input x to a single output y. In Figure 4.12 we show the result of training a network with five hidden units having 'tanh' activation functions given by (4.11). The data sets each consist of 50 data points generated by a variety of functions, and the network has a single linear output unit and was trained for 1000 epochs using the BFGS quasi-Newton algorithm described in Section 7.10. We see that the same network can generate a wide variety of different functions simply by choosing different values for the weights and biases.

The above proofs were concerned with demonstrating that a network with a

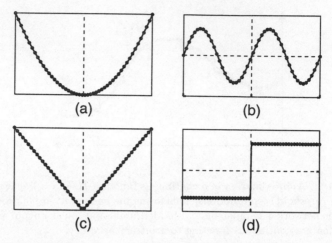

Figure 4.12. Examples of sets of data points (circles) together with the corresponding functions represented by a multi-layer perceptron network which has been trained using the data. The data sets were generated by sampling the following functions: (a) x^2, (b) $\sin(2\pi x)$ (c) $|x|$ which is continuous but with a discontinuous first derivative, and (d) the step function $\theta(x) \equiv \mathrm{sign}(x)$, which is discontinuous.

sufficiently large number of hidden units could approximate a particular mapping. White (1990) and Gallant and White (1992) considered the conditions under which a network will actually learn a given mapping from a finite data set, showing how the number of hidden units must grow as the size of the data set grows.

If we try to approximate a given function $h(\mathbf{x})$ with a network having a finite number M of hidden units, then there will be a residual error. Jones (1992) and Barron (1993) have shown that this error decreases as $\mathcal{O}(1/M)$ as the number M of hidden units is increased.

Since we know that, with a single hidden layer, we can approximate any mapping to arbitrary accuracy we might wonder if there is anything to be gained by using any other network topology, for instance one having several hidden layers. One possibility is that by using extra layers we might find more efficient approximations in the sense of achieving the same level of accuracy with fewer weights and biases in total. Very little is currently known about this issue. However, later chapters discuss situations in which there are other good reasons to consider networks with more complex topologies, including networks with several hidden layers, and networks with only partial connectivity between layers.

4.4 Weight-space symmetries

Consider a two-layer network having M hidden units, with 'tanh' activation functions given by (4.11), and full connectivity in both layers. If we change the sign of all of the weights and the bias feeding into a particular hidden unit, then, for a given input pattern, the sign of the activation of the hidden unit will be reversed, since (4.11) is an odd function. This can be compensated by changing the sign of all of the weights leading out of that hidden unit. Thus, by changing the signs of a particular group of weights (and a bias), the input–output mapping function represented by the network is unchanged, and so we have found two different weight vectors which give rise to the same mapping function. For M hidden units, there will be M such 'sign-flip' symmetries, and thus any given weight vector will be one of a set 2^M equivalent weight vectors (Chen *et al.*, 1993).

Similarly, imagine that we interchange the values of all of the weights (and the bias) leading into and out of a particular hidden unit with the corresponding values of the weights (and bias) associated with a different hidden unit. Again, this clearly leaves the network input–output mapping function unchanged, but it corresponds to a different choice of weight vector. For M hidden units, any given weight vector will have $M!$ equivalent weight vectors associated with this interchange symmetry, corresponding to the $M!$ different orderings of the hidden units (Chen *et al.*, 1993). The network will therefore have an overall weight-space symmetry factor of $M!2^M$. For networks with more than two layers of weights, the total level of symmetry will be given by the product of such factors, one for each layer of hidden units.

It turns out that these factors account for all of the symmetries in weight space (except for possible accidental symmetries due to specific choices for the weight values). Furthermore, the existence of these symmetries is not a particular property of the 'tanh' function, but applies to a wide range of activation functions (Sussmann, 1992; Chen *et al.*, 1993; Albertini and Sontag, 1993; Kůrková and Kainen, 1994). In many cases, these symmetries in weight space are of little practical consequence. However, we shall encounter an example in Section 10.6 where we need to take them into account.

4.5 Higher-order networks

So far in this chapter we have considered units for which the output is given by a non-linear activation function acting on a *linear* combination of the inputs of the form

$$a_j = \sum_i w_{ji} x_i + w_{j0}. \tag{4.16}$$

We have seen that networks composed of such units can in principle approximate any functional mapping to arbitrary accuracy, and therefore constitute a universal class of parametrized multivariate non-linear mappings. Nevertheless, there is still considerable interest in studying other forms of processing unit. Chapter 5

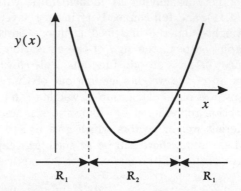

Figure 4.13. A one-dimensional input space x with decision regions $\mathcal{R}_1$ (which is disjoint) and $\mathcal{R}_2$. A linear discriminant function cannot generate the required decision boundaries, but a quadratic discriminant $y(x)$, shown by the solid curve, can. The required decision rule then assigns an input x to class $\mathcal{C}_1$ if $y(x) > 0$ and to class $\mathcal{C}_2$ otherwise.

for instance is devoted to a study of networks containing units whose activations depend on the *distance* of an input vector from the weight vector. Here we consider some extensions of the linear expression in (4.16) which therefore contain (4.16) as a special case.

As discussed in Chapter 3, a network consisting of a single layer of units of the form (4.16) can only produce decision boundaries which take the form of piecewise hyperplanes in the input space. Such a network is therefore incapable of generating decision regions which are concave or which are multiply connected. Consider the one-dimensional input space x illustrated in Figure 4.13. We wish to find a discriminant function which will divide the space into the decision regions $\mathcal{R}_1$ and $\mathcal{R}_2$ as shown. A linear discriminant function is not sufficient since the region $\mathcal{R}_1$ is disjoint. However, the required decision boundaries can be generated by a quadratic discriminant of the form

$$y(x) = w_2 x^2 + w_1 x + w_0 \tag{4.17}$$

provided the weights w_2, w_1 and w_0 are chosen appropriately.

We can generalize this idea to higher orders than just quadratic, and to several input variables (Ivakhnenko, 1971; Barron and Barron, 1988). This leads to *higher-order* processing units (Giles and Maxwell, 1987; Ghosh and Shin, 1992), also known as *sigma-pi* units (Rumelhart *et al.*, 1986). For second-order units the generalization of (4.16) takes the form

$$a_j = w_j^{(0)} + \sum_{i_1=1}^{d} w_{ji_1}^{(1)} x_{i_1} + \sum_{i_1=1}^{d} \sum_{i_2=1}^{d} w_{ji_1i_2}^{(2)} x_{i_1} x_{i_2} \qquad (4.18)$$

where the sums run over all inputs, or units, which send connections to unit j. As before, this sum is then transformed using a non-linear activation function to give $z_j = g(a_j)$. If terms up to degree M are retained, this will be known as an Mth-order unit. Clearly (4.18) includes the conventional linear (first-order) unit (4.16) as a special case. The similarity to the higher-order polynomials discussed in Section 1.7 is clear. Note that the summations in (4.18) can be constrained to allow for the permutation symmetry of the higher-order terms. For instance, the term $x_{i_1} x_{i_2}$ is equivalent to the term $x_{i_2} x_{i_1}$ and so we need only retain one of these in the summation. The total number of independent parameters in a higher-order expression such as (4.18) is discussed in Exercises 1.6–1.8.

If we introduce an extra input $z_0 = +1$ then, for an Mth-order unit we can absorb all of the terms up to the Mth-order within the Mth-order term. For instance, if we consider second-order units we can write (4.18) in the equivalent form

$$a_j = \sum_{i_1=0}^{d} \sum_{i_2=0}^{d} w_{ji_1i_2}^{(2)} z_{i_1} z_{i_2} \qquad (4.19)$$

with similar generalizations to higher orders.

We see that there will typically be many more weight parameters in a higher-order unit than there are in a first-order unit. For example, if we consider an input dimensionality of $d = 10$ then a first-order unit will have 11 weight parameters (including the bias), a second-order unit will have 66 independent weights, and a third-order unit will have 572 independent weights. This explosion in the number of parameters is the principal difficulty with such higher-order units. The compensating benefit is that it is possible to arrange for the response of the unit to be invariant to various transformations of the input. In Section 8.7.4 it is shown how a third-order unit can be simultaneously invariant to translations, rotations and scalings of the input patterns when these are drawn from pixels in a two-dimensional image. This is achieved by imposing constraints on the weights, which also greatly reduce the number of independent parameters, and thereby makes the use of such units a tractable proposition. Higher-order units are generally used only in the first layer of a network, with subsequent layers being composed of conventional first-order units.

4.6 Projection pursuit regression and other conventional techniques

Statisticians have developed a variety of techniques for classification and regression which can be regarded as complementary to the multi-layer perceptron. Here we give a brief overview of the most prominent of these approaches, and indicate their relation to neural networks. One of the most closely related is that of *projection pursuit regression* (Friedman and Stuetzle, 1981; Huber, 1985). For a single output variable, the projection pursuit regression mapping can be written in the form

$$y = \sum_{j=1}^{M} w_j \phi_j (\mathbf{u}_j^T \mathbf{x} + u_{j0}) + w_0 \tag{4.20}$$

which is remarkably similar to a two-layer feed-forward neural network. The parameters $\mathbf{u}_j$ and u_{j0} define the projection of the input vector $\mathbf{x}$ onto a set of planes labelled by $j = 1, \ldots, M$, as in the multi-layer perceptron. These projections are transformed by non-linear 'activation functions' ϕ_j and these in turn are linearly combined to form the output variable y. Determination of the parameters in the model is done by minimizing a sum-of-squares error function. One important difference is that each 'hidden unit' in projection pursuit regression is allowed a different activation function, and these functions are not prescribed in advance, but are determined from the data as part of the training procedure.

Another difference is that typically all of the parameters in a neural network are optimized simultaneously, while those in projection pursuit regression are optimized cyclically in groups. Specifically, training in the projection pursuit regression network takes place for one hidden unit at a time, and for each hidden unit the second-layer weights are optimized first, followed by the activation function, followed by the first-layer weights. The process is repeated for each hidden unit in turn, until a sufficiently small value for the error function is achieved, or until some other stopping criterion is satisfied. Since the output y in (4.20) depends linearly on the second-layer parameters, these can be optimized by linear least-squares techniques, as discussed in Section 3.4. Optimization of the activation functions ϕ_j represents a problem in one-dimensional curve-fitting for which a variety of techniques can be used, such as cubic splines (Press *et al.*, 1992). Finally, the optimization of the first-layer weights requires non-linear techniques of the kind discussed in Chapter 7.

Several generalizations to more than one output variable are possible (Ripley, 1994) depending on whether the outputs share common basis functions ϕ_j, and if not, whether the separate basis functions ϕ_{jk} (where k labels the outputs) share common projection directions. In terms of representational capability, we can regard projection pursuit regression as a generalization of the multi-layer perceptron, in that the activation functions are more flexible. It is therefore not surprising that projection pursuit regression should have the same 'universal' approximation capabilities as multi-layer perceptrons (Diaconis and Shahshahani, 1984; Jones, 1987). Projection pursuit regression is compared with multi-layer perceptron networks in Hwang *et al.* (1994).

Another framework for non-linear regression is the class of *generalized additive models* (Hastie and Tibshirani, 1990) which take the form

$$y = g \left(\sum_{i=1}^{d} \phi_i(x_i) + w_0 \right) \tag{4.21}$$

where the $\phi_i(\cdot)$ are non-linear functions and $g(\cdot)$ represents the logistic sigmoid function (4.10). This is actually a very restrictive class of models, since it does not allow for interactions between the input variables. Thus a function of the form $x_1 x_2$, for example, cannot be modelled. They do, however, have an advantage in terms of the interpretation of the trained model, since the individual univariate functions $\phi_i(\cdot)$ can be plotted.

An extension of the additive models which allows for interactions is given by the technique of *multivariate adaptive regression splines* (MARS) (Friedman, 1991) for which the mapping function can be written

$$y = \sum_{j=1}^{M} w_j \prod_{k=1}^{K_j} \phi_{jk}(x_{\nu(k,j)}) + w_0 \tag{4.22}$$

where the jth basis function is given by a product of some number K_j of one-dimensional spline functions ϕ_{jk} (Press *et al.*, 1992) each of which depends on one of the input variables x_ν, where the particular input variable used in each case is governed by a label $\nu(k, j)$. The basis functions are adaptive in that the number of factors K_j, the labels $\nu(k, j)$, and the knots for the one-dimensional spline functions are all determined from the data. Basis functions are added incrementally during learning, using the technique of sequential forward selection discussed in Section 8.5.3.

An alternative framework for learning non-linear multivariate mappings involves partitioning the input space into regions, and fitting a different mapping within each region. In many such algorithms, the partitions are formed from hyperplanes which are parallel to the input variable axes, as indicated in Figure 4.14. In the simplest case the output variable is taken to be constant within each region. A common technique is to form a binary partition in which the input space is divided into two regions, and then each of these is divided in turn, and so on. This form of partitioning can then be described by a binary tree structure, in which each leaf represents one of the regions. Successive branches can be added to the tree during learning, with the locations of the hyperplanes being determined by the data. Procedures are often also devised for pruning the tree structure as a way of controlling the effective complexity of the model. Two of the best known algorithms of this kind are *classification and regression trees* (CART) (Breiman *et al.*, 1984) and ID3 (Quinlan, 1986). A detailed discussion of these algorithms would, however, take us too far afield.

4.7 Kolmogorov's theorem

There is a theorem due to Kolmogorov (1957) which, although of no direct practical significance, does have an interesting relation to neural networks. The theo-

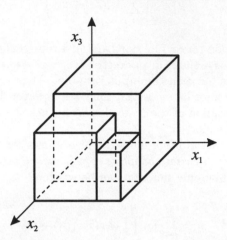

Figure 4.14. An example of the partitioning of a space by hyperplanes which are parallel to the coordinate axes. Such partitions form the basis of a number of algorithms for solving classification and regression problems.

rem has its origins at the end of the nineteenth century when the mathematician Hilbert compiled a list of 23 unsolved problems as a challenge for twentieth century mathematicians (Hilbert, 1900). Hilbert's thirteenth problem concerns the issue of whether functions of several variables can be represented in terms of superpositions of functions of fewer variables. He conjectured that there exist continuous functions of three variables which cannot be represented as superpositions of functions of two variables. The conjecture was disproved by Arnold (1957). However, a much more general result was obtained by Kolmogorov (1957) who showed that every continuous function of several variables (for a closed and bounded input domain) can be represented as the superposition of a small number of functions of one variable. Improved versions of Kolmogorov's theorem have been given by Sprecher (1965), Kahane (1975) and Lorentz (1976). In neural network terms this theorem says that any continuous mapping $y(\mathbf{x})$ from d input variables x_i to an output variable y can be represented exactly by a three-layer neural network having $d(2d+1)$ units in the first hidden layer and $(2d+1)$ units in the second hidden layer. The network topology is illustrated, for the case of a single output, in Figure 4.15. Each unit in the first hidden layer computes a function of one of the input variables x_i given by $h_j(x_i)$ where $j = 1, \ldots, 2d+1$ and the h_j are strictly monotonic functions. The activation of the jth unit in the second hidden layer is given by

$$z_j = \sum_{i=1}^{d} \lambda_i h_j(x_i) \tag{4.23}$$

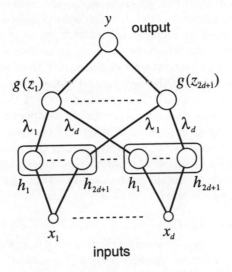

y output

$g(z_1)$ $g(z_{2d+1})$

λ_1 λ_d λ_1 λ_d

h_1 h_{2d+1} h_1 h_{2d+1}

x_1 x_d

inputs

Figure 4.15. Network topology to implement Kolmogorov's theorem.

where $0 < \lambda_i < 1$ are constants. The output y of the network is then given by

$$y = \sum_{j=1}^{2d+1} g(z_j) \tag{4.24}$$

where the function g is real and continuous. Note that the function g depends on the particular function $y(\mathbf{x})$ which is to be represented, while the functions h_j do not. This expression can be extended to a network with more that one output unit simply by modifying (4.24) to give

$$y_k = \sum_{j=1}^{2d+1} g_k(z_j). \tag{4.25}$$

Note that the theorem only guarantees the existence of a suitable network. No actual examples of functions h_j or g are known, and there is no known constructive technique for finding them.

While Kolmogorov's theorem is remarkable, its relevance to practical neural computing is at best limited (Girosi and Poggio, 1989; Kůrková, 1991; Kůrková, 1992). There are two reasons for this. First, the functions h_j are far from being smooth. Indeed, it has been shown that if the functions h_j are required to be smooth then the theorem breaks down (Vitushkin, 1954). The presence of non-smooth functions in a network would lead to problems of extreme sensitivity to the input variables. Smoothness of the network mapping is an important property in connection with the generalization performance of a network, as is discussed in greater detail in Section 9.2. The second reason is that the function g depends on the particular function $y(\mathbf{x})$ which we wish to represent. This is the converse of the situation which we generally encounter with neural networks. Usually, we consider fixed activation functions, and then adjust the number of hidden units, and the values of the weights and biases, to give a sufficiently close representation of the desired mapping. In Kolmogorov's theorem the number of hidden units is fixed, while the activation functions depend on the mapping. In general, if we are trying to represent an arbitrary continuous function then we cannot hope to do this exactly with a finite number of fixed activation functions since the finite number of adjustable parameters represents a finite number of degrees of freedom, and a general continuous function has effectively infinitely many degrees of freedom.

4.8 Error back-propagation

So far in this chapter we have concentrated on the representational capabilities of multi-layer networks. We next consider how such a network can learn a suitable mapping from a given data set. As in previous chapters, learning will be based on the definition of a suitable error function, which is then minimized with respect to the weights and biases in the network.

Consider first the case of networks of threshold units. The final layer of weights in the network can be regarded as a perceptron with inputs given by the outputs of the last layer of hidden units. These weights could therefore be chosen using the perceptron learning rule introduced in Chapter 3. Such an approach cannot, however, be used to determine the weights in earlier layers of the network. Although such layers could in principle be regarded as being like single-layer perceptrons, we have no procedure for assigning target values to their outputs, and so the perceptron procedure cannot be applied. This is known as the *credit assignment problem*. If an output unit produces an incorrect response when the network is presented with an input vector we have no way of determining which of the hidden units should be regarded as responsible for generating the error, so there is no way of determining which weights to adjust or by how much.

The solution to this credit assignment problem is relatively simple. If we consider a network with differentiable activation functions, then the activations of the output units become differentiable functions of both the input variables, and of the weights and biases. If we define an error function, such as the sum-of-squares error introduced in Chapter 1, which is a differentiable function of the network outputs, then this error is itself a differentiable function of the weights. We can therefore evaluate the derivatives of the error with respect to the weights, and these derivatives can then be used to find weight values which minimize the error function, by using either gradient descent or one of the more powerful optimization methods discussed in Chapter 7. The algorithm for evaluating the derivatives of the error function is known as *back-propagation* since, as we shall see, it corresponds to a propagation of errors backwards through the network. The technique of back-propagation was popularized in a paper by Rumelhart, Hinton and Williams (1986). However, similar ideas had been developed earlier by a number of researchers including Werbos (1974) and Parker (1985).

It should be noted that the term back-propagation is used in the neural computing literature to mean a variety of different things. For instance, the multi-layer perceptron architecture is sometimes called a back-propagation network. The term back-propagation is also used to describe the training of a multi-layer perceptron using gradient descent applied to a sum-of-squares error function. In order to clarify the terminology it is useful to consider the nature of the training process more carefully. Most training algorithms involve an iterative procedure for minimization of an error function, with adjustments to the weights being made in a sequence of steps. At each such step we can distinguish between two distinct stages. In the first stage, the derivatives of the error function with respect to the weights must be evaluated. As we shall see, the important contribution of the back-propagation technique is in providing a computationally efficient method for evaluating such derivatives. Since it is at this stage that errors are propagated backwards through the network, we shall use the term back-propagation specifically to describe the evaluation of derivatives. In the second stage, the derivatives are then used to compute the adjustments to be made to the weights. The simplest such technique, and the one originally considered by Rumelhart *et al.* (1986), involves gradient descent. It is important to recognize that the two stages are distinct. Thus, the first stage process, namely the propagation of errors backwards through the network in order to evaluate derivatives, can be applied to many other kinds of network and not just the multi-layer perceptron. It can also be applied to error functions other that just the simple sum-of-squares, and to the evaluation of other derivatives such as the Jacobian and Hessian matrices, as we shall see later in this chapter. Similarly, the second stage of weight adjustment using the calculated derivatives can be tackled using a variety of optimization schemes (discussed at length in Chapter 7), many of which are substantially more powerful than simple gradient descent.

4.8.1 *Evaluation of error function derivatives*

We now derive the back-propagation algorithm for a general network having arbitrary feed-forward topology, and arbitrary differentiable non-linear activation functions, for the case of an arbitrary differentiable error function. The resulting formulae will then be illustrated using a simple layered network structure having a single layer of sigmoidal hidden units and a sum-of-squares error.

In a general feed-forward network, each unit computes a weighted sum of its inputs of the form

$$a_j = \sum_i w_{ji} z_i \tag{4.26}$$

where z_i is the activation of a unit, or input, which sends a connection to unit

j, and w_{ji} is the weight associated with that connection. The summation runs over all units which send connections to unit j. In Section 4.1 we showed that biases can be included in this sum by introducing an extra unit, or input, with activation fixed at $+1$. We therefore do not need to deal with biases explicitly. The sum in (4.26) is transformed by a non-linear activation function $g(\cdot)$ to give the activation z_j of unit j in the form

$$z_j = g(a_j). \tag{4.27}$$

Note that one or more of the variables z_i in the sum in (4.26) could be an input, in which case we shall denote it by x_i. Similarly, the unit j in (4.27) could be an output unit, in which case we denote its activation by y_k.

As before, we shall seek to determine suitable values for the weights in the network by minimization of an appropriate error function. Here we shall consider error functions which can be written as a sum, over all patterns in the training set, of an error defined for each pattern separately

$$E = \sum_n E^n \tag{4.28}$$

where n labels the patterns. Nearly all error functions of practical interest take this form, for reasons which are explained in Chapter 6. We shall also suppose that the error E^n can be expressed as a differentiable function of the network output variables so that

$$E^n = E^n(y_1, \ldots, y_c). \tag{4.29}$$

Our goal is to find a procedure for evaluating the derivatives of the error function E with respect to the weights and biases in the network. Using (4.28) we can express these derivatives as sums over the training set patterns of the derivatives for each pattern separately. From now on we shall therefore consider one pattern at a time.

For each pattern we shall suppose that we have supplied the corresponding input vector to the network and calculated the activations of all of the hidden and output units in the network by successive application of (4.26) and (4.27). This process is often called *forward propagation* since it can be regarded as a forward flow of information through the network.

Now consider the evaluation of the derivative of E^n with respect to some weight w_{ji}. The outputs of the various units will depend on the particular input pattern n. However, in order to keep the notation uncluttered, we shall omit the superscript n from the input and activation variables. First we note that E^n depends on the weight w_{ji} only via the summed input a_j to unit j. We can therefore apply the chain rule for partial derivatives to give

$$\frac{\partial E^n}{\partial w_{ji}} = \frac{\partial E^n}{\partial a_j}\frac{\partial a_j}{\partial w_{ji}}. \tag{4.30}$$

We now introduce a useful notation

$$\delta_j \equiv \frac{\partial E^n}{\partial a_j} \tag{4.31}$$

where the δ's are often referred to as *errors* for reasons we shall see shortly. Using (4.26) we can write

$$\frac{\partial a_j}{\partial w_{ji}} = z_i. \tag{4.32}$$

Substituting (4.31) and (4.32) into (4.30) we then obtain

$$\frac{\partial E^n}{\partial w_{ji}} = \delta_j z_i. \tag{4.33}$$

Note that this has the same general form as obtained for single-layer networks in Section 3.4. Equation (4.33) tells us that the required derivative is obtained simply by multiplying the value of δ for the unit at the output end of the weight by the value of z for the unit at the input end of the weight (where $z = 1$ in the case of a bias). Thus, in order to evaluate the derivatives, we need only to calculate the value of δ_j for each hidden and output unit in the network, and then apply (4.33).

For the output units the evaluation of δ_k is straightforward. From the definition (4.31) we have

$$\delta_k \equiv \frac{\partial E^n}{\partial a_k} = g'(a_k)\frac{\partial E^n}{\partial y_k} \tag{4.34}$$

where we have used (4.27) with z_k denoted by y_k. In order to evaluate (4.34) we substitute appropriate expressions for $g'(a)$ and $\partial E^n/\partial y$. This will be illustrated with a simple example shortly.

To evaluate the δ's for hidden units we again make use of the chain rule for partial derivatives,

$$\delta_j \equiv \frac{\partial E^n}{\partial a_j} = \sum_k \frac{\partial E^n}{\partial a_k}\frac{\partial a_k}{\partial a_j} \tag{4.35}$$

where the sum runs over all units k to which unit j sends connections. The arrangement of units and weights is illustrated in Figure 4.16. Note that the units labelled k could include other hidden units and/or output units. In writing

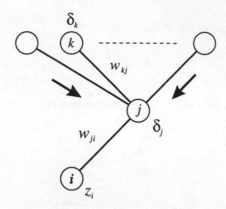

Figure 4.16. Illustration of the calculation of δ_j for hidden unit j by back-propagation of the δ's from those units k to which unit j sends connections.

down (4.35) we are making use of the fact that variations in a_j give rise to variations in the error function only through variations in the variables a_k. If we now substitute the definition of δ given by (4.31) into (4.35), and make use of (4.26) and (4.27), we obtain the following *back-propagation* formula

$$\delta_j = g'(a_j) \sum_k w_{kj}\delta_k \tag{4.36}$$

which tells us that the value of δ for a particular hidden unit can be obtained by propagating the δ's backwards from units higher up in the network, as illustrated in Figure 4.16. Since we already know the values of the δ's for the output units, it follows that by recursively applying (4.36) we can evaluate the δ's for all of the hidden units in a feed-forward network, regardless of its topology.

We can summarize the back-propagation procedure for evaluating the derivatives of the error E^n with respect to the weights in four steps:

1. Apply an input vector $\mathbf{x}^n$ to the network and forward propagate through the network using (4.26) and (4.27) to find the activations of all the hidden and output units.

2. Evaluate the δ_k for all the output units using (4.34).

3. Back-propagate the δ's using (4.36) to obtain δ_j for each hidden unit in the network.

4. Use (4.33) to evaluate the required derivatives.

The derivative of the total error E can then be obtained by repeating the above steps for each pattern in the training set, and then summing over all patterns:

$$\frac{\partial E}{\partial w_{ji}} = \sum_n \frac{\partial E^n}{\partial w_{ji}}. \tag{4.37}$$

In the above derivation we have implicitly assumed that each hidden or output unit in the network has the same activation function $g(\cdot)$. The derivation is easily generalized, however, to allow different units to have individual activation functions, simply by keeping track of which form of $g(\cdot)$ goes with which unit.

4.8.2 A simple example

The above derivation of the back-propagation procedure allowed for general forms for the error function, the activation functions and the network topology. In order to illustrate the application of this algorithm, we shall consider a particular example. This is chosen both for its simplicity and for its practical importance, since many applications of neural networks reported in the literature make use of this type of network. Specifically, we shall consider a two-layer network of the form illustrated in Figure 4.1, together with a sum-of-squares error. The output units have linear activation functions while the hidden units have logistic sigmoid activation functions given by (4.10), and repeated here:

$$g(a) \equiv \frac{1}{1 + \exp(-a)}. \tag{4.38}$$

A useful feature of this function is that its derivative can be expressed in a particularly simple form:

$$g'(a) = g(a)(1 - g(a)). \tag{4.39}$$

In a software implementation of the network algorithm, (4.39) represents a convenient property since the derivative of the activation can be obtained efficiently from the activation itself using two arithmetic operations.

For the standard sum-of-squares error function, the error for pattern n is given by

$$E^n = \frac{1}{2} \sum_{k=1}^c (y_k - t_k)^2 \tag{4.40}$$

where y_k is the response of output unit k, and t_k is the corresponding target, for a particular input pattern $\mathbf{x}^n$.

Using the expressions derived above for back-propagation in a general network, together with (4.39) and (4.40), we obtain the following results. For the output units, the δ's are given by

$$\delta_k = y_k - t_k \tag{4.41}$$

while for units in the hidden layer the δ's are found using

$$\delta_j = z_j(1 - z_j) \sum_{k=1}^{c} w_{kj} \delta_k \qquad (4.42)$$

where the sum runs over all output units. The derivatives with respect to the first-layer and second-layer weights are then given by

$$\frac{\partial E^n}{\partial w_{ji}} = \delta_j x_i, \qquad \frac{\partial E^n}{\partial w_{kj}} = \delta_k z_j. \qquad (4.43)$$

So far we have discussed the evaluation of the derivatives of the error function with respect to the weights and biases in the network. In order to turn this into a learning algorithm we need some method for updating the weights based on these derivatives. In Chapter 7 we discuss several such parameter optimization strategies in some detail. For the moment, we consider the fixed-step gradient descent technique introduced in Section 3.4. We have the choice of updating the weights either after presentation of each pattern (on-line learning) or after first summing the derivatives over all the patterns in the training set (batch learning). In the former case the weights in the first layer are updated using

$$\Delta w_{ji} = -\eta \delta_j x_i \qquad (4.44)$$

while in the case of batch learning the first-layer weights are updated using

$$\Delta w_{ji} = -\eta \sum_n \delta_j^n x_i^n \qquad (4.45)$$

with analogous expressions for the second-layer weights.

4.8.3 *Efficiency of back-propagation*

One of the most important aspects of back-propagation is its computational efficiency. To understand this, let us examine how the number of computer operations required to evaluate the derivatives of the error function scales with the size of the network. Let W be the total number of weights and biases. Then a single evaluation of the error function (for a given input pattern) would require $\mathcal{O}(W)$ operations, for sufficiently large W. This follows from the fact that, except for a network with very sparse connections, the number of weights is typically much greater than the number of units. Thus, the bulk of the computational effort in forward propagation is concerned with evaluating the sums in (4.26), with the evaluation of the activation functions representing a small overhead. Each term in the sum in (4.26) requires one multiplication and one addition, leading to an overall computational cost which is $\mathcal{O}(W)$.

For W weights in total there are W such derivatives to evaluate. If we simply took the expression for the error function and wrote down explicit formulae for the derivatives and then evaluated them numerically by forward propagation, we would have to evaluate W such terms (one for each weight or bias) each requiring $\mathcal{O}(W)$ operations. Thus, the total computational effort required to evaluate all the derivatives would scale as $\mathcal{O}(W^2)$. By comparison, back-propagation allows the derivatives to be evaluated in $\mathcal{O}(W)$ operations. This follows from the fact that both the forward and the backward propagation phases are $\mathcal{O}(W)$, and the evaluation of the derivative using (4.33) also requires $\mathcal{O}(W)$ operations. Thus back-propagation has reduced the computational complexity from $\mathcal{O}(W^2)$ to $\mathcal{O}(W)$ for each input vector. Since the training of MLP networks, even using back-propagation, can be very time consuming, this gain in efficiency is crucial. For a total of N training patterns, the number of computational steps required to evaluate the complete error function for the whole data set is N times larger than for one pattern.

The practical importance of the $\mathcal{O}(W)$ scaling of back-propagation is analogous in some respects to that of the fast Fourier transform (FFT) algorithm (Brigham, 1974; Press *et al.*, 1992) which reduces the computational complexity of evaluating an L-point Fourier transform from $\mathcal{O}(L^2)$ to $\mathcal{O}(L \log_2 L)$. The discovery of this algorithm led to the widespread use of Fourier transforms in a large range of practical applications.

4.8.4 *Numerical differentiation*

An alternative approach to back-propagation for computing the derivatives of the error function is to use finite differences. This can be done by perturbing each weight in turn, and approximating the derivatives by the expression

$$\frac{\partial E^n}{\partial w_{ji}} = \frac{E^n(w_{ji} + \epsilon) - E^n(w_{ji})}{\epsilon} + \mathcal{O}(\epsilon) \tag{4.46}$$

where $\epsilon \ll 1$ is a small quantity. In a software simulation, the accuracy of the approximation to the derivatives can be improved by making ϵ smaller, until numerical roundoff problems arise. The main problem with this approach is that the highly desirable $\mathcal{O}(W)$ scaling has been lost. Each forward propagation requires $\mathcal{O}(W)$ steps, and there are W weights in the network each of which must be perturbed individually, so that the overall scaling is $\mathcal{O}(W^2)$. However, finite differences play an important role in practice, since a numerical comparison of the derivatives calculated by back-propagation with those obtained using finite differences provides a very powerful check on the correctness of any software implementation of the back-propagation algorithm.

The accuracy of the finite differences method can be improved significantly by using symmetrical *central differences* of the form

$$\frac{\partial E^n}{\partial w_{ji}} = \frac{E^n(w_{ji} + \epsilon) - E^n(w_{ji} - \epsilon)}{2\epsilon} + \mathcal{O}(\epsilon^2). \tag{4.47}$$

In this case the $\mathcal{O}(\epsilon)$ corrections cancel, as is easily verified by Taylor expansion on the right-hand side of (4.47), and so the residual corrections are $\mathcal{O}(\epsilon^2)$. The number of computational steps is, however, roughly doubled compared with (4.46).

We have seen that the derivatives of an error function with respect to the weights in a network can be expressed efficiently through the relation

$$\frac{\partial E}{\partial w_{ji}} = \frac{\partial E}{\partial a_j} z_i. \tag{4.48}$$

Instead of using the technique of central differences to evaluate the derivatives $\partial E^n / \partial w_{ji}$ directly, we can use it to estimate $\partial E^n / \partial a_j$ since

$$\frac{\partial E^n}{\partial a_j} = \frac{E^n(a_j + \epsilon) - E^n(a_j - \epsilon)}{2\epsilon} + \mathcal{O}(\epsilon^2) \tag{4.49}$$

We can then make use of (4.48) to evaluate the required derivatives. Because the derivatives with respect to the weights are found from (4.48) this approach is still relatively efficient. Back-propagation requires one forward and one backward propagation through the network, each taking $\mathcal{O}(W)$ steps, in order to evaluate all of the $\partial E/\partial a_i$. By comparison, (4.49) requires $2M$ forward propagations, where M is the number of hidden and output nodes. The overall scaling is therefore proportional to MW, which is typically much less than the $\mathcal{O}(W^2)$ scaling of (4.47), but more than the $\mathcal{O}(W)$ scaling of back-propagation. This technique is called *node perturbation* (Jabri and Flower, 1991), and is closely related to the *madeline III* learning rule (Widrow and Lehr, 1990).

In a software implementation, derivatives should be evaluated using back-propagation, since this gives the greatest accuracy and numerical efficiency. However, the results should be compared with numerical differentiation using (4.47) for a few test cases in order to check the correctness of the implementation.

4.9   The Jacobian matrix

We have seen how the derivatives of an error function with respect to the weights can be obtained by the propagation of errors backwards through the network. The technique of back-propagation can also be applied to the calculation of other derivatives. Here we consider the evaluation of the *Jacobian* matrix, whose elements are given by the derivatives of the network outputs with respect to the inputs

$$J_{ki} \equiv \frac{\partial y_k}{\partial x_i} \tag{4.50}$$

where each such derivative is evaluated with all other inputs held fixed. Note that the term Jacobian matrix is also sometimes used to describe the derivatives of the error function with respect to the network weights, as calculated earlier using back-propagation. The Jacobian matrix provides a measure of the local sensitivity of the outputs to changes in each of the input variables, and is useful in several contexts in the application of neural networks. For instance, if there are known errors associated with the input variables, then the Jacobian matrix allows these to be propagated through the trained network in order to estimate their contribution to the errors at the outputs. Thus, we have

$$\Delta y_k \simeq \sum_i \frac{\partial y_k}{\partial x_i} \Delta x_i. \tag{4.51}$$

In general, the network mapping represented by a trained neural network will be non-linear, and so the elements of the Jacobian matrix will not be constants but will depend on the particular input vector used. Thus (4.51) is valid only for small perturbations of the inputs, and the Jacobian itself must be re-evaluated for each new input vector.

The Jacobian matrix can be evaluated using a back-propagation procedure which is very similar to the one derived earlier for evaluating the derivatives of an error function with respect to the weights. We start by writing the element J_{ki} in the form

$$J_{ki} = \frac{\partial y_k}{\partial x_i} = \sum_j \frac{\partial y_k}{\partial a_j} \frac{\partial a_j}{\partial x_i}$$

$$= \sum_j w_{ji} \frac{\partial y_k}{\partial a_j} \tag{4.52}$$

where we have made use of (4.26). The sum in (4.52) runs over all units j to which the input unit i sends connections (for example, over all units in the first hidden layer in the layered topology considered earlier). We now write down a recursive back-propagation formula to determine the derivatives $\partial y_k / \partial a_j$

$$\frac{\partial y_k}{\partial a_j} = \sum_l \frac{\partial y_k}{\partial a_l} \frac{\partial a_l}{\partial a_j}$$

$$= g'(a_j) \sum_l w_{lj} \frac{\partial y_k}{\partial a_l} \tag{4.53}$$

where the sum runs over all units l to which unit j sends connections. Again, we have made use of (4.26) and (4.27). This back-propagation starts at the output units for which, using (4.27), we have

$$\frac{\partial y_k}{\partial a_{k'}} = g'(a_k)\delta_{kk'} \tag{4.54}$$

where $\delta_{kk'}$ is the Kronecker delta symbol, and equals 1 if $k = k'$ and 0 otherwise. We can therefore summarize the procedure for evaluating the Jacobian matrix as follows. Apply the input vector corresponding to the point in input space at which the Jacobian matrix is to be found, and forward propagate in the usual way to obtain the activations of all of the hidden and output units in the network. Next, for each row k of the Jacobian matrix, corresponding to the output unit k, back-propagate using the recursive relation (4.53), starting with (4.54), for all of the hidden units in the network. Finally, use (4.52) to do the back-propagation to the inputs. The second and third steps are then repeated for each value of k, corresponding to each row of the Jacobian matrix.

The Jacobian can also be evaluated using an alternative *forward* propagation formalism which can be derived in an analogous way to the back-propagation approach given here (Exercise 4.6). Again, the implementation of such algorithms can be checked by using numerical differentiation in the form

$$\frac{\partial y_k}{\partial x_i} = \frac{y_k(x_i + \epsilon) - y_k(x_i - \epsilon)}{2\epsilon} + \mathcal{O}(\epsilon^2). \tag{4.55}$$

4.10 The Hessian matrix

We have shown how the technique of back-propagation can be used to obtain the first derivatives of an error function with respect to the weights in the network. Back-propagation can also be used to evaluate the second derivatives of the error, given by

$$\frac{\partial^2 E}{\partial w_{ji} \partial w_{lk}}. \tag{4.56}$$

These derivatives form the elements of the *Hessian* matrix, which plays an important role in many aspects of neural computing, including the following:

1. Several non-linear optimization algorithms used for training neural networks are based on considerations of the second-order properties of the error surface, which are controlled by the Hessian matrix (Chapter 7).

2. The Hessian forms the basis of a fast procedure for re-training a feedforward network following a small change in the training data (Bishop, 1991a).

3. The inverse of the Hessian has been used to identify the least significant weights in a network as part of network 'pruning' algorithms (Section 9.5.3).

4. The inverse of the Hessian can also be used to assign error bars to the predictions made by a trained network (Section 10.2).

5. Suitable values for regularization parameters can be determined from the eigenvalues of the Hessian (Section 10.4).

6. The determinant of the Hessian can be used to compare the relative probabilities of different network models (Section 10.6).

For many of these applications, various approximation schemes have been used to evaluate the Hessian matrix. However, the Hessian can also be calculated exactly using an extension of the back-propagation technique for evaluating the first derivatives of the error function.

An important consideration for many applications of the Hessian is the efficiency with which it can be evaluated. If there are W parameters (weights and biases) in the network then the Hessian matrix has dimensions $W \times W$ and so the computational effort needed to evaluate the Hessian must scale at least like $\mathcal{O}(W^2)$ for each pattern in the data set. As we shall see, there are efficient methods for evaluating the Hessian whose scaling is indeed $\mathcal{O}(W^2)$.

4.10.1 *Diagonal approximation*

Some of the applications for the Hessian matrix discussed above require the inverse of the Hessian, rather than the Hessian itself. For this reason there has been some interest in using a diagonal approximation to the Hessian, since its inverse is trivial to evaluate. We again shall assume, as is generally the case, that the error function consists of a sum of terms, one for each pattern in the data set, so that $E = \sum_n E^n$. The Hessian can then be obtained by considering one pattern at a time, and then summing the results over all patterns. From (4.26) the diagonal elements of the Hessian, for pattern n, can be written

$$\frac{\partial^2 E^n}{\partial w_{ji}^2} = \frac{\partial^2 E^n}{\partial a_j^2} z_i^2. \tag{4.57}$$

Using (4.26) and (4.27), the second derivatives on the right-hand side of (4.57) can be found recursively using the chain rule of differential calculus, to give a back-propagation equation of the form

$$\frac{\partial^2 E^n}{\partial a_j^2} = g'(a_j)^2 \sum_k \sum_{k'} w_{kj} w_{k'j} \frac{\partial^2 E^n}{\partial a_k \partial a_{k'}} + g''(a_j) \sum_k w_{kj} \frac{\partial E^n}{\partial a_k}. \tag{4.58}$$

If we now neglect off-diagonal elements in the second derivative terms we obtain (Becker and Le Cun, 1989; Le Cun *et al.*, 1990)

$$\frac{\partial^2 E^n}{\partial a_j^2} = g'(a_j)^2 \sum_k w_{kj}^2 \frac{\partial^2 E^n}{\partial a_k^2} + g''(a_j) \sum_k w_{kj} \frac{\partial E^n}{\partial a_k}. \tag{4.59}$$

Due to the neglect of off-diagonal terms on the right-hand side of (4.59), this approach only gives an approximation to the diagonal terms of the Hessian.

However, the number of computational steps is reduced from $\mathcal{O}(W^2)$ to $\mathcal{O}(W)$.

Ricotti *et al.* (1988) also used the diagonal approximation to the Hessian, but they retained all terms in the evaluation of $\partial^2 E^n / \partial a_j^2$ and so obtained exact expressions for the diagonal terms. Note that this no longer has $\mathcal{O}(W)$ scaling. The major problem with diagonal approximations, however, is that in practice the Hessian is typically found to be strongly non-diagonal, and so these approximations, which are driven mainly be computational convenience, must be treated with great care.

4.10.2 *Outer product approximation*

When neural networks are applied to regression problems, it is common to use a sum-of-squares error function of the form

$$E = \frac{1}{2} \sum_n (y^n - t^n)^2 \tag{4.60}$$

where we have considered the case of a single output in order to keep the notation simple (the extension to several outputs is straightforward). We can then write the elements of the Hessian in the form

$$\frac{\partial^2 E}{\partial w_{ji} \partial w_{lk}} = \sum_n \frac{\partial y^n}{\partial w_{ji}} \frac{\partial y^n}{\partial w_{lk}} + \sum_n (y^n - t^n) \frac{\partial^2 y^n}{\partial w_{ji} \partial w_{lk}}. \tag{4.61}$$

If the network has been trained on the data set and its outputs y^n happen to be very close to the target values t^n then the second term in (4.61) will be small and can be neglected. If the data are noisy, however, such a network mapping is severely over-fitted to the data, and is not the kind of mapping we seek in order to achieve good generalization (see Chapters 1 and 9). Instead we want to find a mapping which averages over the noise in the data. It turns out that for such a solution we may still be able to neglect the second term in (4.61). This follows from the fact that the quantity $(y^n - t^n)$ is a random variable with zero mean, which is uncorrelated with the value of the second derivative term on the right-hand side of (4.61). This whole term will therefore tend to average to zero in the summation over n (Hassibi and Stork, 1993). A more formal derivation of this result is given in Section 6.1.4.

By neglecting the second term in (4.61) we arrive at the Levenberg–Marquardt approximation (Levenberg, 1944; Marquardt, 1963) or *outer product* approximation (since the Hessian matrix is built up from a sum of outer products of vectors), given by

$$\frac{\partial^2 E}{\partial w_{ji} \partial w_{lk}} = \sum_n \frac{\partial y^n}{\partial w_{ji}} \frac{\partial y^n}{\partial w_{lk}}. \tag{4.62}$$

Its evaluation is straightforward as it only involves first derivatives of the error function, which can be evaluated efficiently in $\mathcal{O}(W)$ steps using standard back-propagation. The elements of the matrix can then be found in $\mathcal{O}(W^2)$ steps by simple multiplication. It is important to emphasize that this approximation is only likely to be valid for a network which has been trained correctly on the same data set used to evaluate the Hessian, or on one with the same statistical properties. For a general network mapping, the second derivative terms on the right-hand side of (4.61) will typically not be negligible.

4.10.3 *Inverse Hessian*

Hassibi and Stork (1993) have used the outer product approximation to develop a computationally efficient procedure for approximating the inverse of the Hessian. We first write the outer product approximation in matrix notation as

$$\mathbf{H}_N = \sum_{n=1}^{N} \mathbf{g}^n (\mathbf{g}^n)^{\mathrm{T}} \tag{4.63}$$

where N is the number of patterns in the data set, and the vector $\mathbf{g} \equiv \nabla_{\mathbf{w}} E$ is the gradient of the error function. This leads to a sequential procedure for building up the Hessian, obtained by separating off the contribution from data point $N + 1$ to give

$$\mathbf{H}_{N+1} = \mathbf{H}_N + \mathbf{g}^{N+1} (\mathbf{g}^{N+1})^{\mathrm{T}}. \tag{4.64}$$

In order to evaluate the inverse of the Hessian we now consider the matrix identity (Kailath, 1980)

$$(\mathbf{A} + \mathbf{BC})^{-1} = \mathbf{A}^{-1} - \mathbf{A}^{-1}\mathbf{B}(\mathbf{I} + \mathbf{CA}^{-1}\mathbf{B})^{-1}\mathbf{CA}^{-1} \tag{4.65}$$

where $\mathbf{I}$ is the unit matrix. If we now identify $\mathbf{H}_N$ with $\mathbf{A}$, $\mathbf{g}^{N+1}$ with $\mathbf{B}$, and $(\mathbf{g}^{N+1})^{\mathrm{T}}$ with $\mathbf{C}$, then we can apply (4.65) to (4.64) to obtain

$$\mathbf{H}_{N+1}^{-1} = \mathbf{H}_N^{-1} - \frac{\mathbf{H}_N^{-1}\mathbf{g}^{N+1}(\mathbf{g}^{N+1})^{\mathrm{T}}\mathbf{H}_N^{-1}}{1 + (\mathbf{g}^{N+1})^{\mathrm{T}}\mathbf{H}_N^{-1}\mathbf{g}^{N+1}}. \tag{4.66}$$

This represents a procedure for evaluating the inverse of the Hessian using a single pass through the data set. The initial matrix $\mathbf{H}_0$ is chosen to be $\alpha\mathbf{I}$, where α is a small quantity, so that the algorithm actually finds the inverse of $\mathbf{H} + \alpha\mathbf{I}$. The results are not particularly sensitive to the precise value of α. Extension of this algorithm to networks having more than one output is straightforward (Exercise 4.9).

   We note here that the Hessian matrix can sometimes be calculated indirectly as part of the network training algorithm. In particular, quasi-Newton non-linear optimization algorithms gradually build up an approximation to the inverse of the Hessian during training. Such algorithms are discussed in detail in

Section 7.10.

4.10.4 Finite differences

As with first derivatives of the error function, we can find the second derivatives by using finite differences, with accuracy limited by the numerical precision of our computer. If we perturb each possible pair of weights in turn, we obtain

$$
\frac{\partial^2 E}{\partial w_{ji} \partial w_{lk}} = \frac{1}{4\epsilon^2} \{ E(w_{ji} + \epsilon, w_{lk} + \epsilon) - E(w_{ji} + \epsilon, w_{lk} - \epsilon)
$$

$$
- E(w_{ji} - \epsilon, w_{lk} + \epsilon) + E(w_{ji} - \epsilon, w_{lk} - \epsilon) \} + \mathcal{O}(\epsilon^2). \quad (4.67)
$$

Again, by using a symmetrical central differences formulation, we ensure that the residual errors are $\mathcal{O}(\epsilon^2)$ rather than $\mathcal{O}(\epsilon)$. Since there are W^2 elements in the Hessian matrix, and since the evaluation of each element requires four forward propagations each needing $\mathcal{O}(W)$ operations (per pattern), we see that this approach will require $\mathcal{O}(W^3)$ operations to evaluate the complete Hessian. It therefore has very poor scaling properties, although in practice it is very useful as a check on the software implementation of back-propagation methods.

A more efficient version of numerical differentiation can be found by applying central differences to the first derivatives of the error function, which are themselves calculated using back-propagation. This gives

$$
\frac{\partial^2 E}{\partial w_{ji} \partial w_{lk}} = \frac{1}{2\epsilon} \left\{ \frac{\partial E}{\partial w_{ji}} (w_{lk} + \epsilon) - \frac{\partial E}{\partial w_{ji}} (w_{lk} - \epsilon) \right\} + \mathcal{O}(\epsilon^2). \quad (4.68)
$$

Since there are now only W weights to be perturbed, and since the gradients can be evaluated in $\mathcal{O}(W)$ steps, we see that this method gives the Hessian in $\mathcal{O}(W^2)$ operations.

4.10.5 Exact evaluation of the Hessian

So far we have considered various approximation schemes for evaluating the Hessian matrix. We now describe an algorithm for evaluating the Hessian exactly, which is valid for a network of arbitrary feed-forward topology, of the kind illustrated schematically in Figure 4.3 (Bishop, 1991a, 1992). The algorithm is based on an extension of the technique of back-propagation used to evaluate first derivatives, and shares many of its desirable features including computational efficiency. It can be applied to any differentiable error function which can be expressed as a function of the network outputs, and to networks having arbitrary differentiable activation functions. The number of computational steps needed to evaluate the Hessian scales like $\mathcal{O}(W^2)$. Similar algorithms have also been considered by Buntine and Weigend (1993). As before, we shall consider one pattern at a time. The complete Hessian is then obtained by summing over all patterns.

Consider the general expression (4.33) for the derivative of the error function with respect to an arbitrary weight w_{lk}, which we reproduce here for convenience

$$\frac{\partial E^n}{\partial w_{lk}} = \delta_l z_k. \tag{4.69}$$

Differentiating this with respect to some other weight w_{ji} we obtain

$$\frac{\partial^2 E^n}{\partial w_{ji} \partial w_{lk}} = \frac{\partial a_j}{\partial w_{ji}} \frac{\partial}{\partial a_j} \left(\frac{\partial E^n}{\partial w_{lk}} \right) = z_i \frac{\partial}{\partial a_j} \left(\frac{\partial E^n}{\partial w_{lk}} \right) \tag{4.70}$$

where we have used (4.26). Here we have assumed that the weight w_{ji} does not occur on any forward propagation path connecting unit l to the outputs of the network. We shall return to this point shortly.

Making use of (4.69), together with the relation $z_k = g(a_k)$, we can write (4.70) in the form

$$\frac{\partial^2 E^n}{\partial w_{ji} \partial w_{lk}} = z_i \delta_l g'(a_k) h_{kj} + z_i z_k b_{lj} \tag{4.71}$$

where we have defined the quantities

$$h_{kj} \equiv \frac{\partial a_k}{\partial a_j} \tag{4.72}$$

$$b_{lj} \equiv \frac{\partial \delta_l}{\partial a_j}. \tag{4.73}$$

The quantities $\{h_{kj}\}$ can be evaluated by forward propagation as follows. Using the chain rule for partial derivatives we have

$$h_{kj} = \sum_r \frac{\partial a_k}{\partial a_r} \frac{\partial a_r}{\partial a_j} \tag{4.74}$$

where the sum runs over all units r which send connections to unit k. In fact, contributions only arise from units which lie on paths connecting unit j to unit k. From (4.26) and (4.27) we then obtain the forward propagation equation

$$h_{kj} = \sum_r g'(a_r) w_{kr} h_{rj}. \tag{4.75}$$

The initial conditions for evaluating the $\{h_{kj}\}$ follow from the definition (4.72), and can be stated as follows. For each unit j in the network, (except for input units, for which the corresponding $\{h_{kj}\}$ are not required), set $h_{jj} = 1$ and set

$h_{kj} = 0$ for all units $k \neq j$ which do not lie on any forward propagation path starting from unit j. The remaining elements of h_{kj} can then be found by forward propagation using (4.75).

Similarly, we can derive a back-propagation equation which allows the $\{b_{lj}\}$ to be evaluated. We have already seen that the quantities δ_l can be found by back-propagation

$$\delta_l = g'(a_l) \sum_s w_{sl}\delta_s. \tag{4.76}$$

Substituting this into the definition of b_{lj} in (4.73) we obtain

$$b_{lj} = \frac{\partial}{\partial a_j} \left\{ g'(a_l) \sum_s w_{sl}\delta_s \right\} \tag{4.77}$$

which gives

$$b_{lj} = g''(a_l)h_{lj} \sum_s w_{sl}\delta_s + g'(a_l) \sum_s w_{sl}b_{sj} \tag{4.78}$$

where the sums run over all units s to which unit l sends connections. Note that, in a software implementation, the first summation in (4.78) will already have been computed in evaluating the $\{\delta_l\}$ in (4.76).

There is one subtlety which needs to be considered. The derivative $\partial/\partial a_j$ which appears in (4.77) arose from the derivative $\partial/\partial w_{ji}$ in (4.70). This transformation, from w_{ji} to a_j, is valid provided w_{ji} does not appear explicitly within the brackets on the right-hand side of (4.77). In other words, the weight w_{ji} should not lie on any of the forward-propagation paths from unit l to the outputs of the network, since these are also the paths used to evaluate δ_l by back-propagation. In practice the problem is easily avoided as follows. If w_{ji} does occur in the sequence of back-propagations needed to evaluate δ_l, then we simply consider instead the diagonally opposite element of the Hessian matrix for which this problem will not arise (since the network has a feed-forward topology). We then make use of the fact that the Hessian is a symmetric matrix.

The initial conditions for the back-propagation in (4.78) follow from (4.72) and (4.73), together with the initial conditions (4.34) for the δ's, to give

$$b_{kj} = \sum_{k'} H_{kk'} h_{k'j} \tag{4.79}$$

where we have defined

$$H_{kk'} \equiv \frac{\partial^2 E^n}{\partial a_k \partial a'_k}. \tag{4.80}$$

This algorithm represents a straightforward extension of the usual forward and backward propagation procedures used to find the first derivatives of the error function. We can summarize the algorithm in five steps:

1. Evaluate the activations of all of the hidden and output units, for a given input pattern, by using the usual forward propagation equations. Similarly, compute the initial conditions for the h_{kj} and forward propagate through the network using (4.75) to find the remaining non-zero elements of h_{kj}.
2. Evaluate δ_k for the output units in the usual way. Similarly, evaluate the H_k for all the output units using (4.80).
3. Use the standard back-propagation equations to find δ_j for all hidden units in the network. Similarly, back-propagate to find the $\{b_{lj}\}$ by using (4.78) with initial conditions given by (4.79).
4. Evaluate the elements of the Hessian for this input pattern using (4.71).
5. Repeat the above steps for each pattern in the training set, and then sum to obtain the full Hessian.

In a practical implementation, we substitute appropriate expressions for the error function and the activation functions. For the sum-of-squares error function and linear output units, for example, we have

$$\delta_k = y_k - t_k, \qquad\qquad H_{kk'} = \delta_{kk'} \qquad\qquad (4.81)$$

where $\delta_{kk'}$ is the Kronecker delta symbol.

4.10.6 *Exact Hessian for two-layer network*

As an illustration of the above algorithm, we consider the specific case of a layered network having two layers of weights. We can then use the results obtained above to write down explicit expressions for the elements of the Hessian matrix. We shall use indices i and i' to denote inputs, indices j and j' to denoted units in the hidden layer, and indices k and k' to denote outputs. Using the previous results, the Hessian matrix for this network can then be considered in three separate blocks as follows.

1. Both weights in the second layer:

$$\frac{\partial^2 E^n}{\partial w_{kj} \partial w_{k'j'}} = z_j z_{j'} \delta_{kk'} H_{kk}. \qquad\qquad (4.82)$$

2. Both weights in the first layer:

$$\frac{\partial^2 E^n}{\partial w_{ji} \partial w_{j'i'}} = x_i x_{i'} g''(a_{j'}) \delta_{jj'} \sum_k w_{kj'} \delta_k$$

$$+ x_i x_{i'} g'(a_{j'}) g'(a_j) \sum_k w_{kj'} w_{kj} H_{kk}. \qquad\qquad (4.83)$$

3. One weight in each layer:

$$\frac{\partial^2 E^n}{\partial w_{ji} \partial w_{kj'}} = x_i g'(a_j) \left\{ \delta_k \delta_{jj'} + z_{j'} w_{kj} H_{kk} \right\}. \tag{4.84}$$

If one or both of the weights is a bias term, then the corresponding expressions are obtained simply by setting the appropriate activation(s) to 1.

4.10.7 Fast multiplication by the Hessian

In some applications of the Hessian, the quantity of interest is not the Hessian matrix $\mathbf{H}$ itself, but the product of $\mathbf{H}$ with some vector $\mathbf{v}$. We have seen that the evaluation of the Hessian takes $\mathcal{O}(W^2)$ operations, and it also requires storage which is $\mathcal{O}(W^2)$. The vector $\mathbf{v}^{\mathrm{T}}\mathbf{H}$ which we wish to calculate itself only has W elements, so instead of computing the Hessian as an intermediate step, we can instead try to find an efficient approach to evaluating $\mathbf{v}^{\mathrm{T}}\mathbf{H}$ directly, which requires only $\mathcal{O}(W)$ operations.

We first note that

$$\mathbf{v}^{\mathrm{T}}\mathbf{H} \equiv \mathbf{v}^{\mathrm{T}}\nabla(\nabla E) \tag{4.85}$$

where ∇ denotes the gradient operator in weight space. We can then estimate the right-hand side of (4.85) using finite differences to give

$$\mathbf{v}^{\mathrm{T}}\nabla(\nabla E) = \frac{\nabla E(\mathbf{w} + \epsilon\mathbf{v}) - \nabla E(\mathbf{w})}{\epsilon} + \mathcal{O}(\epsilon). \tag{4.86}$$

Thus, the quantity $\mathbf{v}^{\mathrm{T}}\mathbf{H}$ can be found by forward propagating first with the original weights, and then with the weights perturbed by the small vector $\epsilon\mathbf{v}$. This procedure therefore takes $\mathcal{O}(W)$ operations. It was used by Le Cun et al. (1993) as part of a technique for on-line estimation of the learning rate parameter in gradient descent.

Note that the residual error in (4.86) can again be reduced from $\mathcal{O}(\epsilon)$ to $\mathcal{O}(\epsilon^2)$ by using central differences of the form

$$\mathbf{v}^{\mathrm{T}}\nabla(\nabla E) = \frac{\nabla E(\mathbf{w} + \epsilon\mathbf{v}) - \nabla E(\mathbf{w} - \epsilon\mathbf{v})}{2\epsilon} + \mathcal{O}(\epsilon^2) \tag{4.87}$$

which again scales as $\mathcal{O}(W)$.

The problem with a finite-difference approach is one of numerical inaccuracies. This can be resolved by adopting an analytic approach (Møller, 1993a; Pearlmutter, 1994). Suppose we write down standard forward-propagation and back-propagation equations for the evaluation of ∇E. We can then apply (4.85) to these equations to give a set of forward-propagation and back-propagation equations for the evaluation of $\mathbf{v}^{\mathrm{T}}\mathbf{H}$. This corresponds to acting on the original forward-propagation and back-propagation equations with a differential operator

$\mathbf{v}^{\mathrm{T}}\nabla$. Pearlmutter (1994) used the notation $\mathcal{R}\{\cdot\}$ to denote the operator $\mathbf{v}^{\mathrm{T}}\nabla$ and we shall follow this notation. The analysis is straightforward, and makes use of the usual rules of differential calculus, together with the result

$$\mathcal{R}\{\mathbf{w}\} = \mathbf{v}. \tag{4.88}$$

The technique is best illustrated with a simple example, and again we choose a two-layer network with linear output units and a sum-of-squares error function. As before, we consider the contribution to the error function from one pattern in the data set. The required vector is then obtained as usual by summing over the contributions from each of the patterns separately. For the two-layer network, the forward-propagation equations are given by

$$a_j = \sum_i w_{ji} x_i \tag{4.89}$$

$$z_j = g(a_j) \tag{4.90}$$

$$y_k = \sum_j w_{kj} z_j. \tag{4.91}$$

We now act on these equations using the $\mathcal{R}\{\cdot\}$ operator to obtain a set of forward propagation equations in the form

$$\mathcal{R}\{a_j\} = \sum_i v_{ji} x_i \tag{4.92}$$

$$\mathcal{R}\{z_j\} = g'(a_j)\mathcal{R}\{a_j\} \tag{4.93}$$

$$\mathcal{R}\{y_k\} = \sum_j w_{kj}\mathcal{R}\{z_j\} + \sum_j v_{kj} z_j \tag{4.94}$$

where v_{ji} is the element of the vector $\mathbf{v}$ which corresponds to the weight w_{ji}. Quantities of the form $\mathcal{R}\{z_j\}$, $\mathcal{R}\{a_j\}$ and $\mathcal{R}\{y_k\}$ are to be regarded as new variables whose values are found using the above equations.

Since we are considering a sum-of-squares error function, we have the following standard back-propagation expressions:

$$\delta_k = y_k - t_k \tag{4.95}$$

$$\delta_j = g'(a_j)\sum_k w_{kj}\delta_k. \tag{4.96}$$

Again we act on these equations with the $\mathcal{R}\{\cdot\}$ operator to obtain a set of back-propagation equations in the form

$$\mathcal{R}\{\delta_k\} = \mathcal{R}\{y_k\} \tag{4.97}$$

$$\mathcal{R}\{\delta_j\} = g''(a_j)\mathcal{R}\{a_j\} \sum_k w_{kj}\delta_k$$

$$+ g'(a_j) \sum_k v_{kj}\delta_k$$

$$+ g'(a_j) \sum_k w_{kj}\mathcal{R}\{\delta_k\}. \tag{4.98}$$

Finally, we have the usual equations for the first derivatives of the error

$$\frac{\partial E}{\partial w_{kj}} = \delta_k z_j \tag{4.99}$$

$$\frac{\partial E}{\partial w_{ji}} = \delta_j x_i \tag{4.100}$$

and acting on these with the $\mathcal{R}\{\cdot\}$ operator we obtain expressions for the elements of the vector $\mathbf{v}^T\mathbf{H}$:

$$\mathcal{R}\left\{\frac{\partial E}{\partial w_{kj}}\right\} = \mathcal{R}\{\delta_k\}z_j + \delta_k\mathcal{R}\{z_j\} \tag{4.101}$$

$$\mathcal{R}\left\{\frac{\partial E}{\partial w_{ji}}\right\} = x_i\mathcal{R}\{\delta_j\}. \tag{4.102}$$

The implementation of this algorithm involves the introduction of additional variables $\mathcal{R}\{a_j\}$, $\mathcal{R}\{z_j\}$ and $\mathcal{R}\{\delta_j\}$ for the hidden units, and $\mathcal{R}\{\delta_k\}$ and $\mathcal{R}\{y_k\}$ for the output units. For each input pattern, the values of these quantities can be found using the above results, and the elements of $\mathbf{v}^T\mathbf{H}$ are then given by (4.101) and (4.102). An elegant aspect of this technique is that the structure of the equations for evaluating $\mathbf{v}^T\mathbf{H}$ mirror closely those for standard forward and backward propagation, and so software implementation is straightforward.

If desired, the technique can be used to evaluate the full Hessian matrix by choosing the vector $\mathbf{v}$ to be given successively by a series of unit vectors of the form $(0, 0, \ldots, 1, \ldots, 0)$ each of which picks out one column of the Hessian. This leads to a formalism which is analytically equivalent to the back-propagation procedure of Bishop (1992), as described in Section 4.10.5, though with some loss of efficiency in a software implementation due to redundant calculations.

Exercises

4.1 ($\star$) In Section 4.4 we showed that, for networks with 'tanh' hidden unit activation functions, the network mapping is invariant if all of the weights and the bias feeding into and out of a unit have their signs changed. Demonstrate the corresponding symmetry for hidden units with logistic sigmoidal activation functions.

4.2 ($\star$) Consider a second-order network unit of the form (4.19). Use the symmetry properties of this term, together with the results of Exercises 1.7 and 1.8, to find an expression for the number of independent weight parameters and show that this is the same result as that obtained by applying symmetry considerations to the equivalent form (4.18).

4.3 ($\star$) Show, for a feed-forward network with 'tanh' hidden unit activation functions, and a sum-of-squares error function, that the origin in weight space is a stationary point of the error function.

4.4 ($\star$) Consider a layered network with d inputs, M hidden units and c output units. Write down an expression for the total number of weights and biases in the network. Consider the derivatives of the error function with respect to the weights for one input pattern only. Using the fact that these derivatives are given by equations of the form $\partial E^n / \partial w_{kj} = \delta_k z_j$, write down an expression for the number of independent derivatives.

4.5 ($\star$) Consider a layered network having second-order units of the form (4.19) in the first layer and conventional units in the remaining layers. Derive a back-propagation formalism for evaluating the derivatives of the error function with respect to any weight or bias in the network. Extend the result to general Mth-order units in the first layer.

4.6 ($\star$) In Section 4.9, a formalism was developed for evaluating the Jacobian matrix by a process of back-propagation. Derive an alternative formalism for obtaining the Jacobian matrix using *forward* propagation equations.

4.7 ($\star$) Consider a two-layer network having 20 inputs, 10 hidden units, and 5 outputs, together with a training set of 2000 patterns. Calculate roughly how long it would take to perform one evaluation of the Hessian matrix using (a) central differences based on direct error function evaluations; (b) central differences based on gradient evaluations using back-propagation; (c) the analytic expressions given in (4.82), (4.83) and (4.84). Assume that the workstation can perform 5×10^7 floating point operations per second, and that the time taken to evaluate an activation function or its derivatives can be neglected.

4.8 ($\star$) Verify the identity (4.65) by pre- and post-multiplying both sides by $\mathbf{A} + \mathbf{BC}$.

4.9 ($\star$) Extend the expression (4.63) for the outer product approximation of the Hessian to the case of $c > 1$ output units. Hence derive a recursive expression analogous to (4.64) for incrementing the number N of patterns, and a similar expression for incrementing the number c of outputs. Use these results, together with the identity (4.65), to find sequential update expressions analogous (4.66) for finding the inverse of the Hessian by incrementally including both extra patterns and extra outputs.

4.10 ($\star\star$) Verify that the results (4.82), (4.83) and (4.84) for the Hessian matrix of a two-layer network follow from the general expressions for calculating the Hessian matrix for a network of arbitrary topology given in Section 4.10.5.

4.11 ($\star\star$) Derive the results (4.82), (4.83) and (4.84) for the exact evaluation of the Hessian matrix for a two-layer network by direct differentiation of the forward-propagation and back-propagation equations.

4.12 ($\star\star\star$) Write a software implementation of the forward and backward propagation equations for a two-layer network with 'tanh' hidden unit activation function and linear output units. Generate a data set of random input and target vectors, and set the network weights to random values. For the case of a sum-of-squares error function, evaluate the derivatives of the error with respect to the weights and biases in the network by using the central differences expression (4.47). Compare the results with those obtained using the back-propagation algorithm. Experiment with different values of ϵ, and show numerically that, for values of ϵ in an appropriate range, the two approaches give almost identical results. Plot graphs of the logarithm of the evaluation times for these two algorithms versus the logarithm of the number W of weights in the network, for networks having a range of different sizes (including networks with relatively large values of W). Hence verify the scalings with W discussed in Section 4.8.

4.13 ($\star\star\star$) Extend the software implementation of the previous exercise to include the forward and backward propagation equations for the $\mathcal{R}\{\cdot\}$ variables, described in Section 4.10.7. Use this implementation to evaluate the complete Hessian matrix by setting the vector $\mathbf{v}$ in the $\mathcal{R}\{\cdot\}$ operator to successive unit vectors of the form $(0, 0, \ldots, 1, \ldots, 0)$ each of which picks out one column of the Hessian. Also implement the central differences approach for evaluation of the Hessian given by (4.67). Show that the results from the $\mathcal{R}\{\cdot\}$ operator and central difference methods agree closely, provided ϵ is chosen appropriately. Again, plot graphs of the logarithm of the evaluation time versus the logarithm of the number of weights in the network, for networks having a range of different sizes, for both of these approaches to evaluation of the Hessian, and verify the scalings with W of the two algorithms, as discussed in the text.

4.14 ($\star\star\star$) Extend further the software implementation of Exercise 4.12 by implementing equations (4.82), (4.83) and (4.84) for computing the elements of the Hessian matrix. Show that the results agree with those from the $\mathcal{R}\{\cdot\}$-operator approach, and extend the graph of the previous exercise to include the logarithm of the computation times for this algorithm.

4.15 ($\star\star$) Consider a feed-forward network which has been trained to a minimum of some error function E, corresponding to a set of weights $\{w_j\}$, where for convenience we have labelled all of the weights and biases in the network with a single index j. Suppose that all of the input values x_i^n and target values t_k^n in the training set are perturbed by small amounts Δx_i^n and Δt_k^n respectively. This causes the minimum of the error function to change to a new set of weight values given by $\{w_j + \Delta w_j\}$. Write down the Taylor expansion of the new error function $E(\{w_j + \Delta w_j\}, \{x_i^n + \Delta x_i^n\}, \{t_k^n + \Delta t_k^n\})$ to second order in the Δ's. By minimizing this expression with respect to the $\{\Delta w_j\}$, show that the new set of weights which minimizes the error function can be calculated from the original set of weights by adding corrections Δw_j which are given by solutions of the following equation

$$\sum_j H_{lj} \Delta w_j = -\Delta T_l, \tag{4.103}$$

where H_{lj} are the elements of the Hessian matrix, and we have defined

$$\Delta T_l \equiv \sum_n \sum_i \frac{\partial^2 E^n}{\partial x_i^n \partial w_l} \Delta x_i^n + \sum_n \sum_k \frac{\partial^2 E^n}{\partial w_l \partial t_k^n} \Delta t_k^n. \tag{4.104}$$

RADIAL BASIS FUNCTIONS

The network models discussed in Chapters 3 and 4 are based on units which compute a non-linear function of the scalar product of the input vector and a weight vector. Here we consider the other major class of neural network model, in which the activation of a hidden unit is determined by the *distance* between the input vector and a prototype vector.

An interesting and important property of these radial basis function networks is that they form a unifying link between a number of disparate concepts as we shall demonstrate in this chapter. In particular, we shall motivate the use of radial basis functions from the point of view of function approximation, regularization, noisy interpolation, density estimation, optimal classification theory, and potential functions.

One consequence of this unifying viewpoint is that it motivates procedures for training radial basis function networks which can be substantially faster than the methods used to train multi-layer perceptron networks. This follows from the interpretation which can be given to the internal representations formed by the hidden units, and leads to a two-stage training procedure. In the first stage, the parameters governing the basis functions (corresponding to hidden units) are determined using relatively fast, unsupervised methods (i.e. methods which use only the input data and not the target data). The second stage of training then involves the determination of the final-layer weights, which requires the solution of a linear problem, and which is therefore also fast.

5.1 Exact interpolation

Radial basis function methods have their origins in techniques for performing exact interpolation of a set of data points in a multi-dimensional space (Powell, 1987). The exact interpolation problem requires every input vector to be mapped exactly onto the corresponding target vector, and forms a convenient starting point for our discussion of radial basis function networks.

Consider a mapping from a d-dimensional input space $\mathbf{x}$ to a one-dimensional target space t. The data set consists of N input vectors $\mathbf{x}^n$, together with corresponding targets t^n. The goal is to find a function $h(\mathbf{x})$ such that

$$h(\mathbf{x}^n) = t^n, \qquad n = 1, \ldots, N. \tag{5.1}$$

The radial basis function approach (Powell, 1987) introduces a set of N *basis functions*, one for each data point, which take the form $\phi(\|\mathbf{x} - \mathbf{x}^n\|)$ where $\phi(\cdot)$ is some non-linear function whose form will be discussed shortly. Thus the nth such function depends on the distance $\|\mathbf{x} - \mathbf{x}^n\|$, usually taken to be Euclidean, between $\mathbf{x}$ and $\mathbf{x}^n$. The output of the mapping is then taken to be a linear combination of the basis functions

$$h(\mathbf{x}) = \sum_n w_n \phi(\|\mathbf{x} - \mathbf{x}^n\|). \tag{5.2}$$

We recognize this as having the same form as the generalized linear discriminant function considered in Section 3.3. The interpolation conditions (5.1) can then be written in matrix form as

$$\boldsymbol{\Phi}\mathbf{w} = \mathbf{t} \tag{5.3}$$

where $\mathbf{t} \equiv (t^n)$, $\mathbf{w} \equiv (w_n)$, and the square matrix $\boldsymbol{\Phi}$ has elements $\Phi_{nn'} = \phi(\|\mathbf{x}^n - \mathbf{x}^{n'}\|)$. Provided the inverse matrix $\boldsymbol{\Phi}^{-1}$ exists we can solve (5.3) to give

$$\mathbf{w} = \boldsymbol{\Phi}^{-1}\mathbf{t}. \tag{5.4}$$

It has been shown (Micchelli, 1986) that, for a large class of functions $\phi(\cdot)$, the matrix $\boldsymbol{\Phi}$ is indeed non-singular provided the data points are distinct. When the weights in (5.2) are set to the values given by (5.4), the function $h(\mathbf{x})$ represents a continuous differentiable surface which passes exactly through each data point.

Both theoretical and empirical studies (Powell, 1987) show that, in the context of the exact interpolation problem, many properties of the interpolating function are relatively insensitive to the precise form of the non-linear function $\phi(\cdot)$. Several forms of basis function have been considered, the most common being the Gaussian

$$\phi(x) = \exp\left(-\frac{x^2}{2\sigma^2}\right) \tag{5.5}$$

where σ is a parameter whose value controls the smoothness properties of the interpolating function. The Gaussian (5.5) is a *localized* basis function with the property that $\phi \to 0$ as $|x| \to \infty$. Another choice of basis function with the same property is the function

$$\phi(x) = \left(x^2 + \sigma^2\right)^{-\alpha}, \qquad \alpha > 0. \tag{5.6}$$

It is not, however, necessary for the functions to be localized, and other possible choices are the thin-plate spline function

$$\phi(x) = x^2 \ln(x), \tag{5.7}$$

the function

$$\phi(x) = \left(x^2 + \sigma^2\right)^\beta, \qquad 0 < \beta < 1, \tag{5.8}$$

which for $\beta = 1/2$ is known as the multi-quadric function, the cubic

$$\phi(x) = x^3, \tag{5.9}$$

and the 'linear' function

$$\phi(x) = x \tag{5.10}$$

which all have the property that $\phi \to \infty$ as $x \to \infty$. Note that (5.10) linear in $x = \|\mathbf{x} - \mathbf{x}^n\|$ and so is still a non-linear function of the components of $\mathbf{x}$. In one dimension, it leads to a piecewise-linear interpolating function which represents the simplest form of exact interpolation. As we shall see, in the context of neural network mappings there are reasons for considering localized basis functions. We shall focus most of our attention on Gaussian basis functions since, as well as being localized, they have a number of useful analytical properties. The technique of radial basis functions for exact interpolation is illustrated in Figure 5.1 for a simple one-input, one-output mapping.

The generalization to several output variables is straightforward. Each input vector $\mathbf{x}^n$ must be mapped exactly onto an output vector $\mathbf{t}^n$ having components t_k^n so that (5.1) becomes

$$h_k(\mathbf{x}^n) = t_k^n, \qquad n = 1, \ldots, N \tag{5.11}$$

where the $h_k(\mathbf{x})$ are obtained by linear superposition of the same N basis functions as used for the single-output case

$$h_k(\mathbf{x}) = \sum_n w_{kn} \phi(\|\mathbf{x} - \mathbf{x}^n\|). \tag{5.12}$$

The weight parameters are obtained by analogy with (5.4) in the form

$$w_{kn} = \sum_{n'} (\mathbf{\Phi}^{-1})_{nn'} t_k^{n'}. \tag{5.13}$$

Note that in (5.13) the same matrix $\mathbf{\Phi}^{-1}$ is used for each of the output functions.

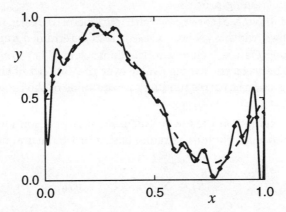

Figure 5.1. A simple example of exact interpolation using radial basis functions. A set of 30 data points was generated by sampling the function $y = 0.5 + 0.4 \sin(2\pi x)$, shown by the dashed curve, and adding Gaussian noise with standard deviation 0.05. The solid curve shows the interpolating function which results from using Gaussian basis functions of the form (5.5) with width parameter $\sigma = 0.067$ which corresponds to roughly twice the spacing of the data points. Values for the second-layer weights were found using matrix inversion techniques as discussed in the text.

5.2 Radial basis function networks

The radial basis function mappings discussed so far provide an interpolating function which passes exactly through every data point. As the example in Figure 5.1 illustrates, the exact interpolating function for noisy data is typically a highly oscillatory function. Such interpolating functions are generally undesirable. As discussed in Section 1.5.1, when there is noise present on the data, the interpolating function which gives the best generalization is one which is typically much smoother and which averages over the noise on the data. An additional limitation of the exact interpolation procedure discussed above is that the number of basis functions is equal to the number of patterns in the data set, and so for large data sets the mapping function can become very costly to evaluate.

By introducing a number of modifications to the exact interpolation procedure we obtain the radial basis function neural network model (Broomhead and Lowe, 1988; Moody and Darken, 1989). This provides a smooth interpolating function in which the number of basis functions is determined by the complexity of the mapping to be represented rather than by the size of the data set. The modifications which are required are as follows:

1. The number M of basis functions need not equal the number N of data points, and is typically much less than N.
2. The centres of the basis functions are no longer constrained to be given by

input data vectors. Instead, the determination of suitable centres becomes part of the training process.

3. Instead of having a common width parameter σ, each basis function is given its own width σ_j whose value is also determined during training.

4. Bias parameters are included in the linear sum. They compensate for the difference between the average value over the data set of the basis function activations and the corresponding average value of the targets, as discussed in Section 3.4.3.

When these changes are made to the exact interpolation formula (5.12), we arrive at the following form for the radial basis function neural network mapping

$$y_k(\mathbf{x}) = \sum_{j=1}^{M} w_{kj}\phi_j(\mathbf{x}) + w_{k0}. \tag{5.14}$$

If desired, the biases w_{k0} can be absorbed into the summation by including an extra basis function ϕ_0 whose activation is set to 1. For the case of Gaussian basis functions we have

$$\phi_j(\mathbf{x}) = \exp\left(-\frac{\|\mathbf{x} - \boldsymbol{\mu}_j\|^2}{2\sigma_j^2}\right) \tag{5.15}$$

where $\mathbf{x}$ is the d-dimensional input vector with elements x_i, and $\boldsymbol{\mu}_j$ is the vector determining the centre of basis function ϕ_j and has elements μ_{ji}. Note that the Gaussian basis functions in (5.15) are not normalized, as was the case for Gaussian density models in Chapter 2 for example, since any overall factors can be absorbed into the weights in (5.14) without loss of generality. This mapping function can be represented as a neural network diagram as shown in Figure 5.2. Note that more general topologies of radial basis function network (more than one hidden layer for instance) are not normally considered.

In discussing the representational properties of multi-layer perceptron networks in Section 4.3.1, we appealed to intuition to suggest that a linear superposition of localized functions, as in (5.14) and (5.15), is capable of universal approximation. Hartman *et al.* (1990) give a formal proof of this property for networks with Gaussian basis functions in which the widths of the Gaussians are treated as adjustable parameters. A more general result was obtained by Park and Sandberg (1991) who show that, with only mild restrictions on the form of the kernel functions, the universal approximation property still holds. Further generalizations of this results are given in (Park and Sandberg, 1993). As with the corresponding proofs for multi-layer perceptron networks, these are existence proofs which rely on the availability of an arbitrarily large number of hidden units, and they do not offer practical procedures for constructing the networks. Nevertheless, these theorems are crucial in providing a theoretical foundation on which practical applications can be based with confidence.

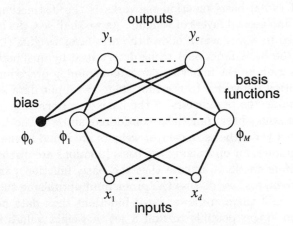

Figure 5.2. Architecture of a radial basis function neural network, corresponding to (5.14). Each basis function acts like a hidden unit. The lines connecting basis function ϕ_j to the inputs represent the corresponding elements μ_{ji} of the vector μ_j. The weights w_{kj} are shown as lines from the basis functions to the output units, and the biases are shown as weights from an extra 'basis function' ϕ_0 whose output is fixed at 1.

Girosi and Poggio (1990) have shown that radial basis function networks possess the property of *best approximation*. An approximation scheme has this property if, in the set of approximating functions (i.e. the set of functions corresponding to all possible choices of the adjustable parameters) there is one function which has minimum approximating error for any given function to be approximated. They also showed that this property is not shared by multi-layer perceptrons.

The Gaussian radial basis functions considered above can be generalized to allow for arbitrary covariance matrices Σ_j, as discussed for normal probability density functions in Section 2.1.1. Thus we take the basis functions to have the form

$$\phi_j(\mathbf{x}) = \exp\left\{-\frac{1}{2}(\mathbf{x} - \mu_j)^{\mathrm{T}}\Sigma_j^{-1}(\mathbf{x} - \mu_j)\right\}. \tag{5.16}$$

Since the covariance matrices Σ_j are symmetric, this means that each basis function has $d(d+3)/2$ independent adjustable parameters (where d is the dimensionality of the input space), as compared with the $(d+1)$ independent parameters for the basis functions (5.15). In practice there is a trade-off to be considered between using a smaller number of basis with many adjustable parameters and a larger number of less flexible functions.

5.3   Network training

A key aspect of radial basis function networks is the distinction between the roles of the first and second layers of weights. As we shall see, the basis functions can be interpreted in a way which allows the first-layer weights (i.e. the parameters governing the basis functions) to be determined by unsupervised training techniques. This leads to the following two-stage training procedure for training radial basis function networks. In the first stage the input data set $\{\mathbf{x}^n\}$ alone is used to determine the parameters of the basis functions (e.g. $\boldsymbol{\mu}_j$ and σ_j for the spherical Gaussian basis functions considered above). The basis functions are then kept fixed while the second-layer weights are found in the second phase of training. Techniques for optimizing the basis functions are discussed at length in Section 5.9. Here we shall assume that the basis function parameters have already been chosen, and we discuss the problem of optimizing the second-layer weights. Note that, if there are fewer basis functions than data points, then in general it will no longer possible to find a set of weight values for which the mapping function fits the data points exactly.

We begin by considering the radial basis function network mapping in (5.14) and we absorb the bias parameters into the weights to give

$$y_k(\mathbf{x}) = \sum_{j=0}^{M} w_{kj}\phi_j(\mathbf{x}) \tag{5.17}$$

where ϕ_0 is an extra 'basis function' with activation value fixed at $\phi_0 = 1$. This can be written in matrix notation as

$$\mathbf{y}(\mathbf{x}) = \mathbf{W}\boldsymbol{\phi} \tag{5.18}$$

where $\mathbf{W} = (w_{kj})$ and $\boldsymbol{\phi} = (\phi_j)$. Since the basis functions are considered fixed, the network is equivalent to a single-layer network of the kind considered in Section 3.3 in the context of classification problems, where it is termed a generalized linear discriminant. As discussed in earlier chapters, we can optimize the weights by minimization of a suitable error function. It is particularly convenient, as we shall see, to consider a sum-of-squares error function given by

$$E = \frac{1}{2}\sum_{n}\sum_{k}\{y_k(\mathbf{x}^n) - t_k^n\}^2 \tag{5.19}$$

where t_k^n is the target value for output unit k when the network is presented with input vector $\mathbf{x}^n$. Since the error function is a quadratic function of the weights, its minimum can be found in terms of the solution of a set of linear equations. This problem was discussed in detail in Section 3.4.3, from which we see that the weights are determined by the linear equations

$$\boldsymbol{\Phi}^{\mathrm{T}}\boldsymbol{\Phi}\mathbf{W}^{\mathrm{T}} = \boldsymbol{\Phi}^{\mathrm{T}}\mathbf{T} \tag{5.20}$$

where $(\mathbf{T})_{nk} = t_k^n$ and $(\boldsymbol{\Phi})_{nj} = \phi_j(\mathbf{x}^n)$. The formal solution for the weights is given by

$$\mathbf{W}^{\mathrm{T}} = \boldsymbol{\Phi}^{\dagger}\mathbf{T} \tag{5.21}$$

where the notation $\boldsymbol{\Phi}^{\dagger}$ denotes the pseudo-inverse of $\boldsymbol{\Phi}$ (Section 3.4.3). In practice, the equations (5.20) are solved using singular value decomposition, to avoid problems due to possible ill-conditioning of the matrix $\boldsymbol{\Phi}$. Thus, we see that the second-layer weights can be found by fast, linear matrix inversion techniques.

For the most part we shall consider radial basis function networks in which the dependence of the network function on the second-layer weights is linear, and in which the error function is given by the sum-of-squares. It is possible to consider the use of non-linear activation functions applied to the output units, or other choices for the error function. However, the determination of the second-layer weights is then no longer a linear problem, and hence a non-linear optimization of these weights is then required. As we have indicated, one of the major advantages of radial basis function networks is the possibility of avoiding the need for such an optimization during network training.

As a simple illustration of the use of radial basis function networks, we return to the data set shown in Figure 5.1 and consider the mapping obtained by using a radial basis function network in which the number of basis functions is smaller than the number of data points, as shown in Figure 5.3

The width parameter σ in Figure 5.3 was chosen to be roughly twice the average spacing between the basis functions. Techniques for setting the basis function parameters, including σ_j, are discussed in detail in Section 5.9. Here we simply note the effect of poor choices of σ. Figure 5.4 shows the result of choosing too small a value for σ, while the effect of having σ too large is illustrated in Figure 5.5.

5.4 Regularization theory

An alternative motivation for radial basis function expansions comes from the theory of regularization (Poggio and Girosi, 1990a, 1990b). In Section 1.6 the technique of regularization was introduced as a way of controlling the smoothness properties of a mapping function. It involves adding to the error function an extra term which is designed to penalize mappings which are not smooth. For simplicity of notation we shall consider networks having a single output y, so that with a sum-of-squares error, the total error function to be minimized becomes

$$E = \frac{1}{2}\sum_n \{y(\mathbf{x}^n) - t^n\}^2 + \frac{\nu}{2}\int |Py|^2\,d\mathbf{x} \tag{5.22}$$

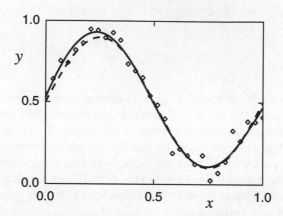

Figure 5.3. This shows the same set of 30 data points as in Figure 5.1, together with a network mapping (solid curve) in which the number of basis functions has been set to 5, which is significantly fewer than the number of data points. The centres of the basis functions have been set to a random subset of the data set input vectors, and the width parameters of the basis functions have been set to a common value of $\sigma = 0.4$, which again is roughly equal to twice the average spacing between the centres. The second-layer weights are found by minimizing a sum-of-squares error function using singular value decomposition.

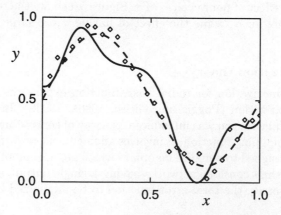

Figure 5.4. As in Figure 5.3, but in which the width parameter has been set to $\sigma = 0.08$. The resulting network function is insufficiently smooth and gives a poor representation of the underlying function which generated the data.

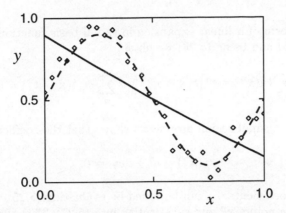

Figure 5.5. As in Figure 5.3, but in which the width parameter has been set to $\sigma = 10.0$. This leads to a network function which is over-smoothed, and which again gives a poor representation of the underlying function which generated the data.

where P is some differential operator, and ν is called a regularization parameter. Network mapping functions $y(\mathbf{x})$ which have large curvature will typically give rise to large values of $|Py|^2$ and hence to a large penalty in the total error function. The value of ν controls the relative importance of the regularization term, and hence the degree of smoothness of the function $y(\mathbf{x})$.

We can solve the regularized least-squares problem of (5.22) by using calculus of variations (Appendix D) as follows. Setting the functional derivative of (5.22) with respect to $y(\mathbf{x})$ to zero we obtain

$$\sum_n \{y(\mathbf{x}^n) - t^n\}\delta(\mathbf{x} - \mathbf{x}^n) + \nu \widehat{P}Py(\mathbf{x}) = 0 \tag{5.23}$$

where $\widehat{P}$ is the *adjoint* differential operator to P and $\delta(\mathbf{x})$ is the Dirac delta function. The equations (5.23) are the *Euler–Lagrange* equations corresponding to (5.22). A formal solution to these equations can be written down in terms of the *Green's functions* of the operator $\widehat{P}P$, which are the functions $G(\mathbf{x}, \mathbf{x}')$ which satisfy

$$\widehat{P}PG(\mathbf{x}, \mathbf{x}') = \delta(\mathbf{x} - \mathbf{x}'). \tag{5.24}$$

If the operator P is translationally and rotationally invariant, then the Green's functions depend only on the distance $\|\mathbf{x} - \mathbf{x}'\|$, and hence they are radial functions. The formal solution to (5.23) can then be written as

$$y(\mathbf{x}) = \sum_n w_n G(\|\mathbf{x} - \mathbf{x}^n\|) \tag{5.25}$$

which has the form of a linear expansion in radial basis functions. Substituting (5.25) into (5.23) and using (5.24) we obtain

$$\sum_n \{y(\mathbf{x}^n) - t^n\}\delta(\mathbf{x} - \mathbf{x}^n) + \nu \sum_n w_n \delta(\mathbf{x} - \mathbf{x}^n) = 0 \tag{5.26}$$

Integrating over a small region around $\mathbf{x}^n$ shows that the coefficients w_n satisfy

$$y(\mathbf{x}^n) - t^n + \nu w_n = 0. \tag{5.27}$$

Values for the coefficients w_n can be found by evaluating (5.25) at the values of the training data points $\mathbf{x}^n$ and substituting into (5.27). This gives the values of w_n as the solutions of the linear equation

$$(\mathbf{G} + \nu\mathbf{I})\mathbf{w} = \mathbf{t} \tag{5.28}$$

where $(\mathbf{G})_{nn'} = G(\|\mathbf{x}^{n'} - \mathbf{x}^n\|)$, $(\mathbf{w})_n = w_n$, $(\mathbf{t})_n = t^n$ and $\mathbf{I}$ denotes the unit matrix.

If the operator P is chosen to have the particular form

$$\int |Py|^2 d\mathbf{x} = \sum_{l=0}^{\infty} \frac{\sigma^{2l}}{l! 2^l} \int |D^l y(\mathbf{x})|^2 \, d\mathbf{x} \tag{5.29}$$

where $D^{2l} = (\nabla^2)^l$ and $D^{2l+1} = \nabla(\nabla^2)^l$, with ∇ and ∇^2 denoting the gradient and Laplacian operators respectively, then the Green's functions are Gaussians with width parameters σ (Exercise 5.3).

We see that there is a very close similarity between this form of basis function expansion, and the one discussed in the context of exact interpolation in Section 5.1. Here the Greens functions $G(\|\mathbf{x} - \mathbf{x}^n\|)$ correspond to the basis functions $\phi(\|\mathbf{x} - \mathbf{x}^n\|)$, and there is one such function centred on each data point in the training set. Also, we see that (5.28) reduces to the exact interpolation result (5.3) when the regularization parameter ν is zero. When the regularization parameter is greater than zero, however, we no longer have an exact interpolating function. The effect of the regularization term is to force a smoother network mapping function, as illustrated in Figure 5.6.

In practice, regularization can also be applied to radial basis function networks in which the basis functions are not constrained to be centred on the data points, and in which the number of basis functions need not equal the number of data points. Also, regularization terms can be considered for which the basis functions are not necessarily the Green's functions. Provided the regularization term is a quadratic function of the network mapping, the second-layer weights

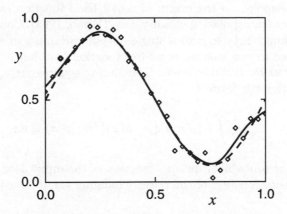

Figure 5.6. This shows the same data set as in Figure 5.1, again with one basis function centred on each data point, and a width parameter $\sigma = 0.067$. In this case, however, a regularization term is used, with coefficient $\nu = 40$, leading to a smoother mapping (shown by the solid curve) which no longer gives an exact fit to the data, but which now gives a much better approximation to the underlying function which generated the data (shown by the dashed curve).

can again be found by the solution of a set of linear equations which minimize a sum-of-squares error. For example, the regularizer

$$\frac{\nu}{2} \sum_n \sum_k \sum_i \left(\frac{\partial^2 y_k^n}{\partial x_i^2} \right)^2 \tag{5.30}$$

penalizes mappings which have large curvature (Bishop, 1991b). This regularizer leads to second-layer weights which are found by solution of

$$\mathbf{MW} = \mathbf{\Phi}^{\mathrm{T}} \mathbf{T} \tag{5.31}$$

where

$$(\mathbf{M})_{jj'} = \sum_n \left\{ \phi_j^n \phi_{j'}^n + \nu \sum_i \left(\frac{\partial^2 \phi_j^n}{\partial x_i^2} \frac{\partial^2 \phi_{j'}^n}{\partial x_i^2} \right) \right\} \tag{5.32}$$

and $\mathbf{\Phi} = (\phi_j^n)$ as before. When $\nu = 0$ (5.31) reduces to the previous result (5.20). The inclusion of the regularization term adds little to the computational cost, since most of the time is spent in solving the coupled linear equations (5.31).

5.5   Noisy interpolation theory

Yet another viewpoint on the origin of radial basis function expansions comes
from the theory of interpolation of noisy data (Webb, 1994). Consider a mapping
from a single input variable x to a single output variable y in which the target
data is generated from a smooth noise-free function $h(x)$ but in which the *input*
data is corrupted by additive noise. The sum-of-squares error, in the limit of
infinite data, takes the form

$$E = \frac{1}{2} \int\!\!\int \{y(x + \xi) - h(x)\}^2 \widetilde{p}(\xi) p(x) \, d\xi \, dx \tag{5.33}$$

where $p(x)$ is the probability density function of the input data, and $\widetilde{p}(\xi)$ is the
probability density function of the noise. Changing variables using $z = x + \xi$ we
have

$$E = \frac{1}{2} \int\!\!\int \{y(z) - h(x)\}^2 \widetilde{p}(z - x) p(x) \, dz \, dx. \tag{5.34}$$

A formal expression for the minimum of the error can then be obtained using
variational techniques (Appendix D) by setting the functional derivative of E
with respect to $y(z)$ to zero, to give

$$y(z) = \frac{\int h(x) \widetilde{p}(z - x) p(x) \, dx}{\int \widetilde{p}(z - x) p(x) \, dx}. \tag{5.35}$$

If we consider the case of a finite number of data points $\{x^n\}$ drawn from
the distribution $p(x)$, we can approximate (5.35) by

$$y(x) = \frac{\sum_n h(x^n) \widetilde{p}(x - x^n)}{\sum_n \widetilde{p}(x - x^n)} \tag{5.36}$$

which we recognize as being an expansion in radial basis functions, in which
$h(x^n)$ are the expansion coefficients, and the basis functions are given by

$$\phi(x - x^n) = \frac{\widetilde{p}(x - x^n)}{\sum_n \widetilde{p}(x - x^n)}. \tag{5.37}$$

Since the function $h(x)$ is unknown, the coefficients $h(x^n)$ should be regarded
as parameters to be determined from the data. To do this we note that $h(x)$ is
noise-free and so we have $h(x^n) = t^n$. Thus (5.36) becomes an expansion in basis
functions in which the coefficients are given by the target values. Note that this
form of basis function expansion differs from that introduced in (5.14) and (5.15)

in that the basis functions are normalized (Moody and Darken, 1989). Strictly speaking, the normalization in (5.36) would require lateral connections between different hidden units in a network diagram. If the distribution of the noise is normal, so that $\widetilde{p}(\xi) \propto \exp(-\xi^2/2\sigma^2)$, then we obtain an expansion in Gaussian basis functions

$$y(x) = \frac{\sum_n h(x^n) \exp\{-(x-x^n)^2/2\sigma^2\}}{\sum_n \exp\{-(x-x^n)^2/2\sigma^2\}}. \tag{5.38}$$

The extension of this result to several output variables is straightforward and gives

$$y_k(x) = \frac{\sum_n h_k(x^n) \exp\{-(x-x^n)^2/2\sigma^2\}}{\sum_n \exp\{-(x-x^n)^2/2\sigma^2\}}. \tag{5.39}$$

Note that (5.36) will only be a good approximation to (5.35) if the integrand is sufficiently smooth. This implies that the width of the basis functions should be large in relation to the spacing of the data, which is a useful rule of thumb when designing networks with good generalization properties.

5.6 Relation to kernel regression

Further motivation for the use of radial basis functions for function approximation comes from the theory of kernel regression (Scott, 1992). This is a technique for estimating regression functions from noisy data, based on the methods of kernel density estimation discussed in Section 2.5.3. Consider a mapping from an input vector $\mathbf{x}$ to an output vector $\mathbf{y}$, and suppose we are given a set of training data $\{\mathbf{x}^n, \mathbf{t}^n\}$ where $n = 1, \ldots, N$. A complete description of the statistical properties of the generator of the data is given by the probability density $p(\mathbf{x}, \mathbf{t})$ in the joint input-target space. We can model this density by using a Parzen kernel estimator constructed from the data set. If we consider Gaussian kernel functions, this estimator takes the form

$$\widehat{p}(\mathbf{x}, \mathbf{t}) = \frac{1}{N} \sum_{n=1}^{N} \frac{1}{(2\pi h^2)^{(d+c)/2}} \exp\left\{ -\frac{\|\mathbf{x} - \mathbf{x}^n\|^2}{2h^2} - \frac{\|\mathbf{t} - \mathbf{t}^n\|^2}{2h^2} \right\} \tag{5.40}$$

where d and c are the dimensionalities of the input and output spaces respectively. This is illustrated schematically, for the case of one input variable and one output variable, in Figure 5.7.

As we have already seen, the goal of learning is to find a smooth mapping from $\mathbf{x}$ to $\mathbf{y}$ which captures the underlying systematic aspects of the data, without fitting the noise on the data. In Section 6.1.3 it is shown that, under many circumstances, the optimal mapping is given by forming the regression, or conditional average $\langle \mathbf{t}|\mathbf{x}\rangle$, of the target data, conditioned on the input variables. This

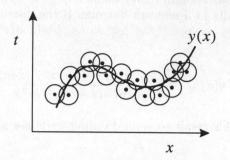

Figure 5.7. Schematic illustration of the use of a kernel estimator to model the joint probability density in the input-output space. The dots show the data points, and the circles represent Gaussian kernel functions centred on the data points, while the curve shows the regression function given by the conditional average of t as a function of x.

can be expressed in terms of the conditional density $p(t|x)$, and hence in terms of the joint density $p(x, t)$, as follows:

$$y(x) = \langle t|x \rangle$$

$$= \int t p(t|x)\, dt$$

$$= \frac{\int t p(x, t)\, dt}{\int p(x, t)\, dt}. \tag{5.41}$$

If we now substitute our density estimate (5.40) into (5.41) we obtain the following expression for the regression of the target data

$$y(x) = \frac{\sum_n t^n \exp\left\{-\|x - x^n\|^2 / 2h^2\right\}}{\sum_n \exp\left\{-\|x - x^n\|^2 / 2h^2\right\}}. \tag{5.42}$$

This is known as the *Nadaraya–Watson* estimator (Nadaraya, 1964; Watson, 1964), and has been re-discovered relatively recently in the context of neural networks (Specht, 1990; Schiøler and Hartmann, 1992). We see that (5.42) has the form of a normalized expansion in Gaussian radial basis functions defined in the input space, and should be compared with the form (5.38) obtained earlier from the perspective of additive noise on the input data. Each basis function is centred on a data point, and the coefficients in the expansion are given by the target values t^n. Note that this construction provides values for the hidden-to-output unit weights which are just given by the target data values.

This approach can be extended by replacing the kernel estimator with an adaptive mixture model, as discussed in Section 2.6. The parameters of the mixture model can be found using, for instance, the EM (expectation–maximization) algorithm (Section 2.6.2). For a mixture of M spherical Gaussian functions, we can write the joint density in the form

$$\widehat{p}(\mathbf{x}, \mathbf{t}) = \sum_{j=1}^{M} P(j) \frac{1}{(2\pi h^2)^{(d+c)/2}} \exp\left\{ -\frac{\|\mathbf{x} - \boldsymbol{\mu}_j\|^2}{2h^2} - \frac{\|\mathbf{t} - \boldsymbol{\nu}_j\|^2}{2h^2} \right\}. \quad (5.43)$$

Following the same line of argument as before, we arrive at the following expression for the regression:

$$\mathbf{y}(\mathbf{x}) = \frac{\sum_j P(j) \boldsymbol{\nu}_j \exp\left\{ -\|\mathbf{x} - \boldsymbol{\mu}_j\|^2/2h^2 \right\}}{\sum_j P(j) \exp\left\{ -\|\mathbf{x} - \boldsymbol{\mu}_j\|^2/2h^2 \right\}} \quad (5.44)$$

which can be viewed as a normalized radial basis function expansion in which the number of basis functions is typically much smaller than the number of data points, and in which the basis function centres are no longer constrained to coincide with the data points. This result can be extended to Gaussian functions with general covariance matrices (Ghahramani and Jordan, 1994b).

5.7 Radial basis function networks for classification

A further key insight into the nature of the radial basis function network is obtained by considering the use of such networks for classification problems (Lowe, 1995). Suppose we have a data set which falls into three classes as shown in Figure 5.8. A multi-layer perceptron can separate the classes by using hidden units which form hyperplanes in the input space, as indicated in Figure 5.8(a). An alternative approach is to model the separate class distributions by local kernel functions, as indicated in (b). This latter type of representation is related to the radial basis function network.

Suppose we model the data in each class $\mathcal{C}_k$ using a single kernel function, which we write as $p(\mathbf{x}|\mathcal{C}_k)$. In a classification problem our goal is to model the posterior probabilities $p(\mathcal{C}_k|\mathbf{x})$ for each of the classes. These probabilities can be obtained through Bayes' theorem, using prior probabilities $p(\mathcal{C}_k)$, as follows:

$$P(\mathcal{C}_k|\mathbf{x}) = \frac{p(\mathbf{x}|\mathcal{C}_k)P(\mathcal{C}_k)}{p(\mathbf{x})} \quad (5.45)$$

$$= \frac{p(\mathbf{x}|\mathcal{C}_k)P(\mathcal{C}_k)}{\sum_{k'} p(\mathbf{x}|\mathcal{C}_{k'})P(\mathcal{C}_{k'})}. \quad (5.46)$$

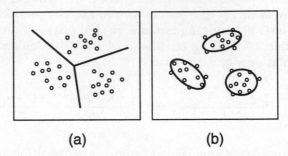

(a)   **(b)**

Figure 5.8. Schematic example of data points in two dimensions which fall into three distinct classes. One way to separate the classes is to use hyperplanes, shown in (a), as used in a multi-layer perceptron. An alternative approach, shown in (b), is to fit each class with a kernel function, which gives the type of representation formed by a radial basis function network.

This can be viewed as a simple form of basis function network with normalized basis functions given by

$$\phi_k(\mathbf{x}) = \frac{p(\mathbf{x}|\mathcal{C}_k)}{\sum_{k'} p(\mathbf{x}|\mathcal{C}_{k'})P(\mathcal{C}_{k'})} \tag{5.47}$$

and second-layer connections which consist of one weight from each hidden unit going to the corresponding output unit, with value $p(\mathcal{C}_k)$. The outputs of this network represent approximations to the posterior probabilities.

In most applications a single kernel function will not give a particularly good representation of the class-conditional distributions $p(\mathbf{x}|\mathcal{C}_k)$. A better representation could be obtained by using a separate mixture model to represent each of the conditional densities. However, a computationally more efficient approach, and one which may help to reduce the number of adjustable parameters in the model, is to use a common pool of M basis functions, labelled by an index j, to represent all of the class-conditional densities. Thus, we write

$$p(\mathbf{x}|\mathcal{C}_k) = \sum_{j=1}^{M} p(\mathbf{x}|j)P(j|\mathcal{C}_k). \tag{5.48}$$

An expression for the unconditional density $p(\mathbf{x})$ can be found from (5.48) by summing over all classes

$$p(\mathbf{x}) = \sum_{k} p(\mathbf{x}|\mathcal{C}_k)P(\mathcal{C}_k) \tag{5.49}$$

$$= \sum_{j=1}^{M} p(\mathbf{x}|j)P(j) \tag{5.50}$$

where we have defined priors for the basis functions given by

$$P(j) = \sum_{k} P(j|\mathcal{C}_k)P(\mathcal{C}_k). \tag{5.51}$$

Again, the quantities we are interested in are the posterior probabilities of class membership. These can be obtained by substituting the expressions (5.48) and (5.50) into Bayes' theorem (5.45) to give

$$P(\mathcal{C}_k|\mathbf{x}) = \frac{\sum_{j=1}^{M} P(j|\mathcal{C}_k)p(\mathbf{x}|j)P(\mathcal{C}_k)}{\sum_{j'=1}^{M} p(\mathbf{x}|j')P(j')} \frac{P(j)}{P(j)} \tag{5.52}$$

$$= \sum_{j=1}^{M} w_{kj}\phi_j(\mathbf{x}) \tag{5.53}$$

where we have inserted an extra factor of $1 = P(j)/P(j)$ into (5.52). The expression (5.53) represents a radial basis function network, in which the normalized basis functions are given by

$$\phi_j(\mathbf{x}) = \frac{p(\mathbf{x}|j)P(j)}{\sum_{j'=1}^{M} p(\mathbf{x}|j')P(j')} \tag{5.54}$$

$$= P(j|\mathbf{x}) \tag{5.55}$$

and the second-layer weights are given by

$$w_{kj} = \frac{P(j|\mathcal{C}_k)P(\mathcal{C}_k)}{P(j)} \tag{5.56}$$

$$= P(\mathcal{C}_k|j). \tag{5.57}$$

Thus, the activations of the basis functions can be interpreted as the posterior probabilities of the presence of corresponding features in the input space, and the weights can similarly be interpreted as the posterior probabilities of class membership, given the presence of the features. The activations of the hidden units in a multi-layer perceptron (with logistic sigmoid activation functions) can be given a similar interpretation as posterior probabilities of the presence of features, as discussed in Section 6.7.1.

Note from (5.50) that the unconditional density of the input data is expressed

in terms of a mixture model, in which the component densities are given by
the basis functions. This motivates the use of mixture density estimation as a
procedure for finding the basis function parameters, as discussed in Section 5.9.4.

It should be emphasized that the outputs of this network also have a precise
interpretation as the posterior probabilities of class membership. The ability to
interpret network outputs in this way is of central importance in the effective
application of neural networks, and is discussed at length in Chapter 6.

Finally, for completeness, we point out that radial basis functions are also
closely related to the method of *potential functions* (Aizerman *et al.*, 1964; Niranjan *et al.*, 1989). This is a way of finding a linear discriminant function from
a training set of data points, based on an analogy with electrostatics. Imagine
we place a unit of positive charge at each point in input space at which there is a
training vector from class C_1, and a unit of negative charge at each point where
there is a training vector from class C_2. These charges give rise to an electro-
static potential field which can be treated as a discriminant function. The kernel
function which is used to compute the contribution to the potential from each
charge need not be that of conventional electrostatics, but can be some other
function of the radial distance from the data point.

5.8   Comparison with the multi-layer perceptron

Radial basis function networks and multi-layer perceptrons play very similar roles
in that they both provide techniques for approximating arbitrary non-linear functional mappings between multidimensional spaces. In both cases the mappings
are expressed in terms of parametrized compositions of functions of single variables. The particular structures of the two networks are very different, however,
and so it is interesting to compare them in more detail. Some of the important
differences between the multi-layer perceptron and radial basis function networks
are as follows:

1. The hidden unit representations of the multi-layer perceptron depend on
    weighted linear summations of the inputs, transformed by monotonic acti-
    vation functions. Thus the activation of a hidden unit in a multi-layer per-
    ceptron is constant on surfaces which consist of parallel $(d-1)$-dimensional
    hyperplanes in d-dimensional input space. By contrast, the hidden units
    in a radial basis function network use distance to a prototype vector fol-
    lowed by transformation with a (usually) localized function. The activation
    of a basis function is therefore constant on concentric $(d-1)$-dimensional
    hyperspheres (or more generally on $(d-1)$-dimensional hyperellipsoids).

2. A multi-layer perceptron can be said to form a *distributed representation* in
    the space of activation values for the hidden units since, for a given input
    vector, many hidden units will typically contribute to the determination
    of the output value. During training, the functions represented by the hid-
    den units must be such that, when linearly combined by the final layer
    of weights, they generate the correct outputs for a range of possible input
    values. The interference and cross-coupling between the hidden units which

this requires results in the network training process being highly non-linear with problems of local minima, or nearly flat regions in the error function arising from near cancellations in the effects of different weights. This can lead to very slow convergence of the training procedure even with advanced optimization strategies. By contrast, a radial basis function network with localized basis functions forms a representation in the space of hidden units which is *local* with respect to the input space because, for a given input vector, typically only a few hidden units will have significant activations.

3. A multi-layer perceptron often has many layers of weights, and a complex pattern of connectivity, so that not all possible weights in any given layer are present. Also, a variety of different activation functions may be used within the same network. A radial basis function network, however, generally has a simple architecture consisting of two layers of weights, in which the first layer contains the parameters of the basis functions, and the second layer forms linear combinations of the activations of the basis functions to generate the outputs.

4. All of the parameters in a multi-layer perceptron are usually determined at the same time as part of a single global training strategy involving supervised training. A radial basis function network, however, is typically trained in two stages, with the basis functions being determined first by unsupervised techniques using the input data alone, and the second-layer weights subsequently being found by fast linear supervised methods.

5.9 Basis function optimization

One of the principal advantages of radial basis function neural networks, as compared with the multi-layer perceptron, is the possibility of choosing suitable parameters for the hidden units without having to perform a full non-linear optimization of the network. In this section we shall discuss several possible strategies for selecting the parameters of the basis functions. The problem of selecting the appropriate number of basis functions, however, is discussed in the context of model order selection and generalization in Chapter 9.

We have motivated radial basis functions from the perspectives of function approximation, regularization, noisy interpolation, kernel regression, and the estimation of posterior class probabilities for classification problems. All of these viewpoints suggest that the basis function parameters should be chosen to form a representation of the probability density of the input data. This leads to an unsupervised procedure for optimizing the basis function parameters which depends only on the input data from the training set, and which ignores any target information. The basis function centres μ_j can then be regarded as *prototypes* of the input vectors. In this section we discuss a number of possible strategies for optimizing the basis functions which are motivated by these considerations.

There are many potential applications for neural networks where unlabelled input data is plentiful, but where labelled data is in short supply. For instance, it may be easy to collect examples of raw input data for the network, but the labelling of the data with target variables may require the time of a human expert which therefore limits the amount of data which can be labelled in a reasonable time. With such applications, the two-stage training process for a radial basis function network can be particularly advantageous since the determination of the non-linear representation given by first layer of the network can be done using a large quantity of unlabelled data, leaving a relatively small number of parameters in the second layer to be determined using the labelled data. At each stage of the training process, we can ensure that the number of data points is large compared with the number of parameters to be determined, as required for good generalization.

One of the major potential difficulties with radial basis function networks, however, also stems from the localized nature of the hidden unit representation. It concerns the way in which such a network addresses the curse of dimensionality discussed in Section 1.4. There we saw that the number of hypercubes which are needed to fill out a compact region of a d-dimensional space grows exponentially with d. When the data is confined to some lower-dimensional sub-space, d is to be interpreted as the effective dimensionality of the sub-space, known as the *intrinsic dimensionality* of the data. If the basis function centres are used to fill out the sub-space then the number of basis function centres will be an exponential function of d (Hartman *et al.*, 1990). As well as increasing the computation time, a large number of basis functions leads to a requirement for large numbers of training patterns in order to ensure that the network parameters are properly determined.

The problem is particularly severe if there are input variables which have significant variance but which play little role in determining the appropriate output variables. Such irrelevant inputs are not uncommon in practical applications. When the basis function centres are chosen using the input data alone, there is no way to distinguish relevant from irrelevant inputs. This problem is illustrated in Figure 5.9 where we see a variable y which is a non-linear function of an input variable x_1. We wish to use radial basis function network network to approximate this function. The basis functions are chosen to cover the region of the x_1 axis where data is observed. Suppose that a second input variable x_2 is introduced which is uncorrelated with x_1. Then the number of basis functions needed to cover the required region of input space increases dramatically as indicated in Figure 5.10. If y is independent of x_2 then these extra basis functions have no useful role in determining the value of y. Simulations using artificial data (Hartman *et al.*, 1990), in which 19 out of 20 input variables consisted of noise uncorrelated with the output, showed that a multi-layer perceptron could learn to ignore the irrelevant inputs and obtain accurate results with a small number of hidden units, while radial basis function networks showed large error which decreased only slowly as the number of hidden units was increased.

Problems arising from the curse of dimensionality may be much less severe if basis functions with full covariance matrices are used, as in (5.16), rather than spherical basis functions of the form (5.15). However, the number of parameters per basis function is then much greater.

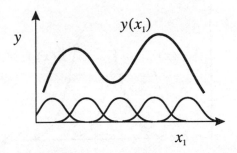

Figure 5.9. A schematic example of a function $y(x_1)$ of an input variable x_1 which has been modelled using a set of radial basis functions.

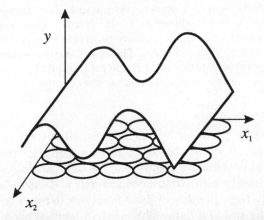

Figure 5.10. As in Figure 5.9, but in which an extra, irrelevant variable x_2 has been introduced. Note that the number of basis functions, whose locations are determined using the input data alone, has increased dramatically, even though x_2 carries no useful information for determining the output variable.

We have provided compelling reasons for using unsupervised methods to determine the first-layer parameters in a radial basis function network by modelling the density of input data. Such method have also proven to be very powerful in practice. However, it should be emphasized that the optimal choice of basis function parameters for density estimation need not be optimal for representing the mapping to the output variables. Figure 5.11 shows a simple example of a problem for which the use of density estimation to set the basis function parameters clearly gives a sub-optimal solution.

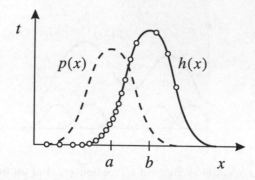

Figure 5.11. A simple example to illustrate why the use of unsupervised methods based on density estimation to determine the basis function parameters
need not be optimal for approximating the target function. Data in one dimension (shown by the circles) is generated from a Gaussian distribution $p(x)$
shown by the dashed curve. Unsupervised training of one Gaussian basis function would cause it to be centred at $x = a$, giving a good approximation to
$p(x)$. Target values for the input data are generated from a Gaussian function
centred at b shown by the solid curve. The basis function centred at a can only
give a very poor representation of $h(x)$. By contrast, if the basis function were
centred at b it could represent the function $h(x)$ exactly.

5.9.1 Subsets of data points

One simple procedure for selecting the basis function centres μ_j is to set them
equal to a random subset of the input vectors from the training set, as was
done for the example shown in Figure 5.3. Clearly this is not an optimal procedure so far as density estimation is concerned, and may also lead to the use
of an unnecessarily large number of basis functions in order to achieve adequate
performance on the training data. This method is often used, however, to provide a set of starting values for many of the iterative adaptive procedures to be
discussed shortly.

   Another approach is to start with all data points as basis functions centres
and then selectively remove centres in such a way as to have minimum disruption
on the performance of the system. Such an approach was introduced into the
K-nearest-neighbour classification scheme by Devijver and Kittler (1982) and
applied to radial basis function networks used for classification by Kraaijveld
and Duin (1991). A procedure for selecting a subset of the basis functions so as
to preserve the best estimator of the unconditional density is given in Fukunaga
and Hayes (1989).

   These techniques only set the basis function centres, and the width parameters σ_j must be chosen using some other procedure. One heuristic approach is
to choose all the σ_j to be equal and to be given by some multiple of the average
distance between the basis function centres. This ensures that the basis func-

tions overlap to some degree and hence give a relatively smooth representation of the distribution of training data. We might also recognize that the optimal width may be different for basis functions in different regions of input space. For instance, the widths may be determined from the average distance of each basis function to its L nearest neighbours, where L is typically small. Such *ad hoc* procedures for choosing the basis function parameters are very fast, and allow a radial basis function network to be set up very quickly, but are likely to be significantly sub-optimal.

5.9.2 *Orthogonal least squares*

A more principled approach to selecting a sub-set of the data points as basis function centres is based on the technique of *orthogonal least squares*. To motivate this approach consider the following procedure for selecting basis functions. We start by considering a network with just one basis function. For each data point in turn we set the basis function centre to the input vector for that data point, and then set the second-layer weights by pseudo-inverse techniques using the complete training set of N data points. The basis function centre which gives rise to the smallest residual error is retained. In subsequent steps of the algorithm, the number of basis functions is then increased incrementally. If at some point in the algorithm l of the data points have been selected as basis function centres, then $N - l$ networks are trained in which each of the remaining $N - l$ data points in turn is selected as the centre for the additional basis function. The extra basis function which gives the smallest value for the residual sum-of-squares error is then retained, and the algorithm proceeds to the next stage.

Such an approach would be computationally intensive since at each step it would be necessary to obtain a complete pseudo-inverse solution for each possible choice of basis functions. A much more efficient procedure for achieving the same result is that of *orthogonal least squares* (Chen *et al.*, 1989, 1991). In outline, the algorithm involves the sequential addition of new basis functions, each centred on one of the data points, as described above. This is done by constructing a set of orthogonal vectors in the space S spanned by the vectors of hidden unit activations for each pattern in the training set (Section 3.4.2). It is then possible to calculate directly which data point should be chosen as the next basis function centre in order to produce the greatest reduction in residual sum-of-squares error. Values for the second-layer weights are also determined at the same time. If the algorithm is continued long enough then all data points will be selected, and the residual error will be zero. In order to achieve good generalization, the algorithm must be stopped before this occurs. This is the problem of model-order selection, and is discussed at length in Chapters 9 and 10.

5.9.3 *Clustering algorithms*

As an improvement on simply choosing a subset of the data points as the basis function centres, we can use clustering techniques to find a set of centres which more accurately reflects the distribution of the data points. Moody and Darken (1989) use the *K-means clustering algorithm*, in which the number K of centres must be decided in advance. The algorithm involves a simple re-estimation procedure, as follows. Suppose there are N data points $\mathbf{x}^n$ in total, and we wish to find a set of K representative vectors $\boldsymbol{\mu}_j$ where $j = 1, \ldots, K$. The algorithm seeks to partition the data points $\{\mathbf{x}^n\}$ into K disjoint subsets $\mathcal{S}_j$ containing N_j data points, in such a way as to minimize the sum-of-squares clustering function given by

$$J = \sum_{j=1}^{K} \sum_{n \in \mathcal{S}_j} \|\mathbf{x}^n - \boldsymbol{\mu}_j\|^2 \tag{5.58}$$

where $\boldsymbol{\mu}_j$ is the mean of the data points in set $\mathcal{S}_j$ and is given by

$$\boldsymbol{\mu}_j = \frac{1}{N_j} \sum_{n \in \mathcal{S}_j} \mathbf{x}^n. \tag{5.59}$$

The batch version of K-means (Lloyd, 1982) begins by assigning the points at random to K sets and then computing the mean vectors of the points in each set. Next, each point is re-assigned to a new set according to which is the nearest mean vector. The means of the sets are then recomputed. This procedure is repeated until there is no further change in the grouping of the data points. It can be shown (Linde *et al.*, 1980) that at each such iteration the value of J will not increase. The calculation of the means can also be formulated as a stochastic on-line process (MacQueen, 1967; Moody and Darken, 1989). In this case, the initial centres are randomly chosen from the data points, and as each data point $\mathbf{x}^n$ is presented, the nearest $\boldsymbol{\mu}_j$ is updated using

$$\Delta \boldsymbol{\mu}_j = \eta(\mathbf{x}^n - \boldsymbol{\mu}_j) \tag{5.60}$$

where η is the learning rate parameter. Note that this is simply the Robbins–Monro procedure (Section 2.4.1) for finding the root of a regression function given by the derivative of J with respect to $\boldsymbol{\mu}_j$. Once the centres of the basis functions have been found in this way, the covariance matrices of the basis functions can be set to the covariances of the points assigned to the corresponding clusters.

Another unsupervised technique which has been used for assigning basis function centres is the Kohonen topographic feature map, also called a *self-organizing feature map* (Kohonen, 1982). This algorithm leads to placement of a set of prototype vectors in input space, each of which corresponds to a point on a regular grid in a (usually two-dimensional) feature-map space. When the algorithm has converged, prototype vectors corresponding to nearby points on the feature map grid have nearby locations in input space. This leads to a number of applications for this algorithm including the projection of data into a two-dimensional space for visualization purposes. However, the imposition of the topographic property, particularly if the data is not intrinsically two-dimensional (Section 8.6.1), may lead to suboptimal placement of vectors.

5.9.4 *Gaussian mixture models*

We have already discussed a number of heuristic procedures for setting the basis function parameters such that the basis functions approximate the distribution of the input data. A more principled approach, however, is to recognize that this is essentially the mixture density estimation problem, which is discussed at length in Section 2.6. The basis functions of the neural network can be regarded as the components of a mixture density model, whose parameters are to be optimized by maximum likelihood. We therefore model the density of the input data by a mixture model of the form

$$p(\mathbf{x}) = \sum_{j=1}^{M} P(j)\phi_j(\mathbf{x}) \tag{5.61}$$

where the parameters $P(j)$ are the mixing coefficients, and $\phi_j(\mathbf{x})$ are the basis functions of the network. Note that the mixing coefficients can be regarded as prior probabilities for the data points to have been generated from the jth component of the mixture. The likelihood function is given by

$$\mathcal{L} = \prod_n p(\mathbf{x}^n) \tag{5.62}$$

and is maximized both with respect to the mixing coefficients $P(j)$, and with respect to the parameters of the basis functions. This maximization can be performed by computing the derivatives of $\mathcal{L}$ with respect to the parameters and using these derivatives in standard non-linear optimization algorithms (Chapter 7). Alternatively, the parameters can be found by re-estimation procedures based on the EM (expectation–maximization) algorithm, described in Section 2.6.2.

Once the mixture model has been optimized, the mixing coefficients $P(j)$ can be discarded, and the basis functions then used in the radial basis function network in which the second-layer weights are found by supervised training. By retaining the mixing coefficients, however, the density model $p(\mathbf{x})$ in (5.61) can be used to assign error bars to the network outputs, based on the degree of *novelty* of the input vectors (Bishop, 1994b).

It is interesting to note that the K-means algorithm can be seen as a particular limit of the EM optimization of a Gaussian mixture model. From Section 2.6.2, the EM update formula for a basis function centre is given by

$$\mu_j^{\text{new}} = \frac{\sum_n P(j|\mathbf{x}^n)\mathbf{x}^n}{\sum_{n'} P(j|\mathbf{x}^{n'})} \tag{5.63}$$

where $P(j|\mathbf{x})$ is the posterior probability of basis function j, and is given in terms of the basis functions and the mixing coefficients, using Bayes' theorem, in the form

$$P(j|\mathbf{x}) = \frac{P(j)\phi_j(\mathbf{x})}{p(\mathbf{x})} \tag{5.64}$$

where $p(\mathbf{x})$ is given by (5.61). Suppose we consider spherical Gaussian basis functions having a common width parameter σ. Then the ratio of the posterior probabilities of two of the basis functions, for a particular data point $\mathbf{x}^n$, is given by

$$\frac{P(j|\mathbf{x}^n)}{P(k|\mathbf{x}^n)} = \exp\left\{ -\frac{\|\mathbf{x}^n - \boldsymbol{\mu}_j\|^2}{2\sigma^2} + \frac{\|\mathbf{x}^n - \boldsymbol{\mu}_k\|^2}{2\sigma^2} \right\} \frac{P(j)}{P(k)}. \tag{5.65}$$

If we now take the limit $\sigma \to 0$, we see that

$$\frac{P(j|\mathbf{x}^n)}{P(k|\mathbf{x}^n)} \to 0 \quad \text{if} \quad \|\mathbf{x}^n - \boldsymbol{\mu}_j\|^2 > \|\mathbf{x}^n - \boldsymbol{\mu}_k\|^2. \tag{5.66}$$

Thus, the probabilities for all of the kernels is zero except for the kernel whose centre vector $\boldsymbol{\mu}_k$ is closest to $\mathbf{x}^n$. In this limit, therefore, the EM update formula (5.63) reduces to the K-means update formula (5.59).

5.10 Supervised training

As we have already remarked, the use of unsupervised techniques to determine the basis function parameters is not in general an optimal procedure so far as the subsequent supervised training is concerned. The difficulty arises because the setting up of the basis functions using density estimation on the input data takes no account of the target labels associated with that data. In order to set the parameters of the basis functions to give optimal performance in computing the required network outputs we should include the target data in the training procedure. That is, we should perform supervised, rather than unsupervised, training.

The basis function parameters for regression can be found by treating the basis function centres and widths, along with the second-layer weights, as adaptive parameters to be determined by minimization of an error function. For the case of the sum-of-squares error (5.19), and spherical Gaussian basis functions (5.15), we obtain the following expressions for the derivatives of the error function with respect to the basis function parameters

$$\frac{\partial E}{\partial \sigma_j} = \sum_n \sum_k \{y_k(\mathbf{x}^n) - t_k^n\} w_{kj} \exp\left(-\frac{\|\mathbf{x}^n - \boldsymbol{\mu}_j\|^2}{2\sigma_j^2} \right) \frac{\|\mathbf{x}^n - \boldsymbol{\mu}_j\|^2}{\sigma_j^3} \tag{5.67}$$

$$\frac{\partial E}{\partial \mu_{ji}} = \sum_n \sum_k \{y_k(\mathbf{x}^n) - t_k^n\} w_{kj} \exp\left(-\frac{\|\mathbf{x}^n - \boldsymbol{\mu}_j\|^2}{2\sigma_j^2}\right) \frac{(x_i^n - \mu_{ji})}{\sigma_j^2} \quad (5.68)$$

where μ_{ji} denotes the ith component of $\boldsymbol{\mu}_j$. These expressions for the derivatives can then be used in conjunction with one of the standard optimization strategies discussed in Chapter 7.

The setting of the basis function parameters by supervised learning represents a non-linear optimization problem which will typically be computationally intensive and may be prone to finding local minima of the error function. However, provided the basis functions are reasonably well localized, any given input vector will only generate a significant activation in a small fraction of the basis functions, and so only these functions will be significantly updated in response to that input vector. Training procedures can therefore be speeded up significantly by identifying the relevant basis functions and thereby avoiding unnecessary computation. Techniques for finding these units efficiently are described by Omohundro (1987). Also, one of the unsupervised techniques described above can be used to initialize the basis function parameters, after which they can be 'fine tuned' using supervised procedures. However, one of the drawbacks of supervised training of the basis functions is that there is no guarantee that they will remain localized. Indeed, in numerical simulations it is found that a subset of the basis functions may evolve to have very broad responses (Moody and Darken, 1989). Also, some of the main advantages of radial basis function networks, namely fast two-stage training, and interpretability of the hidden unit representation, are lost if supervised training is adopted.

Exercises

5.1 ($\star$) Consider a radial basis function network represented by (5.14) with Gaussian basis functions having full covariance matrices of the form (5.16). Derive expressions for the elements of the Jacobian matrix given by

$$J_{ki} = \frac{\partial y_k}{\partial x_i}. \quad (5.69)$$

5.2 ($\star\star$) Consider a radial basis function network with spherical Gaussian basis of the form (5.15), network outputs given by (5.17) and a sum-of-squares error function of the form (5.19). Derive expressions for elements of the Hessian matrix given by

$$H_{rs} = \frac{\partial^2 E}{\partial w_r \partial w_s} \quad (5.70)$$

where w_r and w_s are any two parameters in the network. Hint: the results can conveniently be set out as six equations, one for each possible pair of weight types (basis function centres, basis function widths, or second-layer weights).

5.3 (⋆⋆) Consider the functional derivative (Appendix D) of the regularization functional given by (5.29), with respect to the function $y(\mathbf{x})$. By using successive integration by parts, and making use of the identities

$$\nabla(ab) = a\nabla b + b\nabla a \tag{5.71}$$

$$\nabla \cdot (a\nabla b) = a\nabla^2 b + \nabla b \cdot \nabla a \tag{5.72}$$

show that the operator $\widehat{P}P$ is given by

$$\widehat{P}Py = \sum_{l=0}^{\infty} \frac{\sigma^{2l}}{l!2^l}(-1)^l(\nabla^2)^l y. \tag{5.73}$$

It should be assumed that 'boundary' terms arising from the integration by parts can be neglected. Now find the Green's function $G(\|\mathbf{x} - \mathbf{x}'\|)$ of this operator, defined by (5.24), as follows. First introduce the multidimensional Fourier transform of G, in the form

$$G(\|\mathbf{x} - \mathbf{x}'\|) = \int \widetilde{G}(\mathbf{s}) \exp\left\{-i\mathbf{s}^{\mathrm{T}}(\mathbf{x} - \mathbf{x}')\right\} d\mathbf{s}. \tag{5.74}$$

By substituting (5.74) into (5.73), and using the following form for the Fourier transform of the delta function

$$\delta(\mathbf{x} - \mathbf{x}') = \frac{1}{(2\pi)^d} \int \exp\left\{-i\mathbf{s}^{\mathrm{T}}(\mathbf{x} - \mathbf{x}')\right\} d\mathbf{s} \tag{5.75}$$

where d is the dimensionality of $\mathbf{x}$ and $\mathbf{s}$, show that the Fourier transform of the Green's function is given by

$$\widetilde{G}(\mathbf{s}) = \exp\left\{-\frac{\sigma^2}{2}\|\mathbf{s}\|^2\right\}. \tag{5.76}$$

Now substitute this result into (5.74) and, by using the results given in Appendix B, show that the Green's function is given by

$$G(\|\mathbf{x} - \mathbf{x}'\|) = \frac{1}{(2\pi\sigma^2)^{d/2}} \exp\left\{-\frac{1}{2\sigma^2}\|\mathbf{x} - \mathbf{x}'\|^2\right\}. \tag{5.77}$$

5.4 (⋆) Consider general Gaussian basis functions of the form (5.16) and suppose that all of the basis functions in the network share a common covariance matrix $\boldsymbol{\Sigma}$. Show that the mapping represented by such a network is equivalent to that of a network of spherical Gaussian basis functions of the form (5.15), with a common variance parameter $\sigma^2 = 1$, provided the input vector $\mathbf{x}$ is first transformed by an appropriate linear transformation. By making use of the results of Appendix A, find expressions relating the transformed input vector $\widetilde{\mathbf{x}}$ and transformed basis function centres $\widetilde{\boldsymbol{\mu}}_j$ to the corresponding original vectors $\mathbf{x}$ and $\boldsymbol{\mu}_j$.

5.5 ($\star$) In a multi-layer perceptron a hidden unit has a constant activation for input vectors which lie on a hyperplanar surface in input space given by $\mathbf{w}^{\mathrm{T}}\mathbf{x} + w_0 = \text{const.}$, while for a radial basis function network, with basis functions given by (5.15), a hidden unit has constant activation on a hyperspherical surface defined by $\|\mathbf{x} - \boldsymbol{\mu}\|^2 = \text{const.}$ Show that, for suitable choices of the parameters, these surfaces coincide if the input vectors are normalized to unit length, so that $\|\mathbf{x}\| = 1$. Illustrate this equivalence geometrically for vectors in a three-dimensional input space.

5.6 ($\star\star\star$) Write a numerical implementation of the K-means clustering algorithm described in Section 5.9.3 using both the batch and on-line versions. Illustrate the operation of the algorithm by generating data sets in two dimensions from a mixture of Gaussian distributions, and plotting the data points together with the trajectories of the estimated means during the course of the algorithm. Investigate how the results depend on the value of K in relation to the number of Gaussian distributions, and how they depend on the variances of the distributions in relation to their separation. Study the performance of the on-line version of the algorithm for different values of the learning rate parameter η in (5.60), and compare the algorithm with the batch version.

5.7 ($\star\star\star$) Implement a radial basis function network for one input variable, one output variable and Gaussian basis functions having a common variance parameter σ^2. Generate a set of data by sampling the function $h(x) = 0.5 + 0.4\sin(2\pi x)$ with added Gaussian noise, and with x values taken randomly from a uniform distribution in the interval $(0, 1)$. Set the basis function centres to a random subset of the x values, and use singular value decomposition (Press *et al.*, 1992) to find the network weights which minimize the sum-of-squares error function. Investigate the dependence of the network function on the number of basis function centres and on the value of the variance parameter. Plot graphs of the form shown in Figure 5.3 to illustrate the results.

5.8 ($\star\star\star$) Write down an analytic expression for the regularized matrix $\mathbf{M}$ in (5.32) for the case of Gaussian basis functions given by (5.15). Extend the software implementation of the previous exercise to include this form of regularization. Consider the case in which the number of basis functions equals the number of data points and in which σ is equal to roughly twice the average separation of the input values. Investigate the effect of using different values for the regularization coefficient λ, and show that, if the value of λ is either too small or too large, then the resulting network mapping gives a poor approximation to the function $h(x)$ from which the data was generated.

6

ERROR FUNCTIONS

In previous chapters we have made use of the sum-of-squares error function, which was motivated primarily by analytical simplicity. There are many other possible choices of error function which can also be considered, depending on the particular application. In this chapter we shall describe a variety of different error functions and discuss their relative merits.

For regression problems we shall see that the basic goal is to model the conditional distribution of the output variables, conditioned on the input variables. This motivates the use of a sum-of-squares error function, and several important properties of this error function will be explored in some detail.

For classification problems the goal is to model the posterior probabilities of class membership, again conditioned on the input variables. Although the sum-of-squares error function can be used for classification (and can approximate the posterior probabilities) we shall see that there are other, more appropriate, error functions which can be considered. Generally speaking, Sections 6.1 to 6.4 are concerned with error functions for regression problems, while the remaining sections are concerned primarily with error functions for classification.

As we have stressed several times, the central goal in network training is not to memorize the training data, but rather to model the *underlying generator* of the data, so that the best possible predictions for the output vector $\mathbf{t}$ can be made when the trained network is subsequently presented with a new value for the input vector $\mathbf{x}$. The most general and complete description of the generator of the data is in terms of the probability density $p(\mathbf{x}, \mathbf{t})$ in the joint input-target space. For associative prediction problems of the kind we are considering, it is convenient to decompose the joint probability density into the product of the conditional density of the target data, conditioned on the input data, and the unconditional density of input data, so that

$$p(\mathbf{x}, \mathbf{t}) = p(\mathbf{t}|\mathbf{x})p(\mathbf{x}) \tag{6.1}$$

where $p(\mathbf{t}|\mathbf{x})$ denotes the probability density of $\mathbf{t}$ *given* that $\mathbf{x}$ takes a particular value, while $p(\mathbf{x})$ represents the unconditional density of $\mathbf{x}$ and is given by

$$p(\mathbf{x}) = \int p(\mathbf{t}, \mathbf{x}) \, d\mathbf{t}. \tag{6.2}$$

The density $p(\mathbf{x})$ plays an important role in several aspects of neural networks, including procedures for choosing the basis function parameters in a radial basis function network (Section 5.9). However, for the purposes of making predictions of $\mathbf{t}$ for new values of $\mathbf{x}$, it is the conditional density $p(\mathbf{t}|\mathbf{x})$ which we need to model.

Most of the error functions which will be considered in this chapter can be motivated from the principle of maximum likelihood (Section 2.2). For a set of training data $\{\mathbf{x}^n, \mathbf{t}^n\}$, the likelihood can be written as

$$\mathcal{L} = \prod_n p(\mathbf{x}^n, \mathbf{t}^n)$$

$$= \prod_n p(\mathbf{t}^n|\mathbf{x}^n)p(\mathbf{x}^n) \tag{6.3}$$

where we have assumed that each data point $(\mathbf{x}^n, \mathbf{t}^n)$ is drawn independently from the same distribution, and hence we can multiply the probabilities. Instead of maximizing the likelihood, it is generally more convenient to minimize the negative logarithm of the likelihood. These are equivalent procedures, since the negative logarithm is a monotonic function. We therefore minimize

$$E = -\ln \mathcal{L} = -\sum_n \ln p(\mathbf{t}^n|\mathbf{x}^n) - \sum_n \ln p(\mathbf{x}^n) \tag{6.4}$$

where E is called an *error function*. As we shall see, a feed-forward neural network can be regarded as a framework for modelling the conditional probability density $p(\mathbf{t}|\mathbf{x})$. The second term in (6.4) does not depend on the network parameters, and so represents an additive constant which can be dropped from the error function. We therefore have

$$E = -\sum_n \ln p(\mathbf{t}^n|\mathbf{x}^n). \tag{6.5}$$

Note that the error function takes the form of a sum over patterns of an error term for each pattern separately. This follows from the assumed independence of the data points under the given distribution. Different choices of error function arise from different assumptions about the form of the conditional distribution $p(\mathbf{t}|\mathbf{x})$. For interpolation problems, the targets $\mathbf{t}$ consist of continuous quantities whose values we are trying to predict, while for classification problems they represent labels defining class membership or, more generally, estimates of the probabilities of class membership.

6.1 Sum-of-squares error

Consider the case of c target variables t_k where $k = 1, \ldots, c$, and suppose that the distributions of the different target variables are independent, so that we can write

$$p(\mathbf{t}|\mathbf{x}) = \prod_{k=1}^{c} p(t_k|\mathbf{x}). \tag{6.6}$$

We shall further assume that the distribution of the target data is Gaussian. More specifically, we assume that the target variable t_k is given by some deterministic function of $\mathbf{x}$ with added Gaussian noise ϵ, so that

$$t_k = h_k(\mathbf{x}) + \epsilon_k. \tag{6.7}$$

We now assume that the errors ϵ_k have a normal distribution with zero mean, and standard a deviation σ which does not depend on $\mathbf{x}$ or on k. Thus, the distribution of ϵ_k is given by

$$p(\epsilon_k) = \frac{1}{(2\pi\sigma^2)^{1/2}} \exp\left(-\frac{\epsilon_k^2}{2\sigma^2}\right). \tag{6.8}$$

We now seek to model the functions $h_k(\mathbf{x})$ by a neural network with outputs $y_k(\mathbf{x}; \mathbf{w})$ where $\mathbf{w}$ is the set of weight parameters governing the neural network mapping. Using (6.7) and (6.8) we see that the probability distribution of target variables is given by

$$p(t_k|\mathbf{x}) = \frac{1}{(2\pi\sigma^2)^{1/2}} \exp\left(-\frac{\{y_k(\mathbf{x}; \mathbf{w}) - t_k\}^2}{2\sigma^2}\right) \tag{6.9}$$

where we have replaced the unknown function $h_k(\mathbf{x})$ by our model $y_k(\mathbf{x}; \mathbf{w})$. Together with (6.6) and (6.5) this leads to the following expression for the error function

$$E = \frac{1}{2\sigma^2} \sum_{n=1}^{N} \sum_{k=1}^{c} \{y_k(\mathbf{x}^n; \mathbf{w}) - t_k^n\}^2 + Nc\ln\sigma + \frac{Nc}{2}\ln(2\pi). \tag{6.10}$$

We note that, for the purposes of error minimization, the second and third terms on the right-hand side of (6.10) are independent of the weights $\mathbf{w}$ and so can be omitted. Similarly, the overall factor of $1/\sigma^2$ in the first term can also be omitted. We then finally obtain the familiar expression for the sum-of-squares error function

$$E = \frac{1}{2} \sum_{n=1}^{N} \sum_{k=1}^{c} \{y_k(\mathbf{x}^n; \mathbf{w}) - t_k^n\}^2 \tag{6.11}$$

$$= \frac{1}{2} \sum_{n=1}^{N} \|\mathbf{y}(\mathbf{x}^n; \mathbf{w}) - \mathbf{t}^n\|^2 . \tag{6.12}$$

Having found a set of values $\mathbf{w}^*$ for the weights which minimizes the error, the optimum value for σ can then by found by minimization of E in (6.10) with respect to σ. This minimization is easily performed analytically with the explicit, and intuitive, result

$$\sigma^2 = \frac{1}{Nc} \sum_{n=1}^{N} \sum_{k=1}^{c} \{y_k(\mathbf{x}^n; \mathbf{w}^*) - t_k^n\}^2 \tag{6.13}$$

which says that the optimal value of σ^2 is proportional to the residual value of the sum-of-squares error function at its minimum. We shall return to this result later.

We have derived the sum-of-squares error function from the principle of maximum likelihood on the assumption of Gaussian distributed target data. Of course the use of a sum-of-squares error does not *require* the target data to have a Gaussian distribution. Later in this chapter we shall consider the least-squares solution for an example problem with a strongly non-Gaussian distribution. However, as we shall see, if we use a sum-of-squares error, then the results we obtain cannot distinguish between the true distribution and any other distribution having the same mean and variance.

Note that it is sometimes convenient to assess the performance of networks using a different error function from that used to train them. For instance, in an interpolation problem the networks might be trained using a sum-of-squares error function of the form

$$E = \frac{1}{2} \sum_{n} \|\mathbf{y}(\mathbf{x}^n; \mathbf{w}) - \mathbf{t}^n\|^2 \tag{6.14}$$

where the sum runs over all N patterns in the training set, whereas for network testing it would be more convenient to use a root-mean-square (RMS) error of the form

$$E^{\text{RMS}} = \frac{\sum_{n} \|\mathbf{y}(\mathbf{x}^n; \mathbf{w}^*) - \mathbf{t}^n\|^2}{\sum_{n} \|\mathbf{t}^n - \overline{\mathbf{t}}\|^2} \tag{6.15}$$

where $\mathbf{w}^*$ denotes the weight vector of the trained network, and the sums now run over the N' patterns in the test set. Here $\overline{\mathbf{t}}$ is defined to be the average test set target vector

$$\overline{\mathbf{t}} = \frac{1}{N'} \sum_{n=1}^{N'} \mathbf{t}^n. \tag{6.16}$$

The RMS error (6.15) has the advantage, unlike (6.14), that its value does not grow with the size of the data set. If it has a value of unity then the network is predicting the test data 'in the mean' while a value of zero means perfect prediction of the test data.

6.1.1 Linear output units

The mapping function of a multi-layer perceptron or a radial basis function network can be written in the form

$$y_k(\mathbf{x}; \mathbf{w}) = g(a_k) \tag{6.17}$$

$$a_k = \sum_{j=0}^{M} w_{kj} z_j(\mathbf{x}; \widetilde{\mathbf{w}}) \tag{6.18}$$

where $g(\cdot)$ denotes the activation function of the output units, $\{w_{kj}\}$ denotes the set of weights (and biases) which connect directly to the output units, and $\widetilde{\mathbf{w}}$ denotes the set of all other weights (and biases) in the network. The derivative of the sum-of-squares error (6.11) with respect to a_k can be written as

$$\frac{\partial E}{\partial a_k} = \sum_n g'(a_k^n)(y_k^n - t_k^n). \tag{6.19}$$

If we choose the activation function for the output units to be linear, $g(a) = a$, then this derivative takes a particularly simple form

$$\frac{\partial E}{\partial a_k} = \sum_n (y_k^n - t_k^n). \tag{6.20}$$

This allows the minimization with respect to the weights $\{w_{kj}\}$ (with the weights $\widetilde{\mathbf{w}}$ held fixed) to be expressed as a linear optimization problem, which can be solved in closed form as discussed in Section 3.4.3. Here we shall follow a similar analysis, except that we shall find it convenient to make the bias parameters explicit and deal with them separately.

We first write the network mapping in the form

$$y_k = \sum_{j=1}^{M} w_{kj} z_j + w_{k0}. \tag{6.21}$$

Minimizing the sum-of-squares error (6.11) with respect to the biases first, we then obtain

$$\frac{\partial E}{\partial w_{k0}} = \sum_{n=1}^{N} \left\{ \sum_{j=1}^{c} w_{kj} z_j^n + w_{k0} - t_k^n \right\} = 0 \tag{6.22}$$

which can be solved explicitly for the biases to give

$$w_{k0} = \bar{t}_k - \sum_{j=1}^{M} w_{kj} \bar{z}_j \tag{6.23}$$

where we have defined the following average quantities:

$$\bar{t}_k = \frac{1}{N} \sum_{n=1}^{N} t_k^n, \qquad \bar{z}_j = \frac{1}{N} \sum_{n=1}^{N} z_j^n. \tag{6.24}$$

The result (6.23) shows that the role of the biases is to compensate for the difference between the averages (over the data set) of the target values, and the weighted sums of the averages of the hidden unit outputs.

If we back-substitute the expression (6.23) into the sum-of-squares error we obtain

$$E = \frac{1}{2} \sum_{n=1}^{N} \sum_{k=1}^{c} \left\{ \sum_{j=1}^{M} w_{kj} \tilde{z}_j^n - \tilde{t}_k^n \right\}^2 \tag{6.25}$$

where we have defined

$$\tilde{t}_k^n = t_k^n - \bar{t}_k, \qquad \tilde{z}_j^n = z_j^n - \bar{z}_j. \tag{6.26}$$

We can now minimize this error with respect to the output weights w_{kj} to give

$$\frac{\partial E}{\partial w_{kj}} = \sum_{n=1}^{N} \left\{ \sum_{j'=1}^{M} w_{kj'} \tilde{z}_{j'}^n - \tilde{t}_k^n \right\} \tilde{z}_j^n = 0. \tag{6.27}$$

It is convenient at this point to introduce a matrix notation so that $(\mathbf{T})_{nk} = \tilde{t}_k^n$, $(\mathbf{W})_{kj} = w_{kj}$ and $(\mathbf{Z})_{nj} = \tilde{z}_j^n$. We can then write (6.27) in the form

$$\mathbf{Z}^{\mathrm{T}} \mathbf{Z} \mathbf{W}^{\mathrm{T}} - \mathbf{Z}^{\mathrm{T}} \mathbf{T} = 0 \tag{6.28}$$

where $\mathbf{Z}^T$ denotes the transpose of $\mathbf{Z}$. We can write an explicit solution for the weight matrix as

$$\mathbf{W}^T = \mathbf{Z}^\dagger \mathbf{T} = 0 \tag{6.29}$$

where $\mathbf{Z}^\dagger$ is the pseudo-inverse of the matrix $\mathbf{Z}$ given by

$$\mathbf{Z}^\dagger \equiv (\mathbf{Z}^T \mathbf{Z})^{-1} \mathbf{Z}^T. \tag{6.30}$$

Here we have assumed that the matrix $(\mathbf{Z}^T \mathbf{Z})$ is non-singular. A more general discussion of the properties of the pseudo-inverse can be found in Section 3.4.3. For a single-layer network, this represents the optimal solution for the weights, which can therefore be calculated explicitly. In the present case, however, this expression for the weights depends on the activations of the hidden units which themselves depend on the weights $\widetilde{\mathbf{w}}$. Thus, as the weights $\widetilde{\mathbf{w}}$ change during learning, so the optimal values for the weights $\{w_{kj}\}$ will also change. Nevertheless, it is still possible to exploit the linear nature of the partial optimization with respect to the output unit weights as part of an overall strategy for error minimization, as discussed in Section 7.3.

6.1.2 *Linear sum rules*

The use of a sum-of-squares error function to determine the weights in a network with linear output units implies an interesting sum rule for the network outputs (Lowe and Webb, 1991). Suppose that the target patterns used to train the network satisfy an exact linear relation, so that for each pattern n we have

$$\mathbf{u}^T \mathbf{t}^n + u_0 = 0 \tag{6.31}$$

where $\mathbf{u}$ and u_0 are constants. We now show that, if the final-layer weights are determined by the optimal least-squares procedure outlined above, then the outputs of the network will satisfy the same linear constraint for arbitrary input patterns.

Summing over all patterns n in (6.31) we find that the average target vector $\bar{\mathbf{t}}$ satisfies the relation $u_0 = -\mathbf{u}^T \bar{\mathbf{t}}$ where the components of $\bar{\mathbf{t}}$ are given by (6.24). Thus, the linear relation (6.31) can be written in the form

$$\mathbf{u}^T \mathbf{t}^n = \mathbf{u}^T \bar{\mathbf{t}}. \tag{6.32}$$

The network outputs, given by (6.21), can be written in vector notation as

$$\mathbf{y} = \mathbf{Wz} + \mathbf{w}_0. \tag{6.33}$$

Similarly, the solution for the optimal biases given by (6.23) can be written as

$$\mathbf{w}_0 = \bar{\mathbf{t}} - \mathbf{W}\bar{\mathbf{z}}. \tag{6.34}$$

Now consider the scalar product of $\mathbf{y}$ with the vector $\mathbf{u}$, for an arbitrary input pattern. Using the optimal weights given by (6.29), together with (6.33) and (6.34), we have

$$\mathbf{u}^{\mathrm{T}}\mathbf{y} = \mathbf{u}^{\mathrm{T}}(\mathbf{w}_0 + \mathbf{W}\mathbf{z})$$

$$= \mathbf{u}^{\mathrm{T}}\bar{\mathbf{t}} + \mathbf{u}^{\mathrm{T}}\mathbf{T}^{\mathrm{T}}(\mathbf{Z}^{\dagger})^{\mathrm{T}}(\mathbf{z} - \bar{\mathbf{z}}) \tag{6.35}$$

where we have used the following property of matrix transposes $(\mathbf{AB})^{\mathrm{T}} = \mathbf{B}^{\mathrm{T}}\mathbf{A}^{\mathrm{T}}$. From (6.32), however, it follows that

$$(\mathbf{u}^{\mathrm{T}}\mathbf{T}^{\mathrm{T}})_n = \mathbf{u}^{\mathrm{T}}\tilde{\mathbf{t}}^n = \mathbf{u}^{\mathrm{T}}(\mathbf{t}^n - \bar{\mathbf{t}}) = 0 \tag{6.36}$$

where we have used the linear constraint (6.32). Combining (6.35) and (6.36) we obtain

$$\mathbf{u}^{\mathrm{T}}\mathbf{y} = \mathbf{u}^{\mathrm{T}}\bar{\mathbf{t}} \tag{6.37}$$

and so the network outputs exactly satisfy the same linear sum rule as the target data. We shall see an application of this result in the next section. More generally, if a set of targets satisfies several linear constraints simultaneously, then so will the outputs of the network (Exercise 6.3).

6.1.3 *Interpretation of network outputs*

We next derive an important result for the interpretation of the outputs of a network trained by minimizing a sum-of-squares error function. In particular, we will show that the outputs approximate the conditional averages of the target data. This is a central result which has several important consequences for practical applications of neural networks. An understanding of its implications can help to avoid some common mistakes, and lead to more effective use of network network techniques.

Consider the limit in which the size N of the training data set goes to infinity. In this limit we can replace the finite sum over patterns in the sum-of-squares error with an integral of the form

$$E = \lim_{N \to \infty} \frac{1}{2N} \sum_{n=1}^{N} \sum_{k} \{y_k(\mathbf{x}^n; \mathbf{w}) - t_k^n\}^2 \tag{6.38}$$

$$= \frac{1}{2} \sum_{k} \int\int \{y_k(\mathbf{x}; \mathbf{w}) - t_k\}^2 p(t_k, \mathbf{x}) \, dt_k \, d\mathbf{x} \tag{6.39}$$

where we have introduced an extra factor of $1/N$ into the definition of the sum-of-squares error in order to make the limiting process meaningful. We now factor the joint distributions $p(t_k, \mathbf{x})$ into the product of the unconditional density function for the input data $p(\mathbf{x})$, and the target data density conditional on the input vector $p(t_k|\mathbf{x})$, as in (6.1), to give

$$E = \frac{1}{2} \sum_k \iint \{y_k(\mathbf{x}; \mathbf{w}) - t_k\}^2 \, p(t_k|\mathbf{x})p(\mathbf{x}) \, dt_k \, d\mathbf{x}. \tag{6.40}$$

Next we define the following conditional averages of the target data

$$\langle t_k|\mathbf{x}\rangle \equiv \int t_k p(t_k|\mathbf{x}) \, dt_k \tag{6.41}$$

$$\langle t_k^2|\mathbf{x}\rangle \equiv \int t_k^2 p(t_k|\mathbf{x}) \, dt_k. \tag{6.42}$$

We now write the term in brackets in (6.40) in the form

$$\{y_k - t_k\}^2 = \{y_k - \langle t_k|\mathbf{x}\rangle + \langle t_k|\mathbf{x}\rangle - t_k\}^2 \tag{6.43}$$

$$= \{y_k - \langle t_k|\mathbf{x}\rangle\}^2 + 2\{y_k - \langle t_k|\mathbf{x}\rangle\}\{\langle t_k|\mathbf{x}\rangle - t_k\}$$

$$+ \{\langle t_k|\mathbf{x}\rangle - t_k\}^2 \tag{6.44}$$

Next we substitute (6.44) into (6.40) and make use of (6.41) and (6.42). The second term on the right-hand side of (6.44) then vanishes as a consequence of the integration over t_k. The sum-of-squares error can then be written in the form

$$E = \frac{1}{2} \sum_k \int \{y_k(\mathbf{x}; \mathbf{w}) - \langle t_k|\mathbf{x}\rangle\}^2 p(\mathbf{x}) \, d\mathbf{x}$$

$$+ \frac{1}{2} \sum_k \int \{\langle t_k^2|\mathbf{x}\rangle - \langle t_k|\mathbf{x}\rangle^2\} p(\mathbf{x}) \, d\mathbf{x}. \tag{6.45}$$

We now note that the second term in (6.45) is independent of the network mapping function $y_k(\mathbf{x}; \mathbf{w})$ and hence is independent of the network weights $\mathbf{w}$. For the purposes of determining the network weights by error minimization, this term can be neglected. Since the integrand in the first term in (6.45) is non-negative, the absolute minimum of the error function occurs when this first term vanishes, which corresponds to the following result for the network mapping

$$y_k(\mathbf{x}; \mathbf{w}^*) = \langle t_k|\mathbf{x}\rangle \tag{6.46}$$

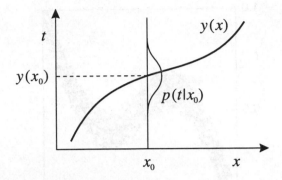

Figure 6.1. A schematic illustration of the property (6.46) that the network mapping which minimizes a sum-of-squares error function is given by the conditional average of the target data. Here we consider a mapping from a single input variable x to a single target variable t. At any given value x_0 of the input variable, the network output $y(x_0)$ is given by the average of t with respect to the distribution $p(t|x_0)$ of the target variable, for that value of x.

where $\mathbf{w}^*$ is the weight vector at the minimum of the error function. Equation (6.46) is a key result and says that the network mapping is given by the conditional average of the target data, in other words by the *regression* of t_k conditioned on $\mathbf{x}$. This result is illustrated schematically in Figure 6.1, and by a simple example in Figure 6.2.

Before discussing the consequences of this important result we note that it is dependent on three key assumptions. First, the data set must be sufficiently large that it approximates an infinite data set. Second, the network function $y_k(\mathbf{x}; \mathbf{w})$ must be sufficiently general that there exists a choice of parameters which makes the first term in (6.45) sufficiently small. This second requirement implies that the number of adaptive weights (or equivalently the number of hidden units) must be sufficiently large. It is important that the two limits of large data set and large number of weights must be approached in a coupled way in order to achieve the desired result. This important issue is discussed in Section 9.1 in the context of generalization and the trade-off between bias and variance. The third caveat is that the optimization of the network parameters is performed in such a way as to find the appropriate minimum of the cost function. Techniques for parameter optimization in neural networks are discussed in Chapter 7.

Note that the derivation of the result (6.46) did not depend on the choice of network architecture, or even whether we were using a neural network at all. It only required that the representation for the non-linear mapping be sufficiently general. The importance of neural networks is that they provide a practical framework for approximating arbitrary non-linear multivariate mappings, and can therefore in principle approximate the conditional average to arbitrary accuracy.

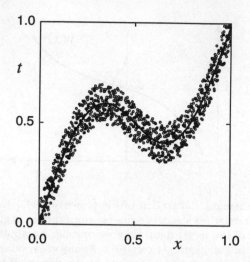

Figure 6.2. A simple example of a network mapping which approximates the conditional average of the target data (shown by the circles) generated from the function $t = x + 0.3\sin(2\pi x) + \epsilon$ where ϵ is a random variable drawn from a uniform distribution in the range $(-0.1, 0.1)$. The solid curve shows the result of training a multi-layer perceptron network with five hidden units using a sum-of-squares error function. The network approximates the conditional average of the target data, which gives a good representation of the function from which the data was generated.

We can easily see why the minimum of a sum-of-squares error is given by the average value of the target data by considering the simple error function

$$E(y) = (y - a)^2 + (y - b)^2 \tag{6.47}$$

where a and b are constants. Differentiation of $E(y)$ with respect to y shows that the minimum occurs at

$$y^{\min} = (a + b)/2 \tag{6.48}$$

In other words, the minimum is given by the average of the target data. The more general property (6.46) is simply the extension of this result to conditional averages.

We can also derive (6.46) in a more direct way as follows. If we take the sum-of-squares error in the form (6.39) and set the functional derivative (Appendix D) of E with respect to $y_k(\mathbf{x})$ to zero we obtain

$$\frac{\delta E}{\delta y_k(\mathbf{x})} = \int \{y_k(\mathbf{x}) - t_k\} p(t_k|\mathbf{x}) p(\mathbf{x}) \, dt_k = 0. \tag{6.49}$$

If we make use of (6.41) we then obtain (6.46) directly. The use of a functional derivative here is equivalent to the earlier assumption that the class of functions $y_k(\mathbf{x})$ is very general.

For many regression problems, the form of network mapping given by the conditional average (6.46) can be regarded as optimal. If the data is generated from a set of deterministic functions $h_k(\mathbf{x})$ with superimposed zero-mean noise ϵ_k then the target data is given by

$$t_k^n = h_k(\mathbf{x}^n) + \epsilon_k^n. \tag{6.50}$$

The network outputs, given by the conditional averages of the target data, then take the form

$$y_k(\mathbf{x}) = \langle t_k|\mathbf{x}\rangle = \langle h_k(\mathbf{x}) + \epsilon_k|\mathbf{x}\rangle = h_k(\mathbf{x}) \tag{6.51}$$

since $\langle \epsilon^n \rangle = 0$. Thus the network has averaged over the noise on the data and discovered the underlying deterministic function. Not all regression problems are as simple as this, however, as we shall see later.

Note that the first integral in (6.45) is weighted by the unconditional density $p(\mathbf{x})$. We therefore see that the network function $y_k(\mathbf{x})$ pays a significant penalty for departing from the conditional average $\langle t_k|\mathbf{x}\rangle$ in regions of input space where the density $p(\mathbf{x})$ of input data is high. In regions where $p(\mathbf{x})$ is small, there is little penalty if the network output is a poor approximation to the conditional average. This forms the basis of a simple procedure for assigning error bars to network predictions, based on an estimate of the density $p(\mathbf{x})$ (Bishop, 1994b).

If we return to (6.45) we see that the second term can be written in the form

$$\frac{1}{2} \sum_k \int \sigma_k^2(\mathbf{x}) p(\mathbf{x}) \, d\mathbf{x} \tag{6.52}$$

where $\sigma_k^2(\mathbf{x})$ represents the variance of the target data, as a function of $\mathbf{x}$, and is given by

$$\sigma_k^2(\mathbf{x}) = \langle t_k^2|\mathbf{x}\rangle - \langle t_k|\mathbf{x}\rangle^2 \tag{6.53}$$

$$= \langle (t_k - \langle t_k|\mathbf{x}\rangle)^2|\mathbf{x}\rangle \tag{6.54}$$

$$= \int \{t_k - \langle t_k|\mathbf{x}\rangle\}^2 p(t_k|\mathbf{x}) \, dt_k. \tag{6.55}$$

If the network mapping function is given by the conditional average (6.46), so that the first term in (6.45) vanishes, then the residual error is given by (6.52). The value of the residual error is therefore be a measure of the average variance of the target data. This is equivalent to the earlier result (6.13) obtained for a finite data set. It should be emphasized, however, that these are *biased* estimates of the variance, as discussed in Section 2.2, and so they should be treated with care in practical applications.

We originally derived the sum-of-squares error function from the principle of maximum likelihood by assuming that the distribution of the target data could be described by a Gaussian function with an **x**-dependent mean, and a single global variance parameter. As we noted earlier, the sum-of-squares error does not require that the distribution of target variables be Gaussian. If a sum-of-squares error is used, however, the quantities which can be determined are the **x**-dependent mean of the distribution (given by the outputs of the trained network) and a global averaged variance (given by the residual value of the error function at its minimum). Thus, the sum-of-squares error function cannot distinguish between the true distribution, and a Gaussian distribution having the same **x**-dependent mean and average variance.

6.1.4 *Outer product approximation for the Hessian*

In Section 4.10.2 we discussed a particular approximation to the Hessian matrix (the matrix of second derivatives of the error function with respect to the network weights) for a sum-of-squares error function. This approximation is based on a sum of outer products of first derivatives. Here we show that the approximation is exact in the infinite data limit, provided we are at the global minimum of the error function. Consider the error function in the form (6.45). Taking the second derivatives with respect to two weights w_r and w_s we obtain

$$\frac{\partial^2 E}{\partial w_r \partial w_s} = \sum_k \int \left\{ \frac{\partial y_k}{\partial w_r} \frac{\partial y_k}{\partial w_s} \right\} p(\mathbf{x}) \, d\mathbf{x}$$

$$+ \sum_k \int \left\{ \frac{\partial^2 y_k}{\partial w_r \partial w_s} (y_k - \langle t_k | \mathbf{x} \rangle) \right\} p(\mathbf{x}) \, d\mathbf{x}. \tag{6.56}$$

Using the result (6.46) that the outputs $y_k(\mathbf{x})$ of the trained network represent the conditional averages of the target data, we see that the second term in (6.56) vanishes. The Hessian is therefore given by an integral of terms involving only the products of first derivatives. For a finite data set, we can write this result in the form

$$\frac{\partial^2 E}{\partial w_r \partial w_s} = \frac{1}{N} \sum_{n=1}^{N} \sum_k \frac{\partial y_k^n}{\partial w_r} \frac{\partial y_k^n}{\partial w_s}. \tag{6.57}$$

6.1.5 *Inverse problems*

The fact that a least-squares solution approximates the conditional average of the target data has an important consequence when neural networks are used to solve *inverse* problems. Many potential applications of neural networks fall into this category. Examples include the analysis of spectral data, tomographic reconstruction, control of industrial plant, and robot kinematics. For such problems there exists a well-defined *forward* problem which is characterized by a *functional* (i.e. single-valued) mapping. Often this corresponds to causality in a physical system. In the case of spectral reconstruction, for example, the forward problem corresponds to the evaluation of the spectrum when the parameters (locations, widths and amplitudes) of the spectral lines are prescribed. In practical applications we generally have to solve the corresponding inverse problem in which the roles of input and output variables are interchanged. In the case of spectral analysis, this corresponds to the determination of the spectral line parameters from an observed spectrum. For inverse problems, the mapping can be often be multi-valued, with values of the inputs for which there are several valid values for the outputs. For example, there may be several choices for the spectral line parameters which give rise to the same observed spectrum. If a least-squares approach is applied to an inverse problem, it will approximate the conditional average of the target data, and this will frequently lead to extremely poor performance (since the average of several solutions is not necessarily itself a solution).

As a simple illustration of this problem, consider the data set shown earlier in Figure 6.2 where we saw how a network which approximates the conditional average of the target data gives a good representation of the underlying generator of the data. Suppose we now reverse the roles of the input and target variables. Figure 6.3 shows the result of training a network of the same type as before on the same data set, but with input and output variables interchanged. The network again tries to approximate the conditional average of the target data, but this time the conditional average gives a very poor description of the generator of the data. The problem can be traced to the intermediate values of x in Figure 6.3 where the target data is multi-valued. Predictions made by the trained network in this region can be very poor. The problem cannot be solved by modifying the network architecture or the training algorithm, since it is a fundamental consequence of using a sum-of-squares error function. For problems involving many input and output variables, where visualization of the data is not straightforward, it can be very difficult to ascertain whether there are regions of input space for which the target data is multi-valued. One approach to such problems is to go beyond the Gaussian description of the distribution of target variables, and to find a more general model for the conditional density, as will be discussed in Section 6.4.

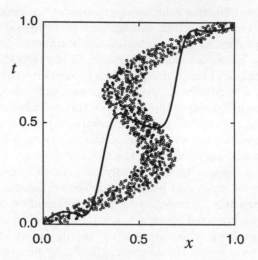

Figure 6.3. An illustration of the problem which can arise when a least-squares approach is applied to an inverse problem. This shows the same data set as in Figure 6.2 but with the roles of input and output variables interchanged. The solid curve shows the result of training the same neural network as in Figure 6.2, again using a sum-of-squares error. This time the network gives a very poor fit to the data, as it again tries to represent the conditional average of the target values.

6.2 Minkowski error

We have derived the sum-of-squares error function from the principle of maximum likelihood on the assumption of a Gaussian distribution of target data. We can obtain more general error functions by considering a generalization of the Gaussian distribution of the form

$$p(\epsilon) = \frac{R\beta^{1/R}}{2\Gamma(1/R)} \exp\left(-\beta|\epsilon|^R\right) \tag{6.58}$$

where $\Gamma(a)$ is the gamma function (defined on page 28), the parameter β controls the variance of the distribution, and the pre-factor in (6.58) ensures that $\int p(\epsilon)\,d\epsilon = 1$. For the case of $R = 2$ this distribution reduces to a Gaussian. We now consider the negative log-likelihood of a data set, given by (6.5) and (6.6), under the distribution (6.58). Omitting irrelevant constants, we obtain an error function of the form

$$E = \sum_n \sum_{k=1}^c |y_k(\mathbf{x}^n; \mathbf{w}) - t_k^n|^R \tag{6.59}$$

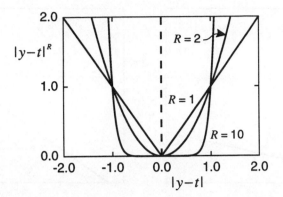

Figure 6.4. Plot of the function $|y - t|^R$ against $|y - t|$ for various values of R. This function forms the basis for the definition of the Minkowski-R error measure.

called the *Minkowski-R* error. This reduces to the usual sum-of-squares error when $R = 2$. For the case of $R = 1$, the distribution function (6.58) is a *Laplacian*, and the corresponding Minkowski-R measure (6.59) is called the *city block* metric (because the distance between two points on a plane measured by this metric is equal to the Euclidean distance covered by moving between the two points along segments of lines parallel to the axes, as if moving along blocks in a city). More generally, the distance metric $|y - t|^R$ is known as the L_R norm. The function $|y - t|^R$ is plotted against $|y - t|$ for various values of R in Figure 6.4.

The derivatives of the Minkowski-R error function with respect to the weights in the network are given by

$$\frac{\partial E}{\partial w_{ji}} = \sum_n \sum_k |y_k(\mathbf{x}^n; \mathbf{w}) - t_k^n|^{R-1} \text{sign}(y_k(\mathbf{x}^n; \mathbf{w}) - t_k^n) \frac{\partial y_k^n}{\partial w_{ji}}. \qquad (6.60)$$

These derivatives can be evaluated using the standard back-propagation procedure, discussed in Section 4.8. Examples of the application of the Minkowski-R error to networks trained using back-propagation are given in Hanson and Burr (1988) and Burrascano (1991).

One of the potential difficulties of the standard sum-of-squares error is that it receives the largest contributions from the points which have the largest errors. If there are long tails on the distributions then the solution can be dominated by a very small number of points called *outliers* which have particularly large errors. This is illustrated by a simple example in Figure 6.5.

A similarly severe problem can also arise from incorrectly labelled data. For instance, one single data point for which the target value has been incorrectly labelled by a large amount can completely invalidate the least-squares solution.

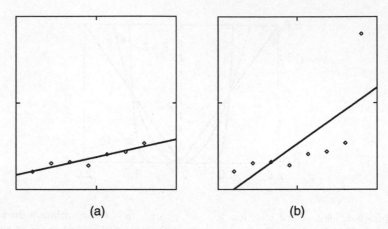

(a)   (b)

Figure 6.5. Example of fitting a linear polynomial through a set of noisy data
points by minimizing a sum-of-squares error. In (a) the line gives a good representation of the systematic aspects of the data. In (b) a single extra data
point has been added which lies well away from the other data points, showing
how it dominates the fitting of the line.

Techniques which attempt to solve this problem are referred to as *robust statistics*, and a review in the context of conventional statistical methods can be found
in Huber (1981). The use of the Minkowski error with an R value less than 2
reduces the sensitivity to outliers. For instance, with $R = 1$, the minimum error
solution computes the conditional *median* of the data, rather than the conditional mean (Exercise 6.5). The reason for this can be seen by considering the
simple error

$$E(y) = \sum_n |y - t^n|. \tag{6.61}$$

Minimizing $E(y)$ with respect to y gives

$$\sum_n \text{sign}(y - t^n) = 0 \tag{6.62}$$

which is satisfied when y is the median of the points $\{t^n\}$ (i.e. the value for which
the same number of points t^n have values greater than y as have values less than
y). If one of the t^n is taken to some very large value, this has no effect on the
solution for y.

6.3 Input-dependent variance

So far we have assumed that the variance of the target data can be described by a single global parameter σ. In many practical applications, this will be a poor assumption, and we now discuss more general models for the target data distribution. The sum-of-squares error is easily extended to allow each output to be described by its own variance parameter σ_k. More generally, we might wish to determine how the variance of the data depends on the input vector $\mathbf{x}$ (Nix and Weigend, 1994). This can be done by adopting a more general description for the conditional distribution of the target data, and then writing down the negative log-likelihood in order to obtain a suitable error function. Thus, we write the conditional distribution of the target variables in the form

$$p(t_k|\mathbf{x}) = \frac{1}{(2\pi)^{1/2}\sigma_k(\mathbf{x})} \exp\left(-\frac{\{y_k(\mathbf{x};\mathbf{w}) - t_k\}^2}{2\sigma_k^2(\mathbf{x})}\right). \tag{6.63}$$

Forming the negative logarithm of the likelihood function as before, and omitting additive constants, we obtain

$$E = \sum_{n=1}^{N}\sum_{k}\left(\ln\sigma_k(\mathbf{x}^n) + \frac{\{y_k(\mathbf{x}^n) - t_k^n\}^2}{2\sigma_k^2(\mathbf{x}^n)}\right). \tag{6.64}$$

If we now multiply by $1/N$ as before, and take the infinite-data limit, we obtain the error function in the form

$$E = \sum_{k}\iint\left(\ln\sigma_k(\mathbf{x}) + \frac{\{y_k(\mathbf{x}) - t_k\}^2}{2\sigma_k^2(\mathbf{x})}\right)p(t_k|\mathbf{x})p(\mathbf{x})\,dt_k\,d\mathbf{x}. \tag{6.65}$$

The functions $\sigma_k(\mathbf{x})$ can be modelled by adding further outputs to the neural network. We shall not consider this approach further, as it is a special case of a much more general technique for modelling the full conditional distribution, which will be discussed shortly.

An alternative approach to determining an input-dependent variance (Satchwell, 1994) is based on the result (6.46) that the network mapping which minimizes a sum-of-squares error is given by the conditional expectation of the target data. First a network is trained in the usual way by minimizing a sum-of-squares error in which the t_k^n form the targets. The outputs of this network, when presented with the training data input vectors $\mathbf{x}^n$, correspond to the conditional averages of the target data. These averages are subtracted from the target values and the results are then squared and used as targets for a second network which is also trained using a sum-of-squares error function. The outputs of this network then represent the conditional averages of $\{t_k - \langle t_k|\mathbf{x}\rangle\}^2$ and thus approximate the variances $\sigma_k^2(\mathbf{x})$ given by (6.55).

This procedure can be justified directly as follows. Consider the infinite data limit again, for which we can write the error function in the form (6.65). If we again assume that the functions $y_k(\mathbf{x})$ and $\sigma_k(\mathbf{x})$ have unlimited flexibility then we can first minimize E with respect to the y_k by functional differentiation to give

$$\frac{\delta E}{\delta y_k(\mathbf{x})} = 0 = p(\mathbf{x}) \int \frac{\{y_k(\mathbf{x}) - t_k\}}{\sigma_k^2(\mathbf{x})} p(t_k|\mathbf{x}) \, dt_k \qquad (6.66)$$

which, after some rearrangement, gives the standard result

$$y_k(\mathbf{x}) = \langle t_k|\mathbf{x} \rangle \qquad (6.67)$$

as before. We can similarly minimize E independently with respect to the functions $\sigma_k(\mathbf{x})$ to give

$$\frac{\delta E}{\delta \sigma_k(\mathbf{x})} = 0 = p(\mathbf{x}) \int \left(\frac{1}{\sigma_k(\mathbf{x})} - \frac{\{y_k(\mathbf{x}) - t_k\}^2}{\sigma_k(\mathbf{x})^3} \right) p(t_k|\mathbf{x}) \, dt_k \qquad (6.68)$$

which is easily solved for $\sigma_k^2(\mathbf{x})$ to give

$$\sigma_k^2(\mathbf{x}) = \langle \{t_k - \langle t_k|\mathbf{x} \rangle\}^2 |\mathbf{x} \rangle \qquad (6.69)$$

where we have used (6.67). We can then interpret (6.69) in terms of the two-stage two-network approach described above. This technique is simple and can make use of standard neural network software. Its principal limitation is that it still assumes a Gaussian form for the distribution function (since it makes use only of the second-order statistics of the target data).

Since these approaches are based on maximum likelihood, they will give a biased estimate of the variances as discussed above, and so will tend to underestimate the true variance. In extreme cases, such methods can discover pathological solutions in which the variance goes to zero, corresponding to an infinite likelihood, as discussed in the context of unconditional density estimation in Section 2.5.5.

6.4 Modelling conditional distributions

We can view the basic goal in training a feed-forward neural network as that of modelling the statistical properties of the generator of the data, expressed in terms of a conditional distribution function $p(\mathbf{t}|\mathbf{x})$. For the sum-of-squares error function, this corresponds to modelling the conditional distribution of the target data in terms of a Gaussian distribution with a global variance parameter and an $\mathbf{x}$-dependent mean. However, if the data has a complex structure, as for example in Figure 6.3, then this particular choice of distribution can lead to a very poor representation of the data. We therefore seek a general framework for modelling conditional probability distributions.

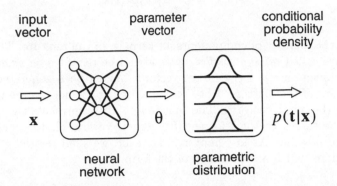

input vector

parameter vector

conditional probability density

x $\qquad$ θ $\qquad$ $p(\mathbf{t}|\mathbf{x})$

neural network

parametric distribution

Figure 6.6. We can represent general conditional probability densities $p(\mathbf{t}|\mathbf{x})$ by considering a parametric model for the distribution of **t** whose parameters are determined by the outputs of a neural network which takes **x** as its input vector.

In Chapter 2 we discussed a number of parametric techniques for modelling unconditional distributions. Suppose we use one of these techniques to model the distribution $p(\mathbf{t}|\boldsymbol{\theta})$ of target variables **t**, where $\boldsymbol{\theta}$ denotes the set of parameters which govern the model distribution. If we allow the parameters $\boldsymbol{\theta}$ to be functions of the input vector **x**, then we can model conditional distributions. We can achieve this by letting the components of $\boldsymbol{\theta}(\mathbf{x})$ be given by the outputs of a feed-forward neural network which takes **x** as input. This leads to the combined density model and neural network structure shown in Figure 6.6. Provided we consider a sufficiently general density model, and a sufficiently flexible network, we have a framework for approximating arbitrary conditional distributions.

For different choices of the parametric model, we obtain different representations for the conditional densities. For example, a single Gaussian model for $p(\mathbf{t}|\boldsymbol{\theta})$ corresponds to the procedure described above in Section 6.3. Another possibility is to use a linear combination of a fixed set of kernel functions. In this case the outputs of the network represent the coefficients in the linear combination (Bishop and Legleye, 1995), and we must ensure that the coefficients are positive and sum to one in order to preserve the positivity and normalization of the conditional density. We do not discuss this approach further as it is a special case of the more general technique which we consider next.

A powerful, general framework for modelling unconditional distributions, based on the use of *mixture models*, was introduced in Section 2.6. Mixture models represent a distribution in terms of a linear combination of adaptive kernel functions. If we apply this technique to the problem of modelling conditional distributions we have

$$p(\mathbf{t}|\mathbf{x}) = \sum_{j=1}^{M} \alpha_j(\mathbf{x})\phi_j(\mathbf{t}|\mathbf{x}) \tag{6.70}$$

where M is the number of components, or kernels, in the mixture. The parameters $\alpha_j(\mathbf{x})$ are called *mixing coefficients*, and can be regarded as *prior* probabilities (conditioned on $\mathbf{x}$) of the target vector $\mathbf{t}$ having been generated from the jth component of the mixture. Note that the mixing coefficients are taken to be functions of the input vector $\mathbf{x}$. The function $\phi_j(\mathbf{t}|\mathbf{x})$ represents the conditional density of the target vector $\mathbf{t}$ for the jth kernel. Various choices for the kernel functions are possible. As in Chapter 2, however, we shall restrict attention to kernel functions which are Gaussian of the form

$$\phi_j(\mathbf{t}|\mathbf{x}) = \frac{1}{(2\pi)^{c/2}\sigma_j^c(\mathbf{x})} \exp\left\{ -\frac{\|\mathbf{t} - \boldsymbol{\mu}_j(\mathbf{x})\|^2}{2\sigma_j^2(\mathbf{x})} \right\} \tag{6.71}$$

where the vector $\boldsymbol{\mu}_j(\mathbf{x})$ represents the centre of the jth kernel, with components μ_{jk}, and c is the dimensionality of $\mathbf{t}$. In (6.71) we have assumed that the components of the output vector are statistically independent within each of the kernel functions, and can be described by a common variance $\sigma_j^2(\mathbf{x})$. This assumption can be relaxed in a straightforward way by introducing full covariance matrices for each Gaussian kernel, at the expense of a more complex formalism. In principle, however, such a complication is not necessary, since a Gaussian mixture model, with kernels given by (6.71), can approximate any given density function to arbitrary accuracy, provided the mixing coefficients and the Gaussian parameters (means and variances) are correctly chosen (McLachlan and Basford, 1988). Thus, the representation given by (6.70) and (6.71) is completely general. In particular, it does not assume that the components of $\mathbf{t}$ are statistically independent, in contrast to the single-Gaussian representation used in (6.6) and (6.9) to derive the sum-of-squares error.

For any given value of $\mathbf{x}$, the mixture model (6.70) provides a general formalism for modelling an arbitrary conditional density function $p(\mathbf{t}|\mathbf{x})$. We now take the various parameters of the mixture model, namely the mixing coefficients $\alpha_j(\mathbf{x})$, the means $\boldsymbol{\mu}_j(\mathbf{x})$ and the variances $\sigma_j^2(\mathbf{x})$, to be governed by the outputs of a conventional neural network which takes $\mathbf{x}$ as its input. This technique was introduced in the form of the *mixture-of-experts* model (Jacobs *et al.*, 1991) described in Section 9.7, and has since been discussed by other authors (Bishop, 1994a; Liu, 1994; Neuneier *et al.*, 1994). By choosing a mixture model with a sufficient number of kernel functions, and a neural network with a sufficient number of hidden units, this model can approximate as closely as desired any conditional density function $p(\mathbf{t}|\mathbf{x})$. The original motivation for the mixture-of-experts model was to provide a mechanism for partitioning the solution to a problem between several networks. This was achieved by using a separate network to determine the parameters of each kernel function, with a further network to determine the mixing coefficients. For some applications this modular approach offers a number of advantages, and is discussed further in Section 9.7.

The neural network in Figure 6.6 can be any standard feed-forward network structure with universal approximation capabilities. Here we consider a multi-layer perceptron, with a single hidden layer of sigmoidal units and an output layer of linear units. For M components in the mixture model (6.70), the network will have M outputs denoted by z_j^α which determine the mixing coefficients, M outputs denoted by z_j^σ which determine the kernel widths σ_j, and $M \times c$ outputs denoted by z_{jk}^μ which determine the components μ_{jk} of the kernel centres $\boldsymbol{\mu}_j$. The total number of network outputs is given by $(c+2) \times M$, as compared with the usual c outputs for a network used with a sum-of-squares error function.

In order to ensure that the mixing coefficients $\alpha_j(\mathbf{x})$ can be interpreted as probabilities, they must satisfy the constraints

$$\sum_{j=1}^{M} \alpha_j(\mathbf{x}) = 1 \tag{6.72}$$

$$0 \leq \alpha_j(\mathbf{x}) \leq 1. \tag{6.73}$$

The first constraint also ensures that the distribution is correctly normalized, so that $\int p(\mathbf{t}|\mathbf{x})\, d\mathbf{t} = 1$. These constraints can be satisfied by choosing $\alpha_j(\mathbf{x})$ to be related to the corresponding networks outputs by a *softmax* function (Bridle, 1990; Jacobs *et al.*, 1991)

$$\alpha_j = \frac{\exp(z_j^\alpha)}{\sum_{l=1}^{M} \exp(z_l^\alpha)}. \tag{6.74}$$

We shall encounter the softmax function again in the next section when we discuss error functions for classification problems.

The variances σ_j represent *scale* parameters and so it is convenient to represent them in terms of the exponentials of the corresponding network outputs

$$\sigma_j = \exp(z_j^\sigma). \tag{6.75}$$

In a Bayesian framework (Exercise 10.13) this would correspond to the choice of a *non-informative prior*, assuming the corresponding network outputs z_j^σ had uniform probability distributions (Jacobs *et al.*, 1991; Nowlan and Hinton, 1992). This representation also has the additional benefit of helping to avoid pathological configurations in which one or more of the variances goes to zero, since this would require the corresponding $z_j^\sigma \to -\infty$. The possibility of such results is discussed in Section 2.6.1 in the context of mixture models for unconditional density estimation.

The centres μ_j represent *location* parameters, and again the notion of a non-informative prior (Exercise 10.12) suggests that these be represented directly by the network outputs

$$\mu_{jk} = z_{jk}^{\mu}. \tag{6.76}$$

As before, we can construct an error function from the likelihood by using (6.5) to give

$$E = -\sum_n \ln \left\{ \sum_{j=1}^{M} \alpha_j(\mathbf{x}^n) \phi_j(\mathbf{t}^n|\mathbf{x}^n) \right\} \tag{6.77}$$

with $\phi_j(\mathbf{t}|\mathbf{x})$ given by (6.71). The minimization of this error function with respect to the parameters of the neural network leads to a model for the conditional density of the target data. From this density function, any desired statistic involving the output variables can in principle be computed.

In order to minimize the error function, we need to calculate the derivatives of the error E with respect to the weights in the neural network. These can be evaluated by using the standard back-propagation procedure, provided we obtain suitable expressions for the derivatives of the error with respect to the outputs of the network. Since the error function (6.77) is composed of a sum of terms $E = \sum_n E^n$, one for each pattern, we can consider the derivatives $\delta_k^n = \partial E^n/\partial z_k$ for a particular pattern n and then find the derivatives of E by summing over all patterns. Note that, since the network output units have linear activation functions $g(a) = a$, the quantities δ_k^n can also be written as $\partial E^n/\partial a_k$, and so are equivalent to the 'errors' introduced in the discussion of error back-propagation in Section 4.8. These errors can be back-propagated through the network to find the derivatives with respect to the network weights.

We have already remarked that the ϕ_j can be regarded as conditional density functions, with prior probabilities α_j. As with the mixture models discussed in Section 2.6, it is convenient to introduce the corresponding *posterior* probabilities, which we obtain using Bayes' theorem,

$$\pi_j(\mathbf{x}, \mathbf{t}) = \frac{\alpha_j \phi_j}{\sum_{l=1}^{M} \alpha_l \phi_l}, \tag{6.78}$$

as this leads to some simplification of the subsequent analysis. Note that, from (6.78), the posterior probabilities sum to unity:

$$\sum_{j=1}^{M} \pi_j = 1. \tag{6.79}$$

Consider first the derivatives of E^n with respect to those network outputs which correspond to the mixing coefficients α_j. Using (6.77) and (6.78) we obtain

$$\frac{\partial E^n}{\partial \alpha_k} = -\frac{\pi_k}{\alpha_k}. \tag{6.80}$$

We now note that, as a result of the softmax transformation (6.74), the value of α_k depends on all of the network outputs which contribute to the mixing coefficients, and so differentiating (6.74) we have

$$\frac{\partial \alpha_k}{\partial z_j^\alpha} = \delta_{jk}\alpha_k - \alpha_j\alpha_k. \tag{6.81}$$

From the chain rule we have

$$\frac{\partial E^n}{\partial z_j^\alpha} = \sum_k \frac{\partial E^n}{\partial \alpha_k}\frac{\partial \alpha_k}{\partial z_j^\alpha}. \tag{6.82}$$

Combining (6.80), (6.81) and (6.82) we then obtain

$$\frac{\partial E^n}{\partial z_j^\alpha} = \alpha_j - \pi_j \tag{6.83}$$

where we have used (6.79).

For the derivatives corresponding to the σ_j parameters we make use of (6.77) and (6.78), together with (6.71), to give

$$\frac{\partial E^n}{\partial \sigma_j} = -\pi_j \left\{ \frac{\|\mathbf{t} - \boldsymbol{\mu}_j\|^2}{\sigma_j^3} - \frac{c}{\sigma_j} \right\}. \tag{6.84}$$

Using (6.75) we have

$$\frac{\partial \sigma_j}{\partial z_j^\sigma} = \sigma_j. \tag{6.85}$$

Combining these together we then obtain

$$\frac{\partial E^n}{\partial z_j^\sigma} = -\pi_j \left\{ \frac{\|\mathbf{t} - \boldsymbol{\mu}_j\|^2}{\sigma_j^2} - c \right\}. \tag{6.86}$$

Finally, since the parameters μ_{jk} are given directly by the z_{jk}^μ network outputs, we have, using (6.77) and (6.78), together with (6.71),

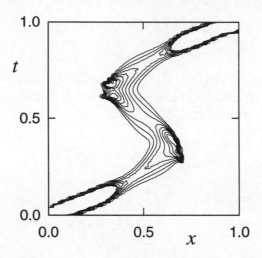

Figure 6.7. Plot of the contours of the conditional probability density of the target data obtained from a multi-layer perceptron network trained using the same data as in Figure 6.3, but using the error function (6.77). The network has three Gaussian kernel functions, and uses a two-layer multi-layer perceptron with five 'tanh' sigmoidal units in the hidden layer, and nine outputs.

$$\frac{\partial E^n}{\partial z_{jk}^\mu} = \pi_j \left\{ \frac{\mu_{jk} - t_k}{\sigma_j^2} \right\}. \tag{6.87}$$

An example of the application of these techniques to the estimation of conditional densities is given in Figure 6.7, which shows the contours of conditional density corresponding to the data set shown in Figure 6.3.

The outputs of the neural network, and hence the parameters in the mixture model, are necessarily continuous single-valued functions of the input variables. However, the model is able to produce a conditional density which is unimodal for some values of x and trimodal for other values, as in Figure 6.7, by modulating the amplitudes of the mixing components, or priors, $\alpha_j(\mathbf{x})$. This can be seen in Figure 6.8 which shows plots of the three priors $\alpha_j(x)$ as functions of x. It can be seen that for $x = 0.2$ and $x = 0.8$ only one of the three kernels has a non-zero prior probability. At $x = 0.5$, however, all three kernels have significant priors.

Once the network has been trained it can predict the conditional density function of the target data for any given value of the input vector. This conditional density represents a complete description of the generator of the data, so far as the problem of predicting the value of the output vector is concerned. From this density function we can calculate more specific quantities which may be of interest in different applications. One of the simplest of these is the mean, corresponding to the conditional average of the target data, given by

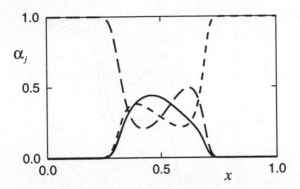

Figure 6.8. Plot of the priors $\alpha_j(x)$ as a function of x for the three kernel functions from the network used to plot Figure 6.7. At both small and large values of x, where the conditional probability density of the target data is unimodal, only one of the kernels has a prior probability which differs significantly from zero. At intermediate values of x, where the conditional density is trimodal, the three kernels have comparable priors.

$$\langle \mathbf{t}|\mathbf{x} \rangle = \int \mathbf{t}p(\mathbf{t}|\mathbf{x})\, d\mathbf{t} \tag{6.88}$$

$$= \sum_j \alpha_j(\mathbf{x}) \int \mathbf{t}\phi_j(\mathbf{t}|\mathbf{x})\, d\mathbf{t} \tag{6.89}$$

$$= \sum_j \alpha_j(\mathbf{x})\boldsymbol{\mu}_j(\mathbf{x}) \tag{6.90}$$

where we have used (6.70) and (6.71). This is equivalent to the function computed by a standard network trained by least squares, and so this network can reproduce the conventional least-squares result as a special case. We can likewise evaluate the variance of the density function about the conditional average, to give

$$s^2(\mathbf{x}) = \left\langle \|\mathbf{t} - \langle \mathbf{t}|\mathbf{x} \rangle\|^2 \,\big|\, \mathbf{x} \right\rangle \tag{6.91}$$

$$= \sum_j \alpha_j(\mathbf{x}) \left\{ \sigma_j(\mathbf{x})^2 + \left\| \boldsymbol{\mu}_j(\mathbf{x}) - \sum_l \alpha_l(\mathbf{x})\boldsymbol{\mu}_l(\mathbf{x}) \right\|^2 \right\} \tag{6.92}$$

where we have used (6.70), (6.71) and (6.90). This is more general than the corresponding least-squares result since this variance is allowed to be a general function of $\mathbf{x}$. Similar results can be obtained for other moments of the condi-

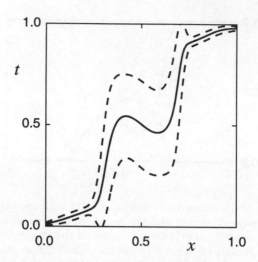

Figure 6.9. This shows a plot of $\langle t|x \rangle$ against x (solid curve) calculated from the conditional density in Figure 6.7 using (6.90), together with corresponding plots of $\langle t|x \rangle \pm s(x)$ (dashed curves) obtained using (6.92).

tional distribution. Plots of the mean and variance, obtained from the conditional distribution in Figure 6.7, are shown in Figure 6.9.

For some applications, the distribution of the target data will consist of a limited number of distinct branches, as is the case for the data shown in Figure 6.3. In such cases we may be interested in finding an output value corresponding to just one of the branches (as would be the case in many control applications for example). The most probable branch is the one which has the greatest associated 'probability mass'. Since each component of the mixture model is normalized, $\int \phi_j(\mathbf{t}|\mathbf{x})\,d\mathbf{t} = 1$, the most probable branch of the solution, assuming the components are well separated and have negligible overlap, is given by

$$\arg \max_j \{\alpha_j(\mathbf{x})\}. \tag{6.93}$$

In the mixture-of-experts model (Jacobs *et al.*, 1991) this corresponds to selecting the output of one of the component network modules. The required value of $\mathbf{t}$ is then given by the corresponding centre $\boldsymbol{\mu}_j$. Figure 6.10 shows the most probable branch of the solution, as a function of x, for the same network as used to plot Figure 6.7.

Again, one of the limitations of using maximum likelihood techniques to determine variance-like quantities such as the σ_j, is that it is biased (Section 2.2). In particular, it tends to underestimate the variance in regions where there is limited data.

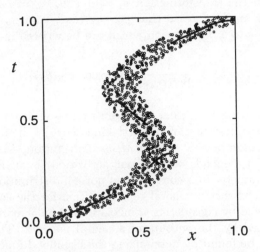

Figure 6.10. Plot of the central value of the most probable kernel as a function of x from the network used to plot Figure 6.7. This gives a discontinuous functional mapping from x to t which at every value of x lies well inside a region of significant probability density. The diagram should be compared with the corresponding continuous mapping in Figure 6.3 obtained from standard least squares.

6.4.1 *Periodic variables*

So far we have considered the problem of 'regression' for variables which live on the real axis $(-\infty, \infty)$. However, a number of applications involve angle-like output variables which live on a finite interval, usually $(0, 2\pi)$ and which are intrinsically periodic. Due to the periodicity, the techniques described so far cannot be applied directly. Here we show how the general framework discussed above can be extended to estimate the conditional distribution $p(\theta|\mathbf{x})$ of a periodic variable θ, conditional on an input vector $\mathbf{x}$ (Bishop and Legleye, 1995).

The approach is again based on a mixture of kernel functions , but in this case the kernel functions themselves are periodic, thereby ensuring that the overall density function will be periodic. To motivate this approach, consider the problem of modelling the distribution of a velocity vector $\mathbf{v}$ in two dimensions. Since $\mathbf{v}$ lives in a Euclidean plane, we can model the density function $p(\mathbf{v})$ using a mixture of conventional spherical Gaussian kernels, where each kernel has the form

$$\phi(v_x, v_y) = \frac{1}{2\pi\sigma^2} \exp\left\{ -\frac{(v_x - \mu_x)^2}{2\sigma^2} - \frac{(v_y - \mu_y)^2}{2\sigma^2} \right\} \tag{6.94}$$

where (v_x, v_y) are the Cartesian components of $\mathbf{v}$, and (μ_x, μ_y) are the components of the centre $\boldsymbol{\mu}$ of the kernel. From this we can extract the conditional distribution of the polar angle θ of the vector $\mathbf{v}$, given a value for $v = \|\mathbf{v}\|$. This is easily done with the transformation $v_x = v\cos\theta$, $v_y = v\sin\theta$, and defining θ_0 to be the polar angle of $\boldsymbol{\mu}$, so that $\mu_x = \mu\cos\theta_0$ and $\mu_y = \mu\sin\theta_0$, where $\mu = \|\boldsymbol{\mu}\|$. This leads to a distribution which can be written in the form

$$\phi(\theta) = \frac{1}{2\pi I_0(m)} \exp\{m\cos(\theta - \theta_0)\} \tag{6.95}$$

where the normalization coefficient has been expressed in terms of the zeroth-order modified Bessel function of the first kind, $I_0(m)$. The distribution (6.95) is known as a *circular normal* or *von Mises* distribution (Mardia, 1972). The parameter m (which depends on v in our derivation) is analogous to the (inverse) variance parameter in a conventional normal distribution. Since (6.95) is periodic, we can construct a general representation for the conditional density of a periodic variable by considering a mixture of circular normal kernels, with parameters governed by the outputs of a neural network. The weights in the network can again be found by maximizing the likelihood function defined over a set of training data.

An example of the application of these techniques to the determination of wind direction from satellite radar scatterometer data is given in Bishop and Legleye (1995). This is an inverse problem in which the target data is multi-valued. For problems involving periodic variables in which the target data is effectively single-valued with respect to the input vector, then a single circular normal kernel can be used.

An alternative approach to modelling conditional distributions of periodic variables is discussed in Exercise 6.8.

6.5 Estimating posterior probabilities

So far in this chapter we have focused on 'regression' problems in which the target variable are continuous. We now turn to a consideration of error functions for classification problems in which the target variables represent discrete class labels (or, more generally, the probabilities of class membership).

When we use a neural network to solve a classification problem, there are two distinct ways in which we can view the objectives of network training. At the simpler level, we can arrange for the network to represent a non-linear discriminant function so that, when a new input vector is presented to the trained network, the outputs provide a classification directly. The second approach, which is more general and more powerful, is to use the network to model the posterior probabilities of class membership. Typically there is one output unit for each possible class, and the activation of each output unit represents the corresponding posterior probability $p(\mathcal{C}_k|\mathbf{x})$, where $\mathcal{C}_k$ is the kth class, and $\mathbf{x}$ is the input vector. These probabilities can then be used in a subsequent decision-making stage to arrive at a classification.

By arranging for the network outputs to approximate posterior probabilities, we can exploit a number of results which are not available if the network is used simply as a non-linear discriminant (Richard and Lippmann, 1991). These include:

Minimum error-rate decisions

From the discussion of optimal classification in Section 1.9 we know that, to minimize the probability of misclassification, a new input vector should be assigned to the class having the largest posterior probability. Note that the network outputs need not be close to 0 or 1 if the class-conditional density functions are overlapping. Heuristic procedures, such as applying extra training using those patterns which fail to generate outputs close to the target values, will be counterproductive, since this alters the distributions and makes it less likely that the network will generate the correct Bayesian probabilities.

Outputs sum to 1

Since the network outputs approximate posterior probabilities they should sum to unity. This can be enforced explicitly as part of the choice of network structure as we shall see. Also, the average of each network output over all patterns in the training set should approximate the corresponding prior class probabilities, since

$$P(\mathcal{C}_k) = \int P(\mathcal{C}_k|\mathbf{x})p(\mathbf{x})\, d\mathbf{x} \simeq \frac{1}{N}\sum_n P(\mathcal{C}_k|\mathbf{x}^n). \tag{6.96}$$

These estimated priors can be compared with the sample estimates of the priors obtained from the fractions of patterns in each class within the training data set. Differences between these two estimates are an indication that the network is not modelling the posterior probabilities accurately (Richard and Lippmann, 1991).

Compensating for different prior probabilities

In some of the conventional approaches to pattern classification discussed in Chapter 1, the posterior probabilities were expressed through Bayes' theorem in the form

$$P(\mathcal{C}_k|\mathbf{x}) = \frac{p(\mathbf{x}|\mathcal{C}_k)P(\mathcal{C}_k)}{p(\mathbf{x})} \tag{6.97}$$

and the prior probabilities $P(\mathcal{C}_k)$ and class-conditional densities $p(\mathbf{x}|\mathcal{C}_k)$ were estimated separately. The neural network approach, by contrast, provides direct estimates of the posterior probabilities. Sometimes the prior probabilities expected when the network is in use differ from those represented by the training set. It is then it is a simple matter to use Bayes' theorem (6.97) to make the necessary corrections to the network outputs. This is achieved simply by dividing the network outputs by the prior probabilities corresponding to the training set, multiplying them by the new prior probabilities, and then normalizing the results. Changes in the prior probabilities can therefore be accommodated without re-training the network. The prior probabilities for the training set may be estimated simply by evaluating the fraction of the training set data points in each class. Prior probabilities corresponding to the network's operating environment can often be obtained very straightforwardly since only the class labels are needed and no input data is required. As an example, consider the problem of classifying medical images into 'normal' and 'tumour'. When used for screening purposes, we would expect a very small prior probability of 'tumour'. To obtain a good variety of tumour images in the training set would therefore require huge numbers of training examples. An alternative is to increase artificially the proportion of tumour images in the training set, and then to compensate for the different priors on the test data as described above. The prior probabilities for tumours in the general population can be obtained from medical statistics, without having to collect the corresponding images. Correction of the network outputs is then a simple matter of multiplication and division.

Combining the outputs of several networks

Rather than using a single network to solve a complete problem, there is often benefit in breaking the problem down into smaller parts and treating each part with a separate network. By dividing the network outputs by the prior probabilities used during training, the network outputs become likelihoods scaled by the unconditional density of the input vectors. These scaled likelihoods can be multiplied together on the assumption that the input vectors for the various networks are independent. Since the scaling factor is independent of class, a classifier based on the product of scaled likelihoods will give the same results as one based on the true likelihoods. This approach has been successfully applied to problems in speech recognition (Bourlard and Morgan, 1990; Singer and Lippmann, 1992).

Minimum risk

As discussed in Chapter 1, the goal of a classification system may not always be to minimize the probability of misclassification. Different misclassifications may carry different penalties, and we may wish to minimize the overall loss or risk (Section 1.10). Again the medical screening application provides a good example. It may be far more serious to mis-classify a tumour image as normal than to mis-classify a normal image as that of a tumour. In this case, the posterior probabilities from the network can be combined with a suitable matrix of loss coefficients to allow the minimum risk decision to be made. Again, no network re-training is required to achieve this. However, if the required loss matrix elements are known before the network is trained, then it may be better to modify the error function as will be discussed for the case of a sum-of-squares error in Section 6.6.2.

Rejection thresholds

In Section 1.10.1 we introduced the concept of a rejection threshold, which is such that if all of the posterior probabilities fall below this threshold then no classification decision is made. Alternative classification techniques can then be applied to the rejected cases. This reflects the costs associated with making the wrong decisions balanced against the cost of alternative classification procedures. In the medical image classification problem, for instance, it may be better not to try to classify doubtful images automatically, but instead to have a human expert provide a decision. Rejection of input vectors can be achieved in a principled way, provided the network outputs represent posterior probabilities of class membership.

In subsequent sections of this chapter we show how the outputs of a network can be interpreted as approximations to posterior probabilities, provided the error function used for network training is carefully chosen. We also show that some error functions allow networks to represent non-linear discriminants, even though the output values themselves need not correspond to probabilities.

6.6 Sum-of-squares for classification

In the previous section we showed that, for a network trained by minimizing a sum-of-squares error function, the network outputs approximate the conditional averages of the target data

$$y_k(\mathbf{x}) = \langle t_k | \mathbf{x} \rangle = \int t_k p(t_k | \mathbf{x}) \, dt_k. \tag{6.98}$$

In the case of a classification problem, every input vector in the training set is labelled by its class membership, represented by a set of target values t_k^n. The targets can be chosen according to a variety of schemes, but the most convenient is the 1-of-c coding in which, for an input vector $\mathbf{x}^n$ from class $\mathcal{C}_l$, we have $t_k^n = \delta_{kl}$ where δ_{kl} is the Kronecker delta symbol defined on page xiii. In this case the target values are precisely known and the density function in target space becomes singular and can be written as

$$p(t_k | \mathbf{x}) = \sum_{l=1}^{c} \delta(t_k - \delta_{kl}) P(\mathcal{C}_l | \mathbf{x}) \tag{6.99}$$

since $P(\mathcal{C}_l | \mathbf{x})$ is the probability that $\mathbf{x}$ belongs to class $\mathcal{C}_l$. If we now substitute (6.99) into (6.98) we obtain

$$y_k(\mathbf{x}) = P(\mathcal{C}_k | \mathbf{x}) \tag{6.100}$$

so that the outputs of the network correspond to Bayesian posterior probabilities (White, 1989; Richard and Lippmann, 1991).

If the network outputs represent probabilities, then they should lie in the range $(0, 1)$ and should sum to 1. For a network with linear output units, trained by minimizing a sum-of-squares error function, it was shown in Section 6.1.2 that if the target values satisfy a linear constraint, then the network outputs will satisfy the same constraint for an arbitrary input vector. In the case of a 1-of-c coding scheme, the target values sum to unity for each pattern, and so the network outputs will also always sum to unity. However, there is no guarantee that they will lie in the range $(0, 1)$. In fact, the sum-of-squares error function is not the most appropriate for classification problems. It was derived from maximum likelihood on the assumption of Gaussian distributed target data. However, the target values for a 1-of-c coding scheme are binary, and hence far from having a Gaussian distribution. Later we discuss error measures which are more appropriate for classification problems. However, there are advantages in using a sum-of-squares error, including the fact that the determination of the output weights in a network represents a linear optimization problem. The significance of this result for radial basis function networks was described in Chapter 5. We therefore discuss the use of a sum-of-squares error for classification problems in more detail before considering alternative choices of error function.

For a two-class problem, the 1-of-c target coding scheme described above leads to a network with two output units, one for each class, whose activations represent the corresponding probabilities of class membership. An alternative approach, however, is to use a single output y and a target coding which sets $t^n = 1$ if $\mathbf{x}^n$ is from class $\mathcal{C}_1$ and $t^n = 0$ if $\mathbf{x}^n$ is from class $\mathcal{C}_2$. In this case, the distribution of target values is given by

$$p(t_k|\mathbf{x}) = \delta(t - 1)P(\mathcal{C}_1|\mathbf{x}) + \delta(t)P(\mathcal{C}_2|\mathbf{x}). \qquad (6.101)$$

Substituting this into (6.98) gives

$$y(\mathbf{x}) = P(\mathcal{C}_1|\mathbf{x}) \qquad (6.102)$$

and so the network output $y(\mathbf{x})$ represents the posterior probability of the input vector $\mathbf{x}$ belonging to class $\mathcal{C}_1$. The corresponding probability for class $\mathcal{C}_2$ is then given by $P(\mathcal{C}_2|\mathbf{x}) = 1 - y(\mathbf{x})$.

6.6.1   Interpretation of hidden units

In Section 6.1.1 we derived the expression (6.29) for the final-layer weights which minimizes a sum-of-squares error, for networks with linear output units. By substituting this result back into the error function we obtain an expression in which the only adaptive parameters are those associated with hidden units, which we denote by $\widetilde{\mathbf{w}}$. This expression sheds light on the nature of the hidden unit representation which a network learns, and indicates why multi-layer non-linear neural networks can be effective as pattern classification systems (Webb and Lowe, 1990).

Writing (6.25) in matrix notation we obtain

$$E = \frac{1}{2}\mathrm{Tr}\{(\mathbf{ZW}^{\mathrm{T}} - \mathbf{T})(\mathbf{ZW}^{\mathrm{T}} - \mathbf{T})^{\mathrm{T}}\} \tag{6.103}$$

where $\mathbf{Z}$, $\mathbf{W}$ and $\mathbf{T}$ are defined on page 199. We now substitute the solution (6.29) for the optimal weights into (6.103) to give

$$E = \frac{1}{2}\mathrm{Tr}\{(\mathbf{ZZ}^{\dagger}\mathbf{T} - \mathbf{T})(\mathbf{ZZ}^{\dagger}\mathbf{T} - \mathbf{T})^{\mathrm{T}}\}. \tag{6.104}$$

By using some matrix manipulation (Exercise 6.9) we can write this in the form

$$E = \frac{1}{2}\mathrm{Tr}\{\mathbf{T}^{\mathrm{T}}\mathbf{T} - \mathbf{S}_B\mathbf{S}_T^{-1}\} \tag{6.105}$$

Here $\mathbf{S}_T$ is given by

$$\mathbf{S}_T = \mathbf{Z}^{\mathrm{T}}\mathbf{Z} = \sum_n (\mathbf{z}^n - \bar{\mathbf{z}})(\mathbf{z}^n - \bar{\mathbf{z}})^{\mathrm{T}} \tag{6.106}$$

and the components of $\bar{\mathbf{z}}$ are defined by (6.24). We see that this can be interpreted as the total covariance matrix for the activations at the output of the final layer of hidden units with respect to the training data set. Similarly, $\mathbf{S}_B$ in (6.105) is given by

$$\mathbf{S}_B = \mathbf{Z}^{\mathrm{T}}\mathbf{TT}^{\mathrm{T}}\mathbf{Z} \tag{6.107}$$

which can be interpreted (as we shall see) as a form of between-class covariance matrix.

Since the first term in the curly brackets in (6.105) depends only on the target data it is independent of the remaining weights $\tilde{\mathbf{w}}$ in the network. Thus, minimizing the sum-of-squares error is equivalent to maximizing a particular discriminant function defined with respect to the activations of the final-layer hidden units given by

$$J = \frac{1}{2}\mathrm{Tr}\{\mathbf{S}_B\mathbf{S}_T^{-1}\}. \tag{6.108}$$

Note that, if the matrix $\mathbf{S}_T$ is ill-conditioned, then the inverse matrix $\mathbf{S}_T^{-1}$ should be replaced by the pseudo-inverse $\mathbf{S}_T^{\dagger}$. The criterion (6.108) has a clear similarity to the Fisher discriminant function which is discussed in Section 3.6. Nothing here is specific to the multi-layer perceptron, or indeed to neural networks. The same result is obtained regardless of the functions $z_j(\mathbf{x}; \tilde{\mathbf{w}})$ and applies to any generalized linear discriminant in which the basis functions contain adaptive parameters.

The role played by the hidden units can now be stated as follows. The weights in the final layer are adjusted to produce an optimum discrimination of the classes of input vectors by means of a linear transformation. Minimizing the error of this linear discriminant requires that the input data undergo a non-linear transformation into the space spanned by the activations of the hidden units in such a way as to maximize the discriminant function given by (6.108).

Further insight into the nature of the matrix $\mathbf{S}_B$ is obtained by considering a particular target coding scheme. For the 1-of-c target coding scheme we can write (6.107) in the form (Exercise 6.10)

$$\mathbf{S}_B = \sum_k N_k^2 (\overline{\mathbf{z}}^k - \overline{\mathbf{z}})(\overline{\mathbf{z}}^k - \overline{\mathbf{z}})^{\mathrm{T}} \tag{6.109}$$

where N_k is the number of patterns in class $\mathcal{C}_k$ and $\overline{\mathbf{z}}^k$ is the mean activation vector of the hidden units for all training patterns in class $\mathcal{C}_k$, and is defined by

$$\overline{\mathbf{z}}^k = \frac{1}{N_k} \sum_{n \in \mathcal{C}_k} \mathbf{z}^n. \tag{6.110}$$

Note that $\mathbf{S}_B$ in (6.109) differs from the conventional between-class covariance matrix introduced in Section 3.6 by having factors of N_k^2 instead of N_k in the sum over classes. This represents a strong weighting of the feature extraction criterion in favour of classes with larger numbers of patterns. If there is a significant difference between the prior probabilities for the training and test data sets, then this effect may be undesirable, and we shall shortly see how to correct for it by modifying the sum-of-squares error measure. As discussed in Section 3.6, there are several ways to generalize Fisher's original two-class discriminant criterion to several classes, all of which reduce to the original Fisher result as a special case. In general, there is no way to decide which of these will yield the best results. For a two-class problem, the between-class covariance matrix given in (6.109) differs from the conventional one only by a multiplicative constant, so in this case the network criterion is equivalent to the original Fisher expression.

In earlier work, Gallinari *et al.* (1988, 1991) showed that, for a network of *linear* processing units with a 1-of-c target coding, the minimization of a sum-of-squares error gave a set of input-to-hidden weights which maximized a criterion which took the form of a ratio of determinants of between-class and total covariance matrices defined at the outputs of the hidden units. The results of Webb and Lowe (1990) contain this result as a special case.

6.6.2 *Weighted sum-of-squares*

We have seen that, for networks with linear output units, minimization of a sum-of-squares error at the network outputs maximizes a particular non-linear feature extraction criterion

$$J = \frac{1}{2}\text{Tr}\{\mathbf{S}_B\mathbf{S}_T^{-1}\} \tag{6.111}$$

at the hidden units. For the 1-of-c coding scheme, the corresponding between-class covariance matrix, given by (6.109), contains coefficients which depend on N_k, the number of patterns in class C_k. Thus, the hidden unit representation obtained by maximizing this discriminant function will only be optimal for a particular set of prior probabilities N_k/N. If the prior probabilities differ between training and test sets, then the feature extraction need not be optimal.

A related difficulty arises if there are different costs associated with different misclassifications, so that a general loss matrix needs to be considered. It has been suggested (Lowe and Webb, 1990, 1991) that modifications to the form of the sum-of-squares error to take account of the loss matrix can lead to improved feature extraction by the hidden layer, and hence to improved classification performance.

To deal with different prior probabilities between the training set and the test set, Lowe and Webb (1990) modify the sum-of-squares error by introducing a weighting factor κ_n for each pattern n so that the error function becomes

$$E = \frac{1}{2}\sum_n \sum_k \kappa_n \{y_k(\mathbf{x}^n) - t^n\}^2 \tag{6.112}$$

where the weighting factors are given by

$$\kappa_n = \frac{\widetilde{P}(C_k)}{P_k} \qquad \text{for pattern } n \text{ in class } C_k \tag{6.113}$$

where $\widetilde{P}(C_k)$ is the prior probability of class C_k for the *test* data, and $P_k = N_k/N$ is the corresponding (sample estimate of the) prior probability for the training data. It is straightforward to show (Exercise 6.12) that the total covariance matrix $\mathbf{S}_T$ then becomes

$$\mathbf{S}_T = \sum_k \frac{\widetilde{P}(C_k)}{P_k} \sum_{n \in C_k} (\mathbf{z}^n - \overline{\mathbf{z}})(\mathbf{z}^n - \overline{\mathbf{z}})^\text{T} \tag{6.114}$$

which is the sample-based estimate of the total covariance matrix for data with prior class probabilities $\widetilde{P}(C_k)$. In (6.114) the $\overline{\mathbf{z}}$ are given by

$$\overline{\mathbf{z}} = \sum_k \frac{\widetilde{P}(C_k)}{N_k} \sum_{n \in C_k} \mathbf{z}^n \tag{6.115}$$

which again is the sample-based estimate of the value which $\overline{\mathbf{z}}$ would take for data having the prior probabilities $\widetilde{P}(C_k)$. Similarly, assuming a 1-of-c target coding scheme, the between-class covariance matrix is modified to become

$$\mathbf{S}_B = \sum_k N^2 \widetilde{P}(\mathcal{C}_k)^2 (\overline{\mathbf{z}}^k - \overline{\mathbf{z}})(\overline{\mathbf{z}}^k - \overline{\mathbf{z}})^{\mathrm{T}} \tag{6.116}$$

which is the sample-based estimate of the between-class covariance matrix for data with prior probabilities $\widetilde{P}(\mathcal{C}_k)$.

The effects of an arbitrary loss matrix can similarly be taken into account by modifying the target coding scheme so that, for a pattern n which is labelled as belonging to class $\mathcal{C}_l$, the target vector has components $t_k^n = 1 - L_{lk}$, where L_{lk} represents the loss in assigning a pattern from class $\mathcal{C}_l$ to class $\mathcal{C}_k$. The total covariance matrix is unaltered, while the between-class covariance matrix becomes (Exercise 6.13)

$$\mathbf{S}_B = \sum_k \left\{ \sum_l (1 - L_{lk}) N_l (\overline{\mathbf{z}}_l - \overline{\mathbf{z}}) \right\} \left\{ \sum_{l'} (1 - L_{l'k}) N_{l'} (\overline{\mathbf{z}}_{l'} - \overline{\mathbf{z}})^{\mathrm{T}} \right\} \tag{6.117}$$

which reduces to the usual expression when $L_{lk} = 1 - \delta_{lk}$. Examples of the application of these techniques to a problem in medical prognosis are given in Lowe and Webb (1990).

6.7 Cross-entropy for two classes

We have seen that, for a 1-of-c target coding scheme, the outputs of a network trained by minimizing a sum-of-squares error function approximate the posterior probabilities of class membership, conditioned on the input vector. However, the sum-of-squares error was obtained from the maximum likelihood principle by assuming the target data was generated from a smooth deterministic function with added Gaussian noise. This is clearly a sensible starting point for regression problems. For classification problems, however, the targets are binary variables, and the Gaussian noise model does not provide a good description of their distribution. We therefore seek more appropriate choices of error function.

To start with, we consider problems involving two classes. One approach to such problems would be to use a network with two output units, one for each class. This type of representation is discussed in Section 6.9. Here we discuss an alternative approach in which we consider a network with a single output y. We would like the value of y to represent the posterior probability $P(\mathcal{C}_1|\mathbf{x})$ for class $\mathcal{C}_1$. The posterior probability of class $\mathcal{C}_2$ will then by given by $P(\mathcal{C}_2|\mathbf{x}) = 1 - y$. This can be achieved if we consider a target coding scheme for which $t = 1$ if the input vector belongs to class $\mathcal{C}_1$ and $t = 0$ if it belongs to class $\mathcal{C}_2$. We can combine these into a single expression, so that the probability of observing either target value is

$$p(t|\mathbf{x}) = y^t (1 - y)^{1-t} \tag{6.118}$$

which is a particular case of the binomial distribution called the Bernoulli distribution. With this interpretation of the output unit activations, the likelihood of observing the training data set, assuming the data points are drawn independently from this distribution, is then given by

$$\prod_n (y^n)^{t^n} (1 - y^n)^{1-t^n}. \tag{6.119}$$

As usual, it is more convenient to minimize the negative logarithm of the likelihood. This leads to the *cross-entropy* error function (Hopfield, 1987; Baum and Wilczek, 1988; Solla *et al.*, 1988; Hinton, 1989; Hampshire and Pearlmutter, 1990) in the form

$$E = -\sum_n \{t^n \ln y^n + (1 - t^n) \ln(1 - y^n)\}. \tag{6.120}$$

We shall discuss the meaning of the term 'entropy' in Section 6.10. For the moment let us consider some elementary properties of this error function.

Differentiating the error function with respect to y^n we obtain

$$\frac{\partial E}{\partial y^n} = \frac{(y^n - t^n)}{y^n(1 - y^n)}. \tag{6.121}$$

The absolute minimum of the error function occurs when

$$y^n = t^n \qquad \text{for all } n. \tag{6.122}$$

In Section 3.1.3 we showed that, for a network with a single output $y = g(a)$ whose value is to be interpreted as a probability, it is appropriate to consider the logistic activation function

$$g(a) = \frac{1}{1 + \exp(-a)} \tag{6.123}$$

which has the property

$$g'(a) = g(a)(1 - g(a)). \tag{6.124}$$

Combining (6.121) and (6.124) we see that the derivative of the error with respect to a takes the simple form

$$\delta^n \equiv \frac{\partial E}{\partial a^n} = y^n - t^n. \tag{6.125}$$

Here δ^n is the 'error' quantity which is back-propagated through the network in order to compute the derivatives of the error function with respect to the network weights (Section 4.8). Note that (6.125) has the same form as obtained for the sum-of-squares error function and linear output units. We see that there is a natural pairing of error function and output unit activation function which gives rise to this simple form for the derivative. Use of the logistic form of activation function also leads to corresponding simplifications when evaluating the Hessian matrix (the matrix of second derivatives of the error function).

From (6.120) and (6.122), the value of the cross-entropy error function at its minimum is given by

$$E_{\min} = -\sum_n \left\{ t^n \ln t^n + (1 - t^n) \ln(1 - t^n) \right\}. \tag{6.126}$$

For the 1-of-c coding scheme this vanishes. However, the error function (6.120) is also the correct one to use when t^n is a continuous variable in the range $(0, 1)$ representing the probability of the input vector $\mathbf{x}^n$ belonging to class $\mathcal{C}_1$ (see Section 6.10 and Exercise 6.15). In this case the minimum value (6.126) of the error need not vanish, and so it is convenient to subtract off this value from the original error function to give a modified error of the form

$$E = -\sum_n \left\{ t^n \ln \frac{y^n}{t^n} + (1 - t^n) \ln \frac{(1 - y^n)}{(1 - t^n)} \right\}. \tag{6.127}$$

Since (6.126) is independent of the network outputs this does not affect the location of the minimum and so has no effect on network training. The modified error (6.127) always has its minimum at 0, irrespective of the particular training set.

As a simple illustration of the interpretation of network outputs as probabilities, we consider a simple two-class problem with one input variable in which the class-conditional densities are given by the Gaussian mixture functions shown in Figure 6.11. A multi-layer perceptron with five hidden units having 'tanh' activation functions, and one output unit having a logistic sigmoid activation function, was trained by minimizing a cross-entropy error using 100 cycles of the BFGS quasi-Newton algorithm (Section 7.10). The resulting network mapping function is shown, along with the true posterior probability calculated using Bayes' theorem, in Figure 6.12.

6.7.1 Sigmoid activation functions

In Section 3.1.3, the logistic sigmoid activation function was motivated for a single-layer network by the goal of ensuring that the network outputs represent posterior probabilities, with the assumption that the class-conditional densities can be approximated by normal distributions. We can apply a similar argument to the network outputs in the case of multi-layered networks (Rumelhart *et*

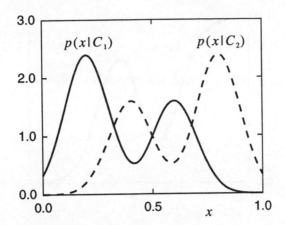

Figure 6.11. Plots of the class-conditional densities used to generate a data set
to demonstrate the interpretation of network outputs as posterior probabilities.
A total of 2000 data points were generated from these densities, using equal
prior probabilities.

al., 1995). In this case we need to consider the distributions of the outputs of
the hidden units, represented here by the vector $\mathbf{z}$ for the two classes. We can
generalize the discussion by assuming that these class-conditional densities are
described by

$$p(\mathbf{z}|\mathcal{C}_k) = \exp\left\{A(\boldsymbol{\theta}_k) + B(\mathbf{z}, \boldsymbol{\phi}) + \boldsymbol{\theta}_k^{\mathrm{T}}\mathbf{z}\right\} \qquad (6.128)$$

which is a member of the *exponential family* of distributions (which includes
many of the common distributions as special cases such as Gaussian, binomial,
Bernoulli, Poisson, and so on). The parameters $\boldsymbol{\theta}_k$ and $\boldsymbol{\phi}$ control the form of the
distribution. In writing (6.128) we are implicitly assuming that the distributions
differ only in the parameters $\boldsymbol{\theta}_k$ and not in $\boldsymbol{\phi}$. An example would be two Gaussian
distributions with different means, but with common covariance matrices.

Using Bayes' theorem, we can write the posterior probability for class $\mathcal{C}_1$ in
the form

$$P(\mathcal{C}_1|\mathbf{z}) = \frac{p(\mathbf{z}|\mathcal{C}_1)P(\mathcal{C}_1)}{p(\mathbf{z}|\mathcal{C}_1)P(\mathcal{C}_1) + p(\mathbf{z}|\mathcal{C}_2)P(\mathcal{C}_2)}$$

$$= \frac{1}{1 + \exp(-a)} \qquad (6.129)$$

which is a logistic sigmoid function, in which

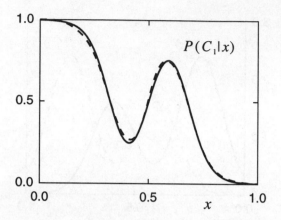

Figure 6.12. The result of training a multi-layer perceptron on data generated from the density functions in Figure 6.11. The solid curve shows the output of the trained network as a function of the input variable x, while the dashed curve shows the true posterior probability $P(C_1|x)$ calculated from the class-conditional densities using Bayes' theorem.

$$a = \ln \frac{p(\mathbf{z}|C_1)P(C_1)}{p(\mathbf{z}|C_2)P(C_2)} \tag{6.130}$$

Using (6.128) we can write this in the form

$$a = \mathbf{w}^{\mathrm{T}}\mathbf{z} + w_0 \tag{6.131}$$

where we have defined

$$\mathbf{w} = \boldsymbol{\theta}_1 - \boldsymbol{\theta}_2 \tag{6.132}$$

$$w_0 = A(\boldsymbol{\theta}_1) - A(\boldsymbol{\theta}_2) + \ln \frac{P(C_1)}{P(C_2)}. \tag{6.133}$$

Thus the network output is given by a logistic sigmoid activation function acting on a weighted linear combination of the outputs of those hidden units which send connections to the output unit.

It is clear that we can apply the above arguments to the activations of hidden units in a network. Provided such units use logistic sigmoid activation functions, we can interpret their outputs as probabilities of the presence of corresponding 'features' conditioned on the inputs to the units.

6.7.2 *Properties of the cross-entropy error*

Suppose we write the network output, for a particular pattern n, in the form $y^n = t^n + \epsilon^n$. Then the cross-entropy error function (6.127) can be written as

$$E = -\sum_n \{t^n \ln(1 + \epsilon^n/t^n) + (1 - t^n)\ln(1 - \epsilon^n/(1 - t^n))\} \qquad (6.134)$$

so that the error function depends on the *relative* errors of the network outputs. This should be compared with the sum-of-squares error function which depends on the (squares of the) absolute errors. Minimization of the cross-entropy error function will therefore tend to result in similar relative errors on both small and large target values. By contrast, the sum-of-squares error function tends to give similar absolute errors for each pattern, and will therefore give large relative errors for small output values. This suggests that the cross-entropy error function is likely to perform better than sum-of-squares at estimating small probabilities.

For binary targets, with $t^n = 1$ for an input vector $\mathbf{x}^n$ from class $\mathcal{C}_1$ and $t^n = 0$ for inputs from class $\mathcal{C}_2$, we can write the cross-entropy error function (6.134) in the form

$$E = -\sum_{n \in \mathcal{C}_1} \ln(1 + \epsilon^n) - \sum_{n \in \mathcal{C}_2} \ln(1 - \epsilon^n) \qquad (6.135)$$

where we have used $z \ln z \to 0$ for $z \to 0$. If we suppose that ϵ^n is small, then the error function becomes

$$E \simeq \sum_n |\epsilon^n| \qquad (6.136)$$

where we have expanded the logarithms using $\ln(1 + z) \simeq z$ and noted that if $y \in (0, 1)$ then $\epsilon^n < 0$ for inputs from class $\mathcal{C}_1$ and $\epsilon^n > 0$ for inputs from class $\mathcal{C}_2$. The result (6.136) has the form of the Minkowski-R error function for $R = 1$, discussed earlier. Compared to the sum-of-squares error function, this gives much stronger weight to smaller errors.

We have obtained the cross-entropy function by requiring that the network output y represents the probability of an input vector $\mathbf{x}$ belonging to class $\mathcal{C}_1$. We can now confirm the consistency of this requirement by considering the minimum of the error function for an infinitely large data set, for which we can write (6.120) in the form

$$E = -\iint \{t \ln y(\mathbf{x}) + (1 - t)\ln(1 - y(\mathbf{x}))\} \, p(t|\mathbf{x})p(\mathbf{x}) \, dt \, d\mathbf{x}. \qquad (6.137)$$

Since the network function $y(\mathbf{x})$ is independent of the target value t we can write (6.137) in the form

$$E = -\int \{\langle t|\mathbf{x}\rangle \ln y(\mathbf{x}) + (1 - \langle t|\mathbf{x}\rangle)\ln(1 - y(\mathbf{x}))\}\, p(\mathbf{x})\, d\mathbf{x} \tag{6.138}$$

where, as before, we have defined the conditional average of the target data as

$$\langle t|\mathbf{x}\rangle = \int t p(t|\mathbf{x})\, dt. \tag{6.139}$$

If we now set the functional derivative (Appendix D) of (6.138) with respect to $y(\mathbf{x})$ to zero we see that the minimum of the error function occurs when

$$y(\mathbf{x}) = \langle t|\mathbf{x}\rangle \tag{6.140}$$

so that, as for the sum-of-squares error, the output of the network approximates the conditional average of the target data for the given input vector. For the target coding scheme which we have adopted we have

$$p(t|\mathbf{x}) = \delta(t - 1)P(\mathcal{C}_1|\mathbf{x}) + \delta(t)P(\mathcal{C}_2|\mathbf{x}). \tag{6.141}$$

Substituting (6.141) into (6.139) we find

$$y(\mathbf{x}) = P(\mathcal{C}_1|\mathbf{x}) \tag{6.142}$$

as required.

6.8 Multiple independent attributes

In all of the classification problems which we have considered so far, the aim has been to assign new vectors to one of c mutually exclusive classes. However, in some applications we may wish to use a network to determine the probabilities of the presence or absence of a number of attributes which need not be mutually exclusive. In this case the network has multiple outputs, and the value of the output variable y_k represents the probability that the kth attribute is present. If we treat the attributes as independent, then the distribution of target values will satisfy

$$p(\mathbf{t}|\mathbf{x}) = \prod_{k=1}^{c} p(t_k|\mathbf{x}). \tag{6.143}$$

We can now use (6.118) for each of the conditional distributions to give

$$p(\mathbf{t}|\mathbf{x}) = \prod_{k=1}^{c} y_k^{t_k}(1 - y_k)^{t_k}. \tag{6.144}$$

If we now construct the likelihood function and take the negative logarithm in the usual way, we obtain the error function in the form

$$E = -\sum_n \sum_{k=1}^c \{t_k^n \ln y_k^n + (1 - t_k^n) \ln(1 - y_k^n)\}. \tag{6.145}$$

With this choice of error function, the network outputs should each have a logistic sigmoidal activation function of the form (6.123). Again, for binary target variables t_k^n, this error function vanishes at its minimum. If the t_k^n are probabilities in the range $(0, 1)$, the minimum of the error will depend on the particular data set, and so it is convenient to subtract off this minimum value to give

$$E = -\sum_n \sum_{k=1}^c \left\{ t_k^n \ln \left(\frac{y_k^n}{t_k^n} \right) + (1 - t_k^n) \ln \left(\frac{1 - y_k^n}{1 - t_k^n} \right) \right\} \tag{6.146}$$

which always has an absolute minimum value with respect to the $\{y_k^n\}$ of zero.

6.9 Cross-entropy for multiple classes

We now return to the conventional classification problem involving mutually exclusive classes, and consider the form which the error function should take when the number of classes is greater than two. Consider a network with one output y_k for each class, and target data which has a 1-of-c coding scheme, so that $t_k^n = \delta_{kl}$ for a pattern n from class C_l. The probability of observing the set of target values $t_k^n = \delta_{kl}$, given an input vector $\mathbf{x}^n$, is just $p(C_l|\mathbf{x}) = y_l$. The value of the conditional distribution for this pattern can therefore be written as

$$p(\mathbf{t}^n|\mathbf{x}^n) = \prod_{k=1}^c (y_k^n)^{t_k^n}. \tag{6.147}$$

If we form the likelihood function, and take the negative logarithm as before, we obtain an error function of the form

$$E = -\sum_n \sum_{k=1}^c t_k^n \ln y_k^n. \tag{6.148}$$

The absolute minimum of this error function with respect to the $\{y_k^n\}$ occurs when $y_k^n = t_k^n$ for all values of k and n. At the minimum the error function takes the value

$$E_{\min} = -\sum_n \sum_{k=1}^c t_k^n \ln t_k^n. \tag{6.149}$$

For a 1-of-c coding scheme this minimum value is 0. However, the error function (6.148) is still valid, as we shall see, when t_k^n is a continuous variable in the range $(0, 1)$ representing the probability that input $\mathbf{x}^n$ belongs to class $\mathcal{C}_k$. In this case the minimum of the error function need not vanish (it represents the entropy of the distribution of target variables, as will be discussed shortly). It is then convenient to subtract off this minimum value, and hence obtain the error function in the form

$$E = -\sum_n \sum_{k=1}^c t_k^n \ln \left(\frac{y_k^n}{t_k^n} \right) \tag{6.150}$$

which is non-negative, and which equals zero when $y_k^n = t_k^n$ for all k and n.

We now consider the corresponding activation function which should be used for the network output units. If the output values are to be interpreted as probabilities they must lie in the range $(0, 1)$, and they must sum to unity. This can be achieved by using a generalization of the logistic sigmoid activation function which takes the form

$$y_k = \frac{\exp(a_k)}{\sum_{k'} \exp(a_{k'})} \tag{6.151}$$

which is known as the normalized exponential, or *softmax* activation function (Bridle, 1990). The term softmax is used because this activation function represents a smooth version of the *winner-takes-all* activation model in which the unit with the largest input has output $+1$ while all other units have output 0. If the exponentials in (6.151) are modified to have the form $\exp(\beta a_k)$, then the winner-takes-all activation is recovered in the limit $\beta \to \infty$. The softmax activation function can be regarded as a generalization of the logistic function, since it can be written in the form

$$y_k = \frac{1}{1 + \exp(-A_k)} \tag{6.152}$$

where A_k is given by

$$A_k = a_k - \ln \left\{ \sum_{k' \neq k} \exp(a_{k'}) \right\}. \tag{6.153}$$

As with the logistic sigmoid, we can give a very general motivation for the softmax activation function by considering the posterior probability that a hidden unit activation vector $\mathbf{z}$ belongs to class $\mathcal{C}_k$, in which the class-conditional densities are assumed to belong to the family of exponential distributions of the general form

$$p(\mathbf{z}|\mathcal{C}_k) = \exp\left\{A(\boldsymbol{\theta}_k) + B(\mathbf{z}, \boldsymbol{\phi}) + \boldsymbol{\theta}_k^{\mathrm{T}}\mathbf{z}\right\}. \tag{6.154}$$

From Bayes' theorem, the posterior probability of class $\mathcal{C}_k$ is given by

$$p(\mathcal{C}_k|\mathbf{z}) = \frac{p(\mathbf{z}|\mathcal{C}_k)P(\mathcal{C}_k)}{\sum_{k'} p(\mathbf{z}|\mathcal{C}_{k'})P(\mathcal{C}_{k'})}. \tag{6.155}$$

Substituting (6.154) into (6.155) and re-arranging we obtain

$$p(\mathcal{C}_k|\mathbf{z}) = \frac{\exp(a_k)}{\sum_{k'} \exp(a_{k'})} \tag{6.156}$$

where

$$a_k = \mathbf{w}_k^{\mathrm{T}}\mathbf{z} + w_{k0} \tag{6.157}$$

and we have defined

$$\mathbf{w}_k = \boldsymbol{\theta}_k \tag{6.158}$$

$$w_{k0} = A(\boldsymbol{\theta}_k) + \ln P(\mathcal{C}_k). \tag{6.159}$$

The result (6.156) represents the final layer of a network with softmax activation functions, and shows that (provided the distribution (6.154) is appropriate) the outputs can be interpreted as probabilities of class membership, conditioned on the outputs of the hidden units.

In evaluating the derivatives of the softmax error function we need to consider the inputs to all output units, and so we have (for pattern n)

$$\frac{\partial E^n}{\partial a_k} = \sum_{k'} \frac{\partial E^n}{\partial y_{k'}} \frac{\partial y_{k'}}{\partial a_k}. \tag{6.160}$$

From (6.151) we have

$$\frac{\partial y_{k'}}{\partial a_k} = y_{k'}\delta_{kk'} - y_{k'}y_k \tag{6.161}$$

while from (6.150) we have

$$\frac{\partial E^n}{\partial y_{k'}} = -\frac{t_{k'}}{y_{k'}}. \tag{6.162}$$

Substituting (6.161) and (6.162) into (6.160) we find

$$\frac{\partial E^n}{\partial a_k} = y_k - t_k \qquad (6.163)$$

which is the same result as found for both the sum-of-squares error (with a linear activation function) and the two-class cross-entropy error (with a logistic activation function). Again, we see that there is a natural pairing of error function and activation function.

6.10 Entropy

The concept of entropy was originally developed by physicists in the context of equilibrium thermodynamics and later extended through the development of statistical mechanics. It was introduced into information theory by Shannon (1948). An understanding of basic information theory leads to further insights into the entropy-based error measures discussed in this section. It also paves the way for an introduction to the minimum description length framework in Section 10.10. Here we consider two distinct but related interpretations of entropy, the first based on *degree of disorder* and the second based on *information content*.

Consider a probability density function $p(x)$ for a single random variable x. It is convenient to represent the density function as a histogram in which the x-axis has been divided into bins labelled by the integer i. Imagine constructing the histogram by putting a total of N identical discrete objects into the bins, such that the ith bin contains N_i objects. We wish to count the number of distinct ways in which objects can be arranged, while still giving rise to the same histogram. Since there are N ways of choosing the first object, $(N-1)$ ways of choosing the second object, and so on, there a total of $N!$ ways to select the N objects. However, we do not wish to count rearrangements of objects within a single bin. For the ith bin there are $N_i!$ such rearrangements and so the total number of distinct ways to arrange the objects, known as the multiplicity, is given by

$$W = \frac{N!}{\prod_i N_i!}. \qquad (6.164)$$

The entropy is defined as (a constant times) the negative logarithm of the multiplicity

$$S = -\frac{1}{N}\ln W = -\frac{1}{N}\{\ln N! - \sum_i \ln N_i!\}. \qquad (6.165)$$

We now consider the limit $N \to \infty$, and make use of Stirling's approximation $\ln N! \simeq N \ln N - N$ together with the relation $\sum_i N_i = N$, to give

$$S = -\lim_{N\to\infty}\sum_i \left(\frac{N_i}{N}\right)\ln\left(\frac{N_i}{N}\right) = -\sum_i p_i \ln p_i \qquad (6.166)$$

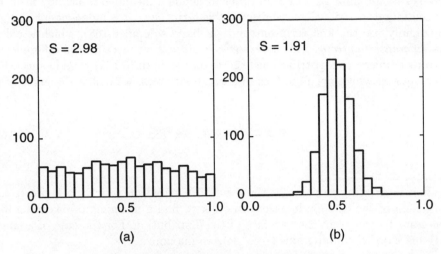

Figure 6.13. Examples of two histograms, together with their entropy values defined by (6.166). The histograms were generated by sampling two Gaussian functions with variance parameters $\sigma = 0.4$ and $\sigma = 0.08$, and each contain 1000 points. Note that the more compact distribution has a lower entropy.

where $p_i = N_i/N$ (as $N \to \infty$) represents the probability corresponding to the ith bin. The entropy therefore gives a measure of the number of different *microstates* (arrangements of objects in the bins) which can give rise to a given *macrostate* (i.e. a given set of probabilities p_i). A very sharply peaked distribution has a very low entropy, whereas if the objects are spread out over many bins the entropy is much higher. The smallest value for the entropy is 0 and occurs when all of the probability mass is concentrated in one bin (so that one of the p_i is 1 and all the rest are 0). Conversely the largest entropy arises when all of the bins contain equal probability mass, so that $p_i = 1/M$ where M is the total number of bins. This is easily seen by maximizing (6.166) subject to the constraint $\sum_i p_i = 1$ using a Lagrange multiplier (Appendix C). An example of two histograms, with their respective entropies, is shown in Figure 6.13.

For continuous distributions (rather than histograms) we can take the limit in which the number M of bins goes to infinity. If Δ is the width of each bin, then the probability mass in the ith bin is $p_i = p(x_i)\Delta$, and so the entropy can be written in the form

$$S = \lim_{M \to \infty} \sum_{i=1}^{M} p(x_i)\Delta \ln \{p(x_i)\Delta\} \qquad (6.167)$$

$$= \int p(x) \ln p(x) \, dx + \lim_{M \to \infty} \ln \Delta \qquad (6.168)$$

where we have used $\int p(x)\,dx = 1$. The second term on the right-hand side diverges in the limit $M \to \infty$. In order to define a meaningful entropy measure for continuous distributions we discard this term, since it is independent of $p(x)$, and simply use the first term on the right-hand side of (6.168), which is called the *differential entropy*. This is reasonable, since if we measure the difference in entropy between two distributions, the second term in (6.168) would cancel. For distributions which are functions of several variables, we define the entropy to be

$$S = -\int p(\mathbf{x}) \ln p(\mathbf{x})\,d\mathbf{x} \tag{6.169}$$

where $\mathbf{x} \equiv (x_1, \ldots, x_d)^{\mathrm{T}}$.

It is interesting to consider the form of distribution which gives rise to the maximum of the entropy function. In order to find a meaningful maximum it is necessary to constrain the variance of the distribution. For the case of a single variable x on the infinite axis $(-\infty, \infty)$, we maximize

$$S = -\int_{-\infty}^{\infty} p(x) \ln p(x)\,dx \tag{6.170}$$

subject to the constraints that the distribution be normalized and that the mean and variance of the distribution have specified values

$$\int_{-\infty}^{\infty} p(x)\,dx = 1 \tag{6.171}$$

$$\int_{-\infty}^{\infty} x p(x)\,dx = \mu \tag{6.172}$$

$$\int_{-\infty}^{\infty} (x - \mu)^2 p(x)\,dx = \sigma^2. \tag{6.173}$$

Introducing Lagrange multipliers λ_1, λ_2 and λ_3 (Appendix C) for each of the constraints, we can use calculus of variations (Appendix D) to maximize the functional

$$\int_{-\infty}^{\infty} p(x) \left\{ \ln p(x) + \lambda_1 + \lambda_2 x + \lambda_3 (x - \mu)^2 \right\}\,dx - \lambda_1 - \lambda_2 \mu - \lambda_3 \sigma^2 \tag{6.174}$$

which leads to

$$p(x) = \exp\left\{ -1 - \lambda_1 - \lambda_2 x - \lambda_3 (x - \mu)^2 \right\}. \tag{6.175}$$

We can solve for the Lagrange multipliers by back-substituting this expression into the constraint equations. This finally gives the expression for the maximizing distribution in the form

$$p(x) = \frac{1}{(2\pi\sigma^2)^{1/2}} \exp\left\{-\frac{(x-\mu)^2}{2\sigma^2}\right\}. \tag{6.176}$$

Thus we see that the distribution having maximum entropy, for given mean and variance, is the Gaussian.

As a second viewpoint on the interpretation of entropy, let us consider the amount of information, or equivalently the 'degree of surprise', which is obtained when we learn that a particular event has occurred. We expect that the information will depend on the probability p of the event, since if $p = 1$ then the event is certain to occur, and there is no surprise when the event is found to occur (and so no information is received). Conversely, if the probability is low, then there is a large degree of surprise in learning that it has occurred. We are therefore looking for a measure of information $s(p)$ which is a continuous, monotonically increasing function of p and which is such that $s(1) = 0$. An appropriate expression can be obtained as follows. Consider two independent events A and B, with probabilities p_A and p_B. If we know that both events have occurred then the total information is $s(p_A p_B)$. If, however, we are first told that A has occurred, then the residual information on learning that B has occurred must be $s(p_A p_B) - s(p_A)$, which must equal $s(p_B)$ since knowledge that A has occurred should not affect the information resulting from learning that B occurred (since the events are independent). This leads to the following condition

$$s(p_A p_B) = s(p_A) + s(p_B). \tag{6.177}$$

From this we can deduce that $s(p^2) = 2s(p)$ and by induction that $s(p^N) = Ns(p)$ for integer N. Similarly, $s(p) = s([p^{1/N}]^N) = Ns(p^{1/N})$ and by extension $s(p^{M/N}) = (M/N)s(p)$. This implies that

$$s(p^x) = xs(p) \tag{6.178}$$

for rational x and hence, by continuity, for real x. If we define $z = -\log_2 p$, so that $p = (1/2)^z$, then

$$s(p) = s((1/2)^z) = zs(1/2) = -s(1/2)\log_2(p). \tag{6.179}$$

It is conventional to choose $s(1/2) = 1$. The information is then expressed in *bits* (binary digits). From now on we shall consider logarithms to base e (natural logarithms) in which case the information is expressed in *nats*. We see that the amount of information is proportional to the logarithm of the probability. This arises essentially because, for independent events, probabilities are multiplicative, while information is additive.

Consider a random variable α which can take values α_k with probabilities $p(\alpha_k)$. If a sender wishes to transmit the value of α to a receiver, then the amount of information (in bits) which this requires is $-\ln p(\alpha_k)$ if the variable takes the value α_k. Thus, the expected (average) information needed to transmit the value of α is given by

$$S(\alpha) = -\sum_k p(\alpha_k) \ln p(\alpha_k) \qquad (6.180)$$

which is the entropy of the random variable α. Thus $S(\alpha)$ as the average amount of information received when the value of α is observed. The average length of a binary message (in nats) needed to transmit the value of α is at least equal to the entropy of α. This is known as the *noiseless coding theorem* (Shannon, 1948; Viterbi and Omura, 1979).

Returning to the case of continuous variables, denoted by the vector $\mathbf{x}$, we note that in practice we do not know the true distribution $p(\mathbf{x})$. If we encode the value of $\mathbf{x}$ for transmission to a receiver, then we must (implicitly or explicitly) choose a distribution $q(\mathbf{x})$ from which to construct the coding. The information needed to encode a value of $\mathbf{x}$ under this distribution is just $-\ln q(\mathbf{x})$. If the variable $\mathbf{x}$ is drawn from a true distribution $p(\mathbf{x})$ then the average information needed to encode $\mathbf{x}$ is given by

$$-\int p(\mathbf{x}) \ln q(\mathbf{x}) \, d\mathbf{x} \qquad (6.181)$$

which is the *cross-entropy* between the distributions $q(\mathbf{x})$ and $p(\mathbf{x})$. Comparison with (2.68) shows that this equals the negative log likelihood under the model distribution $q(\mathbf{x})$ when the true distribution is $p(\mathbf{x})$. It is also equal to the sum of the Kullback–Leibler distance between $p(\mathbf{x})$ and $q(\mathbf{x})$, given by (2.70), and the entropy of $p(\mathbf{x})$ since

$$-\int p(\mathbf{x}) \ln q(\mathbf{x}) \, d\mathbf{x} = -\int p(\mathbf{x}) \ln \frac{q(\mathbf{x})}{p(\mathbf{x})} \, d\mathbf{x} - \int p(\mathbf{x}) \ln p(\mathbf{x}) \, d\mathbf{x}. \qquad (6.182)$$

We can easily show that, of all possible distributions $q(\mathbf{x})$, the choice which gives the smallest average information, i.e. the smallest value for the cross-entropy, is the true distribution $p(\mathbf{x})$ (Exercise 6.21). Since the entropy of $p(\mathbf{x})$ is independent of the distribution $q(\mathbf{x})$, we see from (6.182) that minimization of the cross-entropy is equivalent to minimization of the Kullback–Leibler distance.

We can apply the concept of cross-entropy to the training of neural networks. For a variable α which takes a discrete set of values α_k we can write (6.181) in the form

$$-\sum_k P(\alpha_k) \ln Q(\alpha_k). \tag{6.183}$$

Consider first a network with c outputs $y_k(\mathbf{x})$ representing the model probabilities for $\mathbf{x}$ to belong to the corresponding classes C_k. We shall suppose that we also have a set of target variables t_k representing the corresponding true probabilities. Then the cross-entropy becomes

$$-\sum_{k=1}^{c} t_k \ln y_k(\mathbf{x}). \tag{6.184}$$

For a set of N data points which are assumed to be drawn independently from a common distribution, the information is additive and hence the total cross-entropy is given by

$$-\sum_{n=1}^{N} \sum_{k=1}^{c} t_k^n \ln y_k(\mathbf{x}^n) \tag{6.185}$$

which can be used as an error function for network training. We see that this form of error function is valid not only when the targets t_k^n have a one-of-c coding (representing precise knowledge of the true classes of the data) but also when they lie anywhere in the range $0 \leq t_k^n \leq 1$, subject to the constraint $\sum_k t_k^n = 1$, corresponding to probabilities of class membership.

For two classes, we can consider a network with a single output y representing the model probability for membership of class C_1, with corresponding true probability t. The model probability for membership of class C_2 is then $1 - y$, and the corresponding true probability is $1 - t$. Following the same line of argument as above we then arrive at the cross-entropy error function for two classes and N data points in the form

$$-\sum_{n=1}^{N} \left\{ t^n \ln y(\mathbf{x}^n) + (1 - t^n) \ln(1 - y(\mathbf{x}^n)) \right\}. \tag{6.186}$$

6.11 General conditions for outputs to be probabilities

So far, we have considered three different error measures (sum-of-squares, cross-entropy for a single output, and cross-entropy for softmax networks) all of which allow the network outputs to be interpreted as probabilities. We may therefore wonder what conditions an error measure should satisfy in order that the network outputs have this property. The discussion given here is based on that of Hampshire and Pearlmutter (1990).

All of the error measures we are considering take the form of a sum over patterns of an error term for each pattern $E = \sum_n E^n$. We shall also take the error to be a sum over terms for each output unit separately. This corresponds to the assumption that the distributions of different target variables are statistically independent (which is not satisfied by the Gaussian mixture based error considered earlier, or by the softmax error, for instance). Thus we write

$$E^n = \sum_{k=1}^{c} f(y_k^n, t_k^n) \tag{6.187}$$

where $f(\cdot, \cdot)$ is some function to be determined. We shall also assume that f depends only on the magnitude of the difference between y_k and t_k, so that $f(y_k^n, t_k^n) = f(|y_k^n - t_k^n|)$. In the limit of an infinite data set, we can write the average (or expected) per-pattern error in the form

$$\langle E \rangle = \sum_{k=1}^{c} \iint f(|y_k - t_k|) p(\mathbf{t}|\mathbf{x}) p(\mathbf{x}) \, d\mathbf{t} \, d\mathbf{x}. \tag{6.188}$$

If we use a 1-of-c target coding scheme, then from (6.99) we can write the conditional distribution of the target variables in the form

$$p(\mathbf{t}|\mathbf{x}) = \prod_{k=1}^{c} \left\{ \sum_{l=1}^{c} \delta(t_k - \delta_{kl}) P(\mathcal{C}_l|\mathbf{x}) \right\}. \tag{6.189}$$

We now substitute (6.189) into (6.188) and evaluate the integrals over the t_k variables (which simply involves integrals of δ-functions) to give

$$\langle E \rangle = \sum_{k=1}^{c} \int \left\{ f(1 - y_k) P(\mathcal{C}_k|\mathbf{x}) + f(y_k) \left[1 - P(\mathcal{C}_k|\mathbf{x}) \right] \right\} p(\mathbf{x}) \, d\mathbf{x} \tag{6.190}$$

where we have used $\sum_k P(\mathcal{C}_k|\mathbf{x}) = 1$, and assumed that $0 \leq y_k \leq 1$ so that the modulus signs can be omitted. The condition that the average per-pattern error in (6.190) be minimized with respect to the $y_k(\mathbf{x})$ is given by setting the functional derivative of $\langle E \rangle$ (Appendix D) to zero

$$\frac{\delta \langle E \rangle}{\delta y_k(\mathbf{x})} = -f'(1 - y_k) P(\mathcal{C}_k|\mathbf{x}) + f'(y_k) \left[1 - P(\mathcal{C}_k|\mathbf{x}) \right] = 0 \tag{6.191}$$

which gives

$$\frac{f'(1 - y_k)}{f'(y_k)} = \frac{1 - P(\mathcal{C}_k|\mathbf{x})}{P(\mathcal{C}_k|\mathbf{x})}. \tag{6.192}$$

If the outputs of the network are to represent probabilities, so that $y_k(\mathbf{x}) = P(\mathcal{C}_k|\mathbf{x})$, then the function f must satisfy the condition

$$\frac{f'(1-y)}{f'(y)} = \frac{1-y}{y}. \tag{6.193}$$

A class of functions f which satisfies this condition is given by

$$f(y) = \int y^r (1-y)^{r-1} \, dy. \tag{6.194}$$

This includes two important error functions which we have encountered already. For $r = 1$ we obtain $f(y) = y^2/2$ which gives the sum-of-squares error function. Similarly, for $r = 0$ we obtain $f(y) = -\ln(1-y) = -\ln(1-|y|)$ which gives rise to the cross-entropy error function. To see this, consider a single output and note that $f(y,t) = -\ln(1-|y-t|) = -\ln(y)$ if $t = 1$ and $f(y,t) = -\ln(1-|y-t|) = -\ln(1-y)$ if $t = 0$. These can be combined into a single expression of the form

$$-\{t \ln y + (1-t) \ln(1-y)\}. \tag{6.195}$$

Summing over all outputs, as in (6.187), and then over all patterns gives the cross-entropy error for multiple independent attributes in the form (6.145).

As an example of an error function which does not satisfy (6.193), consider the Minkowski-R error measure which is given by $f(y) = y^R$. Substituting this into (6.193) gives

$$y^{R-2} = (1-y)^{R-2} \tag{6.196}$$

which is only satisfied if $R = 2$, corresponding to the sum-of-squares error. For $R \neq 2$, the outputs of the network do not correspond to posterior probabilities. They do, however, represent non-linear discriminant functions, so that the minimum probability of mis-classification is obtained by assigning patterns to the class for which the corresponding network output is largest. To see this, substitute $f(y) = y^R$ into the condition (6.192) satisfied by the network outputs at the minimum of the error function, to give

$$y_k(\mathbf{x}) = \frac{P(\mathcal{C}_k|\mathbf{x})^{1/(R-1)}}{P(\mathcal{C}_k|\mathbf{x})^{1/(R-1)} + [1 - P(\mathcal{C}_k|\mathbf{x})]^{1/(R-1)}}. \tag{6.197}$$

We see that the y_k only represent the posterior probabilities when $R = 2$, corresponding to the sum-of-squares error. However, the decision boundaries correspond to the minimum mis-classification rate discriminant for all values of R since the y_k are monotonic functions of the posterior probabilities $P(\mathcal{C}_k|\mathbf{x})$.

Exercises

6.1 (⋆) Throughout this chapter we have considered data in which the input
vectors **x** are known exactly, but the target vectors **t** are noisy. Consider
instead the situation in which the target data is generated from a smooth
function **h(x)** but where the input data is corrupted by additive noise
(Webb, 1994). Show that the sum-of-squares error, in the infinite data
limit, can be written as

$$E = \frac{1}{2} \int\int \|\mathbf{y}(\mathbf{x} + \boldsymbol{\xi}) - \mathbf{h}(\mathbf{x})\|^2 \, p(\mathbf{x}, \boldsymbol{\xi}) \, d\mathbf{x} \, d\boldsymbol{\xi}. \tag{6.198}$$

By changing variables to $\mathbf{z} = \mathbf{x} + \boldsymbol{\xi}$, and using functional differentiation
(Appendix D), show that the least squares solution is given by

$$\mathbf{y}(\mathbf{z}) = \int \mathbf{h}(\mathbf{z} - \boldsymbol{\xi}) p(\boldsymbol{\xi}|\mathbf{z}) \, d\boldsymbol{\xi} \tag{6.199}$$

so that the optimum solution is again given by the conditional expectation
of the target data.

6.2 (⋆) Consider a model in which the target data is taken to have the form

$$\mathbf{t}^n = \mathbf{y}(\mathbf{x}^n; \mathbf{w}) + \boldsymbol{\epsilon}^n \tag{6.200}$$

where $\boldsymbol{\epsilon}^n$ is drawn from a zero mean Gaussian distribution having a fixed
covariance matrix $\boldsymbol{\Sigma}$. Derive the likelihood function for a data set drawn
from this distribution, and hence write down the error function. The use
of such an error function is called *generalized least squares*, and the usual
sum-of-squares error function corresponds to the special case $\boldsymbol{\Sigma} = \sigma^2 \mathbf{I}$
where $\mathbf{I}$ is the identity matrix.

6.3 (⋆) Consider a network with linear output units whose final-layer weights
are obtained by minimization of a sum-of-squares error function using the
pseudo-inverse matrix. Show that, if the target values for each training
pattern satisfy several linear constraints of the form (6.31) simultaneously,
then the outputs of the trained network will satisfy the same constraints
exactly for an arbitrary input vector.

6.4 (⋆) Verify the normalization of the probability density function in (6.58).
Use the result $\Gamma(1/2) = \sqrt{\pi}$ to show that the Gaussian distribution is a
special case corresponding to $R = 2$.

6.5 (⋆) Write down an expression for the Minkowski-R error function (6.59) with
$R = 1$ in infinite data limit, and hence show that the network mapping
which minimizes the error is given by the conditional *median* of the target
data.

6.6 (⋆⋆) Write down an expression for the conditional mixture density error
function (6.77) in the limit of an infinite data set. Hence, by using functional
differentiation (Appendix D), find expressions satisfied by the quantities

$\alpha_j(\mathbf{x})$, $\mu_j(\mathbf{x})$ and $\sigma_j^2(\mathbf{x})$, in terms of conditional averages, at the minimum of this error. Note that the constraint $\sum_j \alpha_j = 1$ should be enforced by using a Lagrange multiplier (Appendix C). Discuss the interpretation of these expressions.

6.7 ($\star$) Consider the circular normal distribution given by (6.95) and show that, for $\theta - \theta_0 \ll 1$, the shape of the distribution is approximately Gaussian.

6.8 ($\star\star$) In Section 6.4.1 we discussed a technique for modelling the conditional density $p(\theta|\mathbf{x})$ of a periodic variable θ based on a mixture of circular normal distributions. Here we investigate an alternative approach which involves finding a transformation from the periodic variable $\theta \in (0, 2\pi)$ to a Euclidean variable $\chi \in (-\infty, \infty)$, and then applying the Gaussian mixture technique of Section 6.4 to the estimation of the conditional density $\widetilde{p}(\theta|\mathbf{x})$ in χ-space (Bishop and Legleye, 1995). Consider the density function defined by the transformation

$$p(\theta|\mathbf{x}) = \sum_{L=-\infty}^{\infty} \widetilde{p}(\theta + L2\pi|\mathbf{x}) \tag{6.201}$$

where $\widetilde{p}(\chi|\mathbf{x})$ is a density function in χ-space. Show that (6.201) satisfies the periodicity requirement $p(\theta + 2\pi|\mathbf{x}) = p(\theta|\mathbf{x})$. Also, show that, if the density function $\widetilde{p}(\chi|\mathbf{x})$ is normalized on the interval $(-\infty, \infty)$, then the density $p(\theta|\mathbf{x})$ will be normalized on $(0, 2\pi)$. The density function $\widetilde{p}(\chi|\mathbf{x})$ can now be modelled using a mixture of Gaussians $\phi_j(\chi|\mathbf{x})$ of the form

$$\widetilde{p}(\chi|\mathbf{x}) = \sum_{j=1}^{M} \alpha_j(\mathbf{x})\phi_j(\chi|\mathbf{x}). \tag{6.202}$$

Write down the error function given by the negative logarithm of the likelihood of a set of data points $\{\mathbf{x}^n, \theta^n\}$, and find expressions for the derivatives of the error function with respect to the means and variances of the Gaussian components. Assuming that the mixing coefficients α_j are determined by a softmax function of the form (6.74), find the derivatives of the error function with respect to the corresponding network output variables z_j^α. Note that, in a practical implementation, it is necessary to restrict the summation over L to a limited range. Since the Gaussian functions $\phi_j(\chi|\mathbf{x})$ have exponentially decaying tails, this can represent an extremely good approximation in almost all cases.

6.9 ($\star$) Using the definition of the pseudo-inverse matrix given by (6.30), verify that the result (6.105) follows from the pseudo-inverse formula (6.104).

6.10 ($\star$) Verify that, for a 1-of-c target coding scheme, the between-class covariance matrix given by (6.107) reduces to the form (6.109).

6.11 ($\star$) The result (6.108) shows that minimizing a sum-of-squares error function for a network with linear output units, maximizes a particular nonlinear discriminant function defined over the space of activations of the hidden units. Show that if, instead of using 0 and 1 as the network targets, the values 0 and $1/\sqrt{N_k}$ are used, where N_k is the number of patterns in class $\mathcal{C}_k$, then the between-class covariance matrix, given by (6.107) becomes

$$\mathbf{S}_B = \sum_k N_k(\overline{\mathbf{z}}^k - \overline{\mathbf{z}})(\overline{\mathbf{z}}^k - \overline{\mathbf{z}})^\mathrm{T} \tag{6.203}$$

where $\overline{\mathbf{z}}^k$ is defined by (6.110). This is now the standard between-class covariance matrix as introduced in Section 3.6.

6.12 ($\star\star$) Consider a weighted sum-of-squares error function of the form (6.112) in which the network outputs y_k are given by (6.21). Show that the solution for the biases which minimizes the error function is given by

$$w_{k0} = \overline{t}_k - \sum_{j=1}^M w_{kj}\overline{z}_j \tag{6.204}$$

where we have introduced the following weighted averages

$$\overline{t}_k = \frac{\sum_{n=1}^N \kappa_n t_k^n}{\sum_{n=1}^N \kappa_n}, \qquad \overline{z}_j = \frac{\sum_{n=1}^N \kappa_n z_j^n}{\sum_{n=1}^N \kappa_n}. \tag{6.205}$$

Use this result to show that the error function, with the biases set to their optimal values, can be written in the form

$$E = \frac{1}{2}\mathrm{Tr}\{(\mathbf{Z}\mathbf{W}^\mathrm{T} - \mathbf{T})^\mathrm{T}\mathbf{K}^\mathrm{T}\mathbf{K}(\mathbf{Z}\mathbf{W}^\mathrm{T} - \mathbf{T})\} \tag{6.206}$$

where $\mathbf{K} = \mathrm{diag}(\kappa_n^{1/2})$, $(\mathbf{T})_{nk} = \tilde{t}_k^n$, $(\mathbf{W})_{kj} = w_{kj}$ and $(\mathbf{Z})_{nj} = \tilde{z}_j^n$, and we have defined

$$\tilde{t}_k^n = t_k^n - \overline{t}_k, \qquad \tilde{z}_j^n = z_j^n - \overline{z}_j. \tag{6.207}$$

Show that (6.206) has the same form as the error function in (6.103) but with $\mathbf{Z}$ and $\mathbf{T}$ pre-multiplied by $\mathbf{K}$. Hence show that the value of $\mathbf{W}$ which minimizes this error function is given by

$$\mathbf{W}^\mathrm{T} = (\mathbf{K}\mathbf{Z})^\dagger\mathbf{K}\mathbf{T} \tag{6.208}$$

Hence show that minimization of the error (6.206) is equivalent to maximization of a criterion of the form

$$J = \frac{1}{2}\mathrm{Tr}\{\mathbf{S}_B\mathbf{S}_T^{-1}\} \tag{6.209}$$

in which

$$\mathbf{S}_B = \mathbf{Z}^\mathrm{T}\mathbf{K}\mathbf{T}\mathbf{T}^\mathrm{T}\mathbf{K}\mathbf{Z} \tag{6.210}$$

$$\mathbf{S}_T = \mathbf{Z}^T \mathbf{K} \mathbf{Z}. \tag{6.211}$$

Show that, for a 1-of-c target coding scheme, and for weighting factors κ_n given by (6.113), the total covariance matrix $\mathbf{S}_T$ is given by (6.114) and the between-class covariance matrix $\mathbf{S}_B$ is given by (6.116).

6.13 ($\star$) Suppose that, in Exercise 6.11, the target values had been set to $t_k^n = 1 - L_{lk}$ for a pattern n belonging class $\mathcal{C}_l$, where L_{lk} represents the loss associated with assigning such a pattern to class $\mathcal{C}_k$ (loss matrices are introduced in Section 1.10). Show that the between-class covariance matrix given by (6.107) takes the form (6.117). Verify that this reduces to the form (6.109) when $L_{lk} = 1 - \delta_{lk}$.

6.14 ($\star$) Consider the Hessian matrix for the cross-entropy error function (6.120) for two classes and a single network output. Show that, in the limit of an infinite data set, the terms involving second derivatives of the network outputs, as well as some of the terms involving first derivatives, vanish at the minimum of the error function as a consequence of the fact that the network outputs equal the conditional averages of the target data. Extend this result to the cross-entropy error (6.145) corresponding to several independent attributes.

6.15 ($\star$) Show that the entropy measure in (6.145), which was derived for targets $t_k = 0, 1$, applies also in the case where the targets are probabilities with values in the range $(0, 1)$. Do this by considering an extended data set in which each pattern t_k^n is replaced by a set of M patterns of which a fraction $M t_k^n$ are set to 1 and the remainder are set to 0, and then applying (6.145) to this extended data set.

6.16 ($\star$) Consider the error function (6.148), together with a network whose outputs are given by a softmax activation function (6.151), in the limit of an infinite data set. Show that the network output functions $y_k(\mathbf{x})$ which minimize the error are given by the conditional averages of the target data $\langle t_k | \mathbf{x} \rangle$. Hint: since the $\{y_k\}$ are not independent, as a result of the constraint $\sum_k y_k = 1$, consider the functional derivative (Appendix D) with respect to $a_k(\mathbf{x})$ instead.

6.17 ($\star$) Consider the Hessian matrix for the error function (6.148) and a network with a softmax output activation function (6.151) so that $\sum_k y_k(\mathbf{x}) = 1$. Show that the terms involving second derivatives of the network outputs vanish in the limit of infinite data, provided the network has been trained to a minimum of the error function. Hint: make use of the result of Exercise 6.16.

6.18 ($\star$) Consider a classification network in which the targets for training are given by $t_k^n = 1 - L_{lk}$ for an input vector $\mathbf{x}^n$ from class $\mathcal{C}_l$, where L_{lk} are the elements of a loss matrix, as discussed in Section 1.10. Use the general result $y_k(\mathbf{x}) = \langle t_k | \mathbf{x} \rangle$ for the network outputs at the minimum of the error function to show that the outputs are given by weighted posterior probabilities such that selection of the largest output corresponds to the minimum-risk classification.

6.19 ($\star\star$) Generate histograms of the kind shown in Figure 6.13 for a discrete variable by sampling from a distribution consisting of a mixture of two Gaussians. Evaluate numerically the entropy of the histograms using (6.166) and explore the dependence of the entropy on the parameters of the mixture model.

6.20 ($\star$) Using the technique of functional differentiation (Appendix D), together with Lagrange multipliers (Appendix C), show that the probability density function $p(x)$ which maximizes the entropy

$$S = \int p(x) \ln p(x) \, dx \tag{6.212}$$

subject to the constraints

$$\int p(x) \, dx = 1 \tag{6.213}$$

$$\int x p(x) \, dx = \mu \tag{6.214}$$

$$\int |x - \mu|^R p(x) \, dx = \sigma^R \tag{6.215}$$

is given by

$$p(x) = \frac{R^{1-1/R}}{2\sigma\Gamma(1/R)} \exp\left(-\frac{|x - \mu|^R}{R\sigma^R}\right) \tag{6.216}$$

where $\Gamma(a)$ is the gamma function defined on page 28.

6.21 ($\star$) Show that the choice of distribution $q(\mathbf{x})$ which minimizes the cross-entropy (6.181) is given by $q(\mathbf{x}) = p(\mathbf{x})$. To do this, consider the functional derivative (Appendix D) of (6.181) with respect to $q(\mathbf{x})$. This derivative needs to be evaluated subject to the constraint

$$\int q(\mathbf{x}) \, d\mathbf{x} = 1 \tag{6.217}$$

which can be imposed by using a Lagrange multiplier (Appendix C).

6.22 ($\star$) By substituting (6.189) into (6.188) and evaluating the integral over $\mathbf{t}$, derive the result (6.190).

7

PARAMETER OPTIMIZATION ALGORITHMS

In previous chapters, the problem of learning in neural networks has been formulated in terms of the minimization of an error function E. This error is a function of the adaptive parameters (weights and biases) in the network, which we can conveniently group together into a single W-dimensional weight vector $\mathbf{w}$ with components $w_1 \ldots w_W$.

In Chapter 4 it was shown that, for a multi-layer perceptron, the derivatives of an error function with respect to the network parameters can be obtained in a computationally efficient way using back-propagation. We shall see that the use of such gradient information is of central importance in finding algorithms for network training which are sufficiently fast to be of practical use for large-scale applications.

The problem of minimizing continuous, differentiable functions of many variables is one which has been widely studied, and many of the conventional approaches to this problem are directly applicable to the training of neural networks. In this chapter we shall review several of the most important practical algorithms. One of the simplest of these is gradient descent, which has been described briefly in earlier chapters. Here we investigate gradient descent in more detail, and discuss its limitations. We then describe a number of heuristic modifications to gradient descent which aim to improve its performance. Next we review an important class of conventional optimization algorithms based on the concept of conjugate gradients, including a relatively recent variation called scaled conjugate gradients. We then describe the other major class of conventional optimization algorithms known as quasi-Newton methods. Finally, we discuss the powerful Levenberg–Marquardt algorithm which is applicable specifically to a sum-of-squares error function. There are many standard textbooks which cover non-linear optimization techniques, including Polak (1971), Gill *et al.* (1981), Dennis and Schnabel (1983), Luenberger (1984), and Fletcher (1987).

It is sometimes argued that learning algorithms for neural networks should be local (in the sense of the network diagram) so that the computations needed to update each weight can be performed using information available locally to that weight. This requirement may be motivated by interest in modelling biological neural systems or by the desire to implement network algorithms in parallel hardware. Although the locality issue is relevant both to biological plausibility and to hardware implementation, it represents only one facet of these issues, and much more careful analyses are required. Since our goal is to find the most

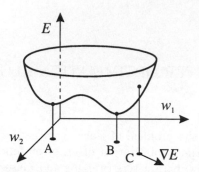

Figure 7.1. Geometrical picture of the error function $E(\mathbf{w})$ as a surface sitting above weight space. Points A and B represent minima of the error function. At any point C, the local gradient of the error surface is given by the vector ∇E.

effective techniques for pattern recognition, there is little point in introducing unnecessary restrictions. We shall therefore regard the issue of locality as irrelevant in the present context.

Most of the algorithms which are described in this chapter are ones which have been found to have good performance in a wide range of applications. However, different algorithms will perform best on different problems and it is therefore not possible to recommend a single universal optimization algorithm. Instead, we highlight the relative advantages and limitations of different algorithms as they are discussed.

7.1 Error surfaces

The problem addressed in this chapter is to find a weight vector $\mathbf{w}$ which minimizes an error function $E(\mathbf{w})$. It is useful to have a simple geometrical picture of the error minimization process, which can be obtained by viewing $E(\mathbf{w})$ as an *error surface* sitting above *weight space*, as shown in Figure 7.1. For networks having a single layer of weights, linear output-unit activation functions, and a sum-of-squares error, the error function will be a quadratic function of the weights. In this case the error surface will have a general multidimensional parabolic form. There is then a single minimum (or possibly a single continuum of degenerate minima), which can be located by solution of a set of coupled linear equations, as discussed in detail in Section 3.4.3.

However, for more general networks, in particular those with more than one layer of adaptive weights, the error function will typically be a highly non-linear function of the weights, and there may exist many minima all of which satisfy

$$\nabla E = 0 \tag{7.1}$$

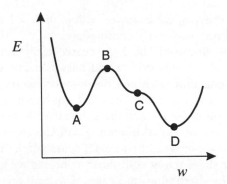

Figure 7.2. A schematic error function for a single parameter w, showing four stationary points at which the local gradient of the error function vanishes. Point A is a local minimum, point B is a local maximum, point C is a saddle-point, and point D is the global minimum.

where ∇E denotes the gradient of E in weight space. The minimum for which the value of the error function is smallest is called the *global minimum* while other minima are called *local minima*. There may also be other points which satisfy the condition (7.1) such as local maxima or saddlepoints. Any vector $\mathbf{w}$ for which this condition is satisfied is called a *stationary point*, and the different kinds of stationary point are illustrated schematically in Figure 7.2.

As a consequence of the non-linearity of the error function, it is not in general possible to find closed-form solutions for the minima. Instead, we consider algorithms which involve a search through weight space consisting of a succession of steps of the form

$$\mathbf{w}^{(\tau+1)} = \mathbf{w}^{(\tau)} + \Delta \mathbf{w}^{(\tau)} \tag{7.2}$$

where τ labels the iteration step. Different algorithms involve different choices for the weight vector increment $\Delta \mathbf{w}^{(\tau)}$. For some algorithms, such as conjugate gradients and the quasi-Newton algorithms discussed later, the error function is guaranteed not to increase as a result of a change to the weights (and hopefully will decrease). One potential disadvantage of such algorithms is that if they reach a local minimum they will remain there forever, as there is no mechanism for them to escape (as this would require a temporary increase in the error function). The choice of initial weights for the algorithm then determines which minimum the algorithm will converge to. Also, the presence of saddlepoints, or regions where the error function is very flat, can cause some iterative algorithms to become 'stuck' for extensive periods of time, thereby mimicking local minima.

Different algorithms can exhibit different behaviour in the neighbourhood of a minimum. If $\epsilon^{(\tau)}$ denotes the distance to the minimum at step τ, then convergence often has the general form

$$\epsilon^{(\tau+1)} \propto (\epsilon^{(\tau)})^L \tag{7.3}$$

where L governs the *order of convergence*. Values of $L = 1$ and $L = 2$ are known respectively as linear and quadratic convergence.

In Section 4.4 we discussed the high degree of symmetry which exists in the weight space of a multi-layered neural network. For instance, a two-layer network with M hidden units exhibits a symmetry factor of $M!2^M$. Thus, for any point in weight space, there will be $M!2^M$ equivalent points which generate the same network mapping, and which therefore give rise to the same value for the error function. Any local or global minimum will therefore be replicated a large number of times throughout weight space. Of course, in a practical application it is irrelevant which of these many equivalent solutions we use. Furthermore, the algorithms we shall be discussing make use of a local stepwise search through weight space, and will be completely unaffected by the presence of the numerous equivalent points elsewhere in weight space.

In Section 6.1.3 we showed that the sum-of-squares error function, in the limit of an infinite data set, can be written as the sum of two terms

$$E = \frac{1}{2} \sum_k \int \{y_k(\mathbf{x}; \mathbf{w}) - \langle t_k | \mathbf{x} \rangle\}^2 p(\mathbf{x})\, d\mathbf{x}$$

$$+ \frac{1}{2} \sum_k \int \{\langle t_k^2 | \mathbf{x} \rangle - \langle t_k | \mathbf{x} \rangle^2\} p(\mathbf{x})\, d\mathbf{x} \tag{7.4}$$

where $y_k(\mathbf{x}; \mathbf{w})$ denotes the activation of output unit k when the network is presented with input vector $\mathbf{x}$, and $\langle t_k | \mathbf{x} \rangle$ denotes the conditional average of the corresponding target variable given by

$$\langle t_k | \mathbf{x} \rangle = \int t_k p(t_k | \mathbf{x})\, dt_k. \tag{7.5}$$

Since only the first term in (7.4) depends on the network weights, the global minimum of the error is obtained when $y_k(\mathbf{x}; \mathbf{w}) = \langle t_k | \mathbf{x} \rangle$. This can be regarded as the optimal solution, as discussed in Section 6.1.3. In practice we must deal with finite data sets, however. If the network is relatively complex (for instance if it has a large number of adaptive parameters) then the best generalization performance might be obtained from a local minimum, or from some other point in weight space which is not a minimum of the error. This leads to a consideration of techniques in which the generalization performance is monitored as a function of time during the training, and the training is halted when the optimum generalization is achieved. Such methods are discussed briefly in Section 9.2.4.

7.2 Local quadratic approximation

A considerable degree of insight into the optimization problem, and into the various techniques for solving it, can be obtained by considering a local quadratic approximation to the error function. Consider the Taylor expansion of $E(\mathbf{w})$ around some point $\widehat{\mathbf{w}}$ in weight space

$$E(\mathbf{w}) = E(\widehat{\mathbf{w}}) + (\mathbf{w} - \widehat{\mathbf{w}})^{\mathrm{T}}\mathbf{b} + \frac{1}{2}(\mathbf{w} - \widehat{\mathbf{w}})^{\mathrm{T}}\mathbf{H}(\mathbf{w} - \widehat{\mathbf{w}}) \qquad (7.6)$$

where $\mathbf{b}$ is defined to be the gradient of E evaluated at $\widehat{\mathbf{w}}$

$$\mathbf{b} \equiv \nabla E|_{\widehat{\mathbf{w}}} \qquad (7.7)$$

and the Hessian matrix $\mathbf{H}$ is defined by

$$(\mathbf{H})_{ij} \equiv \frac{\partial E}{\partial w_i \partial w_j}\bigg|_{\widehat{\mathbf{w}}} . \qquad (7.8)$$

From (7.6), the corresponding local approximation for the gradient is given by

$$\nabla E = \mathbf{b} + \mathbf{H}(\mathbf{w} - \widehat{\mathbf{w}}). \qquad (7.9)$$

For points $\mathbf{w}$ which are close to $\widehat{\mathbf{w}}$, these expressions will give reasonable approximations for the error and its gradient, and they form the basis for much of the subsequent discussion of optimization algorithms.

Consider the particular case of a local quadratic approximation around a point $\mathbf{w}^*$ which is a minimum of the error function. In this case there is no linear term, since $\nabla E = 0$ at $\mathbf{w}^*$, and (7.6) becomes

$$E(\mathbf{w}) = E(\mathbf{w}^*) + \frac{1}{2}(\mathbf{w} - \mathbf{w}^*)^{\mathrm{T}}\mathbf{H}(\mathbf{w} - \mathbf{w}^*) \qquad (7.10)$$

where the Hessian is evaluated at $\mathbf{w}^*$. In order to interpret this geometrically, consider the eigenvalue equation for the Hessian matrix

$$\mathbf{H}\mathbf{u}_i = \lambda_i \mathbf{u}_i \qquad (7.11)$$

where the eigenvectors $\mathbf{u}_i$ form a complete orthonormal set (Appendix A) so that

$$\mathbf{u}_i^{\mathrm{T}}\mathbf{u}_j = \delta_{ij}. \qquad (7.12)$$

We now expand $(\mathbf{w} - \mathbf{w}^*)$ as a linear combination of the eigenvectors in the form

$$\mathbf{w} - \mathbf{w}^* = \sum_i \alpha_i \mathbf{u}_i. \qquad (7.13)$$

Substituting (7.13) into (7.10), and using (7.11) and (7.12), allows the error function to be written in the form

$$E(\mathbf{w}) = E(\mathbf{w}^*) + \frac{1}{2} \sum_i \lambda_i \alpha_i^2. \qquad (7.14)$$

Equation (7.13) can be regarded as a transformation of the coordinate system in which the origin is translated to the point $\mathbf{w}^*$, and the axes are rotated to align with the eigenvectors (through the orthogonal matrix whose columns are the $\mathbf{u}_i$). This transformation is discussed in more detail in Appendix A.

A matrix $\mathbf{H}$ is said to be *positive definite* if

$$\mathbf{v}^{\mathrm{T}} \mathbf{H} \mathbf{v} > 0 \qquad \text{for all } \mathbf{v}. \qquad (7.15)$$

Since the eigenvectors $\{\mathbf{u}_i\}$ form a complete set, an arbitrary vector $\mathbf{v}$ can be written

$$\mathbf{v} = \sum_i \beta_i \mathbf{u}_i \qquad (7.16)$$

From (7.11) and (7.12) we then have

$$\mathbf{v}^{\mathrm{T}} \mathbf{H} \mathbf{v} = \sum_i \beta_i^2 \lambda_i \qquad (7.17)$$

and so $\mathbf{H}$ will be positive definite if all of its eigenvalues are positive. In the new coordinate system whose basis vectors are given by the eigenvectors $\{\mathbf{u}_i\}$, the contours of constant E are ellipses centred on the origin, whose axes are aligned with the eigenvectors and whose lengths are inversely proportional to the square roots of the eigenvalues, as indicated in Figure 7.3. For a one-dimensional weight space, a stationary point w^* will be a minimum if

$$\partial E / \partial w|_{w^*} > 0. \qquad (7.18)$$

The corresponding result in d-dimensions is that the Hessian matrix, evaluated at $\mathbf{w}^*$, should be positive definite (Exercise 7.1).

7.2.1   *Use of gradient information*

For most of the network models and error functions which are discussed in earlier chapters, it is possible to evaluate the gradient of the error function relatively efficiently, for instance by means of the back-propagation procedure. The use of

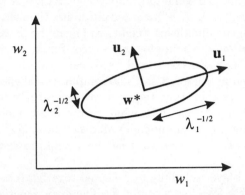

Figure 7.3. In the neighbourhood of a minimum $\mathbf{w}^*$, the error function can be approximated by a quadratic function. Contours of constant error are then ellipses whose axes are aligned with the eigenvectors $\mathbf{u}_i$ of the Hessian matrix, with lengths that are inversely proportional to the square roots of the corresponding eigenvectors λ_i.

this gradient information can lead to significant improvements in the speed with which the minima of the error function can be located. We can easily see why this is so, as follows.

In the quadratic approximation to the error function, given in (7.6), the error surface is specified by the quantities $\mathbf{b}$ and $\mathbf{H}$, which contain a total of $W(W+3)/2$ independent terms (since the matrix $\mathbf{H}$ is symmetric), where W is the dimensionality of $\mathbf{w}$ (i.e. the total number of adaptive parameters in the network). The location of the minimum of this quadratic approximation therefore depends on $\mathcal{O}(W^2)$ parameters, and we should not expect to be able to locate the minimum until we have gathered $\mathcal{O}(W^2)$ independent pieces of information. If we do not make use of gradient information, we would expect to have to perform at least $\mathcal{O}(W^2)$ function evaluations, each of which would require $\mathcal{O}(W)$ steps. Thus, the computational effort needed to find the minimum would scale like $\mathcal{O}(W^3)$.

Now compare this with an algorithm which makes use of the gradient information. Since each evaluation of ∇E brings W items of information, we might hope to find the minimum of the function in $\mathcal{O}(W)$ gradient evaluations. Using back-propagation, each such evaluation takes only $\mathcal{O}(W)$ steps and so the minimum could now be found in $\mathcal{O}(W^2)$ steps. This dramatically improved scaling with W strongly suggests that gradient information should be exploited, as is the case for the optimization algorithms discussed in this chapter.

7.3 Linear output units

As discussed at length in Section 3.4.3, if a sum-of-squares error function is used, and the network mapping depends linearly on the weights, then the minimization of the error function represents a linear problem, which can be solved exactly in a single step using singular value decomposition (SVD). If we consider a more general multi-layer network with linear output units, then the dependence of the network mapping on the final-layer weights will again be linear. This means that the partial optimization of a sum-of-squares error function with respect to these weights (with all other parameters held fixed) can again be performed by linear methods, as discussed in Section 3.4.3. The computational effort involved in SVD is often very much less than that required for general non-linear optimization, which suggests that it may be worthwhile to use linear methods for the final-layer weights, and non-linear methods for all other parameters. This leads to the following hybrid procedure for optimizing the weights in such networks (Webb and Lowe, 1988).

Suppose the final-layer weights are collected together into a vector $\mathbf{w}_L$, with the remaining weights forming a vector $\widetilde{\mathbf{w}}$. The error function can then be expressed as $E(\mathbf{w}_L, \widetilde{\mathbf{w}})$, which is a quadratic function of $\mathbf{w}_L$. For any given value of $\widetilde{\mathbf{w}}$ we can perform a one-step exact minimization with respect to the $\mathbf{w}_L$ using SVD, in which $\widetilde{\mathbf{w}}$ is held fixed. We denote the optimum $\mathbf{w}_L$ by $\mathbf{w}_L(\widetilde{\mathbf{w}})$. A conventional non-linear optimization method (such as conjugate gradients, or the quasi-Newton methods to be described later) is used to minimize E with respect to $\widetilde{\mathbf{w}}$. Every time the value of $\widetilde{\mathbf{w}}$ is changed, the weights $\mathbf{w}_L$ are recomputed. We can therefore regard the final layer weights $\mathbf{w}_L$ as evolving on a fast time-scale compared to the remaining weights $\widetilde{\mathbf{w}}$. Effectively, the non-linear optimization is attempting to minimize a function $\widetilde{E}(\mathbf{w}_L(\widetilde{\mathbf{w}}), \widetilde{\mathbf{w}})$ with respect to $\widetilde{\mathbf{w}}$. An obvious advantage of this method is that the dimensionality of the effective search space for the non-linear algorithm is reduced, and we might hope that this would reduce the number of training iterations which is required to find a good solution. However, this is offset to some extent by the greater computational effort required at each such step. Webb and Lowe (1988) show that, for some problems, this hybrid approach can yield better solutions, or can require less computational effort, than full non-linear optimization of the complete network.

7.4 Optimization in practice

In order to apply the algorithms described in this chapter to real problems, we need to address a variety of practical issues. Here we discuss procedures for initializing the weights in a network, criteria used to terminate training, and normalized error functions for assessing the performance of trained networks.

All of the training algorithms which we consider in this chapter begin by initializing the weights in the network to some randomly chosen values. We have already seen that optimization algorithms which proceed by a steady monotonic reduction in the error function can become stuck in local minima. A suitable choice of initial weights is therefore potentially important in allowing the training algorithm to produce a good set of weights, and in addition may lead to improvements in the speed of training. Even stochastic algorithms such as gradient descent, which have the possibility of escaping from local minima, can show strong sensitivity to the initial conditions. The initialization of weights for radial basis function networks has already been dealt with in Chapter 6. Here we shall concern ourselves with multi-layer perceptrons having sigmoidal hidden-unit activation functions.

The majority of initialization procedures in current use involve setting the weights to randomly chosen small values. Random values are used in order to avoid problems due to symmetries in the network. The initial weight values are chosen to be small so that sigmoidal activation functions are not driven into the saturation regions where $g'(a)$ is very small (which would lead to small ∇E, and consequently a very flat error surface). If the weights are too small, however, all of the sigmoidal activation functions will be approximately linear, which can again lead to slow training. This suggests that the summed inputs to the sigmoidal functions should be of order unity. A random initialization of the weights requires that some choice be made for the distribution function from which the weights are generated. We now examine the choice of this distribution in a little more detail.

We shall suppose that the input values to the network $x_1, \ldots x_d$ have been rescaled so as to have zero mean $\langle x_i \rangle = 0$ and unit variance $\langle x_i^2 \rangle = 1$, where the notation $\langle \cdot \rangle$ will be used to denote an average both over the training data set and over all the choices of initial network weights. The pre-processing of input data prior to network training, in order to achieve this normalization, is discussed in more detail in Section 8.2. The weights are usually generated from a simple distribution, such as a spherically symmetric Gaussian, for convenience, and this is generally taken to have zero mean, since there is no reason to prefer any other specific point in weight space. The choice of variance σ^2 for the distribution can be important, however. For a unit in the first hidden layer, the activation is given by $y = g(a)$ where

$$a = \sum_{i=0}^{d} w_i x_i. \tag{7.19}$$

Since the choice of weight values is uncorrelated with the inputs, the average of a is zero

$$\langle a \rangle = \sum_{i=0}^{d} \langle w_i x_i \rangle = \sum_{i=0}^{d} \langle w_i \rangle \langle x_i \rangle = 0 \tag{7.20}$$

since $\langle x_i \rangle = 0$. Next consider the variance of a

$$\langle a^2 \rangle = \left\langle \left(\sum_{i=0}^{d} w_i x_i \right) \left(\sum_{j=0}^{d} w_j x_j \right) \right\rangle = \sum_{i=0}^{d} \langle w_i^2 \rangle \langle x_i^2 \rangle = \sigma^2 d \tag{7.21}$$

where σ^2 is the variance of the distribution of weights, and we have used the fact that the weight values are uncorrelated and hence $\langle w_i w_j \rangle = \delta_{ij} \sigma^2$, together with $\langle x_i^2 \rangle = 1$. As we have discussed already, we would like a to be of order unity so that the activations of the hidden units are determined by the non-linear part of the sigmoids, without saturating. From (7.21) this suggests that the standard deviation of the distribution used to generate the initial weights should scale like $\sigma \propto d^{-1/2}$. A similar argument can be applied to the weights feeding into any other unit in the network, if we assume that the outputs of hidden units are appropriately distributed.

Since a particular training run is sensitive to the initial conditions for the weights, it is common practice to train a particular network many times using different weight initializations. This leads to a set of different networks whose generalization performance can be compared by making use of independent data. In this case it is possible to keep the best network and simply discard the remainder. However, improved prediction capability can often be achieved by forming a *committee* of networks from amongst the better ones found during the training process, as discussed in Section 9.6. The use of multiple training runs also plays a related role in building a mixture model for the distribution of weight values in the Bayesian framework, as discussed in Section 10.7.

When using non-linear optimization algorithms, some choice must be made of when to stop the training process. Some of the possible choices are listed below:

1. Stop after a fixed number of iterations. The problem with this approach is that it is difficult to know in advance how many iterations would be appropriate, although an approximate idea can be obtained from some preliminary tests. If several networks are being trained (e.g. with various numbers of hidden units) then the appropriate number of iterations may be different for different networks.

2. Stop when a predetermined amount of CPU (central processing unit) time has been used. Again, it is difficult to know what constitutes a suitable time unless some preliminary tests are performed first. Some adjustment for different architectures may again be necessary.

3. Stop when the error function falls below some specified value. This suffers from the problem that the specified value may never be reached, so some limit on CPU time may also be required.

4. Stop when the relative change in error function falls below some specified value. This may lead to premature termination if the error function decreases relatively slowly during some part of the training run.

5. Stop training when the error measured using an independent validation set starts to increase. This approach is generally used as part of a strategy to optimize the generalization performance of the network, and will be discussed further in Section 9.2.4.

In practice some combination of the above methods may be employed as part of a largely empirical process of parameter optimization.

Since the value of the error function depends on the number of patterns, it is useful to consider a normalized error function for the purposes of assessing the performance of a trained network. For a sum-of-squares error, an appropriate choice would be the normalized error function given by

$$\widetilde{E} = \sqrt{\frac{\sum_n \|\mathbf{y}(\mathbf{x}^n) - \mathbf{t}^n\|^2}{\sum_n \|\mathbf{\bar{t}} - \mathbf{t}^n\|^2}} \tag{7.22}$$

where $\mathbf{\bar{t}}$ is the mean of the target data over the test set (Webb *et al.*, 1988). This error function equals unity when the model is as good a predictor of the target data as the simple model $\mathbf{y} = \mathbf{\bar{t}}$, and equals zero if the model predicts the data values exactly. A value of $\widetilde{E}$ of 0.1 will often prove adequate for simple classification problems, while for regression applications a significantly smaller value may be needed. For reasons introduced in Chapter 1, and discussed at greater length in Chapter 9, the performance of the trained network should be assessed using a data set which is independent of the training data.

For classification problems, it is appropriate to test the performance of the trained network by assessing the number of misclassifications, or more generally the value of the total loss (Section 1.10).

7.5 Gradient descent

One of the simplest network training algorithms, and one which we have already encountered several times in previous chapters, is gradient descent, sometimes also known as *steepest descent*. In the *batch* version of gradient descent, we start with some initial guess for the weight vector (which is often chosen at random) denoted by $\mathbf{w}^{(0)}$. We then iteratively update the weight vector such that, at step τ, we move a short distance in the direction of the greatest rate of decrease of the error, i.e. in the direction of the negative gradient, evaluated at $\mathbf{w}^{(\tau)}$:

$$\Delta\mathbf{w}^{(\tau)} = -\eta \left.\nabla E\right|_{\mathbf{w}^{(\tau)}}. \tag{7.23}$$

Note that the gradient is re-evaluated at each step. In the *sequential*, or *pattern-based*, version of gradient descent, the error function gradient is evaluated for just one pattern at a time, and the weights updated using

$$\Delta\mathbf{w}^{(\tau)} = -\eta \left.\nabla E^n\right|_{\mathbf{w}^{(\tau)}} \tag{7.24}$$

where the different patterns n in the training set can be considered in sequence, or selected at random. The parameter η is called the *learning rate*, and, provided its value is sufficiently small, we expect that, in the batch version (7.23) of gradient descent, the value of E will decrease at each successive step, eventually leading to a weight vector at which the condition (7.1) is satisfied.

For the sequential update (7.24) we might also hope for a steady reduction in error since, for sufficiently small η, the average direction of motion in weight space should approximate the negative of the local gradient. In order to study this

more carefully, we note that sequential gradient descent (7.24) is reminiscent of
the Robbins–Monro procedure (Section 2.4.1) for finding the zero of a regression
function (in this case the error function gradient). The analogy becomes precise,
and we are assured of convergence, if the learning rate parameter η is made to
decrease at each step of the algorithm in accordance with the requirements of the
theorem (Luo, 1991). These can be satisfied by choosing $\eta^{(\tau)} \propto 1/\tau$, although
such a choice leads to very slow convergence. In practice, a constant value of η is
often used as this generally leads to better results even though the guarantee of
convergence is lost. There is still a serious difficulty with this approach, however.
If η is too large, the algorithm may overshoot leading to an increase in E and
possibly to divergent oscillations resulting in a complete breakdown in the algorithm. Conversely, if η is chosen to be too small the search can proceed extremely
slowly, leading to very long computation times. Furthermore, the optimum value
for η will typically change during the course of the minimization.

An important advantage of the sequential approach over batch methods arises
if there is a high degree of redundant information in the data set. As a simple example, suppose that we create a larger training set from the original one simply
by replicating the original data set ten times. Every evaluation of E then takes
ten times as long, and so a batch algorithm will take ten times as long to find a
given solution. By contrast, the sequential algorithm updates the weights after
each pattern presentation, and so will be unaffected by the replication of data.
Later in this chapter we describe a number of powerful optimization algorithms
(such as conjugate gradients and quasi-Newton methods) which are intrinsically
batch techniques. For such algorithms it is still possible to gain some of the
advantages of sequential techniques by grouping the data into blocks and presenting the blocks sequentially as if each of them was representative of the whole
data set. Some experimentation may be needed to determine a suitable size for
the blocks.

Another potential advantage of the sequential approach is that, since it is a
stochastic algorithm, it has the possibility of escape from local minima. Later
in this chapter we shall discuss a number of algorithms which have the property
that each step of the algorithm is guaranteed not to produce an increase in the
error function. If such an algorithm finds its way into a local minimum it will
typically remain there indefinitely.

7.5.1 Convergence

As we have already indicated, one of the limitations of the gradient descent
technique is the need to choose a suitable value for the learning rate parameter
η. The problems with gradient descent do not stop there, however. Figure 7.4
depicts the contours of E, for a hypothetical two-dimensional weight space, in
which the curvature of E varies significantly with direction. At most points on the
error surface, the local gradient does not point directly towards the minimum.
Gradient descent then takes many small steps to reach the minimum, and is
clearly a very inefficient procedure.

We can gain deeper insight into the nature of this problem by considering

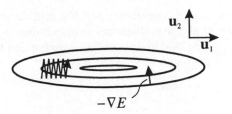

$$-\nabla E$$

Figure 7.4. Schematic illustration of fixed-step gradient descent for an error function which has substantially different curvatures along different directions. Ellipses depict contours of constant E, so that the error surface has the form of a long valley. The vectors $\mathbf{u}_1$ and $\mathbf{u}_2$ represent the eigenvectors of the Hessian matrix. Note that, for most points in weight space, the local negative gradient vector $-\nabla E$ does not point towards the minimum of the error function. Successive steps of gradient descent can oscillate across the valley, with very slow progress along the valley towards the minimum.

the quadratic approximation to the error function in the neighbourhood of the minimum, discussed earlier in Section 7.2. From (7.10), (7.11) and (7.13), the gradient of the error function in this approximation can be written as

$$\nabla E = \sum_i \alpha_i \lambda_i \mathbf{u}_i. \tag{7.25}$$

From (7.13) we also have

$$\Delta \mathbf{w} = \sum_i \Delta \alpha_i \mathbf{u}_i. \tag{7.26}$$

Combining (7.25) with (7.26) and the gradient descent formula (7.23), and using the orthonormality relation (7.12) for the eigenvectors of the Hessian, we obtain the following expression for the change in α_i at each step of the gradient descent algorithm

$$\Delta \alpha_i = -\eta \lambda_i \alpha_i \tag{7.27}$$

from which it follows that

$$\alpha_i^{\text{new}} = (1 - \eta \lambda_i) \alpha_i^{\text{old}} \tag{7.28}$$

where 'old' and 'new' denote values before and after a weight update. Using the orthonormality relation (7.12) for the eigenvectors, together with (7.13), we have

$$\mathbf{u}_i^T(\mathbf{w} - \mathbf{w}^*) = \alpha_i \tag{7.29}$$

and so α_i can be interpreted as the distance to the minimum along the direction $\mathbf{u}_i$. From (7.28) we see that these distances evolve independently such that, at each step, the distance along the direction of $\mathbf{u}_i$ is multiplied by a factor $(1-\eta\lambda_i)$. After a total of T steps we have

$$\alpha_i^{(T)} = (1 - \eta\lambda_i)^T \alpha_i^{(0)} \tag{7.30}$$

and so, provided $|1 - \eta\lambda_i| < 1$, the limit $T \to \infty$ leads to $\alpha_i = 0$, which from (7.29) shows that $\mathbf{w} = \mathbf{w}^*$ and so the weight vector has reached the minimum of the error. Note that (7.30) demonstrates that gradient descent leads to linear convergence in the neighbourhood of a minimum. Also, convergence to the stationary point requires that all of the λ_i be positive, which in turn implies that the stationary point is indeed a minimum (Exercise 7.1).

By making η larger we can make the factor $(1 - \eta\lambda_i)$ smaller and hence improve the speed of convergence. There is a limit to how large η can be made, however. We can permit $(1-\eta\lambda_i)$ to go negative (which gives oscillating values of α_i) but we must ensure that $|1-\eta\lambda_i| < 1$ otherwise the α_i values will diverge. This limits the value of η to $\eta < 2/\lambda_{\max}$ where $\lambda_{\max}$ is the largest of the eigenvalues. The rate of convergence, however, is dominated by the smallest eigenvalue, so with η set to its largest permitted value, the convergence along the direction corresponding to the smallest eigenvalue (the long axis of the ellipse in Figure 7.4) will be governed by

$$\left(1 - \frac{2\lambda_{\min}}{\lambda_{\max}}\right) \tag{7.31}$$

where $\lambda_{\min}$ is the smallest eigenvalue. If the ratio $\lambda_{\min}/\lambda_{\max}$ (whose reciprocal is known as the *condition number* of the Hessian) is very small, corresponding to highly elongated elliptical error contours as in Figure 7.4, then progress towards the minimum will be extremely slow. From our earlier discussion of quadratic error surfaces, we might expect to be able to find the minimum exactly using as few as $W(W + 3)/2$ error function evaluations. Gradient descent is an extremely inefficient algorithm for error function minimization, since the number of function evaluations can easily be very much greater than this. Later we shall encounter algorithms which are guaranteed to find the minimum of a quadratic error surface exactly in a small, fixed number of steps which is $\mathcal{O}(W^2)$.

The gradient descent procedure we have described so far involves taking a succession of finite steps through weight space. We can instead imagine the evolution of the weight vector taking place continuously as a function of time τ. The gradient descent rule is then replaced by a set of coupled non-linear ordinary differential equations of the form

$$\frac{dw_i}{d\tau} = -\eta \frac{\partial E}{\partial w_i} \tag{7.32}$$

where w_i represents any weight parameter in the network. These equations correspond to the motion of a massless particle with position vector $\mathbf{w}$ moving in a potential field $E(\mathbf{w})$ subject to viscous drag with viscosity coefficient η^{-1}. They represent a set of *stiff* differential equations (ones characterized by several widely differing time-scales) as a consequence of the fact that the Hessian matrix often has widely differing eigenvalues. The simple gradient descent formula (7.23) represents a 'fixed-step forward Euler' technique for solving (7.32), which is a particularly inefficient approach for stiff equations. Application of specialized techniques for solving stiff ordinary differential equations (Gear, 1971) to the system in (7.32) can give significant improvements in convergence time (Owens and Filkin, 1989).

7.5.2 *Momentum*

One very simple technique for dealing with the problem of widely differing eigenvalues is to add a *momentum* term to the gradient descent formula (Plaut *et al.*, 1986). This effectively adds inertia to the motion through weight space (Exercise 7.3) and smoothes out the oscillations depicted in Figure 7.4. The modified gradient descent formula is given by

$$\Delta \mathbf{w}^{(\tau)} = -\eta \, \nabla E|_{\mathbf{w}^{(\tau)}} + \mu \Delta \mathbf{w}^{(\tau-1)} \tag{7.33}$$

where μ is called the momentum parameter.

To understand the effect of the momentum term, consider first the motion through a region of weight space for which the error surface has relatively low curvature, as indicated in Figure 7.5. If we make the approximation that the gradient is unchanging, then we can apply (7.33) iteratively to a long series of weight updates, and then sum the resulting arithmetic series to give

$$\Delta \mathbf{w} = -\eta \nabla E\{1 + \mu + \mu^2 + \ldots\} \tag{7.34}$$

$$= -\frac{\eta}{1-\mu} \nabla E \tag{7.35}$$

and we see that the result of the momentum term is to increase the effective learning rate from η to $\eta/(1-\mu)$.

By contrast, in a region of high curvature in which the gradient descent is oscillatory, as indicated in Figure 7.6, successive contributions from the momentum term will tend to cancel, and the effective learning rate will be close to η. Thus, the momentum term can lead to faster convergence towards the minimum without causing divergent oscillations. A schematic illustration of the effect of a momentum term is shown in Figure 7.7. From (7.35) we see that μ must lie between in the range $0 \le \mu \le 1$.

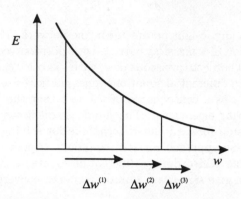

Figure 7.5. With a fixed learning rate parameter, gradient descent down a surface with low curvature leads to successively smaller steps (linear convergence). In such a situation, the effect of a momentum term is similar to an increase in the effective learning rate parameter.

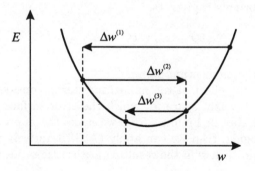

Figure 7.6. For a situation in which successive steps of gradient descent are oscillatory, a momentum term has little influence on the effective value of the learning rate parameter.

The inclusion of momentum generally leads to a significant improvement in the performance of gradient descent. Nevertheless, the algorithm remains relatively inefficient. The inclusion of momentum also introduces a second parameter μ whose value needs to be chosen, in addition to that of the learning rate parameter η.

7.5.3 Enhanced gradient descent

As we have seen, gradient descent, even with a momentum term included, is not a particularly efficient algorithm for error function minimization. There have been numerous attempts in recent years to improve the performance of basic gradient

Figure 7.7. Illustration of the effect of adding a momentum term to the gradient descent algorithm, showing the more rapid progress along the valley of the error function, compared with the unmodified gradient descent shown in Figure 7.4.

descent for neural network training by making various *ad hoc* modifications. We shall not attempt to review them all here as the literature is much too extensive, and we will shortly be considering several robust, theoretically well-founded optimization algorithms. Instead we consider a few illustrative examples of such techniques which attempt to address various deficiencies of the basic gradient descent procedure.

One obvious problem with simple gradient descent plus momentum is that it contains two parameters, η and μ, whose values must be selected by trial and error. The optimum values for these parameters will depend on the particular problem, and will typically vary during training. We might therefore seek some procedure for setting these automatically as part of the training algorithm. One such approach is the *bold driver* technique (Vogl *et al.*, 1988; Battiti, 1989). Consider the situation without a momentum term first. The idea is to check whether the error function has actually decreased after each step of the gradient descent. If it has increased then the algorithm must have overshot the minimum (i.e. the minimum along the direction of the weight change) and so the learning rate parameter must have been too large. In this case the weight change is undone, and the learning rate is decreased. This process is repeated until a decrease in error is found. If, however, the error decreased at a given step, then the new weight values are accepted. However, the learning rate might have been too small, and so its value is increased. This leads to the following prescription for updating the learning rate parameter:

$$\eta_{\text{new}} = \begin{cases} \rho\eta_{\text{old}} & \text{if } \Delta E < 0 \\ \sigma\eta_{\text{old}} & \text{if } \Delta E > 0. \end{cases} \tag{7.36}$$

The parameter ρ is chosen to be slightly larger than unity (a typical value might be $\rho = 1.1$) in order to avoid frequent occurrences of an error increase, since in such cases the error evaluation is wasted. The parameter σ is taken to be significantly less than unity ($\sigma = 0.5$ is typical) so that the algorithm quickly reverts to finding a step which decreases the error, again to minimize wasted computation. Many variations of this heuristic are possible, such as increasing η

linearly (by a fixed increment) rather than exponentially (by a fixed factor). If we include momentum in the bold driver algorithm, the momentum coefficient can be set to some fixed value (selected in an *ad hoc* fashion), but the weight update is usually reset along the negative gradient direction after every occurrence of an error function increase, which is equivalent to setting the momentum coefficient temporarily to zero (Vogl *et al.*, 1988).

A more principled approach to setting the optimal learning rate parameter was introduced by Le Cun *et al.* (1993). In Section 7.5.1 we showed that the largest value which can be used for the learning rate parameter was given by $\eta_{max} = 2/\lambda_{max}$, where λ_{max} is the largest eigenvalue of the Hessian matrix. It is easily shown (Exercise 7.5) that if an arbitrary vector is alternately normalized and then multiplied by the Hessian, it eventually converges to λ_{max} times the corresponding eigenvector. The length of this vector then gives λ_{max} itself. Evaluation of the product of the Hessian with a vector can be performed efficiently by using the $\mathcal{R}\{\cdot\}$-operator technique discussed in Section 4.10.7. Once a suitable value for the learning rate has been determined, the standard gradient descent technique is applied.

We have already noted that the (negative) gradient vector need not point towards the error function minimum, even for a quadratic error surface, as indicated in Figure 7.4. In addition, we have seen that long narrow valleys in the error function, characterized by a Hessian matrix with widely differing eigenvalues, can lead to very slow progress down the valley, as a consequence of the need to keep the learning rate small in order to avoid divergent oscillations across the valley. One approach that has been suggested for dealing with this problem (Jacobs, 1988) is to introduce a separate learning rate for each weight in the network, with procedures for updating these learning rates during the training process. The gradient descent rule then becomes

$$\Delta w_i^{(\tau)} = -\eta_i^{(\tau)} \frac{\partial E}{\partial w_i^{(\tau)}}. \tag{7.37}$$

Heuristically, we might wish to increase a particular learning rate when the derivative of E with respect to the corresponding parameter has the same sign on consecutive steps since this weight is moving steadily in the downhill direction. Conversely, if the sign of the gradient changes on consecutive steps, this signals oscillation, and the learning rate parameter should be decreased.

One way to implement this is to take

$$\Delta\eta_i^{(\tau)} = \gamma g_i^{(\tau)} g_i^{(\tau-1)} \tag{7.38}$$

where

$$g_i^{(\tau)} = \frac{\partial E}{\partial w_i^{(\tau)}} \tag{7.39}$$

and $\gamma > 0$ is a step-size parameter. This prescription is called the *delta-delta* rule (since, in Jacobs (1988) the notation δ_i was used instead of g_i to denote the components of the local gradient vector). For the case of a quadratic error surface, it can be derived by minimizing the error with respect to the learning rate parameters (Exercise 7.6). This rule does not work well in practice since it can lead to negative values for the learning rate, which results in uphill steps, unless the value of γ is set very small, in which case the algorithm exhibits little improvement over conventional gradient descent. A modification to the algorithm, known as the *delta-bar-delta* rule is to take

$$\Delta \eta_i^{(\tau)} = \begin{cases} \kappa & \text{if } \bar{g}_i^{(\tau-1)} g_i^{(\tau)} > 0 \\ -\phi \eta_i^{(\tau)} & \text{if } \bar{g}_i^{(\tau-1)} g_i^{(\tau)} < 0 \end{cases} \tag{7.40}$$

where

$$\bar{g}_i^{(\tau)} = (1 - \theta) g_i^{(\tau)} + \theta \bar{g}_i^{(\tau-1)} \tag{7.41}$$

so that $\bar{g}$ is an exponentially weighted average of the current and previous values of g. This algorithm appears to work moderately well in practice, at least for some problems. One of its obvious drawbacks, however, is that it now contains four parameters (θ, ϕ, κ and μ) if we include momentum. A more serious difficulty is that the algorithm rests on the assumption that we can regard the weight parameters as being relatively independent. This would be the case for a quadratic error function if the Hessian matrix were diagonal (so that the major axes of the ellipse in Figure 7.3 were aligned with the weight axes). In practice, the weights in a typical neural network are strongly coupled, leading to a Hessian matrix which is often far from diagonal. The solution to this problem lies in a number of standard optimization algorithms which we shall discuss shortly.

Another heuristic scheme, known as *quickprop* (Fahlman, 1988), also treats the weights as if they were quasi-independent. The idea is to approximate the error surface, as a function of each of the weights, by a quadratic polynomial (i.e. a parabola), and then to use two successive evaluations of the error function, and an evaluation of its gradient, to determine the coefficients of the polynomial. At the next step of the iteration, the weight parameter is moved to the minimum of the parabola. This leads to an expression for the weight update at step τ given by (Exercise 7.7)

$$\Delta w_i^{(\tau+1)} = \frac{g_i^{(\tau)}}{g_i^{(\tau-1)} - g_i^{(\tau)}} \Delta w_i^{(\tau)}. \tag{7.42}$$

The algorithm can be started using a single step of gradient descent. This assumes that the result of the local quadratic fit is to give a parabola with a minimum. If instead it leads to a parabola with a maximum, the algorithm can take an uphill step. Also, some bound on the maximum size of step needs to be imposed to deal with the problem of a nearly flat parabola, and several other fixes are needed in order to get the algorithm to work in practice.

7.6 Line search

The algorithms which are described in this chapter involve taking a sequence of steps through weight space. It is convenient to consider each of these steps in two parts. First we must decide the direction in which to move, and second, we must decide how far to move in that direction. With simple gradient descent, the direction of each step is given by the local negative gradient of the error function, and the step size is determined by an arbitrary learning rate parameter. We might expect that a better procedure would be to move along the direction of the negative gradient to find the point at which the error is minimized. More generally we can consider some *search direction* in weight space, and then find the minimum of the error function along that direction. This procedure is referred to as a *line search*, and it forms the basis for several algorithms which are considerably more powerful than gradient descent. We first consider how line searches can be implemented in practice.

Suppose that at step τ in some algorithm the current weight vector is $\mathbf{w}^{(\tau)}$, and we wish to consider a particular search direction $\mathbf{d}^{(\tau)}$ through weight space. The minimum along the search direction then gives the next value for the weight vector:

$$\mathbf{w}^{(\tau+1)} = \mathbf{w}^{(\tau)} + \lambda^{(\tau)}\mathbf{d}^{(\tau)} \tag{7.43}$$

where the parameter $\lambda^{(\tau)}$ is chosen to minimize

$$E(\lambda) = E(\mathbf{w}^{(\tau)} + \lambda\mathbf{d}^{(\tau)}). \tag{7.44}$$

This gives us an automatic procedure for setting the step length, once we have chosen the search direction.

The line search represents a one-dimensional minimization problem. A simple approach would be to proceed along the search direction in small steps, evaluating the error function at each new position, and stop when the error starts to increase (Hush and Salas, 1988). It is possible, however, to find very much more efficient approaches (Press *et al.*, 1992). Consider first the issue of whether to make use of gradient information in performing a line search. We have already argued that there is generally a substantial advantage to be gained from using gradient information for the general problem of seeking the minimum of the error function E in the W-dimensional weight space. For the sub-problem of line search, however, the argument is somewhat different. Since this is now a one-dimensional problem, both the value of the error function and the gradient of the error function each represent just one piece of information. An error function calculation requires one forward propagation and hence needs $\sim 2NW$ operations,

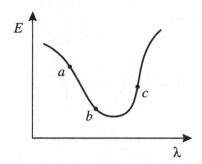

Figure 7.8. An example of an error function which depends on a parameter λ governing distance along the search direction, showing a minimum which has been bracketed. The three points $a < b < c$ are such that $E(a) > E(b)$ and $E(c) > E(b)$. This ensures that the minimum lies somewhere in the interval (a, c).

where N is the number of patterns in the data set. An error function gradient evaluation, however, requires a forward propagation, a backward propagation, and a set of multiplications to form the derivatives. It therefore needs $\sim 5NW$ operations, although it does allow the error function itself to be evaluated as well. On balance, the line search is slightly more efficient if it makes use of error function evaluations only.

Each line search proceeds in two stages. The first stage is to *bracket* the minimum by finding three points $a < b < c$ along the search direction such that $E(a) > E(b)$ and $E(c) > E(b)$, as shown in Figure 7.8. Since the error function is continuous, this ensures that there is a minimum somewhere in the interval (a, c) (Press *et al.*, 1992). The second stage is to locate the minimum itself. Since the error function is smooth and continuous, this can be achieved by a process of parabolic interpolation. This involves fitting a quadratic polynomial to the error function evaluated at three successive points, and then moving to the minimum of the parabola, as illustrated in Figure 7.9. The process can be repeated by evaluating the error function at the new point, and then fitting a new parabola to this point and two of the previous points. In practice, several refinements are also included, leading to the very robust *Brent's* algorithm (Brent, 1973). Line-search algorithms, and termination criteria, are reviewed in Luenberger (1984).

An important issue concerns the accuracy with which the line searches are performed. Depending on the particular algorithm in which the line search is to be used, it may be wasteful to invest too much computational time in evaluating the minimum along each search direction to high accuracy. We shall return to this point later. For the moment, we make one comment regarding the limit of accuracy which can be achieved in a line search. Near a minimum at λ_0, the error function along the search direction can be approximated by

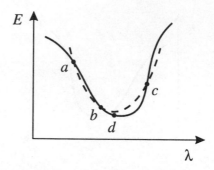

Figure 7.9. An illustration of the process of parabolic interpolation used to perform line-search minimization. The solid curve depicts the error as a function of distance λ along the search direction, and the error is evaluated at three points $a < b < c$ which are such that $E(a) > E(b)$ and $E(c) > E(b)$. A parabola (shown dotted) is fitted to the three points a, b, c. The minimum of the parabola, at d, gives an approximation to the minimum of $E(\lambda)$. The process can be repeated by fitting another parabola through three points given by d and whichever of two of the previous points have the smallest error values (b and c in this example).

$$E(\lambda) = E(\lambda_0) + \frac{1}{2}E''(\lambda_0)(\lambda - \lambda_0)^2. \tag{7.45}$$

Thus $\lambda - \lambda_0$ must typically be at least of the order of the *square root* of the machine precision before the difference between $E(\lambda)$ and $E(\lambda_0)$ is significant. This limits the accuracy with which the minimum can be found. For double-precision arithmetic this implies that the minimum can only be found to a relative accuracy of approximately 3×10^{-8}. In practice is may be better to settle for much lower accuracy than this.

7.7   Conjugate gradients

In the previous section we considered procedures for line-search minimization along a specified search direction. To apply line search to the problem of error function minimization we need to choose a suitable search direction at each stage of the algorithm. Suppose we have already minimized along a search direction given by the local negative gradient vector. We might suppose that the search direction at the next iteration should be given by the negative gradient vector at the new position. However, the use of successive gradient vectors turns out in general not to represent the best choice of search direction. To see why, we note that at the minimum of the line search we have, from (7.44)

$$\frac{\partial}{\partial \lambda} E(\mathbf{w}^{(\tau)} + \lambda \mathbf{d}^{(\tau)}) = 0 \tag{7.46}$$

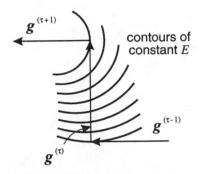

Figure 7.10. After a line minimization, the new gradient is orthogonal to the line-search direction. Thus, if the search directions are always chosen to co-incide with the negative gradients of the error function, as indicated here, then successive search directions will be orthogonal, and the error function minimization will typically proceed very slowly.

which gives

$$\mathbf{g}^{(\tau+1)\mathrm{T}}\mathbf{d}^{(\tau)} = 0 \tag{7.47}$$

where $\mathbf{g} \equiv \nabla E$. Thus, the gradient at the new minimum is orthogonal to the previous search direction, as illustrated geometrically in Figure 7.10. Choosing successive search directions to be the local (negative) gradient directions can lead to the problem already indicated in Figure 7.4 in which the search point oscillates on successive steps while making little progress towards the minimum. The algorithm can then take many steps to converge, even for a quadratic error function.

The solution to this problem lies in choosing the successive search directions $\mathbf{d}^{(\tau)}$ such that, at each step of the algorithm, the component of the gradient parallel to the previous search direction, which has just been made zero, is un-altered (to lowest order). This is illustrated in Figure 7.11. Suppose we have already performed a line minimization along the direction $\mathbf{d}^{(\tau)}$, starting from the point $\mathbf{w}^{(\tau)}$, to give the new point $\mathbf{w}^{(\tau+1)}$. Then at the point $\mathbf{w}^{(\tau+1)}$ we have

$$\mathbf{g}(\mathbf{w}^{(\tau+1)})^{\mathrm{T}}\mathbf{d}^{(\tau)} = 0. \tag{7.48}$$

We now choose the next search direction $\mathbf{d}^{(\tau+1)}$ such that, along this new direc-tion, we retain the property that the component of the gradient parallel to the previous search direction remains zero (to lowest order). Thus we require that

$$\mathbf{g}(\mathbf{w}^{(\tau+1)} + \lambda\mathbf{d}^{(\tau+1)})^{\mathrm{T}}\mathbf{d}^{(\tau)} = 0 \tag{7.49}$$

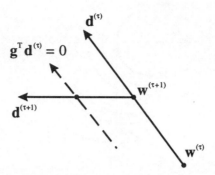

Figure 7.11. This diagram illustrates the concept of conjugate directions. Suppose a line search has been performed along the direction $\mathbf{d}^{(\tau)}$ starting from the point $\mathbf{w}^{(\tau)}$, to give an error minimum along the search path at the point $\mathbf{w}^{(\tau+1)}$. The direction $\mathbf{d}^{(\tau+1)}$ is said to be conjugate to the direction $\mathbf{d}^{(\tau)}$ if the component of the gradient parallel to the direction $\mathbf{d}^{(\tau)}$, which has just been made zero, remains zero (to lowest order) as we move along the direction $\mathbf{d}^{(\tau+1)}$.

as shown in Figure 7.11. If we now expand (7.49) to first order in λ, and note that the zeroth-order term vanishes as a consequence of (7.48), we obtain

$$\mathbf{d}^{(\tau+1)\mathrm{T}}\mathbf{H}\mathbf{d}^{(\tau)} = 0 \qquad (7.50)$$

where $\mathbf{H}$ is the Hessian matrix evaluated at the point $\mathbf{w}^{(\tau+1)}$. If the error surface is quadratic, this relation holds for arbitrary values of λ in (7.49) since the Hessian matrix is constant, and higher-order terms in the expansion of (7.49) in powers of λ vanish. Search directions which satisfy (7.50) are said to be *non-interfering* or *conjugate*. In fact, we shall see that it is possible to construct a sequence of successive search directions $\mathbf{d}^{(\tau)}$ such that each direction is conjugate to all previous directions, up to the dimensionality W of the search space. This leads naturally to the conjugate gradient optimization algorithm.

7.7.1   Quadratic error function

In order to introduce the conjugate gradient algorithm, we follow Johansson *et al.* (1992) and consider first the case of a quadratic error function of the form

$$E(\mathbf{w}) = E_0 + \mathbf{b}^{\mathrm{T}}\mathbf{w} + \frac{1}{2}\mathbf{w}^{\mathrm{T}}\mathbf{H}\mathbf{w} \qquad (7.51)$$

in which the parameters $\mathbf{b}$ and $\mathbf{H}$ are constant, and $\mathbf{H}$ is assumed to be positive definite. The local gradient of this error function is given by

$$\mathbf{g}(\mathbf{w}) = \mathbf{b} + \mathbf{H}\mathbf{w} \qquad (7.52)$$

and the error function (7.51) is minimized at the point $\mathbf{w}^*$ given, from (7.52), by

$$\mathbf{b} + \mathbf{H}\mathbf{w}^* = 0. \tag{7.53}$$

Suppose we can find a set of W vectors (where W is the dimensionality of the weight space) which are mutually conjugate with respect to $\mathbf{H}$ so that

$$\mathbf{d}_j^{\mathrm{T}}\mathbf{H}\mathbf{d}_i = 0 \qquad j \neq i \tag{7.54}$$

then it is easily shown that these vectors will be linearly independent if $\mathbf{H}$ is positive definite (Exercise 7.8). Such vectors therefore form a complete, but non-orthogonal, basis set in weight space. Suppose we are starting from some point $\mathbf{w}_1$, and we wish to get to the minimum $\mathbf{w}^*$ of the error function. The difference between the vectors $\mathbf{w}_1$ and $\mathbf{w}^*$ can be written as a linear combination of the conjugate direction vectors in the form

$$\mathbf{w}^* - \mathbf{w}_1 = \sum_{i=1}^{W} \alpha_i \mathbf{d}_i. \tag{7.55}$$

Note that, if we define

$$\mathbf{w}_j = \mathbf{w}_1 + \sum_{i=1}^{j-1} \alpha_i \mathbf{d}_i \tag{7.56}$$

then (7.55) can be written as an iterative equation in the form

$$\mathbf{w}_{j+1} = \mathbf{w}_j + \alpha_j \mathbf{d}_j. \tag{7.57}$$

This represents a succession of steps parallel the conjugate directions, with step lengths controlled by the parameters α_j.

In order to find expressions for the α's we multiply (7.55) by $\mathbf{d}_j^{\mathrm{T}}\mathbf{H}$ and make use of (7.53) to give

$$-\mathbf{d}_j^{\mathrm{T}}(\mathbf{b} + \mathbf{H}\mathbf{w}_1) = \sum_{i=1}^{W} \alpha_i \mathbf{d}_j^{\mathrm{T}}\mathbf{H}\mathbf{d}_i. \tag{7.58}$$

We now see the significance of using mutually conjugate directions, since (7.54) shows that the terms on the right-hand side of (7.58) decouple, allowing an explicit solution for the α's in the form

$$\alpha_j = -\frac{\mathbf{d}_j^{\mathrm{T}}(\mathbf{b} + \mathbf{H}\mathbf{w}_1)}{\mathbf{d}_j^{\mathrm{T}}\mathbf{H}\mathbf{d}_j}. \tag{7.59}$$

Figure 7.12. Schematic illustration of the application of the conjugate gradient algorithm to the minimization of a two-dimensional quadratic error function. The algorithm moves to the minimum of the error after two steps. This should be compared with Figures 7.4 and 7.7.

Without this property, (7.58) would represent a set of coupled equations for the α_i.

We can write (7.59) in a more convenient form as follows. From (7.56) we have

$$\mathbf{d}_j^T \mathbf{H} \mathbf{w}_j = \mathbf{d}_j^T \mathbf{H} \mathbf{w}_1 \tag{7.60}$$

where we have again used the conjugacy condition (7.54). This allows the numerator on the right-hand side of (7.59) to be written in the form

$$\mathbf{d}_j^T (\mathbf{b} + \mathbf{H} \mathbf{w}_1) = \mathbf{d}_j^T (\mathbf{b} + \mathbf{H} \mathbf{w}_j) = \mathbf{d}_j^T \mathbf{g}_j \tag{7.61}$$

where $\mathbf{g}_j \equiv \mathbf{g}(\mathbf{w}_j)$, and we have made use of (7.52). Thus, α_j can be written in the form

$$\alpha_j = -\frac{\mathbf{d}_j^T \mathbf{g}_j}{\mathbf{d}_j^T \mathbf{H} \mathbf{d}_j}. \tag{7.62}$$

We now give a simple inductive argument to show that, if the weights are incremented using (7.57) with the α_j given by (7.62) then the gradient vector $\mathbf{g}_j$ at the jth step is orthogonal to all previous conjugate directions. It therefore follows that after W steps the components of the gradient along all directions have been made zero, and so we will have arrived at the minimum of the quadratic form. This is illustrated schematically for a two-dimensional space in Figure 7.12. To derive the orthogonality property, we note from (7.52) that

$$\mathbf{g}_{j+1} - \mathbf{g}_j = \mathbf{H}(\mathbf{w}_{j+1} - \mathbf{w}_j) = \alpha_j \mathbf{H} \mathbf{d}_j \tag{7.63}$$

where we have used (7.57). We now take the scalar product of this equation with $\mathbf{d}_j$, and use the definition of α_j given by (7.62), to give

$$\mathbf{d}_j^{\mathrm{T}}\mathbf{g}_{j+1} = 0. \tag{7.64}$$

Similarly, from (7.63), we have

$$\mathbf{d}_k^{\mathrm{T}}(\mathbf{g}_{j+1} - \mathbf{g}_j) = \alpha_j \mathbf{d}_k^{\mathrm{T}}\mathbf{H}\mathbf{d}_j = 0 \qquad \text{for all } k < j \leq W. \tag{7.65}$$

Applying the technique of induction to (7.64) and (7.65) we obtain the result that

$$\mathbf{d}_k^{\mathrm{T}}\mathbf{g}_j = 0 \qquad \text{for all } k < j \leq W \tag{7.66}$$

as required.

The next problem is how to construct a set of mutually conjugate directions. This can be achieved by selecting the first direction to be the negative gradient $\mathbf{d}_1 = -\mathbf{g}_1$, and then choosing each successive direction to be a linear combination of the current gradient and the previous search direction

$$\mathbf{d}_{j+1} = -\mathbf{g}_{j+1} + \beta_j \mathbf{d}_j. \tag{7.67}$$

The coefficients β_j can be found by imposing the conjugacy condition (7.54) which gives

$$\beta_j = \frac{\mathbf{g}_{j+1}^{\mathrm{T}}\mathbf{H}\mathbf{d}_j}{\mathbf{d}_j^{\mathrm{T}}\mathbf{H}\mathbf{d}_j}. \tag{7.68}$$

In fact, it is easily shown by induction (Exercise 7.9) that successive use of the construction given by (7.67) and (7.68) generates a set of W mutually conjugate directions.

From (7.67) it follows that $\mathbf{d}_k$ is given by a linear combination of all previous gradient vectors

$$\mathbf{d}_k = -\mathbf{g}_k + \sum_{l=1}^{k-1} \gamma_l \mathbf{g}_l. \tag{7.69}$$

Using (7.66) we then have

$$\mathbf{g}_k^{\mathrm{T}}\mathbf{g}_j = \sum_{l=1}^{k-1} \gamma_l \mathbf{g}_l^{\mathrm{T}}\mathbf{g}_j \qquad \text{for all } k < j \leq W. \tag{7.70}$$

Since the initial search direction is just $\mathbf{d}_1 = -\mathbf{g}_1$, we can use (7.66) to show that $\mathbf{g}_1^{\mathrm{T}}\mathbf{g}_j = 0$, so that the gradient at step j is orthogonal to the initial gradient. If we apply induction to (7.70) we find that the current gradient is orthogonal to all previous gradients

$$\mathbf{g}_k^T \mathbf{g}_j = 0 \qquad \text{for all } k < j \leq W. \tag{7.71}$$

We have now developed an algorithm for finding the minimum of a general quadratic error function in at most W steps. Starting from a randomly chosen point $\mathbf{w}_1$, successive conjugate directions are constructed using (7.67) in which the parameters β_j are given by (7.68). At each step the weight vector is incremented along the corresponding direction using (7.57) in which the parameter α_j is given by (7.62).

7.7.2 *The conjugate gradient algorithm*

So far our discussion of conjugate gradients has been limited to quadratic error functions. For a general non-quadratic error function, the error in the neighbourhood of a given point will be approximately quadratic, and so we may hope that repeated application of the above procedure will lead to effective convergence to a minimum of the error. The step length in this procedure is governed by the coefficient α_j given by (7.62), and the search direction is determined by the coefficient β_j given by (7.68). These expressions depend on the Hessian matrix $\mathbf{H}$. For a non-quadratic error function, the Hessian matrix will depend on the current weight vector, and so will need to be re-evaluated at each step of the algorithm. Since the evaluation of $\mathbf{H}$ is computationally costly for non-linear neural networks, and since its evaluation would have to be done repeatedly, we would like to avoid having to use the Hessian. In fact, it turns out that the coefficients α_j and β_j can be found without explicit knowledge of $\mathbf{H}$. This leads to the *conjugate gradient algorithm* (Hestenes and Stiefel, 1952; Press *et al.*, 1992).

Consider first the coefficient β_j. If we substitute (7.63) into (7.68) we obtain

$$\beta_j = \frac{\mathbf{g}_{j+1}^T (\mathbf{g}_{j+1} - \mathbf{g}_j)}{\mathbf{d}_j^T (\mathbf{g}_{j+1} - \mathbf{g}_j)} \tag{7.72}$$

which is known as the *Hestenes–Stiefel* expression. From (7.66) and (7.67) we have

$$\mathbf{d}_j^T \mathbf{g}_j = -\mathbf{g}_j^T \mathbf{g}_j \tag{7.73}$$

which, together with a further use of (7.66), allows (7.72) to be written in the *Polak–Ribiere* form

$$\beta_j = \frac{\mathbf{g}_{j+1}^T (\mathbf{g}_{j+1} - \mathbf{g}_j)}{\mathbf{g}_j^T \mathbf{g}_j}. \tag{7.74}$$

Similarly, we can use the orthogonality property (7.71) for the gradients to simplify (7.74) further, resulting in the *Fletcher–Reeves* form

$$\beta_j = \frac{\mathbf{g}_{j+1}^{\mathrm{T}} \mathbf{g}_{j+1}}{\mathbf{g}_j^{\mathrm{T}} \mathbf{g}_j}. \tag{7.75}$$

Note that these three expressions for β_j are equivalent provided the error function is exactly quadratic. In practice, the error function will not be quadratic, and these different expressions for β_j can give different results. The Polak–Ribiere form is generally found to give slightly better results than the other expressions. This is probably due to the fact that, if the algorithm is making little progress, so that successive gradient vectors are very similar, the Polak–Ribiere form gives a small value for β_j so that the search direction in (7.67) tends to be reset to the negative gradient direction, which is equivalent to restarting the conjugate gradient procedure.

We also wish to avoid the use of the Hessian matrix to evaluate α_j. In fact, in the case of a quadratic error function, the correct value of α_j can be found by performing a line minimization along the search direction. To see this, consider a quadratic error (7.51) as a function of the parameter α along the search direction $\mathbf{d}_j$, starting at the point $\mathbf{w}_j$, given by

$$E(\mathbf{w}_j + \alpha \mathbf{d}_j) = E_0 + \mathbf{b}^{\mathrm{T}}(\mathbf{w}_j + \alpha \mathbf{d}_j) + \frac{1}{2}(\mathbf{w}_j + \alpha \mathbf{d}_j)^{\mathrm{T}} \mathbf{H}(\mathbf{w}_j + \alpha \mathbf{d}_j). \tag{7.76}$$

If we set the derivative of this expression with respect to α equal to zero we obtain

$$\alpha_j = -\frac{\mathbf{d}_j^{\mathrm{T}} \mathbf{g}_j}{\mathbf{d}_j^{\mathrm{T}} \mathbf{H} \mathbf{d}_j} \tag{7.77}$$

where we have used the expression in (7.52) for the local gradient in the quadratic approximation. We see that the result in (7.77) is equivalent to that found in (7.62). Thus, we can replace the explicit evaluation of α_j by a numerical procedure involving a line minimization along the search direction $\mathbf{d}_j$.

We have seen that, for a quadratic error function, the conjugate gradient algorithm finds the minimum after at most W line minimizations, without calculating the Hessian matrix. This clearly represents a significant improvement on the simple gradient descent approach which could take a very large number of steps to minimize even a quadratic error function. In practice, the error function may be far from quadratic. The algorithm therefore generally needs to be run for many iterations until a sufficiently small error is obtained or until some other termination criterion is reached. During the running of the algorithm, the conjugacy of the search directions tends to deteriorate, and so it is common practice to restart the algorithm after every W steps by resetting the search vector to the negative gradient direction. More sophisticated restart procedures are described in Powell (1977).

The conjugate gradient algorithm has been derived on the assumption of a quadratic error function with a positive-definite Hessian matrix. For general non-linear error functions, the local Hessian matrix need not be positive definite. The search directions defined by the conjugate gradient algorithm need not then be descent directions (Shanno, 1978). In practice, the use of robust line minimization techniques ensures that the error can not increase at any step, and such algorithms are generally found to have good performance in real applications.

As we have seen, the conjugate gradient algorithm provides a minimization technique which requires only the evaluation of the error function and its derivatives, and which, for a quadratic error function, is guaranteed to find the minimum in at most W steps. Since the derivation has been relatively complex, we now summarize the key steps of the algorithm:

1. Choose an initial weight vector $\mathbf{w}_1$.
2. Evaluate the gradient vector $\mathbf{g}_1$, and set the initial search direction $\mathbf{d}_1 = -\mathbf{g}_1$.
3. At step j, minimize $E(\mathbf{w}_j + \alpha \mathbf{d}_j)$ with respect to α to give $\mathbf{w}_{j+1} = \mathbf{w}_j + \alpha_{\min} \mathbf{d}_j$.
4. Test to see if the stopping criterion is satisfied.
5. Evaluate the new gradient vector $\mathbf{g}_{j+1}$.
6. Evaluate the new search direction using (7.67) in which β_j is given by the Hestenes–Stiefel formula (7.72), the Polak–Ribiere formula (7.74) or the Fletcher–Reeves formula (7.75).
7. Set $j = j + 1$ and go to 3.

Empirical results from the training of multi-layer perceptron networks using conjugate gradients can be found in Watrous (1987), Webb *et al.* (1988), Kramer and Sangiovanni-Vincentelli (1989), Makram-Ebeid *et al.* (1989), Barnard (1992) and Johansson *et al.* (1992).

The batch form of gradient descent with momentum, discussed in Section 7.5, involves two arbitrary parameters λ and μ, where λ determines the step length, and μ controls the momentum, i.e. the fraction of the previous step to be included in the current step. A major problem with gradient descent is how to determine values for λ and μ, particularly since the optimum values will typically vary from one iteration to the next. The conjugate gradient method can be regarded as a form of gradient descent with momentum, in which the parameters λ and μ are determined automatically at each iteration. The effective learning rate is determined by line minimization, while the momentum is determined by the parameter β_j in (7.72), (7.74) or (7.75) since this controls the search direction through (7.67).

7.8 Scaled conjugate gradients

We have seen how the use of a line search allows the step size in the conjugate gradient algorithm to be chosen without having to evaluate the Hessian matrix. However, the line search itself introduces some problems. In particular, every line minimization involves several error function evaluations, each of which is computationally expensive. Also, the line-search procedure itself necessarily involves some parameter whose value determines the termination criterion for each line search. The overall performance of the algorithm can be sensitive to the value of this parameter since a line search which is insufficiently accurate implies that the value of α_j is not being determined correctly, while, an excessively accurate line search can represent a good deal of wasted computation.

Møller (1993b) introduced the *scaled conjugate gradient* algorithm as a way of avoiding the line-search procedure of conventional conjugate gradients. First, note that the Hessian matrix enters the formula (7.62) for α_j only in the form of the Hessian multiplied by a vector $\mathbf{d}_j$. We saw in Section 4.10.7 that, for the multi-layer perceptron, and indeed for more general networks, the product of the Hessian with an arbitrary vector could be computed efficiently, in $\mathcal{O}(W)$ steps (per training pattern), by using central differences or, more accurately, by using the $\mathcal{R}\{\cdot\}$-operator technique.

This suggests that, instead of using line minimization, which typically involves several error function evaluations, each of which takes $\mathcal{O}(W)$ operations, we simply evaluate $\mathbf{Hd}_j$ using the methods of Section 4.10.7. This simple approach fails, however, because, in the case of a non-quadratic error function, the Hessian matrix need not be positive definite. In this case, the denominator in (7.62) can become negative, and the weight update can lead to an increase in the value of the error function. The problem can be overcome by modifying the Hessian matrix to ensure that it is positive definite. This is achieved by adding to the Hessian some multiple of the unit matrix, so that the Hessian becomes

$$\mathbf{H} + \lambda \mathbf{I} \tag{7.78}$$

where $\mathbf{I}$ is the unit matrix, and $\lambda \geq 0$ is a scaling coefficient. Provided λ is sufficiently large, this modified Hessian is guaranteed to be positive definite. The formula for the step length is then given by

$$\alpha_j = -\frac{\mathbf{d}_j^{\mathrm{T}} \mathbf{g}_j}{\mathbf{d}_j^{\mathrm{T}} \mathbf{H}_j \mathbf{d}_j + \lambda_j \|\mathbf{d}_j\|^2} \tag{7.79}$$

where the suffix j on λ_j reflects the fact that the optimum value for this parameter can vary from one iteration to the next. For large values of λ_j the step size becomes small. Techniques such as this are well known in standard optimization theory, where they are called *model trust region* methods, because the model is effectively only trusted in a small region around the current search point. The size of the trust region is governed by the parameter λ_j, so that for large λ_j the trust region is small. The model-trust-region technique is considered in more detail in the context of the Levenberg–Marquardt algorithm later in this chapter.

We now have to find a way to choose an appropriate value for λ_j. From the discussion in Section 7.7.2 we know that the expression (7.79) with $\lambda_j = 0$ will move the weight vector to the minimum along the search direction provided (i) the error function can be represented by a quadratic form, and (ii) the denominator is positive (corresponding to a positive-definite Hessian). If either of these conditions is not satisfied then the value of λ_j needs to be increased accordingly.

Consider first the problem of a Hessian which is not positive definite. The denominator in the expression (7.79) for the α_j can be written as

$$\delta_j = \mathbf{d}_j^T \mathbf{H}_j \mathbf{d}_j + \lambda_j \|\mathbf{d}_j\|^2. \tag{7.80}$$

For a positive-definite Hessian we have $\delta_j > 0$. If, however, $\delta_j < 0$ then we can increase the value of λ_j in order to make $\delta_j > 0$. Let the raised value of λ_j be called $\overline{\lambda}_j$. Then the corresponding raised value of δ_j is given by

$$\overline{\delta}_j = \delta_j + (\overline{\lambda}_j - \lambda_j)\|\mathbf{d}_j\|^2. \tag{7.81}$$

This will be positive if $\overline{\lambda}_j > \lambda_j - \delta_j/\|\mathbf{d}_j\|^2$. Møller (1993b) chooses to set

$$\overline{\lambda}_j = 2\left(\lambda_j - \frac{\delta_j}{\|\mathbf{d}_j\|^2}\right). \tag{7.82}$$

Substituting (7.82) into (7.81) gives

$$\overline{\delta}_j = -\delta_j + \lambda_j\|\mathbf{d}_j\|^2 = -\mathbf{d}_j^T \mathbf{H}_j \mathbf{d}_j \tag{7.83}$$

which is therefore now positive. This value is used as the denominator in (7.79) to compute the value of the step-size parameter α_j.

We now consider the effects of the local quadratic assumption. In regions where the quadratic approximation is good, the value of λ_j should be reduced, while if the quadratic approximation is poor, λ_j should be increased, so that the size of the trust region reflects the accuracy of the local quadratic approximation. This can be achieved by considering the comparison parameter defined by (Fletcher, 1987)

$$\Delta_j = \frac{E(\mathbf{w}_j) - E(\mathbf{w}_j + \alpha_j \mathbf{d}_j)}{E(\mathbf{w}_j) - E_Q(\mathbf{w}_j + \alpha_j \mathbf{d}_j)} \tag{7.84}$$

where $E_Q(\mathbf{w})$ is the local quadratic approximation to the error function in the neighbourhood of the point $\mathbf{w}_j$, given by

$$E_Q(\mathbf{w}_j + \alpha_j \mathbf{d}_j) = E(\mathbf{w}_j) + \alpha_j \mathbf{d}_j^T \mathbf{g}_j + \frac{1}{2}\alpha_j^2 \mathbf{d}_j^T \mathbf{H}_j \mathbf{d}_j. \tag{7.85}$$

From (7.84) we see that Δ_j gives a measure of the accuracy of the quadratic approximation. If Δ_j is close to 1 then the approximation is a good one and the value of λ_j can be decreased. Conversely a small value of Δ_j is an indication that λ_j should be increased. Substituting (7.85) into (7.84), and using the definition

(7.62) for α_j, we obtain

$$\Delta_j = \frac{2\{E(\mathbf{w}_j) - E(\mathbf{w}_j + \alpha_j \mathbf{d}_j)\}}{\alpha_j \mathbf{d}_j^{\mathrm{T}} \mathbf{g}_j}. \tag{7.86}$$

The value of λ_j can then be adjusted using the following prescription (Fletcher, 1987):

$$\text{if } \Delta_j > 0.75 \text{ then } \lambda_{j+1} = \lambda_j/2 \tag{7.87}$$

$$\text{if } \Delta_j < 0.25 \text{ then } \lambda_{j+1} = 4\lambda_j \tag{7.88}$$

otherwise set $\lambda_{j+1} = \lambda_j$. Note that, if $\Delta_j < 0$ so that the step would actually lead to an increase in the error, then the weights are not updated, but instead the value of λ_j is increased in accordance with (7.88), and Δ_j is re-evaluated. Eventually an error decrease will be obtained since, for sufficiently large λ_j, the algorithm will be taking a small step in the direction of the negative gradient. The two stages of increasing λ_j (if necessary) to ensure that $\bar{\delta}_j$ is positive, and adjusting λ_j according to the validity of the local quadratic approximation, are applied in succession after each weight update.

Detailed step-by-step descriptions of the algorithm can be found in Møller (1993b) and Williams (1991). Results from software simulations indicate that this algorithm can sometimes offer a significant improvement in speed compared to conventional conjugate gradient algorithms.

7.9 Newton's method

In the conjugate gradient algorithm, implicit use was made of second-order information about the error surface, represented by the local Hessian matrix. We now turn to a class of algorithms which make explicit use of the Hessian.

Using the local quadratic approximation, we can obtain directly an expression for the location of the minimum (or more generally the stationary point) of the error function. From (7.10) the gradient at any point $\mathbf{w}$ is given by

$$\mathbf{g} = \nabla E = \mathbf{H}(\mathbf{w} - \mathbf{w}^*) \tag{7.89}$$

and so the weight vector $\mathbf{w}^*$ corresponding to the minimum of the error function satisfies

$$\mathbf{w}^* = \mathbf{w} - \mathbf{H}^{-1}\mathbf{g}. \tag{7.90}$$

The vector $-\mathbf{H}^{-1}\mathbf{g}$ is known as the *Newton direction* or the *Newton step*, and forms the basis for a variety of optimization strategies. Unlike the local gradient vector, the Newton direction for a quadratic error surface, evaluated at any $\mathbf{w}$, points directly at the minimum of the error function, as illustrated in Figure 7.13.

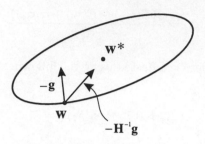

Figure 7.13. Illustration of the Newton direction for a quadratic error surface. The local negative gradient vector $-\mathbf{g}(\mathbf{w})$ does not in general point towards the minimum of the error function, whereas the Newton direction $-\mathbf{H}^{-1}\mathbf{g}(\mathbf{w})$ does.

Since the quadratic approximation used to obtain (7.90) is not exact it would be necessary to apply (7.90) iteratively, with the Hessian being re-evaluated at each new search point. From (7.90), we see that the gradient descent procedure (7.23) corresponds to one step of the Newton formula (7.90), with the inverse Hessian approximated by the unit matrix times η, where η is the learning rate parameter.

There are several difficulties with such an approach, however. First, the exact evaluation of the Hessian for non-linear networks is computationally demanding, since it requires $\mathcal{O}(NW^2)$ steps, where W is the number of weights in the network and N is the number of patterns in the data set. This evaluation would be prohibitively expensive if done at each stage of an iterative algorithm. Second, the Hessian must be inverted, which requires $\mathcal{O}(W^3)$ steps, and so is also computationally demanding. Third, the Newton step in (7.90) may move towards a maximum or a saddlepoint rather than a minimum. This occurs if the Hessian is not positive definite, so that there exist directions of negative curvature. Thus, the error is not guaranteed to be reduced at each iteration. Finally, the step size predicted by (7.90) may be sufficiently large that it takes us outside the range of validity of the quadratic approximation. In this case the algorithm could become unstable.

Nevertheless, by making various modifications to the full Newton rule it can be turned into a practical optimization method. Note first that, if the Hessian is positive definite (as is the case close to a minimum), then the Newton direction always represents a descent direction, as can be seen by considering the local directional derivative of the error function in the Newton direction evaluated at some point $\mathbf{w}$

$$\frac{\partial}{\partial\lambda}E(\mathbf{w}+\lambda\mathbf{d})\bigg|_{\lambda=0} = \mathbf{d}^{\mathrm{T}}\mathbf{g} = -\mathbf{g}^{\mathrm{T}}\mathbf{H}^{-1}\mathbf{g} < 0 \qquad (7.91)$$

where we have used the Newton step formula $\mathbf{d} = -\mathbf{H}^{-1}\mathbf{g}$.

Away from the neighbourhood of a minimum, the Hessian matrix need not be positive definite. The problem can be resolved by adopting the *model trust region* approach, discussed earlier in Section 7.8, and described in more detail in Section 7.11. This involves adding to the Hessian a positive-definite symmetric matrix which comprises the unit matrix $\mathbf{I}$ times a constant factor λ. Provided λ is sufficiently large, the new matrix

$$\mathbf{H} + \lambda\mathbf{I} \tag{7.92}$$

will be positive definite. The corresponding step direction is a compromise between the Newton direction and the negative gradient direction. For very small values of λ we recover the Newton direction, while for large values of λ the direction approximates the negative gradient

$$-(\mathbf{H} + \lambda\mathbf{I})^{-1}\mathbf{g} \simeq -\frac{1}{\lambda}\mathbf{g}. \tag{7.93}$$

This still leaves the problem of computing and inverting the Hessian matrix. One approach is to approximate the Hessian by neglecting the off-diagonal terms (Becker and Le Cun, 1989; Ricotti *et al.*, 1988). This has the advantages that the inverse of the Hessian is trivial to compute, and the Newton update equations (7.90) decouple into separate equations for each weight. The problem of negative curvatures is dealt with by the simple heuristic of taking the modulus of the second derivative. This gives a Newton update for a weight w_i in the form

$$\Delta w_i = -\left(\left|\frac{\partial^2 E}{\partial w_i^2}\right| + \lambda\right)^{-1}\frac{\partial E}{\partial w_i} \tag{7.94}$$

where λ is treated as a small positive constant. For the multi-layer perceptron, the diagonal terms in the Hessian matrix can be computed by a back-propagation procedure as discussed in Section 4.10.1. A major drawback of this approach, however, is that the Hessian matrix for many neural network problems is typically far from diagonal.

7.10 Quasi-Newton methods

We have already argued that a direct application of the Newton method, as given by (7.90), would be computationally prohibitive since it would require $\mathcal{O}(NW^2)$ operations to evaluate the Hessian matrix and $\mathcal{O}(W^3)$ operations to compute its inverse. Alternative approaches, known as *quasi-Newton* or *variable metric* methods, are based on (7.90), but instead of calculating the Hessian directly, and then evaluating its inverse, they build up an approximation to the inverse Hessian over a number of steps. As with conjugate gradients, these methods can find the minimum of a quadratic form in at most W steps, giving an overall computational cost which is $\mathcal{O}(NW^2)$.

The quasi-Newton approach involves generating a sequence of matrices $\mathbf{G}^{(\tau)}$ which represent increasingly accurate approximations to the inverse Hessian $\mathbf{H}^{-1}$, using only information on the first derivatives of the error function. The problems arising from Hessian matrices which are not positive definite are solved by starting from a positive-definite matrix (such as the unit matrix) and ensuring that the update procedure is such that the approximation to the inverse Hessian is guaranteed to remain positive definite.

From the Newton formula (7.90) we see that the weight vectors at steps τ and $\tau + 1$ are related to the corresponding gradients by

$$\mathbf{w}^{(\tau+1)} - \mathbf{w}^{(\tau)} = -\mathbf{H}^{-1}(\mathbf{g}^{(\tau+1)} - \mathbf{g}^{(\tau)}) \tag{7.95}$$

which is known as the quasi-Newton condition. The approximation $\mathbf{G}$ of the inverse Hessian is constructed so as to satisfy this condition also.

The two most commonly used update formulae are the *Davidson–Fletcher–Powell* (DFP) and the *Broyden–Fletcher–Goldfarb–Shanno* (BFGS) procedures. Here we give only the BFGS expression, since this is generally regarded as being superior:

$$\mathbf{G}^{(\tau+1)} = \mathbf{G}^{(\tau)} + \frac{\mathbf{p}\mathbf{p}^{\mathrm{T}}}{\mathbf{p}^{\mathrm{T}}\mathbf{v}} - \frac{(\mathbf{G}^{(\tau)}\mathbf{v})\mathbf{v}^{\mathrm{T}}\mathbf{G}^{(\tau)}}{\mathbf{v}^{\mathrm{T}}\mathbf{G}^{(\tau)}\mathbf{v}} + (\mathbf{v}^{\mathrm{T}}\mathbf{G}^{(\tau)}\mathbf{v})\mathbf{u}\mathbf{u}^{\mathrm{T}} \tag{7.96}$$

where we have defined the following vectors:

$$\mathbf{p} = \mathbf{w}^{(\tau+1)} - \mathbf{w}^{(\tau)} \tag{7.97}$$

$$\mathbf{v} = \mathbf{g}^{(\tau+1)} - \mathbf{g}^{(\tau)} \tag{7.98}$$

$$\mathbf{u} = \frac{\mathbf{p}}{\mathbf{p}^{\mathrm{T}}\mathbf{v}} - \frac{\mathbf{G}^{(\tau)}\mathbf{v}}{\mathbf{v}^{\mathrm{T}}\mathbf{G}^{(\tau)}\mathbf{v}}. \tag{7.99}$$

Derivations of this expression can be found in many standard texts on optimization methods such as Polak (1971), or Luenberger (1984). It is straightforward to verify by direct substitution that (7.96) does indeed satisfy the quasi-Newton condition (7.95).

Initializing the procedure using the identity matrix corresponds to taking the first step in the direction of the negative gradient. At each step of the algorithm, the direction $-\mathbf{G}\mathbf{g}$ is guaranteed to be a descent direction, since the matrix $\mathbf{G}$ is positive definite. However, the full Newton step given by (7.90) may take the search outside the range of validity of the quadratic approximation. The solution is to use a line-search algorithm (Section 7.6), as used with conjugate gradients, to find the minimum of the error function along the search direction. Thus, the weight vector is updated using

$$\mathbf{w}^{(\tau+1)} = \mathbf{w}^{(\tau)} + \alpha^{(\tau)} \mathbf{G}^{(\tau)} \mathbf{g}^{(\tau)} \qquad (7.100)$$

where $\alpha^{(\tau)}$ is found by line minimization.

A significant advantage of the quasi-Newton approach over the conjugate gradient method is that the line search does not need to be performed with such great accuracy since it does not form a critical factor in the algorithm. For conjugate gradients, the line minimizations need to be performed accurately in order to ensure that the system of conjugate directions and orthogonal gradients is set up correctly.

A potential disadvantage of the quasi-Newton method is that it requires the storage and update of a matrix $\mathbf{G}$ of size $W \times W$. For small networks this is of little consequence, but for networks with more than a few thousand weights it could lead to prohibitive memory requirements. In such cases, techniques such as conjugate gradients, which require only $\mathcal{O}(W)$ storage, have a significant advantage.

For an W-dimensional quadratic form, the sequence of matrices $\mathbf{G}^{(\tau)}$ is guaranteed to converge exactly to the true Hessian after W steps, and the quasi-Newton algorithm would find the exact minimum of the quadratic form after W steps, assuming the line minimizations were performed exactly. Results from the application of quasi-Newton methods to the training of neural networks can be found in Watrous (1987), Webb *et al.* (1988), and Barnard (1992).

7.10.1 *Limited memory quasi-Newton methods*

Shanno (1978) investigated the accuracy needed for line searches in both conjugate gradient and quasi-Newton algorithms, and concluded that conjugate gradient algorithms require relatively accurate line searches, while quasi-Newton methods remain robust even if the line searches are only performed to relatively low accuracy. This implies that, for conjugate gradient methods, significant computational effort needs to be expended on each line minimization.

The advantage of conjugate gradient algorithms, however, is that they require $\mathcal{O}(W)$ storage rather than the $\mathcal{O}(W^2)$ storage needed by quasi-Newton methods. The question therefore arises as to whether we can find an algorithm which uses $\mathcal{O}(W)$ storage but which does not require accurate line searches (Shanno, 1978). One way to reduce the storage requirement of quasi-Newton methods is to replace the approximate inverse Hessian matrix $\mathbf{G}$ at each step by the unit matrix. If we make this substitution into the BFGS formula in (7.96), and multiply the resulting approximate inverse Hessian by the current gradient $\mathbf{g}^{(\tau+1)}$, we obtain the following expression for the search direction

$$\mathbf{d}^{(\tau+1)} = -\mathbf{g}^{(\tau+1)} + A\mathbf{p} + B\mathbf{v} \qquad (7.101)$$

where the scalars A and B are defined by

$$A = -\left(1 + \frac{\mathbf{v}^T\mathbf{v}}{\mathbf{p}^T\mathbf{v}}\right)\frac{\mathbf{p}^T\mathbf{g}^{(\tau+1)}}{\mathbf{p}^T\mathbf{v}} + \frac{\mathbf{v}^T\mathbf{g}^{(\tau+1)}}{\mathbf{p}^T\mathbf{v}} \tag{7.102}$$

$$B = \frac{\mathbf{p}^T\mathbf{g}^{(\tau+1)}}{\mathbf{p}^T\mathbf{v}} \tag{7.103}$$

and the vectors $\mathbf{p}$ and $\mathbf{v}$ are defined in (7.97) and (7.98). If exact line searches are performed, then (7.101) produces search directions which are mutually conjugate (Shanno, 1978). The difference compared with standard conjugate gradients is that if approximate line searches are used, the algorithm remains well behaved. As with conjugate gradients, the algorithm is restarted in the direction of the negative gradient every W steps. This is known as the *limited memory BFGS* algorithm, and has been applied to the problem of neural network training by Battiti (1989).

7.11 The Levenberg–Marquardt algorithm

Many of the optimization algorithms we have discussed up to now have been general-purpose methods designed to work with a wide range of error functions. We now describe an algorithm designed specifically for minimizing a sum-of-squares error.

Consider the sum-of-squares error function in the form

$$E = \frac{1}{2}\sum_n(\epsilon^n)^2 = \frac{1}{2}\|\boldsymbol{\epsilon}\|^2 \tag{7.104}$$

where ϵ^n is the error for the nth pattern, and $\boldsymbol{\epsilon}$ is a vector with elements ϵ^n. Suppose we are currently at a point $\mathbf{w}_{\text{old}}$ in weight space and we move to a point $\mathbf{w}_{\text{new}}$. If the displacement $\mathbf{w}_{\text{new}} - \mathbf{w}_{\text{old}}$ is small then we can expand the error vector $\boldsymbol{\epsilon}$ to first order in a Taylor series

$$\boldsymbol{\epsilon}(\mathbf{w}_{\text{new}}) = \boldsymbol{\epsilon}(\mathbf{w}_{\text{old}}) + \mathbf{Z}(\mathbf{w}_{\text{new}} - \mathbf{w}_{\text{old}}) \tag{7.105}$$

where we have defined the matrix $\mathbf{Z}$ with elements

$$(\mathbf{Z})_{ni} \equiv \frac{\partial \epsilon^n}{\partial w_i}. \tag{7.106}$$

The error function (7.104) can then be written as

$$E = \frac{1}{2}\|\boldsymbol{\epsilon}(\mathbf{w}_{\text{old}}) + \mathbf{Z}(\mathbf{w}_{\text{new}} - \mathbf{w}_{\text{old}})\|^2. \tag{7.107}$$

If we minimize this error with respect to the new weights $\mathbf{w}_{\text{new}}$ we obtain

$$\mathbf{w}_{\text{new}} = \mathbf{w}_{\text{old}} - (\mathbf{Z}^T \mathbf{Z})^{-1} \mathbf{Z}^T \boldsymbol{\epsilon}(\mathbf{w}_{\text{old}}). \tag{7.108}$$

Note that this has the same structure as the pseudo-inverse formula for linear networks introduced in Section 3.4.3, as we would expect, since we are indeed minimizing a sum-of-squares error function for a linear model.

For the sum-of-squares error function (7.104), the elements of the Hessian matrix take the form

$$(\mathbf{H})_{ik} = \frac{\partial^2 E}{\partial w_i \partial w_k} = \sum_n \left\{ \frac{\partial \epsilon^n}{\partial w_i} \frac{\partial \epsilon^n}{\partial w_k} + \epsilon^n \frac{\partial^2 \epsilon^n}{\partial w_i \partial w_k} \right\}. \tag{7.109}$$

If we neglect the second term, then the Hessian can be written in the form

$$\mathbf{H} = \mathbf{Z}^T \mathbf{Z}. \tag{7.110}$$

For a linear network (7.110) is exact. We therefore see that (7.108) involves the inverse Hessian, as we might expect since it corresponds to the Newton step applied to the linearized model in (7.105). For non-linear networks it represents an approximation, although we note that in the limit of an infinite data set the expression (7.110) is exact at the global minimum of the error function, as discussed in Section 6.1.4. Recall that in this approximation the Hessian is relatively easy to compute, since first derivatives with respect to network weights can be obtained very efficiently using back-propagation as shown in Section 4.8.3.

In principle, the update formula (7.108) could be applied iteratively in order to try to minimize the error function. The problem with such an approach is that the step size which is given by (7.108) could turn out to be relatively large, in which case the linear approximation (7.107) on which it is based would no longer be valid. In the *Levenberg–Marquardt* algorithm (Levenberg, 1944; Marquardt, 1963), this problem is addressed by seeking to minimize the error function while at the same time trying to keep the step size small so as to ensure that the linear approximation remains valid. This is achieved by considering a modified error function of the form

$$\widetilde{E} = \frac{1}{2} \|\boldsymbol{\epsilon}(\mathbf{w}_{\text{old}}) + \mathbf{Z}(\mathbf{w}_{\text{new}} - \mathbf{w}_{\text{old}})\|^2 + \lambda \|\mathbf{w}_{\text{new}} - \mathbf{w}_{\text{old}}\|^2 \tag{7.111}$$

where the parameter λ governs the step size. For large values of λ the value of $\|\mathbf{w}_{\text{new}} - \mathbf{w}_{\text{old}}\|^2$ will tend to be small. If we minimize the modified error (7.111) with respect to $\mathbf{w}_{\text{new}}$, we obtain

$$\mathbf{w}_{\text{new}} = \mathbf{w}_{\text{old}} - (\mathbf{Z}^T \mathbf{Z} + \lambda \mathbf{I})^{-1} \mathbf{Z}^T \boldsymbol{\epsilon}(\mathbf{w}_{\text{old}}) \tag{7.112}$$

where $\mathbf{I}$ is the unit matrix. For very small values of the parameter λ we recover the Newton formula, while for large values of λ we recover standard gradient descent. In this latter case the step length is determined by λ^{-1}, so that it is clear that, for sufficiently large values of λ, the error will necessarily decrease since (7.112) then generates a very small step in the direction of the negative gradient. The Levenberg–Marquardt algorithm is an example of a *model trust region* approach in which the model (in this case the linearized approximation for the error function) is trusted only within some region around the current search point. The size of this region is governed by the value of λ.

In practice a value must be chosen for λ and this value should vary appropriately during the minimization process. One common approach for setting λ is to begin with some arbitrary value such as $\lambda = 0.1$, and at each step monitor the change in error E. If the error decreases after taking the step predicted by (7.112) the new weight vector is retained, the value of λ is decreased by a factor of 10, and the process repeated. If, however, the error increases, then λ is increased by a factor of 10, the old weight vector is restored, and a new weight update computed. This is repeated until a decrease in E is obtained. Comparisons of the Levenberg–Marquardt algorithm with other methods for training multi-layer perceptrons are given in Webb *et al.* (1988).

Exercises

7.1 ($\star$) Show that the stationary point $\mathbf{w}^*$ of quadratic error surface of the form (7.10) is a unique global minimum if, and only if, the Hessian matrix is positive definite, so that all of its eigenvalues are positive.

7.2 ($\star\star$) Consider a quadratic error error function in two-dimensions of the form

$$E = \frac{1}{2}\lambda_1 w_1^2 + \frac{1}{2}\lambda_2 w_2^2 \tag{7.113}$$

Verify that λ_1 and λ_2 are the eigenvalues of the Hessian matrix. Write a numerical implementation of the gradient descent algorithm, and apply it to the minimization of this error function for the case where the ratio of the eigenvalues λ_2/λ_1 is large (say 10:1). Explore the convergence properties of the algorithm for various values of the learning rate parameter, and verify that the largest value of η which still leads to a reduction in E is determined by the ratio of the two eigenvalues, as discussed in Section 7.5.1. Now include a momentum term and explore the convergence behaviour as a function of both the learning rate and momentum parameters. For each experiment, plot trajectories of the evolution of the weight vector in the two-dimensional weight space, superimposed on contours of constant error.

7.3 ($\star$) Take the continuous-time limit of (7.33) and show that leads to the following equation of motion

$$m\frac{d^2\mathbf{w}}{d\tau^2} + \nu\frac{d\mathbf{w}}{d\tau} = -\nabla E \tag{7.114}$$

where

$$m = \frac{\mu \Delta^2}{\eta^2}, \qquad \nu = \frac{(1 - \mu)\Delta}{\eta} \qquad (7.115)$$

and τ is the continuous time variable. The equation of motion (7.114) corresponds to the motion of a massive particle (i.e. one having inertia) with mass m moving downhill under a force $-\nabla E$, subject to viscous drag with viscosity coefficient ν. This is the origin of the term 'momentum' in (7.33).

7.4 (⋆) In (7.35) we considered the effect of a momentum term on gradient descent through a region of weight space in which the error function gradient could be taken to be approximately constant. This was based on summing an arithmetic series after an infinite number of steps. Repeat this analysis more carefully for a finite number L of steps, by expressing the resulting finite series as the difference of two infinite series. Hence obtain an expression for the weight vector $\mathbf{w}^{(L)}$ in terms of the initial weight vector $\mathbf{w}^{(0)}$, the error gradient ∇E (assumed constant) and the parameters η and μ. Show that (7.35) is obtained in the limit $L \to \infty$.

7.5 (⋆) Consider an arbitrary vector $\mathbf{v}$ and suppose that we first normalize $\mathbf{v}$ so that $\|\mathbf{v}\| = 1$ and then multiply the resulting vector by a real symmetric matrix $\mathbf{H}$. Show that, if this process of normalization and multiplication by $\mathbf{H}$ is repeated many times, the resulting vector will converge towards $\lambda_{\max} \mathbf{u}_{\max}$ where $\lambda_{\max}$ is the largest eigenvalue of $\mathbf{H}$ and $\mathbf{u}_{\max}$ is the corresponding eigenvector. (Assume that the initial vector $\mathbf{v}$ is not orthogonal to $\mathbf{u}_{\max}$).

7.6 (⋆) Consider a single-layer network having a mapping function given by

$$y_k = \sum_i w_{ki} x_i \qquad (7.116)$$

and a sum-of-squares error function of the form

$$E = \frac{1}{2} \sum_n \sum_k (y_k^n - t_k^n)^2 \qquad (7.117)$$

with n labels the patterns, and k labels the output units. Suppose the weights are updated by a gradient descent rule in which each weight w_{ki} has its own learning rate parameter η_{ki}, so that the value of w_{ki} at time step τ is given by

$$w_{ki}^{(\tau)} = w_{ki}^{(\tau-1)} - \eta_{ki}^{(\tau)} \frac{\partial E}{\partial w_{ki}^{(\tau-1)}}. \qquad (7.118)$$

Use the above equations to find an expression for the error at step τ in terms of the weight values at step $\tau - 1$ and the learning rate parameters $\eta_{ki}^{(\tau)}$. Show that the derivative of the error function with respect to $\eta_{ki}^{(\tau)}$ is given by the delta-delta expression

$$\frac{\partial E}{\partial \eta_{ki}^{(\tau)}} = -g_{ki}^{(\tau)} g_{ki}^{(\tau-1)} \qquad (7.119)$$

where

$$g_{ki}^{(\tau)} \equiv \frac{\partial E}{\partial w_{ki}^{(\tau)}}. \qquad (7.120)$$

7.7 $(\star)$ Derive the quickprop weight update formula (7.42) by following the discussion given in the text.

7.8 $(\star)$ Consider a symmetric, positive-definite $W \times W$ matrix $\mathbf{H}$, and suppose there exists a set of W mutually conjugate directions $\mathbf{d}_i$ satisfying

$$\mathbf{d}_j^{\mathrm{T}} \mathbf{H} \mathbf{d}_i = 0, \qquad j \neq i. \qquad (7.121)$$

Show that the vectors $\mathbf{d}_i$ must be linearly independent (i.e. that $\mathbf{d}_i$ cannot be expressed as a linear combination of $\{\mathbf{d}_j\}$ where $j = 1, \ldots, W$ with $j \neq i$).

7.9 $(\star)$ The purpose of this exercise is to show by induction that if successive search directions are constructed from (7.67) using the conjugacy condition (7.68), that the first W such directions will all be mutually conjugate. We know by construction that $\mathbf{d}_2^{\mathrm{T}} \mathbf{H} \mathbf{d}_1 = 0$. Now suppose that $\mathbf{d}_j^{\mathrm{T}} \mathbf{H} \mathbf{d}_i = 0$ for some given $j < W$ and for all i satisfying $i < j$. Since $\mathbf{d}_{j+1}^{\mathrm{T}} \mathbf{H} \mathbf{d}_j = 0$ by construction, we need to show that $\mathbf{d}_{j+1}^{\mathrm{T}} \mathbf{H} \mathbf{d}_i = 0$ for all $i < j + 1$. Using (7.67) we have

$$\mathbf{d}_{j+1}^{\mathrm{T}} \mathbf{H} \mathbf{d}_i = -\mathbf{g}_{j+1}^{\mathrm{T}} \mathbf{H} \mathbf{d}_i + \beta_j \mathbf{d}_j^{\mathrm{T}} \mathbf{H} \mathbf{d}_i. \qquad (7.122)$$

The second term in (7.122) vanishes by assumption. Show that the first term also vanishes, by making use of (7.63) and (7.71). This completes the proof.

7.10 $(\star)$ Verify by direct substitution that the BFGS update formula (7.96) satisfies the Newton condition (7.95).

7.11 $(\star)$ Verify that replacement of the approximate inverse Hessian matrix $\mathbf{G}^{(\tau)}$ by the unit matrix $\mathbf{I}$ in the BFGS formula (7.96) leads to a Newton step $-\mathbf{G}^{(\tau+1)}\mathbf{g}$ given by the limited memory BFGS expression (7.101).

8

PRE-PROCESSING AND FEATURE EXTRACTION

Since neural networks can perform essentially arbitrary non-linear functional mappings between sets of variables, a single neural network could, in principle, be used to map the raw input data directly onto the required final output values. In practice, for all but the simplest problems, such an approach will generally give poor results for a number of reasons which we shall discuss below. For most applications it is necessary first to transform the data into some new representation before training a neural network. To some extent, the general-purpose nature of a neural network mapping means that less emphasis has to be placed on careful optimization of this pre-processing than would be the case with simple linear techniques, for instance. Nevertheless, in many practical applications the choice of pre-processing will be one of the most significant factors in determining the performance of the final system.

In the simplest case, pre-processing may take the form of a linear transformation of the input data, and possibly also of the output data (where it is sometimes termed post-processing). More complex pre-processing may involve reduction of the dimensionality of the input data. The fact that such dimensionality reduction can lead to improved performance may at first appear somewhat paradoxical, since it cannot increase the information content of the input data, and in most cases will reduce it. The resolution is related to the curse of dimensionality discussed in Section 1.4.

Another important way in which network performance can be improved, sometimes dramatically, is through the incorporation of *prior knowledge*, which refers to relevant information which might be used to develop a solution and which is additional to that provided by the training data. Prior knowledge can either be incorporated into the network structure itself or into the pre-processing and post-processing stages. It can also be used to modify the training process through the use of regularization, as discussed in Sections 9.2 and 10.1.2.

A final aspect of data preparation arises from the fact that real data often suffers from a number of deficiencies such as missing input values or incorrect target values.

In this chapter we shall focus primarily on classification problems. It should be emphasized, however, that most of the same general principles apply equally to regression problems.

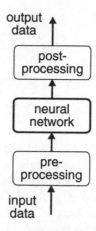

Figure 8.1. Schematic illustration of the use of data pre-processing and post-processing in conjunction with a neural network mapping.

8.1 Pre-processing and post-processing

In Chapter 1 we formulated the problem of pattern recognition in terms of a non-linear mapping from a set of input variables to a set of output variables. We have already seen that a feed-forward neural network can in principle represent an arbitrary functional mapping between spaces of many dimensions, and so it would appear that we could use a single network to map the raw input data directly onto the required output variables. In practice it is nearly always advantageous to apply pre-processing transformations to the input data before it is presented to a network. Similarly, the outputs of the network are often post-processed to give the required output values. These steps are indicated in Figure 8.1. The pre-processing and post-processing steps may consist of simple fixed transformations determined by hand, or they may themselves involve some adaptive processes which are driven by the data. For practical applications, data pre-processing is often one of the most important stages in the development of solution, and the choice of pre-processing steps can often have a significant effect on generalization performance.

Since the training of the neural network may involve an iterative algorithm, it will generally be convenient to process the whole training set using the pre-processing transformations, and then use this transformed data set to train the network. With applications involving on-line learning, each new data point must first be pre-processed before it is passed to the network. If post-processing of the network outputs is used, then the target data must be transformed using the inverse of the post-processing transformation in order to generate the target values for the network outputs. When subsequent data is processed by the trained network, it must first be passed through the pre-processing stage, then through the network, and finally through the post-processing transformation.

One of the most important forms of pre-processing involves a reduction in the dimensionality of the input data. At the simplest level this could involve discarding a subset of the original inputs. Other approaches involve forming linear or non-linear combinations of the original variables to generate inputs for the network. Such combinations of inputs are sometimes called *features*, and the process of generating them is called *feature extraction*. The principal motivation for dimensionality reduction is that it can help to alleviate the worst effects of the curse of dimensionality (Section 1.4). A network with fewer inputs has fewer adaptive parameters to be determined, and these are more likely to be properly constrained by a data set of limited size, leading to a network with better generalization properties. In addition, a network with fewer weights may be faster to train.

As a rather extreme example, consider the hypothetical character recognition problem discussed in Section 1.1. A 256×256 image has a total of $65\,536$ pixels. In the most direct approach we could take each pixel as the input to a single large neural network, which would give $65\,537$ adaptive weights (including the bias) for every unit in the first hidden layer. This implies that a very large training set would be needed to ensure that the weights were well determined, and this in turn implies that huge computational resources would be needed in order to find a suitable minimum of the error function. In practice such an approach is clearly impractical. One technique for dimensionality reduction in this case is *pixel averaging* which involves grouping blocks of pixels together and replacing each of them with a single effective pixel whose grey-scale value is given by the average of the grey-scale values of the original pixels in the block. It is clear that information is discarded by this process, and that if the blocks of pixels are too large, then there will be insufficient information remaining in the pixel averaged image for effective classification. These averaged pixels are examples of *features*, that is modified inputs formed from collections of the original inputs which might be combined in linear or non-linear ways. For an image interpretation problem it will often be possible to identify more appropriate features which retain more of the relevant information in the original image. For a medical classification problem, such features might include various measures of textures, while for a problem involving detecting objects in images, it might be more appropriate to extract features involving geometrical parameters such as the lengths of edges or the areas of contiguous regions.

Clearly in most situations a reduction in the dimensionality of the input vector will result in loss of information. One of the main goals in designing a good pre-processing strategy is to ensure that as much of the relevant information as possible is retained. If too much information is lost in the pre-processing stage then the resulting reduction in performance more than offsets any improvement arising from a reduction in dimensionality. Consider a classification problem in which an input vector $\mathbf{x}$ is to be assigned to one of c classes C_k where $k = 1, \ldots, c$. The minimum probability of misclassification is obtained by assigning each input vector $\mathbf{x}$ to the class C_k having the largest posterior probability $P(C_k|\mathbf{x})$. We can regard these probabilities as examples of features. Since there are c such features, and since they satisfy the relation $\sum_k P(\mathcal{C}_k|\mathbf{x}) = 1$, we see that in principle $c-1$ independent features are sufficient to give the optimal classifier. In practice, of course, we will not be able to obtain these probabilities easily, otherwise we would already have solved the problem. We may therefore need to retain a much larger number of features in order to ensure that we do not discard too much useful information. This discussion highlights the rather artificial distinction between the pre-processing stage and the classification or regression stage. If we can perform sufficiently clever pre-processing then the remaining operations become trivial. Clearly there is a balance to be found in the extent to which data processing is performed in the pre-processing and post-processing stages, and the extent to which it is performed by the network itself.

8.2   Input normalization and encoding

One of the most common forms of pre-processing consists of a simple linear rescaling of the input variables. This is often useful if different variables have typical values which differ significantly. In a system monitoring a chemical plant, for instance, two of the inputs might represent a temperature and a pressure respectively. Depending on the units in which each of these is expressed, they may have values which differ by several orders of magnitude. Furthermore, the typical sizes of the inputs may not reflect their relative importance in determining the required outputs.

By applying a linear transformation we can arrange for all of the inputs to have similar values. To do this, we treat each of the input variables independently, and for each variable x_i we calculate its mean $\overline{x}_i$ and variance σ_i^2 with respect to the training set, using

$$\overline{x}_i = \frac{1}{N} \sum_{n=1}^{N} x_i^n$$

$$\sigma_i^2 = \frac{1}{N-1} \sum_{n=1}^{N} (x_i^n - \overline{x}_i)^2 \tag{8.1}$$

where $n = 1, \ldots, N$ labels the patterns. We then define a set of re-scaled variables given by

$$\widetilde{x}_i^n = \frac{x_i^n - \overline{x}_i}{\sigma_i}. \tag{8.2}$$

It is easy to see that the transformed variables given by the $\widetilde{x}_i^n$ have zero mean and unit standard deviation over the transformed training set. In the case of regression problems it is often appropriate to apply a similar linear rescaling to the target values.

Note that the transformation in (8.2) is linear and so, for the case of a multi-layer perceptron, it is in principle redundant since it could be combined with the linear transformation in the first layer of the network. In practice, however, input normalization ensures that all of the input and target variables are of order unity, in which case we expect that the network weights should also be of order unity. The weights can then be given a suitable random initialization prior to network training. Without the linear rescaling, we would need to find a solution for the weights in which some weight values had markedly different values from others.

Note that, in the case of a radial basis function network with spherically-symmetric basis functions, it is particularly important to normalize the input variables so that they span similar ranges. This is a consequence of the fact that the activation of a basis function is determined by the Euclidean distance l between the input vector $\mathbf{x}$ and the basis function centre $\boldsymbol{\mu}_j$ given by

$$l^2 = \|\mathbf{x} - \boldsymbol{\mu}_j\|^2 = \sum_{i=1}^{d} \{x_i - \mu_{ji}\}^2 \tag{8.3}$$

where d is the dimensionality of the input space. If one of the input variables has a much smaller range of values than the others, the value of l^2 will be very insensitive to this variable. In principle, an alternative to normalization of the input data is to use basis functions with more general covariance matrices.

The simple linear rescaling in (8.2) treats the variables as independent. We can perform a more sophisticated linear rescaling, known as *whitening*, which allows also for correlations amongst the variables (Fukunaga, 1990). For convenience we group the input variables x_i into a vector $\mathbf{x} = (x_1, \ldots, x_d)^{\mathrm{T}}$, which has sample mean vector and covariance matrix with respect to the N data points of the training set given by

$$\bar{\mathbf{x}} = \frac{1}{N} \sum_{n=1}^{N} \mathbf{x}^n$$

$$\boldsymbol{\Sigma} = \frac{1}{N-1} \sum_{n=1}^{N} (\mathbf{x}^n - \bar{\mathbf{x}})(\mathbf{x}^n - \bar{\mathbf{x}})^{\mathrm{T}}. \tag{8.4}$$

If we introduce the eigenvalue equation for the covariance matrix

$$\boldsymbol{\Sigma} \mathbf{u}_j = \lambda_j \mathbf{u}_j \tag{8.5}$$

then we can define a vector of linearly transformed input variables given by

$$\tilde{\mathbf{x}}^n = \boldsymbol{\Lambda}^{-1/2} \mathbf{U}^{\mathrm{T}} (\mathbf{x}^n - \bar{\mathbf{x}}) \tag{8.6}$$

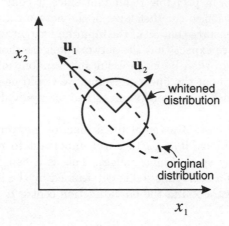

Figure 8.2. Schematic illustration of the use of the eigenvectors $\mathbf{u}_j$ (together with their corresponding eigenvalues λ_j) of the covariance matrix of a distribution to whiten the distribution so that its covariance matrix becomes the unit matrix.

where we have defined

$$\mathbf{U} = (\mathbf{u}_1, \ldots, \mathbf{u}_d) \tag{8.7}$$

$$\mathbf{\Lambda} = \mathrm{diag}(\lambda_1, \ldots, \lambda_d). \tag{8.8}$$

Then it is easy to verify that, in the transformed coordinates, the data set has zero mean and a covariance matrix which is given by the unit matrix. This is illustrated schematically in Figure 8.2.

8.2.1 *Discrete data*

So far we have discussed data which takes the form of continuous variables. We may also have to deal with data taking on discrete values. In such cases it is convenient to distinguish between *ordinal* variables which have a natural ordering, and *categorical* variables which do not. An example of an ordinal variable would be a person's age in years. Such data can simply be transformed directly into the corresponding values of a continuous variable. An example of a categorical variable would be a measurement which could take one of the values red, green or blue. If these were to be represented as, for instance, the values 0.0, 0.5 and 1.0 of a single continuous input variable, this would impose an artificial ordering on the data. One way around this is to use a 1-of-c coding for the input data, similar to that discussed for target data in classification problems in Section 6.6. In the above example this requires three input variables, with the three colours represented by input values of $(1, 0, 0)$, $(0, 1, 0)$ and $(0, 0, 1)$.

8.3 Missing data

In practical applications it sometimes happens that the data suffers from deficiencies which should be remedied before the data is used for network training. A common problem is that some of the input values may be missing from the data set for some of the pattern vectors (Little and Rubin, 1987; Little, 1992). If the quantity of data available is sufficiently large, and the proportion of patterns affected is small, then the simplest solution is to discard those patterns from the data set. Note that this approach is implicitly assuming that the mechanism which is responsible for the omission of data values is independent of the data itself. If the values which are missing depend on the data, then this approach will modify the effective data distribution. An example would be a sensor which always fails to produce an output signal when the signal value exceeds some threshold.

When there is too little data to discard the deficient examples, or when the proportion of deficient points is too high, it becomes important to make full use of the information which is potentially available from the incomplete patterns. Consider first the problem of unconditional density estimation, for the case of a parametric model based on a single Gaussian distribution. A common heuristic for estimating the model parameters would be the following. The components μ_i of the mean vector $\boldsymbol{\mu}$ are estimated from the values of x_i for all of the data points for which this value is available, irrespective of whether other input values are present. Similarly, the (i, j) element of the covariance matrix $\boldsymbol{\Sigma}$ is found using all pairs of data points for which values of both x_i and x_j are available. Such an approach, however, can lead to poor results (Ghahramani and Jordan, 1994b), as indicated in Figure 8.3.

Various heuristics have also been proposed for dealing with missing input data in regression and classification problems. For example, it is common to 'fill in' the missing input values first (Hand, 1981), and then train a feed-forward network using some standard method. For example, each missing value might be replaced by the mean of the corresponding variable over those patterns for which its value is available. This is prone to serious problems as discussed above. A more elaborate approach is to express any variable which has missing values in terms of a regression over the other variables using the available data, and then to use the regression function to fill in the missing values. Again, this approach tends to cause problems as it underestimates the covariance in the data since the regression function is noise-free.

Missing data in density estimation problems can be dealt with in a principled way by seeking a maximum likelihood solution, and using the expectation–maximization, or EM, algorithm to deal with missing data. In Section 2.6.2, the EM algorithm was introduced as a technique for finding maximum likelihood solutions for mixture models, in which hypothetical variables describing which component was responsible for generating each data point were introduced and treated as 'missing data'. The EM algorithm can similarly be applied to the problem of variables missing from the data itself (Ghahramani and Jordan, 1994b).

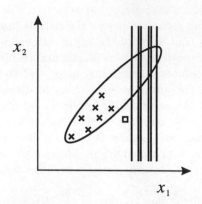

Figure 8.3. Schematic illustration of a set of data points in two dimensions. For some of the data points (shown by the crosses) the values of both variables are present, while for others (shown by the vertical lines) only the values of x_1 are known. If the mean vector of the distribution is estimated using the available values of each variable separately, then the result is a poor estimate, as indicated by the square.

In fact the two problems can be tackled together, so that the parameters of a mixture model can be estimated, even when there is missing data. Such techniques can be applied to the determination of the basis function parameters in a radial basis function network, as discussed in Section 5.9.4. They can also be used to determine the density $p(\mathbf{x}, \mathbf{t})$ in the joint input-target space. From this density, the conditional density $p(\mathbf{t}|\mathbf{x})$ can be evaluated, as can the regression function $\langle \mathbf{t}|\mathbf{x}\rangle$.

In general, missing values should be treated by integration over the corresponding variables (Ahmad and Tresp, 1993), weighted by the appropriate distribution (Exercise 8.4). This requires that the input distribution itself be modelled. A related approach is to fill in the missing data points with values drawn at random from this distribution (Lowe and Webb, 1990). It is then possible to generate many different 'completions' of a given input pattern which has missing variables. This can be regarded as a simple Monte Carlo approximation to the required integration over the input distribution (Section 10.9).

8.4 Time series prediction

Many potential applications of neural networks involve data $\mathbf{x} = \mathbf{x}(\tau)$ which varies as a function of time τ. The goal is often to predict the value of $\mathbf{x}$ a short time into the future. Techniques based on feed-forward networks, of the kind described in earlier chapters, can be applied directly to such problems provided the data is appropriately pre-processed first. Consider for simplicity a single variable $x(\tau)$. One common approach is to sample $x(\tau)$ at regular intervals to generate a series of discrete values $x_{\tau-1}, x_\tau, x_{\tau+1}$ and so on. We can take a set

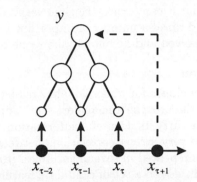

Figure 8.4. Sampling of a time series at discrete steps can be used to generate a set of training data for a feed-forward network. Successive values of the time-dependent variable $x(\tau)$, given by $x_{\tau-d+1}, \ldots, x_{\tau}$, form the inputs to a feed-forward network, and the corresponding target value is given by $x_{\tau+1}$.

of d such values $x_{\tau-d+1}, \ldots, x_{\tau}$ to be the inputs to a feed-forward network, and use the next value $x_{\tau+1}$ as the target for the output of the network, as indicated in Figure 8.4. By stepping along the time axis, we can create a training data set consisting of many sets of input values with corresponding target values. Once the network has been trained, it can be presented with a set of observed values $x_{\tau'-d+1}, \ldots, x_{\tau'}$ and used to make a prediction for $x_{\tau'+1}$. This is called *one step ahead* prediction. If the predictions themselves are cycled around to the inputs of the network, then predictions can be made at further points $x_{\tau'+2}$ and so on. This is called *multi-step ahead* prediction, and is typically characterized by a rapidly increasing divergence between the predicted and observed values as the number of steps ahead is increased due to the accumulation of errors. The above approach is easily generalized to deal with several time-dependent variables in the form of a time-dependent vector $\mathbf{x}(\tau)$.

One drawback with this technique is the need to choose the time increment between successive inputs, and this may require some empirical optimization. Another problem is that the time series may show an underlying trend, such as a steadily increasing value, with more complex structure superimposed. This can be removed by fitting a simple (e.g. linear) function of time to the data, and then subtracting off the predictions of this simple model. Such pre-processing is called *de-trending*, and without it, a trained network would be forced to extrapolate when presented with new data, and would therefore have poor performance.

There is a key assumption which is implicit in this approach to time series prediction, which is that the statistical properties of the generator of the data (after de-trending) are time-independent. Provided this is the case, then the pre-processing described above has mapped the time series problem onto a static function approximation problem, to which a feed-forward network can be applied.

If, however, the generator of the data itself evolves with time, then this approach is inappropriate and it becomes necessary for the network model to adapt to the data continuously so that it can 'track' the time variation. This requires on-line learning techniques, and raises a number of important issues, many of which are at present largely unresolved and lie outside the scope of this book.

8.5 Feature selection

One of the simplest techniques for dimensionality reduction is to select a subset of the inputs, and to discard the remainder. This approach can be useful if there are inputs which carry little useful information for the solution of the problem, or if there are very strong correlations between sets of inputs so that the same information is repeated in several variables. It can be applied not only to the original data, but also to a set of candidate features constructed by some other means. For convenience we shall talk of feature selection, even though the features might simply be the original input variables. Many of the ideas are equally applicable to conventional approaches to pattern recognition, and are covered in a number of the standard books in this area including Hand (1981), Devijver and Kittler (1982) and Fukunaga (1990), and are reviewed in Siedlecki and Sklansky (1988).

Any procedure for feature selection must be based on two components. First, a criterion must be defined by which it is possible to judge whether one subset of features is better than another. Second, a systematic procedure must be found for searching through candidate subsets of features. In principle the selection criterion should be the same as will be used to assess the complete system (such as misclassification rate for a classification problem or sum-of-squares error for a regression problem). Similarly, the search procedure could simply consist of an exhaustive search of all possible subsets of features since this is in general the only approach which is guaranteed to find the optimal subset. In a practical application, however, we are often forced to consider simplified selection criteria as well as non-exhaustive search procedures in order to limit the computational complexity of the search process. We begin with a discussion of possible selection criteria.

8.5.1 *Selection criteria*

It is clear that the optimal subset of features selected from a given starting set will depend, among other things, on the particular form of model (neural network or otherwise) with which they are to be used. Ideally the selection criterion would be obtained by training the network on the given subset of features, and then evaluating its performance on an independent set of test data. If the network training procedure involves non-linear optimization, such an approach is likely to be impractical since the training and testing process would have to be repeated for each new choice of feature subset, and the computational requirements would become too great. It is therefore common to use a simpler model, such as a linear mapping, in order to select the features, and then use these features with the more sophisticated non-linear model. The simplified model is chosen so that it can be trained relatively quickly (using linear matrix methods for instance) thereby permitting a relatively large number of feature combinations to be explored. It should be emphasized, however, that the feature selection and the classification (or regression) stages should be ideally be optimized together, and that it is only because of practical constraints that we are often forced to treat them independently.

For regression problems, we can take the simple model to be a linear mapping given by a single-layer network with linear output units, which is equivalent to matrix multiplication with the addition of a bias vector. If the error function for network training is given by a sum-of-squares, we can use this same measure for feature selection. In this case, the optimal values for the weights and biases in the linear mapping can be expressed in terms of a set of linear equations whose solution can be found quickly by using singular value decomposition (Section 3.4.3).

For classification problems, the selection criterion should ideally be taken to be the probability of misclassification, or more generally as the expected total loss or risk. This could in principle be calculated by using either parametric or non-parametric techniques to estimate the posterior probabilities for each class (Hand, 1981). In practice, evaluation of this criterion directly is generally too complex, and we have to resort instead to simpler criteria such as those based on class separability. We expect that a set of variables in which the classes are best separated will be a good set of variables for input to a neural network or other classifier. Appropriate criteria for class separability, based on covariance matrices, were discussed in Section 3.6 in the context of the Fisher discriminant and its generalizations.

If we were able to use the full criterion of misclassification rate, we would expect that, as we reduce the number of features which are retained, the generalization performance of the system would improve (a consequence of the curse of dimensionality) until some optimal subset of features is reached, and that if fewer features are retained the performance will degrade. One of the limitations of many simple selection criteria, such as those based on class separability, is that they are incapable of modelling this phenomenon. For example, the Mahalanobis distance Δ^2 (Section 2.1.1) always increases as extra variables are added. In general such measures J satisfy a monotonicity property such that

$$J(X^+) \geq J(X) \tag{8.9}$$

where X denotes a set of features, and X^+ denotes a larger set of features which contains the set X as a subset. This property is shared by criteria based on covariance matrices. The inequality simply says that deleting features cannot reduce the error rate. As a consequence, criteria which satisfy the monotonicity constraint cannot be used to determine the optimum size for a set of variables and so cannot be used to compare sets of different sizes. However, they do offer a useful way to compare sets of variables having the same number of elements. In practice the removal of features can improve the error rate when we take account of the effects of a finite size data set. One approach to the set size problem is to use conventional statistical tests to measure the significance of the improvement in discrimination resulting from inclusion of extra variables (Hand, 1981). Another approach is to apply cross-validation techniques (Section 9.8.1) to compare models trained using different numbers of features, where the particular feature subset used for each model is determined by one of the approaches discussed here.

8.5.2   Search procedures

If we have a total of d possible features, then since each feature can be present or absent, there are a total of 2^d possible feature subsets which could be considered. For a relatively small number of features we might consider simply using exhaustive search. With 10 input variables, for example, there are 1024 possible subsets which it might be computationally feasible to consider. For large numbers of input variables, however, exhaustive search becomes prohibitively expensive. Thus with 100 inputs there are over 10^{30} possible subsets, and exhaustive search is impossible. If we have already decided that we want to extract precisely $\tilde{d}$ features then the number of combinations of features is given by

$$\frac{d!}{(d - \tilde{d})!\tilde{d}!} \tag{8.10}$$

which can be significantly smaller than 2^d, but which may still be impractically large in many applications.

In principle it may be necessary to consider all possible subsets of features, since combinations of variables can provide significant information which is not available in any of the individual variables separately. This is illustrated for two classes, and two features x_1 and x_2, in Figure 8.5. Either feature taken alone gives strong overlap between the two classes, while if the two features are considered together then the classes form well-separated clusters. A similar effect can occur with an arbitrary number of features so that, in the most general case, the only way to find the optimum subset is to perform exhaustive search.

If we are using a criterion which satisfies the monotonicity relation in (8.9) then there exists an accelerated search procedure known as *branch and bound* (Narendra and Fukunaga, 1977). This method can also be applied in many other areas such as cluster analysis and searching for nearest neighbours. In the present context it will guarantee to find the best subset of given size, without needing to evaluate all possible subsets. To understand this technique, we begin by discussing the exhaustive search procedure, which we set out as a tree structure. Consider an original set of d features x_i where $i = 1, \ldots, d$, and denote the indices of the $M = d - \tilde{d}$ features which have been discarded by $z_1, \ldots, z_M$, where each z_k can take the value $1, \ldots, d$. However, no two z_k should take the same value, since that would represent a single feature being eliminated twice.

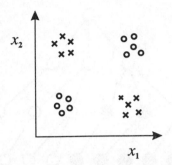

Figure 8.5. Example of data from two classes (represented by the crosses and the circles respectively) as described by two feature variables x_1 and x_2. If the data was described by either feature alone then there would be strong overlap of the two classes, while with if both features are used, as shown here, then the classes are well separated.

Also, the order of the z_k's is irrelevant in defining the feature subset. A sufficient condition for satisfying these constraints is that the z_k should satisfy

$$z_1 < z_2 < \ldots < z_M. \tag{8.11}$$

This allows us to construct a search tree, as shown in Figure 8.6 for the case of five original features from which we wish to select a subset of two. The features are indexed by the labels 1, 2, 3, 4, 5, and the number next to each node denotes the feature which is eliminated at that node. Each possible subset of two features selected from a total of five is represented by one of the nodes at the bottom of the tree. At the first level down from the top of the tree, the highest value of z_k which is considered is 3, since any higher value would not allow the constraint (8.11) to be satisfied. Similar arguments are used to construct the rest of the tree. Now suppose that we wish to maximize a criterion $J(\widetilde{d})$ and that the value of J corresponding to the node shown at A is recorded as a threshold. If at any point in the search an intermediate node is encountered, such as that shown at B, for which the value of J is smaller than the threshold, then there is no need to evaluate any of the sets which lie below this node on the tree, since, as a consequence of the monotonicity relation (8.9), such nodes necessarily have values of the criterion which are smaller than the threshold. Thus, the nodes shown as solid circles in Figure 8.6 need not be evaluated. If at any point in the search a final-layer node is encountered which has a larger value for the criterion, then this value becomes the new threshold. The algorithm terminates when every final-layer node has either been evaluated or excluded using the monotonicity relation. Note that, unlike exhaustive search applied to all possible subsets of $\widetilde{d}$ variables, this method requires evaluation of some of the intermediate sub-sets

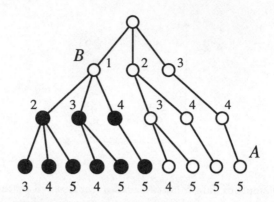

Figure 8.6. A search tree for feature subset selection, for the case of a set of five feature variables from which we wish to pick out the optimum subset of two variables. If a strictly monotonic selection criterion is being used, and a node such as that at B is found which has a lower value for the criterion than some final-level node such as that at A, then all nodes below B (shown as solid black nodes) can be eliminated from the search.

which contain more than $\widetilde{d}$ variables. However, this is more than offset by the savings in not having to evaluate final-layer subsets which are excluded using the monotonicity property. The basic branch and bound algorithm can be modified to generate a tree in which nodes with smaller values of the selection criterion tend to have larger numbers of successive branches (Fukunaga, 1990). This can lead to improvements in computational efficiency since nodes with smaller values of the criterion are more likely to be eliminated from the search tree.

8.5.3 Sequential search techniques

The branch and bound algorithm for monotonic selection criteria is generally faster than exhaustive search but is still guaranteed to find the feature subset (of given size) which maximizes the criterion. In some applications, such an approach is still computationally too expensive, and we are then forced to consider techniques which are significantly faster but which may give suboptimal solutions. The simplest method would be to select those $\widetilde{d}$ features which are individually the best (obtained by evaluating the selection criterion using one feature at a time). This method, however, is likely to be highly unreliable, and would only be optimal for selection criteria which can be expressed as the sum, or the product, of the criterion evaluated for each feature individually, and it would therefore only be appropriate if the features were completely independent.

A better approach, known as *sequential forward selection*, is illustrated in Figure 8.7. The procedure begins by considering each of the variables individually and selecting the one which gives the largest value for the selection criterion. At each successive stage of the algorithm, one additional feature is added to the set,

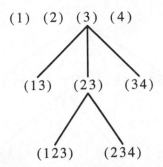

Figure 8.7. Sequential forward selection illustrated for a set of four input features, denoted by 1, 2, 3 and 4. The single best feature variable is chosen first, and then features are added one at a time such that at each stage the variable chosen is the one which produces the greatest increase in the criterion function.

again chosen on the basis of which of the possible candidates at that stage gives rise to the largest increase in the value of the selection criterion. One obvious difficulty with this approach is that, if there are two feature variables of the kind shown in Figure 8.5, such that either feature alone provides little discrimination, but where both features together are very effective, then the forward selection procedure may never find this combination since either feature alone would never be selected.

An alternative is to start with the full set of d features and to eliminate them one at a time. This gives rise to the technique of *sequential backward elimination* illustrated in Figure 8.8. At each stage of the algorithm, one feature is deleted from the set, chosen from amongst all available candidates as the one which gives the smallest reduction in the value of the selection criterion. This overcomes the problem with the forward selection approach highlighted above, but is still not guaranteed to be optimal. The backward elimination algorithm requires a greater number of evaluations, however, since it considers numbers of features greater than or equal to $\tilde{d}$ while the forward selection procedure considers numbers of features less than or equal to $\tilde{d}$.

These algorithms can be generalized in various ways in order to allow small subsets of features which are collectively useful to be selected (Devijver and Kittler, 1982). For example, at the kth stage of the algorithm, we can add l features using the sequential forward algorithm and then eliminate r features using the sequential backwards algorithm. Clearly there are many variations on this theme giving a range of algorithms which search a larger range of feature subsets at the price of increased computation.

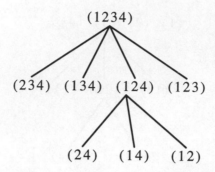

Figure 8.8. Sequential backward elimination of variables, again illustrated for the case of four features. Starting with the complete set, features are eliminated one at a time, such that at each stage the feature chosen for elimination is the one corresponding to the smallest reduction in the value of the selection criterion.

8.6 Principal component analysis

We have already discussed the problems which can arise in attempts to perform pattern recognition in high-dimensional spaces, and the potential improvements which can be achieved by first mapping the data into a space of lower dimensionality. In general, a reduction in the dimensionality of the input space will be accompanied by a loss of some of the information which discriminates between different classes (or, more generally, which determines the target values). The goal in dimensionality reduction is therefore to preserve as much of the relevant information as possible. We have already discussed one approach to dimensionality reduction based on the selection of a subset of a given set of features or inputs. Here we consider techniques for combining inputs together to make a (generally smaller) set of features. The procedures we shall discuss in this section rely entirely on the input data itself without reference to the corresponding target data, and can be regarded as a form of *unsupervised* learning. While they are of great practical significance, the neglect of the target data information implies they can also be significantly sub-optimal, as we discuss in Section 8.6.3.

We begin our discussion of unsupervised techniques for dimensionality reduction by restricting our attention to linear transformations. Our goal is to map vectors $\mathbf{x}^n$ in a d-dimensional space $(x_1, \ldots, x_d)$ onto vectors $\mathbf{z}^n$ in an M-dimensional space $(z_1, \ldots, z_M)$, where $M < d$. We first note that the vector $\mathbf{x}$ can be represented, without loss of generality, as a linear combination of a set of d orthonormal vectors $\mathbf{u}_i$

$$\mathbf{x} = \sum_{i=1}^{d} z_i \mathbf{u}_i \tag{8.12}$$

where the vectors $\mathbf{u}_i$ satisfy the orthonormality relation

$$\mathbf{u}_i^T \mathbf{u}_j = \delta_{ij} \qquad (8.13)$$

in which δ_{ij} is the Kronecker delta symbol defined on page xiii. Explicit expressions for the coefficients z_i in (8.12) can be found by using (8.13) to give

$$z_i = \mathbf{u}_i^T \mathbf{x} \qquad (8.14)$$

which can be regarded as a simple rotation of the coordinate system from the original x's to a new set of coordinates given by the z's (Appendix A). Now suppose that we retain only a subset $M < d$ of the basis vectors $\mathbf{u}_i$, so that we use only M coefficients z_i. The remaining coefficients will be replaced by constants b_i so that each vector $\mathbf{x}$ is approximated by an expression of the form

$$\widetilde{\mathbf{x}} = \sum_{i=1}^{M} z_i \mathbf{u}_i + \sum_{i=M+1}^{d} b_i \mathbf{u}_i. \qquad (8.15)$$

This represents a form of dimensionality reduction since the original vector $\mathbf{x}$ which contained d degrees of freedom must now be approximated by a new vector $\mathbf{z}$ which has $M < d$ degrees of freedom. Now consider a whole data set of N vectors $\mathbf{x}^n$ where $n = 1, \ldots, N$. We wish to choose the basis vectors $\mathbf{u}_i$ and the coefficients b_i such that the approximation given by (8.15), with the values of z_i determined by (8.14), gives the best approximation to the original vector $\mathbf{x}$ on average for the whole data set. The error in the vector $\mathbf{x}^n$ introduced by the dimensionality reduction is given by

$$\mathbf{x}^n - \widetilde{\mathbf{x}}^n = \sum_{i=M+1}^{d} (z_i^n - b_i)\mathbf{u}_i. \qquad (8.16)$$

We can then define the best approximation to be that which minimizes the sum of the squares of the errors over the whole data set. Thus, we minimize

$$E_M = \frac{1}{2} \sum_{n=1}^{N} \|\mathbf{x}^n - \widetilde{\mathbf{x}}^n\|^2 = \frac{1}{2} \sum_{n=1}^{N} \sum_{i=M+1}^{d} (z_i^n - b_i)^2 \qquad (8.17)$$

where we have used the orthonormality relation (8.13). If we set the derivative of E_M with respect to b_i to zero we find

$$b_i = \frac{1}{N} \sum_{n=1}^{N} z_i^n = \mathbf{u}_i^T \overline{\mathbf{x}} \qquad (8.18)$$

where we have defined the mean vector $\overline{\mathbf{x}}$ to be

$$\overline{\mathbf{x}} = \frac{1}{N} \sum_{n=1}^{N} \mathbf{x}^n. \qquad (8.19)$$

Using (8.14) and (8.18) we can write the sum-of-squares error (8.17) as

$$E_M = \frac{1}{2} \sum_{i=M+1}^{d} \sum_{n=1}^{N} \left\{ \mathbf{u}_i^{\mathrm{T}} (\mathbf{x}^n - \overline{\mathbf{x}}) \right\}^2$$

$$= \frac{1}{2} \sum_{i=M+1}^{d} \mathbf{u}_i^{\mathrm{T}} \Sigma \mathbf{u}_i \qquad (8.20)$$

where Σ is the covariance matrix of the set of vectors $\{\mathbf{x}^n\}$ and is given by

$$\Sigma = \sum_n (\mathbf{x}^n - \overline{\mathbf{x}})(\mathbf{x}^n - \overline{\mathbf{x}})^{\mathrm{T}}. \qquad (8.21)$$

There now remains the task of minimizing E_M with respect to the choice of basis vectors $\mathbf{u}_i$. It is shown in Appendix E that the minimum occurs when the basis vectors satisfy

$$\Sigma \mathbf{u}_i = \lambda_i \mathbf{u}_i \qquad (8.22)$$

so that they are the eigenvectors of the covariance matrix. Note that, since the covariance matrix is real and symmetric, its eigenvectors can indeed be chosen to be orthonormal as assumed. Substituting (8.22) into (8.20), and making use of the orthonormality relation (8.13), we obtain the value of the error criterion at the minimum in the form

$$E_M = \frac{1}{2} \sum_{i=M+1}^{d} \lambda_i. \qquad (8.23)$$

Thus, the minimum error is obtained by choosing the $d-M$ smallest eigenvalues, and their corresponding eigenvectors, as the ones to discard.

The linear dimensionality reduction procedure derived above is called the *Karhunen–Loéve transformation* or *principal component analysis* and is discussed at length in Jollife (1986). Each of the eigenvectors $\mathbf{u}_i$ is called a *principal component*. The technique is illustrated schematically in Figure 8.9 for the case of data points in two dimensions.

In practice, the algorithm proceeds by first computing the mean of the vectors $\mathbf{x}^n$ and then subtracting off this mean. Then the covariance matrix is calculated

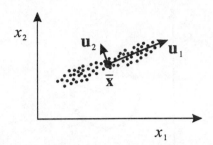

Figure 8.9. Schematic illustration of principal component analysis applied to data in two dimensions. In a linear projection down to one dimension, the optimum choice of projection, in the sense of minimizing the sum-of-squares error, is obtained by first subtracting off the mean $\overline{x}$ of the data set, and then projecting onto the first eigenvector u_1 of the covariance matrix.

and its eigenvectors and eigenvalues are found. The eigenvectors corresponding to the M *largest* eigenvalues are retained and the input vectors x^n are projected onto the eigenvectors to give the components of the transformed vectors z^n in the M-dimensional space. Thus, in Figure 8.9, each two-dimensional data point is transformed to a single variable z_1 representing the projection of the data point onto the eigenvector u_1.

The error introduced by a dimensionality reduction using principal component analysis can be evaluated using (8.23). In some applications the original data has a very high dimensionality and we wish only to retain the first few principal components. In such cases use can be made of efficient algorithms which allow only the required eigenvectors, corresponding to the largest few eigenvalues, to be evaluated (Press *et al.*, 1992).

We have considered linear dimensionality reduction based on the sum-of-squares error criterion. It is possible to consider other criteria including data covariance measures and population entropy. These give rise to the same result for the optimal dimensionality reduction in terms of projections onto the eigenvectors of Σ corresponding to the largest eigenvalues (Fukunaga, 1990).

8.6.1 Intrinsic dimensionality

Suppose we are given a set of data vectors in a d-dimensional space, and we apply principal component analysis and discover that the first d' eigenvalues have significantly larger values than the remaining $d-d'$ eigenvalues. This tells us that the data can be represented to a relatively high accuracy by projection onto the first d' eigenvectors. We therefore discover that the effective dimensionality of the data is less than the apparent dimensionality d, as a result of correlations within the data. However, principal component analysis is limited by virtue of being a linear technique. It may therefore be unable to capture more complex non-linear correlations, and may therefore overestimate the true dimensionality

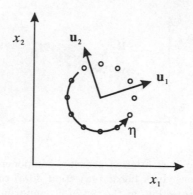

Figure 8.10. Example of a data set in two dimensions which has an intrinsic dimensionality $d' = 1$. The data can be specified not only in terms of the two variables x_1 and x_2, but also in terms of the single parameter η. However, a linear dimensionality reduction technique, such as principal component analysis, is unable to detect the lower dimensionality.

of the data. This is illustrated schematically in Figure 8.10, for data points which lie around the perimeter of a circle. Principal component analysis would give two eigenvectors with equal eigenvalues (as a result of the symmetry of the data). In fact, however, the data could be described equally well by a single parameter η as shown. More generally, a data set in d dimensions is said to have an *intrinsic dimensionality* equal to d' if the data lies entirely within a d'-dimensional subspace (Fukunaga, 1982).

Note that if the data is slightly noisy, then the intrinsic dimensionality may be increased. Figure 8.11 shows some data in two dimensions which is corrupted by a small level of noise. Strictly the data now lives in a two-dimensional space, but can nevertheless by represented to high accuracy by a single parameter.

8.6.2 *Neural networks for dimensionality reduction*

Multi-layer neural networks can themselves be used to perform non-linear dimensionality reduction, thereby overcoming some of the limitations of linear principal component analysis. Consider first a multi-layer perceptron of the form shown in Figure 8.12, having d inputs, d output units and M hidden units, with $M < d$ (Rumelhart *et al.*, 1986). The targets used to train the network are simply the input vectors themselves, so that the network is attempting to map each input vector onto itself. Due to the reduced number of units in the first layer, a perfect reconstruction of all input vectors is not in general possible. The network can be trained by minimizing a sum-of-squares error of the form

$$E = \frac{1}{2} \sum_{n=1}^{N} \sum_{k=1}^{d} \{y_k(\mathbf{x}^n) - x_k^n\}^2. \tag{8.24}$$

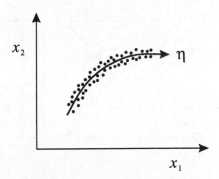

Figure 8.11. Addition of a small level of noise to data in two dimensions having an intrinsic dimensionality of 1 can increase its intrinsic dimensionality to 2. Nevertheless, the data can be represented to a good approximation by a single variable η and for practical purposes can be regarded as having an intrinsic dimensionality of 1.

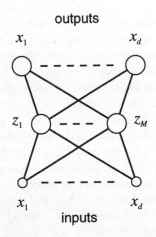

Figure 8.12. An auto-associative multi-layer perceptron having two layers of weights. Such a network is trained to map input vectors onto themselves by minimization of a sum-of-squares error. Even with non-linear units in the hidden layer, such a network is equivalent to linear principal component analysis. Biases have been omitted for clarity.

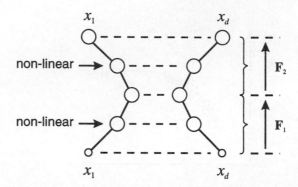

Figure 8.13. Addition of extra hidden layers of non-linear units to the network of Figure 8.12 gives an auto-associative network which can perform a general non-linear dimensionality reduction. Biases have been omitted for clarity.

Such a network is said to form an *auto-associative* mapping. Error minimization in this case represents a form of unsupervised training, since no independent target data is provided. If the hidden units have linear activations functions, then it can be shown that the error function has a unique global minimum, and that at this minimum the network performs a projection onto the M-dimensional sub-space which is spanned by the first M principal components of the data (Bourlard and Kamp, 1988; Baldi and Hornik, 1989). Thus, the vectors of weights which lead into the hidden units in Figure 8.12 form a basis set which spans the principal sub-space. (Note, however, that these vectors need not be orthogonal or normalized.) This result is not surprising, since both principal component analysis and the neural network are using linear dimensionality reduction and are minimizing the same sum-of-squares error function.

It might be thought that the limitations of a linear dimensionality reduction could be overcome by using non-linear (sigmoidal) activation functions for the hidden units in the network in Figure 8.12. However, it was shown by Bourlard and Kamp (1988) that such non-linearities make no difference, and that the minimum error solution is again given by the projection onto the principal component sub-space. There is therefore no advantage in using two-layer neural networks to perform dimensionality reduction. Standard techniques for principal component analysis (based on singular value decomposition) are guaranteed to give the correct solution in finite time, and also generate an ordered set of eigenvalues with corresponding orthonormal eigenvectors.

The situation is different, however, if additional hidden layers are permitted in the network. Consider the four-layer auto-associative network shown in Figure 8.13. Again the output units are linear, and the M units in the second hidden layer can also be linear. However, the first and third hidden layers have sigmoidal non-linear activation functions. The network is again trained by min-

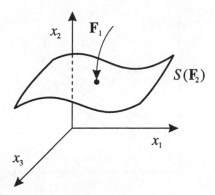

Figure 8.14. Geometrical interpretation of the mappings performed by the network in Figure 8.13.

imization of the error in (8.24). We can view this network as two successive functional mappings $\mathbf{F}_1$ and $\mathbf{F}_2$. The first mapping $\mathbf{F}_1$ projects the original d-dimensional data onto an M-dimensional sub-space S defined by the activations of the units in the second hidden layer. Because of the presence of the first hidden layer of non-linear units, this mapping is essentially arbitrary, and in particular is not restricted to being linear. Similarly the second half of the network defines an arbitrary functional mapping from the M-dimensional space back into the original d-dimensional space. This has a simple geometrical interpretation, as indicated for the case $d = 3$ and $M = 2$ in Figure 8.14. The function $\mathbf{F}_2$ maps from an M-dimensional space S into a d-dimensional space and therefore defines the way in which the space S is embedded within the original $\mathbf{x}$-space. Since the mapping $\mathbf{F}_2$ can be non-linear, the sub-space S can be non-planar, as indicated in the figure. The mapping $\mathbf{F}_1$ then defines a projection of points in the original d-dimensional space into the M-dimensional sub-space S.

Such a network effectively performs a non-linear principal component analysis. It has the advantage of not being limited to linear transformations, although it contains standard principal component analysis as a special case. However, the minimization of the error function is now a non-linear optimization problem, since the error function in (8.24) is no longer a quadratic function of the network parameters. Computationally intensive non-linear optimization techniques must be used (Chapter 7), and there is the risk of finding a sub-optimal local minimum of the error function. Also, the dimensionality of the sub-space must be specified in advance of training the network, so that in practice it may be necessary to train and compare several networks having different values of M. An example of the application of this approach is given in Kramer (1991).

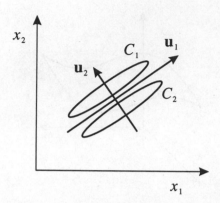

Figure 8.15. An example of a simple classification problem for which principal component analysis would discard the discriminatory information. Two-dimensional data is taken from two Gaussian classes C_1 and C_2 depicted by the two ellipses. Dimensionality reduction to one dimension using principal component analysis would give a projection of the data onto the vector $\mathbf{u}_1$ which would remove all ability to discriminate the two classes. The full discriminatory capability can be preserved if instead the data is projected onto the vector $\mathbf{u}_2$, which is the direction which would be obtained from linear discriminant analysis.

8.6.3 *Limitations of unsupervised techniques*

We have described both linear and non-linear unsupervised techniques for dimensionality reduction. These can lead to significant improvements in the performance of subsequent regression or classification systems. It should be emphasized, however, that methods based on unsupervised techniques take no account of the target data, and can therefore give results which are substantially less than optimal. A reduction in dimensionality generally involves the loss of some information, and it may happen that this information is very important for the subsequent regression or classification phase, even though it is of relatively little importance for representation of the input data itself.

As a simple example, consider a classification problem involving input data in two dimensions taken from two Gaussian-distributed classes as shown in Figure 8.15. Principal component analysis applied to this data would give the eigenvectors $\mathbf{u}_1$ and $\mathbf{u}_2$ as shown. If the dimensionality of the data were to be reduced to one dimension using principal component analysis, then the data would be projected onto the vector $\mathbf{u}_1$ since this has the larger eigenvalue. However, this would lead to a complete loss of all discriminatory information, and the classes would have identical distributions in the one-dimensional space. By contrast, a projection onto the vector $\mathbf{u}_2$ would give optimal class separation with no loss of discriminatory information. Clearly this is an extreme example, and in practice dimensionality reduction by unsupervised techniques can prove useful in many applications.

Note that in the example of Figure 8.15, a reduction of dimensionality using Fisher's linear discriminant (Section 3.6) would yield the optimal projection vector u_2. This is a consequence of the fact that it takes account of the class information in selecting the projection vector. However, as we saw in Section 3.6, for a problem with c classes, Fisher's linear technique can only find $c - 1$ independent directions. For problems with few classes and high input dimensionality this may result in too drastic a reduction of dimensionality. Techniques such as principal component analysis do not suffer from this limitation and are able to extract any number of orthogonal directions up to the dimensionality of the original space.

It is worth noting that there is an additional link between principal component analysis and a class of linear neural network models which make use of modifications of the *Hebb learning rule* (Hebb, 1949). This form of learning involves making changes to the value of a weight parameter in proportion to the activation values of the two units which are linked by that weight. Such networks can be made to perform principal component analysis of the data (Oja, 1982, 1989; Linsker, 1988; Sanger, 1989), and furthermore it can be arranged that the weights converge to orthonormal vectors along the principal component directions. For practical applications, however, there would appear to be little advantage in using such approaches compared with standard numerical analysis techniques such as those described earlier.

8.7 Invariances and prior knowledge

Throughout this book we are considering the problem of setting up a multivariate mapping (for regression or classification) on the basis of a set of training data. In many practical situations we have, in addition to the data itself, some general information about the form which the mapping should take or some constraints which it should satisfy. This is referred to as *prior knowledge*, and its inclusion in the network design process can often lead to substantial improvements in performance.

We have already encountered one form of prior knowledge expressed as prior probabilities of class membership in a classification problem (Section 1.8). These can be taken into account in an optimal way by direct use of Bayes' theorem, or by introducing weighting factors in a sum-of-squares error function (Section 6.6.2). Here we concentrate on forms of prior knowledge concerned with various kinds of invariance. As we shall see, the required invariance properties can be built into the pre-processing stage, or they can be included in the network structure itself. While the latter option does not strictly constitute part of the pre-processing, it is discussed in this chapter for convenience.

8.7.1 *Invariances*

In many practical applications it is known that the outputs in a classification or regression problem should be unchanged, or *invariant*, when the input is subject to various transformations. An important example is the classification of objects in two-dimensional images. A particular object should be assigned the same classification even if it is rotated or translated within the image or if it is linearly scaled (corresponding to the object moving towards or away from the camera). Such transformations produce significant changes in the raw data (expressed in terms of the intensities at each of the pixels in the image) and yet should give rise to the same output from the classification system. We shall use this object recognition example to illustrate the use of invariances in neural networks. It should be borne in mind, however, that the same general principles apply to any problem for which it is desired to incorporate invariance with respect to a set of transformations.

Broadly we can identify three basic approaches to the construction of invariant classification (or regression) systems based on neural networks (Barnard and Casasent, 1991):

1. The first approach is to train a network by example. This involves including within the training set a sufficiently large number of examples of the effects of the various transformations. Thus, for translation invariance, the training set should include examples of objects at many different positions. If suitable training data is not readily available then it can be generated by applying the transformations to the existing data, for example by translating a single image to generate several images of the same object at different locations.

2. The second approach involves making a choice of pre-processing which incorporates the required invariance properties. If features are extracted from the raw data which are themselves invariant, then any subsequent regression or classification system will necessarily also respect these invariances.

3. The final option is to build the invariance properties into the network structure itself. One way to achieve this is through the use of shared weights, and we shall consider two specific examples involving local receptive fields and higher-order networks.

While approach 1 is relatively straightforward, it suffers from the disadvantage of being inefficient in requiring a substantially expanded data set. It will also result in a network which only approximately respects the invariance. Furthermore, the network will be unable to deal with new inputs in which the range of the transformation exceeds that encountered during training, as this represents an extrapolation of the network inputs. Methods 2 and 3 achieve the required invariance properties without needing unnecessarily large data sets. In the context of translation invariance, for instance, a network which has been trained to recognize an object correctly at one position within an image can recognize the same object correctly at any position. In contrast to a network trained by method 1, such a network is able to extrapolate to new inputs if they differ from the training data primarily by virtue of one of the transformations.

An alternative approach which also involves incorporating invariances through training, but which does not require artificial expansion of the data set, is the technique of *tangent prop* (Simard *et al.*, 1992). Consider the effect of a trans-

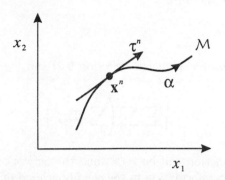

Figure 8.16. Illustration of a two-dimensional input space showing the effect of a continuous transformation on a particular input vector $\mathbf{x}^n$. A one-dimensional transformation, parametrized by the continuous variable α, applied to $\mathbf{x}^n$ causes it to sweep out a one-dimensional manifold $\mathcal{M}$. Locally, the effect of the transformation can be approximated by the tangent vector τ^n.

formation on a particular input pattern vector $\mathbf{x}^n$. Provided the transformation is continuous (such as translation or rotation, but not mirror reflection for instance) then the transformed pattern will sweep out a manifold $\mathcal{M}$ within the d-dimensional input space. This is illustrated in Figure 8.16, for the case of $d = 2$ for simplicity. Suppose the transformation is governed by a single parameter α (which might be rotation angle for instance). Then the sub-space $\mathcal{M}$ swept out by $\mathbf{x}^n$ will be one-dimensional, and will be parametrized by α. Let the vector which results from acting on $\mathbf{x}^n$ by this transformation be denoted by $\mathbf{s}(\alpha, \mathbf{x}^n)$ which is defined so that $\mathbf{s}(0, \mathbf{x}^n) = \mathbf{x}^n$. Then the tangent to the curve $\mathcal{M}$ is given by the directional derivative $\tau = \partial \mathbf{s}/\partial \alpha$, and the tangent vector at the point $\mathbf{x}^n$ is given by

$$\tau^n = \left. \frac{\partial \mathbf{s}(\alpha, \mathbf{x}^n)}{\partial \alpha} \right|_{\alpha=0}. \tag{8.25}$$

Under a transformation of the input vector, the network output vector will, in general, change. The derivative of the activation of output unit k with respect to α is given by

$$\frac{\partial y_k}{\partial \alpha} = \sum_{i=1}^{d} \frac{\partial y_k}{\partial x_i} \frac{\partial x_i}{\partial \alpha} = \sum_{i=1}^{d} J_{ki} \tau_i \tag{8.26}$$

where J_{ki} is the (k, i) element of the Jacobian matrix $\mathbf{J}$, as discussed in Section 4.9. The result (8.26) can be used to modify the standard error function, so as to encourage local invariance in the neighbourhood of the data points, by the addition to the usual error function E of a regularization function Ω to give a total error function of the form

$$\widetilde{E} = E + \nu\Omega \tag{8.27}$$

where ν is a regularization coefficient (Section 9.2) and

$$\Omega = \frac{1}{2}\sum_n\sum_k\left(\sum_{i=1}^d J_{ki}^n \tau_i^n\right)^2. \tag{8.28}$$

The regularization function will be zero when the network mapping function is invariant under the transformation in the neighbourhood of each pattern vector, and the value of the parameter ν determines the balance between the network fitting the training data and the network learning the invariance property.

In a practical implementation, the tangent vector τ^n can be approximated by finite differences, by subtracting the original vector $\mathbf{x}^n$ from the corresponding vector after transformation using a small value of α, and dividing by α. Some smoothing of the data may also be required. The regularization function depends on the network weights through the Jacobian $\mathbf{J}$. A back-propagation formalism for computing the derivatives of the regularizer with respect to the network weights is easily obtained (Exercise 8.6) by extension of the techniques introduced in Chapter 4.

If the transformation is governed by L parameters (e.g. $L = 2$ for the case of translation in a two-dimensional image) then the space $\mathcal{M}$ will have dimensionality L, and the corresponding regularizer is given by the sum of terms of the form (8.28), one for each transformation. If several transformations are considered at the same time, and the network mapping is made invariant to each separately, then it will be (locally) invariant to combinations of the transformations (Simard *et al.*, 1992). A related technique, called *tangent distance*, can be used to build invariance properties into distance-based methods such as nearest-neighbour classifiers (Simard *et al.*, 1993).

8.7.2 *Invariance through pre-processing*

The second approach which we shall consider for incorporating invariance properties into neural network mappings is by a suitable choice of pre-processing. One such technique involves the extraction of features from the original input data which are invariant under the required transformations. Such features are often based on *moments* of the original data. For inputs which consist of a two-dimensional image, the moments are defined by

$$\iint x(u,v)K(u,v)\,du\,dv \tag{8.29}$$

where (u, v) are Cartesian coordinates describing locations within the image, $x(u, v)$ represents the intensity of the image at location (u, v), and $K(u, v)$ is called a *kernel* and is a fixed function whose form determines the particular moments under consideration. In practice, an image is specified in terms of a finite array of pixels, and so the integrals in (8.29) are replaced by discrete sums

$$\sum_i \sum_j x(u_i, v_j) K(u_i, v_j) \Delta u_i \Delta v_j. \tag{8.30}$$

When the kernel function takes the form of simple powers we have *regular moments* which, in continuous notation, can be written

$$M_{lm} = \iint x(u, v) u^l v^m \, du \, dv \tag{8.31}$$

where l and m are non-negative integers. We can define a corresponding set of translation-invariant features, called *central moments*, by first subtracting off the means of u and v

$$\widehat{M}_{lm} = \iint x(u, v)(u - \overline{u})^l (v - \overline{v})^m \, du \, dv \tag{8.32}$$

where $\overline{u} = M_{10}/M_{00}$ and $\overline{v} = M_{01}/M_{00}$. Under a translation of the image $x(u, v) \rightarrow x(u + \Delta u, v + \Delta v)$, and it is easy to verify that the moments defined in (8.32) are invariant. Note that this neglects edge effects and assumes that the integrals in (8.32) run over $(-\infty, \infty)$. In practice, the use of moments in the discrete form (8.30) will give only approximate invariance under such transformations.

Similarly, under a change of scale we have $x(u, v) \rightarrow x(\alpha u, \alpha v)$. We can make the central moments invariant to scale by normalizing them to give

$$\mu_{lm} = \frac{\widehat{M}_{lm}}{\widehat{M}_{00}^{1+(l+m)/2}} \tag{8.33}$$

and again it is easy to verify that the normalized moments in (8.33) are simultaneously invariant to translations and scaling. Similarly, we can use the moments in (8.33) in turn to construct moments which are simultaneously invariant to translation, scale and rotation (Exercise 8.7). For instance, the quantity

$$\mu_{20} + \mu_{02} \tag{8.34}$$

has this property (Schalkoff, 1989). Other forms of moments can also be considered which are based on different forms for the kernel function $K(u, v)$ (Khotanzad and Hong, 1990).

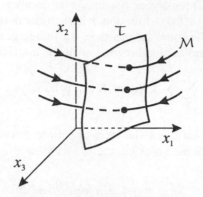

Figure 8.17. Illustration of a three-dimensional input space showing trajectories, such as $\mathcal{M}$, which patterns sweep out under the action of transformations to which the network outputs should be invariant. A suitably chosen set of constraints will define a sub-space $\mathcal{T}$ which intersects each trajectory precisely once. If new inputs are mapped onto this surface using the transformations then invariance is guaranteed.

One problem with the use of moments as input features is that considerable computational effort may be required for their evaluation, and this computation must be repeated for each new input image. A second problem is that a lot of information is discarded in evaluating any particular moment, and so many moments may be required in order to give good discrimination.

An alternative, related approach to invariant pre-processing is to transform any new inputs so as to satisfy some appropriately chosen set of constraints (Barnard and Casasent, 1991). This is illustrated schematically in Figure 8.17 for a set of one-parameter transformations. Under the action of the transformations, each input vector sweeps out a trajectory $\mathcal{M}$ as discussed earlier. Those patterns which satisfy the constraints live on a sub-space $\mathcal{T}$ which intersects the trajectories. Note that the constraints must be chosen so that each trajectory intersects the constraint surface at precisely one point. Any new input vector is first transformed (thus moving it along its trajectory) until it reaches the constraint surface. This transformed vector is then used as the input to the network. As an example, suppose we wish to impose invariance to translations and changes of scale. The constraints might then take the form that the zeroth and first moments M_{00}, M_{10} and M_{01}, given by (8.31), should have specified values. Every image (for the training set or test set) is first transformed by translation and scaling until the constraints are satisfied.

8.7.3 Shared weights

The third approach to dealing with invariances, discussed above, involves structuring the network itself in such a way that the network mapping respects the

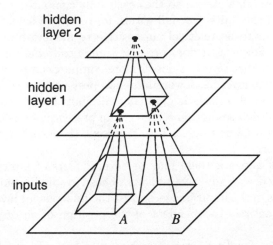

Figure 8.18. Schematic architecture of a network for translation-invariant object recognition in two-dimensional images. In a practical system there may be more than two layers between the input image and the outputs.

invariances. While, strictly, this is not a form of pre-processing, it is treated here for convenience. Again, we introduce this concept in the context of networks designed for object recognition in two-dimensional images.

Consider the network structure shown in Figure 8.18. The inputs to the network are given by the intensities at each of the pixels in a two-dimensional array. Units in the first and second layers are similarly arranged in two-dimensional sheets to reflect the geometrical structure of the problem. Instead of having full interconnections between adjacent layers, each hidden unit receives inputs only from units in a small region in the previous layer, known as a *receptive field*. This reflects the results of experiments in conventional image processing which have demonstrated the advantage of extracting local features from an image and then combining them together to form higher-order features. Note that it also imitates some aspects of the mammalian visual processing system. The network architecture is typically chosen so that there is some overlap between adjacent receptive fields.

The technique of *shared weights* can then be used to build in some degree of translation invariance into the response of the network (Rumelhart *et al.*, 1986; Le Cun *et al.*, 1989; Lang *et al.*, 1990). In the simplest case this involves constraining the weights from each receptive field to be equal to the corresponding weights from all of the receptive fields of the other units in the same layer. Consider an object which falls within receptive field shown at A in Figure 8.18, corresponding to a unit in hidden layer 1, and which produces some activation level in that unit. If the same object falls at the corresponding position in receptive field B, then, as a consequence of the shared weights, the corresponding unit in hidden layer 1 will have the same activation level. The units in the second layer have fixed weights chosen so that each unit computes a simple average of the activations of the units that fall within its receptive field. This allows units in the second layer to be relatively insensitive to moderate translations within the input image. However, it does preserve some positional information thereby allowing units in higher layers to detect more complex composite features. Typically each successive layer has fewer units than previous layers, as information on the spatial location of objects is gradually eliminated. This corresponds to the use of a relatively high resolution to detect the presence of a feature in an earlier layer, while using a lower resolution to represent the location of that feature in a subsequent layer.

In a practical network there may be several pairs of layers, with alternate layers having fixed and adaptive weights. These gradually build up increasing tolerance to shifts in the input image, so that the final output layer has a response which is almost entirely independent of the position of an object in the input field.

As described so far, this network architecture has only one kind of receptive field in each layer. In order to be able to extract several different kinds of feature is necessary to provide several 'planes' of units in each hidden layer, with all units in a given plane sharing the same weights. Weight sharing can be enforced during learning by initializing corresponding weights to the same (random) values and then averaging the weight changes for all of the weights in one group and updating all of the corresponding weights by the same amount using the averaged weight change.

Network architectures of this form have been used in the zip code recognition system of Le Cun *et al.* (1989), and in the *neocognitron* of Fukushima *et al.* (1983) and Fukushima (1988), for translation-invariant recognition of handwritten digits.

The use of receptive fields can dramatically reduce the number of weights present in the network compared with a fully connected architecture. This makes it practical to treat pixel values in an image directly as inputs to a network. In addition, the use of shared weights means that the number of independent parameters in the network is much less than the number of weights, which allows much smaller data sets to be used than would otherwise be necessary.

8.7.4 *Higher-order networks for encoding invariances*

In Section 4.5 we introduced the concept of a higher-order network based on units whose outputs are given by

$$z_j = g \left(w_j + \sum_{i_1=1}^{d} w_{ji_1} x_{i_1} + \sum_{i_1=1}^{d} \sum_{i_2=1}^{d} w_{ji_1 i_2} x_{i_1} x_{i_2} + \cdots \right) \qquad (8.35)$$

where x_i is an input, $g(\cdot)$ is a non-linear activation function and the w's represent the weights. We have already remarked that such networks can have a

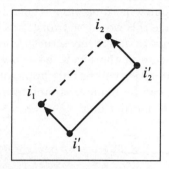

Figure 8.19. We can impose translation invariance on a second-order network if we ensure that, for each hidden unit separately, weights from any pair of points i_1 and i_2 are constrained to equal those from any other pair i_1' and i_2', where the line i_1'–i_2' can be obtained from the line i_1–i_2 by translation.

proliferation of weight parameters and are therefore impractical for many applications. (The number of independent parameters per unit is the same as for the corresponding multivariate polynomial, and is discussed in Exercises 1.6–1.8.) However, we can exploit the structure of a higher-order network to impose invariances, and at the same time reduce significantly the number of independent weights in the network, by using a form of weight sharing (Giles and Maxwell, 1987; Perantonis and Lisboa, 1992). Consider the problem of incorporating translation invariance into a higher-order network. This can be achieved by using a second-order network of the form

$$z_j = g\left(\sum_{i_1}\sum_{i_2} w_{ji_1i_2}x_{i_1}x_{i_2}\right). \tag{8.36}$$

Under a translation, the value of the intensity in pixel i_1 will go from its original value x_{i_1} to a new value x_{i_1}' given by $x_{i_1}' = x_{i_1}$, where the translation can be described by a vector from pixel i_1' to pixel i_1. Thus the argument of the activation function $g(\cdot)$ in (8.36) will be invariant if, for each unit j in the first hidden layer, we have

$$w_{ji_1i_2} = w_{ji_1'i_2'}. \tag{8.37}$$

This has a simple geometrical interpretation as indicated in Figure 8.19. Each unit in the first hidden layer takes inputs from two pixels in the image, such as those labelled i_1 and i_2 in the figure. The constraint in (8.37) requires that, for each unit in the first hidden layer, and for each possible pair of points in the image, the weights from any other pair of points, such as those at i_1' and i_2' which can be obtained from i_1 and i_2 by translation, must be equal. Note that such an approach would not work with a first-order network, since the constraint on the weights would force all weights into any given unit to be equal. Each unit would therefore take as input something proportional to the average of all of the input pixel values and, while this would be translation invariant, there would be no freedom left for the units to detect any structure in the image. Edge effects, as well as the discrete nature of the pixels, have been neglected here, and in practice the invariance properties will be only approximately realized.

Higher-order networks can be made invariant to more complex transformations. Consider a general Kth-order unit

$$\sum_{i_1} \cdots \sum_{i_K} w_{ji_1,\cdots,i_K} x_{i_1}, \cdots, x_{i_K}. \tag{8.38}$$

Under a particular geometrical transformation, $x_{i_l} \to x'_{i_l} = x_{i'_l}$ where the pixel at i_l is replaced by the pixel at i'_l. It follows that the expression in (8.38) will be invariant provided

$$w_{ji'_1,\cdots,i'_K} = w_{ji_1,\cdots,i_K}. \tag{8.39}$$

As well as allowing invariances to be built into the network structure, the imposition of the constraints in (8.39) can greatly reduce the number of free parameters in the network, and thereby dramatically reduce the size of data set needed to determine those weights.

Simultaneous translation and scale invariance can be built into a second-order network by demanding that, for each unit in the first hidden layer, and for each pair of inputs i_1 and i_2, the weights from i_1 and i_2 are constrained to equal those from any other pair i'_1 and i'_2 where the pair i'_1–i'_2 can be obtained from i_1–i_2 by a combination of translation and scaling. This selects all pairs of points such that the line i'_1–i'_2 is parallel to the line i_1–i_2. There is a slight complication in the case of scaling arising from the fact that the input image consists of discrete pixels. If a given geometrical object is scaled by a factor λ then the number of pixels which it occupies is scaled by a factor λ^2. If the image consists of black pixels (value $+1$) on a white background (value 0) for instance, then the number of active pixels will be scaled by λ^2, which would spoil the scale invariance. The problem can be avoided by normalizing the image, e.g. to a vector of unit length. Note that this then gives fractional values for the inputs.

If we consider simultaneous translation, rotation and scale invariance, we see that any pair of points can be mapped to any other pair by a combination of such transformations. Thus a second-order network would be constrained to have all weights to any hidden unit equal, which would again cause the activation of each unit to be simply proportional to the average of the input values. We therefore need to go to a third-order network. In this case, each unit takes inputs from three pixels in the image, and the weights must satisfy the constraint that, for every triplet of pixels, and for every hidden unit, the weights must equal those

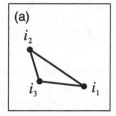
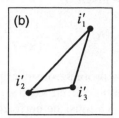

Figure 8.20. Simultaneous translation, rotation and scale invariance can be built into a third-order network provided weights from triplets of points which correspond to similar triangles, such as those shown in (a) and (b), are constrained to be equal.

emanating from any other triplet which can be obtained by any combination of translations, rotations and scalings (Reid *et al.*, 1989). This means that corresponding triplets lie at the vertices of *similar* triangles, in other words triangles which have the same values of the angles encountered in the same order when traversing the triangle in, say, a clockwise direction. This is illustrated in Figure 8.20. Although the incorporation of constraints greatly reduces the number of free parameters in higher-order networks, the use of such networks is not widespread.

Exercises

8.1 (⋆) Verify that the whitened input vector, given by (8.6), has zero mean and a covariance matrix given by the identity matrix.

8.2 (⋆) Consider a radial basis function network with spherical Gaussian basis functions in which the jth basis function is governed by a mean μ_j and a variance parameter σ_j^2 (Section 5.2). Show that the effect of applying the whitening transformation (8.6) to the original input data is equivalent to a special case of the same network with general Gaussian basis functions governed by a general covariance matrix Σ_j in which the original un-whitened data is used. Obtain an expression for the corresponding mean $\widetilde{\mu}_j$ and covariance matrix $\widetilde{\Sigma}_j$ in terms of the parameters of the original basis functions and of the whitening transformation.

8.3 (⋆⋆) Generate sets of data points in two dimensions using a variety of distributions including Gaussian (with general covariance matrix) and mixtures of Gaussians. For each data set, apply the whitening transformation (Section 8.2) and produce scatter plots of the data points before and after transformation.

8.4 (⋆) Consider a trained classifier which can produce the posterior probabilities $P(\mathcal{C}_k|\mathbf{x})$ for a new input vector $\mathbf{x}$. Suppose that some of the values of the input vector are missing, so that $\mathbf{x}$ can be partitioned into a subvector $\mathbf{x}_m$ of components whose values are missing, and a remaining vector

$\widehat{\mathbf{x}}$ whose values are present. Show that posterior probabilities, given only the data $\widehat{\mathbf{x}}$, are given by

$$P(C_k|\widehat{\mathbf{x}}) = \frac{1}{p(\widehat{\mathbf{x}})} \int P(C_k|\widehat{\mathbf{x}}, \mathbf{x}_m) p(\widehat{\mathbf{x}}, \mathbf{x}_m) \, d\mathbf{x}_m. \tag{8.40}$$

8.5 ($\star$) Consider the problem of selecting M feature variables from a total of d candidate variables. Find expressions for the number of criterion function evaluations which must be performed for (i) exhaustive search, (ii) sequential forward selection, and (iii) sequential backward elimination. Consider the case of choosing 10 features out of a set of 50 candidates, and evaluate the corresponding expressions for the number of evaluations by these three methods.

8.6 ($\star\star$) Consider a multi-layer perceptron with arbitrary feed-forward topology, which is to be trained by minimizing the 'tangent prop' error function (8.27) in which the regularizing function is given by (8.28). Show that the regularization term Ω can be written as a sum over patterns of terms of the form

$$\Omega^n = \frac{1}{2} \sum_k (\mathcal{D}y_k)^2 \tag{8.41}$$

where $\mathcal{D}$ is a differential operator defined by

$$\mathcal{D} \equiv \sum_i \tau_i \frac{\partial}{\partial x_i}. \tag{8.42}$$

By acting on the forward propagation equations

$$z_j = g(a_j), \qquad a_j = \sum_i w_{ji} z_i \tag{8.43}$$

with the operator $\mathcal{D}$, show that Ω^n can be evaluated by forward propagation using the following equations:

$$\xi_j = g'(a_j)\alpha_j, \qquad \alpha_j = \sum_i w_{ji}\xi_i. \tag{8.44}$$

where we have defined the new variables

$$\xi_j \equiv \mathcal{D}z_j, \qquad \alpha_j \equiv \mathcal{D}a_j. \tag{8.45}$$

Now show that the derivatives of Ω^n with respect to a weight w_{rs} in the network can be written in the form

$$\frac{\partial \Omega^n}{\partial w_{rs}} = \sum_k \xi_k \left\{ \phi_r^k z_s + \delta_r^k \xi_s \right\} \tag{8.46}$$

where we have defined

$$\delta_r^k \equiv \frac{\partial y_k}{\partial a_r}, \qquad \phi_r^k \equiv \mathcal{D}\delta_r^k. \qquad (8.47)$$

Write down the back-propagation equations for δ_r^k, and hence derive a set of back-propagation equations for the evaluation of the ϕ_r^k.

8.7 ($\star$) We have seen that the normalized moments μ_{lm} defined by (8.33) are simultaneously invariant to translation and scaling. It follows that any combination of such moments will also satisfy the same invariances. Show that the moment defined in (8.34) is, additionally, invariant under rotation $\theta \to \theta + \Delta\theta$. Hint: this is most easily done by representing the moments using polar coordinates centred on the point $(\overline{u}, \overline{v})$, so that the central moments become

$$\widehat{M}_{lm} = \int\int x(r, \theta)(r\cos\theta)^l (r\sin\theta)^m r\, dr\, d\theta, \qquad (8.48)$$

and then making use of the relation $\sin^2\theta + \cos^2\theta = 1$. Which of the following moments are rotation invariant?

$$\text{(a)} \qquad (\mu_{20} - \mu_{02})^2 + 4\mu_{11}^2 \qquad (8.49)$$

$$\text{(b)} \qquad (\mu_{20} + \mu_{02})^2 - 4\mu_{11}^2 \qquad (8.50)$$

$$\text{(c)} \qquad (\mu_{30} + 3\mu_{12})^2 - (3\mu_{21} + \mu_{03})^2 \qquad (8.51)$$

$$\text{(d)} \qquad (\mu_{30} - 3\mu_{12})^2 + (3\mu_{21} - \mu_{03})^2. \qquad (8.52)$$

9

LEARNING AND GENERALIZATION

As we have emphasized in several other chapters, the goal of network training is not to learn an exact representation of the training data itself, but rather to build a statistical model of the process which generates the data. This is important if the network is to exhibit good generalization, that is, to make good predictions for new inputs. In Section 1.5, we introduced the simple analogy of curve fitting using polynomials, and showed that a polynomial with too few coefficients gives poor predictions for new data, i.e. poor generalization, since the polynomial function has too little flexibility. Conversely, a polynomial with too many coefficients also gives poor generalization since it fits too much of the noise on the training data. The number of coefficients in the polynomial controls the effective flexibility, or complexity, of the model.

This highlights the need to optimize the complexity of the model in order to achieve the best generalization. Considerable insight into this phenomenon can be obtained by introducing the concept of the bias–variance trade-off, in which the generalization error is decomposed into the sum of the *bias* squared plus the *variance*. A model which is too simple, or too inflexible, will have a large bias, while one which has too much flexibility in relation to the particular data set will have a large variance. Bias and variance are complementary quantities, and the best generalization is obtained when we have the best compromise between the conflicting requirements of small bias and small variance.

In order to find the optimum balance between bias and variance we need to have a way of controlling the effective complexity of the model. In the case of neural networks, the complexity can be varied by changing the number of adaptive parameters in the network. This is called *structural stabilization*. One way to implement this in practice is to compare a range of models having different different numbers of hidden units. Alternatively, we can start with a relatively large network and prune out the least significant connections, either by removing individual weights or by removing complete units. Similarly, we can start with a small network, and add units during the learning process, with the goal of arriving at an optimal network structure. Yet another way to reduce variance is to combine the outputs of several networks together to form a committee.

The second principal approach to controlling the complexity of a model is through the use of *regularization* which involves the addition of a penalty term to the error function. We can control the degree of regularization, and hence the effective complexity of the model, by scaling the regularization term by an adjustable multiplicative parameter.

In a practical application, we have to optimize the model complexity for the given training data set. One of the most important techniques for doing this is called *cross-validation*.

In Chapter 10 we discuss the Bayesian framework which provides a complimentary viewpoint to the one presented in this chapter. The bias–variance trade-off is then no longer relevant, and we can in principle consider networks of arbitrarily high complexity without encountering over-fitting.

9.1 Bias and variance

In Section 1.5 we discussed the problem of curve fitting using polynomial functions, and we showed that there is an optimal number of coefficients for the polynomial, for a given training set, in order to obtain the best representation of the underlying systematic properties of the data, and hence to obtain the best generalization on new data. This represents a trade-off between achieving a good fit to the training data, and obtaining a reasonably smooth function which is not over-fitted to the data. Similar considerations apply to the problem of density estimation, discussed in Chapter 2, where various smoothing parameters arise which control the trade-off between smoothing the model density function and fitting the data set. The same issues also arise in the supervised training of neural networks.

A key insight into this trade-off comes from the decomposition of error into *bias* and *variance* components (Geman *et al.*, 1992). We begin with a mathematical treatment of the bias–variance decomposition, and then discuss its implications.

It is convenient to consider the particular case of a model trained using a sum-of-squares error function, although our conclusions will be much more general. Also, for notational simplicity, we shall consider a network having a single output y, although again this is not a significant limitation. We showed in Section 6.1.3 that the sum-of-squares error, in the limit of an infinite data set, can be written in the form

$$E = \frac{1}{2} \int \{y(\mathbf{x}) - \langle t|\mathbf{x}\rangle\}^2 p(\mathbf{x})\, dx$$

$$+ \frac{1}{2} \int \{\langle t^2|\mathbf{x}\rangle - \langle t|\mathbf{x}\rangle^2\} p(\mathbf{x})\, dx \tag{9.1}$$

in which $p(\mathbf{x})$ is the unconditional density of the input data, and $\langle t|\mathbf{x}\rangle$ denotes the conditional average, or regression, of the target data given by

$$\langle t|\mathbf{x}\rangle \equiv \int tp(t|\mathbf{x})\, dt \tag{9.2}$$

where $p(t|\mathbf{x})$ is the conditional density of the target variable t conditioned on the input vector $\mathbf{x}$. Similarly

$$\langle t^2|\mathbf{x}\rangle \equiv \int t^2 p(t|\mathbf{x})\, dt. \tag{9.3}$$

Note that the second term in (9.1) is independent of the network function $y(\mathbf{x})$ and hence is independent of the network weights. The optimal network function $y(\mathbf{x})$, in the sense of minimizing the sum-of-squares error, is the one which makes the first term in (9.1) vanish, and is given by $y(\mathbf{x}) = \langle t|\mathbf{x}\rangle$. The second term represents the intrinsic noise in the data and sets a lower limit on the error which can be achieved.

In a practical situation we must deal with the problems arising from a finite-size data set. Suppose we consider a training set D consisting of N patterns which we use to determine our network model $y(\mathbf{x})$. Now consider a whole ensemble of possible data sets, each containing N patterns, and each taken from the same fixed joint distribution $p(\mathbf{x}, t)$. We have already argued that the optimal network mapping is given by the conditional average $\langle t|\mathbf{x}\rangle$. A measure of how close the actual mapping function $y(\mathbf{x})$ is to the desired one is given by the integrand of the first term in (9.1):

$$\{y(\mathbf{x}) - \langle t|\mathbf{x}\rangle\}^2. \tag{9.4}$$

The value of this quantity will depend on the particular data set D on which it is trained. We can eliminate this dependence by considering an average over the complete ensemble of data sets, which we write as

$$\mathcal{E}_D[\{y(\mathbf{x}) - \langle t|\mathbf{x}\rangle\}^2] \tag{9.5}$$

where $\mathcal{E}_D[\cdot]$ denotes the expectation, or ensemble average, and we recall that the function $y(\mathbf{x})$ depends on the particular data set D which is used for training. Note that this expression is itself a function of $\mathbf{x}$.

If the network function were always a perfect predictor of the regression function $\langle t|\mathbf{x}\rangle$ then this error would be zero. As we shall see, a non-zero error can arise for essentially two distinct reasons. It may be that the network function is on average different from the regression function. This is called *bias*. Alternatively, it may be that the network function is very sensitive to the particular data set D, so that, at a given $\mathbf{x}$, it is larger than the required value for some data sets, and smaller for other data sets. This is called *variance*. We can make the decomposition into bias and variance explicit by writing (9.5) in somewhat different, but mathematically equivalent, form. First we expand the term in curly brackets in (9.5) to give

$$\{y(\mathbf{x}) - \langle t|\mathbf{x}\rangle\}^2 = \{y(\mathbf{x}) - \mathcal{E}_D[y(\mathbf{x})] + \mathcal{E}_D[y(\mathbf{x})] - \langle t|\mathbf{x}\rangle\}^2$$

$$= \{y(\mathbf{x}) - \mathcal{E}_D[y(\mathbf{x})]\}^2 + \{\mathcal{E}_D[y(\mathbf{x})] - \langle t|\mathbf{x}\rangle\}^2$$

$$+2\{y(\mathbf{x}) - \mathcal{E}_D[y(\mathbf{x})]\}\{\mathcal{E}_D[y(\mathbf{x})] - \langle t|\mathbf{x}\rangle\}. \qquad (9.6)$$

In order to compute the expression in (9.5) we take the expectation of both sides of (9.6) over the ensemble of data sets D. We see that the third term on the right-hand side of (9.6) vanishes, and we are left with

$$\mathcal{E}_D[\{y(\mathbf{x}) - \langle t|\mathbf{x}\rangle\}^2]$$

$$= \underbrace{\{\mathcal{E}_D[y(\mathbf{x})] - \langle t|\mathbf{x}\rangle\}^2}_{(\text{bias})^2} + \underbrace{\mathcal{E}_D[\{y(\mathbf{x}) - \mathcal{E}_D[y(\mathbf{x})]\}^2]}_{\text{variance}}. \qquad (9.7)$$

It is worth studying the expressions in (9.7) closely. The bias measures the extent to which the average (over all data sets) of the network function differs from the desired function $\langle t|\mathbf{x}\rangle$. Conversely the variance measures the extent to which the network function $y(\mathbf{x})$ is sensitive to the particular choice of data set. Note that the expressions for bias and variance are functions of the input vector $\mathbf{x}$. We can also introduce corresponding average values for bias and variance by integrating over all $\mathbf{x}$. By referring back to (9.1) we see that the appropriate weighting for this integration is given by the unconditional density $p(\mathbf{x})$, so that

$$(\text{bias})^2 = \frac{1}{2} \int \{\mathcal{E}_D[y(\mathbf{x})] - \langle t|\mathbf{x}\rangle\}^2 p(\mathbf{x}) \, d\mathbf{x} \qquad (9.8)$$

$$\text{variance} = \frac{1}{2} \int \mathcal{E}_D[\{y(\mathbf{x}) - \mathcal{E}_D[y(\mathbf{x})]\}^2] p(\mathbf{x}) \, d\mathbf{x}. \qquad (9.9)$$

The meaning of the bias and variance terms can be illustrated by considering two extreme limits for the choice of functional form for $y(\mathbf{x})$. We shall suppose that the target data for network training is generated from a smooth function $h(\mathbf{x})$ to which zero mean random noise ϵ is added, so that

$$t^n = h(\mathbf{x}^n) + \epsilon^n. \qquad (9.10)$$

Note that the optimal mapping function in this case is given by $\langle t|\mathbf{x}\rangle = h(\mathbf{x})$. One choice of model for $y(\mathbf{x})$ would be some fixed function $g(\mathbf{x})$ which is completely independent of the data set D, as indicated in Figure 9.1. It is clear that the variance term in (9.7) will vanish, since $\mathcal{E}_D[y(\mathbf{x})] = g(\mathbf{x}) = y(\mathbf{x})$. However, the bias term will typically be high since no attention at all was paid to the data, and so unless we have some prior knowledge which helps us to choose the function $g(\mathbf{x})$ we are making a wild guess.

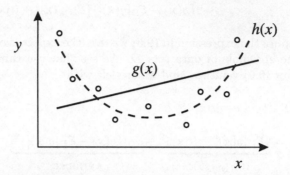

Figure 9.1. A schematic illustration of the meaning of bias and variance. Circles denote a set of data points which have been generated from an underlying function $h(x)$ (dashed curve) with the addition of noise. The goal is to try to approximate $h(x)$ as closely as possible. If we try to model the data by a fixed function $g(x)$, then the bias will generally be high while the variance will be zero.

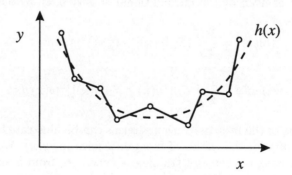

Figure 9.2. As in Figure 9.1, but in which a model is used which is a simple exact interpolant of the data points. In this case the bias is low but the variance is high.

The opposite extreme is to take a function which fits the training data perfectly, such as the simple exact interpolant indicated in Figure 9.2. In this case the bias term vanishes at the data points themselves since

$$\mathcal{E}_D[y(\mathbf{x})] = \mathcal{E}_D[h(\mathbf{x}) + \epsilon] = h(\mathbf{x}) = \langle t|\mathbf{x}\rangle \tag{9.11}$$

and the bias will typically be small in the neighbourhood of the data points. The variance, however, will be significant since

$$\mathcal{E}_D[\{y(\mathbf{x}) - \mathcal{E}_D[y(\mathbf{x})]\}^2] = \mathcal{E}_D[\{y(\mathbf{x}) - h(\mathbf{x})\}^2] = \mathcal{E}_D[\epsilon^2] \qquad (9.12)$$

which is just the variance of the noise on the data, which could be substantial.

We see that there is a natural trade-off between bias and variance. A function which is closely fitted to the data set will tend to have a large variance and hence give a large expected error. We can decrease the variance by smoothing the function, but if this is taken too far then the bias becomes large and the expected error is again large. This trade-off between bias and variance plays a crucial role in the application of neural network techniques to practical problems. We shall give a simple example of the dependence of bias and variance on the effective model complexity in Section 9.8.1.

9.1.1 *Minimizing bias and variance*

We have seen that, for any given size of data set, there is some optimal balance between bias and variance which gives the smallest average generalization error. In order to improve the performance of the network further we need to be able to reduce the bias while at the same time also reducing the variance. One way to achieve this is to use more data points. As we increase the number of data points we can afford to use more complex models, and therefore reduce bias, while at the same time ensuring that each model is more heavily constrained by the data, thereby also reducing variance. If we increase the number of data points sufficiently rapidly in relation to the model complexity we can find a sequence of models such that both bias and variance decrease. Models such as feed-forward neural networks can in principle provide *consistent* estimators of the regression function, meaning that they can approximate the regression to arbitrary accuracy in the limit as the number of data points goes to infinity. This limit requires a subtle balance of network complexity against number of data points to ensure that at each step both bias and variance are decreased. Consistency has been widely studied in the context of conventional techniques for statistical pattern recognition. For feed-forward networks, White (1990) has shown how the complexity of a two-layer network must grow in relation to the size of the data set in order to be consistent. This does not, however, tell us the complexity required for any given number of data points. It also requires that the parameter optimization algorithms are capable of finding the global minimum of the error function. Note that, even if both bias and variance can be reduced to zero, the error on new data will still be non-zero as a result of the intrinsic noise on the data given by the second term in (9.1).

In practice we are often limited in the number of training patterns available, and in many applications this may indeed be a severe limitation. An alternative approach to reducing both bias and variance becomes possible if we have some prior knowledge concerning the unknown function $h(\mathbf{x})$. Such knowledge can be used to constrain the model function $y(\mathbf{x})$ in a way which is consistent with $h(\mathbf{x})$ and which therefore does not give rise to increased bias. Note that the bias–variance problem implies that, for example, a simple linear model (single-layer network) might, in some applications involving relatively small data sets, give superior performance to a more general non-linear model (such as a multi-layer network) even though the latter contains the linear model as a special case.

9.2 Regularization

In Section 1.5 we saw that a polynomial with an excess of free coefficients tends to generate mappings which have a lot of curvature and structure, as a result of over-fitting to the noise on the training data. Similar behaviour also arises with more complex non-linear neural network models. The technique of regularization encourages smoother network mappings by adding a penalty Ω to the error function to give

$$\widetilde{E} = E + \nu\Omega. \tag{9.13}$$

Here E is one of the standard error functions as discussed in Chapter 6, and the parameter ν controls the extent to which the penalty term Ω influences the form of the solution. Training is performed by minimizing the total error function $\widetilde{E}$, which requires that the derivatives of Ω with respect to the network weights can be computed efficiently. A function $\mathbf{y}(\mathbf{x})$ which provides a good fit to the training data will give a small value for E, while one which is very smooth will give a small value for Ω. The resulting network mapping is a compromise between fitting the data and minimizing Ω. Regularization is discussed in the context of radial basis function networks in Section 5.4, and is given a Bayesian interpretation in Section 10.1.

In this section we shall consider various forms for the regularization term Ω. Regularization techniques have been extensively studied in the context of linear models for $\mathbf{y}(\mathbf{x})$. For the case of one input variable x and one output variable y, the class of *Tikhonov* regularizers takes the form

$$\Omega = \frac{1}{2} \sum_{r=0}^{R} \int_a^b h_r(x) \left(\frac{d^r y}{dx^r}\right)^2 dx \tag{9.14}$$

where $h_r \geq 0$ for $r = 0, \ldots, R - 1$, and $h_R > 0$ (Tikhonov and Arsenin, 1977). Regularization has also been widely studied in the context of vision systems (Poggio *et al.*, 1985).

9.2.1 *Weight decay*

One of the simplest forms of regularizer is called *weight decay* and consists of the sum of the squares of the adaptive parameters in the network

$$\Omega = \frac{1}{2} \sum_i w_i^2 \tag{9.15}$$

where the sum runs over all weights and biases. In conventional curve fitting, the use of this form of regularizer is called *ridge regression*. It has been found empirically that a regularizer of this form can lead to significant improvements in network generalization (Hinton, 1987). Some heuristic justification for the weight-decay regularizer can be given as follows. We know that to produce an over-fitted mapping with regions of large curvature requires relatively large values for the weights. For small values of the weights the network mapping represented by a multi-layer perceptron is approximately linear, since the central region of a sigmoidal activation function can be approximated by a linear transformation. By using a regularizer of the form (9.15), the weights are encouraged to be small.

Many network training algorithms make use of the derivatives of the total error function with respect to the network weights, which from (9.13) and (9.15) are given by

$$\nabla \widetilde{E} = \nabla E + \nu \mathbf{w}. \tag{9.16}$$

Suppose that the data term E is absent and we consider training by simple gradient descent in the continuous-time limit. The weight vector $\mathbf{w}(\tau)$ then evolves with time τ according to

$$\frac{d\mathbf{w}}{d\tau} = -\eta \nabla E = -\eta \nu \mathbf{w} \tag{9.17}$$

where η is the learning rate parameter. This equation has solution

$$\mathbf{w}(\tau) = \mathbf{w}(0) \exp(-\eta \nu \tau) \tag{9.18}$$

and so all of the weights decay exponentially to zero, which is the reason for the use of the term 'weight decay'.

We can gain some further insight into the behaviour of the weight-decay regularizer by considering the particular case of a quadratic error function. A general quadratic error can be written in the form

$$E(\mathbf{w}) = E_0 + \mathbf{b}^{\mathrm{T}} \mathbf{w} + \frac{1}{2} \mathbf{w}^{\mathrm{T}} \mathbf{H} \mathbf{w} \tag{9.19}$$

where the Hessian $\mathbf{H}$ and the vector $\mathbf{b}$ are constants. The minimum of this error function occurs at the point $\mathbf{w}^*$ which, by differentiating (9.19), satisfies

$$\mathbf{b} + \mathbf{H}\mathbf{w}^* = 0. \tag{9.20}$$

In the presence of the regularization term, the minimum moves to a point $\widetilde{\mathbf{w}}$ which, from (9.13), satisfies

$$\mathbf{b} + \mathbf{H}\widetilde{\mathbf{w}} + \nu \widetilde{\mathbf{w}} = 0. \tag{9.21}$$

We can better interpret the effect of the weight-decay term if we rotate the axes in weight space so as to diagonalize the Hessian matrix $\mathbf{H}$ (Appendix A). This is done by considering the eigenvector equation for the Hessian given by

$$\mathbf{H}\mathbf{u}_j = \lambda_j \mathbf{u}_j. \tag{9.22}$$

We can now expand $\mathbf{w}^*$ and $\widetilde{\mathbf{w}}$ in terms of the eigenvectors to give

$$\mathbf{w}^* = \sum_j w_j^* \mathbf{u}_j, \qquad \widetilde{\mathbf{w}} = \sum_j \widetilde{w}_j \mathbf{u}_j. \tag{9.23}$$

Combining (9.20), (9.21) and (9.23), and using the orthonormality of the $\{\mathbf{u}_j\}$, we obtain the following relation between the minima of the original and the regularized error functions

$$\widetilde{w}_j = \frac{\lambda_j}{\lambda_j + \nu} w_j^*. \tag{9.24}$$

The eigenvectors $\mathbf{u}_j$ represent the principal directions of the quadratic error surface. Along those directions for which the corresponding eigenvalues are relatively large, so that $\lambda_j \gg \nu$, (9.24) shows that $\widetilde{w}_j \simeq w_j^*$, and so the minimum of the error function is shifted very little. Conversely, along directions for which the eigenvalues are relatively small, so that $\lambda_j \ll \nu$, (9.24) shows that $|\widetilde{w}_j| \ll |w_j^*|$, and so the corresponding components of the minimum weight vector are suppressed. This effect is illustrated in Figure 9.3.

9.2.2 Consistency of weight decay

One of the limitations of simple weight decay in the form (9.15) is that is inconsistent with certain scaling properties of network mappings. To illustrate this, consider a multi-layer perceptron network having a single hidden layer and linear output units, which performs a mapping from a set of input variables x_i to a set of output variables y_k. The activation of a hidden unit in the first hidden layer is given by

$$z_j = g\left(\sum_i w_{ji} x_i + w_{j0}\right) \tag{9.25}$$

while the activations of the output units are given by

$$y_k = \sum_j w_{kj} z_j + w_{k0}. \tag{9.26}$$

Suppose we perform a linear transformation on the input data of the form

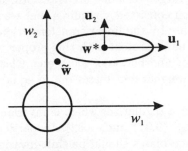

Figure 9.3. Illustration of the effect of a simple weight-decay regularizer on a quadratic error function. The circle represents a contour along which the weight-decay term is constant, and the ellipse represents a contour of constant unregularized error. Note that the axes in weight space have been rotated to be parallel with the principal axes of the original error surface, determined by the eigenvectors of the corresponding Hessian matrix. The effect of the regularizer is to shift the minimum of the error function from $\mathbf{w}^*$ to $\widetilde{\mathbf{w}}$. This reduces the value of w_1 at the minimum significantly since this corresponds to a small eigenvalue, while the value of w_2, which corresponds to a large eigenvalue, is hardly affected.

$$x_i \rightarrow \widetilde{x}_i = ax_i + b. \tag{9.27}$$

Then we can arrange for the mapping performed by the network to be unchanged by making a corresponding linear transformation of the weights and biases from the inputs to the units in the hidden layer of the form

$$w_{ji} \rightarrow \widetilde{w}_{ji} = \frac{1}{a} w_{ji} \tag{9.28}$$

$$w_{j0} \rightarrow \widetilde{w}_{j0} = w_{j0} - \frac{b}{a} \sum_i w_{ji}. \tag{9.29}$$

Similarly, a linear transformation of the output variables of the network of the form

$$y_k \rightarrow \widetilde{y}_k = cy_k + d \tag{9.30}$$

can be achieved by making a transformation of the second-layer weights using

$$w_{kj} \rightarrow \widetilde{w}_{kj} = cw_{kj} \tag{9.31}$$

$$w_{k0} \rightarrow \widetilde{w}_{k0} = cw_{k0} + d. \tag{9.32}$$

If we train one network using the original data and one network using data for which the input and/or target variables are transformed by one of the above linear transformations, then consistency requires that we should obtain equivalent networks which differ only by the linear transformation of the weights as given. Any regularizer should be consistent with this property, otherwise it arbitrarily favours one solution over another, equivalent one. Clearly, simple weight decay (9.15) which treats all weights and biases on an equal footing does not satisfy this property.

We therefore look for a regularizer which is invariant under the linear transformations (9.28), (9.29), (9.31) and (9.32). In particular, the weights should be scale-invariant and the biases should be shift-invariant. Such a regularizer is given by

$$\frac{\nu_1}{2} \sum_{w \in \mathcal{W}_1} w^2 + \frac{\nu_2}{2} \sum_{w \in \mathcal{W}_2} w^2 \tag{9.33}$$

where $\mathcal{W}_1$ denotes the set of weights in the first layer, $\mathcal{W}_2$ denotes the set of weights in the second layer, and biases are excluded from the summations. Under the linear transformations of the weights given by (9.28), (9.29), (9.31) and (9.32), the regularizer will remain unchanged provided the parameters ν_1 and ν_2 are suitably rescaled.

In Section 3.4.3 we showed that the role of the biases in the final layer of a network with linear outputs, trained by minimizing a sum-of-squares error function, is to compensate for the difference between the mean (over the data set) of the output vector from the network and the corresponding mean of the target values. It is therefore reasonable to exclude the biases from the regularizer as we do not wish systematically to distort the mean network output. The output is then equal to the sample mean of the target data, and provides an unbiased estimate of the true target mean.

Weight-decay regularizers can be motivated in the context of linear models by considering the sensitivity of the model predictions to noise on the input vectors. Minimization of this sensitivity leads naturally to a weight-decay regularizer, in which the biases are excluded from the sum over weights (Exercise 9.2). The more general case of non-linear networks is covered in detail later, when we consider the training of networks with additive noise on the inputs.

9.2.3 *A simple illustration of weight decay*

As an illustration of the use of weight decay, we return to the example used in Section 5.1 of modelling a noisy sine function using a radial basis function network. In Figure 9.4 we show an example of a data set together with the network function obtained by minimizing a sum-of-squares error. Here data was generated by sampling the function $h(x)$ given by

$$h(x) = 0.5 + 0.4 \sin(2\pi x) \tag{9.34}$$

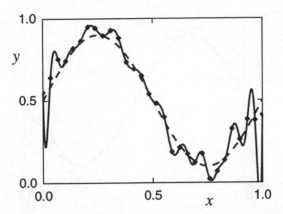

Figure 9.4. Example of data generated by sampling the function $h(x)$, defined by (9.34), and adding Gaussian distributed random noise with standard deviation of 0.05. The dashed curve shows the function $h(x)$ and the solid curve shows the result of fitting a radial basis function network without regularization. There is one Gaussian basis function for each of the 30 data points, and the result is a strongly over-fitted network mapping. (This figure is identical to Figure 5.1, and is reproduced here for ease of comparison.)

and adding Gaussian distributed random noise with zero mean and standard deviation $\sigma = 0.05$. There is one basis function centred on each data point, and consequently the network gives a strongly over-fitted solution.

We now include a weight-decay regularizer of the form (9.15) with the bias parameter excluded from the summation, for reasons discussed above. Figure 9.5 shows the effect of using a regularization coefficient of $\nu = 40$. The network mapping is now much smoother and gives a much closer representation of the underlying function from which the data was generated (shown by the dashed curve). The degree of smoothing is controlled by the regularization coefficient ν, and too large a value of ν leads to over-smoothing, as illustrated for $\nu = 1000$ in Figure 9.6.

9.2.4 *Early stopping*

An alternative to regularization as a way of controlling the effective complexity of a network is the procedure of *early stopping*. The training of non-linear network models corresponds to an iterative reduction of the error function defined with respect to a set of training data. During a typical training session, this error generally decreases as a function of the number of iterations in the algorithm. For many of the algorithms described in Chapter 7 (such as conjugate gradients) the error is a monotonically decreasing function of the iteration index. However, the error measured with respect to independent data, generally called a validation set, often shows a decrease at first, followed by an increase as the network starts

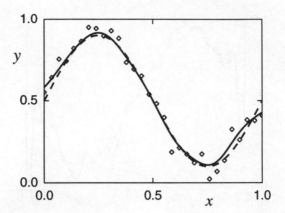

Figure 9.5. As in Figure 9.4 but with a weight-decay regularizer and a regularization coefficient $\nu = 40$, showing the much smoother network mapping and the correspondingly closer agreement with the underlying generator of the data, shown by the dashed curve.

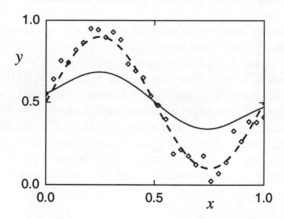

Figure 9.6. As in Figure 9.5 but with $\nu = 1000$, showing the effect of having too large a value for the regularization coefficient.

to over-fit. Training can therefore be stopped at the point of smallest error with respect to new data, as indicated in Figure 9.7, since this gives a network which is expected to have the best generalization performance.

The behaviour of the network in this case is sometimes explained qualitatively in terms of the effective number of degrees of freedom in the network. This number is suppose to start out small and then to grow during the train-

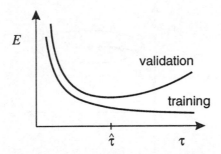

Figure 9.7. A schematic illustration of the behaviour of training and validation set errors during a typical training session, as a function of the iteration step τ. The goal of achieving the best generalization performance suggests that training should be stopped at the point $\hat{\tau}$ corresponding to the minimum of the validation set error.

ing process, corresponding to a steady increase in the effective complexity of the model. Halting training before a minimum of the training error has been reached then represents a way of limiting the effective network complexity.

In the case of a quadratic error function, early stopping should give rise to similar behaviour to regularization using a simple weight-decay term. This can be understood from Figure 9.8. The axes in weight space have been rotated to be parallel to the eigenvectors of the Hessian matrix. If, in the absence of weight decay, the weight vector starts at the origin and proceeds during training along a path which follows the local negative gradient vector, then the weight vector will move initially parallel to the w_2 axis to a point corresponding roughly to $\widetilde{\mathbf{w}}$ and then move towards the minimum of the error function $\mathbf{w}^*$. This follows from the shape of the error surface and the widely differing eigenvalues of the Hessian. Stopping at a point near $\widetilde{\mathbf{w}}$ is therefore similar to weight decay. The relationship between early stopping and weight decay can be made quantitative, as discussed in Exercise 9.1, thereby showing that the quantity $\tau\eta$ (where τ is the iteration index, and η is the learning rate parameter) plays the role of the reciprocal of the regularization parameter ν. This exercise also shows that the effective number of parameters in the network (i.e. the number of weights whose values differ significantly from zero) grows during the course of training.

9.2.5 *Curvature-driven smoothing*

We have seen that over-fitted solutions are generally characterized by mappings which have a lot of structure and relatively high curvature. This provided some indirect motivation for weight-decay regularizers as a way of reducing the curvature of the network function. A more direct approach is to consider a regularizer which penalizes curvature explicitly. Since the curvature is governed by the second derivatives of the network function, we can consider a regularizer of the form

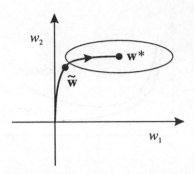

Figure 9.8. A schematic illustration of why early stopping can give similar results to weight decay in the case of a quadratic error function. The ellipse shows a contour of constant error, and $\mathbf{w}^*$ denotes the minimum of the error function. If the weight vector starts at the origin and moves according to the local negative gradient direction, then it will follow the path shown by the curve. By stopping training early, a weight vector $\widetilde{\mathbf{w}}$ is found which is qualitatively similar to that obtained with a simple weight-decay regularizer and training to the new minimum of the error, as can be seen by comparing with Figure 9.3. A precise quantitative relationship between early stopping and weight-decay regularization can be demonstrated formally for the case of quadratic error surfaces (Exercise 9.1).

$$\Omega = \frac{1}{2} \sum_{n=1}^{N} \sum_{i=1}^{d} \sum_{k=1}^{c} \left(\frac{\partial^2 y_k^n}{\partial x_i^2} \right)^2. \tag{9.35}$$

Note that this regularizer is a discrete version of the Tikhonov form (9.14). Regularizers involving second derivatives also form the basis of the conventional interpolation technique of cubic splines (Wahba and Wold, 1975; De Boor, 1978). The derivatives of (9.35) with respect to the weights for a multi-layer perceptron can be obtained by an extension of the back-propagation procedure (Bishop, 1993).

9.3 Training with noise

We have discussed two approaches to controlling the effective complexity of a network mapping, based respectively on limiting the number of adaptive parameters and on regularization. A third approach is the technique of training with noise, which involves the addition of noise to the input vectors during the training process. For sequential training algorithms, this can be done by adding a new random vector to each input pattern before it is presented to the network, so that, if the patterns are being recycled, a different random vector is added each time. For batch methods, a similar effect can be achieved by replicating each data point a number of times and adding new random vectors onto each copy.

Heuristically, we might expect that the noise will 'smear out' each data point and make it difficult for the network to fit individual data points precisely, and hence will reduce over-fitting. In practice, it has been demonstrated that training with noise can indeed lead to improvements in network generalization (Sietsma and Dow, 1991). We now show that training with noise is closely related to the technique of regularization (Bishop, 1995).

Suppose we describe the noise on the inputs by the random vector ξ, governed by some probability distribution $\widetilde{p}(\xi)$. If we consider the limit of an infinite number of data points, we can write the error function, in the absence of noise, in the form

$$E = \frac{1}{2} \sum_k \int\int \{y_k(\mathbf{x}) - t_k\}^2 p(t_k|\mathbf{x})p(\mathbf{x})\,d\mathbf{x}\,dt_k \qquad (9.36)$$

as discussed in Section 6.1.3. If we now consider an infinite number of copies of each data point, each of which is perturbed by the addition of a noise vector, then the mean error function defined over this expanded data set can be written as

$$\widetilde{E} = \frac{1}{2} \sum_k \int\int\int \{y_k(\mathbf{x}+\xi) - t_k\}^2 p(t_k|\mathbf{x})p(\mathbf{x})\widetilde{p}(\xi)\,d\mathbf{x}\,dt_k\,d\xi. \qquad (9.37)$$

We now assume that the noise amplitude is small, and expand the network function as a Taylor series in powers of ξ to give

$$y_k(\mathbf{x}+\xi) = y_k(\mathbf{x}) + \sum_i \xi_i \left.\frac{\partial y_k}{\partial x_i}\right|_{\xi=0} + \frac{1}{2}\sum_i\sum_j \xi_i\xi_j \left.\frac{\partial^2 y_k}{\partial x_i \partial x_j}\right|_{\xi=0} + \mathcal{O}(\xi^3). \qquad (9.38)$$

The noise distribution is generally chosen to have zero mean, and to be uncorrelated between different inputs. Thus we have

$$\int \xi_i \widetilde{p}(\xi)\,d\xi = 0 \qquad \int \xi_i\xi_j \widetilde{p}(\xi)\,d\xi = \nu\delta_{ij} \qquad (9.39)$$

where the parameter ν represents the variance of the noise distribution. Substituting the Taylor series expansion (9.38) into the error function (9.37), and making use of (9.39) to integrate over the noise distribution, we obtain

$$\widetilde{E} = E + \nu\Omega \qquad (9.40)$$

where E is the standard sum-of-squares error given by (9.36), and the extra term Ω is given by

$$\Omega = \frac{1}{2} \sum_k \sum_i \iint \left\{ \left(\frac{\partial y_k}{\partial x_i} \right)^2 + \frac{1}{2} \{ y_k(\mathbf{x}) - t_k \} \frac{\partial^2 y_k}{\partial x_i^2} \right\} p(t_k|\mathbf{x}) p(\mathbf{x}) \, d\mathbf{x} \, dt_k.$$

(9.41)

This has the form of a regularization term added to the usual sum-of-squares error, with the coefficient of the regularizer determined by the noise variance ν (Webb, 1994).

Provided the noise amplitude is small, so that the neglect of higher-order terms in the Taylor expansion is valid, the minimization of the sum-of-squares error with noise added to the input data is equivalent to the minimization of the regularized sum-of-squares error (9.40), with a regularization term given by (9.41), without the addition of noise. It should be noted, however, that the second term in the regularization function (9.41) involves second derivatives of the network function, and so evaluation of the gradients of this error with respect to network weights will be computationally demanding. Furthermore, this term is not positive definite, and so the error function is not *a priori* bounded below, and is therefore unsuitable for use as the basis of a training algorithm.

We now consider the minimization of the regularized error (9.40) with respect to the network function $\mathbf{y}(\mathbf{x})$, which allows us to show that the second derivative terms can be neglected. This result is analogous to the one obtained for the outer product approximation for the Hessian matrix in Section 6.1.4, in which we showed that similar second-derivative terms also vanish. Thus, we will see that the use of the regularization function (9.41) for network training is equivalent, for small values of the noise amplitude, to the use of a positive-definite regularization function which is of standard Tikhonov form and which involves only *first* derivatives of the network function (Bishop, 1995).

As discussed at length in Section 6.1.3, the network function which minimizes the sum-of-squares error is given by the conditional average $\langle t_k|\mathbf{x}\rangle$ of the target values t_k. From (9.40) we see that, in the presence of the regularization term, the network function which minimizes the total error will have the form

$$y_k(\mathbf{x}) = \langle t_k|\mathbf{x}\rangle + \mathcal{O}(\nu).$$

(9.42)

Now consider the second term in equation (9.41) which depends on the second derivatives of the network function. Making use of the definition of the conditional average of the target data, given in equation (9.2), we can rewrite this term in the form

$$\frac{1}{4} \sum_k \sum_i \int \left(\{ y_k(\mathbf{x}) - \langle t_k|\mathbf{x}\rangle \} \frac{\partial^2 y_k}{\partial x_i^2} \right) p(\mathbf{x}) \, d\mathbf{x}.$$

(9.43)

Using (9.42) we see that, to lowest order in ν, this term vanishes at the minimum of the total error function. Thus, only the first term in equation (9.41) needs to be retained. It should be emphasized that this result is a consequence of the average over the target data, and so it does not require the individual terms

$y_k - t_k$ to be small, only that their (conditional) average over t_k be small.

The minimization of the sum-of-squares error with noise is therefore equivalent (to first order in ν) to the minimization of a regularized sum-of-squares error without noise, where the regularizer, given by the first term in equation (9.41), has the form

$$\Omega = \frac{1}{2} \sum_k \sum_i \int \left(\frac{\partial y_k}{\partial x_i} \right)^2 p(\mathbf{x}) \, d\mathbf{x} \tag{9.44}$$

where we have integrated out the t_k variables. Note that the regularization function in equation (9.44) is not in general equivalent to that given in equation (9.41). However, the total regularized error in each case is minimized by the same network function $\mathbf{y}(\mathbf{x})$, and hence by the same set of network weight values. Thus, for the purposes of network training, we can replace the regularization term in equation (9.41) with the one in equation (9.44). In practice, we approximate (9.44) by a sum over a finite set of N data points of the form

$$\Omega = \frac{1}{2N} \sum_{n=1}^{N} \sum_k \sum_i \left(\frac{\partial y_k^n}{\partial x_i^n} \right)^2 . \tag{9.45}$$

Derivatives of this regularizer with respect to the network weights can be found using an extended back-propagation algorithm (Bishop, 1993).

This regularizer involves first derivatives of the network mapping function. A related approach has been proposed by Drucker and Le Cun (1992) based on a sum of derivatives of the error function itself with respect to the network inputs. This choice of regularizer leads to a computationally efficient algorithm for evaluating the gradients of the regularization function with respect to the network weights. The algorithm is equivalent to forward and backward propagation through an extended network architecture, and is termed *double back-propagation*.

9.4 Soft weight sharing

One way to reduce the effective complexity of a network with a large number of weights is to constrain weights within certain groups to be equal. This is the technique of weight sharing which was discussed in Section 8.7.3 as a way of building translation invariance into networks used for image interpretation. It is only applicable, however, to particular problems in which the form of the constraints can be specified in advance. Here we consider a form of *soft weight sharing* (Nowlan and Hinton, 1992) in which the hard constraint of equal weights is replaced by a form of regularization in which groups of weights are encouraged to have similar values. Furthermore, the division of weights into groups, the mean weight value for each group, and the spread of values within the groups, are all determined as part of the learning process.

As discussed at length in Chapter 6, an error function can be regarded as the negative logarithm of a likelihood function. Thus, the simple weight-decay regularizer (9.15) represents the negative logarithm of the likelihood of the given set of weight values under a Gaussian distribution centred on the origin. To see this, consider a Gaussian of the form

$$p(w) = \frac{1}{(2\pi)^{1/2}} \exp\left\{-\frac{w^2}{2}\right\}. \tag{9.46}$$

Then the likelihood of the set of weight values under this distribution is given by

$$\mathcal{L} = \prod_{i=1}^{W} p(w_i) = \frac{1}{(2\pi)^{W/2}} \exp\left\{-\frac{1}{2}\sum_i w_i^2\right\} \tag{9.47}$$

where W is the total number of weights. Taking the negative logarithm then gives the weight-decay regularizer, up to an irrelevant additive constant. As we have seen, the weight-decay term has the effect of encouraging the weight values to form a cluster with values close to zero.

We can encourage the weight values to form several groups, rather than just one group, by considering a probability distribution which is a *mixture* of Gaussians. An introduction to Gaussian mixture models and their basic properties is given in Section 2.6. The centres and variances of the Gaussian components, as well as the mixing coefficients, will be considered as adjustable parameters to be determined as part of the learning process. Thus, we have a probability density of the form

$$p(w) = \sum_{j=1}^{M} \alpha_j \phi_j(w) \tag{9.48}$$

where α_j are the mixing coefficients, and the component densities $\phi_j(w)$ are Gaussians of the form

$$\phi_j(w) = \frac{1}{(2\pi\sigma_j^2)^{1/2}} \exp\left\{-\frac{(w - \mu_j)^2}{2\sigma_j^2}\right\}. \tag{9.49}$$

Forming the likelihood function in the usual way, and then taking the negative logarithm, leads to a regularizing function of the form

$$\Omega = -\sum_i \ln\left(\sum_{j=1}^{M} \alpha_j \phi_j(w_i)\right). \tag{9.50}$$

The total error function is then given by

$$\tilde{E} = E + \nu\Omega \tag{9.51}$$

where ν is the regularization coefficient. This error is minimized both with respect to the weights w_i and with respect to the parameters α_j, μ_j and σ_j of the mixture model. If the weights were constant, then the parameters of the mixture model could be determined by using the EM re-estimation procedure discussed in Section 2.6.2. However, the distribution of weights is itself evolving during the learning process, and so to avoid numerical instability a joint optimization is performed simultaneously over the weights and the mixture model parameters. This can be done using one of the standard algorithms, such as the conjugate gradient or quasi-Newton methods, described in Chapter 7. The parameter ν, however, cannot be optimized in this way, since this would give $\nu \to 0$ and an over-fitted solution, but must be found using techniques such as cross-validation to be discussed later.

In order to minimize the total error function it is necessary to be able to evaluate its derivatives with respect to the various adjustable parameters. To do this it is convenient to regard the α_j's as *prior* probabilities, and to introduce the corresponding posterior probabilities given by Bayes' theorem in the form

$$\pi_j(w) = \frac{\alpha_j\phi_j(w)}{\sum_k \alpha_k\phi_k(w)}. \tag{9.52}$$

The derivatives of the total error function with respect to the weights are then given by

$$\frac{\partial\tilde{E}}{\partial w_i} = \frac{\partial E}{\partial w_i} + \nu\sum_j \pi_j(w_i)\frac{(w_i - \mu_j)}{\sigma_j^2}. \tag{9.53}$$

The effect of the regularization term is thus to pull each weight towards the centre of the jth Gaussian, with a force proportional to the posterior probability of that Gaussian for the given weight. This is precisely the kind of effect which we are seeking.

Derivatives of the error with respect to the centres of the Gaussians are also easily computed to give

$$\frac{\partial\tilde{E}}{\partial\mu_j} = \nu\sum_i \pi_j(w_i)\frac{(\mu_i - w_j)}{\sigma_j^2} \tag{9.54}$$

which has a simple intuitive interpretation, since it drives μ_j towards an average of the weight values, weighted by the posterior probabilities that the respective weights were generated by component j. Similarly, the derivatives with respect to the variances are given by

$$\frac{\partial \widetilde{E}}{\partial \sigma_j} = \nu \sum_i \pi_j(w_i) \left(\frac{1}{\sigma_j} - \frac{(w_i - \mu_j)^2}{\sigma_j^3} \right) \tag{9.55}$$

which drives σ_j towards the weighted average of the squared deviations of the weights around the corresponding centre μ_j, where the weighting coefficients are again given by the posterior probability that each weight is generated by component j. Note that, in a practical implementation, new variables η_j defined by

$$\sigma_j^2 = \exp(\eta_j) \tag{9.56}$$

are introduced, and the minimization is performed with respect to the η_j. This ensures that the parameters σ_j remain positive. It also has the effect of discouraging pathological solutions in which one or more of the σ_j goes to zero, corresponding to a Gaussian component collapsing onto one of the weight parameter values. Such solutions are discussed in more detail in the context of Gaussian mixture models in Section 2.6. From a Bayesian perspective, the use of a transformation of the form (9.56) can be motivated by a consideration of *non-informative priors* (Section 10.4 and Exercise 10.13).

For the derivatives with respect to the mixing coefficients α_j, we need to take account of the constraints

$$\sum_j \alpha_j = 1, \qquad 0 \le \alpha_i \le 1 \tag{9.57}$$

which follow from the interpretation of the α_j as prior probabilities. This can be done by expressing the mixing coefficients in terms of a set of auxiliary variables $\{\gamma_j\}$ using the *softmax* function given by

$$\alpha_j = \frac{\exp(\gamma_j)}{\sum_{k=1}^M \exp(\gamma_k)}. \tag{9.58}$$

We can now minimize the error function with respect to the $\{\gamma_j\}$. To find the derivatives of $\widetilde{E}$ with respect to γ_j we make use of

$$\frac{\partial \alpha_k}{\partial \gamma_j} = \delta_{jk}\alpha_j - \alpha_j\alpha_k \tag{9.59}$$

which follows from (9.58). Using the chain rule in the form

$$\frac{\partial \widetilde{E}}{\partial \gamma_j} = \sum_k \frac{\partial \widetilde{E}}{\partial \alpha_k} \frac{\partial \alpha_k}{\partial \gamma_j} \tag{9.60}$$

together with (9.50), (9.52) and (9.59), we then obtain the required derivatives in the form

$$\frac{\partial \widetilde{E}}{\partial \gamma_j} = \sum_i \{\alpha_j - \pi_j(w_i)\} \tag{9.61}$$

where we have made use of $\sum_j \alpha_j = 1$. We see that α_j is therefore driven towards the average posterior probability for component j.

In practice it is necessary to take some care over the initialization of the weights in order to ensure that good solutions are found. One approach is to choose the initial weights from a uniform distribution over a finite interval, and then initialize the components $\phi_j(w)$ to have means which are equally spaced over this interval, with equal priors, and variances equal to the spacing between the adjacent means. This ensures that, for most of the weights, there is little initial contribution to the error gradient from the regularization term, and so the initial evolution of the weights is primarily data-driven. Also, the posterior probabilities have roughly equal contributions over the complete set of weights, which helps to avoid problems due to priors going to zero early in the optimization. Results on several test problems (Nowlan and Hinton, 1992) show that this method can lead to significantly better generalization than simple weight decay.

9.5 Growing and pruning algorithms

The architecture of a neural network (number of units and topology of connections) can have a significant impact on its performance in any particular application. Various techniques have therefore been developed for optimizing the architecture, in some cases as part of the network training process itself. It is important to distinguish between two distinct aspects of the architecture selection problem. First, we need a systematic procedure for exploring some space of possible architectures, and this forms the subject of this section. Second, we need some way of deciding which of the architectures considered should be selected. This is usually determined by the requirement of achieving the best possible generalization, and is discussed at length in Section 9.8.

The simplest approach to network structure optimization involves exhaustive search through a restricted class of network architectures. We might for instance consider the class of multi-layer perceptrons having two layers of weights with full connectivity between adjacent layers and no direct input-output connections. The only aspect of the architecture which remains to be specified is the number M of hidden units, and so we train a set of networks having a range of values of M, and select the one which gives the best value for our performance criterion. This approach can require significant computational effort and yet it only searches a very restricted class of network models. If we expand the range of models (by having multiple hidden layers and partial connectivity for example) we quickly reach the point of having insufficient computational resources for a complete search. Note, however, that this is the approach which is most widely adopted in practice. Some justification can be found in the fact that, for the two-layer architecture, we know that we can approximate any continuous functional mapping to arbitrary accuracy (Section 4.3) provided M is sufficiently large.

An obvious drawback of such an approach is that many different networks have to be trained. This can in principle be avoided by considering a network which is initially relatively small and allowing new units and connections to be added during training. A simple example of this would be to consider the class of networks having two layers of weights with full connections in each layer, and to start with a few hidden units and then add one unit at a time. Such an approach was considered by Bello (1992) who used the weights from one network as the initial guess for training the next network (with the extra weights initialized randomly). Techniques of this form are called *growing algorithms* and we shall consider some examples for networks of threshold units, and then discuss the *cascade correlation* algorithm which uses sigmoidal units.

An alternative approach is to start with a relatively large network and gradually remove either connections or complete units. These are known as *pruning algorithms* and we shall consider several specific examples. Note that, if weight sharing is used, then several weights may be controlled by a single parameter, and if the parameter is set to zero then all the corresponding weights are deleted.

A further possible approach to the design of network topology is to construct a complex network from several simpler network modules. We consider two important examples of this, called *network committees* and *mixtures of experts*. The latter allows a problem to be decomposed automatically into a number of sub-problems, each of which is tackled by a separate network.

9.5.1 Exact Boolean classification

As we emphasize at several points in this book, the goal in training a neural network is usually to achieve the best generalization on new data rather than to learn the training set accurately. However, for completeness we give here a brief review of two approaches to network construction algorithms which can learn a finite set of Boolean patterns exactly. We consider networks having threshold units and a single output, for binary input patterns belonging to two classes.

Before discussing these algorithms in detail, we need first to consider a modification to the usual perceptron learning algorithm known as the *pocket algorithm* (Gallant, 1986b) designed to deal with data sets which are not linearly separable. The simple perceptron learning algorithm (Section 3.5) is guaranteed to find an exact classification of the training data set if it is linearly separable. If the data set is not linearly separable, then the algorithm does not converge. The pocket algorithm involves retaining a copy ('in one's pocket') of the set of weights which has so far survived unchanged for the longest number of pattern presentations. It can be shown that, for a sufficiently long training time, this gives, with probability arbitrarily close to unity, the set of weight values which produces the smallest

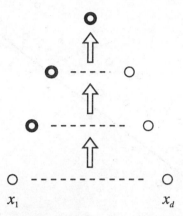

x_1 $\qquad\qquad\qquad\qquad\quad$ x_d

Figure 9.9. The tiling algorithm builds a network in successive layers. In each layer, the first unit added is the master unit (shown as the heavier circle) which plays a special role. Successive layers are fully connected, and there are no other interconnections in the network.

possible number of misclassifications. Note, however, that no upper bound on the training time needed for this to occur is known.

The *tiling algorithm* (Mezard and Nadal, 1989) builds a network in successive layers with each layer having fewer units than the previous layer, as indicated in Figure 9.9. Note that the only interconnections in the network are between adjacent layers. When a new layer is constructed, a single unit, called the master unit, is added and trained using the pocket algorithm. One requirement for the network is that each layer must form a 'faithful' representation of the data set, in other words two input patterns which belong to different classes must not be mapped onto the same pattern of activations in any layer, otherwise it will be impossible for successive layers to separate them. This is achieved by adding further ancillary units to the layer, one at a time, leaving the weights to the master unit and any other ancillary units in that layer fixed. The geometrical interpretation of this procedure is indicated in Figure 9.10. If the representation at any stage is not faithful then there must exist patterns from different classes which give rise to the same set of activations in that layer. The group of all input patterns which give rise to those activations are identified and an extra ancillary unit is added and trained (again using the pocket algorithm) on that group. The process of searching for ambiguities, and adding ancillary units, is repeated until the representation is faithful. The whole process is repeated with the next layer. It can be shown that at each layer the master unit produces fewer misclassifications than the master unit in the previous layer. Thus, eventually one of the master units produces correct classification of all of the patterns, and so the algorithm converges with a network of finite size.

We next consider the *upstart algorithm* (Frean, 1990) which is also guaranteed

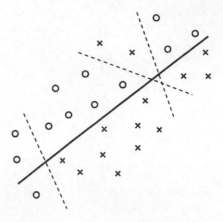

Figure 9.10. Illustration of the role of the ancillary units in the tiling algorithm. The circles and crosses represent the patterns of activations of units in a particular layer when the network is presented with input patterns from two different classes. The master unit in the next layer (whose decision boundary is represented by the solid line) is trained to find the best linear separator of the classes, and then ancillary units (with decision boundaries given by the dashed lines) are added so as to separate those patterns which are misclassified.

to find a finite network which gives complete classification of a finite data set. However, it builds the network by adding extra units between existing units and the inputs, as indicated in Figure 9.11. All units take their inputs directly from the inputs to the network, and have binary threshold activation functions. The algorithm begins by training a single unit using the pocket algorithm. This 'parent' unit will typically mis-classify some of the patterns, and so two 'offspring' units are added, one to deal with the patterns for which the parent is incorrectly off, and the other to deal with the patterns for which the parent is incorrectly on. These units are connected to their parent with sufficiently large negative and positive weights respectively that they can reverse the output of the parent when they are activated. The weights to the parent are frozen and the offspring are trained to produce the correct output for the corresponding incorrect patterns, while at the same time not spoiling the classification of the patterns which were correct. The algorithm is called upstart because the offspring correct the mistakes of their parents! We can always choose the weights and bias of an offspring unit such that it only generates a non-zero output for one particular pattern, and so it will then reduce the number of errors of the parent by one. In practice, the units are trained by the pocket algorithm and may do much better than just correct one pattern. Once trained, the offspring weights are frozen, and they become parents for another layer of offspring, and so on.

Since the addition of each offspring unit reduces the number of errors of its parent by at least one, it is clear that the network must eventually classify

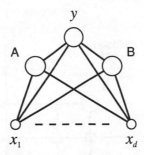

Figure 9.11. The upstart algorithm adds new offspring units, at A and B, to correct the mistakes made by the parent unit. The offspring themselves generate offspring units, leading eventually to a network having a binary tree structure.

all patterns correctly using a finite number of units. This occurs because the number of mistakes which successive offspring have to correct diminishes until eventually an offspring gets all of its patterns correct, which implies that its parent produces the correct patterns, and so on all the way back up the network to the output unit. The final network has the form of a binary tree, although some branches might be missing if they are not needed. However, this architecture can be reorganized into a two-layer network by removing the output connections from the units and moving all units into a single hidden layer (leaving their input connections unchanged). A new output unit is then created, and new hidden-to-output connections added. These connections can be learned with the perceptron algorithm or found by explicit construction in a way which guarantees correct classification of all patterns (Frean, 1990). In simulations it is found that the upstart algorithm produces networks having fewer units than those found with the tiling algorithm. Other algorithms for tackling the Boolean classification problem have been described by Gallant (1986a), Nadal (1989) and Marchand *et al.* (1990).

9.5.2 *Cascade correlation*

A different approach to network construction, applicable to problems with continuous output variables, is known as *cascade-correlation* (Fahlman and Lebiere, 1990) and is based on networks of sigmoidal hidden units. The form of the network architecture is shown in Figure 9.12. To begin with there are no hidden units, and every input is connected to every output unit by adjustable connections (the crosses in Figure 9.12). The output units may be linear or may have sigmoidal non-linearities depending on the application. At this stage the network has a single layer of weights and can be trained by a number of different algorithms, as discussed in Chapters 3 and 7. Fahlman and Lebiere use the quickprop algorithm (Section 7.5.3). The network is trained for a period of time governed by some user-defined parameter (whose value is set empirically)

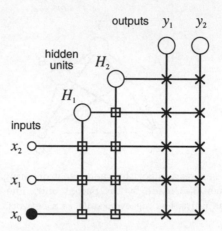

Figure 9.12. Architecture of the cascade-correlation network. Large circles denote processing units, small circles denote inputs, and the bias input is shown in black. Squares represent weights which are trained and then frozen, while the crosses show weights which are retrained after the addition of each hidden unit. Hidden unit H_1 is added first, and then hidden unit H_2, and so on.

and then a sigmoidal hidden unit is added to the network. This is followed by further network training, alternating with the addition of hidden units, until a sufficiently small error is achieved. The addition of hidden units is done in such a way that, at each stage of the algorithm, only a single-layer system is being trained. Each new hidden unit takes inputs from all of the inputs to the network plus the outputs of all existing hidden units, leading to the cascade structure of Figure 9.12. The hidden unit weights are first determined, and then the unit is added to the network. These weights are found by maximizing the correlation between the output of the unit and the residual error of the network outputs prior to the addition of that unit. This correlation (actually the covariance) is defined by

$$S = \sum_k \left| \sum_{n=1}^{N} (z^n - \bar{z}) \left(\epsilon_k^n - \bar{\epsilon}_k \right) \right| \tag{9.62}$$

where $\epsilon_k = (y_k - t_k)$ is the error of network output k, and z denotes the output of the unit given by

$$z = g\left(\sum_i w_i x_i \right) \tag{9.63}$$

where the sum runs over all inputs and all existing hidden units. In (9.62) the following average quantities are defined over the whole training set

$$\bar{z} = \frac{1}{N} \sum_{n=1}^{N} z^n, \qquad \bar{\epsilon}_k = \frac{1}{N} \sum_{n=1}^{N} \epsilon_k^n. \tag{9.64}$$

The derivative of S with respect to the weights of the new hidden unit are easily found in the form

$$\frac{\partial S}{\partial w_i} = \pm \sum_k \sum_n (\epsilon_k^n - \bar{\epsilon}_k) \, g' x_i^n \tag{9.65}$$

where the sign corresponds to the sign of the covariance inside the modulus bars in (9.62). These derivatives can then be used with the quickprop algorithm to optimize the weights for the new hidden unit. Once this has been done the unit is added to the network and is connected to all output units by adaptive weights. All output-layer weights are now retrained (with all hidden unit weights fixed). Again, this corresponds to a single-layer training problem, and is performed using quickprop. These single-layer training problems can be expected to converge very rapidly. For linear output units, the output-layer weights, which minimize a sum-of-squares error, can be found quickly by pseudo-inverse techniques (Section 3.4.3). Note that, because the hidden unit weights are never changed, the activations of the hidden units (for each of the input vectors from the training set) can be evaluated once for the whole of the training set, and these values re-used repeatedly in the remainder of the algorithm, saving considerable computational effort. Benchmark results from this algorithm can be found in Fahlman and Lebiere (1990).

9.5.3 *Saliency of weights*

We turn now to pruning algorithms which start with a relatively large network and then remove connections in order to arrive at a suitable network architecture. Several of the approaches to network pruning are based on the following general procedure. First, a relatively large network is trained using one of the standard training algorithms. This network might for instance have a high degree of connectivity. Then the network is examined to assess the relative importance of the weights, and the least important are deleted. Typically this is followed by some further training of the pruned network, and the procedure of pruning and training may be repeated for several cycles. Clearly, there are various choices to be made concerning how much training is applied at each stage, what fraction of the weights are pruned and so on. Usually these choices are made on a heuristic basis. The most important consideration, however, is how to decide which weights should be removed.

In the case of simple models it may be clear in which order the parameters should be deleted. With a polynomial, for instance, the higher-order coefficients would generally be deleted first since we expect the function we are trying to represent to be relatively smooth. In the case of a neural network it is not obvious *a priori* which weights will be the least significant. We therefore need some measure of the relative importance, or *saliency*, of different weights.

The simplest concept of saliency is to suppose that small weights are less important than large weights, and to use the magnitude $|w|$ of a weight value as a measure of its importance. Such an approach clearly requires that the input and output variables are normalized appropriately (Section 8.2). However, it has little theoretical motivation, and performs poorly in practice. We consider instead how to find a measure of saliency with a more principled justification.

Since network training is defined in terms of the minimization of an error function, it is natural to use the same error function to find a definition of saliency. In particular, we could define the saliency of a weight as the change in the error function which results from deletion (setting to zero) of that weight. This could be implemented by direct evaluation, so that, for each weight in the (trained) network in turn, the weight is temporarily set to zero and the error function re-evaluated. However, such an approach would be computationally demanding (Exercise 9.7).

Consider instead the change in the error function due to small changes in the values of the weights (Le Cun *et al.*, 1990). If the weight w_i is changed to $w_i + \delta w_i$ then the corresponding change in the error function E is given by

$$\delta E = \sum_i \frac{\partial E}{\partial w_i} \delta w_i + \frac{1}{2} \sum_i \sum_j H_{ij} \delta w_i \delta w_j + \mathcal{O}(\delta w^3) \qquad (9.66)$$

where the H_{ij} are the elements of the Hessian matrix

$$H_{ij} = \frac{\partial^2 E}{\partial w_i \partial w_j}. \qquad (9.67)$$

If we assume that the training process has converged, then the first term in (9.66) will vanish. Le Cun *et al.* (1990) approximate the Hessian by discarding the non-diagonal terms. Techniques for calculating the diagonal terms of the Hessian for a multi-layer perceptron were described in Section 4.10.1. Neglecting the higher-order terms in the expansion then reduces (9.66) to the form

$$\delta E = \frac{1}{2} \sum_i H_{ii} \delta w_i^2. \qquad (9.68)$$

If a weight having an initial value w_i is set to zero, then the increase in error will be given approximately by (9.68) with $\delta w_i = w_i$, and so the saliency values of the weights are given approximately by the quantities $H_{ii} w_i^2 / 2$. A practical implementation would typically consist of the following steps:

1. Choose a relatively large initial network architecture.
2. Train the network in the usual way until some stopping criterion is satisfied.
3. Compute the second derivatives H_{ii} for each of the weights, and hence evaluate the saliencies $H_{ii}w_i^2/2$.
4. Sort the weights by saliency and delete some of the low-saliency weights.
5. Go to 2 and repeat until some overall stopping criterion is reached.

This approach to weight elimination has been termed *optimal brain damage* (Le Cun *et al.*, 1990). In an application to the problem of recognition of handwritten zip codes, the technique allowed the number of free parameters in a network to be reduced by about a factor of 4 (from a network initially having over 10 000 free parameters) while giving a small increase in generalization performance and a substantial increase in the speed of the trained network.

The assumption that the Hessian for a network is diagonal, however, is frequently a poor one. A procedure for determining the saliency of weights, known as *optimal brain surgeon*, which does not make the assumption of a diagonal Hessian, was introduced by Hassibi and Stork (1993). This method also computes corrections to the remaining weights after deletion of a particular weight and so reduces the need for network retraining during the pruning phase. Suppose a weight w_i is to be set to zero. The remaining weights are then adjusted so as to minimize the increase in error resulting from the deletion. We can write the total change in the weight vector in the form $\delta\mathbf{w}$. Again, assuming the network is already trained to a minimum of the error function, and neglecting third-order terms, the change in the error resulting from this change to the weight vector can be written

$$\delta E = \frac{1}{2}\delta\mathbf{w}^{\mathrm{T}}\mathbf{H}\delta\mathbf{w}. \tag{9.69}$$

The change in the weight vector must satisfy

$$\mathbf{e}_i^{\mathrm{T}}\delta\mathbf{w} + w_i = 0 \tag{9.70}$$

where $\mathbf{e}_i$ is a unit vector in weight space parallel to the w_i axis. We need to find the $\delta\mathbf{w}$ which minimizes δE in (9.69), subject to the constraint (9.70). This is most easily done by introducing a Lagrange multiplier (Exercise 9.8 and Appendix C), giving the following result for the optimal change in the weight vector

$$\delta\mathbf{w} = -\frac{w_i}{[\mathbf{H}^{-1}]_{ii}}\mathbf{H}^{-1}\mathbf{e}_i \tag{9.71}$$

and the corresponding value for the increase in the error in the form

$$\delta E_i = \frac{1}{2}\frac{w_i^2}{[\mathbf{H}^{-1}]_{ii}}. \tag{9.72}$$

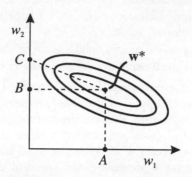

Figure 9.13. A schematic illustration of the error contours for a network having a non-diagonal Hessian matrix, for two of the weights w_1 and w_2. The network is initially trained to the error minimum at $\mathbf{w}^*$. Weight pruning based on the magnitude of the weights would take the weight vector to the point A by elimination of the smaller weight w_2. Conversely, optimal brain damage leads to removal of w_1 and moves the weight vector to B. Finally, optimal brain surgeon removes w_1 and also computes a correction to the remaining weight w_2 and hence moves the weight vector to C.

Note that, if the Hessian is in fact diagonal, then these results reduce to the corresponding results for the optimal brain damage technique discussed above. The inverse Hessian is evaluated using the sequential technique discussed in Section 4.10.3 which is itself based on the outer product approximation for the Hessian, discussed in Section 4.10.2. In a practical implementation, the optimal brain surgeon algorithm proceeds by the following steps:

1. Train a relatively large network to a minimum of the error function.
2. Evaluate the inverse Hessian $\mathbf{H}^{-1}$.
3. Evaluate δE_i for each value of i using (9.72) and select the value of i which gives the smallest increase in error.
4. Update all of the weights in the network using the weight change evaluated from (9.71).
5. Go to 3 and repeat until some stopping criterion is reached.

A comparison of pruning by weight magnitude, optimal brain damage and optimal brain surgeon is shown schematically in Figure 9.13. Note that the weight changes are evaluated in the quadratic approximation. Since the true error function will be non-quadratic, it will be necessary to retrain the network after a period of weight pruning. Simulation results confirm that the optimal brain surgeon technique is superior to optimal brain damage which is in turn superior to magnitude-based pruning (Le Cun *et al.*, 1990; Hassibi and Stork, 1993).

9.5.4 *Weight elimination*

In Section 9.2.1 we discussed the use of a simple weight-decay term as a form of regularization, to give a total error function of the form

$$\widetilde{E} = E + \frac{\nu}{2} \sum_i w_i^2. \tag{9.73}$$

This regularization term favours small weights, and so network training based on minimization of (9.73) will tend to reduce the magnitude of those weights which are not contributing significantly to a reduction in the error E. One procedure for pruning weights from a network would therefore be to train the network using the regularized error (9.73), and then remove weights whose values fall below some threshold.

One of the difficulties of the simple penalty term in (9.73), from the point of view of network pruning, is that it tends to favour many small weights rather than a few large ones. To see this, consider two weights w_1 and w_2 feeding into a unit from identical inputs, so that the weights are performing redundant tasks. The unregularized error E will be identical if we have two equal weights $w_1 = w_2 = w/2$, or if we have one larger weight $w_1 = w$, and one zero weight $w_2 = 0$. In the first case, the weight-decay term $\sum_i w_i^2 = w^2/2$ while in the second case $\sum_i w_i^2 = w^2$.

This problem can be overcome by using a modified decay term of the form (Hanson and Pratt, 1989; Lang and Hinton, 1990; Weigend *et al.*, 1990)

$$\widetilde{E} = E + \nu \sum_i \frac{w_i^2}{\widehat{w}^2 + w_i^2} \tag{9.74}$$

where $\widehat{w}$ is a parameter which sets a scale and is usually chosen to be of order unity. Use of this form of regularizer has been called *weight elimination*. As shown in Exercise 9.9, for weight values somewhat larger than $\widehat{w}$ this penalty term will tend favour a few large weights rather than many small ones, and so is more likely to eliminate weights from the network than is the simple weight-decay term in (9.73). This leads to a form of network pruning which is combined with the training process itself, rather than alternating with it. In practice weight values will typically not be reduced to zero, but it would be possible to remove weights completely if their values fell below some small threshold. Note that this algorithm involves the scale parameter $\widehat{w}$ whose value must be chosen by hand.

9.5.5 *Node pruning*

Instead of pruning individual weights from a network we can prune complete units, and several techniques for achieving this have been suggested. Mozer and Smolensky (1989) adopt an algorithm based on alternate phases of training and removal of units. This requires a measure of the saliency s_i of a unit, of which the most natural definition would be the increase in the error function (measured with respect to the training set) as a result of deleting a unit j

$$s_j = E(\text{without unit } j) - E(\text{with unit } j). \tag{9.75}$$

As with individual weights, such a measure is relatively slow to evaluate since it requires a complete pass through the data set for each unit, although it is clearly less computationally expensive to repeat the error measurement for each unit than it is for each weight. To find a convenient approximation, we can introduce a factor α_j which multiplies the summed input to each unit (except the output units), so that the forward propagation equations become

$$z_j = g\left(\alpha_j \sum_i w_{ji} z_i\right) \tag{9.76}$$

where the activation function $g(\cdot)$ is defined such that $g(0) = 0$, as would be the case for $g(a) = \tanh a$, for example. Then with $\alpha_j = 0$ the unit is absent, and with $\alpha_j = 1$ the unit is present. Then (9.75) can be written as

$$s_j = E(\alpha_j = 1) - E(\alpha_j = 0) \tag{9.77}$$

which can then be approximated by the derivative with respect to α_j:

$$\widehat{s}_j = -\left.\frac{\partial E}{\partial \alpha_j}\right|_{\alpha_j = 1}. \tag{9.78}$$

These derivatives are easily evaluated using an extension of the back-propagation algorithm (Exercise 9.10). Note that the α_j do not actually appear in the forward propagation equations, but are introduced simply as a convenient way to define, and evaluate, the s_j. In order to make this approach work in practice, Mozer and Smolensky (1989) found they had to use a Minkowski-R error with $R = 1$ (Section 6.2), together with an exponentially weighted running average estimate of s_j to smooth out fluctuations. Other forms of node-pruning algorithm have been considered by Hanson and Pratt (1989), Chauvin (1989) and Ji *et al.* (1990).

9.6 Committees of networks

It is common practice in the application of neural networks to train many different candidate networks and then to select the best, on the basis of performance on an independent validation set for instance, and to keep only this network and to discard the rest. There are two disadvantages with such an approach. First, all of the effort involved in training the remaining networks is wasted. Second, the generalization performance on the validation set has a random component due to the noise on the data, and so the network which had best performance on the validation set might not be the one with the best performance on new test data.

These drawbacks can be overcome by combining the networks together to form a *committee* (Perrone and Cooper, 1993; Perrone, 1994). The importance of such an approach is that it can lead to significant improvements in the predictions on new data, while involving little additional computational effort. In fact the performance of a committee can be better than the performance of the best single network used in isolation. For notational convenience we consider networks with a single output y, although the generalization to several outputs is straightforward. Suppose we have a set of L trained network models $y_i(\mathbf{x})$ where $i = 1, \ldots, L$. This set might contain networks having different numbers of hidden units, or networks with the same architecture but trained to different local minima of the error function. It might even include different kinds of network models or a mixture of network and conventional models. We denote the true regression function which we are seeking to approximate by $h(\mathbf{x})$. Then we can write the mapping function of each network as the desired function plus an error:

$$y_i(\mathbf{x}) = h(\mathbf{x}) + \epsilon_i(\mathbf{x}). \tag{9.79}$$

The average sum-of-squares error for model $y_i(\mathbf{x})$ can be written as

$$E_i = \mathcal{E}[\{y_i(\mathbf{x}) - h(\mathbf{x})\}^2] = \mathcal{E}[\epsilon_i^2] \tag{9.80}$$

where $\mathcal{E}[\cdot]$ denotes the expectation, and corresponds to an integration over $\mathbf{x}$ weighted by the unconditional density of $\mathbf{x}$ so that

$$\mathcal{E}[\epsilon_i^2] \equiv \int \epsilon_i^2(\mathbf{x}) p(\mathbf{x}) \, d\mathbf{x}. \tag{9.81}$$

From (9.80) the average error made by the networks acting individually is given by

$$E_{\mathrm{AV}} = \frac{1}{L} \sum_{i=1}^{L} E_i = \frac{1}{L} \sum_{i=1}^{L} \mathcal{E}[\epsilon_i^2]. \tag{9.82}$$

We now introduce a simple form of committee. This involves taking the output of the committee to be the average of the outputs of the L networks which comprise the committee. Thus, we write the committee prediction in the form

$$y_{\mathrm{COM}}(\mathbf{x}) = \frac{1}{L} \sum_{i=1}^{L} y_i(\mathbf{x}). \tag{9.83}$$

The error due to the committee can then be written as

$$E_{\text{COM}} = \mathcal{E}\left[\left(\frac{1}{L}\sum_{i=1}^{L} y_i(\mathbf{x}) - h(\mathbf{x})\right)^2\right] = \mathcal{E}\left[\left(\frac{1}{L}\sum_{i=1}^{L} \epsilon_i\right)^2\right]. \tag{9.84}$$

If we now make the assumption that the errors $\epsilon_i(\mathbf{x})$ have zero mean and are uncorrelated, so that

$$\mathcal{E}[\epsilon_i] = 0, \qquad \mathcal{E}[\epsilon_i\epsilon_j] = 0 \qquad \text{if } j \neq i \tag{9.85}$$

then, using (9.82), we can relate the committee error (9.84) to the average error of the networks acting separately as follows:

$$E_{\text{COM}} = \frac{1}{L^2}\sum_{i=1}^{L}\mathcal{E}\left[\epsilon_i^2\right] = \frac{1}{L}E_{\text{AV}}. \tag{9.86}$$

This represents the apparently rather dramatic result that the sum-of-squares error can be reduced by a factor of L simply by averaging the predictions of L networks. In practice, the reduction in error is generally much smaller than this, because the errors $\epsilon_i(\mathbf{x})$ of different models are typically highly correlated, and so assumption (9.85) does not hold. However, we can easily show that the committee averaging process cannot produce an increase in the expected error by making use of Cauchy's inequality in the form

$$\left(\sum_{i=1}^{L}\epsilon_i\right)^2 \leq L\sum_{i=1}^{L}\epsilon_i^2 \tag{9.87}$$

which gives the result

$$E_{\text{COM}} \leq E_{\text{AV}}. \tag{9.88}$$

Typically, some useful reduction in error is generally obtained, and the method has the advantage of being trivial to implement. There is a significant reduction in processing speed for new data, but in many applications this will be irrelevant.

The reduction in error can be viewed as arising from reduced variance due to the averaging over many solutions. This suggests that the members of the committee should not individually be chosen to have optimal trade-off between bias and variance, but should have relatively smaller bias, since the extra variance can be removed by averaging.

The simple committee discussed so far involves averaging the predictions of the individual networks. However, we might expect that some members of the committee will typically make better predictions than other members. We would therefore expect to be able to reduce the error still further if we give greater weight to some committee members than to others. Thus, we consider a generalized committee prediction given by a weighted combination of the predictions of the members of the form

$$y_{\text{GEN}}(\mathbf{x}) = \sum_{i=1}^{L} \alpha_i y_i(\mathbf{x}) \tag{9.89}$$

$$= h(\mathbf{x}) + \sum_{i=1}^{L} \alpha_i \epsilon_i(\mathbf{x}) \tag{9.90}$$

where the parameters α_i will be determined shortly. We now introduce the error correlation matrix $\mathbf{C}$ with elements given by

$$C_{ij} = \mathcal{E}[\epsilon_i(\mathbf{x})\epsilon_j(\mathbf{x})]. \tag{9.91}$$

This allows the error due to the generalized committee to be written as

$$E_{\text{GEN}} = \mathcal{E}\left[\{y_{\text{GEN}}(\mathbf{x}) - h(\mathbf{x})\}^2\right] \tag{9.92}$$

$$= \mathcal{E}\left[\left(\sum_{i=1}^{L} \alpha_i \epsilon_i\right)\left(\sum_{j=1}^{L} \alpha_j \epsilon_j\right)\right] \tag{9.93}$$

$$= \sum_{i=1}^{L}\sum_{j=1}^{L} \alpha_i \alpha_j C_{ij}. \tag{9.94}$$

We can now determine optimal values for the α_i by minimization of E_{GEN}. In order to find a non-trivial minimum (i.e. a solution other than $\alpha_i = 0$ for all i) we need to constrain the α_i. This is most naturally done by requiring

$$\sum_{i=1}^{L} \alpha_i = 1. \tag{9.95}$$

The motivation for the form of this form of constraint will be discussed shortly. Using a Lagrange multiplier λ (Appendix C) to enforce this constraint, we see that the minimum of (9.94) occurs when

$$2\sum_{j=1}^{L} \alpha_j C_{ij} + \lambda = 0 \tag{9.96}$$

which has the solution

$$\alpha_i = -\frac{\lambda}{2} \sum_{j=1}^{L} (\mathbf{C}^{-1})_{ij}. \tag{9.97}$$

We can find the value of λ by substituting (9.97) into the constraint equation (9.95), which gives the solution for the α_i in the form

$$\alpha_i = \frac{\sum_{j=1}^{L} (\mathbf{C}^{-1})_{ij}}{\sum_{k=1}^{L} \sum_{j=1}^{L} (\mathbf{C}^{-1})_{kj}}. \tag{9.98}$$

Substituting (9.98) into (9.94) we find that the value of the error at the minimum is given by

$$E_{\text{GEN}} = \left(\sum_{i=1}^{L} \sum_{j=1}^{L} (\mathbf{C}^{-1})_{ij} \right)^{-1}. \tag{9.99}$$

In summary, to set up this generalized committee, we train L network models, and then compute the correlation matrix $\mathbf{C}$ using a finite-sample approximation to (9.91) given by

$$C_{ij} \simeq \frac{1}{N} \sum_{n=1}^{N} (y_i(\mathbf{x}^n) - t^n)(y_j(\mathbf{x}^n) - t^n) \tag{9.100}$$

where t^n is the target value corresponding to input vector $\mathbf{x}^n$. We then find $\mathbf{C}^{-1}$, evaluate the α_i using (9.98), and then use (9.89) to make new predictions.

Since the generalized committee (9.89) is a special case of the simple average committee (9.83) we have the inequality

$$E_{\text{GEN}} \leq E_{\text{COM}}. \tag{9.101}$$

The generalization error of a committee can be decomposed into the sum of two terms (Exercise 9.11) to give (Krogh and Vedelsby, 1995)

$$\mathcal{E}\left[\{y_{\text{GEN}}(\mathbf{x}) - h(\mathbf{x})\}^2 \right] = \sum_i \alpha_i \mathcal{E}\left[\{y_i(\mathbf{x}) - h(\mathbf{x})\}^2 \right]$$

$$- \sum_i \alpha_i \mathcal{E}\left[\{y_i(\mathbf{x}) - y_{\text{GEN}}(\mathbf{x})\}^2 \right] \tag{9.102}$$

which is somewhat analogous to the bias–variance decomposition discussed in Section 9.1. The first term depends only on the errors of individual networks, while the second term depends on the spread of predictions of the committee members relative to the committee prediction itself. As a result of the minus sign in front of the second term on the right-hand side of (9.102) we see that, if we can increase the spread of predictions of the committee members without increasing the errors of the individual members themselves, then the committee error will decrease. Furthermore, since this term is strictly negative, we can use (9.80), (9.82) and (9.102), together with $\alpha_i = 1/L$, to give

$$E_{\text{GEN}} \leq E_{\text{AV}} \tag{9.103}$$

in keeping with (9.88) and (9.101).

One problem with the constraint (9.95) is that it does not prevent the weighting coefficients in the committee from adopting large negative and positive values and hence giving extreme predictions from the committee even when each member of the committee might be making sensible predictions. We might therefore seek to constrain the coefficients further by insisting that, for each value of $\mathbf{x}$, we have $y_{\min}(\mathbf{x}) \leq y_{\text{GEN}}(\mathbf{x}) \leq y_{\max}(\mathbf{x})$. This condition can be satisfied in general by requiring that $\alpha_i \geq 0$ and $\sum_i \alpha_i = 1$ (Exercise 9.12). The minimization of the committee error subject to these two constraints is now a more difficult problem, and can be tackled using techniques of linear programming (Press *et al.*, 1992).

The usefulness of committee averaging is not limited to the sum-of-squares error, but applies to any error function which is *convex* (Exercise 9.13). Section 10.7 shows how the concept of a committee arises naturally in a Bayesian framework.

9.7 Mixtures of experts

Consider the problem of learning a mapping in which the form of the mapping is different for different regions of the input space. Although a single homogeneous network could be applied to this problem, we might expect that the task would be made easier if we assigned different 'expert' networks to tackle each of the different regions, and then used an extra 'gating' network, which also sees the input vector, to decide which of the experts should be used to determine the output.

If the problem has an obvious decomposition of this form, then it may be possible to design the network architecture by hand. However, a more powerful and more general approach would be to discover a suitable decomposition as part of the learning process. This is achieved by the *mixture-of-experts* model (Jacobs *et al.*, 1991), whose architecture is shown in Figure 9.14. All of the expert networks, as well as the gating network, are trained together. The goal of the training procedure is to have the gating network learn an appropriate decomposition of the input space into different regions, with one of the expert networks responsible for generating the outputs for input vectors falling within each region.

The key is in the definition of the error function, which has a similar form to that discussed in Section 6.4 in the context of the problem of modelling con-

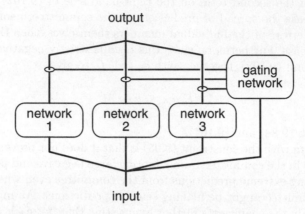

Figure 9.14. Architecture of the mixture-of-experts modular network. The gating network acts as a switch and, for any given input vector, decides which of the expert networks will be used to determine the output.

ditional distributions, and it will be assumed that the reader is already familiar with this material. The error function is given by the negative logarithm of the likelihood with respect to a probability distribution given by a mixture of M Gaussians of the form

$$E = -\sum_n \ln \left\{ \sum_{i=1}^{M} \alpha_i(\mathbf{x}^n)\phi_i(\mathbf{t}^n|\mathbf{x}^n) \right\} \qquad (9.104)$$

where the $\phi_i(\mathbf{t}|\mathbf{x})$ are Gaussian functions given by

$$\phi_i(\mathbf{t}|\mathbf{x}) = \frac{1}{(2\pi)^{c/2}} \exp \left\{ -\frac{\|\mathbf{t} - \boldsymbol{\mu}_i(\mathbf{x})\|^2}{2} \right\}. \qquad (9.105)$$

These Gaussian functions have means $\boldsymbol{\mu}_i(\mathbf{x})$ which are functions of the input vector $\mathbf{x}$, and are taken to have unit covariance matrices. There is one expert network for each Gaussian, and the output of the ith expert network is a vector representing the corresponding mean $\boldsymbol{\mu}_i(\mathbf{x})$ where $\mathbf{x}$ is the input vector. The mixing coefficients $\alpha_i(\mathbf{x})$ are determined by the outputs γ_i of the gating network through a softmax activation function

$$\alpha_i = \frac{\exp(\gamma_i)}{\sum_{j=1}^{M} \exp(\gamma_j)}. \qquad (9.106)$$

Thus, the gating network has one output for each of the expert networks, as indicated in Figure 9.14. This model differs from that discussed in Section 6.4 in two minor respects. First, the variance parameters of the Gaussians here are set to unity, whereas they were taken to be general functions of the input vector $\mathbf{x}$ in Section 6.4, although is it clearly straightforward to incorporate more general Gaussian functions into the present model. Second, different networks are used to model the $\mu_i(\mathbf{x})$ and $\alpha_i(\mathbf{x})$ here, whereas a single network was considered in Section 6.4.

The mixture-of-experts network is trained by minimizing the error function (9.104) simultaneously with respect to the weights in all of the expert networks and in the gating network. When the trained network is used to make predictions for new inputs, the input vector is presented to the gating network and the largest output is used to select one of the expert networks. The input vector is then presented to this expert network whose output $\boldsymbol{\mu}_i(\mathbf{x})$ represents the prediction of the complete system for this input. This corresponds to the selection of the most probable branch of the conditional distribution on the assumption of weakly overlapping Gaussians, as discussed on page 220.

It was also shown in Section 6.4 that the use of an error function based on a mixture of Gaussians leads to an automatic soft clustering of the target vectors into groups associated with the Gaussian components. In the context of the mixture-of-experts architecture it therefore leads to an automatic decomposition of the problem into distinct sub-tasks, each of which is effectively assigned to one of the network modules.

Jacobs *et al.* (1991) demonstrate the performance of this algorithm on a vowel recognition problem and show that it discovers a sensible decomposition of the mapping. Jordan and Jacobs (1994) extend the mixture-of-experts model by considering a hierarchical system in which each expert network can itself consist of a mixture-of-experts model complete with its own gating network. This can be repeated at any number of levels, leading to a tree structure. The hierarchical architecture then allows simple linear networks to be used for the experts at the leaves of the tree, while still allowing the overall system to have flexible modelling capabilities. Jordan and Jacobs (1994) have shown that the EM algorithm (Section 2.6.2) can be extended to provide an effective training mechanism for such networks.

9.8 Model order selection

In this book, we have focused on the minimization of an error function as the basic technique for determining values for the free parameters (the weights and biases) in a neural network. Such an approach, however, is unable to determine the optimum number of such parameters (or equivalently the optimum size of network), because an increase in the number of parameters in a network will generally allow a smaller value of the error to be found. Our goal is to find a network which gives good predictions for new data, and this is typically not the network which gives the smallest error with respect to the training data. In the trade-off between bias and variance discussed in Section 9.1, we saw that there is an optimal degree of complexity in a network model for a given data set. Networks with too little flexibility will smooth out some of the underlying structure in the data (corresponding to high bias), while networks which are too complex will over-fit the data (corresponding to high variance). In either case, the performance of the network on new data will be poor.

Similar considerations apply to the problem of determining the values of continuous parameters such as the regularization coefficient ν in a regularized error function of the form

$$\widetilde{E} = E + \nu\Omega. \tag{9.107}$$

Too large a value for ν leads to a network with large bias (unless the regularization function happens to be completely consistent with the underlying structure of the data) while too small a value allows the network solution to have too high a variance. This was illustrated in Figures 9.4, 9.5 and 9.6. Again, direct minimization of $\widetilde{E}$ cannot be used to find the optimum value for ν, since this gives $\nu = 0$ and an over-fitted solution.

We shall assume that the goal is to find a network having the best generalization performance. This is usually the most difficult part of any pattern recognition problem, and is the one which typically limits the practical application of neural networks. In some cases, however, other criteria might also be important. For instance, speed of operation on a serial computer will be governed by the size of the network, and we might be prepared to trade some generalization capability in return for a smaller network. We shall not discuss these possibilities further, but instead focus exclusively on the problem of generalization.

9.8.1 *Cross-validation*

Since our goal is to find the network having the best performance on new data, the simplest approach to the comparison of different networks is to evaluate the error function using data which is independent of that used for training. Various networks are trained by minimization of an appropriate error function defined with respect to a *training* data set. The performance of the networks is then compared by evaluating the error function using an independent *validation* set, and the network having the smallest error with respect to the validation set is selected. This approach is called the *hold out method*. Since this procedure can itself lead to some over-fitting to the validation set, the performance of the selected network should be confirmed by measuring its performance on a third independent set of data called a *test* set.

The application of this technique is illustrated in Figure 9.15 using the same radial basis function example as used in plotting Figures 9.4, 9.5 and 9.6. Here we have plotted the error on the training set, as well as the generalization error measured with respect to an independent validation set, as functions of the logarithm of the regularization coefficient ν. As expected, the training error decreases steadily with decreasing ν while the validation error shows a minimum at a value of $\ln\nu \simeq 3.7$, and thereafter increases with decreasing ν. Figure 9.5 was plotted using this optimum value of ν, and confirms the expectation that the mapping with the best generalization is one which is closest to the underlying

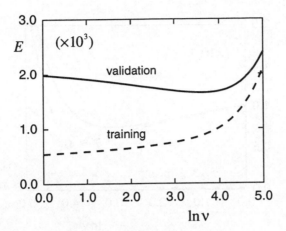

Figure 9.15. Plot of training and validation set errors versus the logarithm of the regularization coefficient, for the example used to plot Figure 9.4. A validation set of 1000 points was used to obtain a good estimate of the generalization error. The validation error shows a minimum at $\ln \nu \simeq 3.7$, which was the value used to plot Figure 9.5.

function from which the data was generated (shown by the dashed curve in Figure 9.5).

This example also provides a convenient opportunity to demonstrate the dependence of bias and variance on the effective network complexity. The values of the average bias and variance were estimated using knowledge of the true underlying generator of the data, given by the sine function $h(x)$ in (9.34). For each value of $\ln \nu$, 100 data sets, each containing 30 points, were generated by sampling $h(x)$ and adding noise. A radial basis function network (with 30 Gaussian basis functions, one centred on each data point as before) was then trained on each of the data sets to give a mapping $y_i(x)$ where $i = 1, \ldots, 100$. The average response of the networks is given by

$$\overline{y}(x) = \frac{1}{100} \sum_{i=1}^{100} y_i(x). \tag{9.108}$$

Estimates of the integrated $(\text{bias})^2$ and variance are then given by

$$(\text{bias})^2 = \sum_n \{\overline{y}(x^n) - h(x^n)\}^2 \tag{9.109}$$

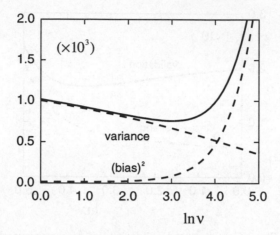

Figure 9.16. Plots of estimated (bias)^2 and variance as functions of the logarithm of the regularization coefficient ν for the radial basis function model used to plot Figure 9.15. Also shown is the sum of (bias)^2 and variance which shows a minimum at a value close to the minimum of the validation error in Figure 9.15.

$$\text{variance} = \sum_n \frac{1}{100} \sum_{i=1}^{100} \{y_i(x^n) - \overline{y}(x^n)\}^2. \tag{9.110}$$

Figure 9.16 shows the (bias)^2 and the variance of the radial basis function model as functions of $\ln \nu$. The minimum of the sum of (bias)^2 and variance occurs at a value of $\ln \nu$ close to that at which the minimum validation error occurs in Figure 9.15 as expected.

In practice, the availability of labelled data may be severely limited and we may not be able to afford the luxury of keeping aside part of the data set for model comparison purposes. In such cases we can adopt the procedure of *cross-validation* (Stone, 1974, 1978; Wahba and Wold, 1975). Here we divide the training set at random into S distinct segments. We then train a network using data from $S-1$ of the segments and test its performance, by evaluating the error function, using the remaining segment. This process is repeated for each of the S possible choices for the segment which is omitted from the training process, and the test errors averaged over all S results. The partitioning of the data set is illustrated in Figure 9.17. Such a procedure allows us to use a high proportion of the available data (a fraction $1 - 1/S$) to train the networks, while also making use of all data points in evaluating the cross-validation error. The disadvantage of such an approach is that it requires the training process to be repeated S times which in some circumstances could lead to a requirement for large amounts of processing time. A typical choice for S might be $S = 10$, although if data is very

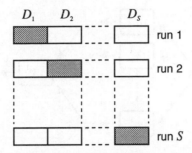

Figure 9.17. Schematic illustration of the partitioning of a data set into S segments for use in cross-validation. A network is trained S times, each time using a version of the data set in which one of the segments (shown shaded) is omitted. Each trained network is then tested on the data from the segment which was omitted during training, and the results averaged over all S networks.

scarce we could go to the extreme limit of $S = N$ for a data set with N data points, which involves N separate training runs per network, each using $(N - 1)$ data points. This limit is known as the *leave-one-out* method.

9.8.2 Stacked generalization

In Section 9.6 we discussed the use of committees as a way of combining the predictions of several trained networks, and we saw how this could lead to reduced errors. The committee techniques are based only on the training data, however, and so do not directly address the issue of model complexity optimization. Conversely, techniques such as cross-validation represent a winner-takes-all strategy in which only the best network is retained. The method of *stacked generalization* (Wolpert, 1992) provides a way of combining trained networks together which uses partitioning of the data set (in a similar way to cross-validation) to find an overall system with usually improved generalization performance.

Consider the modular network system shown in Figure 9.18. Here we see a set of M 'level-0' networks $\mathcal{N}_1^0$ to $\mathcal{N}_M^0$ whose outputs are combined using a 'level-1' network $\mathcal{N}^1$. The idea is to train the level-0 networks first and then examine their behaviour when generalizing. This provides a new training set which is used to train the level-1 network.

The specific procedure for setting up the stacked generalization system is as follows. Let the complete set of available data be denoted by D. We first leave aside a single data point from D as a validation point, and treat the remainder of D as a training set. All level-0 networks are then trained using the training partition and their outputs are measured using the validation data point. This generates a single pattern for a new data set which will be used to train the level-1 network $\mathcal{N}^1$. The inputs of this pattern consist of the outputs of all the level-0 networks, and the target value is the corresponding target value from the original full data set. This process is now repeated with a different choice for

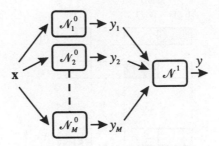

Figure 9.18. Stacked generalization combines the outputs of several 'level-0' networks $\mathcal{N}_1^0, \ldots, \mathcal{N}_M^0$ using a 'level-1' network $\mathcal{N}^1$ to give the final output. The level-1 network corrects for the biases exhibited by the level-0 networks.

the data point which is kept aside. After cycling through the full data set of N points we have N patterns in the new data set, which is now used to train $\mathcal{N}^1$. Finally, all of the level-0 networks are re-trained using the full data set D. Predictions on new data can now be made by presenting new input vectors to the level-0 networks and taking their outputs as the inputs to the level-1 network, whose output constitutes the predicted output. Wolpert (1992) gives arguments to suggest that the level-0 networks should contain a wide variety of different models, while the level-1 network should provide a relatively smooth function and hence should have a relatively simple structure.

There are many possible variations of stacked generalization. For instance, if the data set is large, or if the level-0 networks are computationally intensive to train, we might leave aside a larger fraction of D than just a single data point when training the level-0 networks. Stacking can also be applied in a slightly modified form to improve the generalization of a single network, and it can also be extended to more than two levels of networks (Wolpert, 1992).

9.8.3 Complexity criteria

In conventional statistics, various criteria have been developed, often in the context of linear models, for assessing the generalization performance of trained models without the use of validation data. These include the C_p-statistic (Mallows, 1973), the final prediction error (Akaike, 1969), the Akaike information criterion (Akaike, 1973) and the predicted squared error (Barron, 1984). Such criteria take the general form of a prediction error (PE) which consists of the sum of two terms

$$\text{PE} = \text{training error} + \text{complexity term} \qquad (9.111)$$

where the complexity term represents a penalty which grows as the number of free parameters in the model grows. Thus, if the model is too simple it will give a large value for the criterion because the residual training error is large, while a model which is too complex will have a large value for the criterion because the complexity term is large. The minimum value for the criterion then represents a trade-off between these two competing effects. For a sum-of-squares error a typical form for such a criterion would be

$$\text{PE} = \frac{2E}{N} + \frac{2W}{N}\sigma^2 \tag{9.112}$$

where E is the value of the sum-of-squares error with respect to the training set after training is complete, N is the total number of data points in the training set, W is the number of adjustable parameters (weights) in the model, and σ^2 is the variance of the noise on the data (which must be estimated).

Moody (1992) has generalized such criteria to deal with non-linear models and to allow for the presence of a regularization term. By performing a local linearization of the network mapping function he obtains a criterion, called the *generalized prediction error*, of the form

$$\text{GPE} = \frac{2E}{N} + \frac{2\gamma}{N}\sigma^2 \tag{9.113}$$

where γ is the *effective* number of parameters in the network, which for linear networks is given by

$$\gamma = \sum_{i=1}^{W} \frac{\lambda_i}{\lambda_i + \nu} \tag{9.114}$$

where λ_i are the eigenvalues of the Hessian matrix of the unregularized error evaluated at the error minimum, and ν is the regularization coefficient. The form of γ in (9.114) should be compared to the expression for the minimum of the regularized error given by (9.24). The reason that γ is the effective number of parameters is that eigenvalues which satisfy $\lambda_i \gg \nu$ contribute 1 to the sum in (9.114), while eigenvalues which satisfy $\lambda_i \ll \nu$ contribute 0 to the sum. We shall not discuss the origin of this criterion here, since we give a more general discussion from the Bayesian perspective in Chapter 10.

9.9 Vapnik–Chervonenkis dimension

Some useful insight into generalization is obtained by considering the worst-case performance for a particular trained network. The theory of this has been developed mainly in the context of networks with binary inputs (Baum and Haussler, 1989; Abu-Mostafa, 1989; Hertz *et al.*, 1991). For simplicity we consider networks having a single binary output.

Suppose that the input vectors are generated from some probability distribution $P(\mathbf{x})$ and that the target data is given by a (noiseless) function $h(\mathbf{x})$. For any given model $y(\mathbf{x})$, we can define the average generalization ability $g(y)$ to be the probability that $y(\mathbf{x}) = h(\mathbf{x})$ for the given distribution $P(\mathbf{x})$. This says that, if we pick an input vector $\mathbf{x}$ at random from the distribution $P(\mathbf{x})$, then the probability that the two functions will agree is given by $g(y)$.

In practice, we cannot calculate $g(y)$ directly because we do not know the true probability distribution $P(\mathbf{x})$, nor do we know the function $h(\mathbf{x})$. What we typically do instead is to train a network using a set of N training patterns to give a network function $y(\mathbf{x}; \mathbf{w})$, and then measure the fraction of the training set which the network correctly classifies, which we shall denote by $g_N(y)$. In the limit of an infinite data set $N \to \infty$ we would expect to find $g_N(y) \to g(y)$, by definition of $g(y)$. However, for a finite-size training set the network function $y(\mathbf{x}; \mathbf{w})$ will be partly tuned to the particular training set (the problem of over-fitting) and so we would expect $g_N(y) > g(y)$. For instance, the network might learn the training set perfectly, so that $g_N(y) = 1$, and yet the predictive performance on new data drawn from the same distribution might be poor so that $g(y) \ll 1$. We say that $g_N(y)$ is a biased estimate of $g(y)$, since it is systematically different from the true value. It gives an over-optimistic estimate of the generalization performance of the network.

If we now consider the set of all functions $\{y\}$ which the network can implement, we can study the maximum discrepancy which can occur between the generalization performance estimated from the sample of size N and the true generalization $g(y)$, given by

$$\max_{\{y\}} |g_N(y) - g(y)| \tag{9.115}$$

as this gives a worst-case measure of generalization performance. Given a small quantity ϵ, a theorem due to Vapnik and Chervonenkis (1971) gives an upper bound on the probability of the difference in (9.115) exceeding ϵ, given by

$$\Pr\left(\max_{\{y\}} |g_N(y) - g(y)| > \epsilon\right) \leq 4\Delta(2N)\exp(-\epsilon^2 N/8) \tag{9.116}$$

where $\Delta(N)$ is known as the *growth function* and will be discussed shortly.

Since this result applies to any of the functions y which can be implemented by the network, we can apply it to the particular function $y(\mathbf{x}; \mathbf{w})$ obtained from training the network on the given data set. Then (9.116) gives an upper bound on the discrepancy between our estimate $g_N(y)$ of the prediction error and the true generalization performance $g(y)$. Our aim is to make this bound as small as possible (i.e. make the right-hand side of (9.116) as small as possible), and we can seek to do this by increasing the number N of training patterns. Suppose for instance that we obtained perfect results (zero residual error) on the training data, so that $g_N(y) = 1$. Then, for a given value of ϵ if we could reduce the right-hand side of (9.116) to a small value $\delta = 0.05$, say, we would be 95% certain that $g(y) > 1 - \epsilon$.

The function $\Delta(N)$ in (9.116) gives the number of distinct binary functions

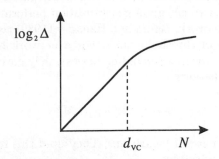

Figure 9.19. General form of the growth function $\Delta(N)$ shown as a plot of $\log_2 \Delta$ versus N. The function initially grows like 2^N up to some critical number of patterns, given by $N = d_{VC}$, at which point the growth slows to become a power law. The value d_{VC} is called the Vapnik–Chervonenkis dimension.

(dichotomies) which can be implemented by the network on a set of N input vectors $\mathbf{x}^n$, where $n = 1, \ldots, N$. The number of potential different patterns is 2^N, and if our network could represent all of these then $\Delta(N) = 2^N$. In this case, it is clear that we cannot make the right-hand side of (9.116) smaller by increasing N. In practice, our network will have a finite capacity, and so for large enough N it will not be capable of representing all possible 2^N patterns. The general form of the function $\Delta(N)$ is shown in Figure 9.19. For small N it grows like 2^N, which says that the network can store exactly all of the training patterns. Beyond some critical number of patterns, however, the growth starts to slow down. This critical number of patterns, denoted d_{VC}, is called the *Vapnik–Chervonenkis* dimension, or VC dimension (Blumer *et al.*, 1989; Abu-Mostafa, 1989) and is a property of the particular network. In fact, it can be shown (Cover, 1965; Vapnik and Chervonenkis, 1971) that the function $\Delta(N)$ is either identically equal to 2^N for all N, or is bounded above by the relation

$$\Delta(N) \leq N^{d_{VC}} + 1. \tag{9.117}$$

Since this now has only polynomial growth, it is clear that we can make the right-hand side of (9.116) arbitrarily small by making N sufficiently large. This is an intuitively reasonable result. If there are so few patterns that the network can store them all perfectly, we cannot expect it to generalize. Only when the network has successfully learned a number of patterns which is much larger than its intrinsic storage capacity for random patterns (as measured by d_{VC}) will the network have captured some of the structure in the data, and only then can we expect it to generalize to new data. Consider a set of data points which are generated at random. The only way to learn all of the patterns in such a data set is for the network to store the training patterns individually, which requires a network with $d_{VC} > N$. For such data sets we cannot expect to find a network which generalizes.

The above results give us some idea of how many patterns we need to use to train a network in order to get good generalization performance in terms of the VC dimension of the network. Baum and Haussler (1989) considered multi-layer feed-forward networks of threshold units. For a network having a total of M units, and a total of W weights (including biases), they gave an upper bound on the VC dimension in the form

$$d_{\text{VC}} \leq 2W \log_2(eM) \tag{9.118}$$

where e is the base of natural logarithms. They used this to show that, if some number N of patterns, given by

$$N \geq \frac{W}{\epsilon} \log_2 \left(\frac{M}{\epsilon} \right) \tag{9.119}$$

can be learned by the network such that a fraction $1 - \epsilon/2$ are correctly classified, where $0 < \epsilon \leq 1/8$, then there is a high probability that the network will correctly classify a fraction $1 - \epsilon$ of future examples drawn from the same distribution.

They also considered the case of networks having two layers of threshold units, and were able to find a lower bound on the VC dimension in the form

$$d_{\text{VC}} \geq 2\lfloor M/2 \rfloor d \tag{9.120}$$

where $\lfloor M/2 \rfloor$ denotes the largest integer which is less than or equal to $M/2$, and d is the number of inputs. For large two-layer networks we typically have $Md \simeq W$ (since most of the weights are in the first layer). From this they derived the approximate rule of thumb that to classify correctly a fraction $1 - \epsilon$ of new examples requires a number of patterns at least equal to

$$N_{\min} \simeq W/\epsilon. \tag{9.121}$$

Thus, for $\epsilon = 0.1$ this suggests that we need around ten times as many training patterns as there are weights in the network.

The VC dimension gives worst-case bounds on generalization. In particular, it only considers which functions can *in principle* be implemented by the network. Thus, it does not depend, for instance, on the presence or absence of a regularizing function, since such a function does not completely rule out any set of weight values. We might hope that in practice we would achieve good generalization with fewer training patterns than the number predicted using the VC dimension.

Exercises

9.1 (⋆⋆) Consider a quadratic error function of the form

$$E = E_0 + \frac{1}{2}(\mathbf{w} - \mathbf{w}^*)^{\mathrm{T}}\mathbf{H}(\mathbf{w} - \mathbf{w}^*) \tag{9.122}$$

where $\mathbf{w}^*$ represents the minimum, and the Hessian matrix $\mathbf{H}$ is positive definite and constant. Suppose the initial weight vector is $\mathbf{w}^{(0)}$ is chosen to be at the origin, and is updated using simple gradient descent

$$\mathbf{w}^{(\tau)} = \mathbf{w}^{(\tau-1)} - \eta \nabla E \tag{9.123}$$

where τ denotes the step number, and η is the learning rate (which is assumed to be small). Show that, after τ steps, the components of the weight vector parallel to the eigenvectors of $\mathbf{H}$ can be written

$$w_j^{(\tau)} = \{1 - (1 - \eta\lambda_j)^\tau\} w_j^* \tag{9.124}$$

where $w_j = \mathbf{w}^{\mathrm{T}}\mathbf{u}_j$, and $\mathbf{u}_j$ and λ_j are the eigenvectors and eigenvalues respectively of $\mathbf{H}$ so that

$$\mathbf{H}\mathbf{u}_j = \lambda_j \mathbf{u}_j. \tag{9.125}$$

Show that, as $\tau \to \infty$ this gives $\mathbf{w}^{(\tau)} \to \mathbf{w}^*$ as expected, provided $|1 - \eta\lambda_j| < 1$. Now suppose that training is halted after a finite number τ of steps. Show that the components of the weight vector parallel to the eigenvectors of the Hessian satisfy

$$w_j^{(\tau)} \simeq w_j^* \quad \text{when } \lambda_j \gg (\eta\tau)^{-1} \tag{9.126}$$

$$|w_j^{(\tau)}| \ll |w_j^*| \quad \text{when } \lambda_j \ll (\eta\tau)^{-1}. \tag{9.127}$$

Compare this result to the corresponding result (9.24) obtained using regularization with simple weight decay, and hence show that $(\eta\tau)^{-1}$ is analogous to the regularization parameter ν. The above results also show that the effective number of parameters in the network, as defined by (9.114), grows as the training progresses.

9.2 (⋆) Consider a linear network model with outputs

$$y_k = \sum_i w_{ki} x_i + w_{k0} \tag{9.128}$$

and a sum-of-squares error function of the form

$$E = \frac{1}{2N} \sum_{n=1}^{N} \sum_k \{y_k(\mathbf{x}^n) - t_k^n\}^2 \tag{9.129}$$

where n labels the patterns from the training set, and t_k^n denotes the target values. Suppose that random noise, with components ϵ_i, is added to the input vectors. By averaging over the noise and assuming $\langle \epsilon_i \rangle = 0$ and $\langle \epsilon_i \epsilon_j \rangle = \delta_{ij} \nu$ show that this is equivalent to the use of a weight-decay regularization term, with the biases w_{k0} omitted, and noise-free data.

9.3 (⋆⋆) Chauvin (1989) considered a regularizer given by the sum of the squares of the activations of all the hidden units in the network. By using the chain rule of calculus, derive a back-propagation algorithm for computing the derivatives of such an error function with respect to the weights and biases in the network.

9.4 (⋆⋆) Consider the cross-entropy error function, in the limit of an infinite data set, given by

$$E = -\sum_k \int\int \{t_k \ln y_k(\mathbf{x}) + (1 - t_k) \ln(1 - y_k(\mathbf{x}))\} p(t_k|\mathbf{x}) p(\mathbf{x}) \, d\mathbf{x} \, dt_k.$$

$$(9.130)$$

Following a similar argument to that given in Section 9.3 for the case of a sum-of-squares error function, show that the addition of noise to the inputs during training is equivalent to the use of a regularizer of the form

$$\Omega = \frac{1}{2} \sum_k \sum_i \int\int \left\{ \left[\frac{1}{y_k(1 - y_k)} - \frac{(y_k - t_k)(1 - 2y_k)}{y_k^2(1 - y_k)^2} \right] \left(\frac{\partial y_k}{\partial x_i} \right)^2 \right.$$

$$\left. + \left[\frac{(y_k - t_k)}{y_k(1 - y_k)} \right] \frac{\partial^2 y_k}{\partial x_i^2} \right\} p(t_k|\mathbf{x}) p(\mathbf{x}) \, d\mathbf{x} \, dt_k. \qquad (9.131)$$

In Section 6.7.2 it was shown that, at the minimum of the unregularized error function, the network output approximates the conditional average of the target data. Use this result to show that the second-derivative term in (9.131), as well as the second term in square brackets, vanishes.

9.5 (⋆⋆) Repeat Exercise 9.4 for the case of the log-likelihood error function of the form

$$E = -\sum_k \int\int t_k \ln y_k(\mathbf{x}) p(t_k|\mathbf{x}) p(\mathbf{x}) \, d\mathbf{x} \, dt_k \qquad (9.132)$$

where the network outputs are given by the softmax function (Section 6.9) so that $\sum_k y_k(\mathbf{x}) = 1$. Again, derive the form of the regularizer, and show, using the result of Exercise 6.16, that the second-derivative term can be neglected when finding the minimum of the regularized error. Hence find the final form of the regularization function.

9.6 (⋆) Consider a regularized error function of the form

$$\widetilde{E} = E + \nu\Omega \qquad (9.133)$$

and suppose that the unregularized error E is minimized by a weight vector $\mathbf{w}^*$. Show that, if the regularization coefficient ν is small, the weight vector $\widetilde{\mathbf{w}}$ which minimizes the regularized error can be written in the form

$$\widetilde{\mathbf{w}} = \mathbf{w}^* - \nu\mathbf{H}^{-1}\nabla\Omega \tag{9.134}$$

where the gradient $\nabla\Omega$ and the Hessian $\mathbf{H} = \nabla\nabla E$ are evaluated at $\mathbf{w} = \mathbf{w}^*$.

9.7 ($\star$) Consider a multi-layer perceptron network with W weights and a training set with N patterns. Find approximate expressions for the number of computational steps required to evaluate the saliency of the weights by (i) temporary deletion of each weight in turn followed by re-evaluation of the error function; (ii) use of the 'optimal brain damage' expression $H_{ii}w_i^2$ for the saliency of the weights in which the diagonal approximation for the Hessian matrix is used (Section 4.10.1); (iii) use of the 'optimal brain surgeon' expression (9.72) together with the sequential update procedure for evaluating the inverse of the Hessian (Section 4.10.3). Evaluate these expressions for the case $W = 300$ and $N = 5000$.

9.8 ($\star$) Use Lagrange multipliers (Appendix C) to verify that minimization of (9.69), subject to the constraint (9.70), leads to the results (9.71) and (9.72) for the change to the weight vector and the increase in error function respectively, for the 'optimal brain surgeon' technique.

9.9 ($\star\star$) Consider the modified weight-decay term in (9.74) for the case of two weights w_1 and w_2 which receive identical inputs and which feed the same unit (so that the weights perform redundant tasks). Change variables to $s = (w_1 + w_2)/\widehat{w}$ and $\alpha = w_2/w_1$. Show analytically that, for fixed s, the value $\alpha = 1$ is a stationary point of the weight-decay term. Plot graphs of the value of the weight-decay term as a function of α for various values of s. Hence show that, for $s = 1$ the regularization term has a single minimum as a function of α at $\alpha \simeq 0.5$, while for $s = 2$ there are two minima at $\alpha = 0$ and $\alpha \to \infty$. We therefore see that, for weight values larger than the characteristic scale $\widehat{w}$, the modified weight-decay term in (9.74) has the desired effect of encouraging a few larger weights in preference to several smaller ones.

9.10 ($\star$) Derive a set of back-propagation equations for evaluation of the derivatives in (9.78), for a network of general feed-forward topology having forward propagation equations given by (9.76).

9.11 ($\star$) Consider a committee defined by (9.89) in which the coefficients satisfy the constraint (9.95). Verify the decomposition of the committee generalization error given by (9.102).

9.12 ($\star$) Consider a committee network of the form

$$y_C(\mathbf{x}) = \sum_i \alpha_i y_i(\mathbf{x}) \tag{9.135}$$

where $y_i(\mathbf{x})$ denote the functions corresponding to the individual networks in the committee. Suppose that, in order to ensure that the committee predictions remain within sensible limits, we require

$$y_{min}(\mathbf{x}) \leq y_C(\mathbf{x}) \leq y_{max}(\mathbf{x}) \tag{9.136}$$

where $y_{min}(\mathbf{x})$ and $y_{max}(\mathbf{x})$ are the minimum and maximum outputs of any members of the committee for that value of $\mathbf{x}$. Show that, if the requirement (9.136) is to be satisfied for any set of network functions $\{y_i(\mathbf{x})\}$, then the necessary and sufficient conditions on the α_i are given by

$$\alpha_i \geq 0, \qquad \sum_i \alpha_i = 1. \tag{9.137}$$

9.13 ($\star$) Use Jensen's inequality (Exercise 2.13) to show that any error function $E(y)$ which is a convex function of the network output y will satisfy the following inequality for committees of networks

$$E_{COM} \leq E_{AV} \tag{9.138}$$

where E_{COM} and E_{AV} are defined in Section 9.6.

9.14 ($\star$) Use the result (9.119) to estimate typical numbers of patterns needed to get good generalization (better than, say, 95% correct on new data) in networks having $d = 10$ inputs and $M = 30$ threshold hidden units.

10

BAYESIAN TECHNIQUES

In this chapter we consider the application of Bayesian inference techniques to neural networks. A simple example of the Bayesian approach was described in Section 2.3 where we considered the problem of inferring the mean of a one-dimensional Gaussian distribution from a set of training data. In the context of neural networks, Bayesian methods offer a number of important features including the following:

1. The conventional training method of error minimization arises from a particular approximation to the Bayesian approach.
2. Regularization can be given a natural interpretation in the Bayesian framework.
3. For regression problems, error bars, or confidence intervals, can be assigned to the predictions generated by a network.
4. Bayesian methods allow the values of regularization coefficients to be selected using only the training data, without the need to use separate training and validation data. Furthermore, the Bayesian approach allows relatively large numbers of regularization coefficients to be used, which would be computationally prohibitive if their values had to be optimized using cross-validation.
5. Similarly, the Bayesian approach allows different models (e.g. networks with different numbers of hidden units, or different network types such as multi-layer perceptrons and radial basis function networks) to be compared using only the training data. More generally, it provides an objective and principled framework for dealing with the issues of model complexity which avoids many of the problems which arise when using maximum likelihood.
6. Bayesian methods allow choices to be made about where in input space new data should be collected in order that it be the most informative (MacKay, 1992c). Such use of the model itself to guide the collection of data during training is known as *active learning*.
7. The relative importance of different inputs can be determined using the Bayesian technique of *automatic relevance determination* (MacKay, 1994a, 1995b; Neal, 1994), based on the use of a separate regularization coefficient for each input. If a particular coefficient acquires a large value, this indicates that the corresponding input is irrelevant and can be eliminated.

Note that, in order to focus on the more basic issues, topics 6 and 7 will not be discussed further.

In earlier chapters network training was based on maximum likelihood which is equivalent to minimization of an error function. We emphasized that, within this framework, a more complex model is typically better able to fit the training data, but that this does not necessarily mean that it will give a smaller error with respect to new data. Models which are either too simple or too complex will give relatively poor approximations to the underlying process from which the data is generated. This was discussed in terms of the bias–variance trade-off in Section 9.1. It is therefore not clear, from the training error alone, which model will give the best generalization, and so we resorted to partitioning of the data set to select an appropriate level of complexity, through such techniques as cross-validation (Section 9.8.1). The Bayesian approach, however, treats the issue of model complexity very differently, and in particular it allows all of the available data to be used for 'training'.

To gain some insight into how this comes about, consider a hypothetical example of three different models, $\mathcal{H}_1$, $\mathcal{H}_2$ and $\mathcal{H}_3$, which we suppose have steadily increasing flexibility, corresponding for instance to a steadily increasing number of hidden units. Thus, each model consists of a specification of the network architecture (number of units, type of activation function, etc.) and is governed by a number of adaptive parameters. By varying the values of these parameters, each model can represent a range of input–output functions. The more complex models, with a greater number of hidden units for instance, can represent a greater range of such functions. Suppose we have a set of input vectors $(\mathbf{x}^1, \ldots, \mathbf{x}^N)$, and a corresponding set of target vectors $D \equiv (\mathbf{t}^1, \ldots, \mathbf{t}^N)$. We can then consider the posterior probability for each of the models, given the observed data set D. From Bayes' theorem this probability can be written in the form

$$p(\mathcal{H}_i|D) = \frac{p(D|\mathcal{H}_i)p(\mathcal{H}_i)}{p(D)}. \tag{10.1}$$

The quantity $p(\mathcal{H}_i)$ represents a prior probability for model $\mathcal{H}_i$. If we have no particular reason to prefer one model over another, then we would assign equal priors to all of the models. Since the denominator $p(D)$ does not depend on the model, we see that different models can be compared by evaluating $p(D|\mathcal{H}_i)$, which is called the *evidence* for the model $\mathcal{H}_i$ (MacKay, 1992a). This is illustrated schematically in Figure 10.1, where we see that the evidence favours models which are neither too simple nor too complex.

This indicates that the Bayesian approach could be used to select a particular model for which the evidence is largest. We might expect that the model with the greatest evidence is also the one which will have the best generalization performance, and we shall discuss this issue in some detail in Section 10.6. However, as we shall see in Section 10.7, the correct Bayesian approach is to make use of the complete set of models. Predicted outputs for new input vectors are obtained

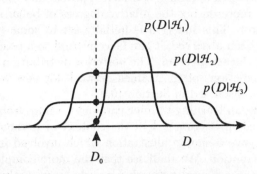

Figure 10.1. Schematic example of three models, $\mathcal{H}_1$, $\mathcal{H}_2$ and $\mathcal{H}_3$, which have successively greater complexity, showing the probability (known as the *evidence*) of different data sets D given each model $\mathcal{H}_i$. We see that more complex models can describe a greater range of data sets. Note, however, that the distributions are normalized. Thus, when a particular data set D_0 is observed, the model $\mathcal{H}_2$ has a greater evidence than either the simpler model $\mathcal{H}_1$ or the more complex model $\mathcal{H}_3$.

by performing a weighted sum over the predictions of all the models, where the weighting coefficients depend on the evidence. More probable models therefore contribute more strongly to the predicted output. Since the evidence can be evaluated using the training data, we see that Bayesian methods are able to deal with the issue of model complexity, without the need to use cross-validation.

An important concept in Bayesian inference is that of *marginalization*, which involves integrating out unwanted variables. Suppose we are discussing a model with two variables w and α. Then the most complete description of these variables is in terms of the joint distribution $p(w, \alpha)$. If we are interested only in the distribution of w then we should integrate out α as follows:

$$p(w) = \int p(w, \alpha) \, d\alpha$$

$$= \int p(w|\alpha)p(\alpha) \, d\alpha. \tag{10.2}$$

Thus the predictive distribution for w is obtained by averaging the conditional distribution $p(w|\alpha)$ with a weighting factor given by the distribution $p(\alpha)$. We shall encounter several examples of marginalization later in this chapter.

10.1 Bayesian learning of network weights

The first problem we shall address is that of learning the weights in a neural network on the basis of a set of training data. In previous chapters we have used maximum likelihood techniques (equivalent to the minimization of an error function) which attempt to find a single set of values for the network weights. By contrast, the Bayesian approach considers a probability distribution function over weight space, representing the relative degrees of belief in different values for the weight vector. This function is initially set to some prior distribution. Once the data has been observed, it can be converted to a posterior distribution through the use of Bayes' theorem. The posterior distribution can then be used to evaluate the predictions of the trained network for new values of the input variables, as will be discussed in Section 10.2.

The use of Bayesian learning to infer parameter values from a set of training data was introduced in Section 2.3 in the context of parametric density estimation. There we gave a simple illustration which involved inferring the mean of a Gaussian distribution. We shall see that the more complex problem of inferring the weights in a neural network proceeds in an analogous manner. For simplicity of notation, we shall consider networks having a single output variable y, although the extension to many output variables is straightforward. Most of the discussion in this chapter will concern function approximation problems, for the case of noise-free input data and noisy target data. The application of Bayesian methods to classification problems will be discussed briefly in Section 10.3. Bayesian inference for noise-free data has been studied by Sibisi (1991), and the problem of interpolating data with noise on both dependent and independent variables has been discussed in the context of straight-line fitting by Gull (1988a).

10.1.1 *Distribution of weights*

We begin by considering the problem of training a network in which the architecture (number of layers, number of hidden units, choice of activation functions etc.) is given. In the conventional maximum likelihood approach, a single 'best' set of weight values is determined by minimization of a suitable error function. In the Bayesian framework, however, we consider a probability distribution over weight values. In the absence of any data, this is described by a prior distribution which we shall denote by $p(\mathbf{w})$, and whose form we shall discuss shortly. Here $\mathbf{w} \equiv (w_1, \ldots, w_W)$ denotes the vector of adaptive weight (and bias) parameters. Let the target data from the training set be denoted by $D \equiv (t^1, \ldots, t^N)$. Once we observe the data D we can write down an expression for the posterior probability distribution for the weights, which we denote by $p(\mathbf{w}|D)$, using Bayes' theorem

$$p(\mathbf{w}|D) = \frac{p(D|\mathbf{w})p(\mathbf{w})}{p(D)} \tag{10.3}$$

where the denominator is a normalization factor which can be written

$$p(D) = \int p(D|\mathbf{w})p(\mathbf{w}) \, d\mathbf{w} \tag{10.4}$$

and which ensures that the left-hand side of (10.3) gives unity when integrated over all weight space. As we shall see shortly, the quantity $p(D|\mathbf{w})$, which represents a model for the noise process on the target data, corresponds to the likelihood function encountered in previous chapters.

Since the data set consists of input as well as target data, the input values should strictly be included in Bayes' theorem (10.3) which should therefore be written in the form

$$p(\mathbf{w}|D, \mathcal{X}) = \frac{p(D|\mathbf{w}, \mathcal{X})p(\mathbf{w}|\mathcal{X})}{p(D|\mathcal{X})} \qquad (10.5)$$

where $\mathcal{X}$ denotes the set of input vectors $(\mathbf{x}^1, \ldots, \mathbf{x}^N)$. As we have already noted in earlier chapters, however, feed-forward networks trained by supervised learning do not in general model the distribution $p(\mathbf{x})$ of the input data. Thus $\mathcal{X}$ always appears as a conditioning variable on the right-hand side of the probabilities in (10.5). We shall therefore continue to omit it from now on in order to simplify the notation.

The picture of learning provided by the Bayesian formalism is as follows. We start with some prior distribution over the weights given by $p(\mathbf{w})$. Since we generally have little idea at this stage of what the weight values should be, the prior might express some rather general properties such as smoothness of the network function, but will otherwise leave the weight values fairly unconstrained. The prior will therefore typically be a rather broad distribution, as indicated schematically in Figure 10.2. Once we have observed the data, this prior distribution can be converted to a posterior distribution using Bayes' theorem in the form (10.3). This posterior distribution will be more compact, as indicated in Figure 10.2, expressing the fact that we have learned something about the extent to which different weight values are consistent with the observed data. In order to evaluate the posterior distribution we need to provide expressions for the prior distribution $p(\mathbf{w})$ and for the likelihood function $p(D|\mathbf{w})$.

10.1.2 *Gaussian prior*

We first consider the prior probability distribution for the weights. This distribution should reflect any prior knowledge we have about the form of network mapping we expect to find. In general, we can write this distribution as an exponential of the form

$$p(\mathbf{w}) = \frac{1}{Z_W(\alpha)} \exp(-\alpha E_W) \qquad (10.6)$$

where $Z_W(\alpha)$ is a normalization factor given by

$$Z_W(\alpha) = \int \exp(-\alpha E_W) \, d\mathbf{w} \qquad (10.7)$$

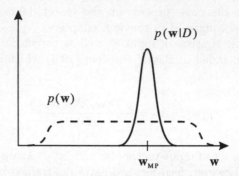

Figure 10.2. Schematic plot of the prior distribution of weights $p(\mathbf{w})$ and the posterior distribution $p(\mathbf{w}|D)$ which arise in the Bayesian inference of network parameters. The most probable weight vector $\mathbf{w}_{\mathrm{MP}}$ corresponds to the maximum of the posterior distribution. In practice the posterior distribution will typically have a complex structure with many local maxima.

which ensures that $\int p(\mathbf{w})\, d\mathbf{w} = 1$. The role of the parameter α will be considered shortly.

The discussion of bias and variance in Section 9.1 indicates that a smooth network function will typically have better generalization than one which is over-fitted to the training data (assuming that the underlying function which we wish to approximate is indeed smooth). This is one of the motivations for regularization techniques designed to encourage smooth network mappings. Such mappings can be achieved by favouring small values for the network weights, and this suggests the following simple form for E_W

$$E_W = \frac{1}{2}\|\mathbf{w}\|^2 = \frac{1}{2}\sum_{i=1}^{W} w_i^2 \tag{10.8}$$

where W is the total number of weights and biases in the network. This corresponds to the use of a simple weight-decay regularizer, as we shall see shortly, and gives a prior distribution of the form

$$p(\mathbf{w}) = \frac{1}{Z_W(\alpha)} \exp\left(-\frac{\alpha}{2}\|\mathbf{w}\|^2\right). \tag{10.9}$$

Thus, when $\|\mathbf{w}\|$ is large, E_W is large, and $p(\mathbf{w})$ is small, and so this choice of prior distribution says that we expect the weight values to be small rather than large.

Since the parameter α itself controls the distribution of other parameters (weights and biases), it is called a *hyperparameter*. To begin with, we shall as-

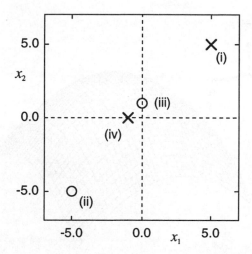

Figure 10.3. A simple data set consisting of two points from class C_1 (circles) and two points from class C_2 (crosses), used to illustrate Bayesian learning in neural networks. The numbers show the order in which the data points are presented to the network.

sume that the value of α is known. We shall discuss how to treat α as part of the learning process in Sections 10.4 and 10.5. A major advantage of the prior in (10.9) is that it is a Gaussian function, which simplifies some of the analysis. Thus, the evaluation of the normalization coefficient $Z_W(\alpha)$ using (10.7) is straightforward, and gives

$$Z_W(\alpha) = \left(\frac{2\pi}{\alpha}\right)^{W/2} \tag{10.10}$$

Many other choices for the prior $p(\mathbf{w})$ can also be considered. Williams (1995) discusses a Laplacian prior of the form (10.6) with $E_W = \sum_i |w_i|$. Several other possibilities, including entropy-based priors, are discussed in Buntine and Weigend (1991). The appropriate selection of priors for very large networks is discussed by Neal (1994).

10.1.3 *Example of Bayesian learning*

We illustrate the concept of Bayesian learning in neural networks by considering a simple example of a single-layer network applied to a classification problem. The input vectors are two-dimensional $\mathbf{x} = (x_1, x_2)$, and the data set consists of four data points, two from each of two classes, as illustrated in Figure 10.3. The network model has a single layer of weights, with a single logistic output given by

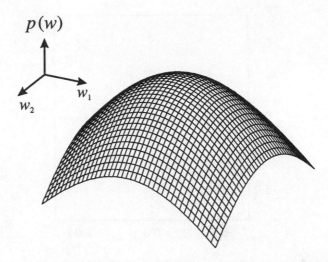

Figure 10.4. Plot of a Gaussian prior shown as a surface over a two-dimensional weight space (w_1, w_2).

$$y(\mathbf{x}; \mathbf{w}) = \frac{1}{1 + \exp(-\mathbf{w}^T \mathbf{x})}. \tag{10.11}$$

Note that the weight vector $\mathbf{w} = (w_1, w_2)$ is two-dimensional, and that there is no bias parameter. We shall choose a Gaussian prior distribution for the weights, given by (10.9), in which the parameter α is given a fixed value of $\alpha = 1$. A surface plot of this prior, as a function of the weight parameters w_1 and w_2, is shown in Figure 10.4.

From Section 6.7.1, we know that the output $y(\mathbf{x}; \mathbf{w})$ of the network in (10.11) can be interpreted as the probability of membership of class $\mathcal{C}_1$, given the input vector $\mathbf{x}$. The probability of membership of class $\mathcal{C}_2$ is then $(1 - y)$. If we assume that the target values are independent and identically distributed, the likelihood function $p(D|\mathbf{w})$ in Bayes' theorem (10.3) will be given by a product of factors, one for each data point, where each factor is either y or $(1 - y)$ according to whether the data point is from class $\mathcal{C}_1$ or $\mathcal{C}_2$.

First, suppose we just consider the data points labelled (i) and (ii) in Figure 10.3. Then we can calculate the posterior distribution of weights using Bayes' theorem (10.3). The resulting distribution is plotted in Figure 10.5. We can understand the form of this distribution by first noting that the network function in (10.11) represents a sigmoidal ridge in which the value $y = 0.5$ (the decision boundary for minimum probability of misclassification) is given by a line passing through the origin in Figure 10.3. The two weight parameters w_1 and w_2 control the orientation of this line and the slope of the sigmoid. Patterns (i) and (ii) cause weight vectors from approximately half of weight space to have extremely

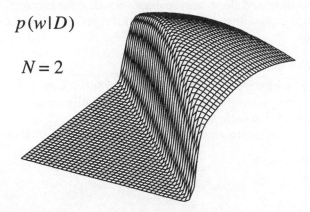

Figure 10.5. Plot of the posterior distribution obtained from the prior in Figure 10.4, using patterns (i) and (ii) from Figure 10.3. (Note that there is a change of vertical scale compared to Figure 10.4.)

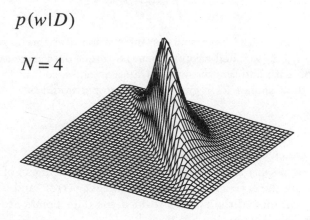

Figure 10.6. Plot of the posterior distribution obtained after using all four patterns from Figure 10.3. (Note that for convenience there is again a change of vertical scale compared to previous figures.)

small probabilities as they represent 'decision surfaces' with the wrong orientation. The remaining weight vectors are largely unaffected and so the shape of the posterior distribution in the corresponding region of weight space then reflects that of the prior distribution in Figure 10.4.

If we now include all four patterns from Figure 10.3, we obtain the posterior distribution shown in Figure 10.6. As a result of the way patterns (iii) and (iv) are labelled, there is now no decision boundary which classifies all four points perfectly. The most probable solution is one in which the sigmoid has a particular orientation and slope, and solutions which differ significantly from this have much lower probability. The posterior distribution of weights is therefore relatively narrow.

10.1.4 *Gaussian noise model*

We turn now to more general architectures of feed-forward network, and to a consideration of 'regression' problems. Later we shall return to a discussion of Bayesian methods for classification.

In general, we can write the likelihood function in Bayes' theorem (10.3) in the form

$$p(D|\mathbf{w}) = \frac{1}{Z_D(\beta)} \exp(-\beta E_D) \qquad (10.12)$$

where E_D is an error function, and β is another example of a hyperparameter which will be discussed shortly. The function $Z_D(\beta)$ is a normalization factor given by

$$Z_D(\beta) = \int \exp(-\beta E_D)\, dD \qquad (10.13)$$

where $\int dD = \int dt^1 \dots dt^N$ represents an integration over the target variables.

As in Section 6.1, we shall assume that the target data is generated from a smooth function with additive zero-mean Gaussian noise, so that the probability of observing a data value t for a given input vector $\mathbf{x}$ would be

$$p(t|\mathbf{x}, \mathbf{w}) \propto \exp\left(-\frac{\beta}{2}\{y(\mathbf{x}; \mathbf{w}) - t\}^2\right) \qquad (10.14)$$

where $y(\mathbf{x}; \mathbf{w})$ represents a network function governing the mean of the distribution, $\mathbf{w}$ represents the corresponding network weight vector, and the parameter β controls the variance of the noise. Provided the data points are drawn independently from this distribution, we have

$$p(D|\mathbf{w}) = \prod_{n=1}^{N} p(t^n|\mathbf{x}^n, \mathbf{w})$$

$$= \frac{1}{Z_D(\beta)} \exp\left(-\frac{\beta}{2} \sum_{n=1}^{N}\{y(\mathbf{x}^n; \mathbf{w}) - t^n\}^2\right) \qquad (10.15)$$

The expression (10.13) for the normalization factor $Z_D(\beta)$ is then the product of N independent Gaussian integrals which are easily evaluated (Appendix B) to give

$$Z_D(\beta) = \left(\frac{2\pi}{\beta}\right)^{N/2} \tag{10.16}$$

For the moment we shall treat β as a fixed, known constant. We shall return to the problem of determining this parameter as part of the learning process in Sections 10.4 and 10.5.

10.1.5 *Posterior distribution of weight values*

Once we have chosen a prior distribution, and an expression for the likelihood function, we can use Bayes' theorem in the form (10.3) and (10.4) to find the posterior distribution of the weights. Using our general expressions (10.6) and (10.12) we obtain the posterior distribution in the form

$$p(\mathbf{w}|D) = \frac{1}{Z_S} \exp(-\beta E_D - \alpha E_W) = \frac{1}{Z_S} \exp(-S(\mathbf{w})) \tag{10.17}$$

where

$$S(\mathbf{w}) = \beta E_D + \alpha E_W \tag{10.18}$$

and

$$Z_S(\alpha, \beta) = \int \exp(-\beta E_D - \alpha E_W) \, d\mathbf{w}. \tag{10.19}$$

Consider first the problem of finding the weight vector $\mathbf{w}_{\mathrm{MP}}$ corresponding to the maximum of the posterior distribution. This can be found by minimizing the negative logarithm of (10.17) with respect to the weights. Since the normalizing factor Z_S in (10.17) is independent of the weights, we see that this is equivalent to minimizing $S(\mathbf{w})$ given by (10.18). For the particular prior distribution given by (10.9) and noise model given by (10.15), this can be written in the form

$$S(\mathbf{w}) = \frac{\beta}{2} \sum_{n=1}^{N} \{y(x^n; \mathbf{w}) - t^n\}^2 + \frac{\alpha}{2} \sum_{i=1}^{W} w_i^2. \tag{10.20}$$

We see that, apart from an overall multiplicative factor, this is precisely the usual sum-of-squares error function with a weight-decay regularization term, as discussed in Section 9.2.1. Note that, if we are only interested in finding the weight vector which minimizes this error function, the effective value of the regularization parameter (the coefficient of the regularizing term) depends only on the ratio α/β, since an overall multiplicative factor is unimportant.

The most probable value for the weight vector, denoted by $\mathbf{w}_{\mathrm{MP}}$, corresponds to the maximum of the posterior probability, or equivalently to the minimum of the right-hand side in (10.20). If we consider a succession of training sets with increasing numbers N of patterns then we see that the first term in (10.20) grows with N while the second term does not. If α and β are fixed, then as N increases, the first term becomes more and more dominant, until eventually the second term becomes insignificant. The maximum likelihood solution is then a very good approximation to the most probable solution $\mathbf{w}_{\mathrm{MP}}$. Conversely, for very small data sets the prior term plays an important role in determining the location of the most probable solution.

10.1.6 *Consistent priors*

We have seen that a quadratic prior, consisting of a sum over all weights (and biases) in the network, corresponds to a simple weight-decay regularizer. In Section 9.2.2, we showed that this regularizer has an intrinsic inconsistency with the known scaling properties of network mappings. This led to a consideration of weight-decay regularizers in which there is a different regularization coefficient for weights in different layers, and in which biases are excluded. For a two-layer network, this suggests a prior of the form

$$p(\mathbf{w}) \propto \exp\left(-\frac{\alpha_1}{2} \sum_{w \in \mathcal{W}_1} w^2 - \frac{\alpha_2}{2} \sum_{w \in \mathcal{W}_2} w^2\right) \tag{10.21}$$

where $\mathcal{W}_1$ denotes the set of weights in the first layer, $\mathcal{W}_2$ denotes the set of weights in the second layer, and biases are excluded from the summations. Note that priors of this form are *improper* (they cannot be normalized) since the bias parameters are unconstrained. The use of improper priors can lead to difficulties in selecting regularization coefficients and in model comparison within the Bayesian framework, since the corresponding evidence is zero. It is therefore common to include separate priors for the biases.

More generally, we can consider priors in which the weights are divided into any number of groups $\mathcal{W}_k$ so that

$$p(\mathbf{w}) \propto \exp\left(-\frac{1}{2} \sum_k \alpha_k \|\mathbf{w}\|_k^2\right) \tag{10.22}$$

where

$$\|\mathbf{w}\|_k^2 = \sum_{w \in \mathcal{W}_k} w^2. \tag{10.23}$$

For simplicity of exposition, we shall continue to use a Gaussian prior of the form (10.9). The extension of the Bayesian analysis to account for the more general prior (10.22) is straightforward, and the reader is led through the relevant analysis in Exercises 10.5 to 10.8.

10.1.7 *Gaussian approximation to the posterior distribution*

Given our particular choices for the noise model and the prior, the expressions (10.17) and (10.20) defining the posterior distribution are exact (although in general the normalization coefficient $Z_S(\alpha, \beta)$ cannot be evaluated analytically). In practice we wish to evaluate the probability distribution of network predictions, as well as the evidences for the hyperparameters and for the model. These require integrations over weight space, and in order to make these integrals analytically tractable, we need to introduce some simplifying approximations. MacKay (1992d) uses a Gaussian approximation for the posterior distribution. This is obtained by considering the Taylor expansion of $S(\mathbf{w})$ around its minimum value and retaining terms up to second order so that

$$S(\mathbf{w}) = S(\mathbf{w}_{\mathrm{MP}}) + \frac{1}{2}(\mathbf{w} - \mathbf{w}_{\mathrm{MP}})^{\mathrm{T}} \mathbf{A} (\mathbf{w} - \mathbf{w}_{\mathrm{MP}}) \tag{10.24}$$

where the linear term has vanished since we are expanding around a minimum of $S(\mathbf{w})$. Here $\mathbf{A}$ is the Hessian matrix of the total (regularized) error function, with elements given by

$$\mathbf{A} = \nabla\nabla S_{\mathrm{MP}}$$

$$= \beta\nabla\nabla E_D^{\mathrm{MP}} + \alpha\mathbf{I}. \tag{10.25}$$

A variety of exact and approximate methods for evaluating the Hessian of the error function E_D were discussed in Section 4.10.

The expansion (10.24) leads to a posterior distribution which is now a Gaussian function of the weights, given by

$$p(\mathbf{w}|D) = \frac{1}{Z_S^*} \exp\left(-S(\mathbf{w}_{\mathrm{MP}}) - \frac{1}{2}\Delta\mathbf{w}^{\mathrm{T}} \mathbf{A} \, \Delta\mathbf{w}\right) \tag{10.26}$$

where $\Delta\mathbf{w} = \mathbf{w} - \mathbf{w}_{\mathrm{MP}}$, and Z_S^* is the normalization constant appropriate to the Gaussian approximation. Some partial justification for this approximation comes from the result of Walker (1969), which says that, under very general circumstances, a posterior distribution will tend to a Gaussian in the limit where the number of data points goes to infinity. For very large data sets we might then expect the Gaussian approximation to be a good one. However, the primary motivation for the Gaussian approximation is that it allows a great deal of progress to be made analytically. Later we shall discuss techniques based on Markov chain Monte Carlo integration which avoid this approximation.

Using the results given in Appendix B, it is now straightforward to evaluate the normalization factor Z_S^* for this Gaussian approximation, in terms of the determinant of the matrix $\mathbf{A}$, to give

$$Z_S^*(\alpha, \beta) = e^{-S(\mathbf{w}_{\mathrm{MP}})} (2\pi)^{W/2} |\mathbf{A}|^{-1/2}. \tag{10.27}$$

For a general non-linear network mapping function $y(\mathbf{x}; \mathbf{w})$, e.g. a multi-layer perceptron, there may be numerous local minima of the error function, some of which may be associated with symmetries in the network. For instance, if we consider a multi-layer perceptron with two layers of weights, M hidden units, and anti-symmetric hidden unit activation functions (e.g. the 'tanh' function), then each distinct local minimum belongs to a family of $2^M M!$ equivalent minima, as discussed in Section 4.4. The weight vectors corresponding to these different minima are related by transformations which interchange the hidden units and reflect the signs of the weights associated with individual hidden units. There may be several families of such minima, where the different families are non-equivalent and are not related by symmetry transformations. The single-Gaussian approximation given by (10.26) clearly does not take multiple minima into account. One approach is to approximate the posterior distribution by a sum of Gaussians, once centred on each of the minima (MacKay, 1992d), and we shall see how to make use of this approximation in Section 10.7.

10.2 Distribution of network outputs

As we have seen, in the Bayesian formalism a 'trained' network is described in terms of the posterior probability distribution of weight values. If we present a new input vector to such a network, then the distribution of weights gives rise to a distribution of network outputs. In addition, there will be a contribution to the output distribution arising from the assumed Gaussian noise on the output variables. Here we shall calculate the distribution of output values, using the single-Gaussian approximation introduced above.

Using the rules of probability, we can write the distribution of outputs, for a given input vector $\mathbf{x}$, in the form

$$p(t|\mathbf{x}, D) = \int p(t|\mathbf{x}, \mathbf{w}) p(\mathbf{w}|D) \, d\mathbf{w} \tag{10.28}$$

where $p(\mathbf{w}|D)$ is the posterior distribution of weights. The distribution $p(t|\mathbf{x}, \mathbf{w})$ is simply the model for the distribution of noise on the target data, for a fixed value of the weight vector, and is given by (10.14).

In order to evaluate this distribution we shall make use of the Gaussian approximation (10.26) for the posterior distribution of weights, together with the expression (10.14) for the distribution of network outputs. This gives

$$p(t|\mathbf{x}, D) \propto \int \exp\left(-\frac{\beta}{2}\{t - y(\mathbf{x}; \mathbf{w})\}^2\right) \exp\left(-\frac{1}{2}\Delta\mathbf{w}^{\mathrm{T}} \mathbf{A} \Delta\mathbf{w}\right) \, d\mathbf{w} \tag{10.29}$$

where we have dropped any constant factors (i.e. factors independent of t). In addition, we shall assume that the width of the posterior distribution (determined by the Hessian matrix $\mathbf{A}$) is sufficiently narrow that we may approximate the network function $y(\mathbf{x}; \mathbf{w})$ by its linear expansion around $\mathbf{w}_{\mathrm{MP}}$

$$y(\mathbf{x}; \mathbf{w}) = y(\mathbf{x}; \mathbf{w}_{\mathrm{MP}}) + \mathbf{g}^{\mathrm{T}} \Delta \mathbf{w} \tag{10.30}$$

where

$$\mathbf{g} \equiv \nabla_{\mathbf{w}} y |_{\mathbf{w}_{\mathrm{MP}}}. \tag{10.31}$$

This allows us to write (10.29) in the form

$$p(t|\mathbf{x}, D) \propto \int \exp\left(-\frac{\beta}{2} \{t - y_{\mathrm{MP}} - \mathbf{g}^{\mathrm{T}} \Delta \mathbf{w}\}^2 - \frac{1}{2} \Delta \mathbf{w}^{\mathrm{T}} \mathbf{A} \Delta \mathbf{w} \right) d\mathbf{w} \tag{10.32}$$

where $y_{\mathrm{MP}} \equiv y(\mathbf{x}; \mathbf{w}_{\mathrm{MP}})$. The integral in (10.32) is easily evaluated (Exercises 10.1 and 10.2) to give a Gaussian distribution of the form

$$p(t|\mathbf{x}, D) = \frac{1}{(2\pi\sigma_t^2)^{1/2}} \exp\left(-\frac{(t - y_{\mathrm{MP}})^2}{2\sigma_t^2} \right) \tag{10.33}$$

where we have restored the normalization factor explicitly. This distribution has a mean given by y_{MP}, and a variance given by

$$\sigma_t^2 = \frac{1}{\beta} + \mathbf{g}^{\mathrm{T}} \mathbf{A}^{-1} \mathbf{g}. \tag{10.34}$$

We can interpret the standard deviation σ_t of the predictive distribution for t as an error bar on the mean value y_{MP}. This error bar has two contributions, one arising from the intrinsic noise on the target data, corresponding to the first term in (10.34), and one arising from the width of the posterior distribution of the network weights, corresponding to the second term in (10.34). When the noise amplitude is large, so that β is small, the noise term dominates, as indicated in Figure 10.7. For a small noise amplitude (large value of β) the variance of the output distribution is dominated by the contribution from the variance of the posterior distribution of weights, as shown in Figure 10.8.

We see that the Bayesian formalism allows us to calculate error bars on the network outputs, instead of just providing a single 'best guess' output. In a practical implementation, we first find the most probable weights $\mathbf{w}_{\mathrm{MP}}$ by minimizing the regularized error function $S(\mathbf{w})$. We can then assign error bars to this network function by evaluating the Hessian matrix and using (10.34). Methods for the exact evaluation of the Hessian, as well as useful approximations, are discussed in Section 4.10.

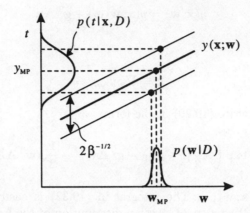

Figure 10.7. The distribution of network outputs in the Bayesian formalism is determined both by the posterior distribution of network weights $p(\mathbf{w}|D)$ and by the variance β^{-1} due to the intrinsic noise on the data. When the posterior distribution of weights is very narrow in relation to the noise variance, as shown here, the width of the distribution of network outputs is determined primarily by the noise.

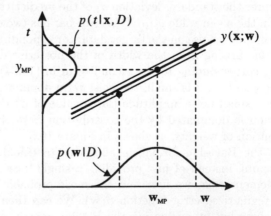

Figure 10.8. As in Figure 10.7, but with a posterior distribution for the weights which is relatively broad in comparison with the intrinsic noise on the data, showing how the width of the distribution over network outputs is now dominated by the distribution of network weights.

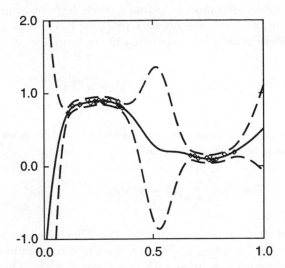

Figure 10.9. A simple example of the application of Bayesian methods to a 'regression' problem. Here 30 data points have been generated by sampling the function (10.35), and the network consists of a multi-layer perceptron with four hidden units having 'tanh' activation functions, and one linear output unit. The solid curve shows the network function with the weight vector set to $\mathbf{w}_{MP}$ corresponding to the maximum of the posterior distribution, and the dashed curves represent the $\pm 2\sigma_t$ error bars from (10.34). Notice how the error bars are larger in regions of low data density.

10.2.1 *Example of Bayesian regression*

As a simple illustration of the application of Bayesian techniques to a 'regression' problem, we consider a one-input one-output example involving data generated from the smooth function

$$h(x) = 0.5 + 0.4\sin(2\pi x) \tag{10.35}$$

with additive Gaussian noise having a standard deviation of $\sigma = 0.05$. Values for x were generated by sampling a Gaussian mixture distribution having two well-separated components. A prior of the form (10.21) was used, and values of α and β were chosen by an on-line re-estimation procedure described in Section 10.4.

The network mapping corresponding to the most probable weight values is shown in Figure 10.9, together with the $\pm 2\sigma_t$ error bars given by (10.34). We see that the width of the error bar depends on the local density of input data, with the error bars increasing in magnitude in regions of input space having low data density. In this example the Hessian matrix was evaluated using exact analytical techniques, as discussed in Section 4.10.

10.2.2   Generalized linear networks

In Section 3.3 we discussed models having a single layer of adaptive weights, so that, for linear output units, the network mapping function is a linear function of the weights. Such models can be written in the form

$$y(\mathbf{x}; \mathbf{w}) = \sum_{j=0}^{M} w_j \phi_j(\mathbf{x}) = \mathbf{w}^{\mathrm{T}} \phi(\mathbf{x}). \tag{10.36}$$

If we continue to use a Gaussian noise model and a Gaussian prior on the weights, then the total error function is given by

$$S(\mathbf{w}) = \frac{\beta}{2} \sum_{n} \{t^n - \mathbf{w}^{\mathrm{T}} \phi(\mathbf{x}^n)\}^2 + \frac{\alpha}{2} \|\mathbf{w}\|^2 \tag{10.37}$$

and hence is a quadratic function of the weights. Thus, the posterior distribution of weights is exactly Gaussian, and only has a single maximum rather than the multiple maxima which can arise with non-linear models. The most probable weight vector $\mathbf{w}_{\mathrm{MP}}$ is described by a set of linear equations, which are easily solved using the techniques described in Section 3.4.3. The network function can then be written, without approximation, in the form

$$y(\mathbf{x}; \mathbf{w}) = y_{\mathrm{MP}} + \phi^{\mathrm{T}} \Delta \mathbf{w} \tag{10.38}$$

where $\Delta \mathbf{w} = \mathbf{w} - \mathbf{w}_{\mathrm{MP}}$ as before. Also, the Hessian matrix $\mathbf{A}$ is given exactly by the outer product expression (Section 4.10.2) in the form

$$\mathbf{A} = \nabla \nabla S(\mathbf{w})|_{\mathbf{w}_{\mathrm{MP}}} = \beta \sum_{n} \phi(\mathbf{x}^n) \phi(\mathbf{x}^n)^{\mathrm{T}} + \alpha \mathbf{I} \tag{10.39}$$

where $\mathbf{I}$ is the unit matrix. The distribution of network outputs is then given by a Gaussian integral of the form

$$p(t|\mathbf{x}, D) \propto \int \exp\left(-\frac{\beta}{2}\{t - \mathbf{w}^{\mathrm{T}}\phi(\mathbf{x})\}^2 - \frac{1}{2}\Delta \mathbf{w}^{\mathrm{T}} \mathbf{A} \Delta \mathbf{w}\right) d\mathbf{w} \tag{10.40}$$

which can be evaluated in the same way as (10.32) to give a distribution for t which is Gaussian with mean y_{MP} and variance

$$\sigma_t^2 = \frac{1}{\beta} + \phi^{\mathrm{T}} \mathbf{A}^{-1} \phi. \tag{10.41}$$

10.3 Application to classification problems

We now return briefly to a discussion of the application of Bayesian methods to classification problems. Following MacKay (1992b) we consider problems involving two classes. As discussed in Section 6.7, the likelihood function for the data given by

$$p(D|\mathbf{w}) = \prod_n y(\mathbf{x}^n)^{t^n} (1 - y(\mathbf{x}^n))^{1-t^n}$$

$$= \exp\left(-G(D|\mathbf{w})\right) \tag{10.42}$$

where G is the cross-entropy error function, given by

$$G(D|\mathbf{w}) = -\sum_n \{t^n \ln y(\mathbf{x}^n) + (1 - t^n) \ln(1 - y(\mathbf{x}^n))\}. \tag{10.43}$$

The distribution (10.42) has the correct normalization since the target data t^n take the values 0 or 1, and so the normalization 'integral' becomes a sum of terms each of which is the product of factors of the form

$$\exp(\ln y) + \exp(\ln(1 - y)) = y + (1 - y) = 1. \tag{10.44}$$

Note that there is no equivalent of the constant β. This is because the targets are assumed to provide perfect class labels, and so there is no uncertainty associated with their values.

As discussed in Section 6.7.1, it is appropriate to choose an output activation function given by the logistic sigmoid of the form

$$y = g(a) \equiv \frac{1}{1 + \exp(-a)} \tag{10.45}$$

where $a = \sum_j w_j z_j$ is the weighted linear sum feeding into the output unit. This activation function allows the network output to be interpreted as the probability $P(\mathcal{C}_1|\mathbf{x})$ that an input vector $\mathbf{x}$ belongs to class $\mathcal{C}_1$.

Again, we can introduce a prior distribution for the network weights in terms of a regularization term E_W, so that the posterior distribution becomes

$$p(\mathbf{w}|D) = \frac{1}{Z_S} \exp\left(-G - \alpha E_W\right) = \frac{1}{Z_S} \exp\left(-S(\mathbf{w})\right). \tag{10.46}$$

As before, this distribution can be approximated by a Gaussian centred on the maximum posterior weight vector $\mathbf{w}_{\mathrm{MP}}$

$$p(\mathbf{w}|D) = \frac{1}{Z_S^*} \exp\left(-S(\mathbf{w}_{MP}) - \frac{1}{2}\Delta\mathbf{w}^T \mathbf{A} \, \Delta\mathbf{w}\right) \qquad (10.47)$$

where Z_S^* is the normalization constant appropriate to the Gaussian approximation, and $\Delta\mathbf{w} = \mathbf{w} - \mathbf{w}_{MP}$.

The probability of membership of class $\mathcal{C}_1$ for a new input vector $\mathbf{x}$ is given in the Bayesian framework by an integration over the distribution of network weights of the form

$$P(\mathcal{C}_1|\mathbf{x}, D) = \int P(\mathcal{C}_1|\mathbf{x}, \mathbf{w})p(\mathbf{w}|D) \, d\mathbf{w} \qquad (10.48)$$

$$= \int y(\mathbf{x}; \mathbf{w})p(\mathbf{w}|D) \, d\mathbf{w}. \qquad (10.49)$$

In the case of regression problems, the distribution of network outputs given by (10.33) is a Gaussian with mean $y_{MP}(\mathbf{x}) = y(\mathbf{x}; \mathbf{w}_{MP})$, so that the marginalized output corresponding to (10.49) coincides with the predictions made by using the most probable weight vector alone (provided the posterior distribution is sufficiently narrow that we can approximate y as a function of $\mathbf{w}$ by a linear function in the neighbourhood of the most probable weight vector). For classification problems, however, this result does not hold, since the network function can no longer be approximated by a linear function of the network weights as a consequence of the sigmoidal activation function $y = g(a)$ on the network outputs. The process of marginalization then introduces some important modifications to the predictions made by the network.

MacKay (1992b) assumes that a (rather than y) is locally a linear function of the weights

$$a(\mathbf{x}; \mathbf{w}) = a_{MP}(\mathbf{x}) + \mathbf{g}^T(\mathbf{x})\Delta\mathbf{w} \qquad (10.50)$$

where $\Delta\mathbf{w} = \mathbf{w} - \mathbf{w}_{MP}$. The distribution of a then takes the form

$$p(a|\mathbf{x}, D) = \int p(a|\mathbf{x}, \mathbf{w})p(\mathbf{w}|D) \, d\mathbf{w} \qquad (10.51)$$

$$= \int \delta(a - a_{MP} - \mathbf{g}^T\Delta\mathbf{w})p(\mathbf{w}|D) \, d\mathbf{w} \qquad (10.52)$$

where $\delta(\cdot)$ is the Dirac delta-function. We now use the Gaussian approximation (10.47) for the posterior distribution $p(\mathbf{w}|D)$. Since the delta-function constraint requires that $\Delta\mathbf{w}$ be linearly related to a, and since the posterior weight distribution is Gaussian, the distribution of a will also be Gaussian. The mean and variance of this Gaussian distribution are easily evaluated (Exercise 10.3) to give

$$p(a|\mathbf{x}, D) = \frac{1}{(2\pi s^2)^{1/2}} \exp\left(-\frac{(a - a_{\text{MP}})^2}{2s^2}\right) \tag{10.53}$$

where the variance s^2 is given by

$$s^2(\mathbf{x}) = \mathbf{g}^T \mathbf{A}^{-1} \mathbf{g}. \tag{10.54}$$

We then have

$$P(\mathcal{C}_1|\mathbf{x}, D) = \int P(\mathcal{C}_1|a)p(a|\mathbf{x}, D)\, da \tag{10.55}$$

$$= \int g(a)p(a|\mathbf{x}, D)\, da \tag{10.56}$$

where $p(a|\mathbf{x}, D)$ is given by (10.53) and $g(a)$ is given by (10.45). Since the integral (10.56) does not have an analytic solution, MacKay (1992b) suggests the following approximation

$$P(\mathcal{C}_1|\mathbf{x}, D) \simeq g(\kappa(s)a_{\text{MP}}) \tag{10.57}$$

where

$$\kappa(s) = \left(1 + \frac{\pi s^2}{8}\right)^{-1/2} \tag{10.58}$$

and s^2 is defined by (10.54).

Now compare the classification decisions obtained using the marginalized output given by (10.56) with those obtained using the output $y_{\text{MP}} = g(a_{\text{MP}})$ corresponding to the most probable weight vector. If the output is used to classify the network input so as to minimize the probability of misclassification, then the decision boundary corresponds to a network output of 0.5 (Section 1.8.1). For the most probable output $y_{\text{MP}} = g(a_{\text{MP}})$, the form of the logistic sigmoid activation function (10.45) shows that $y_{\text{MP}} = 0.5$ corresponds to $a(\mathbf{x}, \mathbf{w}_{\text{MP}}) = 0$. For the marginalized output (10.56) the decision boundary $P(\mathcal{C}_1|\mathbf{x}, D) = 0.5$ also corresponds to $a(\mathbf{x}, \mathbf{w}_{\text{MP}}) = 0$. This follows from (10.56) together with the fact that $g(a) - 0.5$ is anti-symmetric while the Gaussian (10.53) is symmetric. Thus, if the marginalized outputs are used to classify new inputs directly on the basis of the most probable class they will give the same results as would be obtained by using most probable outputs alone.

However, if a more complex loss matrix is introduced or if a 'reject option' is included (Section 1.10), then marginalization can have a significant effect on the decisions made by the network. The effects of marginalization for a simple two-class problem are shown schematically in Figures 10.10 and 10.11 for the

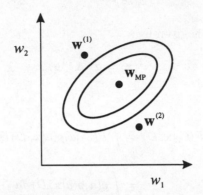

Figure 10.10. A schematic plot of the posterior distribution of weights showing the most probable weight vector $\mathbf{w}_{\mathrm{MP}}$, and also two other weight vectors $\mathbf{w}^{(1)}$ and $\mathbf{w}^{(2)}$ taken from the posterior distribution.

case of a single-layer network. Figure 10.10 shows the posterior distribution of network weights, and Figures 10.11 (a)–(c) show examples of the network outputs obtained by choosing weight vectors from various points in the posterior distribution. The effect of marginalization (integration of the predictions over the posterior distribution) is shown in Figure 10.11 (d). Note that the decision boundary (corresponding to the central $y = 0.5$ line) is the same as for Figure 10.11 (a).

10.4 The evidence framework for α and β

So far in this chapter, we have assumed that the values of the hyperparameters α and β are known. For most applications, however, we will have little idea of suitable values for α and β (in some cases we may have an idea of the noise level β). The treatment of hyperparameters involves Occam's razor (Section 1.6) since the values of hyperparameters which give the best fit to the training data in a maximum likelihood setting represent over-complex or over-flexible models which do not give the best generalization.

As we have discussed already, the correct Bayesian treatment for parameters such as α and β, whose values are unknown, is to integrate them out of any predictions. For example, the posterior distribution of network weights is given by

$$p(\mathbf{w}|D) = \iint p(\mathbf{w}, \alpha, \beta|D)\, d\alpha\, d\beta$$

$$= \iint p(\mathbf{w}|\alpha, \beta, D)p(\alpha, \beta|D)\, d\alpha\, d\beta. \tag{10.59}$$

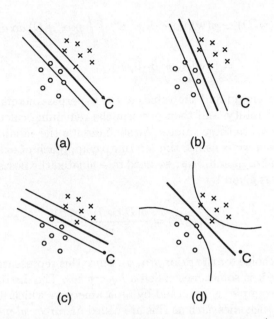

Figure 10.11. Schematic illustration of data from two classes (represented by circles and crosses) showing the predictions made by a classifier with a single layer of weights and a logistic sigmoid output unit. (a) shows the predictions made by the network with the weights set to their most probable values $\mathbf{w}_{MP}$. The three lines correspond to network outputs of 0.1, 0.5 and 0.9. A point such as C, which is well outside the region containing the training data, is classified with great confidence by this network. (b) and (c) show predictions made by the weight vectors corresponding to $\mathbf{w}^{(1)}$ and $\mathbf{w}^{(2)}$ in Figure 10.10. Notice how the point C is classified differently by these two networks. (d) shows the effects of marginalizing over the distribution of weights given in Figure 10.10. We see that the probability contours spread out in regions where there is little data. The point C is now assigned a probability close to 0.5 as we would expect.

Note that we have extended our notation to include dependencies on α and β explicitly in the various probability densities. Two approaches to the treatment of hyperparameters have been discussed in the literature. One of these performs the integrals over α and β analytically, and will be discussed in Section 10.5. An alternative approach, known as the *evidence approximation*, has been discussed by MacKay (1992a, 1992d) and will be considered first. This framework is based on techniques developed by Gull (1988b, 1989) and Skilling (1991). It is computationally equivalent to the *type II maximum likelihood* (ML-II) method of conventional statistics (Berger, 1985).

Let us suppose that the posterior probability distribution $p(\alpha, \beta|D)$ for the hyperparameters in (10.59) is sharply peaked around their most probable values

α_{MP} and β_{MP}. Then (10.59) can be written

$$p(\mathbf{w}|D) \simeq p(\mathbf{w}|\alpha_{\mathrm{MP}}, \beta_{\mathrm{MP}}, D) \int\!\!\int p(\alpha, \beta|D) \, d\alpha \, d\beta \tag{10.60}$$

$$= p(\mathbf{w}|\alpha_{\mathrm{MP}}, \beta_{\mathrm{MP}}, D). \tag{10.61}$$

This says that we should find the values of the hyperparameters which maximize the posterior probability, and then perform the remaining calculations with the hyperparameters set to these values. We shall discuss the validity of this approximation later, when we consider the alternative approach of exact integration.

In order to find α_{MP} and β_{MP}, we need to evaluated the posterior distribution of α and β. This is given by

$$p(\alpha, \beta|D) = \frac{p(D|\alpha, \beta)p(\alpha, \beta)}{p(D)} \tag{10.62}$$

which requires a choice for the prior $p(\alpha, \beta)$. Since this represents a prior over the hyperparameters, it is sometimes called a *hyperprior*. The distribution of weight parameters, for example, is governed by a parameter α which itself is described by a distribution. Schemes such as this are called *hierarchical models* and can be extended to any number of levels. If we have no idea of what would be suitable values for α and β, then we should choose a prior which in some sense gives equal weight to all possible values. Such priors are called *non-informative* and are discussed at length in Berger (1985). They often have the characteristic that they cannot be normalized since the integral of the prior diverges. Priors for which this is the case are called *improper*. An example would be a prior for a parameter α which is taken to be uniform over an infinite interval $(0, \infty)$. In fact, α and β are examples of *scale parameters* since they determine the scale of $\|\mathbf{w}\|^2$ and of the noise respectively. Non-informative priors for scale parameters are generally chosen to be uniform on a logarithmic scale as discussed in Exercise 10.13.

For the moment we shall suppose that the hyperprior $p(\alpha, \beta)$ is chosen to be very insensitive to the values of α and β to reflect the fact that we have little idea of suitable values for these quantities. Later we shall discuss more formally how to choose suitable hyperpriors. Since the denominator in (10.62) is independent of α and β, we see that the maximum-posterior values for these hyperparameters are found by maximizing the likelihood term $p(D|\alpha, \beta)$. This term is called the *evidence* for α and β.

Note that the Bayesian analysis is proceeding in a hierarchical fashion. The first level involves the determination of the distribution of weight values. At the second level we are seeking the distribution of hyperparameter values. The evidence $p(D|\alpha, \beta)$ at this level of the hierarchy is given by the denominator in Bayes' theorem (10.3) from the previous level.

We can easily express the evidence in terms of quantities which we have evaluated already. If we make the dependences on α and β explicit, then we can write (10.4) in the form

$$p(D|\alpha,\beta) = \int p(D|\mathbf{w},\alpha,\beta)p(\mathbf{w}|\alpha,\beta)\,d\mathbf{w} \tag{10.63}$$

$$= \int p(D|\mathbf{w},\beta)p(\mathbf{w}|\alpha)\,d\mathbf{w} \tag{10.64}$$

where we have made use of the fact that the prior is independent of β and the likelihood function is independent of α. Using the exponential forms (10.6) and (10.12) for the prior and likelihood distributions, together with (10.18) and (10.19), we can then write this in the form

$$p(D|\alpha,\beta) = \frac{1}{Z_D(\beta)}\frac{1}{Z_W(\alpha)}\int \exp\left(-S(\mathbf{w})\right)d\mathbf{w}$$

$$= \frac{Z_S(\alpha,\beta)}{Z_D(\beta)Z_W(\alpha)}. \tag{10.65}$$

For our particular choices of noise model and prior on the weights, we have already evaluated Z_D and Z_W in (10.16) and (10.10) respectively. If we make the Gaussian approximation for the posterior distribution of the weights, then Z_S is given by (10.27). The log of the evidence is then given by

$$\ln p(D|\alpha,\beta) = -\alpha E_W^{\text{MP}} - \beta E_D^{\text{MP}} - \frac{1}{2}\ln|\mathbf{A}| \tag{10.66}$$

$$+ \frac{W}{2}\ln\alpha + \frac{N}{2}\ln\beta - \frac{N}{2}\ln(2\pi). \tag{10.67}$$

We first consider the problem of finding the maximum with respect to α. In order to differentiate $\ln|\mathbf{A}|$ with respect to α we first write $\mathbf{A} = \mathbf{H} + \alpha\mathbf{I}$, where $\mathbf{H} = \beta\nabla\nabla E_D$ is the Hessian of the unregularized error function. If $\{\lambda_i\}$ (where $i = 1,\ldots,W$) denote the eigenvalues of $\mathbf{H}$, then $\mathbf{A}$ has eigenvalues $\lambda_i + \alpha$ and we have

$$\frac{d}{d\alpha}\ln|\mathbf{A}| = \frac{d}{d\alpha}\ln\left(\prod_i(\lambda_i + \alpha)\right)$$

$$= \frac{d}{d\alpha}\sum_i\ln(\lambda_i + \alpha)$$

$$= \sum_i \frac{1}{\lambda_i + \alpha} = \text{Tr} \mathbf{A}^{-1} \qquad (10.68)$$

where the last step follows from the fact that the eigenvalues of $\mathbf{A}^{-1}$ are $(\lambda_i + \alpha)^{-1}$. Note that this derivation has implicitly assumed that the eigenvalues λ_i do not themselves depend on α. For an error function E_D which is exactly a quadratic function of the weights (as is the case for a linear network and a sum-of-squares error function), the Hessian will be constant and this assumption will be exact. For non-linear network models, the Hessian $\mathbf{H}$ will be a function of $\mathbf{w}$. Since the Hessian is evaluated at $\mathbf{w}_{\text{MP}}$, and since $\mathbf{w}_{\text{MP}}$ depends on α, we see that the result (10.68) actually neglects terms involving $d\lambda_i/d\alpha$ (MacKay, 1992a).

With this approximation, the maximization of (10.67) with respect to α is then straightforward with the result that, at the maximum,

$$2\alpha E_W^{\text{MP}} = W - \sum_{i=1}^{W} \frac{\alpha}{\lambda_i + \alpha} = \gamma \qquad (10.69)$$

where the quantity γ is defined by

$$\gamma \equiv \sum_{i=1}^{W} \frac{\lambda_i}{\lambda_i + \alpha}. \qquad (10.70)$$

This result can be given a simple and elegant interpretation (Gull, 1989). In the absence of any data, the most probable weight vector would be zero, and $E_W^{\text{MP}} = 0$. The value of E_W^{MP} represents the extent to which the weights are driven away from this value by the data. If we assume for the moment that the eigenvalues λ_i are positive then the quantity $\gamma_i = \lambda_i/(\lambda_i + \alpha)$ is a quantity which lies in the range 0 to 1. This can be interpreted geometrically if we imagine rotating the axes of weight space to align them with the eigenvectors of $\mathbf{H}$ as shown schematically in Figure 10.12. Directions for which $\lambda_i \gg \alpha$ will give a contribution close to one in the sum in (10.70) and the corresponding component of the weight vector is determined primarily by the data. Conversely, directions for which $\lambda_i \ll \alpha$ will make a small contribution to the sum, and the corresponding component of the weight vector is determined primarily by the prior and hence is reduced to a small value. (See also the discussions of weight-decay regularization and early stopping in Sections 9.2.1 and 9.2.4 respectively). Thus γ measures the effective number of weights whose values are controlled by the data rather than by the prior. Such weights are called *well-determined parameters*. The quantity $2\alpha E_W^{\text{MP}}$ can be regarded as a χ^2 (Press *et al.*, 1992) for the weights since it can be written in the form $\sum_i w_i^2/\sigma_W^2$ where $\sigma_W^2 = 1/\alpha$. The criterion (10.70) then says that $\chi_W^2 = \gamma$ so that the χ^2 for the weights is given by the number of well-determined parameters. Note that, since $\mathbf{w}_{\text{MP}}$ corresponds to the minimum of $S(\mathbf{w})$ rather than the minimum of $E_D(\mathbf{w})$, the Hessian $\mathbf{H} = \beta\nabla\nabla E_D$ is not evaluated at the

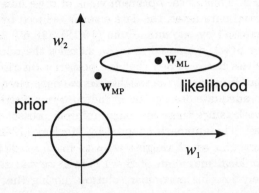

Figure 10.12. Schematic diagram of two directions in weight space after rotation of the axes to align with the eigenvectors of **H**. The circle shows a contour of E_W while the ellipse shows a contour of E_D. In the direction w_1 the eigenvalue λ_1 is small compared with α and so the quantity $\lambda_1/(\lambda_1 + \alpha)$ is close to zero. In the direction w_2 the eigenvalue λ_2 is large compared with α and so the quantity $\lambda_2/(\lambda_2 + \alpha)$ is close to 1.

minimum of E_D, and so there is no guarantee that the eigenvalues λ_i will be positive.

We next consider the maximization of (10.67) with respect to β. Since λ_i are the eigenvalues of $\mathbf{H} = \beta \nabla \nabla E_D$ it follows that λ_i is directly proportional to β and hence

$$\frac{d\lambda_i}{d\beta} = \frac{\lambda_i}{\beta}. \tag{10.71}$$

Thus we have

$$\frac{d}{d\beta} \ln |\mathbf{A}| = \frac{d}{d\beta} \sum_i \ln(\lambda_i + \alpha)$$

$$= \frac{1}{\beta} \sum_i \frac{\lambda_i}{\lambda_i + \alpha}. \tag{10.72}$$

This leads to the following condition satisfied at the maximum of (10.67) with respect to β:

$$2\beta E_D^{\mathrm{MP}} = N - \sum_{i=1}^{W} \frac{\lambda_i}{\lambda_i + \alpha} = N - \gamma. \tag{10.73}$$

Again we can regard $2\beta E_D = \sum_{n=1}^{N}(t^n - y(\mathbf{x}^n; \mathbf{w}))^2/\sigma_D^2$, where $\sigma_D^2 = 1/\beta$, as a χ^2 for the data term. Thus at the optimum value of β we have $\chi_D^2 = N - \gamma$. For every well-determined parameter, the data error is reduced by one unit, and the weight error is increased by one unit. From (10.18), (10.69) and (10.73) we see that the total error $S(\mathbf{w})$, evaluated at $\mathbf{w}_{\text{MP}}$, satisfies the relation $2S_{\text{MP}} = N$.

So far our analysis has assumed that the posterior distribution is described by a single Gaussian function of the weights. As we have already observed, however, this is not an adequate description of the posterior distribution in the case of non-linear networks since there are many minima present in the regularized error function $S(\mathbf{w})$. The approach adopted by MacKay (1992d) is to note that we are using a particular set of weights $\mathbf{w}_{\text{MP}}$ to make predictions, corresponding to a particular local minimum of $S(\mathbf{w})$. Thus, we can set the values of α and β appropriately for this particular solution, noting that different minima may require different values for these hyperparameters. The integral in (10.64) should therefore be interpreted not as an integral over the whole of weight space, but simply as an integral in the neighbourhood of the particular local minimum being considered. By considering a Gaussian approximation to the posterior distribution in the neighbourhood of this minimum, we then arrive at the formalism for determining α and β derived above. Later we shall discuss how to deal with multiple minima.

In a practical implementation of this approach, we need to find the optimum α and β as well as the optimum weight vector $\mathbf{w}_{\text{MP}}$. A simple approach to this problem is to use a standard iterative training algorithm, of the kind described in Chapter 7, to find $\mathbf{w}_{\text{MP}}$, while periodically re-estimating the values of α and β using

$$\alpha^{\text{new}} = \gamma/2E_W \tag{10.74}$$

$$\beta^{\text{new}} = (N - \gamma)/2E_D \tag{10.75}$$

which follow from (10.69) and (10.73). The current estimates of α and β are used to evaluate the quantities on the right-hand sides of (10.74) and (10.75), and the procedure is started by making some initial guess for the values of α and β.

The evidence approach to the determination of α and β is illustrated using the same regression example as in Figure 10.9. The graph shown in Figure 10.13 was obtained by fixing β to its known true value, and shows a plot of γ and $2\alpha E_W$ versus $\ln \alpha$. The value of γ was found by evaluating the Hessian matrix using exact analytic methods described in Section 4.10, and then finding its eigenvalue spectrum. Figure 10.14 shows the corresponding plot of the log evidence for α versus $\ln \alpha$. Comparison of Figures 10.13 and 10.14 shows that the maximum of the evidence occurs approximately when the condition $2\alpha E_W = \gamma$ is satisfied.

As a very rough approximation, we can assume that all of the weight parameters are well determined so that $\gamma = W$, as we would expect to be the case if we have large quantities of data so that $N \gg W$. In this case the re-estimation

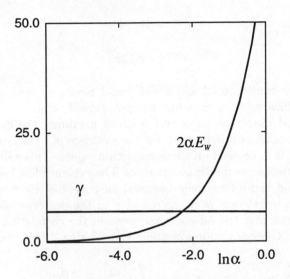

Figure 10.13. This shows a plot of the quantities γ and $2\alpha E_W$ versus $\ln \alpha$ for the example problem shown in Figure 10.9. The parameter β is set to its true value.

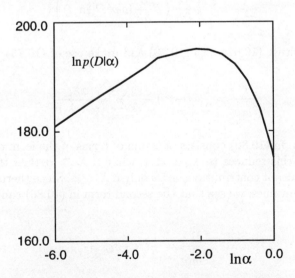

Figure 10.14. This shows a plot of the log evidence for α versus $\ln \alpha$, corresponding to the plots in Figure 10.13. Comparison with Figure 10.13 shows that the maximum of the evidence occurs approximately when the condition $2\alpha E_W = \gamma$ is satisfied. Again the value of β is set to its true value.

formulae of (10.74) and (10.75) reduce to

$$\alpha^{\text{new}} = W/2E_W \tag{10.76}$$

$$\beta^{\text{new}} = N/2E_D \tag{10.77}$$

which are easily implemented and which avoid having to evaluate the Hessian and its eigenvalues, and are therefore computationally fast.

Having found the values of α and β which maximize the evidence, we can construct a Gaussian approximation for the evidence $p(D|\ln\alpha, \ln\beta)$, as a function of $\ln\alpha$ and $\ln\beta$, centred on these maximum values. This will be useful later when we come to discuss model comparison. The evidence has been expressed in terms of $\ln\alpha$ and $\ln\beta$ for reasons discussed on page 408. Here we shall assume that there is no correlation between α and β in the posterior distribution. Exercise 10.11 shows that the off-diagonal terms in the correlation matrix can be neglected in the Gaussian approximation. Considering β first, we write

$$p(D|\ln\beta) = p(D|\ln\beta_{\text{MP}}) \exp\left(-\frac{(\ln\beta - \ln\beta_{\text{MP}})^2}{2\sigma_{\ln\beta}^2}\right). \tag{10.78}$$

From (10.78) it follows that the variance can be calculated using

$$\frac{1}{\sigma_{\ln\beta}^2} = -\beta\frac{\partial}{\partial\beta}\left(\beta\frac{\partial}{\partial\beta}\ln p(D|\ln\beta)\right). \tag{10.79}$$

If we now substitute (10.67) into (10.79) and make use of (10.73) we obtain

$$\frac{1}{\sigma_{\ln\beta}^2} = \frac{1}{2}(N - \gamma) + \frac{1}{2}\sum_{i=1}^{W}\frac{\alpha\lambda_i}{(\alpha + \lambda_i)^2}. \tag{10.80}$$

The second term in (10.80) consists of a sum of terms of the form $\alpha\lambda_i/(\alpha+\lambda_i)^2$. If $\lambda_i \ll \alpha$ then this reduces to $\lambda_i/\alpha \ll 1$, while if $\lambda_i \gg \alpha$ then this reduces to $\alpha/\lambda_i \ll 1$. Significant contributions arise only if $\lambda_i \simeq \alpha$. Since there will typically be few such eigenvalues, we see that the second term in (10.80) can be neglected, and we have

$$\frac{1}{\sigma_{\ln\beta}^2} = \frac{1}{2}(N - \gamma). \tag{10.81}$$

Similarly, we can evaluate the variance of the distribution for $\ln\alpha$ using

$$\frac{1}{\sigma_{\ln\alpha}^2} = -\alpha\frac{\partial}{\partial\alpha}\left(\alpha\frac{\partial}{\partial\alpha}\ln p(D|\ln\alpha)\right). \tag{10.82}$$

Substituting (10.67) into (10.82) and make use of (10.69) we obtain

$$\frac{1}{\sigma_{\ln \alpha}^2} = \frac{\gamma}{2} + \frac{1}{2} \sum_{i=1}^{W} \frac{\alpha \lambda_i}{(\alpha + \lambda_i)^2}. \tag{10.83}$$

Again, the second term can be neglected, for the reasons outlined above, giving

$$\frac{1}{\sigma_{\ln \alpha}^2} = \frac{\gamma}{2}. \tag{10.84}$$

10.5 Integration over hyperparameters

The correct Bayesian treatment for hyperparameters involves marginalization, in other words integration over all possible values. So far we have considered the evidence framework in which this integration is approximated using (10.61), and so the hyperparameters are fixed to their most probable values.

An alternative approach is to perform the integrations over α and β analytically (Buntine and Weigend, 1991; Wolpert, 1993; MacKay, 1994b; Williams, 1995). This can be done by first writing the integral in the form

$$p(\mathbf{w}|D) = \iint p(\mathbf{w}, \alpha, \beta | D) \, d\alpha \, d\beta$$

$$= \frac{1}{p(D)} \iint p(D|\mathbf{w}, \beta) p(\mathbf{w}|\alpha) p(\alpha) p(\beta) \, d\alpha \, d\beta. \tag{10.85}$$

Here we have used Bayes' theorem in the form (10.3). We have then used $p(D|\mathbf{w}, \alpha, \beta) = p(D|\mathbf{w}, \beta)$ since this is the likelihood term and is independent of α. Similarly, $p(\mathbf{w}|\alpha, \beta) = p(\mathbf{w}|\alpha)$ since this is the prior over the weights and hence is independent of β. Finally, we have taken $p(\alpha, \beta) = p(\alpha)p(\beta)$ on the assumption that the two hyperparameters are independent.

To evaluate the integral in (10.85) we need to make specific choices for the priors $p(\alpha)$ and $p(\beta)$. As discussed earlier, these priors should be expressed on logarithmic scales. Thus, we can choose (improper) priors of the form $p(\ln \alpha) = 1$ and $p(\ln \beta) = 1$ which imply

$$p(\alpha) = \frac{1}{\alpha}, \qquad p(\beta) = \frac{1}{\beta}. \tag{10.86}$$

This choice leads to straightforward analytic integrals over the hyperparameters. Consider the integral over α in (10.85). Using (10.6) and (10.10) we have

$$p(\mathbf{w}) = \int_0^\infty p(\mathbf{w}|\alpha) p(\alpha) \, d\alpha$$

$$= \int_0^\infty \frac{1}{Z_W(\alpha)} \exp\left(-\alpha E_W\right) \frac{1}{\alpha} \, d\alpha$$

$$= (2\pi)^{-W/2} \int_0^\infty \exp\left(-\alpha E_W\right) \alpha^{W/2-1} \, d\alpha$$

$$= \frac{\Gamma(W/2)}{(2\pi E_W)^{W/2}} \tag{10.87}$$

where Γ is the standard gamma function (defined on page 28). The integration over β can be performed in exactly the same way with the result

$$p(D|\mathbf{w}) = \frac{\Gamma(N/2)}{(2\pi E_D)^{N/2}}. \tag{10.88}$$

We can now write down the exact (rather than approximate) un-normalized posterior distribution of the weights. The negative logarithm of this posterior, corresponding to an error function, then takes the form

$$-\ln p(\mathbf{w}|D) = \frac{N}{2} \ln E_D + \frac{W}{2} \ln E_W + \text{const.} \tag{10.89}$$

The form (10.89) should be contrasted with the form of the log posterior of the weights for the case in which α and β are assumed to be known. From (10.17) this latter form can be written

$$-\ln p(\mathbf{w}|D) = \beta E_D + \alpha E_W + \text{const.} \tag{10.90}$$

Note that the gradient of (10.90) is given by

$$-\nabla \ln p(\mathbf{w}|D) = \beta \nabla E_D + \alpha \nabla E_W. \tag{10.91}$$

The gradient of (10.89) can be written in an analogous form as

$$-\nabla \ln p(\mathbf{w}|D) = \beta_{\text{eff}} \nabla E_D + \alpha_{\text{eff}} \nabla E_W \tag{10.92}$$

where we have defined

$$\alpha_{\text{eff}} = W/2E_W \tag{10.93}$$

$$\beta_{\text{eff}} = N/2E_D. \tag{10.94}$$

Thus, minimization of the error function of (10.89) could be implemented as a minimization of (10.90) in which the values of β_{eff} and α_{eff} are continuously updated using the re-estimation formulae (10.93) and (10.94) (MacKay, 1994b; Williams, 1995). Notice that this corresponds precisely to the approximation (10.76) and (10.77) to the evidence approach.

10.5.1 *Integration versus maximization*

Formally, Bayesian inference requires that we integrate over the hyperparameters. In practice, one technique which we have considered above, which MacKay (1994b) refers to as the 'MAP' approach (for *maximum posterior*) is to perform this integration analytically. An alternative approach is to use the evidence approximation, which involves finding the values of the hyperparameters which maximize the evidence, and then performing subsequent analysis with the hyperparameters fixed to these values. Since the exact integration is so easily performed, it might appear that this should be the preferred approach (Wolpert, 1993). As well as being exact, it has the advantage of saving the significant computational effort of the evidence approximation, which has to be repeated afresh for each new data set.

However, MacKay (1994b) has argued that in practice the evidence approximation will often be expected to give superior results. The reason that this could in principle be the case, even though formally we should integrate over the hyperparameters, is that in practice with exact integration the remainder of the Bayesian analysis cannot be carried through without introducing further approximations, and these subsequent approximations can lead to much greater inaccuracies than the evidence approach.

Consider the regularization parameter α. We have already seen that the 'effective' value for this parameter differs between the evidence and MAP approaches

$$\alpha_{\text{eff}}^{\text{EV}} = \frac{\gamma}{\sum_i w_i^2}, \qquad \alpha_{\text{eff}}^{\text{MAP}} = \frac{W}{\sum_i w_i^2}. \tag{10.95}$$

Thus, the MAP method effectively estimates an α based on the total number of parameters, while the evidence method makes use of the number of well-determined parameters. MacKay (1994b) attributes this difference to a bias in the MAP approach which is analogous to the distinction between σ_N and σ_{N-1} (Section 2.2).

The MAP approach gives an expression (10.89) for the exact posterior distribution of the weights. In order to make use of this expression in practice, however, it is necessary to make some approximations. Typically, this would involve finding the maximum posterior weight vector $\mathbf{w}_{\text{MP}}$ by a standard non-linear optimization algorithm, and then fitting a Gaussian approximation around this value (Buntine and Weigend, 1991). Clearly the MAP method is capable of finding a true value for $\mathbf{w}_{\text{MP}}$, and so the value found within the evidence approximation must be in error (to the extent that the two approaches differ). However, MacKay (1994b) has argued that the Gaussian approximation found by the evidence approach finds a better representation for most of the *volume* of the posterior probability distribution than does the MAP approach. Since the error bars around the most probable α and β determined from the evidence approximation are given by (10.84) and (10.81), we expect the evidence approximation to be valid when $\gamma \gg 1$ and $N - \gamma \gg 1$. A more thorough discussion of the conditions for the validity of the evidence approximation are given in MacKay (1994b).

10.6 Bayesian model comparison

So far we have considered Bayesian methods for finding the most probable outputs from a neural network, for estimating error bars on these outputs, and for setting the values of regularization coefficients and noise parameters. Our final application for Bayesian methods is to the comparison of different models. As we have already indicated, the Bayesian formalism automatically penalizes highly complex models and so is able to pick out an optimal model without resorting to the use of independent data as in methods such as cross-validation (Section 9.8.1).

Suppose we have a set of models $\mathcal{H}_i$, which might for example include multi-layer perceptron networks with various numbers of hidden units, radial basis function networks and linear models. From Bayes' theorem we can write down the posterior probabilities of the various models $\mathcal{H}_i$, once we have observed the training data set D, in the form

$$P(\mathcal{H}_i|D) = \frac{p(D|\mathcal{H}_i)P(\mathcal{H}_i)}{p(D)} \tag{10.96}$$

where $P(\mathcal{H}_i)$ is the prior probability assigned to model $\mathcal{H}_i$, and the quantity $p(D|\mathcal{H}_i)$, referred to as the *evidence* for $\mathcal{H}_i$ (MacKay, 1992a). This evidence is precisely the denominator in (10.62) in which we have made the conditional dependence on the model $\mathcal{H}_i$ explicit. If we have no reason to assign different priors to different models, then we can compare the relative probabilities of different models on the basis of their evidence. Again, we note the hierarchical nature of this Bayesian framework, with the evidence at this level being given by the denominator of Bayes' theorem at the previous level.

We can provide a simple interpretation of the evidence, and the way it penalizes complex models, as follows (MacKay, 1992a). First, we write the evidence in the form

$$p(D|\mathcal{H}_i) = \int p(D|\mathbf{w}, \mathcal{H}_i) p(\mathbf{w}|\mathcal{H}_i) \, d\mathbf{w}. \tag{10.97}$$

Now consider a single weight parameter w. If the posterior distribution is sharply peaked in weight space around the most probable value w_{MP}, then we can approximate the integral by the value at the maximum times the width $\Delta w_{\text{posterior}}$ of the peak

$$p(D|\mathcal{H}_i) \simeq p(D|w_{\text{MP}}, \mathcal{H}_i) \, p(w_{\text{MP}}|\mathcal{H}_i) \, \Delta w_{\text{posterior}} \tag{10.98}$$

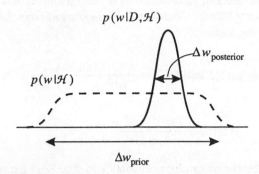

Figure 10.15. An illustration of the Occam factor which arises in the formalism for Bayesian model comparison. The prior probability $p(w|\mathcal{H})$ is taken to be uniform over some large region Δw_{prior}. When the data arrives this collapses to a posterior distribution $p(w|D, \mathcal{H})$ with a width $\Delta w_{\text{posterior}}$. The ratio $\Delta w_{\text{posterior}}/\Delta w_{\text{prior}}$ represents the Occam factor which penalizes the model for having the particular posterior distribution of weights.

as indicated in Figure 10.15. If we take the prior to be uniform over some large interval Δw_{prior} then (10.98) becomes

$$p(D|\mathcal{H}_i) \simeq p(D|w_{\text{MP}}, \mathcal{H}_i) \left(\frac{\Delta w_{\text{posterior}}}{\Delta w_{\text{prior}}} \right). \qquad (10.99)$$

The first term on the right-hand side is the likelihood evaluated for the most probable weight values, while the second term, which is referred to as an Occam factor and which has value < 1, penalizes the network for having this particular posterior distribution of weights. For a model with many parameters, each will generate a similar Occam factor and so the evidence will be correspondingly reduced. Similarly a model in which the parameters have to be finely tuned will also be penalized with a small Occam factor. A model which has a large best-fit likelihood will receive a large contribution to the evidence. However, if the model is also very complex then the Occam factor will be very small. The model with the largest evidence will be determined by the balance between needing large likelihood (to fit the data well) and needing a relatively large Occam factor (so that the model is not too complex).

We can evaluate the evidence more precisely as follows. We first write

$$p(D|\mathcal{H}_i) = \iint p(D|\alpha, \beta, \mathcal{H}_i)p(\alpha, \beta|\mathcal{H}_i) \, d\alpha \, d\beta. \qquad (10.100)$$

The quantity $p(D|\alpha, \beta, \mathcal{H}_i)$ is just the evidence for α and β which we considered earlier (with the dependence on the model again made explicit). Integration over

α and β is easily performed using the Gaussian approximation for the distribution $p(D|\alpha, \beta, \mathcal{H}_i)$ introduced in Section 10.4, in which the variance parameters are given by (10.81) and (10.84). Consider the integration over β. From (10.78) this can be written in the form

$$p(D|\beta_{\mathrm{MP}}) \int \exp\left(-\frac{(\ln\beta - \ln\beta_{\mathrm{MP}})^2}{2\sigma^2_{\ln\beta}}\right) \frac{1}{\ln\Omega} \, d\ln\beta =$$

$$p(D|\beta_{\mathrm{MP}}) \frac{(2\pi)^{1/2}\sigma_{\ln\beta}}{\ln\Omega} \qquad (10.101)$$

where we have taken the prior distribution for $\ln\beta$ to be constant over some large region $\ln\Omega$ which encompasses β_{MP} as well as most of the probability mass of the Gaussian distribution. A similar argument applies to the parameter α. Thus we have

$$p(D|\mathcal{H}_i) \simeq p(D|\alpha_{\mathrm{MP}}, \beta_{\mathrm{MP}}, \mathcal{H}_i) \, 2\pi \, \frac{\sigma_{\ln\alpha}}{\ln\Omega} \frac{\sigma_{\ln\beta}}{\ln\Omega}. \qquad (10.102)$$

We can obtain an expression for $\ln p(D|\alpha_{\mathrm{MP}}, \beta_{\mathrm{MP}}, \mathcal{H}_i)$ by using (10.67) and setting $\alpha = \alpha_{\mathrm{MP}}$ and $\beta = \beta_{\mathrm{MP}}$.

The result (10.67) was obtained by integrating over the posterior distribution $p(\mathbf{w}|D, \mathcal{H}_i)$ represented by a single Gaussian. As we have already remarked, for any given configuration of the weights (corresponding to the mean of the Gaussian) there are many equivalent weight vectors related by symmetries of the network. Here we consider a two-layer network having M hidden units, so that the degree of redundancy is given by $2^M M!$ as discussed in Section 4.4. The Occam factor which we are trying to estimate depends on the ratio of the volume of the posterior distribution in weight space to the volume of the prior. Since our expression for the prior (a Gaussian centred on the origin) already takes account of the many equivalent configurations, we must ensure that our expression for the posterior also takes these into account. Thus, we must include an extra factor of $2^M M!$ in (10.102). Note that this implicitly assumes that there is negligible overlap between the Gaussian functions centred on each such minimum. We shall discuss shortly what to do about the presence of other minima which cannot be related to the current minimum by symmetry transformations.

Rather than evaluate the evidence (10.102) it is more convenient to consider its logarithm. Expressions for $\sigma_{\ln\beta}$ and $\sigma_{\ln\alpha}$ are given by (10.81) and (10.84) respectively. Omitting terms which are the same for different networks, we then obtain

$$\ln p(D|\mathcal{H}_i) = -\alpha_{\mathrm{MP}} E_W^{\mathrm{MP}} - \beta_{\mathrm{MP}} E_D^{\mathrm{MP}} - \frac{1}{2}\ln|\mathbf{A}|$$

$$+ \frac{W}{2} \ln \alpha_{\mathrm{MP}} + \frac{N}{2} \ln \beta_{\mathrm{MP}} + \ln M! + 2 \ln M$$

$$+ \frac{1}{2} \ln \left(\frac{2}{\gamma} \right) + \frac{1}{2} \ln \left(\frac{2}{N - \gamma} \right). \tag{10.103}$$

The new quantity which we need to evaluate here is the determinant of the Hessian matrix $\mathbf{A}$.

In practice the accurate evaluation of the evidence can prove to be very difficult. One of the reasons for this is that the Hessian is given by the product of the eigenvalues and so is very sensitive to such errors. This was not the case for the evaluation of γ used in the optimization of α and β since γ depends on the sum of the eigenvalues and so is less sensitive to errors in the small eigenvalues. Furthermore, the determinant of the Hessian, which measures the volume of the posterior distribution, will be dominated by the small eigenvalues since these correspond to directions in which the distribution is relatively broad. One approach is to take all eigenvalues which are below some (arbitrary) cut-off ϵ and replace them by the value ϵ. A check should then be made to determine if the resulting model comparisons are sensitive to the value of this cut-off. Clearly such an approach is far from satisfactory, and serves to highlight the difficulty of determining the model evidence within the Gaussian approximation framework.

Since the Bayesian approach to model comparison incorporates a mechanism for penalizing over-complex models, we might expect that the model with the largest evidence would give the best results on unseen data, in other words that it would have the best generalization properties. MacKay (1992d) and Thodberg (1993) both report observing empirical (anti) correlation between model evidence and generalization error. However, this correlation is far from perfect. Although we expect some correlation between a model having high evidence and the model generalizing well, the evidence is not measuring the same thing as generalization performance. In particular, we can identify several distinctions between these quantities:

1. The test error is measured on a finite data set and so is a noisy quantity.

2. The evidence provides a quantitative measure of the relative probabilities of different models. Although one particular model may have the highest probability, there may be other models for which the probability is still significant. Thus the model with the highest evidence will not necessarily give the best performance. We shall return to this point shortly when we discuss committees of networks.

3. If we had two different models which happened to give rise to the same most-probable interpolant, then they would necessarily have the same generalization performance, but the more complex model would have a larger Occam factor and hence would have a smaller evidence. Thus, for two models which make the same predictions, the Bayesian approach favours the simpler model.

4. The generalization error, in the form considered above, is measured using a network with weights set to the maximum of the posterior distribution. The evidence, however, takes account of the complete posterior distribution around the most probable value. (As we noted in Section 10.3, however, for the case of a Gaussian posterior distribution, and with a local linearization of the network function, the integration over the posterior has no effect on the network predictions.)

5. The Bayesian analysis implicitly assumes that the set of models under consideration contains the 'truth' as a particular case. If all of the models are poorly matched to the problem then the relative evidences of different models may be misleading. MacKay (1992d) argues that a poor correlation between evidence and generalization error can be used to infer the presence of limitations in the models.

An additional reason why the correlation between evidence and test error may be poor is that there will be inaccuracies in evaluating the evidence. These arise from the use of a Gaussian approximation to the posterior distribution, and are particularly important if the Hessian matrix has one or more very small eigenvalues, as discussed above.

Further insight into the issue of model complexity in the Bayesian framework has been provided by Neal (1994) who has argued that, provided the complete Bayesian analysis is performed without approximation, there is no need to limit the complexity of a model even when there is relatively little training data available. Many real-world applications of neural networks (for example the recognition of handwritten characters) involve a multitude of complications and we do not expect them to be accurately solved by a simple network having a few hidden units. Neal (1994) was therefore led to consider the behaviour of priors over weights in the limit as the number of hidden units tends to infinity. He showed that, provided the parameters governing the priors are scaled appropriately with the number of units, the resulting prior distributions over network functions are well behaved in this limit. Such priors could in principle permit the use of very large networks. In practice, we may wish to limit the complexity in order to ensure that Gaussian assumptions are valid, or that Monte Carlo techniques (discussed in Section 10.9) can produce acceptable answers in reasonable computational time.

10.7 Committees of networks

In Section 9.6 we discussed techniques for combining several network 'modules' together in order to obtain improved performance. Here we shall see how such *committees* of networks arise naturally in the Bayesian framework. When we evaluated the evidence in (10.103) we took account of the multiple solutions due to symmetries in the network. We did not, however, allow for the presence of multiple, non-equivalent minima. If we train our network several times starting from different random initial weight configurations then we will typically discover several such solutions. We can then model the posterior distribution using a set of Gaussians, one centred on each local minimum, in which we assume that there is negligible overlap between the Gaussians.

Consider the predictions made by such a posterior distribution when the network is presented with a new input vector. The posterior distribution of the weights can be represented as

$$p(\mathbf{w}|D) = \sum_i p(m_i, \mathbf{w}|D)$$

$$= \sum_i p(\mathbf{w}|m_i, D)P(m_i|D) \tag{10.104}$$

where m_i denotes one of the non-equivalent minima and all of its symmetric equivalents. This distribution is used to determine other quantities by integration over the whole of weight space. For instance, the mean output predicted by the committee is given by

$$\overline{y} = \int y(\mathbf{x}; \mathbf{w})p(\mathbf{w}|D) \, d\mathbf{w}$$

$$= \sum_i P(m_i|D) \int_{\Gamma_i} y(\mathbf{x}; \mathbf{w})p(\mathbf{w}|m_i, D) \, d\mathbf{w}$$

$$= \sum_i P(m_i|D)\overline{y}_i \tag{10.105}$$

where Γ_i denotes the region of weight space surrounding the ith local minimum, and $\overline{y}_i$ is the corresponding network prediction averaged over this region. Here we have assumed that there is negligible overlap between the distributions centred on each minimum. From (10.105) we see that the predicted output is just a linear combination of the predictions made by each of the networks corresponding to distinct local minima, weighted by the posterior probability of that solution. Note that, strictly speaking, in a practical implementation the weighting for each minimum should be adjusted according to the probability of that minimum being found by the particular parameter optimization algorithm being used, with minima which are more likely to be discovered receiving less weight. For large problems such an approach is infeasible, however, since each minimum will typically only be seen once so that determination of the probabilities of finding the minima will not be possible.

We can extend this result further by considering different models $\mathcal{H}_i$, such as networks with different numbers of hidden units or different kinds of models. In the same way that variables such as hyperparameters are integrated out of the model, so if our model space consists of several distinct models, then Bayesian inference requires that, instead of just picking the most probable model, we should sum over all models. The distribution of some quantity Q, given a data set D, can be written

$$p(Q|D) = \sum_i p(Q, \mathcal{H}_i|D)$$

$$= \sum_i p(Q|D, \mathcal{H}_i)p(\mathcal{H}_i|D) \qquad (10.106)$$

which again is a linear combination of the predictions made by each model separately, where the weighting coefficients are given by the posterior probabilities of the models. We can compute the weighting coefficients by evaluating the evidences, multiplying by the model priors, and then normalizing so that the coefficients sum to 1.

Committees bring two advantages. First they can lead to improved generalization, as was noted in Section 9.6. This is to be expected since the extension from a single Gaussian to a Gaussian mixture provides a more accurate model for the posterior distribution of weights. The second benefit of considering a committee is that the spread of predictions between members of the committee makes a contribution to the estimated error bars on our predictions in addition to those identified already, leading to more accurate estimation of error bars.

In practice, the direct application of such procedures generally leads to poor results since the integral over the Gaussian approximation to the posterior gives only a poor estimation of the evidence (Thodberg, 1993). A more pragmatic approach is to use the evidence simply as a rough indicator, and to select a committee of networks whose members have reasonably high evidence, and then form linear, or non-linear, combinations of the outputs of the committee members using techniques discussed in Section 9.6. Indeed, the method of stacked generalization (Section 9.8.2) can be viewed here as a cross-validatory approach to estimating the posterior probabilities of the members of the committee.

10.8   Practical implementation of Bayesian techniques

Since we have covered a lot of ground in our discussion of Bayesian methods, we summarize here the main steps needed to implement these techniques for practical applications. We restrict attention to the evidence framework with the use of Gaussian approximations.

1. Choose initial values for the hyperparameters α and β. Initialize the weights in the network using values drawn from the prior distribution.

2. Train the network using a standard non-linear optimization algorithm (Chapter 7) to minimize the total error function $S(\mathbf{w})$.

3. Every few cycles of the algorithm, re-estimate values for α and β using (10.74) and (10.75), with γ calculated using (10.70). This requires evaluation of the Hessian matrix (Section 4.10) and evaluation of its eigenvalue spectrum.

4. Repeat steps 1–3 for different random initial choices for the network weights in order to find different local minima. In principle, a check should be made that the different solutions are not simply related by a symmetry transformation of the network (Section 4.4).

5. Repeat steps 1–4 for a selection of different network models, and compare their evidences using (10.103). Eigenvalues which are smaller than a cutoff value are omitted from the sum in evaluating the log determinant of the Hessian. If a committee of networks is to be used it is probably best to choose a selection of the better networks on the basis of their evidences, but then to use the techniques of Section 9.6 to compute suitable weighting coefficients.

Examples of the practical application of Bayesian techniques are given in Thodberg (1993) and MacKay (1995b).

10.9 Monte Carlo methods

In the conventional (maximum likelihood) approach to network training, the bulk of the computational effort is concerned with *optimization*, in order to find the minimum of an error function. By contrast, in the Bayesian approach, the central operations require *integration* over multi-dimensional spaces. For example, the evaluation of the distribution of network outputs involves an integral over weight space given by (10.28). Similarly, the evaluation of the evidence for the hyperparameters also involves an integral over weight space given by (10.64). So far in this chapter, we have concentrated on the use of a Gaussian approximation for the posterior distribution of the weights, which allows these integrals to be performed analytically. This also allows the problem of integration to be replaced again with one of optimization (needed to find the mean of the Gaussian distribution). If we wish to avoid the Gaussian approximation then we might seek numerical techniques for evaluating the corresponding integrals directly.

Many standard numerical integration techniques, which can be used successfully for integrations over a small number of variables, are totally unsuitable for integrals of the kind we are considering, which involve integration over spaces of hundreds or thousands of weight parameters. For instance, if we try to sample weight space on some regular grid then, since the number of grid points grows exponentially with the dimensionality (see the discussion of the 'curse of dimensionality' in Section 1.4), the computational effort would be prohibitive. We resort instead to various forms of random sampling of points in weight space. Such methods are called *Monte Carlo* techniques.

The integrals we wish to evaluate take the form

$$I = \int F(\mathbf{w}) p(\mathbf{w}|D) \, d\mathbf{w} \tag{10.107}$$

where $p(\mathbf{w}|D)$ represents posterior distribution of the weights, and $F(\mathbf{w})$ is some integrand. The basic idea is to approximate (10.107) with the finite sum

$$I \simeq \frac{1}{L} \sum_{i=1}^{L} F(\mathbf{w}_i) \tag{10.108}$$

where $\{\mathbf{w}_i\}$ represents a sample of weight vectors generated from the distribution $p(\mathbf{w}|D)$. The key difficulty is that in general it is very difficult to generate a set of vectors having the required distribution.

One approach would be to consider some simpler distribution $q(\mathbf{w})$ from which we can easily generate suitable vectors. We can then write

$$I = \int F(\mathbf{w}) \frac{p(\mathbf{w}|D)}{q(\mathbf{w})} q(\mathbf{w}) \, d\mathbf{w}$$

$$\simeq \frac{1}{L} \sum_{i=1}^{L} F(\mathbf{w}_i) \frac{p(\mathbf{w}_i|D)}{q(\mathbf{w}_i)} \tag{10.109}$$

which makes use of the fact that we can easily evaluate $p(\mathbf{w}|D)$, even though we cannot easily generate vectors having this distribution. In fact we cannot even normalize $p(\mathbf{w}|D)$, and so we should modify (10.109) slightly and use

$$I \simeq \frac{\sum_{i=1}^{L} F(\mathbf{w}_i) \widetilde{p}(\mathbf{w}_i|D)/q(\mathbf{w}_i)}{\sum_{i=1}^{L} \widetilde{p}(\mathbf{w}_i|D)/q(\mathbf{w}_i)} \tag{10.110}$$

where $\widetilde{p}(\mathbf{w}_i|D)$ is the un-normalized distribution. This approach, which is called *importance sampling*, does not solve our problem, because for neural networks the value of $p(\mathbf{w}|D)$ is typically very small except in extremely narrow regions of weight space. Thus, for any simple choice of $q(\mathbf{w})$, most of the vectors will fall in regions where $p(\mathbf{w}|D)$ is small, and so a prohibitively large sample of vectors would be required to build up an accurate approximation to the integral.

We must therefore face the task of generating a sample of vectors $\mathbf{w}$ representative of the distribution $p(\mathbf{w}|D)$. To do this effectively, we must search through weight space to find regions where $p(\mathbf{w}|D)$ is reasonably large. This can be done by considering a sequence of vectors, where each successive vector depends on the previous vector as well as having a random component. Such techniques are called *Markov chain Monte Carlo* methods, and are reviewed in Neal (1993). The simplest example is a *random walk* in which at successive steps we have

$$\mathbf{w}_{\text{new}} = \mathbf{w}_{\text{old}} + \boldsymbol{\epsilon} \tag{10.111}$$

where $\boldsymbol{\epsilon}$ is some small random vector, chosen for instance from a spherical Gaussian distribution having a small variance parameter. Note that successive vectors generated in this way will no longer be independent. As a result of this dependence, the number of vectors needed to achieve a given accuracy in approximating an integral using (10.108) may be much larger than if the vectors had been independent.

As it stands, such an approach does not yet achieve the desired aim of sampling preferentially the regions where $p(\mathbf{w}|D)$ is large. This can be achieved by a modification to the procedure, known as the *Metropolis* algorithm (Metropolis *et al.*, 1953), which was developed to study the statistical mechanics of physical systems. The idea is to make candidate steps of the form (10.111), but to reject a proportion of the steps which lead to a reduction in the value of $p(\mathbf{w}|D)$. This must be done with great care, however, in order to ensure that resulting sample of weight vectors represents the required distribution. In the Metropolis algorithm this is achieved by using the following criterion:

if $p(\mathbf{w}_{\text{new}}|D) > p(\mathbf{w}_{\text{old}}|D)$ accept

if $p(\mathbf{w}_{\text{new}}|D) < p(\mathbf{w}_{\text{old}}|D)$ accept with probability $\dfrac{p(\mathbf{w}_{\text{new}}|D)}{p(\mathbf{w}_{\text{old}}|D)}$. $\qquad$ (10.112)

In terms of an error function $E = -\ln p$, this can be expressed as

if $E_{\text{new}} < E_{\text{old}}$ accept

if $E_{\text{new}} > E_{\text{old}}$ accept with probability $\exp\{-(E_{\text{new}} - E_{\text{old}})\}$. $\qquad$ (10.113)

The candidate steps are generated in a way which satisfies the principle of *detailed balance*. This requires that, if the current vector is $\mathbf{w}_1$, the probability of generating a candidate vector $\mathbf{w}_2$ must be the same as the probability of generating $\mathbf{w}_1$ as the candidate vector if the current vector is $\mathbf{w}_2$. The random walk formula (10.111), for example, with ϵ governed by spherical Gaussian distribution, clearly satisfies this property. The Metropolis algorithm has been used with great success in many applications. In the case of the Bayesian integrals needed for neural networks, however, it can still prove to be deficient due to the strong correlations in the posterior distribution, as illustrated in Figure 10.16.

This problem can be tackled by taking account of information concerning the gradient of $p(\mathbf{w}|D)$ and using this to choose search directions which favour regions of high posterior probability. For neural networks, the gradient information is easily obtained using back-propagation. Again, great care must be taken to ensure that the gradient information is used in such a way that the distribution of weight vectors which is generated corresponds to the required distribution. A procedure for achieving this, known as *hybrid Monte Carlo*, was developed by Duane *et al.* (1987), and was applied to the Bayesian treatment of neural networks by Neal (1992, 1994).

One of the potential difficulties which still remains is the tendency for such algorithms to spend a long time in the neighbourhood of poor local maxima of the probability (corresponding to local minima of the regularized error function), and so fail to discover good maxima which make a much more significant contribution to the integral. A standard technique for improving the situation is called

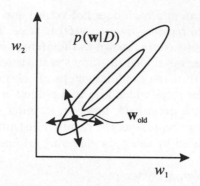

Figure 10.16. When the standard Metropolis algorithm is applied to the evaluation of integrals in the Bayesian treatment of neural networks, a large proportion of the candidate steps are rejected due to the high correlations in the posterior distribution. Starting from the point $\mathbf{w}_{\text{old}}$, almost all potential steps (shown by the arrows) will lead to a decrease in $p(\mathbf{w}|D)$. This problem becomes even more severe in spaces of higher dimensionality.

simulated annealing (following an analogy with physical systems) introduced by Kirkpatrick *et al.* (1983). For the standard Metropolis algorithm, this is achieved by modifying (10.113) to give

$$\text{if } E_{\text{new}} < E_{\text{old}} \text{ accept}$$
$$\text{if } E_{\text{new}} > E_{\text{old}} \text{ accept with probability } \exp\left\{-\frac{(E_{\text{new}} - E_{\text{old}})}{T}\right\} \quad (10.114)$$

where T is a parameter generally referred to as *temperature*. This algorithm leads to a sequence of vectors which asymptotically represent the distribution $\exp\{-E(\mathbf{w}|D)/T\}$. For $T = 1$ we recover the desired distribution. For $T \gg 1$, however, the system can explore weight space much more freely, and can readily escape from local error function minima. Simulated annealing involves starting with a large value for T and then gradually reducing its value during the course of the simulation, giving the system a much better chance to settle into a region of high probability. The application of simulated annealing to the Monte Carlo algorithm for the Bayesian treatment of neural networks has been considered by Neal (1992, 1994) although was not found to be essential.

By using the hybrid Monte Carlo algorithm it is possible to generate a suitable sample of weight vectors $\mathbf{w}_i$ for practical applications of neural networks in reasonable computational time. For a given test input vector $\mathbf{x}$, the corresponding network predictions $y(\mathbf{x}; \mathbf{w}_i)$ represent a sample from the distribution $p(y|\mathbf{x}, D)$. This allows the uncertainties on the network outputs, associated with a new input vector, to be assessed. The estimation of the evidence, however, remains a difficult problem. Another significant problem with Monte Carlo methods is the difficulty in defining a suitable termination criterion. Despite these drawbacks, Monte Carlo techniques offer a promising approach to Bayesian inference in the context of neural networks.

10.10 Minimum description length

An alternative framework for discussing model complexity is provided by the *minimum description length* principle (Rissanen, 1978). Although conceptually very different, this approach leads to a formalism which is essentially identical to the Bayesian one. Imagine that a 'sender' wishes to transmit a data set D to a 'receiver', as indicated in Figure 10.17, using a message of the shortest possible length (where the length of the message might be measured by the number of bits, for instance). One approach would be simply to transmit a suitably encoded form of the data set itself using some fixed coding scheme with the assumption that the data points are independent. However, if there are systematic aspects to the data, the details of which are not known to the receiver in advance of seeing the data, then we would expect to be able to use a shorter message if we first transmit information specifying some model $\mathcal{H}$ which captures those aspects, using a message of length $L(\mathcal{H})$, and then send a second message specifying how the actual data set differs from that predicted by the model. We can regard $L(\mathcal{H})$ as a measure of the complexity of the model, since a more complex model will require more information to describe it. The message needed to send the discrepancy information has length denoted by $L(D|\mathcal{H})$, which can be viewed as an error term. We shall suppose that the input data values are known already to the receiver, since we are not trying to predict the input data, only the output data. Thus the total length of the message which is sent is given by

$$\text{description length} = \underbrace{L(D|\mathcal{H})}_{\text{error}} + \underbrace{L(\mathcal{H})}_{\text{complexity}} \qquad (10.115)$$

We can see that the goal of choosing the shortest description length leads to a natural form of Occam's razor. A very simple model will be a poor predictor of the data, and so the errors will be large and this will lead to a large error term in (10.115). Allowing for a more complex model can lead to a reduction in the error contribution, but too complex a model will require a lot of information to specify and hence will lead to a large complexity term in (10.115). Intuitively we expect the shortest description length to occur when the model $\mathcal{H}$ gives an accurate representation of the statistical process which generated the data, and we also expect that, on average, this model will have the best generalization properties.

In Section 6.10 we showed that, to transmit information about a quantity x efficiently, a sender and receiver should agree on a suitable probability distribution $p(x)$. The minimum amount of information, in bits, needed to transmit the value of x is then given by $-\log_2 p(x)$. If $p(x)$ happens to be the true distribution for x then this minimum amount of information will take a smaller value than for

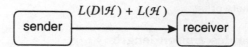

Figure 10.17. Illustration of the concept of minimum description length. A data set D can be transmitted from a sender to a receiver by first sending a prescription for a model $\mathcal{H}$, using a message of length $L(\mathcal{H})$, and then transmitting the discrepancies between the data predicted by $\mathcal{H}$ and the actual data, which represents a message of length $L(D|\mathcal{H})$. The principle of minimum description length then selects as optimal that model which minimizes the total information transmitted.

any other choice of distribution. For convenience we shall measure information using logarithms to base e in which case the information, given by $-\ln p(x)$, is measured in 'nats'. This allows us to write the description length in (10.115) in the form

$$\text{description length} = -\ln p(D|\mathcal{H}) - \ln p(\mathcal{H}) = -\ln p(\mathcal{H}|D) - \ln p(D) \quad (10.116)$$

so that the description length is equivalent, up to an additive constant $-\ln p(D)$, to the negative logarithm of the posterior probability of the model given the data set.

We now consider the problem of determining the values for the weights in a network model. Suppose that we consider a particular weight vector, which we can regard as a 'most probable' set of weights. The cost of transmitting the weights and the data given the model can be written as the sum of two terms

$$L(\mathbf{w}, D|\mathcal{H}) = -\ln p(D|\mathbf{w}, \mathcal{H}) - \ln p(\mathbf{w}|\mathcal{H}) \quad (10.117)$$

where the second term on the right-hand side represents the cost of specifying the weights, and the first term is the cost of specifying the data for given values of the weights (i.e. the cost of specifying the errors between the true values for the data and the values predicted by the model with the weights set to the given values). In order to transmit this information, the sender and receiver need to agree on specific forms for the distributions. Suppose we model the distribution of the weights as a zero mean Gaussian with variance α^{-1}

$$p(\mathbf{w}|\mathcal{H}) = \left(\frac{\alpha}{2\pi}\right)^{W/2} \exp\left\{-\frac{\alpha}{2}\|\mathbf{w}\|^2\right\} \quad (10.118)$$

where W is the total number of weight parameters. Similarly let us suppose that we model the distribution of errors by a Gaussian with variance β^{-1} centred on the prediction $y(\mathbf{x}; \mathbf{w})$ made by the model

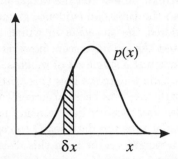

Figure 10.18. When a continuous variable x is encoded to some finite precision δx under a distribution $p(x)$, the information required to describe the value of the variable is given by the negative logarithm of the probability mass under the distribution, shown by the shaded region.

$$p(D|\mathbf{w}, \mathcal{H}) = \left(\frac{\beta}{2\pi}\right)^{N/2} \exp\left\{-\frac{\beta}{2} \sum_{n=1}^{N} (y^n - t^n)^2\right\}. \tag{10.119}$$

Then the description length (10.117) can be written in the form

$$L(D|\mathcal{H}) = \frac{\beta}{2} \sum_{n=1}^{N} (y^n - t^n)^2 + \frac{\alpha}{2}\|\mathbf{w}\|^2 + \text{const.} \tag{10.120}$$

which we recognize as the standard sum-of-squares error function with a weight-decay regularizer.

An additional consideration for continuous variables, which we have so far ignored, is the precision with which they are encoded. We cannot specify a continuous quantity x exactly since that would require an infinite message length, so instead we specify its value to within some small tolerance δx. The message length needed to do this is given by the negative logarithm of the probability mass within this range of uncertainty, as indicated in Figure 10.18. If the tolerance δx is sufficiently small, then this probability mass is given to a good approximation by $p(x)\delta x$.

For the data term $\ln p(D|\mathbf{w}, \mathcal{H})$ the additional contribution from the precision δD of the variables represents an irrelevant constant. For the weights, however, the precision plays an important role, since if the weights are specified to a low precision they can be transmitted with a shorter message, but the errors on the data will then typically be larger and hence will need a longer message to transmit them. Again, there is a trade-off, which leads to an optimal level of precision for the weights. For the case of Gaussian distributions, the calculations can be made explicitly (Wallace and Freeman, 1987). The optimal precision for the weights is related to the posterior uncertainty in the parameters given by

$\mathbf{A}^{-1}$ where $\mathbf{A} = -\nabla\nabla p(\mathbf{w}|D, \mathcal{H})$. The value of the description length with the parameters set to their optimal values, and the weight precision set to its optimal value, is then equivalent to the Bayesian evidence given by (10.67).

So far we have considered the situation in which a 'most probable' set of weight values is transmitted. As we have seen, however, the Bayesian approach requires that we consider not just a single set of weights, but a posterior probability distribution of weights. One way to see how this arises within the description-length framework is through the 'bits back' argument of Hinton and van Camp (1993). Suppose the sender and receiver have already agreed on some prior distribution $p(\mathbf{w}|\mathcal{H})$. The sender uses the data set D to compute the posterior distribution and then picks a weight vector from this distribution, to within some very fine tolerance $\delta\mathbf{w}$, using a string of random bits. This weight vector can be communicated to the receiver by encoding with respect to the prior, with a description length of $-\ln(p(\mathbf{w}|\mathcal{H})\delta\mathbf{w})$. Having sent the weight vector, the data can then be transmitted with description length $-\ln(p(D|\mathbf{w}, \mathcal{H})\delta D)$. Once the data has been received, the receiver can then run the same training algorithm as used by the sender and hence compute the posterior distribution. The receiver can then deduce the string of random bits which were used by the sender to pick the weight vector from the posterior distribution. Since these bits could be used to communicate some other, quite unrelated, message, they should not be included in the description length cost. Thus, there is a 'refund' in the description length given by $+\ln(p(\mathbf{w}|D, \mathcal{H})\delta\mathbf{w})$, which is just the length of the bit string needed to pick the weight vector from the posterior distribution with precision $\delta\mathbf{w}$. The net description length is therefore given by

$$-\ln(p(\mathbf{w}|\mathcal{H})\delta\mathbf{w}) - \ln(p(D|\mathbf{w}, \mathcal{H})\delta D) + \ln(p(\mathbf{w}|D, \mathcal{H})\delta\mathbf{w})$$

$$= -\ln p(D|\mathcal{H}) - \ln \delta D \qquad (10.121)$$

where we have used Bayes' theorem. This is the correct description length for encoding the data, given the model, to precision δD.

In this chapter we have considered two approaches to determining the posterior distribution of the weights. The first is to find the maximum of the posterior distribution, and then to fit a Gaussian function centred on this maximum. The second approach is to express the posterior distribution in terms of a sample of representative vectors, generated using Monte Carlo techniques. We end this chapter by discussing briefly a third approach, known as *ensemble learning*, which again assumes a Gaussian distribution, but in which the mean and the variance are allowed to evolve during the learning process (Hinton and van Camp, 1993). Learning can be expressed in terms of a minimization of the Kullback–Leibler distance (Section 2.5.5) between the model distribution and the true posterior. In general this is not computationally tractable. However, for two-layer networks with linear output units, and with the assumption that the covariance matrix of the model distribution is diagonal, the required derivatives can be evaluated to any desired precision. The hope is that the resulting distribution, which need no longer be centred on the most probable weights, might give a better representation of the posterior distribution. A potentially important limitation of this approach, however, is the neglect of off-diagonal terms in the model distribution.

Exercises

10.1 ($\star\star$) Consider a Gaussian distribution of the form

$$p(t) = \frac{1}{(2\pi\sigma^2)^{1/2}} \exp\left(-\frac{(t - \bar{t})^2}{2\sigma^2}\right) \tag{10.122}$$

and show that this distribution has mean $\bar{t}$ and variance σ^2 so that

$$\int_{-\infty}^{\infty} t\,p(t)\,dt = \bar{t} \tag{10.123}$$

$$\int_{-\infty}^{\infty} (t - \bar{t})^2 p(t)\,dt = \sigma^2. \tag{10.124}$$

Using these results, show that the mean of the distribution (10.32) is given by y_{MP} and that its variance is given by (10.34). (Hint: in each case evaluate the integral over t first, and then evaluate the integral over $\mathbf{w}$ using the techniques of Appendix B).

10.2 ($\star\star$) Use the results derived in Appendix B to evaluate the integral in (10.32) directly. Do this by expanding the square in the exponent and collecting together the terms which are quadratic in $\Delta\mathbf{w}$. Then use the result (B.22) to show that the distribution can be written as a Gaussian of the form

$$p(t|\mathbf{x}, D) = \frac{1}{(2\pi\sigma_t^2)^{1/2}} \exp\left(-\frac{(t - y_{\text{MP}})^2}{2\sigma_t^2}\right) \tag{10.125}$$

in which the mean is given by

$$\bar{t} = y_{\text{MP}} \tag{10.126}$$

and the variance is given by

$$\sigma_t^2 = \frac{1}{\beta - \beta^2 \mathbf{g}^{\mathrm{T}}(\mathbf{A} + \beta\mathbf{g}\mathbf{g}^{\mathrm{T}})^{-1}\mathbf{g}}. \tag{10.127}$$

Simplify this expression for the variance by multiplying numerator and denominator by the factor

$$\mathbf{g}^{\mathrm{T}}(\mathbf{I} + \beta\mathbf{A}^{-1}\mathbf{g}\mathbf{g}^{\mathrm{T}})\mathbf{g} \tag{10.128}$$

where $\mathbf{I}$ is the unit matrix. Hence, using the general result $(\mathbf{BC})^{-1} = \mathbf{C}^{-1}\mathbf{B}^{-1}$, show that the variance can be written in the form

$$\sigma_t^2 = \frac{1}{\beta} + \mathbf{g}^T\mathbf{A}^{-1}\mathbf{g}. \tag{10.129}$$

10.3 ($\star\star$) Use the results (10.123) and (10.124), together with the results obtained in Appendix B, to show that the mean of the distribution (10.52), with $p(\mathbf{w}|D)$ given by (10.47), is given by a_{MP} and that the variance is given by (10.54).

10.4 ($\star\star$) The expressions (10.126) and (10.129) for the mean and variance of the distribution of target values were derived after linearizing the network mapping function around the most probable weights, using (10.30). Consider this expansion taken to next order:

$$y(x;\mathbf{w}) = y(x;\mathbf{w}_{\mathrm{MP}}) + \mathbf{g}^T\Delta\mathbf{w} + \frac{1}{2}\Delta\mathbf{w}^T\mathbf{G}\Delta\mathbf{w} \tag{10.130}$$

where $\mathbf{G} = \nabla\nabla y|_{\mathbf{w}_{\mathrm{MP}}}$. By using (10.123) and (10.124) with $p(t|D)$ given by (10.32), and neglecting terms which are quartic in $\Delta\mathbf{w}$, derive the following results for the mean and variance of the distribution of target values:

$$\bar{t} = y_{\mathrm{MP}} + \frac{1}{2}\mathrm{Tr}(\mathbf{A}^{-1}\mathbf{G}) \tag{10.131}$$

$$\sigma_t^2 = \frac{1}{\beta} + \mathbf{g}^T\mathbf{A}^{-1}\mathbf{g} - \frac{1}{4}\left\{\mathrm{Tr}(\mathbf{A}^{-1}\mathbf{G})\right\}^2. \tag{10.132}$$

10.5 ($\star$) The next four exercises develop the extension of the Bayesian formalism to the case of more general prior distributions given by (10.22) in which the weights are partitioned into groups labelled by k. First, show that the prior (10.22) can be written

$$p(\mathbf{w}) = \frac{1}{Z_W}\exp\left\{-\frac{1}{2}\sum_k \alpha_k\mathbf{w}^T\mathbf{I}_k\mathbf{w}\right\} \tag{10.133}$$

where $\mathbf{I}_k$ is a matrix whose elements are all zero, except for some elements on the leading diagonal $I_{ii} = 1$ where i corresponds to a weight from group k. Show that the normalization coefficient Z_W is given by

$$Z_W = \prod_k \left(\frac{2\pi}{\alpha_k}\right)^{W_k/2} \tag{10.134}$$

where W_k is the number of weights in group k. Verify that the distribution of network outputs is again given by (10.33), with variance given by (10.34) in which the Hessian matrix $\mathbf{A}$ is given by

$$\mathbf{A} = \beta \nabla \nabla E_D + \sum_k \alpha_k \mathbf{I}_k. \qquad (10.135)$$

10.6 ($\star$) Consider a real, symmetric matrix $\mathbf{A}$, whose elements depend on some parameter α. From the results given in Appendix A, we can diagonalize $\mathbf{A}$ by using the eigenvector equation in the form

$$\mathbf{A}\mathbf{v}_j = \eta_j \mathbf{v}_j \qquad (10.136)$$

and then defining the matrix $\mathbf{V} \equiv (\mathbf{v}_1, \ldots, \mathbf{v}_W)$ so that $\mathbf{V}^T \mathbf{A} \mathbf{V} = \mathbf{D}$ where $\mathbf{D} \equiv \mathrm{diag}(\eta_1, \ldots, \eta_W)$. Use this result, together with the fact that $\mathbf{V}$ is an orthogonal matrix so that $\mathbf{V}^T \mathbf{V} = \mathbf{V} \mathbf{V}^T = \mathbf{I}$, to show that

$$\frac{\partial}{\partial \alpha} \ln |\mathbf{A}| = \mathrm{Tr}\left\{ \mathbf{A}^{-1} \frac{\partial}{\partial \alpha} \mathbf{A} \right\}. \qquad (10.137)$$

10.7 ($\star\star$) For the weight prior (10.133) considered in Exercise 10.5, find an expression for the logarithm of the evidence $p(D|\{\alpha_k\}, \beta)$ analogous to the expression given by (10.67). Use the result (10.137) to show that the following conditions are satisfied when this log evidence is maximized with respect to β and α_k:

$$2\beta E_D = N - \gamma \qquad (10.138)$$

$$2\alpha_k E_{Wk} = \gamma_k \qquad (10.139)$$

where $\gamma \equiv \sum_k \gamma_k$, $2E_{Wk} \equiv \mathbf{w}^T \mathbf{I}_k \mathbf{w}$, and

$$\gamma_k = \sum_j \left\{ \frac{\eta_j - \alpha_k}{\eta_j} (\mathbf{V}^T \mathbf{I}_k \mathbf{V})_{jj} \right\}. \qquad (10.140)$$

Here η_j are the eigenvalues of $\mathbf{A}$ as in (10.136) with $\mathbf{A}$ given by (10.135). Verify that, if all of the weights are included in the prior, and all of the coefficients α_k are constrained to a single common value α, then these results reduce to the ones presented in the text for the simple weight-decay prior (10.9). We see that the use of the more general prior (10.133) requires the eigenvectors of the Hessian to be computed, as well as the eigenvalues. The use of the standard weight-decay prior (10.9) requires only the eigenvalues, leading to a saving of computational effort (Press *et al.*, 1992).

10.8 ($\star\star$) By using the results of the previous exercise, together with (10.79) and analogous expressions for the variances $\sigma^2_{\ln \alpha_k}$, show that the Gaussian approximation for the evidence $p(D|\{\alpha_k\}, \beta)$ around the most probable values has variances given approximately by

$$\frac{1}{\sigma^2_{\ln \beta}} = (N - \gamma)/2 \qquad (10.141)$$

$$\frac{1}{\sigma_{\ln \alpha_k}^2} = \gamma_k/2. \tag{10.142}$$

Hence show that the contribution to the logarithm of the model evidence arising from the distribution of values of α_k and β is given by

$$\frac{1}{2} \ln \left(\frac{2}{N - \gamma} \right) + \frac{1}{2} \sum_k \ln \left(\frac{2}{\gamma_k} \right). \tag{10.143}$$

10.9 ($\star$) Show that, for the logistic sigmoid $g(a)$ given by (10.45), the function $g(a) - 0.5$ is anti-symmetric. Hence show that the marginalized network output $P(\mathcal{C}_1|\mathbf{x}, D)$ given by (10.56) is equal to 0.5 when $a_{\mathrm{MP}}(\mathbf{x}) = 0$.

10.10 ($\star\star\star$) Consider the approximation (10.57) to the integral in (10.56). Investigate the accuracy of this approximation by evaluating (10.56) using numerical integration (Press *et al.*, 1992) with $g(a)$ given by (10.45) and $p(a|D)$ given by (10.53). Plot a graph of $P(\mathcal{C}_1|\mathbf{x}, D)$ versus a_{MP} for $s^2 = 4$ by numerical integration of (10.56). Similarly, plot a graph of $P(\mathcal{C}_1|\mathbf{x}, D)$ obtained by evaluating the approximation (10.57), and also plot the difference between these two graphs on a suitably expanded vertical scale.

10.11 ($\star\star$) Consider the Gaussian approximation for the distribution of β given by (10.78), and the analogous result for $p(D|\ln \alpha)$, in which the variances are given by (10.81) and (10.84). In these expressions, any correlation between α and β was neglected. Show that the reciprocal of the off-diagonal term in the inverse covariance matrix for the more general Gaussian distribution $p(D|\ln \alpha, \ln \beta)$ is given by

$$-\beta \frac{\partial}{\partial \beta} \left(\alpha \frac{\partial}{\partial \alpha} \ln p(D|\ln \alpha, \ln \beta) \right). \tag{10.144}$$

Evaluate this term using the expression for the log evidence given by (10.67) together with the results (10.68) and (10.71). Show that this term is negligible compared to the diagonal terms, and hence that the assumption of separable distributions for $\ln \alpha$ and $\ln \beta$ is justified.

10.12 ($\star$) Consider a probability density for a vector $\mathbf{x}$, which is parametrized by a vector $\boldsymbol{\theta}$. If the density takes the form

$$p(\mathbf{x}|\boldsymbol{\theta}) = f(\mathbf{x} - \boldsymbol{\theta}) \tag{10.145}$$

then $\boldsymbol{\theta}$ is said to be a *location* parameter. An example would be the mean vector in a normal distribution. We can obtain a non-informative prior $p(\boldsymbol{\theta})$ for the location parameter by the following argument (Berger, 1985). Suppose that instead of observing $\mathbf{x}$ we observed $\mathbf{x}' = \mathbf{x} + \mathbf{c}$ where $\mathbf{c}$ is a constant (this corresponds to a simple shift of the origin of the coordinate system). Then the density of this new variable is $f(\mathbf{x}' - \boldsymbol{\theta}')$ where $\boldsymbol{\theta}' = \boldsymbol{\theta} + \mathbf{c}$. Since this has the same structure as the original density, it is natural to require that the choice of prior be independent of this change in coordinates. Thus we have

$$\int_\Delta p(\boldsymbol{\theta})\, d\boldsymbol{\theta} = \int_\Delta p'(\boldsymbol{\theta}')\, d\boldsymbol{\theta}' \tag{10.146}$$

where $p'(\boldsymbol{\theta}')$ is the prior for $\boldsymbol{\theta}'$, and Δ is an arbitrary region of $\boldsymbol{\theta}$-space. Show that (10.146) requires that the prior must have the form $p(\boldsymbol{\theta}) =$ const. This is an improper prior, since it cannot be normalized, and it is conventional to take $p(\boldsymbol{\theta}) = 1$.

10.13 ($\star$) If a probability density can be written in the form

$$p(x|s) = \frac{1}{s} f\left(\frac{x}{s}\right) \tag{10.147}$$

then s is known as a *scale* parameter. An example would be the standard deviation parameter σ in a normal distribution of the form

$$p(x|\sigma) = \frac{1}{(2\pi)^{1/2}\sigma} \exp\left\{-\frac{1}{2}\left(\frac{x}{\sigma}\right)^2\right\}. \tag{10.148}$$

We wish to find a non-informative prior $p(s)$ for the scale parameter s (Berger, 1985). Suppose that instead of observing x we observe $x' = cx$ where c is a constant. Show that the density for x' takes the form

$$\frac{1}{s'} f\left(\frac{x'}{s'}\right) \tag{10.149}$$

where $s' = cs$. Since this has the same structure as (10.147) we require that the prior for s', which we denote by $p'(s')$ be the same as the prior for s. Thus we have

$$\int_\Delta p(s)\, ds = \int_\Delta p'(s')\, ds' \tag{10.150}$$

where $\Delta = (a, b)$ is any interval in $(0, \infty)$. Show that this implies that the prior should take the form $p(s) \propto 1/s$. Hence show that the prior for $\ln s$ is constant. This is an improper prior, since it cannot be normalized, and it is conventional to take $p(s) = 1/s$.

10.14 ($\star$) Consider the predictive distribution for a network output variable given by (10.28) and suppose we approximate the integration over weight space by using the Monte Carlo expression (10.108). Show that, for a noise model given by the Gaussian (10.14), the mean and variance of the distribution $p(t|\mathbf{x}, D)$ are given by

$$\bar{t} = \frac{1}{L} \sum_{i=1}^{L} y(\mathbf{x}; \mathbf{w}_i) \tag{10.151}$$

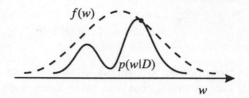

Figure 10.19. An illustration of the technique of rejection sampling for generating values from a distribution $p(w|D)$. Values are generated from a simpler distribution governed by the function $f(w)$ which satisfies $f(w) \geq p(w|D)$. These values are accepted with probability governed by the ratio $p(w|D)/f(w)$ as described in the text.

$$\sigma_t^2 = \frac{1}{\beta} + \frac{1}{L}\sum_{i=1}^{L}\{y(\mathbf{x};\mathbf{w}_i) - \bar{t}\}^2. \tag{10.152}$$

10.15 ($\star\star\star$) This exercise is concerned with the implementation of a simple Monte Carlo method for finding the most probable network interpolant and for estimating corresponding error bars. It is based on the technique of *rejection sampling* (Devroye, 1986; Press *et al.*, 1992) for generating a random sample from a complex distribution. Consider the problem of generating values for a single variable w from a distribution $p(w|D)$. We shall suppose that evaluating $p(w|D)$ is straightforward, while generating values of w directly from this distribution is not. Consider a function $f(w)$ which satisfies $f(w) \geq p(w|D)$ for all w as shown in Figure 10.19, and suppose that values of w are generated at random with a distribution proportional to $f(w)$. Verify that, if these values are accepted with probability given by the ratio $p(w|D)/f(w)$ then the accepted values will be governed by the distribution $p(w|D)$. (Hint: one way to do this is to use Figure 10.19 and to show the result geometrically.) We now apply this technique to the generation of weight vectors from the posterior distribution of network weights. Suppose we choose $f(\mathbf{w}) = Ap(\mathbf{w})$ where A is a constant and $p(\mathbf{w})$ is the prior weight distribution. Consider a likelihood function given by (10.12) and use Bayes' theorem in the form (10.3) to show that the condition $f(\mathbf{w}) \geq p(\mathbf{w}|D)$ can be satisfied by choosing $A^{-1} = Z_D p(D)$ where $p(D)$ is the denominator in (10.3). Hence show that weight vectors can be generated from the posterior distribution simply by selecting them from the prior and then accepting them with probability given by $\exp(-\beta E_D)$. Implement this numerically for a simple regression problem by considering a single-input single-output two-layer network with sigmoidal hidden units and a linear output unit, together with a data set consisting of no more than ten data points. Generate weight vectors from a Gaussian prior given by (10.9) with a fixed suitably-chosen value of α, and select them with a likelihood function $\exp(-\beta E_D)$ having a fixed value of β and a sum-of-squares error E_D until around 10 or 20 weight vectors have been accepted. Techniques for generating numbers with a Gaussian distribution are described in Press *et al.* (1992). Plot the corresponding set of network functions on the same graph, together with the original data points. Use the results of Exercise 10.14 to plot on a separate graph the Monte Carlo estimates of the mean of the predictive distribution, as well as the error bars, as functions of the input variable x. Note that rejection sampling is not suitable as a practical technique for large-scale problems since the time required by this algorithm grows exponentially with the number of data points.

APPENDIX A

SYMMETRIC MATRICES

In several chapters we need to consider the properties of real, symmetric matrices. Examples include Hessian matrices (whose elements are given by the second derivatives of an error function with respect to the network weights) and covariance matrices for Gaussian distributions. Symmetric matrices have the property that $A_{ij} = A_{ji}$, or equivalently $\mathbf{A}^T = \mathbf{A}$ where $\mathbf{A}^T$ denotes the transpose of $\mathbf{A}$.

The inverse of a symmetric matrix is also symmetric. To see this we start from the definition of the inverse given by $\mathbf{A}^{-1}\mathbf{A} = \mathbf{I}$ where $\mathbf{I}$ is the unit matrix, and then use the general result that, for any two matrices $\mathbf{A}$ and $\mathbf{B}$, we have $(\mathbf{AB})^T = \mathbf{B}^T\mathbf{A}^T$. This gives $\mathbf{A}^T(\mathbf{A}^{-1})^T = \mathbf{I}$ which, together with the symmetry property $\mathbf{A}^T = \mathbf{A}$, shows that $(\mathbf{A}^{-1})^T = \mathbf{A}^{-1}$ as required.

Eigenvector equation

We begin by considering the eigenvector equation for a symmetric matrix in the form

$$\mathbf{A}\mathbf{u}_k = \lambda_k\mathbf{u}_k \tag{A.1}$$

where $\mathbf{A}$ is a $W \times W$ matrix, and $k = 1,\ldots,W$. The eigenvector equations (A.1) represent a set of coupled linear algebraic equations for the components u_{ki} of the eigenvectors, and can be written in matrix notation as

$$(\mathbf{A} - \mathbf{D})\mathbf{U} = 0 \tag{A.2}$$

where $\mathbf{D}$ is a diagonal matrix whose elements consist of the eigenvalues λ_k

$$\mathbf{D} = \begin{pmatrix} \lambda_1 & & \\ & \ddots & \\ & & \lambda_W \end{pmatrix} \tag{A.3}$$

and $\mathbf{U}$ is a matrix whose columns consist of the eigenvectors $\mathbf{u}_k$. The necessary and sufficient condition for the set of simultaneous equations represented by (A.2) to have a solution is that the determinant of the matrix of coefficients vanishes, so that

$$|\mathbf{A} - \mathbf{D}| = 0. \tag{A.4}$$

Since this is an Wth order equation it has precisely W roots.

We can show that the eigenvectors can be chosen to form an orthonormal set, as follows. For any pair of eigenvectors $\mathbf{u}_j$ and $\mathbf{u}_k$, it follows from (A.1) that

$$\mathbf{u}_j^\mathrm{T} \mathbf{A} \mathbf{u}_k = \lambda_k \mathbf{u}_j^\mathrm{T} \mathbf{u}_k \tag{A.5}$$

$$\mathbf{u}_k^\mathrm{T} \mathbf{A} \mathbf{u}_j = \lambda_j \mathbf{u}_k^\mathrm{T} \mathbf{u}_j. \tag{A.6}$$

Subtracting these two equations, and using the symmetry property of $\mathbf{A}$ we find

$$(\lambda_k - \lambda_j) \mathbf{u}_k^\mathrm{T} \mathbf{u}_j = 0. \tag{A.7}$$

Thus, for $\lambda_k \neq \lambda_j$, the eigenvectors must be orthogonal. If $\lambda_k = \lambda_j$, then any linear combination of the eigenvectors $\mathbf{u}_j$ and $\mathbf{u}_k$ will also be an eigenvector, and this can be used to choose orthogonal linear combinations. A total of W orthogonal eigenvectors can be found, corresponding to the W solutions of (A.4). Note that, if $\mathbf{u}_k$ is an eigenvector with eigenvalue λ_k, then $\beta \mathbf{u}_k$ is also an eigenvector, for any non-zero β, and has the same eigenvalue. This property can be used to normalize the eigenvectors to unit length, so that they become an orthonormal set satisfying

$$\mathbf{u}_k^\mathrm{T} \mathbf{u}_j = \delta_{kj}. \tag{A.8}$$

If we multiply (A.1) by $\mathbf{A}^{-1}$ we obtain

$$\mathbf{A}^{-1} \mathbf{u}_k = \lambda_k^{-1} \mathbf{u}_k \tag{A.9}$$

so we see that $\mathbf{A}^{-1}$ has the same eigenvectors as $\mathbf{A}$ but with reciprocal eigenvalues.

Diagonalization

The matrix $\mathbf{A}$ can be diagonalized using the matrix $\mathbf{U}$. From (A.1) and (A.8) it follows that

$$\mathbf{U}^\mathrm{T} \mathbf{A} \mathbf{U} = \mathbf{D} \tag{A.10}$$

where $\mathbf{D}$ is defined by (A.3). From (A.8) it follows that the matrix $\mathbf{U}$ is orthogonal, in other words it satisfies

$$\mathbf{U}^\mathrm{T} \mathbf{U} = \mathbf{U} \mathbf{U}^\mathrm{T} = \mathbf{I}. \tag{A.11}$$

Consider a vector $\mathbf{x}$ which is transformed by the orthogonal matrix $\mathbf{U}$ to give a new vector

$$\tilde{\mathbf{x}} = \mathbf{U}^T\mathbf{x}. \tag{A.12}$$

As a consequence of the orthogonality property (A.11), the length of the vector is preserved by this transformation:

$$\|\tilde{\mathbf{x}}\|^2 = \mathbf{x}^T\mathbf{U}\mathbf{U}^T\mathbf{x} = \|\mathbf{x}\|^2. \tag{A.13}$$

Similarly, the angle between two vectors is also preserved

$$\tilde{\mathbf{x}}_1^T\tilde{\mathbf{x}}_2 = \mathbf{x}_1^T\mathbf{U}\mathbf{U}^T\mathbf{x}_2 = \mathbf{x}_1^T\mathbf{x}_2. \tag{A.14}$$

Thus, the effect of multiplication by $\mathbf{U}^T$ is equivalent to a rigid rotation of the coordinate system.

General quadratic form

There are several points in the book where we need to consider quadratic functions of the form

$$F(\mathbf{x}) = \mathbf{x}^T\mathbf{A}\mathbf{x} \tag{A.15}$$

where $\mathbf{A}$ is an arbitrary matrix. Note that we can, without loss of generality, assume that the matrix $\mathbf{A}$ is symmetric, since any anti-symmetric component would vanish on the right-hand side of (A.15). We can diagonalize this quadratic form by using the orthogonal matrix $\mathbf{U}$, whose columns are the eigenvectors of $\mathbf{A}$, as follows:

$$F(\mathbf{x}) = \mathbf{x}^T\mathbf{A}\mathbf{x}$$

$$= \mathbf{x}^T\mathbf{U}\mathbf{U}^T\mathbf{A}\mathbf{U}\mathbf{U}^T\mathbf{x}$$

$$= \tilde{\mathbf{x}}^T\mathbf{D}\tilde{\mathbf{x}}$$

$$= \sum_{i=1}^{W}\lambda_i\tilde{x}_i \tag{A.16}$$

where we have used (A.10), (A.11) and (A.12).

A matrix $\mathbf{A}$ is said to be *positive definite* if $\mathbf{v}^T\mathbf{A}\mathbf{v} > 0$ for any non-zero vector $\mathbf{v}$. It follows from (A.1) and (A.8) that the eigenvalues of a positive-definite matrix are all positive, since

$$\lambda_k = \mathbf{u}_k^T\mathbf{A}\mathbf{u}_k > 0 \tag{A.17}$$

If the matrix $\mathbf{A}$ in the quadratic form (A.15) is positive definite, then it follows from (A.16) that the surfaces of constant $F(\mathbf{x})$ are hyperellipsoids, with principal axes having lengths proportional to $\lambda_k^{-1/2}$.

APPENDIX B

GAUSSIAN INTEGRALS

One variable

We begin by evaluating the following Gaussian integral

$$I = \int_{-\infty}^{\infty} \exp\left(-\frac{\lambda}{2}x^2\right) dx. \tag{B.1}$$

This is easily done by considering the square of the integral, and then transforming to polar coordinates:

$$I^2 = \int_{-\infty}^{\infty} \int_{-\infty}^{\infty} \exp\left(-\frac{\lambda}{2}x^2 - \frac{\lambda}{2}y^2\right) dx\, dy$$

$$= \int_{0}^{\infty} \int_{0}^{2\pi} \exp\left(-\frac{\lambda}{2}r^2\right) r\, dr\, d\theta$$

$$= \pi \int_{0}^{\infty} \exp\left(-\frac{\lambda}{2}u\right) du$$

$$= \frac{2\pi}{\lambda} \tag{B.2}$$

where we have changed variables first using $x = r\cos\theta, y = r\sin\theta$ and then using $r^2 = u$. Taking the square root we finally obtain

$$\int_{-\infty}^{\infty} \exp\left(-\frac{\lambda}{2}x^2\right) dx = \left(\frac{2\pi}{\lambda}\right)^{1/2}. \tag{B.3}$$

Several variables

Consider the evaluation of the W-dimensional Gaussian integral

$$I_W = \int \exp\left(-\frac{1}{2}\mathbf{w}^{\mathrm{T}}\mathbf{A}\mathbf{w}\right) d\mathbf{w} \tag{B.4}$$

where $\mathbf{A}$ is a $W \times W$ real symmetric matrix, $\mathbf{w}$ is a W-dimensional vector, and the integration is over the whole of $\mathbf{w}$-space. In order to evaluate this integral it is convenient to consider the eigenvector equation for $\mathbf{A}$ in the form

$$\mathbf{A}\mathbf{u}_k = \lambda_k \mathbf{u}_k. \tag{B.5}$$

Since $\mathbf{A}$ is real and symmetric, we can choose the eigenvectors to form a complete orthonormal set

$$\mathbf{u}_k^{\mathrm{T}} \mathbf{u}_l = \delta_{kl} \tag{B.6}$$

as discussed in Appendix A. We can then expand the vector $\mathbf{w}$ as a linear combination of the eigenvectors

$$\mathbf{w} = \sum_{k=1}^{W} \alpha_k \mathbf{u}_k. \tag{B.7}$$

The integration over the weight values $dw_1 \ldots dw_W$ can now be replaced by an integration over $d\alpha_1 \ldots d\alpha_W$. The Jacobian of this change of variables is given by

$$J = \det\left(\frac{\partial w_i}{\partial \alpha_k}\right) = \det\left(u_{ki}\right) \tag{B.8}$$

where u_{ki} is the ith element of the vector $\mathbf{u}_k$, and 'det' denotes the determinant. The u_{ki} are also the elements of a matrix $\mathbf{U}$ whose columns are given by the $\mathbf{u}_k$, and which is an orthogonal matrix, i.e. it satisfies $\mathbf{U}^{\mathrm{T}}\mathbf{U} = \mathbf{I}$, since its columns are orthonormal. Thus

$$J^2 = \{\det(\mathbf{U})\}^2 = \det(\mathbf{U}^{\mathrm{T}})\det(\mathbf{U}) = \det(\mathbf{U}^{\mathrm{T}}\mathbf{U}) = \det(\mathbf{I}) = 1 \tag{B.9}$$

and hence $|J| = 1$. Using the orthonormality of the $\mathbf{u}_k$ we have

$$\mathbf{w}^{\mathrm{T}}\mathbf{A}\mathbf{w} = \sum_{k=1}^{W} \lambda_k \alpha_k^2. \tag{B.10}$$

The various integrals over the α_k now decouple, and so we can write

$$I_W = \prod_{k=1}^{W} \int_{-\infty}^{\infty} \exp\left(-\frac{\lambda_k \alpha_k^2}{2}\right) d\alpha_k. \tag{B.11}$$

Using the result (B.3) we obtain

$$I_W = \prod_{k=1}^{W} \left(\frac{2\pi}{\lambda_k} \right)^{1/2} \tag{B.12}$$

Since the determinant of a matrix is given by the product of its eigenvalues,

$$|\mathbf{A}| = \prod_{k=1}^{W} \lambda_k, \tag{B.13}$$

we finally obtain

$$I_W = (2\pi)^{W/2} |\mathbf{A}|^{-1/2}. \tag{B.14}$$

Inclusion of linear term

In deriving the distribution of network outputs within the Bayesian framework in Exercise 10.2, we need to consider a more general form of the Gaussian integral, which has an additional linear term, of the form

$$I_W = \int \exp\left(-\frac{1}{2} \mathbf{w}^{\mathrm{T}} \mathbf{A} \mathbf{w} + \mathbf{h}^{\mathrm{T}} \mathbf{w} \right) d\mathbf{w}. \tag{B.15}$$

Again, it is convenient to work in terms of the eigenvectors of $\mathbf{A}$. We first define h_k to be the projections of $\mathbf{h}$ onto the eigenvectors

$$h_k = \mathbf{h}^{\mathrm{T}} \mathbf{u}_k. \tag{B.16}$$

This again leads to a set of decoupled integrals over the α_k of the form

$$I_W = \prod_{k=1}^{W} \int_{-\infty}^{\infty} \exp\left(-\frac{\lambda_k \alpha_k^2}{2} + h_k \alpha_k \right) d\alpha_k. \tag{B.17}$$

Completing the square in the exponent, we have

$$-\frac{\lambda_k \alpha_k^2}{2} + h_k \alpha_k = -\frac{\lambda_k}{2} \left(\alpha_k - \frac{h_k}{\lambda_k} \right)^2 + \frac{h_k^2}{2\lambda_k}. \tag{B.18}$$

If we now change integration variables to $\widetilde{\alpha}_k = \alpha_k - h_k/\lambda_k$, we again obtain a product of integrals which can be evaluated using (B.3) to give

$$I_W = (2\pi)^{W/2} |\mathbf{A}|^{-1/2} \exp\left(\sum_{k=1}^{W} \frac{h_k^2}{2\lambda_k} \right). \tag{B.19}$$

If we now apply $\mathbf{A}^{-1}$ to both sides of (B.5) we see that $\mathbf{A}^{-1}$ has the same eigenvectors as $\mathbf{A}$, but with eigenvalues λ_k^{-1}:

$$\mathbf{A}^{-1}\mathbf{u}_k = \lambda_k^{-1}\mathbf{u}_k. \tag{B.20}$$

Thus, using (B.6) and (B.16), we see that

$$\mathbf{h}^{\mathrm{T}}\mathbf{A}^{-1}\mathbf{h} = \sum_k \frac{h_k^2}{\lambda_k}. \tag{B.21}$$

Using this result in (B.19) we obtain our final result:

$$I_W = (2\pi)^{W/2}|\mathbf{A}|^{-1/2}\exp\left(\frac{1}{2}\mathbf{h}^{\mathrm{T}}\mathbf{A}^{-1}\mathbf{h}\right). \tag{B.22}$$

APPENDIX C

LAGRANGE MULTIPLIERS

The technique of *Lagrange multipliers*, also sometimes called *undetermined multipliers*, is used to find the stationary points of a function of several variables subject to one or more constraints.

Consider the problem of finding the minimum of a function $f(x_1, x_2)$ subject to a constraint relating x_1 and x_2 which we write in the form

$$g(x_1, x_2) = 0. \tag{C.1}$$

One approach would be to solve the constraint equation (C.1) and thus express x_2 as a function of x_1 in the form $x_2 = h(x_1)$. This can then be substituted into $f(x_1, x_2)$ to give a function of x_1 alone of the form $f(x_1, h(x_1))$. The maximum with respect to x_1 could then be found by differentiation in the usual way, to give the stationary value $x_1^{\min}$, with the corresponding value of x_2 given by $x_2^{\min} = h(x_1^{\min})$.

One problem with this approach is that it may be difficult to find an analytic solution of the constraint equation which allows x_2 to be expressed as an explicit function of x_1. Also, this approach treats x_1 and x_2 differently and so spoils the natural symmetry between these variables.

A more elegant, and often simpler, approach is based on the introduction of a parameter λ called a Lagrange multiplier. We motivate this technique from a geometrical perspective. Consider the case of d variables $x_1, \ldots, x_d$ which we can group into a vector $\mathbf{x}$. The constraint equation $g(\mathbf{x}) = 0$ then represents a surface in $\mathbf{x}$-space as indicated in Figure C.1. At any point P on the constraint surface, the gradient of the function $f(\mathbf{x})$ is given by the vector ∇f. To find the stationary point of $f(\mathbf{x})$ within the surface we can compute the component $\nabla_{\parallel} f$ of ∇f which lies in the surface, and then set $\nabla_{\parallel} f = 0$. Consider the Taylor expansion of the function $g(\mathbf{x})$ when we move a short distance from the point $\mathbf{x}$ in the form

$$g(\mathbf{x} + \boldsymbol{\epsilon}) = g(\mathbf{x}) + \boldsymbol{\epsilon}^{\mathrm{T}} \nabla g(\mathbf{x}). \tag{C.2}$$

If the point $\mathbf{x} + \boldsymbol{\epsilon}$ is chosen to lie within the surface then we have $g(\mathbf{x} + \boldsymbol{\epsilon}) = g(\mathbf{x})$ and hence $\boldsymbol{\epsilon}^{\mathrm{T}} \nabla g(\mathbf{x}) = 0$. Thus we see that the vector ∇g is normal to the surface $g(\mathbf{x}) = 0$. We can then obtain the component $\nabla_{\parallel} f$ which lies in the surface by adding to ∇f some multiple of the normal vector ∇g so that

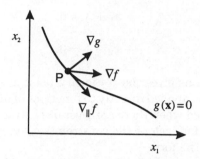

Figure C.1. A geometrical picture of the technique of Lagrange multipliers. The gradient of a function $f(\mathbf{x})$ at a point P is given by a vector ∇f. We wish to find the component of this vector lying within the constraint surface $g(\mathbf{x}) = 0$. This can be done by subtracting from ∇f an appropriate multiple of the vector normal to the constraint surface, given by ∇g.

$$\nabla_{\|} f = \nabla f + \lambda \nabla g \tag{C.3}$$

where λ is a Lagrange multiplier. It is convenient to introduce the Lagrangian function given by

$$L(\mathbf{x}, \lambda) \equiv f(\mathbf{x}) + \lambda g(\mathbf{x}). \tag{C.4}$$

We then see that the vector ∇L is given by the right-hand side of (C.3) and so the required stationarity condition is given by setting $\nabla L = 0$. Furthermore, the condition $\partial L / \partial \lambda = 0$ leads to the constraint equation $g(\mathbf{x}) = 0$.

Thus to find the minimum of a function $f(\mathbf{x})$ subject to the constraint $g(\mathbf{x}) = 0$ we define the Lagrangian function given by (C.4) and we then find the stationary point of $L(\mathbf{x}, \lambda)$ with respect both to $\mathbf{x}$ and λ. For a d-dimensional vector $\mathbf{x}$ this gives $d + 1$ equations which determine both the stationary point $\mathbf{x}^*$ and the value of λ. If we are only interested in $\mathbf{x}^*$ then we can eliminate λ from the stationarity equations without needing to find its value (hence the term 'undetermined multiplier').

As a simple example, suppose we wish to find the stationary point of the function $f(x_1, x_2) \equiv x_1 x_2$ subject to the constraint $g(x_1, x_2) \equiv x_1 + x_2 - 1 = 0$. The corresponding Lagrangian function is given by

$$L(\mathbf{x}, \lambda) = x_1 x_2 + \lambda(x_1 + x_2 - 1). \tag{C.5}$$

The conditions for (C.5) to be stationary with respect to x_1, x_2, and λ then give the following coupled equations:

$$x_2 + \lambda = 0 \qquad\qquad\qquad (C.6)$$

$$x_1 + \lambda = 0 \qquad\qquad\qquad (C.7)$$

$$x_1 + x_2 - 1 = 0. \qquad\qquad\qquad (C.8)$$

Solution of these equations gives the stationary point as $(x_1, x_2) = (\frac{1}{2}, \frac{1}{2})$.

This technique can be applied directly to functions of more than two variables. Similarly it can be applied when there are several constraints simply by using one Lagrange multiplier λ_k for each of the constraints $g_k(\mathbf{x}) = 0$ and constructing a Lagrangian function of the form

$$L(\mathbf{x}, \{\lambda_k\}) = f(\mathbf{x}) + \sum_k \lambda_k g_k(\mathbf{x}). \qquad\qquad (C.9)$$

This Lagrangian is then minimized with respect to $\mathbf{x}$ and $\{\lambda_k\}$. Extensions to constrained functional derivatives (Appendix D) are similarly straightforward.

A more formal discussion of the technique of Lagrange multipliers can be found in Dixon (1972, pages 88–93).

APPENDIX D

CALCULUS OF VARIATIONS

At several points in this book we make use of the technique of *functional differentiation*, also known as *calculus of variations*. Here we give a brief introduction to this topic, using an analogy to conventional differentiation. We can regard a function $f(x)$ as a transformation which takes x as input, and which generates f as output. For this function we can define its derivative df/dx by considering the change in $f(x)$ when the value of x is changed by a small amount δx so that

$$\delta f = \frac{df}{dx}\delta x + \mathcal{O}(\delta x^2). \tag{D.1}$$

A function of many variables $f(x_1, \ldots, x_d)$ can be regarded as a transformation which depends on a discrete set of independent variables. For such a function we have

$$\delta f = \sum_{i=1}^{d} \frac{\partial f}{\partial x_i}\delta x_i + \mathcal{O}(\delta x^2). \tag{D.2}$$

In the same way, we can consider a *functional*, written as $E[f]$, which takes a function $f(x)$ as input and returns a scalar value E. As an example of a functional, consider

$$E[f] = \int \left\{ \left(\frac{df}{dx}\right)^2 + f^2 \right\} dx \tag{D.3}$$

so that the value of $E[f]$ depends on the particular choice of the function $f(x)$. The concept of a functional derivative arises when we consider how much $E[f]$ changes when we make a small change $\delta f(x)$ to the function $f(x)$, where $\delta f(x)$ is a function of x which has small magnitude everywhere but which is otherwise arbitrary. We denote the functional derivative of $E[f]$ with respect to $f(x)$ by $\delta E/\delta f(x)$, and define it by the following relation:

$$\delta E = E[f + \delta f] - E[f] = \int \frac{\delta E}{\delta f(x)}\delta f(x)dx + \mathcal{O}(\delta f^2). \tag{D.4}$$

This can be seen as a natural extension of (D.2) where now $E[f]$ depends on a continuous set of variables, namely the values of f at all points x. As an illustration, we can calculate the derivative of the functional given in (D.3):

$$E[f + \delta f] = E[f] + 2 \int \left\{ \frac{df}{dx} \frac{d}{dx} \delta f + f \delta f \right\} dx + \mathcal{O}(\delta f^2). \qquad (D.5)$$

This can be expressed in the form (D.4) if we integrate by parts, and assume that the boundary term vanishes. We then obtain the following result for the functional derivative:

$$\frac{\delta E}{\delta f(x)} = -2 \frac{d^2 f}{dx^2} + 2f. \qquad (D.6)$$

Note that, from (D.4) we also have the following useful result:

$$\frac{\delta f(x)}{\delta f(x')} = \delta(x - x') \qquad (D.7)$$

where $\delta(x)$ is the Dirac delta function. This result is easily verified by taking $E[f] = f(x)$ and then substituting (D.7) into (D.4).

If we require that, to lowest order in $\delta f(x)$, the functional $E[f]$ be stationary then from (D.4) we have

$$\int \frac{\delta E}{\delta f(x)} \delta f(x) dx = 0. \qquad (D.8)$$

Since this must hold for an arbitrary choice of $\delta f(x)$ we can choose $\delta f(x) = \delta(x - x')$ where $\delta(x)$ is the Dirac delta function. Hence it follows that

$$\frac{\delta E}{\delta f(x)} = 0 \qquad (D.9)$$

so that, requiring the functional to be stationary with respect to arbitrary variations in the function is equivalent to requiring that the functional derivative vanish.

If we define a differential operator $D \equiv d/dx$ then (D.3) can be written as

$$E = \int \left\{ (Df)^2 + f^2 \right\} dx. \qquad (D.10)$$

Following the same argument as before we see that the functional derivative becomes

$$\frac{\delta E}{\delta f(x)} = 2\widehat{D}Df(x) + 2f(x) \tag{D.11}$$

where $\widehat{D} \equiv -d/dx$ is the *adjoint operator* to the operator D. Similar forms of adjoint operator arise in the discussion of radial basis functions and regularization in Section 5.4.

APPENDIX E

PRINCIPAL COMPONENTS

In Section 8.6, we showed that the optimal linear dimensionality reduction procedure (in the sense of least squares) was determined by minimization of the following function:

$$E_M = \frac{1}{2} \sum_{i=M+1}^{d} \sum_{n} \left\{ \mathbf{u}_i^{\mathrm{T}} (\mathbf{x}^n - \overline{\mathbf{x}}) \right\}^2$$

$$= \frac{1}{2} \sum_{i=M+1}^{d} \mathbf{u}_i^{\mathrm{T}} \mathbf{\Sigma} \mathbf{u}_i \tag{E.1}$$

where $\mathbf{\Sigma}$ is the covariance matrix defined by (8.21). We now show that the solution to this problem can be expressed in terms of the eigenvectors and eigenvalues of $\mathbf{\Sigma}$.

It is clear that (E.1) has a non-trivial minimum with respect to the $\mathbf{u}_i$ only if we impose some constraint. A suitable constraint is obtained by requiring the $\mathbf{u}_i$ to be orthonormal, and can be taken into account by the use of a set of Lagrange multipliers μ_{ij} (Appendix C). We therefore minimize the function

$$\widehat{E}_M = \frac{1}{2} \sum_{i=M+1}^{d} \mathbf{u}_i^{\mathrm{T}} \mathbf{\Sigma} \mathbf{u}_i - \frac{1}{2} \sum_{i=M+1}^{d} \sum_{j=M+1}^{d} \mu_{ij} (\mathbf{u}_i^{\mathrm{T}} \mathbf{u}_j - \delta_{ij}). \tag{E.2}$$

This is conveniently written in matrix notation in the form

$$\widehat{E}_M = \frac{1}{2} \mathrm{Tr} \left\{ \mathbf{U}^{\mathrm{T}} \mathbf{\Sigma} \mathbf{U} \right\} - \frac{1}{2} \mathrm{Tr} \left\{ \mathbf{M} (\mathbf{U}^{\mathrm{T}} \mathbf{U} - \mathbf{I} \right\} \tag{E.3}$$

where $\mathbf{M}$ is a matrix with elements μ_{ij}, $\mathbf{U}$ is a matrix whose columns consist of the eigenvectors $\mathbf{u}_i$, and $\mathbf{I}$ is the unit matrix. If we minimize (E.3) with respect to $\mathbf{U}$ we obtain

$$0 = (\mathbf{\Sigma} + \mathbf{\Sigma}^{\mathrm{T}}) \mathbf{U} - \mathbf{U} (\mathbf{M} + \mathbf{M}^{\mathrm{T}}). \tag{E.4}$$

By definition, the matrix $\mathbf{\Sigma}$ is symmetric. Also, the matrix $\mathbf{M}$ can be taken to be symmetric without loss of generality, since the matrix $\mathbf{U}\mathbf{U}^{\mathrm{T}}$ is symmetric as is the unit matrix $\mathbf{I}$, and hence any anti-symmetric component in $\mathbf{M}$ would vanish in (E.3). Thus, we can write (E.4) in the form

$$\boldsymbol{\Sigma}\mathbf{U} = \mathbf{U}\mathbf{M}. \tag{E.5}$$

Since, by construction, $\mathbf{U}$ has orthonormal columns, it is an orthogonal matrix satisfying $\mathbf{U}^{\mathrm{T}}\mathbf{U} = \mathbf{I}$. Thus we can write (E.5) in the equivalent form

$$\mathbf{U}^{\mathrm{T}}\boldsymbol{\Sigma}\mathbf{U} = \mathbf{M}. \tag{E.6}$$

Clearly one solution of this equation is to choose $\mathbf{M}$ to be diagonal so that the columns of $\mathbf{U}$ are the eigenvectors of $\boldsymbol{\Sigma}$ and the elements of $\mathbf{M}$ are its eigenvalues. However, this is not the only possible solution. Consider an arbitrary solution of (E.5). The eigenvector equation for $\mathbf{M}$ can be written

$$\mathbf{M}\boldsymbol{\Psi} = \boldsymbol{\Psi}\boldsymbol{\Lambda} \tag{E.7}$$

where $\boldsymbol{\Lambda}$ is a diagonal matrix of eigenvalues. Since $\mathbf{M}$ is symmetric, the eigenvector matrix $\boldsymbol{\Psi}$ can be chosen to have orthonormal columns. Thus $\boldsymbol{\Psi}$ is an orthogonal matrix satisfying $\boldsymbol{\Psi}^{\mathrm{T}}\boldsymbol{\Psi} = \mathbf{I}$. From (E.7) we then have

$$\boldsymbol{\Lambda} = \boldsymbol{\Psi}^{\mathrm{T}}\mathbf{M}\boldsymbol{\Psi}. \tag{E.8}$$

Substituting (E.6) into (E.8) we obtain

$$\boldsymbol{\Lambda} = \boldsymbol{\Psi}^{\mathrm{T}}\mathbf{U}^{\mathrm{T}}\boldsymbol{\Sigma}\mathbf{U}\boldsymbol{\Psi}$$

$$= (\mathbf{U}\boldsymbol{\Psi})^{\mathrm{T}}\boldsymbol{\Sigma}(\mathbf{U}\boldsymbol{\Psi})$$

$$= \widetilde{\mathbf{U}}^{\mathrm{T}}\boldsymbol{\Sigma}\widetilde{\mathbf{U}} \tag{E.9}$$

where we have defined

$$\widetilde{\mathbf{U}} = \mathbf{U}\boldsymbol{\Psi}. \tag{E.10}$$

Using $\boldsymbol{\Psi}\boldsymbol{\Psi}^{\mathrm{T}} = \mathbf{I}$ we can write

$$\mathbf{U} = \widetilde{\mathbf{U}}\boldsymbol{\Psi}^{\mathrm{T}}. \tag{E.11}$$

Thus, an arbitrary solution to (E.6) can be obtained from the particular solution $\widetilde{\mathbf{U}}$ by application of an orthogonal transformation given by $\boldsymbol{\Psi}$. We now note that the value of the criterion E_M is invariant under this transformation since

$$E_M = \frac{1}{2}\text{Tr}\left\{\mathbf{U}^T\mathbf{\Sigma}\mathbf{U}\right\}$$

$$= \frac{1}{2}\text{Tr}\left\{\mathbf{\Psi}\widetilde{\mathbf{U}}^T\mathbf{\Sigma}\widetilde{\mathbf{U}}\mathbf{\Psi}^T\right\}$$

$$= \frac{1}{2}\text{Tr}\left\{\widetilde{\mathbf{U}}^T\mathbf{\Sigma}\widetilde{\mathbf{U}}\right\} \tag{E.12}$$

where we have used the fact that the trace is invariant to cyclic permutations of its argument, together with $\mathbf{\Psi}^T\mathbf{\Psi} = \mathbf{I}$. Since all of the possible solutions give the same value for the residual error E_M, we can choose whichever is most convenient. We therefore choose the solution given by $\widetilde{\mathbf{U}}$ since, from (E.9), this has columns which are the eigenvectors of $\mathbf{\Sigma}$.

REFERENCES

Abu-Mostafa, Y. S. (1989). The Vapnik-Chervonenkis dimension: information versus complexity in learning. *Neural Computation* **1** (3), 312–317.

Ahmad, S. and V. Tresp (1993). Some solutions to the missing feature problem in vision. In S. J. Hanson, J. D. Cowan, and C. L. Giles (Eds.), *Advances in Neural Information Processing Systems*, Volume 5, pp. 393–400. San Mateo, CA: Morgan Kaufmann.

Aizerman, M. A., E. M. Braverman, and L. I. Rozonoer (1964). The probability problem of pattern recognition learning and the method of potential functions. *Automation and Remote Control* **25**, 1175–1190.

Akaike, H. (1969). Fitting autoregressive models for prediction. *Annals of the Institute of Statistical Mathematics* **21**, 243–247.

Akaike, H. (1973). Information theory and an extension of the maximum likelihood principle. In B. N. Petrov and F. Csáki (Eds.), *2nd International Symposium on Information Theory*, pp. 267–281. Tsahkadsov, Armenia, USSR.

Albertini, F. and E. D. Sontag (1993). For neural networks, function determines form. *Neural Networks* **6** (7), 975–990.

Anderson, J. A. (1982). Logistic discrimination. In P. R. Krishnaiah and L. N. Kanal (Eds.), *Classification, Pattern Recognition and Reduction of Dimensionality*, Volume 2 of *Handbook of Statistics*, pp. 169–191. Amsterdam: North Holland.

Anderson, J. A. and E. Rosenfeld (Eds.) (1988). *Neurocomputing: Foundations of Research*. Cambridge, MA: MIT Press.

Anderson, T. W. (1958). *An Introduction to Multivariate Statistical Analysis*. New York: John Wiley.

Arbib, M. A. (1987). *Brains, Machines, and Mathematics* (Second ed.). New York: Springer-Verlag.

Arnold, V. I. (1957). On functions of three variables. *Doklady Akademiia Nauk SSSR* **114** (4), 679–681.

Baldi, P. and K. Hornik (1989). Neural networks and principal component analysis: learning from examples without local minima. *Neural Networks* **2** (1), 53–58.

Barnard, E. (1992). Optimization for training neural nets. *IEEE Transactions on Neural Networks* **3** (2), 232–240.

Barnard, E. and D. Casasent (1991). Invariance and neural nets. *IEEE Transactions on Neural Networks* **2** (5), 498–508.

Barron, A. R. (1984). Predicted squared error: a criterion for automatic model selection. In S. J. Farlow (Ed.), *Self-Organizing Methods in Modelling*, Volume 54 of *Statistics: Textbooks and Monographs*, pp. 87–103. New York: Marcel Dekker.

Barron, A. R. (1993). Universal approximation bounds for superposition of a sigmoidal function. *IEEE Transactions on Information Theory* **39** (3), 930–945.

Barron, A. R. and R. L. Barron (1988). Statistical learning networks: a unifying view. In E. J. Wegman, D. T. Gantz, and J. J. Miller (Eds.), *Computing Science and Statistics: 20th Symposium on the Interface*, pp. 192–203. Fairfax, Virginia: American Statistical Association.

Battiti, R. (1989). Accelerated backpropagation learning: two optimization methods. *Complex Systems* **3**, 331–342.

Baum, E. B. (1988). On the capabilities of multilayer perceptrons. *Journal of Complexity* **4**, 193–215.

Baum, E. B. and D. Haussler (1989). What size net gives valid generalization? *Neural Computation* **1** (1), 151–160.

Baum, E. B. and F. Wilczek (1988). Supervised learning of probability distributions by neural networks. In D. Z. Anderson (Ed.), *Neural Information Processing Systems*, pp. 52–61. New York: American Institute of Physics.

Becker, S. and Y. Le Cun (1989). Improving the convergence of backpropagation learning with second order methods. In D. Touretzky, G. E. Hinton, and T. J. Sejnowski (Eds.), *Proceedings of the 1988 Connectionist Models Summer School*, pp. 29–37. San Mateo, CA: Morgan Kaufmann.

Bellman, R. (1961). *Adaptive Control Processes: A Guided Tour*. New Jersey: Princeton University Press.

Bello, M. G. (1992). Enhanced training algorithms, and integrated training/architecture selection for multilayer perceptron networks. *IEEE Transactions on Neural Networks* **3** (6), 864–875.

Berger, J. O. (1985). *Statistical Decision Theory and Bayesian Analysis* (Second ed.). New York: Springer-Verlag.

Bishop, C. M. (1991a). A fast procedure for retraining the multilayer perceptron. *International Journal of Neural Systems* **2** (3), 229–236.

Bishop, C. M. (1991b). Improving the generalization properties of radial basis function neural networks. *Neural Computation* **3** (4), 579–588.

Bishop, C. M. (1992). Exact calculation of the Hessian matrix for the multilayer perceptron. *Neural Computation* **4** (4), 494–501.

Bishop, C. M. (1993). Curvature-driven smoothing: a learning algorithm for feedforward networks. *IEEE Transactions on Neural Networks* **4** (5), 882–884.

Bishop, C. M. (1994a). Mixture density networks. Technical Report NCRG 4288, Neural Computing Research Group, Aston University, Birmingham, UK.

Bishop, C. M. (1994b). Novelty detection and neural network validation. *IEE Proceedings: Vision, Image and Signal Processing* **141** (4), 217–222. Special issue on applications of neural networks.

Bishop, C. M. (1995). Training with noise is equivalent to Tikhonov regularization. *Neural Computation* **7** (1), 108–116.

Bishop, C. M. and C. Legleye (1995). Estimating conditional probability densities for periodic variables. In D. S. Touretzky, G. Tesauro, and T. K. Leen (Eds.), *Advances in Neural Information Processing Systems*, Volume 7. Cambridge MA: MIT Press. In press.

Block, H. D. (1962). The perceptron: a model for brain functioning. *Reviews of Modern Physics* **34** (1), 123–135. Reprinted in Anderson and Rosenfeld (1988).

Blum, E. K. and L. K. Li (1991). Approximation theory and feedforward networks. *Neural Networks* **4** (4), 511–515.

Blum, J. R. (1954). Multidimensional stochastic approximation methods. *Annals of Mathematical Statistics* **25**, 737–744.

Blumer, A., A. Ehrenfeucht, D. Haussler, and M. K. Warmuth (1989). Learnability and the Vapnik-Chervonenkis dimension. *Journal of the Association for Computing Machinery* **36** (4), 929–965.

Bourlard, H. and Y. Kamp (1988). Auto-association by multilayer perceptrons and singular value decomposition. *Biological Cybernetics* **59**, 291–294.

Bourlard, H. and N. Morgan (1990). A continuous speech recognition system embedding MLP into HMM. In D. S. Touretzky (Ed.), *Advances in Neural Information Processing Systems*, Volume 2, pp. 186–193. San Mateo, CA: Morgan Kaufmann.

Breiman, L., J. H. Friedman, R. A. Olshen, and C. J. Stone (1984). *Classification and regression trees*. Blemont, CA: Wadsworth.

Brent, R. P. (1973). *Algorithms for Minimization without Derivatives*. Englewood Cliffs, NJ: Prentice-Hall.

Bridle, J. S. (1990). Probabilistic interpretation of feedforward classification network outputs, with relationships to statistical pattern recognition. In F. Fogelman Soulié and J. Hérault (Eds.), *Neurocomputing: Algorithms, Architectures and Applications*, pp. 227–236. New York: Springer-Verlag.

Brigham, E. O. (1974). *The Fast Fourier Transform*. Engelwood Cliffs: Prentice-Hall.

Broomhead, D. S. and D. Lowe (1988). Multivariable functional interpolation and adaptive networks. *Complex Systems* **2**, 321–355.

Buntine, W. L. and A. S. Weigend (1991). Bayesian back-propagation. *Complex Systems* **5**, 603–643.

Buntine, W. L. and A. S. Weigend (1993). Computing second derivatives in feed-forward networks: a review. *IEEE Transactions on Neural Networks* **5** (3), 480–488.

Burrascano, P. (1991). A norm selection criterion for the generalized delta rule. *IEEE Transactions on Neural Networks* **2** (1), 125–130.

Chauvin, Y. (1989). A back-propagation algorithm with optimal use of hidden units. In D. S. Touretzky (Ed.), *Advances in Neural Information Processing Systems*, Volume 1, pp. 519–526. San Mateo, CA: Morgan Kaufmann.

Chen, A. M., H. Lu, and R. Hecht-Nielsen (1993). On the geometry of feedforward neural network error surfaces. *Neural Computation* **5** (6), 910–927.

Chen, S., S. A. Billings, and W. Luo (1989). Orthogonal least squares methods and their application to non-linear system identification. *International Journal of Control* **50** (5), 1873–1896.

Chen, S., C. F. N. Cowan, and P. M. Grant (1991). Orthogonal least squares learning algorithm for radial basis function networks. *IEEE Transactions on Neural Networks* **2** (2), 302–309.

Cheng, B. and D. M. Titterington (1994). Neural networks: a review from a statistical perspective. *Statistical Science* **9** (1), 2–54.

Cotter, N. E. (1990). The Stone-Weierstrass theorem and its application to neural networks. *IEEE Transactions on Neural Networks* **1** (4), 290–295.

Cover, T. M. (1965). Geometrical and statistical properties of systems of linear inequalities with applications in pattern recognition. *IEEE Transactions on Electronic Computers* **14**, 326–334.

Cox, R. T. (1946). Probability, frequency and reasonable expectation. *American Journal of Physics* **14** (1), 1–13.

Cybenko, G. (1989). Approximation by superpositions of a sigmoidal function. *Mathematics of Control, Signals and Systems* **2**, 304–314.

Day, N. E. (1969). Estimating the components of a mixture of normal distributions. *Biometrika* **56** (3), 463–474.

De Boor, C. (1978). *A Practical Guide to Splines*. New York: Springer-Verlag.

Dempster, A. P., N. M. Laird, and D. B. Rubin (1977). Maximum likelihood from incomplete data via the EM algorithm. *Journal of the Royal Statistical Society, B* **39** (1), 1–38.

Dennis, J. E. and R. B. Schnabel (1983). *Numerical Methods for Unconstrained Optimization and Nonlinear Equations*. Englewood Cliffs, NJ: Prentice-Hall.

Devijver, P. A. and J. Kittler (1982). *Pattern Recognition: A Statistical Approach*. Englewood Cliffs, NJ: Prentice-Hall.

Devroye, L. (1986). *Non-Uniform Random Variate Generation*. New York: Springer-Verlag.

Diaconis, P. and M. Shahshahani (1984). On nonlinear functions of linear combinations. *SIAM Journal of Scienctific and Statistical Computing* **5** (1), 175–191.

Dixon, L. C. W. (1972). *Nonlinear Optimisation*. London: English Universities Press.

Drucker, H. and Y. Le Cun (1992). Improving generalization performance using double back-propagation. *IEEE Transactions on Neural Networks* **3** (6), 991–997.

Duane, S., A. D. Kennedy, B. J. Pendleton, and D. Roweth (1987). Hybrid Monte Carlo. *Physics Letters B* **195** (2), 216–222.

Duda, R. O. and P. E. Hart (1973). *Pattern Classification and Scene Analysis.* New York: John Wiley.

Fahlman, S. E. (1988). Faster-learning variations on back-propagation: an empirical study. In D. Touretzky, G. E. Hinton, and T. J. Sejnowski (Eds.), *Proceedings of the 1988 Connectionist Models Summer School*, pp. 38–51. San Mateo, CA: Morgan Kaufmann.

Fahlman, S. E. and C. Lebiere (1990). The cascade-correlation learning architecture. In D. S. Touretzky (Ed.), *Advances in Neural Information Processing Systems*, Volume 2, pp. 524–532. San Mateo, CA: Morgan Kaufmann.

Fisher, R. A. (1936). The use of multiple measurements in taxonomic problems. *Annals of Eugenics* **7**, 179–188. Reprinted in *Contributions to Mathematical Statistics*, John Wiley: New York (1950).

Fletcher, R. (1987). *Practical Methods of Optimization* (Second ed.). New York: John Wiley.

Frean, M. (1990). The upstart algorithm: a method for constructing and training feedforward neural networks. *Neural Computation* **2** (2), 198–209.

Friedman, J. H. (1991). Multivariate adaptive regression splines (with discussion). *Annals of Statistics* **19** (1), 1–141.

Friedman, J. H. and W. Stuetzle (1981). Projection pursuit regression. *Journal of the American Statistical Association* **76** (376), 817–823.

Fukunaga, K. (1982). Intrinsic dimensionality extraction. In P. R. Krishnaiah and L. N. Kanal (Eds.), *Classification, Pattern Recognition and Reduction of Dimensionality*, Volume 2 of *Handbook of Statistics*, pp. 347–360. Amsterdam: North Holland.

Fukunaga, K. (1990). *Introduction to Statistical Pattern Recognition* (Second ed.). San Diego: Academic Press.

Fukunaga, K. and R. R. Hayes (1989). The reduced Parzen classifier. *IEEE Transactions on Pattern Analysis and Machine Intelligence* **11** (4), 423–425.

Fukunaga, K. and P. M. Narendra (1975). A branch and bound algorithm for computing k-nearest neighbors. *IEEE Transactions on Computers* **24**, 750–753.

Fukushima, K. (1988). Neocognitron: a hierarchical neural network capable of visual pattern recognition. *Neural Networks* **1** (2), 119–130.

Fukushima, K., S. Miyake, and T. Ito (1983). Neocognitron: a neural network model for a mechanism of visual pattern recognition. *IEEE Transactions on Systems, Man, and Cybernetics* **13**, 826–834.

Funahashi, K. (1989). On the approximate realization of continuous mappings by neural networks. *Neural Networks* **2** (3), 183–192.

Gallant, A. R. and H. White (1992). On learning the derivatives of an unknown mapping with multilayer feedforward networks. *Neural Networks* **5** (1),

129–138.

Gallant, S. I. (1986a). Optimal linear discriminants. In *Proceedings of the Eighth IEEE International Conference on Pattern Recognition*, Volume 1, pp. 849–852. Washington, DC: IEEE Computer Society.

Gallant, S. I. (1986b). Three constructive algorithms for network learning. In *Proceedings of the Eighth Annual Conference of the Cognitive Science Society*, pp. 652–660. Hillsdale, NJ: Lawrence Erlbaum.

Gallinari, P., S. Thiria, F. Badran, and F. F. Soulie (1991). On the relations between discriminant analysis and multilayer perceptrons. *Neural Networks* **4** (3), 349–360.

Gallinari, P., S. Thiria, and F. F. Soulie (1988). Multi-layer perceptrons and data analysis. In *IEEE International Conference on Neural Networks*, Volume 1, pp. 391–399. San Diego, CA: IEEE.

Gates, G. W. (1972). The reduced nearest neighbor rule. *IEEE Transactions on Information Theory* **18**, 431–433.

Gear, C. W. (1971). *Numerical Initial Value Problems in Ordinary Differential Equations*. Englewood Cliffs, NJ: Prentice-Hall.

Geman, S., E. Bienenstock, and R. Doursat (1992). Neural networks and the bias/variance dilema. *Neural Computation* **4** (1), 1–58.

Ghahramani, Z. and M. I. Jordan (1994a). Learning from incomplete data. Technical Report CBCL 108, Massachusetts Institute of Technology.

Ghahramani, Z. and M. I. Jordan (1994b). Supervised learning from incomplete data via an EM appproach. In J. D. Cowan, G. T. Tesauro, and J. Alspector (Eds.), *Advances in Neural Information Processing Systems*, Volume 6, pp. 120–127. San Mateo, CA: Morgan Kaufmann.

Ghosh, J. and Y. Shin (1992). Efficient higher-order neural networks for classification and function approximation. *International Journal of Neural Systems* **3** (4), 323–350.

Gibson, G. J. and C. F. N. Cowan (1990). On the decision regions of multilayer perceptrons. *Proceedings of the IEEE* **78** (10), 1590–1594.

Giles, C. L. and T. Maxwell (1987). Learning, invariance, and generalization in high-order neural networks. *Applied Optics* **26** (23), 4972–4978.

Gill, P. E., W. Murray, and M. H. Wright (1981). *Practical Optimization*. London: Academic Press.

Girosi, F. and T. Poggio (1989). Representation properties of networks: Kolmogorov's theorem is irrelevant. *Neural Computation* **1** (4), 465–469.

Girosi, F. and T. Poggio (1990). Networks and the best approximation property. *Biological Cybernetics* **63**, 169–176.

Golub, G. and W. Kahan (1965). Calculating the singular values and pseudo-inverse of a matrix. *SIAM Numerical Analysis, B* **2** (2), 205–224.

Gull, S. F. (1988a). Bayesian data analysis – straight-line fitting. In J. Skilling (Ed.), *Maximum Entropy and Bayesian Methods, Cambridge*, pp. 511–518. Dordrecht: Kluwer.

Gull, S. F. (1988b). Bayesian inductive inference and maximum entropy. In G. J. Erickson and C. R. Smith (Eds.), *Maximum-Entropy and Bayesian Methods in Science and Engineering, Vol. 1: Foundations*, pp. 53–74. Dordrecht: Kluwer.

Gull, S. F. (1989). Developments in maximum entropy data analysis. In J. Skilling (Ed.), *Maximum Entropy and Bayesian Methods, Cambridge, 1988*, pp. 53–71. Dordrecht: Kluwer.

Hampshire, J. B. and B. Pearlmutter (1990). Equivalence proofs for multi-layer perceptron classifiers and the Bayesian discriminant function. In D. S. Touretzky, J. L. Elman, T. J. Sejnowski, and G. E. Hinton (Eds.), *Proceedings of the 1990 Connectionist Models Summer School*, pp. 159–172. San Mateo, CA: Morgan Kaufmann.

Hand, D. J. (1981). *Discrimination and Classification*. New York: John Wiley.

Hand, D. J. and B. G. Batchelor (1978). Experiments on the edited condensed nearest neighbour rule. *Information Sciences* **14**, 171–180.

Hanson, S. J. and D. J. Burr (1988). Minkowski-r back-propagation: learning in connectionist models with non-Euclidean error signals. In D. Anderson (Ed.), *Neural Information Processing Systems*, pp. 348–357. New York: American Institute of Physics.

Hanson, S. J. and L. Y. Pratt (1989). Comparing biases for minimal network construction with back-propagation. In D. S. Touretzky (Ed.), *Advances in Neural Information Processing Systems*, Volume 1, pp. 177–185. San Mateo, CA: Morgan Kaufmann.

Hart, P. E. (1968). The condensed nearest neighbor rule. *IEEE Transactions on Information Theory* **14**, 515–516.

Hartman, E. J., J. D. Keeler, and J. M. Kowalski (1990). Layered neural networks with Gaussian hidden units as universal approximations. *Neural Computation* **2** (2), 210–215.

Hassibi, B. and D. G. Stork (1993). Second order derivatives for network pruning: optimal brain surgeon. In S. J. Hanson, J. D. Cowan, and C. L. Giles (Eds.), *Advances in Neural Information Processing Systems*, Volume 5, pp. 164–171. San Mateo, CA: Morgan Kaufmann.

Hastie, T. J. and R. J. Tibshirani (1990). *Generalized Additive Models*. London: Chapman & Hall.

Hebb, D. O. (1949). *The Organization of Behaviour*. New York: John Wiley.

Hecht-Nielsen, R. (1989). Theory of the back-propagation neural network. In *Proceedings of the International Joint Conference on Neural Networks*, Volume 1, pp. 593–605. San Diego, CA: IEEE.

Hertz, J., A. Krogh, and R. G. Palmer (1991). *Introduction to the Theory of Neural Computation*. Redwood City, CA: Addison Wesley.

Hestenes, M. R. and E. Stiefel (1952). Methods of conjugate gradients for solving linear systems. *Journal of Research of the National Bureau of Standards* **49** (6), 409–436.

Hilbert, D. (1900). Mathematische probleme. *Nachrichten der Akademie der Wissenschaften Göttingen*, 290–329.

Hinton, G. E. (1987). Learning translation invariant recognition in massively parallel networks. In J. W. de Bakker, A. J. Nijman, and P. C. Treleaven (Eds.), *Proceedings PARLE Conference on Parallel Architectures and Languages Europe*, pp. 1–13. Berlin: Springer-Verlag.

Hinton, G. E. (1989). Connectionist learning procedures. *Artificial Intelligence* **40**, 185–234.

Hinton, G. E. and D. van Camp (1993). Keeping neural networks simple by minimizing the description length of the weights. In *Proceedings of the Sixth Annual Conference on Computational Learning Theory*, pp. 5–13.

Hopfield, J. J. (1987). Learning algorithms and probability distributions in feed-forward and feed-back networks. *Proceedings of the National Academy of Sciences* **84**, 8429–8433.

Hornik, K. (1991). Approximation capabilities of multilayer feedforward networks. *Neural Networks* **4** (2), 251–257.

Hornik, K., M. Stinchcombe, and H. White (1989). Multilayer feedforward networks are universal approximators. *Neural Networks* **2** (5), 359–366.

Hornik, K., M. Stinchcombe, and H. White (1990). Universal approximation of an unknown mapping and its derivatives using multilayer feedforward networks. *Neural Networks* **3** (5), 551–560.

Huang, W. Y. and R. P. Lippmann (1988). Neural net and traditional classifiers. In D. Z. Anderson (Ed.), *Neural Information Processing Systems*, pp. 387–396. New York: American Institute of Physics.

Huber, P. J. (1981). *Robust Statistics*. New York: John Wiley.

Huber, P. J. (1985). Projection pursuit. *Annals of Statistics* **13** (2), 435–475.

Hush, D. R. and J. M. Salas (1988). Improving the learning rate of back-propagation with the gradient re-use algorithm. In *IEEE International Conference on Neural Networks*, Volume 1, pp. 441–447. San Diego, CA: IEEE.

Hwang, J. N., S. R. Lay, M. Maechler, R. D. Martin, and J. Schimert (1994). Regression modelling in back-propagation and projection pursuit learning. *IEEE Transactions on Neural Networks* **5** (3), 342–353.

Ito, Y. (1991). Representation of functions by superpositions of a step or sigmoid function and their applications to neural network theory. *Neural Networks* **4** (3), 385–394.

Ivakhnenko, A. G. (1971). Polynomial theory of complex systems. *IEEE Transactions on Systems, Man, and Cybernetics* **1** (4), 364–378.

Jabri, M. and B. Flower (1991). Weight perturbation: an optimal architecture and learning technique for analog VLSI feedforward and recurrent multilayer networks. *Neural Computation* **3** (4), 546–565.

Jacobs, R. A. (1988). Increased rates of convergence through learning rate adaptation. *Neural Networks* **1** (4), 295–307.

Jacobs, R. A., M. I. Jordan, S. J. Nowlan, and G. E. Hinton (1991). Adaptive mixtures of local experts. *Neural Computation* **3** (1), 79–87.

Jaynes, E. T. (1986). Bayesian methods: general background. In J. H. Justice (Ed.), *Maximum Entropy and Bayesian Methods in Applied Statistics*, pp. 1–25. Cambridge University Press.

Ji, C., R. R. Snapp, and D. Psaltis (1990). Generalizing smoothness constraints from discrete samples. *Neural Computation* **2** (2), 188–197.

Johansson, E. M., F. U. Dowla, and D. M. Goodman (1992). Backpropagation learning for multilayer feedforward neural networks using the conjugate gradient method. *International Journal of Neural Systems* **2** (4), 291–301.

Jollife, I. T. (1986). *Principal Component Analysis*. New York: Springer-Verlag.

Jones, L. K. (1987). On a conjecture of Huber concerning the convergence of projection pursuit regression. *Annals of Statistics* **15** (2), 880–882.

Jones, L. K. (1990). Constructive approximations for neural networks by sigmoidal functions. *Proceedings of the IEEE* **78** (10), 1586–1589.

Jones, L. K. (1992). A simple lemma on greedy approximation in Hilbert space and convergence rates for projection pursuit regression and neural network training. *Annals of Statistics* **20** (1), 608–613.

Jordan, M. I. and R. A. Jacobs (1994). Hierarchical mixtures of experts and the EM algorithm. *Neural Computation* **6** (2), 181–214.

Kahane, J. P. (1975). Sur le theoreme de superposition de Kolmogorov. *Journal of Approximation Theory* **13**, 229–234.

Kailath, T. (1980). *Linear Systems*. Englewood Cliffs, NJ: Prentice-Hall.

Khotanzad, A. and Y. H. Hong (1990). Invariant image recognition by Zernike moments. *IEEE Transactions on Pattern Analysis and Machine Intelligence* **12** (5), 489–497.

Kiefer, J. and J. Wolfowitz (1952). Stochastic estimation of the maximum of a regression function. *Annals of Mathematical Statistics* **23**, 462–466.

Kirkpatrick, S., C. D. Gelatt, and M. P. Vecchi (1983). Optimization by simulated annealing. *Science* **220** (4598), 671–680.

Kohonen, T. (1982). Self-organized formation of topologically correct feature maps. *Biological Cybernetics* **43**, 59–69. Reprinted in Anderson and Rosenfeld (1988).

Kolmogorov, A. N. (1957). On the representation of continuous functions of several variables by superposition of continuous functions of one variable and addition. *Doklady Akademiia Nauk SSSR* **114** (5), 953–956.

Kraaijveld, M. and R. Duin (1991). Generalization capabilities of minimal kernel-based networks. In *Proceedings of the International Joint Conference on Neural Networks*, Volume 1, pp. 843–848. New York: IEEE.

Kramer, A. H. and A. Sangiovanni-Vincentelli (1989). Efficient parallel learning algorithms for neural networks. In D. S. Touretzky (Ed.), *Advances in*

Neural Information Processing Systems, Volume 1, pp. 40–48. San Mateo, CA: Morgan Kaufmann.

Kramer, M. A. (1991). Nonlinear principal component analysis using autoassociative neural networks. *AIChe Journal* **37** (2), 233–243.

Kreinovich, V. Y. (1991). Arbitrary nonlinearity is sufficient to represent all functions by neural networks: a theorem. *Neural Networks* **4** (3), 381–383.

Krogh, A. and J. Vedelsby (1995). Neural network ensembles, cross validation and active learning. In D. S. Touretzky, G. Tesauro, and T. K. Leen (Eds.), *Advances in Neural Information Processing Systems*, Volume 7. Cambridge MA: MIT Press. In press.

Kullback, S. (1959). *Information Theory and Statistics*. New York: Dover Publications.

Kullback, S. and R. A. Leibler (1951). On information and sufficiency. *Annals of Mathematical Statistics* **22**, 79–86.

Kůrková, V. (1991). Kolmogorov's theorem is relevant. *Neural Computation* **3** (4), 617–622.

Kůrková, V. (1992). Kolmogorov's theorem and multilayer neural networks. *Neural Networks* **5** (3), 501–506.

Kůrková, V. and P. C. Kainen (1994). Functionally equivalent feed-forward neural networks. *Neural Computation* **6** (3), 543–558.

Lang, K. J. and G. E. Hinton (1990). Dimensionality reduction and prior knowledge in E-set recognition. In D. S. Touretzky (Ed.), *Advances in Neural Information Processing Systems*, Volume 2, pp. 178–185. San Mateo, CA: Morgan Kaufmann.

Lang, K. J., A. H. Waibel, and G. E. Hinton (1990). A time-delay neural network architecture for isolated word recognition. *Neural Networks* **3** (1), 23–43.

Lapedes, A. and R. Farber (1988). How neural nets work. In D. Z. Anderson (Ed.), *Neural Information Processing Systems*, pp. 442–456. New York: American Institute of Physics.

Le Cun, Y., B. Boser, J. S. Denker, D. Henderson, R. E. Howard, W. Hubbard, and L. D. Jackel (1989). Backpropagation applied to handwritten zip code recognition. *Neural Computation* **1** (4), 541–551.

Le Cun, Y., J. S. Denker, and S. A. Solla (1990). Optimal brain damage. In D. S. Touretzky (Ed.), *Advances in Neural Information Processing Systems*, Volume 2, pp. 598–605. San Mateo, CA: Morgan Kaufmann.

Le Cun, Y., P. Y. Simard, and B. Pearlmutter (1993). Automatic learning rate maximization by on-line estimation of the Hessian's eigenvectors. In S. J. Hanson, J. D. Cowan, and C. L. Giles (Eds.), *Advances in Neural Information Processing Systems*, Volume 5, pp. 156–163. San Mateo, CA: Morgan Kaufmann.

Levenberg, K. (1944). A method for the solution of certain non-linear problems in least squares. *Quarterly Journal of Applied Mathematics* **II** (2), 164–168.

Lewis, P. M. and C. L. Coates (1967). *Threshold Logic.* New York: John Wiley.

Linde, Y., A. Buzo, and R. M. Gray (1980). An algorithm for vector quantizer design. *IEEE Transactions on Communications* **28** (1), 84–95.

Linsker, R. (1988). Self-organization in a perceptual network. *IEEE Computer* **21**, 105–117.

Lippmann, R. P. (1987). An introduction to computing with neural nets. *IEEE ASSP Magazine,* April, 4–22.

Little, R. J. A. (1992). Regression with missing X's: a review. *Journal of the American Statistical Association* **87** (420), 1227–1237.

Little, R. J. A. and D. B. Rubin (1987). *Statistical Analysis with Missing Data.* New York: John Wiley.

Liu, Y. (1994). Robust parameter estimation and model selection for neural network regression. In J. D. Cowan, G. Tesauro, and J. Alspector (Eds.), *Advances in Neural Information Processing Systems,* Volume 6, pp. 192–199. San Mateo, CA: Morgan Kaufmann.

Lloyd, S. P. (1982). Least squares quantization in PCM. *IEEE Transactions on Information Theory* **28** (2), 129–137.

Lonstaff, I. D. and J. F. Cross (1987). A pattern recognition approach to understanding the multi-layer perceptron. *Pattern Recognition Letters* **5**, 315–319.

Lorentz, G. G. (1976). On the 13th problem of Hilbert. In *Proceedings of Symposia in Pure Mathematics,* pp. 419–429. Providence, RI: American Mathematical Society.

Lowe, D. (1995). Radial basis function networks. In M. A. Arbib (Ed.), *The Handbook of Brain Theory and Neural Networks.* Cambridge, MA: MIT Press. To be published.

Lowe, D. and A. R. Webb (1990). Exploiting prior knowledge in network optimization: an illustration from medical prognosis. *Network: Computation in Neural Systems* **1** (3), 299–323.

Lowe, D. and A. R. Webb (1991). Optimized feature extraction and the Bayes decision in feed-forward classifier networks. *IEEE Transactions on Pattern Analysis and Machine Intelligence* **13** (4), 355–364.

Luenberger, D. G. (1984). *Linear and Nonlinear Programming* (Second ed.). Reading, MA: Addison-Wesley.

Luo, Z. Q. (1991). On the convergence of the LMS algorithm with adaptive learning rate for linear feedforward networks. *Neural Computation* **3** (2), 226–245.

Luttrell, S. P. (1994). Partitioned mixture distribution: an adaptive Bayesian network for low-level image processing. *IEE Proceedings on Vision, Image and Signal Processing* **141** (4), 251–260.

MacKay, D. J. C. (1992a). Bayesian interpolation. *Neural Computation* **4** (3), 415–447.

MacKay, D. J. C. (1992b). The evidence framework applied to classification networks. *Neural Computation* **4** (5), 720–736.

MacKay, D. J. C. (1992c). Information-based objective functions for active data selection. *Neural Computation* **4** (4), 590–604.

MacKay, D. J. C. (1992d). A practical Bayesian framework for back-propagation networks. *Neural Computation* **4** (3), 448–472.

MacKay, D. J. C. (1994a). Bayesian methods for backpropagation networks. In E. Domany, J. L. van Hemmen, and K. Schulten (Eds.), *Models of Neural Networks III*, Chapter 6. New York: Springer-Verlag.

MacKay, D. J. C. (1994b). Hyperparameters: optimise or integrate out? In G. Heidbreder (Ed.), *Maximum Entropy and Bayesian Methods, Santa Barbara 1993*. Dordrecht: Kluwer.

MacKay, D. J. C. (1995a). Bayesian neural networks and density networks. *Nuclear Instruments and Methods in Physics Research, A* **354** (1), 73–80.

MacKay, D. J. C. (1995b). Bayesian non-linear modelling for the 1993 energy prediction competition. In G. Heidbreder (Ed.), *Maximum Entropy and Bayesian Methods, Santa Barbara 1993*. Dordrecht: Kluwer.

MacQueen, J. (1967). Some methods for classification and analysis of multi-variate observations. In L. M. LeCam and J. Neyman (Eds.), *Proceedings of the Fifth Berkeley Symposium on Mathematical Statistics and Probability*, Volume I, pp. 281–297. Berkeley: University of California Press.

Makram-Ebeid, S., J. A. Sirat, and J. R. Viala (1989). A rationalized back-propagation learning algorithm. In *Proceedings of the International Joint Conference on Neural Networks*, Volume 2, pp. 373–380. New Jersey: IEEE.

Mallows, C. L. (1973). Some comments on C_p. *Technometrics* **15**, 661–675.

Marchand, M., M. Golea, and P. Rujan (1990). A convergence theorem for sequential learning in two-layer perceptrons. *Europhysics Letters* **11** (6), 487–492.

Mardia, K. V. (1972). *Statistics of Directional Data*. London: Academic Press.

Marquardt, D. W. (1963). An algorithm for least-squares estimation of non-linear parameters. *Journal of the Society of Industrial and Applied Mathematics* **11** (2), 431–441.

McCulloch, W. S. and W. Pitts (1943). A logical calculus of the ideas immanent in nervous activity. *Bulletin of Mathematical Biophysics* **5**, 115–133. Reprinted in Anderson and Rosenfeld (1988).

McLachlan, G. J. and K. E. Basford (1988). *Mixture Models: Inference and Applications to Clustering*. New York: Marcel Dekker.

Metropolis, N., A. W. Rosenbluth, M. N. Rosenbluth, A. H. Teller, and E. Teller (1953). Equation of state calculations by fast computing machines. *Journal of Chemical Physics* **21** (6), 1087–1092.

Mezard, M. and J. P. Nadal (1989). Learning in feedforward layered networks: The tiling algorithm. *Journal of Physics, A* **22**, 2191–2203.

Micchelli, C. A. (1986). Interpolation of scattered data: distance matrices and conditionally positive definite functions. *Constructive Approximations* **2**, 11–22.

Minsky, M. L. and S. A. Papert (1969). *Perceptrons*. Cambridge, MA: MIT Press. Expanded Edition 1990.

Møller, M. (1993a). Efficient Training of Feed-Forward Neural Networks. Ph.D. thesis, Aarhus University, Denmark.

Møller, M. (1993b). A scaled conjugate gradient algorithm for fast supervised learning. *Neural Networks* **6** (4), 525–533.

Moody, J. and C. J. Darken (1989). Fast learning in networks of locally-tuned processing units. *Neural Computation* **1** (2), 281–294.

Moody, J. E. (1992). The effective number of parameters: an analysis of generalization and regularization in nonlinear learning systems. In J. E. Moody, S. J. Hanson, and R. P. Lippmann (Eds.), *Advances in Neural Information Processing Systems*, Volume 4, pp. 847–854. San Mateo, CA: Morgan Kaufmann.

Mozer, M. C. and P. Smolensky (1989). Skeletonization: a technique for trimming the fat from a network via relevance assessment. In D. S. Touretzky (Ed.), *Advances in Neural Information Processing Systems*, Volume 1, pp. 107–115. San Mateo, CA: Morgan Kaufmann.

Nadal, J. P. (1989). Study of a growth algorithm for a feedforward network. *International Journal of Neural Systems* **1** (1), 55–59.

Nadaraya, É. A. (1964). On estimating regression. *Theory of Probability and its Applications* **9** (1), 141–142.

Narendra, P. M. and K. Fukunaga (1977). A branch and bound algorithm for feature subset selection. *IEEE Transactions on Computers* **26** (9), 917–922.

Neal, R. M. (1992). Bayesian training of backpropagation networks by the hybrid Monte Carlo method. Technical Report CRG-TR-92-1, Department of Computer Science, University of Toronto, Canada.

Neal, R. M. (1993). Probabilistic inference using Markov chain Monte Carlo methods. Technical Report CRG-TR-93-1, Department of Computer Science, University of Toronto, Cananda.

Neal, R. M. (1994). *Bayesian Learning for Neural Networks*. Ph.D. thesis, University of Toronto, Canada.

Neuneier, R., F. Hergert, W. Finnof, and D. Ormoneit (1994). Estimation of conditional densities: a comparison of approaches. In M. Marinaro and P. G. Morasso (Eds.), *Proceedings ICANN*94 International Conference on Artificial Neural Networks*, Volume 1, pp. 689–692. Springer-Verlag.

Nilsson, N. J. (1965). *Learning Machines*. New York: McGraw-Hill. Reprinted as *The Mathematical Foundations of Learning Machines*, Morgan Kaufmann, (1990).

Niranjan, M., A. J. Robinson, and F. Fallside (1989). Pattern recognition with potential functions in the context of neural networks. In M. Pietikäinen and J. Röning (Eds.), *Proceedings Sixth Scandinavian Conference on Image Analysis, Oulu, Finland*, Volume 1, pp. 96–103. Pattern Recognition Society of Finland.

Nix, A. D. and A. S. Weigend (1994). Estimating the mean and variance of the target probability distribution. In *Proceedings of the IEEE International Conference on Neural Networks*, Volume 1, pp. 55–60. New York: IEEE.

Nowlan, S. J. and G. E. Hinton (1992). Simplifying neural networks by soft weight sharing. *Neural Computation* **4** (4), 473–493.

Oja, E. (1982). A simplified neuron model as a principal component analyzer. *Journal of Mathematical Biology* **15**, 267–273.

Oja, E. (1989). Neural networks, principal components, and subspaces. *International Journal of Neural Systems* **1** (1), 61–68.

Omohundro, S. M. (1987). Efficient algorithms with neural network behaviour. *Complex Systems* **1**, 273–347.

Owens, A. J. and D. L. Filkin (1989). Efficient training of the backpropagation network by solving a system of stiff ordinary differential equations. In *Proceedings of the International Joint Conference on Neural Networks*, Volume 2, pp. 381–386. San Diego: IEEE.

Park, J. and I. W. Sandberg (1991). Universal approximation using radial basis function networks. *Neural Computation* **3** (2), 246–257.

Park, J. and I. W. Sandberg (1993). Approximation and radial basis function networks. *Neural Computation* **5** (2), 305–316.

Parker, D. B. (1985). Learning logic. Technical Report TR-47, Cambridge, MA: MIT Center for Research in Computational Economics and Management Science.

Parzen, E. (1962). On estimation of a probability density function and mode. *Annals of Mathematical Statistics* **33**, 1065–1076.

Pearlmutter, B. A. (1994). Fast exact multiplication by the Hessian. *Neural Computation* **6** (1), 147–160.

Perantonis, S. J. and P. J. G. Lisboa (1992). Translation, rotation, and scale invariant pattern recognition by high-order neural networks and moment classifiers. *IEEE Transactions on Neural Networks* **3** (2), 241–251.

Perrone, M. P. (1994). General averaging results for convex optimization. In M. C. Mozer et al. (Eds.), *Proceedings 1993 Connectionist Models Summer School*, pp. 364–371. Hillsdale, NJ: Lawrence Erlbaum.

Perrone, M. P. and L. N. Cooper (1993). When networks disagree: ensemble methods for hybrid neural networks. In R. J. Mammone (Ed.), *Artificial Neural Networks for Speech and Vision*, pp. 126–142. London: Chapman & Hall.

Plaut, D., S. Nowlan, and G. E. Hinton (1986). Experiments on learning by back propagation. Technical Report CMU-CS-86-126, Department of Computer Science, Carnegie Mellon University, Pittsburgh, PA.

Poggio, T. and F. Girosi (1990a). Networks for approximation and learning. *Proceedings of the IEEE* **78** (9), 1481–1497.

Poggio, T. and F. Girosi (1990b). Regularization algorithms for learning that are equivalent to multilayer networks. *Science* **247**, 978–982.

Poggio, T., V. Torre, and C. Koch (1985). Computational vision and regularization theory. *Nature* **317** (26), 314–319.

Polak, E. (1971). *Computational Methods in Optimization: A Unified Approach.* New York: Academic Press.

Powell, M. J. D. (1977). Restart procedures for the conjugate gradient method. *Mathematical Programming* **12**, 241–254.

Powell, M. J. D. (1987). Radial basis functions for multivariable interpolation: a review. In J. C. Mason and M. G. Cox (Eds.), *Algorithms for Approximation*, pp. 143–167. Oxford: Clarendon Press.

Press, W. H., S. A. Teukolsky, W. T. Vetterling, and B. P. Flannery (1992). *Numerical Recipes in C: The Art of Scientific Computing* (Second ed.). Cambridge University Press.

Quinlan, J. R. (1986). Induction of decision trees. *Machine Learning* **1**, 81–106.

Rao, C. R. and S. K. Mitra (1971). *Generalized Inverse of Matrices and Its Applications.* New York: John Wiley.

Redner, R. A. and H. F. Walker (1984). Mixture densities, maximum likelihood and the EM algorithm. *SIAM Review* **26** (2), 195–239.

Reid, M. B., L. Spirkovska, and E. Ochoa (1989). Rapid training of higher-order neural networks for invariant pattern recognition. In *Proceedings of the International Joint Conference on Neural Networks*, Volume 1, pp. 689–692. San Diego, CA: IEEE.

Richard, M. D. and R. P. Lippmann (1991). Neural network classifiers estimate Bayesian a-posteriori probabilities. *Neural Computation* **3** (4), 461–483.

Ricotti, L. P., S. Ragazzini, and G. Martinelli (1988). Learning of word stress in a sub-optimal secondorder backpropagation neural network. In *Proceedings of the IEEE International Conference on Neural Networks*, Volume 1, pp. 355–361. San Diego, CA: IEEE.

Ripley, B. D. (1994). Neural networks and related methods for classification. *Journal of the Royal Statistical Society, B* **56** (3), 409–456.

Rissanen, J. (1978). Modelling by shortest data description. *Automatica* **14**, 465–471.

Robbins, H. and S. Monro (1951). A stochastic approximation method. *Annals of Mathematical Statistics* **22**, 400–407.

Rosenblatt, F. (1962). *Principles of Neurodynamics: Perceptrons and the Theory of Brain Mechanisms.* Washington DC: Spartan.

Rosenblatt, M. (1956). Remarks on some nonparametric estimates of a density function. *Annals of Mathematical Statistics* **27**, 832–837.

Rumelhart, D. E., R. Durbin, R. Golden, and Y. Chauvin (1995). Backpropagation: the basic theory. In Y. Chauvin and D. E. Rumelhart (Eds.), *Backpropagation: Theory, Architectures, and Applications*, pp. 1–34. Hillsdale, NJ: Lawrence Erlbaum.

Rumelhart, D. E., G. E. Hinton, and R. J. Williams (1986). Learning internal representations by error propagation. In D. E. Rumelhart, J. L. McClelland, and the PDP Research Group (Eds.), *Parallel Distributed Processing: Explorations in the Microstructure of Cognition*, Volume 1: Foundations, pp. 318–362. Cambridge, MA: MIT Press. Reprinted in Anderson and Rosenfeld (1988).

Sanger, T. D. (1989). Optimal unsupervised learning in a single-layer linear feed-forward neural network. *Neural Networks* **2** (6), 459–473.

Satchwell, C. (1994). Neural networks for stochastic problems: more than one outcome for the input space. Presentation at the Neural Computing Applications Forum conference, Aston University, September.

Schalkoff, R. J. (1989). *Digital Image Processing and Computer Vision*. New York: John Wiley.

Schiøler, H. and U. Hartmann (1992). Mapping neural network derived from the Parzen window estimator. *Neural Networks* **5** (6), 903–909.

Scott, D. W. (1992). *Multivariate Density Estimation: Theory, Practice, and Visualization*. New York: John Wiley.

Shanno, D. F. (1978). Conjugate gradient methods with inexact searches. *Mathematics of Operations Research* **3** (3), 244–256.

Shannon, C. E. (1948). A mathematical theory of communication. *The Bell System Technical Journal* **27** (3), 379–423 and 623–656.

Sibisi, S. (1991). Bayesian interpolation. In W. T. Grandy and L. H. Schick (Eds.), *Maximum entropy and Bayesian methods, Laramie, 1990*, pp. 349–355. Dordrecht: Kluwer.

Siedlecki, W. and J. Sklansky (1988). On automatic feature selection. *International Journal of Pattern Recognition and Artificial Intelligence* **2** (2), 197–220.

Sietsma, J. and R. J. F. Dow (1991). Creating artificial neural networks that generalize. *Neural Networks* **4** (1), 67–79.

Silverman, B. W. (1986). *Density Estimation for Statistics and Data Analysis*. London: Chapman & Hall.

Simard, P., Y. Le Cun, and J. Denker (1993). Efficient pattern recognition using a new transformation distance. In S. J. Hanson, J. D. Cowan, and C. L. Giles (Eds.), *Advances in Neural Information Processing Systems*, Volume 5, pp. 50–58. San Mateo, CA: Morgan Kaufmann.

Simard, P., B. Victorri, Y. Le Cun, and J. Denker (1992). Tangent prop – a formalism for specifying selected invariances in an adaptive network. In J. E. Moody, S. J. Hanson, and R. P. Lippmann (Eds.), *Advances in Neural*

Information Processing Systems, Volume 4, pp. 895–903. San Mateo, CA: Morgan Kaufmann.

Singer, E. and R. P. Lippmann (1992). Improved hidden Markov model speech recognition using radial basis function networks. In J. E. Moody, S. J. Hanson, and R. P. Lippmann (Eds.), *Advances in Neural Information Processing Systems*, Volume 4, pp. 159–166. San Mateo, CA: Morgan Kaufmann.

Skilling, J. (1991). On parameter estimation and quantified MaxEnt. In W. T. Grandy and L. H. Schick (Eds.), *Maximum Entropy and Bayesian Methods, Laramie, 1990*, pp. 267–273. Dordrecht: Kluwer.

Solla, S. A., E. Levin, and M. Fleisher (1988). Accelerated learning in layered neural networks. *Complex Systems* **2**, 625–640.

Specht, D. F. (1990). Probabilistic neural networks. *Neural Networks* **3** (1), 109–118.

Sprecher, D. A. (1965). On the structure of continuous functions of several variables. *Transactions of the American Mathematical Society* **115**, 340–355.

Stinchecombe, M. and H. White (1989). Universal approximation using feedforward networks with non-sigmoid hidden layer activation functions. In *Proceedings of the International Joint Conference on Neural Networks*, Volume 1, pp. 613–618. San Diego: IEEE.

Stone, M. (1974). Cross-validatory choice and assessment of statistical predictions. *Journal of the Royal Statistical Society, B* **36** (1), 111–147.

Stone, M. (1978). Cross-validation: A review. *Math. Operationsforsch. Statist. Ser. Statistics* **9** (1), 127–139.

Sussmann, H. J. (1992). Uniqueness of the weights for minimal feedforward nets with a given input-output map. *Neural Networks* **5** (4), 589–593.

Tatsuoka, M. M. (1971). *Multivariate Analysis: Techniques for Educational and Psychological Research*. New York: John Wiley.

Thodberg, H. H. (1993). Ace of Bayes: application of neural networks with pruning. Technical Report 1132E, The Danish Meat Research Institute, Maglegaardsvej 2, DK-4000 Roskilde, Denmark.

Tikhonov, A. N. and V. Y. Arsenin (1977). *Solutions of Ill-Posed Problems*. Washington, DC: V. H. Winston.

Titterington, D. M., A. F. M. Smith, and U. E. Makov (1985). *Statistical Analysis of Finite Mixture Distributions*. New York: John Wiley.

Tråvén, H. G. C. (1991). A neural network approach to statistical pattern classification by 'semiparametric' estimation of probability density functions. *IEEE Transactions on Neural Networks* **2** (3), 366–377.

Vapnik, V. N. and A. Y. Chervonenkis (1971). On the uniform convergence of relative frequencies of events to their probabilities. *Theory of Probability and its Applications* **16** (2), 264–280.

Viterbi, A. J. and J. K. Omura (1979). *Principles of Digital Communication and Coding*. New York: McGraw-Hill.

Vitushkin, A. G. (1954). On Hilbert's thirteenth problem. *Doklady Akademiia Nauk SSSR* **95**, 701–704.

Vogl, T. P., J. K. Mangis, A. K. Rigler, W. T. Zink, and D. L. Alkon (1988). Accelerating the convergence of the back-propagation method. *Biological Cybernetics* **59**, 257–263.

Wahba, G. and S. Wold (1975). A completely automatic French curve: fitting spline functions by cross-validation. *Communications in Statistics, Series A* **4** (1), 1–17.

Walker, A. M. (1969). On the asymptotic behaviour of posterior distributions. *Journal of the Royal Statistical Society, B* **31** (1), 80–88.

Wallace, C. S. and P. R. Freeman (1987). Estimation and inference by compact coding. *Journal of the Royal Statistical Society, B* **49** (3), 240–265.

Watrous, R. L. (1987). Learning algorithms for connectionist networks: applied gradient methods of nonlinear optimization. In *Proceedings IEEE First International Conference on Neural Networks*, Volume 2, pp. 619–627. San Diego: IEEE.

Watson, G. S. (1964). Smooth regression analysis. *Sankhyā: The Indian Journal of Statistics. Series A* **26**, 359–372.

Webb, A. R. (1994). Functional approximation by feed-forward networks: a least-squares approach to generalisation. *IEEE Transactions on Neural Networks* **5** (3), 363–371.

Webb, A. R. and D. Lowe (1988). A hybrid optimisation strategy for adaptive feed-forward layered networks. RSRE Memorandum 4193, Royal Signals and Radar Establishment, St Andrews Road, Malvern, UK.

Webb, A. R. and D. Lowe (1990). The optimised internal representation of multilayer classifier networks performs nonlinear discriminant analysis. *Neural Networks* **3** (4), 367–375.

Webb, A. R., D. Lowe, and M. D. Bedworth (1988). A comparison of non-linear optimisation strategies for feed-forward adaptive layered networks. RSRE Memorandum 4157, Royal Signals and Radar Establishment, St Andrew's Road, Malvern, UK.

Weigend, A. S., B. A. Huberman, and D. E. Rumelhart (1990). Predicting the future: a connectionist approach. *International Journal of Neural Systems* **1** (3), 193–209.

Werbos, P. J. (1974). Beyond regression: new tools for prediction and analysis in the behavioural sciences. Ph.D. thesis, Harvard University, Boston, MA.

White, H. (1989). Learning in artificial neural networks: a statistical perspective. *Neural Computation* **1** (4), 425–464.

White, H. (1990). Connectionist nonparametric regression: multilayer feed-forward networks can learn arbitrary mappings. *Neural Networks* **3** (5), 535–549.

Widrow, B. and M. E. Hoff (1960). Adaptive switching circuits. In *IRE WESCON Convention Record*, Volume 4, pp. 96–104. New York. Reprinted in Anderson and Rosenfeld (1988).

Widrow, B. and M. A. Lehr (1990). 30 years of adaptive neural networks: perceptron, madeline, and backpropagation. *Proceedings of the IEEE* **78** (9), 1415–1442.

Wieland, A. and R. Leighton (1987). Geometric analysis of neural network capabilities. In *Proceedings of the First IEEE International Conference on Neural Networks*, Volume 3, pp. 385–392. San Diego, CA: IEEE.

Williams, P. M. (1991). A Marquardt algorithm for choosing the step-size in backpropagation learning with conjugate gradients. Technical Report CSRP 299, University of Sussex, Brighton, UK.

Williams, P. M. (1995). Bayesian regularization and pruning using a Laplace prior. *Neural Computation* **7** (1), 117–143.

Wolpert, D. H. (1992). Stacked generalization. *Neural Networks* **5** (2), 241–259.

Wolpert, D. H. (1993). On the use of evidence in neural networks. In S. J. Hanson, J. D. Cowan, and C. L. Giles (Eds.), *Advances in Neural Information Processing Systems*, Volume 5, pp. 539–546. San Mateo, CA: Morgan Kaufmann.

INDEX